The Ultimate Guide to

Asheville & the Western North Carolina Mountains

Including Boone, Hendersonville, Hickory, Lenoir, Morganton & Waynesville

Updated 2020

Written and Illustrated by

Lee James Pantas

Foreword by

Rick Boyer

Published by R. Brent and Company
Johnson City, Tennessee
robbin@rbrent.com

Editor and publisher: *Robbin Brent*
Original cover design: *Gayle Graham*
Cover design: *jb graphics,*
Design & layout: *Rick Soldin*
Illustrations: *Lee James Pantas*

Publication Data

Pantas, Lee James
the ultimate guide to asheville & the western north carolina mountains: including hendersonville, hickory, lenoir, morganton & waynesville—2018 ed.
p. cm.
ISBN Paperback: 978-0-9910398-5-2
(Previously published by WorldComm®, ISBN 1-56664-129-2, 1st ed.,
ISBN 1-57090-105-8, 2nd ed., 978-0-9910398-0-7, last ed.)
1. Asheville Region (NC)—Guidebooks 2. Blue Ridge Mountains—Guidebooks 3. Great Smoky Mountains National Park (NC and TN)—Guidebooks 4. Hendersonville Region (NC)—Guidebooks
I. Title

Latest Edition.

11 12 13 14 15 5 4 3 2 1

Printed in the United States of America.

Lee James Pantas may be contacted at 828-779-1569 or leepantas@bellsouth.net for ordering information. Visa and MasterCard accepted. This book is also available for order online at ashevilleguidebook.com .

Contents

Section IV: Hendersonville 215

Section V: Western North Carolina 243

List of Maps

List of Illustrations

List of Illustrations *(continued)*

Foreword by Rick Boyer

Why I Live in the "Land of the Sky"

The Today Show, 1982:

On our fourth and final day in New York's NBC studios at Rockefeller Center promoting our new book, *Places Rated Almanac,* Jane Pauley leaned over and asked me the question:

"Okay Mr. Boyer—after doing all this research, after compiling this huge almanac based on facts, figures, and government data—what American city would you relocate to if you had a choice?"

Although I should have been expecting a question like this, I admit it took me somewhat off guard. As we filed out to the studio stage from the "green room" that morning, we were told that between eight and twelve million people would be watching. Now I had been asked to *personally choose* the one metro area in the U.S. out of 330 that had emerged as my *favorite city,* a place I would move to the next day if given the chance.

Where to start, given the fact that I had only a few seconds to come up with an answer? I knew it would not be a major city; I have always loved the countryside and knew that any population center I chose would be small to medium sized, and within an easy drive of farms and wilderness.

Although born and raised in the Middle West, I was sick and tired of the long, cold winters and hot humid summers in that region. Now, having lived in New England (Concord, Massachusetts) for a decade, I found the place charming, but the climate no better. I wanted a more southerly place. But not in the Deep South, where the heat and humidity would stifle me. The semitropical climates of Florida and Southern California, while attractive to so many people, never appealed to me; a place needs some cold weather, I reasoned, not just for variety but for hardiness. Also, places with "paradise climates" like San Diego and Honolulu, where the weather shows hardly any fluctuation from season to season, may be great for people suffering from aching joints, but I knew from experience, both researched and personal, that such monotonous climates have a long-term depressant effect on those confined to them.

The deserts and mountains of the West? Yes, they had always enthralled me. Their scenery and openness were spectacular, and their climates vigorous yet comfortable. Also, the major cities of the region, from Denver and Salt Lake to Boise and Albuquerque, were on the whole quite livable. Still, there was the inevitable drawback of isolation. How and when would I ever get to see my friends and family living like Jeremiah Johnson?

Then somewhere from the back of my mind—sifting through the endless lists and tables that my co-author and I had examined during the past four years, leapt a name. A name of a place small enough that many people outside the region had not heard of it. "I think I would move to Asheville, North Carolina," I answered.

And, less than seven months later, I did.

Basically stated, the reasons were simple: Asheville is not too far north nor too far south. It is in the eastern half of the country, but so far west in the coastal state of North Carolina that it lies directly south of Akron, Ohio. Nestled in a broad valley 2,200 feet high between the Blue Ridge and Smoky Mountains, it is shielded from the cold polar air masses that sweep down from Canada in the winter months, and likewise sheltered from most of the hot, humid air that moves inland from the Gulf and the Atlantic during the summer.

In Chicago, where I grew up, the finest season (the *only* fine season) is the fall. Too bad it only lasts two weeks. In Asheville, fall lasts at least ten weeks: the second half of Sep., all of Oct. and Nov., and usually the first half of Dec. Spring begins on the Ides of Mar. and lasts 'til Jun. The summers, from Jun. until mid-Sep., have warm days and cool nights. For the most part, air conditioning—especially after seven in the evening—is not needed here. Nor are window screens, because there are no mosquitoes!

Although *Places Rated Almanac* is an extremely thorough publication, there was no section in it that "rated" beauty. Therefore, while I was relatively confident that I had made a good choice, *I had never actually seen the place. All my judgments had been made from printed data, not a personal visit.*

Uh oh...

So it was with some apprehension that I boarded the plane in Boston for Asheville to enjoy a paid week (courtesy of the Asheville Chamber of Commerce) in the city that I had chosen on national television as the most livable in the country, but that I had never visited. The chamber put us up in the Grove Park Inn, an historic resort hotel that was destined to triple in size within a decade after "word got out" about Asheville. My co-author and I gave out interviews and spiels in mid-April, when the dogwood blossoms speckled the mountainsides, and mountain warblers sang on every branch (it was still snowing in Boston.) A time, as Thomas Wolfe writes in *Look Homeward Angel:*

"When all the woods are a tender, smokey blur, and birds no bigger than a budding leaf dart through the singing trees...and when the mountain boy brings water to his kinsman laying fence, and as the wind snakes through the grasses hears far in the valley below the long wail of the whistle, and the faint clangor of the bell; and the blue great cup of the hills seems closer, nearer...."

There's a lot more we all like about Asheville: The Biltmore Estate south of town—the grandest, most exquisite chateau ever built, not on the banks of the Loire, but in the valley of the French Broad. The town's architecture, both in her city buildings and her majestic homes set on wide, sycamore-lined avenues. The native mountain people, taciturn at first, funny and kind after a time, and true to their word as a mountain oak.

And always remember this: Every January, there are always three or four days where you can play golf in a sweater....

—Rick Boyer, 2000

Introduction

It is hoped that *The Ultimate Guide to Asheville & the Western North Carolina Mountains* will be just that. A complete resource for you as you visit our area, one that will allow you to make an informed decision as to what you wish to see and do during your stay. Besides being comprehensive in scope and highly factual as any good guidebook should be, *The Ultimate Guide* is unique in that it is filled with pen and ink illustrations that accompany the text. These highly detailed illustrations should also help you to make the right choices for your visit. A picture *can be* worth a thousand words!

I have tried to organize the material in the book into logical sections to help you in thinking about what to do. Section I, "Getting Acquainted," will provide you with an overview as well as vital and useful information to make your stay a successful one. Section II, "The Best of Asheville & Hendersonville," not only represents my personal selections and favorites, but also covers topics of interest to all visitors, from accommodations and restaurants to art and crafts galleries to outdoor recreation. As a longtime resident who lives and works in this area, I am very confident in providing this vital information and very comfortable in making any recommendations, since these come from my firsthand knowledge. Sections Three and Four present the major attractions and things to see and do in "Asheville, All-America City" and "Hendersonville." Section V presents the major attractions in all of "Western North Carolina," realizing that you may wish to stay in Asheville or Hendersonville and venture out into the surrounding mountains on day trips.

I have tried to include in this guidebook everything that would be of interest to visitors. Many of the attractions and features included are very popular and well advertised. Some however are not as well known but just as worthy. It is hoped that my experience of living and working in the Asheville and Hendersonville area has enabled me to do it right, so to speak—to write a guidebook that really is thorough and accurate, not just one that provides superficial or limited information from the perspective of a nonnative.

One of the most delightful surprises along the way, and one I hope you will discover for yourself, is the wonderful friendliness of the many people who work at the places highlighted in *The Ultimate Guide to Asheville & the Western North Carolina Mountains.* There is such a thing as "Southern Hospitality!" The people of the mountains, those whose families have lived here for generations and those who have just arrived, are the true treasures. There are truly beautiful and inspiring places to visit in the mountains, but the folks who greet you at the door make it all the better.

—Lee James Pantas

About the Author

Lee James Pantas, originally from Greenwich, Connecticut, has lived in the Asheville area since 1989. He has a Master's degree in Ecology from the University of Vermont, and has worked as a research scientist, military officer, realtor, lecturer, parapsychologist, marketing director, painter and illustrator in Vermont, Georgia, the orient, Brazil, Colorado, Connecticut and North Carolina. He also was the founder in 1978 of New Covenant House (now known as New Covenant Center) in Stamford, Ct., a soup kitchen for homeless persons. He is active in youth track and field and coaches hurdles for A.C. Reynolds High School.

Well-known throughout North Carolina for his award-winning, exquisitely detailed pen and ink artwork, Mr. Pantas has completed more than 2,500 drawings of private residences, historical buildings, scenes of Western North Carolina and animals. In addition to this illustrated guidebook he is also the author of "Wild & Furry Animals of the Southern Appalachian Mountains", an illustrated book showcasing these animals.

Mr. Pantas is also known for his imaginative visionary and fantasy paintings. His work has been exhibited in New York City, San Francisco and Washington, D.C., and locally in Blue Spiral 1, Broadway Arts and Seven Sisters Gallery, among others, and is found in many private collections.

Correspondence should be directed to:

Lee James Pantas
18 Garren Mountain Lane 828-779-1569
Fairview NC 28730 leepantas@bellsouth.net

Acknowledgements

I am greatly indebted to the many people who offered their time and knowledge and helped to make this book a reality. Many thanks to the management and staff at the various agencies, attractions and other listings in this book for their valuable assistance and input. I am especially grateful to Dini Pickering, Diane LeBeau, Liz Calhoun, Barbara O'Neil, Elizabeth Sims, Marinda Williams and Kathleen Morris of Biltmore Estate; Charlie C. Lytle and Reginna Swimmer of Harrah's Cherokee Casino; Jennifer F. Martin, John H. Horton and Diane Jones of the North Carolina State Preservation Office; Harry Weiss of the Preservation Society of Asheville and Buncombe County; Melody Heltman and Gabby Snyder of the Hendersonville/Flat Rock Visitors Information Center; Angie Chandler, Helen Calloway, Bill Turner, and Angie Briggs of the Asheville Area Chamber of Commerce Visitor Center; Maggie O'Conner of the Historic Resources Commission; Stephen Hill, Susan Weatherford and Ted Mitchell of the Thomas Wolfe Memorial; Maggie Schlubach and David Tomsky of theOmni Grove Park Inn Resort; Rhonda Horton of the Woodfield Inn; Grace Pless, Sara Bissette, and all of the other dedicated volunteers of the Asheville Urban Trail; Susan Michel-Robertson of the Richmond Hill Inn; Gail Gomez of High Country Guild; Roann Bishop of the Historic Johnson Farm; Sherry Masters of the Grovewood Gallery; Cae Gibson of the Flat Rock Playhouse; Joey Moore of the Asheville Arts Alliance; Donna Garrison of the N.C. Department of Transportation; Dick Stanland of Historic Flat Rock Inc.; Weston Utter of the Western North Carolina Nature Center; Patricia R. Crisco and David W. Blynt of the Buncombe County Parks & Recreation Department; Roxanne J. Royer of Office Depot; Sondra McCrary of ARCO Blueprinters; Terry Clevenger of the Asheville Downtown Association; Lisa Smith and Gwen Chalker of the Asheville Convention and Visitors Bureau; Richard Mathews of the Albermarle Park Association; Jerry and Nancy Marstall of The Blue Book; Joan S. Baity of the Old Wilkes Jail Museum; Pam Herrington of The Cove; Mary Alice Murphy of Christmount; Laura Rathbone of Lake Junaluska Assembly; Jim Danielson of Ridgecrest; John Paul Thomas of YMCA Blue Ridge Assembly; Mike Small of UNCA; and Liz Gress of Lutheridge.

Other professionals to whom I am indebted include Lauren Abernathy, Connie Backlund, Harry Bothwell, Bill Bornstein, Irby Brinson, Katherine Caldwell, Wayne Caldwell, Lee Creech, Carol Donnelly, Cheryl Fowler, Jessica Gosnell, Leona Haney, Tom Hardy, Larry Harmon, Carl Hill, Hosey Horton, Dr. Jack Jones, Joy Jones, Elaine McPherson, Rev. Edward

Meeks, Judy and Neil Meyer, Mary Alice Nard, David Olson, Marvin Owings, David Ross, Norm Sanders, Dick Shahan, Chris Smith, David Tate and Barbara Turman.

A special thank you for their encouragement and advice to Annie Ager, Bill and Kathy Agrella, Rem and Isabel Behrer, Larry and Yolanda Bopp, Joe and Bobbi Costy, Greg and Carla Filapelli, Mike and Chris Grier, Mary Herold, Charlotte Harrell, Marge Kavanaugh, John and Agnes Laughter, Roddy Lee, Daniel Lewis, Marilyn and Dick Marino, Elizabeth McAfee, Jane McNeil, Tom and L.J. McPherson, Erich and Liz Pearson, Myra Ramsay, and Phil and Rene Thompson.

I am also grateful to Jim Curwen of the Asheville Track Club for his information about the Track Club and especially for the Kimberly Ave. run; to Mickie Booth, for her wonderful exposition on the Asheville Urban Trail; and to my assistant Kiki Cook for her encouragement and help.

I am thankful to Ralph Roberts, publisher of Alexander Books, for allowing me the opportunity to bring this book to print in the first and second editions, and to Barbara Blood, Gayle Graham, Susan Parker, Vanessa Razzano, Pat Roberts, and Vivian Terrell of Alexander Books for advice and assistance.

A special word of thanks to my mother-in-law, Hazel Nading, and to Art and Martha Nading, Vincent and Maryjean Pantas, Lynne and Bob Boie, and Louise Lea Nading.

I would also like to especially thank both Liza Schillo for her encouragement and review of theOmni Grove Park Inn Resort & Spa, and Robbin Brent Whittington, of R. Brent & Company, for her invaluable guidance and support in bringing the later editions to life. Many thanks also to my star high school hurdler and brilliant student Anu Frempong for her assistance in helping to edit the 2018 edition.

Finally I would like to thank my wife Elizabeth, my son Daniel, and my daughter Susanna for their patience, love, and support.

This book is dedicated in loving memory of my parents
Leo and Alberta Pantas

Icons, Abbreviations & Symbols Used in This Guide

NRHP	Listed in the National Register of Historic Places
NHL	National Historic Landmark
LHL	Local Historic Landmark
See	Sends you to another section of the guide for more information.

Restaurant Price Guide

$	Under $10
$$	$10-$20
$$$	$20-$30
$$$$	Over $30

The typical price for an evening meal for one person, excluding taxes, gratuity, and drinks.

Section I
Getting Acquainted

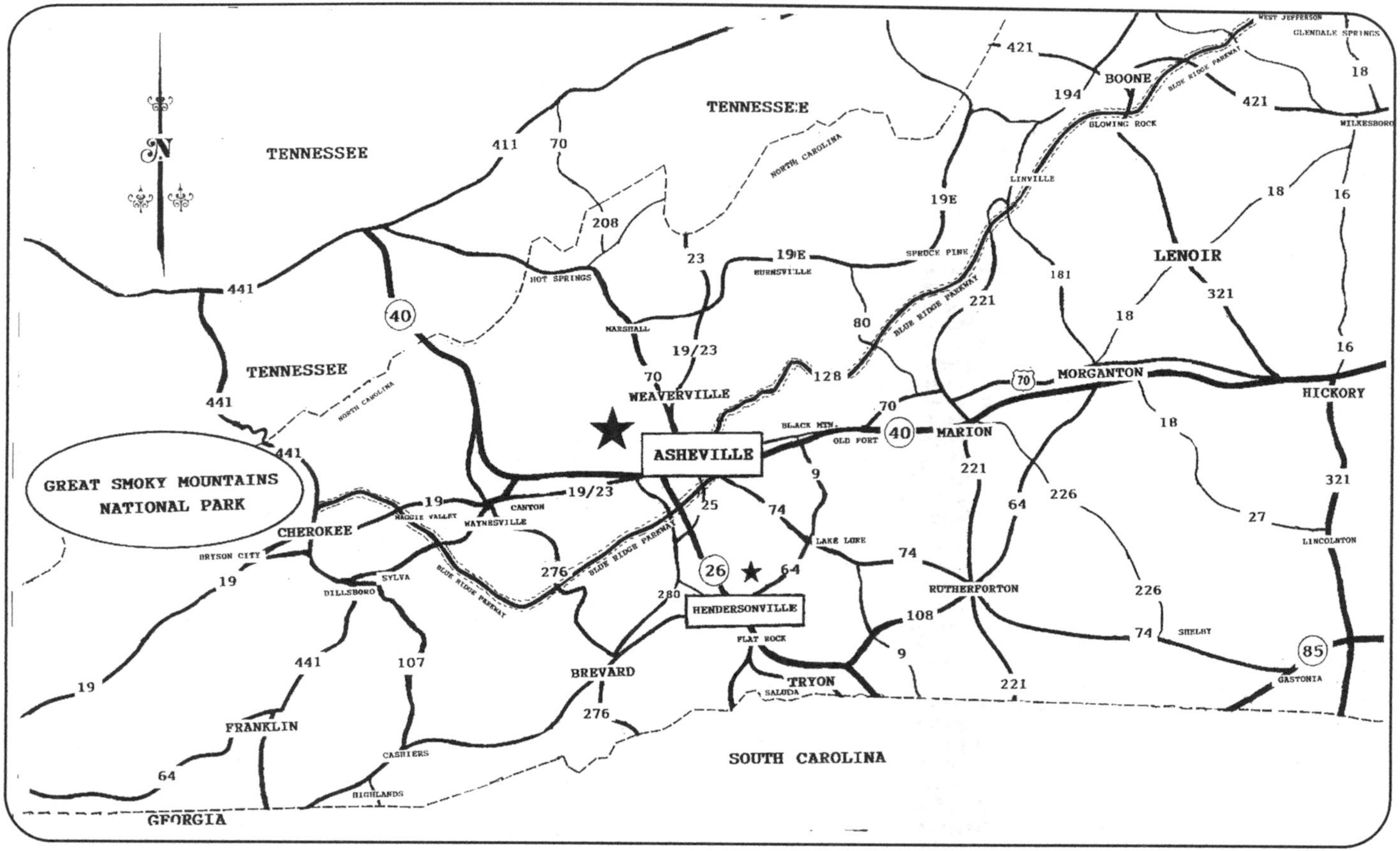

Western North Carolina

Chapter One
Getting Started

Once you arrive in Asheville, one of your first stops should be the visitor center on Montford Ave. (Exit 4C off of I-240 as it passes through downtown). There you will find friendly and informed staff eager to help, a complete array of brochures and tourist-oriented publications, and complimentary maps.

Western North Carolina Basics

Western North Carolina, the region of North Carolina that includes the Appalachian Mountains, is blessed with towering verdant mountains, lovely gentle valleys, flower-filled coves, virgin stands of untouched forest, crystal clear lakes and streams, and vibrant cities and towns. Asheville is the largest city (92,000+) and receives over 11,000,000 visitors each year. It is also home to the famous Biltmore Estate, America's largest private residence and the major tourist attraction in the mountains.

Tourism is the major industry in Western North Carolina, with millions of visitors flocking each year to the mountains for outdoor recreation. The area includes the Great Smoky Mountains National Park, the Nantahala National Forest, the Pisgah National Forest and numerous State Forests. Much of Western North Carolina is wilderness and offers an abundance of recreational opportunities from mountain climbing to whitewater rafting. Other major natural attractions include the Appalachian Scenic National Trail and the Blue Ridge Parkway, both of which pass right through the mountains.

The unique character of the Western North Carolina mountains is such that Congress has even designated them a National Heritage Area and they are now officially recognized as the Blue Ridge National Heritage Area. The 24 counties in Western North Carolina have a total population of over 1,000,000. Western North Carolina covers approximately 11,000 square miles, is roughly the size of the state of Massachusetts and is generally recognized as having four distinct regions: the western, central and northern mountains, and the foothills. In the three mountain regions there are over 80 mountain peaks between 5,000 to 6,000 feet in elevation, and 43 that rise to over 6,000 feet. Major cities are Asheville, Boone, Hendersonville and Waynesville. The foothills region, extending east from the mountains toward the North Carolina Piedmont, is characterized by rolling hills, with much lower elevations, typically between 1,000 and 1,500 feet. Major cities are Hickory, Lenoir and Morganton.

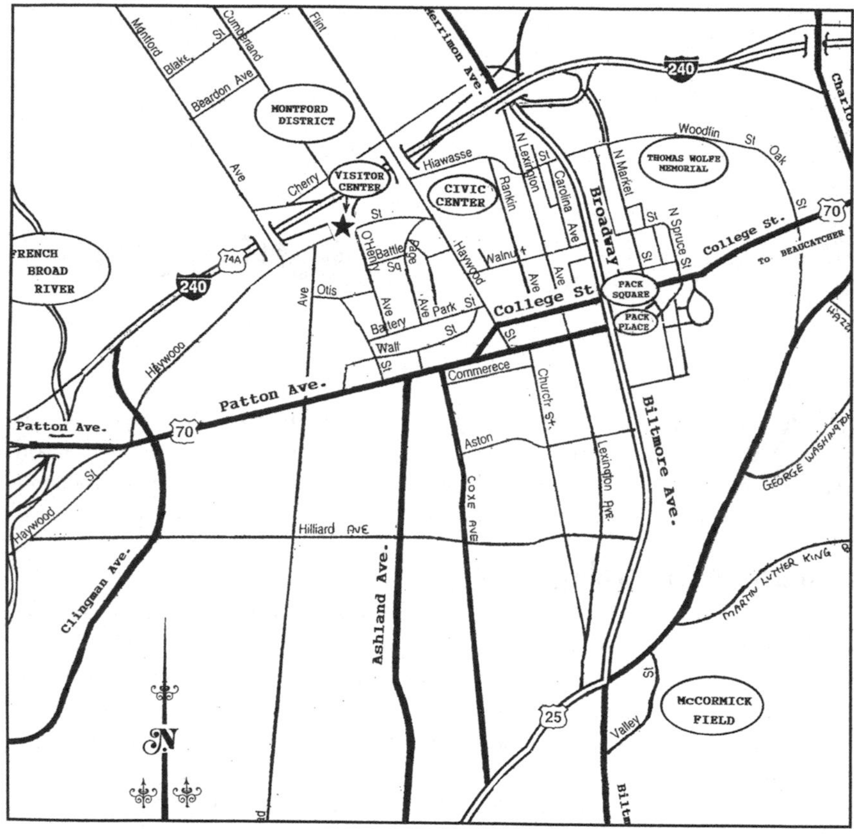

Downtown Asheville

Major Cities in the Mountains

Western North Carolina has seven major cities with populations over 10,000, with Asheville and Hickory the two largest. Some basic facts for these seven mountain cities are presented below. Please refer to the appropriate sections in the book for more detailed information about each city. Asheville, along with nearby Hendersonville, are the two mountain cities that receive the most visitors, and because of that fact, are given more coverage in this book than the other cities and towns. This includes additional and more detailed information about the history, architecture, and local attractions of each city, and listings of more accommodations and restaurants.

Asheville

Location: Central Mountains
Elevation and Population: 2,216 feet, 92,000+
City Hall: 70 Court Plaza, PO Box 7148, Asheville NC 28802; 828-251-1122
City Website: ashevillenc.gov

County: Buncombe County: County Offices, 205 College St., Asheville NC 28801; 828-250-4000; buncombecounty.org

Asheville Area Chamber of Commerce: 36 Montford Ave., Asheville NC 28801; 828-258-6101; ashevillechamber.org

Visitor Center: 36 Montford St., Asheville NC 28801; 800-257-1300; exploreasheville.com

Boone

Location: Northern Mountains, 2 hours northeast of Asheville

Elevation and Population: 3,500 feet, 20,000+

Town Offices: 567 West King St., Boone NC 28607; 828-268-6200

City Website: townofboone.net

City Chamber of Commerce: Boone Area Chamber of Commerce, 870 West King St., Boone NC 28607; 828-264-2225

County: Watauga County: County Offices, 842 West King St., Boone NC 28607; 828-265-8000

County Chamber of Commerce: Boone Area Chamber of Commerce: 208 Howard St., Boone NC 28607; 828-264-2225

Visitor/Welcome Center: 870 West King St., Boone NC 28607; 800-852-9506

Hendersonville

Location: Central Mountains, 30 minutes south of Asheville

Elevation and Population: 2,200 feet, 14,000+

City Hall: 145 5th Ave. East, Hendersonville NC 28792; 828-697-3000

City Website: cityofhendersonville.org

County: Henderson County: County Offices, 1 Historic Courthouse Square, Ste 2, Hendersonville NC 28792; 828-697-4809; hendersoncountync.org

Hendersonville Chamber of Commerce: 204 Kanuga St., Hendersonville NC 28739; 828-692-1413; hendersonvillechamber.org

Visitor Center: 201 South Main St., Hendersonville NC 28792; 800-828-4244; historichendersonville.org

Hendersonville Visitor Center

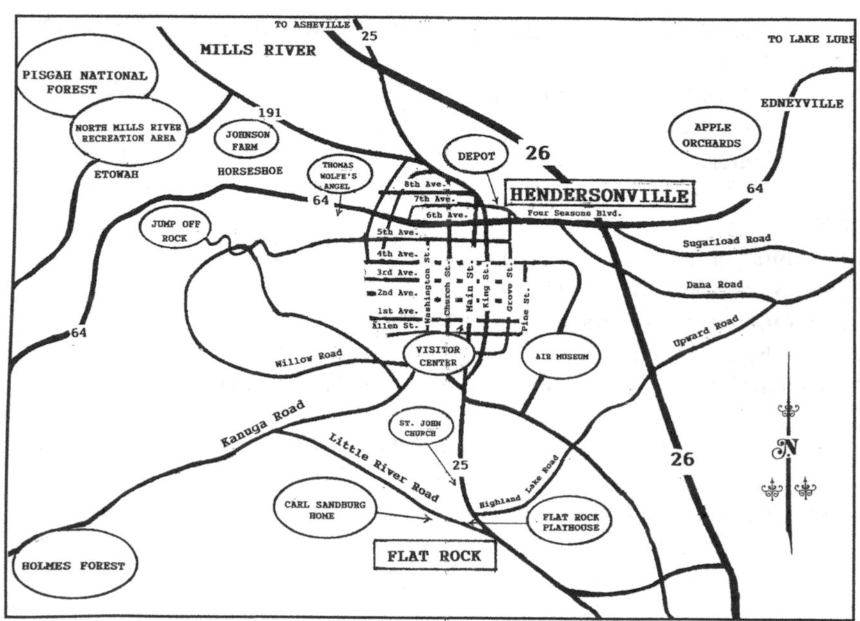

Hendersonville & Flat Rock

Hickory

Location: Foothills, 1 hour and 15 minutes east of Asheville

Elevation and Population: 910 feet, 40,000+

Town Hall: 76 North Center St., Hickory NC 28601; 828-323-7400

City Website: hickorygov.com

County: Catawba County: County Offices, 100-A Southwest Blvd., Newton NC 28658; 828-465-8201

County Chamber of Commerce: 1055 Southgate Corporate Park SW, Hickory NC 28602; 828-328-6111

City Visitor/Welcome Center: Hickory Metro Convention and Visitors Bureau, 1960-A 13th Ave. Dr. SE, Hickory NC 28602; 800-509-2444

County Visitor/Welcome Center: Catawba County Visitor Information Center, 1055 Southgate Corporate Park SW, Hickory NC 28602; 828-328-6111

Lenoir

Location: Foothills, 1.5 hours east of Asheville

Elevation and Population: 1,182 feet, 18,000+

Town Hall: 801 West Ave., Lenoir NC 28645; 828-757-2200

City Website: cityoflenoir.com

County: Caldwell County: County Offices, 905 West Ave. NW, Lenoir NC 28645, 828-757-1300

County Chamber of Commerce: Caldwell County Chamber of Commerce, 1909 Hickory Blvd. SE, Lenoir NC 28645; 828-726-0323

County Visitor/Welcome Center: Caldwell County Chamber of Commerce Visitor Center,1909 Hickory Blvd. SE, Lenoir NC 28645; 828-726-0323

Morganton

Location: Foothills, One hour east of Asheville
Elevation and Population: 1,182 feet, 17,000+
Town Offices: 305 East Union St., Ste A100, Morganton NC 28655; 828-437-8863
City Website: ci.morganton.nc.us
County: Burke County: Burke County Government Center, 200 Avery Ave., Morganton NC 28680; 828-439-4340
County Chamber of Commerce: Burke County Chamber of Commerce, 110 East Meeting St., Morganton NC 28655; 828-437-3021
County Visitor/Welcome Center: Burke County Visitor Center, 110 East Meeting St., Morganton NC 28655; 888-462-2921

Waynesville

Location: Central Mountains, 45 minutes west of Asheville
Elevation and Population: 3,600 feet, 10,000+
Municipal Building: 16 South Main St., Waynesville NC 28786; 828-452-2491
City Website: townofwaynesville.org
County Chamber of Commerce: Haywood County Chamber of Commerce, 28 Walnut St., Waynesville NC 28786; 828-456-3021
County Visitor/Welcome Center: Haywood County Tourism Development Authority Visitor Center, 44 North Main St., Waynesville NC 28786; 828-334-9036

Climate

The mountains surrounding Asheville and Hendersonville serve as a moderating influence from extreme conditions. Major snow storms are rare and annual precipitation is around 50 inches and average annual snowfall is about 15 inches. The mountains serve to keep the area cool during the summer months, and with their higher elevations are usually 10 to 15 degrees cooler than the lowlands of the Carolinas and Georgia. The northern mountains, including the major city of Boone, are at higher elevations and receive more annual snowfall, with slightly cooler year-round temperatures.

Spring in the Appalachians is a wondrous time, with mild days and nights. Wildflowers are blooming in abundance and all chance of snow has virtually disappeared by April. Summer brings more humidity and heat, although nothing like what the lowlands experience. Late afternoon thunderstorms are common and Aug. usually brings a few weeks when it is hot enough for air conditioning. Temperatures can reach over 90 degrees in Asheville and Hendersonville. Such extremes are rare, however, at elevations over 4,000 feet. Winter doesn't make its presence shown until after Christmas, and Jan. and Feb. can be very cold with temperatures dipping down below 20 degrees occasionally. Light snows and ice storms occur frequently, although the snow rarely stays on the ground for more than a few days. Big snowfalls can occur. The Blizzard of 1993 dumped three feet of snow on the ground in less than 24 hours!

Autumn Glory

One of the most beautiful seasons in the mountains is autumn, when the colorful display of fall foliage spreads throughout the area. The peaks and valleys take on deep shades of crimson, brilliant orange, translucent yellow and earth brown every fall during Sep. and Oct. Every year millions of visitors return to the mountains to admire this natural pageant of beauty, and one of the most popular touring routes is the Blue Ridge Parkway with its unbroken vistas and towering mountain peaks.

The fall foliage display usually reaches its height in Oct., but the intensity of color and peak for each area is also determined by elevation. The higher elevations come into color first, followed by the lower ranges. Views from the Parkway can show you various stages of this transformation, with full color above you on the higher peaks and lush green in the valleys far below. If you do plan to visit the mountains during the leaf season, make sure your book your accommodations well in advance.

Chapter Two
Asheville in Two Days

Asheville has such a wealth of attractions and things to see and do that it can be a bit overwhelming in planning your visit. Most people only have a few days, and that narrow time frame only makes choices all the more difficult. If you only have a short time for your visit, here are some recommendations of things to see and do that should be on your list. I have tried to include on this list those attractions and things to do that are unique to Asheville. They are all personal favorites of mine as well!

First and foremost, plan a visit to Biltmore Estate (*See* Section III, Chapter Two). A national treasure, Biltmore House is the largest privately owned residence in America and is the most popular cultural attraction in the mountains. Allow at least 4 to 6 hours minimum to see the house, grounds and related buildings. Also on any list of "must-see" Asheville attractions is the historic Omni Grove Park Inn (*See* Section III, Chapter Five), located on a mountainside overlooking Asheville. Plan to have either lunch or dinner at the hotel. The food is superb and the ambiance even better. My recommendation is the Sunset Terrace with its great views, especially if the weather is good.

For those interested in American literature, my number one choice is the Thomas Wolfe Memorial (*See* Section III, Chapter Two), the childhood home of Asheville author Thomas Wolfe. Conveniently located downtown, it is a state-run historic site and offers a fascinating glimpse into the life of one of America's most famous authors. An alternative choice, and a must if you like arts and crafts is the famous Folk Art Center of the Southern Highland Craft Guild (*See* Section III, Chapter Two) conveniently located inside Asheville city limits at mile marker 382 on the Blue Ridge Parkway. Here you can see and purchase authentic Appalachian crafts. Asheville is noted for its arts and crafts culture, and two commercial craft galleries also of special note are New Morning Gallery in Biltmore Village, and the Grovewood Gallery located near the Omni Grove Park Inn.

If shopping is of interest to you, my top recommendation is to visit Biltmore Village, located near the entrance to Biltmore Estate. Established by George Vanderbilt as a village for his workers while his house was being built, Biltmore Village is full of unique and special shops housed in restored turn of the century houses. It's a fascinating and charming shopping venue! (For more information *See* Section III, Chapter Two). Another great place to shop is the revitalized Lexington St. area located downtown. This section of town boasts a wonderful eclectic array of privately owned shops and restaurants. Here you will find everything from French cuisine to funky art galleries and card shops.

Providing the weather is good, my number one choice for an experience of the vastness and beauty of the mountains is to take a drive on the Blue Ridge Parkway (*See* Section V, Chapter One). You can access the parkway at a number of points as it passes through Asheville. Plan to take at least a half a day and head out first north on the parkway to the Parkway Destination Center at mile-marker 384, just two miles from the Folk Art Center. Here you will get a great overview of the parkway and can further plan your outing. If you decide to go south on the parkway, plan to have lunch or dinner at the historic Pisgah Inn, located at mile marker 408. Going north plan to make Mount Mitchell at mile marker 355 your final destination for lunch or dinner.

Last but not least, the North Carolina Arboretum and the Western North Carolina Nature Center are two great choices for anyone who loves nature. The 426-acre Arboretum, located on the west side of Asheville, is an inter-institutional facility of the University of North Carolina and has wonderful varied gardens, walking trails and natural habitats. The Nature Center, located on the east side and only minutes from downtown, is one of my top recommended attractions in the Asheville area for both kids and grownups alike. *See* Section III, Chapter Two for more information about both of these outstanding attractions.

Chapter Three

Getting Around Asheville

Asheville is located at the junction of Interstates 26 and 40, with an I-240 connector that passes through the downtown district. Hendersonville is located to the south of Asheville off Interstate 26. The Blue Ridge Parkway also passes through the Asheville area with a number of accesses. The major airport is located in Asheville, but many people also choose to fly into the Greenville SC and Charlotte NC airports as well. Asheville is only a two hour drive from either of these cities. There is no railroad passenger service to Asheville.

Airlines

Asheville Regional Airport: 828-684-2226, flyavl.com. The main gateway to the area is the Asheville Regional Airport, 15 miles south of downtown Asheville on I-26. This airport is serviced daily by major carriers with connections to all major cities. The airport has an 8,000-foot runway and modern navigational aids, including a wind shear detection system.

Hendersonville Airport: 828-693-1897, 1232 Shepherd St., Hendersonville NC 28792. Nearby Hendersonville also has a small airport that serves the Hendersonville area, has a 3,200-foot lighted runway, and provides charter service to larger airports.

Bus Travel

Asheville Transit: City bus service, located at 49 Coxe Ave., Asheville NC 28801, Bus service for Asheville. 828-253-5691

Greyhound Bus Lines: Located at 2 Tunnel Rd., Asheville NC 28805, Passenger service. 828-253-8451, 800-231-2222.

Young Transportation: Located at 843 Riverside Dr., Asheville NC 28804, Passenger service and charters. 828-258-0084 or 800-622-5444

Emma Bus Lines Inc.: 1 Stoner Rd., Asheville NC 28803, Charter bus service. 828-274-5719

Limousines

Asheville Limousine: 828-268-3722
Asheville Limo Service: 828-475-8890
Blue Ridge Limousine: 828-232-4046

Taxi Service

Asheville Taxi Company: 828-333-1976
J&J Cab: 828-253-3311
Pegasus Airport Taxi Service: 828-281-4400

Chapter Four

Helpful Information for Asheville & Hendersonville

Bookstores

Asheville:

Barnes and Noble: America's most popular and successful bookseller. Two locations in Asheville: 83 S. Tunnel Rd., Asheville Mall, Asheville NC 28805, 828-296-7335, and 33 Town Square Blvd., Ste 100, Biltmore Park, Asheville NC 28803; 828-687-0681.

Battery Park Book Exchange Champagne Bar: A unique used bookstore and wine bar in the heart of Asheville, across from the Grove Arcade. Peruse thousands of books in dozens of categories while sipping a fine wine, sparkling wine, or champagne. 1 Page Ave., Ste 101, Asheville NC 28801; 828-252-0020.

Downtown Books and News: In business for over 25 years; specializes in used and rare books. Thousands of different genres to choose from with inventory changes every week. They also offer a large selection of micro-published magazines from local and international writers. 67 N. Lexington Ave., Asheville NC 28801; 828-253-8654.

Malaprop's Bookstore and Café: A booklover's paradise, famous locally as well as nationally! An Asheville Institution since 1982. Great books, great food, great coffee. Author readings and community events nearly every night throughout the year. Malaprop's offers a wide variety of coffees and teas as well as baked goods and bagels from local bakeries. 55 Haywood St., Asheville NC 28801, 828-254-6734.

The Captain's Bookshelf: Quality antiquarian bookseller with a deep selection. Also located near the Grove Arcade. 31 Page Ave., Asheville NC 28801; 828-253-6631.

Hendersonville:

Joy of Books: New and used books. Joy of Books is an independent used book seller that sells all types of used book from best-sellers to the classics. They have a small selection of new books that feature local authors and interests, such as waterfalls, hiking, biking, and everything western North Carolina has to offer. They also have an expanded children's section which sells like-new young adult and children's books. 242 Main St., Hendersonville NC 28792; 828-551-7321.

Colleges & Schools

Colleges:

Asheville-Buncombe Technical Community College: 340 Victoria Rd., Asheville NC 28801; 828-398-7900.

Blue Ridge Community College: 180 West Campus Dr., Flat Rock NC 28731; 828-694-1700.

Mars Hill College: 100 Athletic St., Mars Hill NC 28754; 828-689-1307.

South College: 140 Sweeten Creek Rd., Asheville NC 28803; 828-398-2500.

University of North Carolina at Asheville (UNCA): One University Heights, Asheville NC 28804; 828-251-6600.

Warren Wilson College: 701 Warren Wilson Rd., Swannanoa NC 28778; 828-298-3325.

Western Carolina University: 28 Schenck Pkwy, Ste 300, Biltmore Park, Asheville NC 28803; 828-654-6498.

Public Schools:

Asheville City Schools: 828-350-7000, ashevillecityschools.net

Buncombe County Schools: 828-255-5921, buncombe.k12.nc.us

Henderson County Schools: 828-697-4733, henderson.k12.nc.us

Emergency Numbers

Fire, Police and Ambulance: 911

Asheville Police Department Information Center: 828-259-9039

Buncombe County Sheriff's Department: (non-emergency): 828-255-5555

Hendersonville Police Department General Business: 828-697-3025

North Carolina State Hwy. Patrol: 828-298-4253

Hospitals

Buncombe County:

Mission Hospital: 428 and 509 Biltmore Ave., Asheville NC 28801; 828-213-1111.

CarePartners Rehabilitation Hospital: 68 Sweeten Creek Rd., Asheville NC 28803; 828-277-4800.

Park Ridge Hospital: 100 Hospital Dr., Hendersonville NC 28792; 828-684-8501.

V.A. Medical Center in Asheville: Asheville; 1100 Tunnel Rd., Asheville NC 28805; 828-298-7911.

Sisters of Mercy Urgent Care Centers:

Urgent Care South: 1833 Hendersonville Rd., Asheville NC 28803; 828-274-1462.

Urgent Care West: 1201 Patton Ave., Asheville NC 28806; 828-252-4878.

Urgent Care North: 155 Weaver Boulevard, Weaverville NC 28787; 828-645-5088.

Urgent Care Airport: 77 Airport Rd., Arden NC 28704; 828-651-0098.

Henderson County:

Pardee Hospital: 800 North Justice St., Hendersonville NC 28791; 828-696-1000.

Park Ridge Hospital: 100 Hospital Dr., Hendersonville NC 28792; 828-684-8501.

Health and Fitness

Listed below are some of the major health and fitness centers in Asheville and Hendersonville. For a complete list of all centers and spas, visit ashevilleguidebook.com .

Asheville YMCA: 30 Woodfin St., Asheville NC 28801; 828-210-9622; Reuter Family YMCA, 3 Town Square Blvd, Biltmore Park, Asheville NC 28803; 828-651-9622. Woodfin YMCA, 40 N. Merrimon Ave., Ste 101, Asheville NC 28804; 828-505-3990; Fletcher YMCA, 3700 Hendersonville Rd., Fletcher NC 28732; 828-651-9622.

Gold's Gym: 801 Fairview Road, Asheville NC 28803, 828-239-9556; 1046 Patton Avenue, Asheville NC 28806; 828-398-1430; 1815 Hendersonville Rd, Asheville, NC 28803, 828-398-1193.

YWCA of Asheville: 185 South French Broad Ave., Asheville NC 28801; 828-254-7206.

Libraries

Asheville/Buncombe Library System: The main library, Pack Memorial, is located next to the Civic Center downtown. 67 Haywood St., Asheville NC 28801; 828-250-4700; Hours: Mon–Wed: 9:30am–8pm; Thu and Fri: 9:30am–6pm; Sat: 9:30am–5pm.

The Henderson County Public Library: 301 N. Washington St. Hendersonville NC 28739; 828-697-4725. Hours: Mon–Thu: 9am–8pm, Fri–Sat: 9am–5pm.

Movie Theaters

Asheville and Hendersonville have a large number of movie theatres, and your best resources for current movies and reviews is the weekly free publication, the *Mountain*. Both the Hendersonville and Asheville newspapers have daily movie listings as well.

Mountain Xpress: A free weekly independent news, arts, and events newspaper for Western North Carolina. Excellent entertainment coverage, local commentary. Pick up a copy from numerous sidewalk boxes located around Asheville. PO Box 144, Asheville NC 28802; 828-251-1333.

Newspapers & Magazines

Asheville Citizen-Times: The region's largest circulation daily newspaper. 14 OHenry Ave., Asheville NC 28801; 828-252-5610, 800-800-4204. citizen-times.com.

Hendersonville Times-News: Hendersonville's daily newspaper. 106 Henderson Crossing Plaza, Hendersonville NC 28792; 828-692-0505. blueridgenow.com.

Mountain Xpress: A free weekly independent news, arts, and events newspaper for Western North Carolina, with the focus on Asheville. Excellent entertainment coverage, local commentary. PO Box 144, Asheville NC 28802; 828-251-1333. mountainx.com.

Chapter Five

Making the Move to the Mountains

If you are considering a move to the mountains, the following lists should prove to be helpful in your planning. Real estate companies are listed for each city on my guidebook website city pages at ashevilleguidebook.com.

Real Estate Resources

Asheville Board of Realtors: 37 Montford Ave., Asheville NC 28801; 828-255-8505, 800-392-2775.

Asheville Home Builders Association: 14 Mimidis Lane, Rte. 70, Swannanoa NC 28778; 828-299-7001.

Chapter Six

Environmental Issues in Western North Carolina

Paradise is not without its problems, and even though it would seem at first glance that there are really no environmental concerns in the beautiful mountains of Western North Carolina, there are a couple of issues that have just about everyone who lives here worried. Top on the list is an air quality problem that occurs primarily in the summer. On certain days, even the most remote mountains and valleys, especially in the Great Smoky Mountains, have smog that rivals even Los Angeles and other urban centers. The primary culprits are the coal-fired power plants in the Midwest, which spew nitrous oxides and sulfur dioxides into the atmosphere, which are then carried by the prevailing west to east air currents and deposited in our area. A battle to stop this pollution is being fought on a national level, with North Carolina legislators (and those of adjoining states that are similarly affected) in the forefront of the war. Acid rain which harms higher altitude forests is another problem clearly related to this air pollution problem. Of concern also is the increasing number of mountain developments and the consequent loss of habitat.

Western North Carolina Environmental Organizations

Asheville GreenWorks: An affiliate of Keep America Beautiful, is a volunteer-based organization working to achieve a clean and green Asheville and Buncombe County through community organizing, educating and environmental stewardship. Asheville GreenWorks seeks to enhance the environment and quality of life for citizens in Asheville and Buncombe County through community based projects. 357 Depot Street, Asheville NC 28801, 828-254-1776.

Canary Coalition: A non-profit organization dedicated to restoring clean air in Western North Carolina and the southern Appalachian Region. PO Box 653, Sylva NC 287790; 828-631-3447; canarycoalition.org.

Conserving Carolina: Formed by the consolidation of two sister organizations, Carolina Mountain Land Conservancy and Pacolet Area Conservancy. is a non-profit, voluntary organization that works directly to protect the natural diversity and beauty of Western North Carolina by preserving natural lands and scenic areas. They help families meet their conservation and financial goals while preserving their lands for future generations and they provide communities and individuals with a range of conservation tools and tax-saving techniques. Conserving Carolina also fosters a greater understanding and appreciation of our natural heritage. 847 Case Street, Hendersonville, NC 28792; Southeast Office: 2060 Lynn Road, Suite 1, Columbus, NC 28722; 828-697-5777.

Clean Water for North Carolina (CWFNC): formerly the Clean Water Fund of North Carolina) has worked for clean, safe communities and workplaces with hundreds of communities and thousands of North Carolinians. CWFNC is a private non-profit membership organization serving residents across the state of North Carolina. 29 1/2 Page Avenue, Asheville, NC 28801; 828-251-1219

Cradle of Forestry: The Cradle of Forestry in America is a 6,500 acre Historic Site within the Pisgah National Forest, set aside by Congress to commemorate the beginning of forestry conservation in the United States. 828-877-3130, cradleofforestry.com.

Liza's Reef: An art- and science-based resource portal website dedicated to the protection and conservation of coral reefs, other oceanic environments and rain forests. Liza's Reef is also involved in supporting local WNC environmental organizations in their efforts to protect the Western North Carolina mountains. This is also the art and environmental project of Lee Pantas, author of this guidebook. 828-779-1569.

Long Branch Environmental Education Center: The Long Branch Environmental Education Center, Inc. is a small educational institute in Buncombe County's Newfound Mountains, about 18 miles northwest of Asheville, North Carolina. PO Box 369 Leicester NC 28748; 828-683-3662, longbrancheec.org.

North Carolina Interfaith Power and Light: NC IPL works with faith communities to address the causes and consequences of global climate change, and promote practical solutions, through education, outreach, and public policy advocacy. 919-828-6501, ncipl.org

RiverLink: A regional nonprofit spearheading the economic and environmental revitalization of the French Broad River and its tributaries as a place to work, live and play. RiverLink was born in 1987 of simultaneous efforts to address water quality concerns throughout the French Broad River basin, expand public opportunities for access and recreation, and spearhead the economic revitalization of Asheville's dilapidated riverfront district. As expressed in their mission statement, they focus on related issues that directly impact the environmental health of our region's rivers and streams and the growth and sustainability of our economy. 70 Woodfin Place, Asheville, 828-225-0760.

Southern Alliance for Clean Energy: SACE is a nonprofit, nonpartisan organization that promotes responsible energy choices that solve global warming problems and ensure clean, safe, and healthy communities throughout the Southeast. 828-254-6776, cleanenergy.org.

Southern Appalachian Biodiversity Project: SABP's goal is permanent protection for the region's public lands and sustainable management of private lands. Battery Park Ave., Asheville NC 28801; 828-258-2667, sabp.net.

Sustainable Asheville Area Network: The Sustainable Asheville Area Network is comprised of organizations and individuals in the greater Asheville area concerned with sustainability and the environment. sustainableasheville.org.

The Southern Appalachian Highlands Conservancy: Founded in 1974 as a nonprofit charitable organization, the SAHC's mission is to conserve unique plant and animal habitats, clean water, and scenic beauty of the mountains of North Carolina and Tennessee for the benefit of present and future generations. The Conservancy works with individuals and local communities to identify, preserve, and manage the region's important lands. It has helped ensure the protection of more than 21,000 acres throughout the mountain region. 34 Wall St., Suite 802, Asheville, 828-253-0095.

Western North Carolina Alliance: The Western North Carolina Alliance is a grassroots organization that aims to promote a sense of stewardship and caring for the natural environment. 29 N. Market St., Asheville NC 28801; 828-258-8737, wnca.org.

Western North Carolina Green Building Council: WNCGBC is a nonprofit organization whose mission is to promote environmentally sustainable and health-conscious building practices through community education. PO Box 17026, Asheville NC 28816; 828-254-1995, wncgbc.org.

Western North Carolina Nature Center: The Western North Carolina Nature Center is the premier nature center in Western North Carolina.75 Gashes Creek Rd., Asheville NC 28805; 828-298-5600, wildwnc.org.

Section II
The Best of Asheville & Hendersonville

Chapter One

Author's Choice Accommodations

Both Asheville and Hendersonville have a wide variety and number of accommodations, from world-class resort hotels, exotic bed & breakfasts to budget motels. In this section I have presented only the best that our area has to offer in each category. For a complete listing of all the hundreds of Asheville & Hendersonville accommodations by category, visit my guidebook website at ashevilleguidebook.com .

The season of the year has a lot to do with accommodation availability. Summer and the fall leaf season in Oct. are by far the most crowded and busiest times of the year. Also, the weekend around Bele Chere Festival, the Oct. leaf season, and Christmas and New Year's weekends are all high-volume times. Accommodations for these weekends can be hard to find if not booked in advance.

NRHP = Listed on the National Register of Historic Places

Asheville Grand Hotels, Inns & Lodges

AC Hotel Asheville Downtown: Located just a block from Pack Square, this Marriott European and locally inspired design luxury hotel has a restaurant and bar on the 9th floor. Many rooms with sunset views of the mountains. 10 Broadway Street, Asheville NC 28801; 828-258-2522

Aloft Asheville Downtown: Conveniently located in the heart of downtown within short walking distance to restaurants, art galleries and music venues. 51 Biltmore Avenue, Asheville NC 28801; 828-232-2838

Crown Plaza Resort Asheville: Located one mile from downtown on the west side of Asheville, this 274-room, full-service resort offers oversized rooms with Sleep Advantage Deluxe bedding and 30 vacation villas on site. 9-hole golf course, and indoor and outdoor tennis. One Resort Dr., Asheville NC 28806; 800-733-3211, 828-254-3211. crownplaza.com.

Grand Bohemian Hotel Asheville: Located in Biltmore Village opposite the entrance to Biltmore Estate, the Grand Bohemian Hotel has 104 luxurious guestrooms and suites in an atmosphere of gracious, Tudor-inspired style, reminiscent of the grand elegance of the Old World. 11 Boston Way, Asheville NC 28803; 828-505-2949, 877-274-1242 bohemianhotelasheville.com.

The Omni Grove Park Inn (NRHP): Superlative world-class resort hotel owned by Omni Resorts and Hotels. Four-diamond and many other awards. More than 500 rooms, sports center, indoor and outdoor pools, and 18-hole championship golf course. The hotel's world-famous 43,000 sq. ft. subterranean spa is one of the finest in the world and features lush gardens, waterfalls, and a wide range of treatments. 290 Macon Ave., Asheville NC 28804; 800-438-5800 or 828-252-2711. omnigroveparkinn.com.

Haywood Park Hotel & Atrium (NRHP): Four-diamond hotel in the heart of downtown. 33 rooms, all suites, Jacuzzis. Continental breakfast delivered to suite daily. One Battery Park Ave., Asheville NC 28801; 800–228–2522, 828–252-2522.. haywoodpark.com.

Hilton Garden Inn Asheville Downtown: From the brick and glass exterior to the scenic rooftop bar, pressed tin ceiling tiles in the lobby and the rustic vintage design, the Hilton Garden Inn, a pet-friendly hotel, showcases the uniqueness of Asheville. Amenities offered including a modern fitness center, outdoor pool and 24-hour business center. Convenient walking distance to central Pack Square. 309 College St., Asheville, NC 28801; 828-255-0001.

Hotel Indigo Asheville Downtown: Hotel Indigo is a 100-room boutique hotel located in the heart of downtown Asheville, one block from Grove Arcade. The hotel includes a bar and restaurant, off-St. parking and spectacular views. 151 Haywood St., Asheville NC 28801. 828-239-0239. ihg.com/hotelindigo.com.

Hyatt Place Asheville/Downtown: Located within walking distance to more than 200 restaurants, shopping, entertainment venues and all things eclectically Asheville. 199 Haywood Street, Asheville NC 28801: 828-505-8500

Kimpton Hotel Arras: A former bank, this Art Deco inspired boutique hotel is located right on Pack Square in the heart of downtown. 7 Patton Avenue, Asheville NC 28801; 833-221-9044

The Inn on Biltmore Estate: A truly world class deluxe inn with over 200 rooms located on Biltmore Estate grounds, near the Biltmore Estate Winery. Spectacular mountain vistas from porches, balconies, and guest rooms. Guest rooms ranging from deluxe to suites as well as on site dining for breakfast, lunch, and dinner. Four-star rating by both Mobil Travel Guide, Forbes and AAA. One Antler Ridge Rd., Asheville NC 28801; 800-624-1575, 828-225-1600. biltmore.com.

Princess Anne Hotel: (NRHP): Sophistication and grace describe this little gem of a historic hotel. The lovingly restored Princess Anne is characterized by its timeless, classic 1920s appeal with modern luxury and conveniences. The hotel still retains its original ambience and charm. 301 E. Chestnut St., Asheville NC 28801; 866-552-0986, 828-258-0986. princessannehotel.com.

Renaissance Asheville Hotel: Downtown next to Thomas Wolfe Memorial. 281 mountain-view rooms within walking distance everything downtown. Superb dining options, concierge service, 60' indoor pool, whirlpool, and fitness center. 31 Woodfin St., Asheville NC 28801; 800-333-3333, 828-252-8211. marriott.com.

The Foundry Hotel: A restored steel factory, The Foundry Hotel offers a unique, seamless blend of industrial history, local culture, and warm hospitality.51 S Market St, Asheville, NC 28801; 828-552-8545

Village Hotel on Biltmore Estate: An Estate hotel, this casual stay hotel is conveniently located in Antler village on the estate, only a stroll away from outdoor activities, the Winery, shopping and a number of distinctive restaurants. 207 Dairy Rd, Asheville, NC 28803; 866- 336-1245.

Asheville Motels

Airport Area (South of downtown)

Clarion Inn Asheville Airport: 550 New Airport Rd., Fletcher NC 28732; 828-684-1213, 800-465-4329.

Comfort Inn Asheville Airport: 15 Rockwood Rd., Arden NC 28704; 828-687-9199, 800-228-5150.

Econo Lodge Asheville Airport: 196 Underwood Rd., Fletcher NC 28732; 828-684-1200, 800-553-2666.

Fairfield Inn & Suites by Marriott Asheville Airport: 155 Underwood Rd, Fletcher, NC 28732; 828-684-1144

Hampton Inn and Suites I-26: 18 Rockwood Rd., Fletcher NC 28732; 828-687-0806, 800-426-7866.

Holiday Inn & Suites Arden – Asheville Airport: 9 Brian Boulevard, Arden, NC 28704; 828-684-6000

Home2 Suites by Hilton Asheville Airport: 390 New Airport Rd, Arden, NC 28704; 800-445-8667

Asheville Outlet Mall Area (West of downtown)

Comfort Inn Biltmore West: 15 Crowell Rd., Asheville NC 28806; 828-665-6500, 800-228-5150.

Comfort Suites Outlet Center: 890 Brevard Rd., Asheville NC 28806; 828-665-4000, 800-622-4005

Country Inn & Suites by Radisson, Asheville at Asheville Outlet Mall: 845 Brevard Rd., Asheville, NC 28806; 828-670-9000, 800- 456-4000.

Fairfield Inn & Suites by Marriott Asheville Outlets: 11 Rocky Ridge Rd., Asheville NC 28806; 828-665-4242.

Hampton Inn & Suites Asheville Biltmore Area: 835 Brevard Rd., Asheville, NC 28806; 828-575-9593

Hilton Garden Inn Asheville South: 9 Rocky Ridge Rd., Asheville NC 28806: 828-633-6024

Holiday Inn Express & Suites Asheville SW: 12 Rocky Ridge Rd, Asheville, NC 28806; 828-665-6519

Rodeway Inn & Suites Near Outlet Mall Asheville: 9 Wedgewood Dr., Asheville NC 28806; 828-670-8800, 877-354-8800.

Biltmore Park (Southwest of Asheville)

Hilton Asheville Biltmore Park: Located in the heart of Biltmore Park Town Square with a lively shopping, dining, and entertainment scene just steps from the hotel.

Complimentary shuttle service to and from Asheville Regional Airport, located three miles away. This LEED Silver Certified, AAA Four Diamond hotel offers easy access to Interstate 26, Blue Ridge Parkway, and Downtown Asheville. 43 Town Square Blvd., Asheville NC 28803; 828-209-2700. hilton.com.

Biltmore Village Area (Closest to Biltmore Estate)

Baymont by Wyndham Asheville/Biltmore Village: 204 Hendersonville Rd., Asheville NC 28803; 828-274-2022, 800-301-0200.

Brookstone Lodge: 4 Roberts Rd., Asheville NC 28803; 828-398-5888.

Courtyard by Marriott Asheville Biltmore Village: 26 Meadow Road, Asheville NC 28803; 828-782-5000

DoubleTree by Hilton Hotel Asheville - Biltmore: 115 Hendersonville Rd., Asheville NC 28803; 828-274-1800.

Hampton Inn & Suites Asheville -Biltmore Village Area: 117 Hendersonville Road, Asheville, North Carolina, 28803; 828-277-1800

Holiday Inn & Suites Asheville-Biltmore Village Area: 186 Hendersonville Rd, Asheville, NC 28803; 828-277-0026

Home2 Suites by Hilton Asheville Biltmore Village: 61 Thompson St, Asheville, NC 28803; 828-348-1560

Residence Inn by Marriott Asheville Biltmore: 701 Biltmore Ave., Asheville NC 28803; 828-281-3361, 800-331-3131.

Downtown Asheville

Four Points by Sheraton Asheville Downtown: 22 Woodfin St., Asheville NC 28801; 888-854-6897, 828-253-1851.

Cambria Hotel Downtown Asheville: 15 Page Avenue, Asheville, NC, 28801, 623-432-0198.

Country Inn & Suites by Radisson, Asheville Westgate: 22 Westgate Parkway, Asheville NC 28806, 828-772-3188

Element Asheville Downtown: 62 College Place, Asheville, North Carolina 28801; 828-575-5881

The Residences at Biltmore: 700 Biltmore Avenue, Asheville NC 28803, 828-350-8000, 866-433-5594.

East of Downtown

Comfort Inn Tunnel Road East: 1435 Tunnel Rd., Asheville NC 28805; 828-298-4000, 866-949-9914.

Holiday Inn Asheville East: 1450 Tunnel Rd., Asheville NC 28805; 828-298-5611.

Quality Inn and Suites-Biltmore East: 1430 Tunnel Rd., Asheville NC 28805; 828-298-5519, 877-299-5519.

Super 8 by Wyndham Asheville/Biltmore: 1415 Tunnel Rd., Asheville NC 28805, 828- 774-5420

Tru by Hilton Asheville East: 1500 Tunnel Road, Asheville, NC 28805; 828-417-9700

North of Downtown

Days Inn by Wyndham Asheville Downtown North: 3 Reynolds Mountain Blvd., Asheville NC 28804; 828-645-9191; 800-329-7666.

Asheville Mall Tunnel Road Area

Ramada by Wyndham Asheville Southeast: 148 River Ford Pkwy., Asheville NC 28805; 800-836-6732, 828-298-9141.

Candlewood Suites-Innsbruck Hotel: 49 Tunnel Road, Asheville NC 28805: 877-226-3539

Country Inn & Suites by Radisson, Asheville Downtown Tunnel Road: 199 Tunnel Rd., Asheville NC 28805; 828-254-4311, 800-456-4000.

Courtyard by Marriott: 1 Buckstone Place, Asheville NC 28805; 800-321-2211, 828-281-0041.

Days Inn by Wyndham Asheville/Mall: 201 Tunnel Rd., Asheville NC 28805; 828-252-4000; 800-329-7466.

Econo Lodge Biltmore: 190 Tunnel Rd., Asheville NC 28805, 828-254-9521; 800-553-2666.

Extended Stay America Asheville: 6 Kenilworth Knolls, Asheville NC 28805; 828-253-3483, 800-398-7829.

Glo Best Western Asheville Tunnel Road: 501 Tunnel Rd., Asheville NC 28805; 828-298-5562, 888-230–1228.

Hampton Inn Asheville-Tunnel Rd.: 204 Tunnel Rd., Asheville NC 28805; 828-255-9220; 800-426-7866.

Holiday Inn Express & Suites Asheville Downtown: 42 Tunnel Rd., Asheville NC 28805; 828-225-5550, 800-465-4329.

Homewood Suites by Hilton Asheville -Tunnel Road: 88 Tunnel Rd., Asheville NC 28805; 800-225-5466, 828-252-5400.

Springhill Suites by Marriott-Asheville: 2 Buckstone Place, Asheville NC 28805; 828-253-4666, 888-287-9400.

West of Downtown

Country Inn & Suites by Radisson, Asheville West: 1914 Old Haywood Rd., Asheville NC 28806; 828-665-9556.

Country Inn & Suites by Radisson, Asheville Westgate: 22 Westgate Pkwy, Asheville, NC 28806; 828-772-3188

Days Inn by Wyndham Asheville West: 2251 Smokey Park Hwy., Candler NC 28715; 866-665-2031.

Holiday Inn Asheville -Biltmore West: 435 Smokey Park Hwy., Asheville NC 28806; 828-665-2161.

Ramada by Wyndham Asheville / Biltmore West: 275 Smokey Park Hwy., Asheville NC 28806; 800-760-7718.

Rodeway Inn-Asheville: 8 Crowell Rd., Asheville NC 28806; 828-667-8706.

Sleep Inn Asheville - Biltmore West: 1918 Old Haywood Rd., Asheville NC 28806; 828-670-7600, 866-901-1033.

A Bed of Roses, 135 Cumberland Ave.

Asheville Bed & Breakfasts

A Bed of Roses (NRHP): Situated on a quiet, tree-lined St. in the historic Montford district of Asheville, A Bed of Roses was built at the end of the Victorian era by Oliver Davis Revell and meticulously renovated in 2002. Enjoy the comfort of the tastefully decorated 1897 Queen Anne house with its shaded porch and tended gardens. Many of the guest rooms have fireplaces and private baths including Jacuzzi-style tubs. 135 Cumberland Ave., Asheville NC 28801; 828-258-8700, 800-471-4182. abedofroses.com

Abbington Green Bed and Breakfast Inn (NRHP): AAA 4-Diamonds. Richard Sharp Smith designed Colonial Revival-style home. Romantic English flavor that includes antique furnishings, fine rugs, piano, library and fireplaces. Prize-winning English gardens surround the inn. Inside, the stylish guestrooms are named after parks and gardens around London. Each room has a king bed, whirlpool tub with shower, fireplace, HDTV and internet access. Five rooms plus one- and two-bedroom suites. Located in the Montford Historic District. 46 Cumberland Circle, Asheville NC 28801; 828-251-2454, 800-251-2454. abbingtongreen.com

Albemarle Inn (NRHS): The Albemarle Inn is housed in a classic 1907 Southern mansion with English gardens. Period guest rooms offer clawfoot or whirlpool tubs with fragrant bath amenities, fine linens, fresh flowers and evening turndown service. Elegant canopy queen or king-size beds and a private balcony are special features of some rooms. Award winning full gourmet breakfasts are served at private tables on the bright sun porch or cozy period dining room. 86 Edgemont Rd., Asheville NC 28801; 828-255-0027, 800-621-7435. albemarleinn.com

Applewood Manor Inn (NRHP): A Colonial Revival-style house on almost two acres of secluded lawn and shade trees. The inn and its sizeable rooms are accented with fireplaces, private baths and balconies, antiques, art and fresh flowers. Services each day include a full delicious and plentiful 3-course breakfast, afternoon social with beverages and treats and

Albemarle Inn, 86 Edgemont Rd.

turndown service are provide Located in the Montford Historic District. 62 Cumberland Circle, Asheville NC 28801; 828-254-2244, 800-442-2197. applewoodmanor.com

Asheville Seasons Bed and Breakfast: An intimate Inn with only five guest rooms, Asheville Seasons is located in the Montford Historic District. Walk to downtown, enjoy sitting on the front porch, read a book in the parlor or just relax in your room. A delicious breakfast with fruit, a main course, juice, teas, and special blend of gourmet organic fair trade coffee is included. All of the seasonal themed rooms include private baths, king or queen beds and most have working fireplaces. 43 Watauga St., Asheville NC 28801; 828-236-9494. ashevilleseasons.com

At Cumberland Falls Bed and Breakfast Inn (NRHP): Turn-of-the-century home located in Montford Historic District. Grounds are landscaped with waterfalls, koi ponds, and gardens. The inn features quilted maple woodwork and solarium. Guest rooms have wood or gas-burning fireplaces and two-person Jacuzzi tubs surrounded by marble. Gourmet breakfasts, fresh pastries, flowers, and robes in rooms, turndown service with chocolates, massage, and concierge service. 254 Cumberland Ave., Asheville NC 28801; 828-253-4085, 888-743-2557. cumberlandfalls.com

Beaufort House Inn (NRHP): A grand Queen Anne mansion, features wood-burning fireplaces, two-person Jacuzzis, fitness facility and mountain views. Built in 1894, this historic home has been meticulously restored as a romantic bed and breakfast inn with an air of casual luxury and elegance and has a lovely gingerbread porch, with beautifully landscaped grounds that include tea gardens. Popular afternoon tea offered on outdoor porch. 61 North Liberty St., Asheville NC 28801; 828-254-8334, 800-261-2221. beauforthouse.com

Bent Creek Lodge: Bent Creek Lodge is a rustic mountain retreat surrounded by acres of woods and miles of trails and located less than one mile from the North Carolina Arboretum. Built in 1999, the Lodge is an ideal base for biking, hiking, canoeing, and exploring the Asheville area. Features gourmet breakfasts and intimate dinners for guests only. Amenities include a great room with stone fireplace, pool table, spacious decks, and comfortably appointed guest rooms with private baths and air conditioning. 10 Parkway Crescent, Arden NC 28704; 828-654-9040, 877-231-6574. bentcreeknc.com

Biltmore Village Inn: Located in historic Biltmore Village, this lovely BandB is the closest to Biltmore Estate. Large rooms feature Jacuzzis, fireplaces, flat screens, DVD players and wireless Internet access. Meals and conversation are enjoyed on a porch boasting mountain views and sunsets. 119 Dodge St., Asheville NC 28803; 828-274-8707, 866-274-9779. biltmorevillageinn.com

Bunn House Hotel: A small boutique hotel located within walking distance of downtown Asheville. A little gem of refined elegance and timeless design.15 Clayton Street, Asheville NC 28801: 828-333-8700.

Carolina Bed and Breakfast (NRHP): A turn-of-the-century restoration located in the Montford district, this historic house designed in 1900 by Richard Sharp Smith has seven rooms with fireplaces, private baths, and air-conditioning. The rooms are decorated with a blend of antiques and collectibles. Porches and gardens complement the gracious interior. With its pebble dash finish, unique rooflines and abundant porches, this Smith creation blends art and nature in the true Arts and Crafts tradition. 177 Cumberland Ave., Asheville NC 28801; 828-254-3608, 888-254-3608. carolinabb.com

Cedar Crest Inn (NRHP): One of the largest and most opulent residences surviving from Asheville's 1890s boom period, is an 1891 Queen Anne mansion featuring elegant interiors created by Vanderbilt's craftsmen. Romantic guest suites, rooms and beautiful grounds. One of three accommodations in Asheville to be awarded AAA's Four Diamond rating. 674 Biltmore Ave., Asheville NC 28803; 828-252-1389, 800-252-0310. cedarcrestinn.com

Hill House Bed & Breakfast Inn, 120 Hillside St., Asheville

North Lodge Bed & Breakfast, 84 Oakland Rd., Asheville

Chestnut Street Inn (NRHP): A superbly restored Colonial Revival bed and breakfast located in the Chestnut Hill Historic District. The entire grounds are designated a "Treasure Tree" preserve. The 1905 house has been lovingly restored and has some of the most elegant interior woodwork to be found in Asheville. Eclectic furnishings with great porches and all rooms have private baths. Private suite also available. Afternoon tea and breakfast are served on antique china. 176 East Chestnut St., Asheville NC 28801; 828-285-0705, 800-894-2955. chestnutSt.inn.com

Hill House Bed & Breakfast: Located less than a mile from downtown in a lovely residential neighborhood, this 1885 restored house has all of the vintage ambiance of years ago. 120 Hillside Street, Asheville NC 28801; 828-232-0345.

1900 Inn on Montford (NRHP): A 1900 Richard Sharp Smith-designed English country cottage, is furnished with period antiques from 1730 to 1910, oriental rugs and an extensive collection of antique maps. Full breakfast also served daily. Five large and comfortable guest rooms have private in-suite baths, fireplaces, and queen-sized poster beds. A large Southern porch and a massive stone fireplace grace the inn. In Montford Historic District. 296 Montford Ave., Asheville NC 28801; 828-254-9569, 800-254-9569. innonmontford.com

North Lodge on Oakland Bed and Breakfast (NRHP): A lovingly restored 1904 stone and cedar shingle home with private baths and TV in every room. Antiques and contemporary furnishings. Deluxe hot breakfast. No smoking. Fine hotel service at affordable rates. 84 Oakland Rd., Asheville NC 28801; 828-252-6433, 800-282-3602. $$ Moderate. northlodge.com

Oakland Cottage Bed and Breakfast: Circa 1905 BandB with spacious family friendly suites. Breakfast included. This 5,000 square ft "cottage" has been naturally broken into private and roomy Suites. The open common areas create a warm and spacious feel. Conveniently located a short one and a half miles from the entrance of the Biltmore Estate and just two miles from downtown Asheville's Pack Square 74 Oakland Rd., Asheville NC 28801, 828-994-2627, 866-858-0863. vacationinasheville.com

The Black Walnut Bed and Breakfast Inn (NRHP): A finely preserved Shingle-style home which was built in 1899 by Richard Sharp Smith and restored into a bed and breakfast in 1992. The Inn features six rooms in the main house and two brand new, pet friendly suites in the restored carriage house. All rooms have private bath, luxury bedding, and most have fireplaces. Room rates include gourmet three course breakfast and afternoon tea with wine tasting. In Montford Historic District. 288 Montford Ave., Asheville NC 28801; 828-254-3878, 800-381-3878. blackwalnut.com

The Lion and The Rose (NRHP): A Queen Anne/Georgian-style home, was built around 1898. Lovely antique-filled suites and private rooms complete with fresh flowers and linens. 24-hour guest pantry, wireless internet and TV/DVD players in each guest room. Gourmet breakfast served daily in the sunny dining room. In Montford Historic District. 276 Montford Ave., Asheville NC 28801; 828-255-7673, 800-546-6988. lion-rose.com

The Reynolds Mansion Bed and Breakfast (NRHP): The Reynolds Mansion Bed and Breakfast Inn (circa 1847) has graciously restored accommodations that include eight guest rooms in the main house, three guest rooms in the nearby Carriage House and two private Cottages. All guest rooms feature private baths and most offer the warming glow of a fireplace.100 Reynolds Heights, Asheville NC 28804; 828-258-1111, 888-611-1156 thereynoldsmansion.com

Sourwood Inn: Located 10 miles from downtown Asheville on one hundred acres, the Sourwood Inn has 12 guest rooms with wood-burning fireplaces, balconies, and baths. Also available is the charming Sassafras Cabin. Located near the Blue Ridge Parkway in the mountains surrounding Asheville, Sourwood Inn has two miles of walking trails and offers a unique experience of the mountains.810 Elk Mountain Scenic Hwy., Asheville NC 28804; 828-255-0690. sourwoodinn.com

Sweet Biscuit Inn: 1915 Colonial Revival house with rich decorative details throughout, including 11-foot ceilings, tiger oak floors, dramatic formal staircase, and a comfortable full length porch. 3 spacious guest rooms and carriage house with private baths. Located in Kenilworth neighborhood of East Asheville. Casual comfort and unpretentious sophistication are the hallmarks of this sweet and charming B&B. Children welcomed. 77 Kenilworth Rd., Asheville NC 28803; 828-250-0170. sweetbiscuitinn.com

1889 White Gate Inn and Cottage (NRHP): One of Asheville's premier bed and breakfasts, the historic 1889 WhiteGate Inn and Cottage is conveniently located near downtown Asheville. Romance, elegance and tranquility perfectly describe the ambience of this New England-style inn. Sumptuous breakfasts, luxurious spa suites and award-winning gardens, complete with cascading waterfalls and koi ponds, are just part of what make this BandB special. 173 East Chestnut St., Asheville NC 28801; 828-253-2553, 800-485-3045. whitegate.net

1899 Wright Inn and Carriage House NRHP): One of the finest examples of Queen Anne architecture in Asheville, has eight distinctive bedrooms and a luxurious suite with fireplace. All rooms have private baths, cable TV and telephones. The three-bedroom Carriage House is ideal for groups or families. Full breakfast and afternoon tea served daily in the inn. In Montford Historic District. 235 Pearson Dr., Asheville NC 28801; 828-251-0789, 800-552-5724. wrightinn.com

Zen Asheville Inn & Spa Retreat: East meets West at ASIA, a haven of serene privacy, with five luxurious suites. Everything you see, touch, or sense creates an experience of pampering and calm. Japanese Gardens with a fountain, exotic fabrics and finishes! Double Jacuzzis, fireplaces, king beds, robes and slippers, and a mini-bar. 128 Hillside St., Asheville NC 28801, 828-255-0051. $$$ Luxury. ashevillespa.com

Asheville Cabins, Cottages & Chalets

Asheville Cabins of Willow Winds: Twenty-five luxury cabins on delightful 40 acre property with trout pond, stream, waterfall, gardens and fountains. All cabins are tastefully decorated, completely equipped and furnished. Amenities include wood-burning fireplaces, hot tubs, kitchens with dishwashers, linens, towels, cooking utensils, cable television with DVD, free internet, air conditioning, washer/dryer, telephone and private decks with grills. 39 Stockwood Rd. Ext., Asheville NC 28803; 828-277-3948, 800-235-2474. ashevillecabins.com

Asheville Cottages: Luxury cottages complete with a fully equipped kitchens (including breakfast items), wireless internet and satellite TV. Conveniently located near Biltmore Estate, North Carolina Arboretum and many other Asheville area attractions. 29 Brown Rd., Asheville NC 28806, 828-712-1789. ashevillecottages.com

Asheville Swiss Chalets: Pet-friendly. Casual elegance on Beaucatcher Mountain overlooking Asheville. All chalets are smoke free and equipped with heating and air conditioning for year-round comfort. Well appointed and tastefully decorated chalets with every convenience of home with full service kitchens, internet service, cable TV, gas fireplaces and more. 10 N. Delano Rd., Asheville NC 28805; 828-645-8101. ashevilleswisschalets.com

Mountain Springs Cabins: Three Diamond AAA rating. Outstanding country cabins with fireplaces overlooking a rushing mountain stream. Nestled on 30 landscaped, park-like acres just off the Blue Ridge Parkway and 10 minutes west of Asheville. Breathtaking views, a really special place to stay. 27 Emma's Cove Rd., Candler NC 28715; 828-665-1004. rvcoutdoors.com/mountain-springs-cabins

Mountain Springs Cabins & Chalets, 151 Pisgah Hwy., Candler

Pisgah View Ranch: 19 miles southwest of Asheville at the base of Mount Pisgah. 42 cottage rooms with private baths. Famous family style country dining (three meals a day included). Nightly entertainment, swimming, tennis, hiking and horseback riding. Open May through Oct. 70 Pisgah View Ranch Rd., Candler NC 28715; 828-667-9100, 866-252-8361. pisgahviewranch.net

The Pines Cottages: Over 75 years in business at the same location. 15 cottages and cabins to choose from, all with kitchens, some with fireplaces and cable TV. Children welcome. 346 Weaverville Rd., Asheville NC 28804; 828-645-9661, 888-818-6477. ashevillepines.com

Asheville Campgrounds

Campfire Lodgings: Located on Goldview Knob just a ten minute drive outside of Asheville, Campfire Lodgings offers 100 acres of mountaintop camping at its best. Options include RV camping with large, staggered sites to tent sites with water/electric to romantic Yurts, fully furnished log cabins or Cliff House, perfect for a large group. Full hookups. 116 Appalachian Village Rd., Asheville NC 28804; 828-658-8012, 800-933-8012. campfirelodgings.com

French Broad River Campground: Located on the French Broad River, 13 acres with over 2,000 feet of river frontage campground sites. 1030 Old Marshall Hwy., Asheville NC 28804; 828-658-0772. ncrivercamping.com

KOA Asheville-East: Shady RV and tent sites with full and partial hookups. Three bathhouses, 17 cabins and three furnished rental units. Amenities include two fishing lakes, boating, store, laundry, swimming, playground, mini-golf, and LP gas. Free Wi-Fi and Cable 2708 Hwy. 70 East, Swannanoa NC 28778; 828-686-3121, 800-562-5907. koa.com/campgrounds/asheville-east

KOA Asheville-West: Tent sites are beautifully wooded, and our "Big Rig" friendly 50- and 30-amp pull-through sites are large, level, and have cable TV and free Wi-Fi. I-40 Exit 37 and 309 Wiggins Rd., Candler NC 28715; 828-665-7015, 800-562-9015. koa.com/campgrounds/asheville-west

Rutledge Lake RV Park Resort: Friendly professional service, and clean and well-maintained facilities. Lake fishing, boating and canoeing. 170 Rutledge Rd., Fletcher NC 28732; 828 654-7873. rutledgelake.com

Hendersonville Grand Hotels, Inns & Lodges

Echo Mountain Inn: Historic inn with great views. Built in 1896 on Echo Mountain, the inn offers one or two bedroom apartments, rooms with mountain views and fireplaces, private bath, cable TV and telephones. Restaurant, swimming pool and shuffleboard. 2849 Laurel Park Hwy., Hendersonville NC 28739; 828-693-9626, 888-324-6466. echomountaininn.com

Highland Lake Inn: Offers accommodations in the inn, cabins or cottages. Located on scenic Highland Lake and surrounded by 26 wooded acres. A full service resort destination, Highland Lake Inn offers award-winning dining, outdoor pool, walking trails, organic gardens and more. 86 Lily Pad Lane, Flat Rock NC 28731; 828-693-6812, 800-762-1376. hlinn.com

The Henderson: The Henderson is a 17-room bed and breakfast located one block from Main Street. Built between 1919 & 1921, it is listed on the National Historic Register. Their accommodations feature architecture that reflects the Classical Revival Style reminiscent of the roaring 20's. Restaurant and bar on site. 201 3rd Ave. W., Hendersonville, NC 28739; 828-696-2001. thehendersonnc.com

Hendersonville Motels

Best Western Hendersonville Inn: 105 Sugarloaf Rd., Hendersonville NC 28792; 828-692-0521, 800-528-1234.

Cascades Mountain Resort: 201 Sugarloaf Rd. Hendersonville, NC 28792; 828-595-8155

CedarWood Inn: 1510 Greenville Highway, Hendersonville, NC 28792; 828-692-8284

Days Inn by Wyndham Hendersonville: 102 Mitchelle Dr., Hendersonville NC 28792; 828-697-5999.

Hampton Inn Hendersonville: 155 Sugarloaf Rd., Hendersonville NC 28792; 828-697-2333, 800-426-7866.

Holiday Inn Express & Suites Hendersonville SE-Flat Rock: 111 Commercial Blvd., Flat Rock NC 28731; 828-698-8899, 800-465-4329.

Mountain Inn and Suites Flat Rock: 755 Upward Road, Hendersonville NC 28731; 828-692-7772

Mountain Inn and Suites Airport: 447 Naples Rd., Hendersonville NC 28792; 828-684-0040.

Ramada by Wyndham Hendersonville: 150 Sugarloaf Rd., Hendersonville NC 28792; 828-697-0006, 800-272-6232.

Red Roof Inn Hendersonville: 240 Mitchell Dr., Hendersonville NC 28792; 828-697-1223.

Hendersonville Bed & Breakfasts

Aunt Adeline's Bed & Breakfast: Aunt Adeline's, originally a boarding house, was built sometime between 1917 and 1923 and recently updated. It is an active property on the Federal Register of Historic Homes, located in Historic Hyman Heights, a quiet residential district nestled in a grove of mature trees. The original oversized windows (with wavy glass) allow for ample lighting and impressive views of our park-like setting and the surrounding mountains. 1314 Hyman Avenue, Hendersonville, NC 28792; 828-595-4955. Auntadelinesbedandbreakfast.com

Elizabeth Leigh Inn (NRHP): Elegant bed and breakfast in historic 1893 residence. Four suites with king-size beds, private baths and fireplaces. Services and amenities include real estate tours, dinner reservation, massage by appointment, homemade ice cream, guest's pantry, full concierge service and wireless internet access. 908 5th Ave. West, Hendersonville NC 28739; 828-808-5305. elizabethleighinn.com

Melange Bed & Breakfast, 1230 5th Ave. West, Hendersonville

Melange: Newly restored with European flair and charm, is a unique bed and breakfast with a refined atmosphere and museum-quality art and sculpture, oriental rugs, Mediterranean porches, crystal chandeliers and antique furnishings. AC in all rooms, two rooms with Jacuzzis. A gourmet breakfast is served during summer in the Rose Garden and on covered porches and in winter in the formal dining room. 1230 5th Ave. West, Hendersonville NC 28739; 828-697-5253, 800-303-5253. melangebb.com

Northern Lights Bed and Breakfast: Located in historic Flat Rock, a country setting B&B on three acres, complete with ponds, stream and gardens. 163 Northern Lights Lane, Hendersonville NC 28739; 828-284-3258. northernlightsbedandbreakfast.com

Pinebrook Manor: One of the oldest historic estates in Hendersonville, this romantic five-acre property has been lovingly restored to provide the utmost in pampered hospitality for guests. 2701 Kanuga Rd., Hendersonville NC 28739; 828-698-2707, 877-916-2667. pinebrookmanor.com

The Charleston Inn: An historic 1880 house preserved and restored to modern standards. Formerly known as the Claddagh Inn The Charleston Inn is only a short walking distance to downtown. Wonderful front porch and colonial ambiance. Lantern Restaurant on site. 755 North Main Street, Hendersonville NC 28792; 828-693-6737. thecharleston.net

The Henderson: The Henderson is a 17-room bed and breakfast located one block from Main Street. Built between 1919 & 1921, it is listed on the National Historic Register. Their accommodations feature architecture that reflects the Classical Revival Style reminiscent of the roaring 20's. Restaurant and bar on site. 201 3rd Ave. W., Hendersonville, NC 28739; 828-696-2001

1898 Waverly Inn (NRHP): An elegant bed and breakfast established in 1898 that is famous for Southern breakfasts. Fourteen unique guest rooms and one suite, each with private bath, are named for native wildflowers. Special features include four-poster canopy beds, brass beds, claw-foot bathtubs, and pedestal sinks. 783 N. Main St., Hendersonville NC 28792; 800-537-8195. waverlyinn.com

Hendersonville Cabins, Cottages & Chalets

Lakemont Cottages: Located in Flat Rock, Lakemont Cottages features 14 individually decorated units that each sleep from two to six guests. All cottages are furnished, with separate bedrooms, air conditioning, heat, fully equipped kitchens and cable TV. Most have enclosed porches. No pets. 100 Lakemont Dr., Flat Rock NC 28731; 828-693-5174. lakemontcottages.com

Lazy Lake Cabins: Rustic comfort on a six acre hobby farm. Cabins are 750 square feet and all have a fireplace with gas logs, a carpeted loft, a Jacuzzi in the main bathroom, and a full length covered porch with porch furniture. 2322 Sugarloaf Rd., Hendersonville NC 28792; 828-692-5094. lazylakecabins.com

Mountain Lake Cottages: Mountain Lake Inn offers eleven large efficiency cottages available nightly, weekly or seasonally. Each cottage has a well-appointed eat-in kitchen including small stove, fridge, microwave, and coffee maker. All cottages offer private baths, air-conditioning, heat, ceiling fans, television with cable and free wifi. Most cottages offer a separate living room and private porch with chairs. 801 N. Lakeside Dr., Hendersonville NC 28739; 828-692-6269. mountainlakecottages.com

The Cottages of Flat Rock: 13 immaculate one and two bedroom cottages nestled on 2.5 acres. Each cottage has a private front porch with rocking chairs overlooking a one acre park like setting complete with gazebo and quiet stream. Laundry on grounds. 1511 Greenville Hwy., Hendersonville NC 28792; 828-693-8805. the cottagesofflatrock.com

Hendersonville Campgrounds

Apple Valley Travel Park: Apple Valley Travel Park is a seasonal park that is open from April 1st to November 1st. It has 93 campsites which is composed of daily, weekly, monthly and seasonal sites. Each with full hook-up for water, sewer and electric. 1 Apple Orchard Rd., Hendersonville, NC 28792; 828-685-8000. Applevalleytravelpark.com

Blue Ridge Travel Park: Open Apr.–Nov., picnic area. Located on 10 acres in Henderson County's apple growing region. 58 lots all full hookup, with 30-amp electrical service. 3576 Chimney Rock Rd., Hendersonville NC 28792; 828-685-9207. blueridgetravelpark.com

Jaymar Travel Park: Jaymar Travel Park is family-owned and operated and is the largest RV park in the Hendersonville, NC area. This 40-acre park, developed in 1979 is located in an area of rolling hills and apple orchards surrounded by mountain views. Open May-October, 140 Jaymar Park Dr, Hendersonville, NC 28792; 828-685-3771. Jaymartravelpark.com

Lakewood RV Resort: Premier RV resort catering to adults. RV site rentals, amenities include full size pool and deck, shuffleboard, fishing pond, large fully equipped clubhouse, gym and business center. 15 Timmie Lane, Flat Rock NC 28731; 828-697-9523, 888-819-4200. lakewoodrvresort.com

Lazy Boy Travel Trailer Park: Established in 1980, with basketball courts, picnic area, camping. 15 Lazy Boy Lane, Hendersonville, NC 28792; 828-697-7165. lazyboytravel park.net

Park Place RV Park: Located 3 miles from downtown Hendersonville, 48 level sites, all full hookup, 47 are pull-through. Wifi high speed internet now available from campsites. 501 South Allen Rd., Flat Rock NC 28731; 828-693-3831. parkplacervpark.com

Red Gates RV Park and Camping: Located on a gently rolling meadowland with a 2 acre lake and surrounded by beautiful wooded areas. Cottages and 20 large lots with full hookups, hot showers, laundry facilities and sandy swimming beach. 259 Red Gates Lane, Hendersonville NC 28792; 828-685-8787. redgatesrv.com

Rutledge Lake RV Park Resort: Friendly professional service, and clean and well-maintained facilities. Lake fishing, boating and canoeing. 170 Rutledge Rd., Fletcher NC 28732; 828 654-7873. rutledgelake.com

Town Mountain Travel Park: Large shady campsites with full hookups, a patio, and a picnic table. Cable TV is available on some sites and some sites have telephone hook-ups. Also cottage rentals. Located two miles from downtown Hendersonville. 48 Town Mountain Rd., Hendersonville NC 28792; 828-697-6692. townmountaintravelpark.com

Chapter Two

Author's Choice Dining

The choice of restaurants in the Asheville and Hendersonville area is impressive, something you would expect given the hundreds of thousands of visitors who come to the mountains each year. Restaurants of all types and quality abound, and in order to make your vacation in Asheville as enjoyable as possible, I have included a selection of the most popular and established places to eat, including my own favorites. For a complete listing of all Asheville and Hendersonville restaurants, by category, visit my guidebook website at ashevilleguidebook.com .

Pricing Guide

Menu changes affect the pricing of the restaurants listed; however, in an attempt to help you make choices, a basic pricing guide is provided for some idea as to what you can expect to pay for an evening meal for one person, excluding sales tax, gratuity, drinks and dessert.

$	Inexpensive
$$	$20-30 range
$$$	$30–40 range
$$$$	Expensive

Asheville Restaurants

Apollo Flame Bistro and Pizza: MEDITERRANEAN ($$ South and West Asheville). Locally popular for over 40 years. A restaurant does not survive that long unless it's doing things right! Two locations. 485 Hendersonville Rd., Asheville NC 28704; 828-274-3582 and 1025 Brevard Rd., Asheville NC 28806; 828-665-0080. Mon–Sat 11am–10pm, Sun 11am–8pm

Biscuit Head ($$ West Asheville & Downtown): Acclaimed authentic southern cooking, locally sourced, in a casual atmosphere. Indoor and outdoor seating. Two locations: 733 Haywood Rd. Asheville, NC 28806, 828-333-5145 and 417 Biltmore Ave, Ste 4F, Asheville, NC, 28801, 828-505-3449

Blue Ridge Dining Room at The Omni Grove Park Inn: AMERICAN ($$$ Grove Park Inn) Southern Heritage cuisine including shrimp and grits and other southern classics. Enclosed terrace dining with a wonderful sunset view. Omni Grove Park

Inn Resort and Spa, 290 Macon Ave., Asheville NC 28804; 828-252-2711. Reservations recommended. Breakfast: 6:30–11am; Sun Brunch: 10am–2pm Dinner: 3–9:30pm.

12 Bones Smokehouse: SOUTHERN BBQ ($$ River Arts District and South Asheville) An Asheville institution, 12 Bones Smokehouse has two locations, the original down by the French Broad River and another in South Asheville. Serving baby back ribs, pulled pork, beef brisket, and more. Everything is smoked in house and all sides and desserts are made from scratch. Made famous by visits from President and Mrs. Obama. 5 Foundry Street., Asheville NC 28801; 828-253-4499 and 2350 Hendersonville Road, Arden NC 28704; 828-687-1395. Serving lunch Mon through Fri 11am–4pm

Bouchon: FRENCH ($$ Downtown) Superb restaurant offering authentic French "comfort food" (honest ingredients, in season, simply prepared, unpretentiously presented). Wonderful ambiance. 62 North Lexington Ave., Asheville NC 28801; 828-350-1140. Dinner starting at 5pm Seven days a week; St. Food, Mon–Thu 11am–7pm, Fri–Sat 11am–9pm.

Calypso ($$ Downtown): Authentic St. Lucian cuisine in a casual island atmopshere.18 North Lexington Avenue, Asheville NC 28801. 828-575-9494. Monday-Saturday 2:00-9:00 pm.

Carmel's Kitchen and Bar: ECLECTIC ($$ Downtown) Asheville's largest street side outdoor dining patio. Near historic Grove Arcade. 1 Page Ave., Asheville NC 28801; 828-252-8730 Mon–Sat 11am–late, Sun brunch beginning at 11:30am

Chai-Pani: INDIAN ($$ Downtown) Indian St. food, with signature dishes of chaat, quick snacks served by St. vendors in India. 22 Battery Park Ave., Asheville NC 28801, 828-254-4003. 7 days a week: 11:30am–4pm, 5-9pm

City Bakery Café: BAKERY-CAFE ($ Downtown) Family-owned and operated bakery offering European-style organic breads and fresh pastries, all handmade, along with organic coffee, sandwiches, pizza, and salads. Two downtown locations: 88 Charlotte St. (828-254-4289) and 60 Biltmore Ave. (828-252-4426) Asheville NC 28801, Charlotte St. hours: Mon through Sat 7am–6pm; Biltmore Ave. hours: Mon through Sat 7am–7pm, Sun 8am–5pm

Corner Kitchen: SOUTHERN ($$ Biltmore Village): Acclaimed and highly popular bistro offering Southern dishes with an urban twist. 3 Boston Way, Asheville NC 28805; 828-274-2439. Breakfast and Lunch: Mon–Sat 7:30–11am, 11:30am–3pm; Dinner 5pm, Sun Brunch 9am–3pm

Curate: SPANISH TAPAS ($$ Downtown): Traditional Spanish tapas bar and menu, from jamón Ibérico to croquetas de pollo to flan with caramel sauce. 11 Biltmore Ave., Asheville NC, 828-239-2946. Lunch, Dinner and Brunch: Tue–Thu 11:30am–10:30pm, Fri–Sat 11:30am–11pm, Sun 11:30am–10:30pm, Mon closed.

Early Girl Eatery: SOUTHERN (Downtown & West Asheville): Located in two locations, the Early Girl Eatery offers healthy, made-from-scratch cuisine with a regional emphasis. 8 Wall Street, Asheville NC 28801, 828-259-9292; 444 Haywood Rd #101, Asheville, NC 28806, 828-820-2323

El Chapala Mexican Restaurant: MEXICAN ($$ North and West Asheville) Authentic Mexican cuisine: burritos, tacos, enchiladas, tamales and great margaritas. Two Asheville locations: 868 Merrimon Ave., Asheville NC 28803; 828-258-0899; and

282 Smokey Park Hwy., Asheville NC 28806; 828-665-0430. Dinner: Mon–Fri 5–10pm Open Sat and Sun 12–10pm

828 Family Pizzeria: PIZZA ($ North and South Asheville) One of the best pizzerias around since 1933! Fomerly known as Marco's Pizzeria. Wide range of pies. Two locations: 946 Merrimon Ave., Asheville NC 28804; 828-285-0709 and 1854 Hendersonville Rd., Asheville NC 28803; 828-277-0004. Open 7 days a week, 11 30am–9:30pm (9pm on Sun)

Farm Burger: SOUTHERN ($$ Downtown) Farm Burger caters to both regular burger lovers and the non-carnivorous variety, as well. Gluten-free burger buns, vegan burgers and grass-fed, antibiotic+hormone-free, locally raised, fresh meat from local farmers, the Farm Burger has become recognized as a great place not only to eat but eat healthy! 10 Patton Ave., Asheville NC 28801; 828-348-8540. Open 7 days a week.

Fig Bistro: FRENCH ($$ Biltmore Village) Fig is a cozy bistro serving Chef William Klein's modern interpretation of classic, pure, and market-driven French cuisine. Menu changes regularly so they can offer fresh and local ingredients. 18 Brook St., Asheville NC 28803; 828-277-0889. Lunch: Mon–Sat 11am–2pm, Sun 10am–3pm Dinner: Mon–Sat 5–10pm, Sun 5–10pm

Heiwa Shokudo: JAPANESE ($$ Downtown) A little jewel of a Japanese restaurant offering authentic Japanese cuisine. Tempura, teriyaki, sukiyaki, vegetarian dishes and more. 87 North Lexington Ave., Asheville NC 28801; 828-254-7761. Lunch: Mon–Fri 11:30am–2:30pm; Dinner: Mon–Sat 5:30–9:30pm

Homegrown: SOUTHERN ($$ North Asheville) Local eatery, serving local food cooked by local people! Emphasis is on food grown in the mountains, with an eclectic menu. 371 Merrimon Ave., Asheville NC 28801, 828-232-4340. Open 7 days a week from 8am–9pm

Horizons: AMERICAN-CONTINENTAL ($$$$ Grove Park Inn) One of the few area restaurants to be awarded the prestigious DiRoNA Award given by members of the Distinguished Restaurants of North America. Known for its innovative, classic cuisine and extensive wine list.Omni Grove Park Inn Resort and Spa, 290 Macon Ave., Asheville NC 28804; 828-252-2711; reservations required, jacket and tie. Dinner: 6:30–9:30pm

Jerusalem Garden Cafe: MEDITERRANEAN-MIDDLE EASTERN ($$ Downtown) Moroccan and Mediterranean cuisine at its best. And belly dancing with live music every Thu, Fri and Sat night. 78 Patton Ave., Asheville NC 28801; 828-254-0255. Lunch, dinner and Sun Brunch. Mon–Thu 11am–9pm, Fri 11am–10pm, Sat 10am–10pm, Sun 9am–9pm

JandS Cafeteria: CAFETERIA ($$ Outskirts of Asheville) Since 1984, outstanding quality cafeterias. Pleasant decor, friendly service and expansive selection. 3 locations in the Asheville area: River Ridge Mall, 800 Fairview Rd., Asheville NC 28803,828-298-1209; 30 Airport Park Rd., Fletcher NC 28732; 828-684-3418 and Westridge Market Place, 900 Smokey Park Hwy. Enka NC 28792; 828-665-1969. Open seven days a week. Call for hours.

Laughing Seed Cafe: VEGETARIAN ($$ Downtown) Great vegetarian restaurant. Casual atmosphere and sumptuous vegetarian delicacies! 40 Wall St., Asheville NC 28801; 828-252-3445. Mon–Sat 11:30am–9pm; Sun 10am–8pm

Limones: MEXICAN and CALIFORNIAN ($$ Downtown) Innovative Mexican-inspired cuisine served in a romantic setting. Speciality drinks and known for excellent service. 13 Eagle St., Asheville NC 28801; 828-252-2327. Mon–Sun 5–10pm, Sat–Sun brunch 10:30am–2:30pm

Luella's Bar-B-Que: SOUTHERN BBQ ($ North Asheville) Southern BBQ and more. One of the top two BBQ places in Asheville! 505 Merrimon Ave., Asheville NC 28804; 828-505-7427. Open 7 days a week.

Mamacita's Taqueria : MEXICAN ($ Downtown) Mamacita's serves up fresh, made from scratch Mexican cuisine in a casual downtown location. Specializes in hand-crafted burritos, huge fresh salads, quesadillas, Baja-style fish tacos and a number of vegetarian options. 77 Biltmore Ave., Asheville NC 28801; 828-252-2711. Open 7 days a week, 11am–10pm

Mela Indian Restaurant: INDIAN ($$ Downtown) Authentic North and South Indian dishes. 70 N. Lexington Ave., Asheville NC 28801; 828-225-8880. Open 7 days a week, Lunch buffet: 11:30am–2:30pm, Dinner: 5:30–9:30pm or later.

Mellow Mushroom: PIZZA ($ Downtown) Located in an old gas station and featuring an 1960s ambiance, Mellow Mushroom serves up pizzas and calzones made with spring water dough and baked on stone. 50 Broadway, Asheville NC 28801, 828-236-9800. Mon–Thu 11am–11:30pm; Fri–Sat 11am–12:30am; Sun noon-10:30pm

Nine Mile: CARIBBEAN ($$ Montford District) Cozy casual full-service vegetarian-friendly restaurant and bar. Cuisine consists of Caribbean inspired pasta dishes, a handful of traditional pasta dishes and an array of locally made desserts. 233 Montford Ave., Asheville NC 28801. 828-505-3121. Mon–Sun 11;30am–10pm

Posana: SOUTHERN ($$ Downtown) Located on Pack Square, Posana offers breakfast, lunch and dinner, with all dishes prepared from scratch. A certified gluten-free restaurant, their focus is on using local, organic produce. 1 Biltmore Ave., Asheville NC 28801, 828-505-3969. Sun–Wed 7:30am–4pm, Thu–Sat 7:30am–11pm

Red Stag Grill: CONTINENTAL ($$ Biltmore Village) Old-world ambience in Grand Bohemian Hotel, traditional favorites , chops and game. Grand Bohemian Hotel, 11 Boston Way, Asheville NC 28803; 828-717-8756. Open 7 days a week. Breakfast 6:30–10:30am, Lunch 11am–2:30pm, Dinner 5–10pm

Rhubarb: AMERICAN-SOUTHERN ($$$ Downtown) Located right on Pack Square, Rhubarb is known for its exquisite menu, friendly service and great outside patio seating. 7 SW Pack Square, Asheville NC 28801; 828-785-1503. Mon–Thu 11:30am–9:30pm, Fri 11:30am–10:30pm, Sat 10:30am–10:30pm, Sun 10:30am–9:30pm

Salsa's: CUBAN-CARIBBEAN ($$ Downtown) Wonderful blend of Cuban-Caribbean and Mexican cuisine. Innovative and distinctive food that includes such dishes as trout tacos and Mandingo burritos. 6 Patton Ave., Asheville NC 28801; 828-252-9805. Mon–Thu 5–9:30pm; Fri–Sat 5–10pm

Strada Italiano: ITALIAN ($$ Downtown): Authentic Italian fare representing all regions of Italy including many of owner Chef Anthony Cerrato's traditional family recipes. 27 Broadway St., Asheville NC 28801, 828-348-8448. Tue–Sun 11am–3pm, 4–9:30pm Closed Mon.

Sunset Terrace at The Omni Grove Park Inn: AMERICAN ($$$ Grove Park Inn) One of the most beautiful places for dining anywhere in Asheville is the Sunset Terrace at the historic Grove Park Inn. Here you can enjoy the outdoors (weather permitting), have an elegant dinner and experience a magnificent view of the lights of Asheville as darkness falls.Omni Grove Park Inn Resort and Spa, 290 Macon Ave., Asheville NC 28804; 828-252-2711. Dinner: 6–9pm

Sunny Point Cafe: SOUTHERN ($$ West Asheville): Sunny Point offers creative and delicious dishes that shine through with local flavors. Handmade desserts and award-winning breakfasts anytime. Dine on their patio for an *al fresco* experience. 626 Haywood Rd., Asheville NC 28806, 828-252-0055. Tue through Sat 8:30am–9:30pm; Sun and Mon 8:30am–2:30pm

Table: SOUTHERN ($$$ Downtown) American cuisine with focus toward seasonal, organic and local ingredients, and an obsession with freshness. 48 College St., Asheville NC 28801; 828-254-8980, Lunch: 11am–2:30pm Dinner: 5:30–10pm Mon–Sat and Sun brunch: 10:30am–2:30pm, Closed Tue.

Tupelo Honey Café: SOUTHERN ($$) Elegant southern cuisine with an uptown twist. The Tupelo Honey Cafe has an upscale, yet casual environment with touches of an authentic Charleston/New Orleans style. Two locations: 12 College St., Asheville NC 28801, 828-255-4863 and 1829 Hendersonville Rd., Asheville NC 28704; 828-505-7676. Breakfast and Lunch: Tue–Sun 9am–3pm; Dinner: Tue–Thu 5:30–10pm, Fri–Sat 5:30–11pm

The Lobster Trap: SEAFOOD ($$$ Downtown) A local favorite offering fresh seafood and an oyster bar. Famous for flying in fresh seafood from Maine, the Lobster Trap also has live music and their own Oysterhouse Brewing Company microbrewery beer. 35 Patton Ave., Asheville NC 28801; 828-350-0505. Dinner: seven nights a week, from 5pm

The Market Place: SOUTHERN ($$ Downtown) Known for its innovative menu, The Market Place specializes In Farm to Table cuisine and is one of Asheville's best locally sourced restaurants. 20 Wall St., Asheville NC 28801; 828-252-4162. Open 7 days a week for dinner 5:30–Until. Sat and Sun brunch 10:30am–2:30pm

Urban Burrito: CAL-MEX ($ North and East Asheville) Wide selection of California-style burritos, as well as great salsas. Voted best burritos of WNC. 640 Merrimon Ave., #203 Asheville NC 28804; 828-251-1921. Mon–Sat 11am–10pm; Sun 12–10pm

Zambra: SPANISH-MEDITERRANEAN TAPAS ($$ Downtown) Spanish, Portuguese and Moroccan cuisine served in an exotic European setting. Like taking a trip to Spain for dinner. Tapas bar and restaurant. Not to be missed. 85 Walnut St., Asheville NC; 828-232-1060. Dinner: Mon–Thu 5:30–9pm; Fri–Sat 5-until; Sun 5:30–9pm Lounge service menu starts an hour earlier.

Asheville Coffeehouses

Lots of coffeehouses in Asheville, here are some of the best!

BattleCat Coffee Bar: COFFEE BAR (West Asheville) Popular West Asheville hangout, BattleCat has several rooms for lounging, as well as wide covered front porch and front yard with picnic tables. Menu features coffee, tea, yerba mate, and snacks. 373 Haywood Rd., Asheville NC 28807, 828-713-3885. Open 7 days a week 7:30am–8pm

Round Earth Roasters: COFFEEHOUSE (Biltmore Village) Fair Trade coffees that are roasted and brewed in house. Conveniently located near the entrance to Biltmore Estate. 518 Hendersonville Rd, Asheville NC 28803, 828-277-9227

Dobra Tea: COFFEEHOUSE (Downtown) An absolutely unique coffeehouse. Cheaper than taking a trip to China, Nepal, India and Japan. Traditional and authentic teas from around the world. A tearoom, light-fare restaurant and loose-leaf tea shop (100+ varieties) all rolled into one. 78 North Lexington Ave., Asheville NC 28801; 828-575-2424. Open 7 days a week, 11am–11pm

French Broad Chocolate Lounge: CHOCOLATE LOUNGE (Downtown) A sacred space for chocophiles. Handcrafted artisan chocolate truffles, salted honey caramels, beautiful pastries and classic cakes, featuring superb local and organic ingredients. Not to be missed! 10 South Pack Square, Asheville NC 28801; 828-252-4181. Mon–Thu 11am–11pm; Fri–Sat 11am–12 midnight; Sun 1pm-8pm

Green Sage Coffeehouse and Cafe: COFFEEHOUSE (Downtown) A great coffeehouse and cafe offering fair-trade organic coffee, natural and organic food, and operated sustainably as a model ecologically-driven business. The Green Sage is one of Asheville's premier coffeehouses, conveniently located downtown. Other Asheville locations at 633 Merrimon Ave., 1800 Hendersonville Rd. and 70 Westgate Pky. 5 Broadway St., Asheville NC 28801; 828-252-4450. Coffeehouse: Mon through Wed 7:30am–9pm; Thu 7:30am–10pm; Fri 7:30am–11pm; Sat 8am–11pm; Sun 8am–9pm

Malaprop's Bookstore and Café: BOOKSTORE and COFFEEHOUSE (Downtown) A booklover's paradise, famous locally as well as nationally! An Asheville Institution since 1982. Great books, great food, great coffee. Author readings and community events nearly every night throughout the year. Malaprop's offers a wide variety of coffees and teas as well as baked goods and bagels from local bakeries. 55 Haywood St., Asheville NC 28801, 828-254-6734. Mon–Sat 9am–9pm; Sun 9am–7pm malaprops.com

Hendersonville Restaurants

Binion's Roadhouse: COUNTRY-WESTERN ($$ Four Seasons Blvd.) Country style and casual, wild west atmosphere. 1565 Four Seasons Blvd., Hendersonville NC 28792; 828-693-0492. Sun–Thu 11am–10pm; Fri–Sat 11am–11pm

Black Rose Public House: IRISH-AMERICAN ($$ Downtown) Menu features a wide array of great selections, always made from the highest quality ingredients and always made from scratch. 222 N Main St., Hendersonville NC 28792; 828-698-2622. Open seven days a week.

Champa: PAN-ASIAN ($$ Downtown) Full ABC bar, elegant decor, Pan-Asian menu with focus on Thai cuisine. 437 North Main St., Hendersonville NC 28792; 828-696-9800. Lunch: Mon–Fri 11am–3pm, Sat–Sun 12–3pm; Dinner: Mon–Fri 4:30–10pm, Sat–Sun 3-10pm.

Flat Rock Wood Room: ITALIAN ($$ Just south of Downtown) Acclaimed smokehouse serving wood-fired pizzas, pit-cooked BBQ, panini & burgers in a casual setting. 1501 Greenville Hwy, Hendersonville, NC 28792, 828-435-1391.

Hannah Flanagan's Pub and Eatery: IRISH ($$ Downtown): A little bit of Ireland in the mountains. Full menu that ranges from sandwiches to Irish stew and shepherd's pie. Children's menu. Featuring authentic fish and chips every Friday. 300 N. Main St., Hendersonville NC 28739; 828-696-1665. Mon–Wed 11am–1am; Thu–Sat 11am–2am; Sun 11am–midnight.

Haus Heidelburg German Restaurant: GERMAN ($$ South of Downtown) German cuisine prepared only with the freshest ingredients. 630 Greenville Hwy., Hendersonville NC 28792; 828-693-8227. Open for lunch and dinner seven day a week.

Mezzaluna: ITALIAN ($$ Downtown) Breakfast, lunch and dinner. An excellent choice for families with children. 226 N. Main St., Hendersonville NC 28792; 828-697-6575. Sun–Thu 11am–9pm, Fri and Sat 11am–10pm

Mike's on Main St.: SANDWICHES-ICE CREAM ($ Downtown): An old-fashioned ice cream parlor that serves soup, sandwiches and breakfast. Like stepping back into the 1920s! 303 N. Main St., Hendersonville NC 28792; 828-698-1616. Mon–Sat 7:30am–5pm; Sun 12–5pm

Postero: AMERICAN ($$ Downtown) New American cuisine in casual elegant space. 401 N Main St, Hendersonville, NC 28792, 828-595-9676. Lunch and dinner call for hours.

Season's at Highland Lake: AMERICAN ($$$ Highland Lake) World-class, award winning cuisine in a casual, elegant country setting at the Highland Lake Inn. Local, organic produce (much of it grown in the Inn's 2 acre gardens). Lavish family-friendly Sun buffets year-round. 87 Lily Pad Lane, Flat Rock NC 28731; 828-696-9094. Breakfast, lunch, dinner, Sun Brunch Buffet; please call for hours.

Three Chopt Sandwich Shoppe: AMERICAN ($ Downtown): An excellent sandwich shop located downtown. Luncheon only. 103 Third Ave., Hendersonville NC 28792; 828-692-0228. Open Mon–Sat 11am–2:30pm

Hendersonville Coffeehouses

Black Bear Coffee Co.: COFFEE HOUSE (Downtown) Sidewalk seating and great coffee! 318 N. Main St., Hendersonville, 28792; 828-692-6333. Mon–Fri 8am–6pm; Sat 9am–6pm; Sun 11am–5pm

Chapter Three

Festivals & Events

Western North Carolina has a wide range of festivals throughout the year, from small town gatherings to one of the largest street festivals in the South. Most of these occur annually, during the same month each year. However, in planning your visit, be sure to check the festival website to verify exact dates. It is beyond the scope of this book to present each and every festival in the mountains, only the major and more established ones will be presented, month by month. The largest street festival in the mountains is the North Carolina Apple Festival in Hendersonville. For a complete listing of all major mountain festivals and events, visit my guidebook website at ashevilleguidebook.com .

January:

(ASHEVILLE) All That Jazz and Big Band Dance Weekends at the Omni Grove Park Inn: The inn hosts a fabulous lineup of entertainers and events, all jazz-related. 828-252-2711. groveparkinn.com

February:

(ASHEVILLE) Arts & Crafts Conference at the Omni Grove Park Inn: Over 130 exhibitors with arts & crafts, antiques and new works for sale. 800-438-5800

March:

(ASHEVILLE) Heritage Classic DanceSport Championships at the Omni Grove Park Inn: One of the nation's premier dancesport events. 800-438-5800. grove parkinn.com

(ASHEVILLE) Asheville Artisan Bread Baker's Festival: This annual all-day event begins with a bread tasting and sale at the Magnolia Building on the A-B Tech campus in Asheville. Hands-on workshops and lectures will take place from 9am–6pm at the same location. 828-683-2902. ashevillebreadfestival.com

April:

(ASHEVILLE) Festival of Flowers at Biltmore Estate: A celebration that highlights the spring blooming of flowers at Biltmore Estate. Guided tours through the gardens alive with color from more than 50,000 tulips, azaleas, flowering shrubs and much more. Live music and other special events. Ongoing April through May. 800-543-2961, 828-225-1333. biltmore.com

May:

(ASHEVILLE) Asheville Herb Festival: The largest herb festival in the Southeast. More than 50 herb vendors marketing herbs, herb plants and herb products. Held at the Western North Carolina Farmers Market. 828-253-1691. ashevilleherbfestival.com

(BLACK MOUNTAIN) Lake Eden Arts Festival (LEAF): Located at a mountain retreat, Camp Rockmont, LEAF is held twice a year in the spring and fall features music from dozens of national and regionally known musicians as well as crafts, storytelling, drumming, dancing and a healing arts tent. 828-686-8742. theleaf.com

(HOT SPRINGS) French Broad River Festival: Music, whitewater rafting and activities centered around the French Broad River. frenchbroadriverfestival.com

June:

(BAKERSVILLE) North Carolina Rhododendron Festival: St. fair, car show, ducky derby, beauty pageant, 10K run and St. dance are highlights of this local mountain city festival. 828-688-5901. bakersville.com

(BREVARD) Brevard Music Festival: Held at the Brevard Music Center over a seven-week period each summer during Jun., Jul. and Aug., this world-class music festival features over 70 different concerts, from symphony orchestra to Broadway musicals. 828-862-2100. brevardmusic.org

July:

(ASHEVILLE) Shindig on the Green: Held every Sat at sundown during Jul., Aug. and Sep. at Pack Square Park in downtown Asheville. Bluegrass music, dancing, clogging. This festival has been around for over 43 years! 828-2586101. folkheritage.org

(ASHEVILLE) Craft Fair of the Southern Highlands: For four days each Jul. and Oct., the US Cellular Center in Asheville NC comes alive with fine traditional and contemporary crafts. Over 200 craftspeople fill the two levels of the center selling their works of clay, fiber, glass, leather, metal, mixed media, natural materials, paper, wood, and jewelry. 828-298-7928. southernhighlandguild.org

(LINVILLE) Grandfather Mountain Highland Games: Scottish athletes and musicians share their heritage from bagpipes and Celtic music to border collies and sheep herding at the largest gathering of Scottish clans in North America. 828-733-1333. gmgh.org

(WAYNESVILLE) Folkmoot USA: North Carolina's official international festival, Folkmoot USA is a world-class folk festival with international dancers and musicians performing their countries' traditional folk dances. Over 350 performers at numerous venues. 828-452-2997. folkmootusa.org

August:

(ASHEVILLE) Mountain Dance and Folk Festival: The oldest festival in America. For more than 70 years, a celebration of traditional mountain music and dance. Held at various venues in Asheville. 828-258-6101. folkheritage.org

(ASHEVILLE) RiverFest: RiverLink annual celebration of life and leisure in the River Arts District on the French Broad River. This highly popular free festival consists of boats and rafts competitions crafted from various materials and the purpose of the festival is to celebrate RiverLink's ongoing efforts efforts to revitalize this magnificent river. riverlink.org

(ASHEVILLE) Goombay: Since 1982, a St. festival in the historic black business district in downtown Asheville. A celebration of African-Caribbean culture. 828-252-4614. ymicc.org

(ASHEVILLE) Village Art and Craft Fair: A long-standing, premier outdoor art and craft fair that hosts over 100 exhibitors representing all media. Held on the beautiful tree covered grounds of the Cathedral of All Souls in historic Biltmore Village for over 39 years. 828-274-2831

(BLACK MOUNTAIN) Sourwood Festival: Art and crafts, dancing, music, food and games. 828-669-2300. blackmountain.org

(BURNSVILLE) Mt. Mitchell Crafts Fair: The oldest and largest crafts fair in the Blue Ridge with more than 200 artists. Live entertainment and kid's activities. 828-682-7413. yanceychamber.com

(SPRUCE PINE) NC Gem and Mineral Festival: For over sixty years, one of the most popular and oldest running mineral and gem festivals in the country. Indoor and outdoor venues, hundreds of dealers. 828-765-9033 ncgemfest.com.

September:

(ASHEVILLE) North Carolina Mountain State Fair: Great state fair held at the Western North Carolina Agricultural Center. Rides, farm animals and great food. For the whole family. 828-687-1414. mountainfair.org

(ASHEVILLE) Brewgrass Festival: One of the most popular beer and bluegrass festivals in the southeast. American breweries and national and regional bluegrass musicians . brewgrassfestival.com

(HENDERSONVILLE) North Carolina Apple Festival: Another not-to-be-missed festival. A celebration of apples and the fall season. 828-697-4557. ncapplefestival.org

October:

(ASHEVILLE) Craft Fair of the Southern Highlands: For four days each Jul. and Oct., the US Cellular Center in Asheville NC comes alive with fine traditional and contemporary crafts. Over 200 craftspeople fill the two levels of the center selling their works of clay, fiber, glass, leather, metal, mixed media, natural materials, paper, wood, and jewelry. 828-298-7928. southernhighlandguild.org

(ASHEVILLE) Thomas Wolfe Festival: A festival centered on the life and times of the Asheville-born author Thomas Wolfe. Walking tours, concerts, plays, Wolfe workshops, road race and other events centered on Wolfe's life. 828-253-8304. thomaswolfe memorial.com

(BANNER ELK) Woolly Worm Festival: The stripes on the winner of the woolly worm race will be inspected by the town elders. Brown signals a mild winter, black predicts severe weather. Nonstop music, food, crafts, and children's rides. 800-972-2183. woolyworm.com

(BLACK MOUNTAIN) Lake Eden Arts Festival (LEAF): Located at a mountain retreat, Camp Rockmont, LEAF is held twice a year in the spring and fall features music from dozens of national and regionally known musicians as well as crafts, storytelling, drumming, dancing and a healing arts tent.828-686-8742. theleaf.com

November:

(ASHEVILLE) The National Gingerbread House Competition at the Omni Grove Park Inn: In existence for over two decades, this popular event has become one of the nation's most celebrated and competitive holiday events. 800-413-5778. www.omnihotels.com/hotels/asheville-grove-park

(ASHEVILLE) Christmas at Biltmore House: Biltmore House is especially memorable during the Christmas season. During Candlelight Christmas Evenings, Biltmore's doors open to a world of crackling fires, festive music performances, glittering trees and the warm glow of hundreds of candles illuminating the richly decorated rooms. Ongoing during Dec. 800-543-2961, 828-225-1333. biltmore.com

December:

(ASHEVILLE) Christmas at Biltmore House: Biltmore House is especially memorable during the Christmas season. During Candlelight Christmas Evenings, Biltmore's doors open to a world of crackling fires, festive music performances, glittering trees and the warm glow of hundreds of candles illuminating the richly decorated rooms. Ongoing during Dec. 800-543-2961, 828-225-1333. biltmore.com

(ASHEVILLE) Biltmore Village Dickens Festival: Ongoing Christmas festivities in picturesque Biltmore Village during the month of Dec. 828-274-8788. biltmorevillage.com

(ASHEVILLE) Victorian Christmas Celebration at the Smith-McDowell House festivals & events: A celebration of Christmas the old-fashioned way. The Museum's timeline of authentically decorated period rooms showcases the evolution of Christmas celebrations and includes hand-crafted decorations and live trees. 828-253-9231. wnchistory.org

Chapter Four
Beer City USA

Each year since 2009, an American city has been crowned "Beer City USA" as a result of votes cast in a national poll produced by the Brewers Association. Asheville has won this award many times since the poll began, a clear recognition of its growing and vibrant craft beer culture. All of Western North Carolina with its growing number of large and small companies can be considered the brewing capital of the southeast, with Asheville the absolute epicenter. On any given day, a staggering array of craft beers can be purchased on draft or in bottles at local pubs, bars and restaurants, and over 17 craft breweries (and counting) can be found In the Asheville area alone. With the arrival of major companies Sierra Nevada in South Asheville and New Belgium in the River Arts District, Asheville has arrived as a true beer lover's paradise. There are a number of popular beer-centric festivals, the Winter Warmer Beer festival in January, the Beer City Festival in Jun. and the Brewgrass Festival In Sep. all topped off with the Oktoberfest in Oct. A number of local craft breweries, as well as Sierra Nevada and Highland Brewing, also give tours of their facilities. Daily walking, mobile and private tours of Asheville's microbrewery scene is also offered by Asheville Brewery Tours (ashevillebrewerytours.com, 828-233-5006).

Asheville Craft-Brewery Tasting Rooms & Pubs

Asheville Brewing Company

Location: 3 locations
Downtown: 77 Coxe Ave., Asheville NC 28801; 828-255-4077
North Asheville: 675 Merrimon Ave., Asheville NC 28804; 828-254-1281
South Asheville: 1850 Hendersonville Rd., Asheville NC 28803; 828-277-5775
Website: ashevillebrewing.com
Hours: Open daily 11am–12pm
Offers: Hand-crafted beers and ales since 1998.
Notes: Asheville's third oldest brewery. Coxe Ave. location is home of production facility.

Bhramari Brewing Company

Location: Downtown Asheville
Address: 101 S Lexington Ave, Asheville, NC 28801

Telephone: 828-214-7981
Website: bhramaribrewing.com
Hours: Check website
Offers: Creative, innovative beers.

Burial Beer Company

Location: Downtown Asheville
Address: 40 Collier Ave., Asheville NC 28801
Telephone: 828-475-2739
Website: burialbeer.com
Hours: Fri 4–8pm, Sat 2–8pm
Offers: Traditional German lagers and Belgian-style ales.
Notes: Experimental beer making.

Catawba Brewing Company

Location: Biltmore Village and Asheville's South Slope.
South Slope: 32 Banks Ave Asheville, NC 28801; 828-552-3934
Biltmore Village: 63 Brook St. Asheville, NC 28803; 828-424-7290
Website: catawbabrewing.com
Hours: Mon–Fri 4–10pm, Sat–Sun 2–10pm
Offers: Custom craft beers and ales, including their popular Farmer Ted's Cream Ale.
Notes: Asheville branch of the Morganton NC main beer production operation.

French Broad Brewery

Location: South of Asheville near Biltmore Village
Address: 101 Fairview Rd., #D, Asheville NC 28803
Telephone: 828-277-0222
Website: frenchbroadbrewery.com
Hours: Open seven days a week from 1–8pm
Offers: Six+ staple year-round European-style beers, plus seasonal beers
Notes: Since 2001, great tasting room, continental European-style production brewery, and live music on weekends.

Green Man Brewery

Location: Downtown Asheville
Address: 23 Buxton Ave., Asheville NC 28801
Telephone: 828-252-5502
Website: greenmanbrewery.com
Hours: Sun–Thu 3–9pm, Fri–Sat 2–10pm
Offers: English-style ales and beers
Notes: One of Asheville's oldest breweries. Featured also at Jack of the Wood, a popular Celtic-style pub located at 95 Patton Ave. in downtown Asheville, and the original home of Green Man Brewery.

Highland Brewing Company

Location: Southeast Asheville, near Swannanoa River
Address: 12 Old Charlotte Hwy., Ste H, Asheville NC 28803
Telephone: 828-299-3370
Website: highlandbrewing.com
Hours: Brewery tours: Brewery Tours and Tasting Room open 7 days a week. Call for hours.
Offers: Impressive array of ales and beers, including Gaelic Ale a highly popular best seller.
Notes: One of the oldest and premier craft breweries in the Asheville area, since 1994. Brews over 50,000 barrels annually. Tasting room and brewery tours offered at their facility.

Hi-Wire Brewing

Location: Downtown Asheville
Address: 197 Hilliard Ave., Asheville NC 28801
Telephone: 828-575-9675
Website: hiwirebrewing.com
Hours: Seven days a week. Call for hours
Offers: Features 4 year-round "Main Attraction" beers and a rotating selection of seasonal offerings.
Notes: Tasting room.

New Belgium Brewing Company

Location: River Arts District
Address: 21 Craven St, Asheville, NC 28806
Telephone: 828-333-6900
Website: newbelgium.com
Hours: Beer Garden Seating. Usually 12- 8pm daily
Offers: Large selection. New Belgium is a major national beer making company
Notes: See website for tours hours.
Notes: small-batch, hand-crafted nano-brewery and alehouse

One World Brewing

Location: Downtown Asheville
Address: 1 Silverstone Dr., Asheville NC 28801
Telephone: 508-982-3757
Website: oneworldbrewing.com
Hours: Hours vary, call. Usually 4pm–12am weekdays and 12pm–2am weekends
Offers: Six flagship beers and four rotating taps.
Notes: small-batch, hand-crafted nano-brewery and alehouse.

Oyster House Brewing Company

Location: West Asheville
Address: 625 Haywood Rd., Asheville NC 28806
Telephone: 828-575-9370

Website: oysterhousebeers.com
Hours: Open daily at 5pm
Offers: Known for its Moonstone Oyster Stout served with fresh, raw oysters
Notes: Asheville's first nano-brewery devoted to producing high quality, unique ales for beer and seafood lovers.

Sierra Nevada Brewing Company

Location: Mills River area south of Asheville
Address: 100 Sierra Nevada Way, Mills River NC 28732
Telephone: 828-681-5300, Tour Desk 828-708-6176
Website: sierranevada.com
Hours: Taproom and restaurant open daily, call for hours or visit website.
Offers: A myriad of seasonal beers and bottled specialties Sierra Nevada has produced in recent years, as well as an expansion of the brewery's well-known flagship product: Sierra Nevada Pale Ale.
Notes: Daily tours, taproom, and restaurant. Located on 200 acres along the French Broad River. Founded in 1980, Sierra Nevada Brewing Company is one of America's premier craft breweries, highly regarded for using only whole-cone hops and ingredients of the finest quality.

Thirsty Monk Pub & Brewery

Location: 3 locations
Downtown Asheville: 92 Patton Ave., Asheville NC 28801; 828-254-5470
Biltmore Park: 2 Town Square Blvd., Asheville NC 28803; 828-687-3873
North Asheville: 51 North Merrimon Ave., #113 (Reynolds Village), Asheville NC 28804; 828-424-7807
Website: monkpub.com
Hours: Call for hours or visit website
Offers: Huge selection of beers. Over 36 on tap and 150 bottled.
Notes: National recognition as a great beer bar, they tap over 1,200 beers at their four Asheville locations.

Upcountry Brewing Company

Location: West Asheville
Address: 1042 Haywood Rd., Asheville NC 28806
Telephone: 828-575-2400
Website: upcountrybrewing.com
Hours: 2pm–2am seven days a week
Offers: Full spectrum of ales, including IPA, American Pale, Golden Amber, Stout, Porter, and many others
Notes: 20+ taps including beer from other breweries. Weekly live music, dog-friendly, and special events.

Urban Orchard Cider Company

Locations: West Asheville and South Slope
West Asheville: 210 Haywood Rd., Asheville NC 28806; 828-774-5151
South Slope: 24 Buxton Ave, Asheville, NC 28801; 828-505-7243
Website: urbanorchardcider.com
Hours: Call for hours or visit website
Offers: Their own, naturally gluten-free craft hard apple cider on tap year-round with a rotating selection of seasonal and experimental batches. Also local craft beers and wine.
Notes: Family-owned company and tasting room, with the Urban Orchard Cidery located directly beneath the Cider Bar.

Wedge Brewing Company

Locations: Two locations in the River Arts District
5 Foundy Street, Asheville, NC 28801; 828-253-7152
37 Paynes Way, Suite 001 Asheville, NC 28801; 828-505-2792
Website: wedgebrewing.com
Hours: Mon–Thu 4–10pm, Fri 3-10pm, Sat 2–10pm
Offers: Iron Rain IPA and a variety of hand-crafted beers and ales.
Notes: Popular tasting room located in the lower level of the Wedge Studios. Production size of about 1,300 barrels.

Wicked Weed Brewing

Location: Multiple locations in Asheville
Brewpub (Downtown), 91 Biltmore Ave., Asheville NC 28801; 828-575-9599
Funkatorium (South Slope), 147 Coxe Ave. Asheville, NC 28801; 828-552-320
Cultura (South Slope), 147 Coxe Ave., Asheville, NC 28801; 828-417-697
Website: wickedweedbrewing.com
Hours: Call for hours or visit website
Offers: Creative, big-flavor, hop-forward West Coast style beers and Belgian style ales.
Notes: Gastropub offering locally sourced food.

Chapter Five

Author's Favorites

No guidebook would be complete without a list of the author's personal favorite places and attractions. I have included my favorites hoping it will help you in making decisions about what to see and do while visiting our mountains.

Man-Made Awesome Majesty

Biltmore Estate: An absolute stunner. Not to be missed. Breathtaking gardens and grounds. (*See* Section III, Chapter Three)

The Omni Grove Park Inn: Monumental building. Great ambience. Wonderful special events and facilities. (*See* Section III, Chapter Four)

Historical Treasures

Thomas Wolfe Memorial: A fascinating time capsule. Superb restoration. (*See* Section III, Chapter Two)

Smith-McDowell House: A historic gem. Wonderful at Christmas in its Victorian finery. (*See* Section III, Chapter Two)

Thomas Wolfe Angel Statue: In Oakdale Cemetery in Hendersonville. Possible to take a close-up look. (*See* Section IV, Chapter Three)

Architectural Masterpieces

Asheville City Building: An Art Deco masterpiece. (*See* Section III, Chapter Four)

Basilica of St. Lawrence: Wonderful stained glass and interior. Amazing rose gardens in season. Make time to take the self-guided art and architecture tour. (*See* Section III, Chapter Four)

Cathedral of All Souls: Inside and out, this elegant church is truly inspirational. One of the most beautiful buildings in Asheville. (*See* Section III, Chapter Four)

Your Kids Will Thank You!

Western North Carolina Nature Center: Animals from otters to cougars. A must! (*See* Section III, Chapter Two)

Pack Place Education, Arts and Science Center: Fascinating stuff for all ages. (*See* Section III, Chapter Two)

Pisgah National Forest: A perfect day trip in the summer. Take a picnic lunch. Visit Looking Glass Falls, Sliding Rock's natural waterslide, and the National Forest Fish Hatchery to let the kids feed the huge trout. Finish up at the Forest Discovery Center at the Cradle of Forestry. (*See* Section II, Chapter Eight, Waterfalls and Trout)

Sweet Treats

The Chocolate Fetish: 36 Haywood St., Asheville NC 28801. Handmade truffles rated "America's best" by the Los Angeles Times. They're right!

French Broad Chocolate Lounge: 10 South Pack Square., Asheville NC 28801. A sacred space for chocophiles. Handcraft artisan chocolate truffles, salted honey caramels, beautiful pastries and classic cakes, featuring superb local and organic ingredients.

Festivals

Craft Fair of the Southern Highlands in Asheville: World-class arts and crafts show head each Jul. and Oct. 828-298-7928. southernhighlandguild.org

Apple Festival in Hendersonville: Small-town friendliness and wonderful mountain culture. (*See* Section II, Chapter Three)

Unbelievable Views/Natural Wonders

Chimney Rock Park: This place will take your breath away. Take a good pair of walking shoes and go on a clear day. (*See* Section V, Chapter One)

Blue Ridge Parkway: Head out in any direction. Be sure to take a picnic lunch. (*See* Section V, Chapter One)

Graveyard Fields at Milepost 418 on Blue Ridge Parkway: Great easy hiking trails and a wonderful waterfall. Easy to reach and family friendly. (*See* Section V, Chapter One, Waterfalls and Blue Ridge Parkway)

Looking Glass Falls: Pisgah National Forest. One of the most accessible and spectacular waterfalls around. (*See* Section V, Chapter One)

Gardener's Delights

Formal Flower Gardens at Biltmore Estate: World-class. Especially wonderful in Apr.–May during the Festival of Flowers. Will leave you dazzled. (*See* Section III, Chapter Three)

North Carolina Arboretum: Extraordinary gardens and educational center. Inspirational. (*See* Section III, Chapter Two)

Chapter Six

Great Things To Do With Kids

A trip to Western North Carolina doesn't have to be a bore for the kids. Here is a listing of things to do that will bring smiles to the faces of kids and kids-at-heart alike.

Asheville

Asheville's Fun Depot: Kid centered activities, commercial venue but well done. (*See* Section III, Chapter Two)

Asheville Museum of Science: Asheville's premiere museum (See Chapter Two)

Biltmore Estate: Educational, awe-inspiring and fascinating (for older kids). (*See* Section III, Chapter Three)

Folk Art Center: Art and craft exhibits, craft demonstrations. (*See* Section III, Chapter 2)

Lake Julian District Park: Swimming, fishing, boating and picnic area. (*See* Section III, Chapter Nine)

McCormick Field: Asheville Tourists baseball games. (*See* Section III, Chapter Two)

North Carolina Arboretum: Wonderful gardens and botanical exhibits. (*See* Section III, Chapter Two)

Outdoor Activities: The lineup of choices can be found in Section II, Chapter 15.

Western North Carolina Nature Center: Animals of all types, Appalachian nature exhibits, and much more. (*See* Section III, Chapter Two)

Zebulon B. Vance Birthplace: Pioneer history exhibits and demonstrations. (*See* Section V, Chapter Two)

Hendersonville

Carl Sandburg Home: Historical exhibits, goat farm, hiking trails. (*See* Section IV, Chapter Two)

Historic Johnson Farm: Farm animals, exhibits, farm history. (*See* Section IV, Chapter 2)

Holmes Educational Forest: Trails, nature center, exhibits, picnic areas. (*See* Section IV, Chapter Two)

Western North Carolina

Blue Ridge Parkway: (Enter from Asheville area) Picnics, hiking. (*See* Section V, Chapter One)

Cherokee Indian Reservation: (Cherokee) Plan to spend a day. History and fun for kids. (*See* Section V, Chapter Two)

Chimney Rock Park: (Lake Lure) Spectacular hiking trails, nature center. (*See* Section V, Chapter One)

Cradle of Forestry: (Brevard) Educational and inspiring. (*See* Section V, Chapter Two)

Foothills Equestrian Nature Center (FENCE): (Tryon) A great nature center plus horse stuff! (*See* Section V, Chapter Two)

Grandfather Mountain: (Linville) World class mountain park and nature center (*See* Section V, Chapter One)

Great Smoky Mountains Railroad: (Bryson City, Dillsboro) Your kids will love this one! (*See* Section V, Chapter Two)

Lake Lure: (Lake Lure) Swimming, fishing, wonderful boat tours of lake. (*See* Section V, Chapter One)

Joyce Kilmer Memorial Forest: (Robbinsville area) A chance for your children to old growth, huge trees! (*See* Section I, Chapter Two)

Linville Caverns: (Linville) Underground, guided adventure for kids and adults (*See* Section V, Chapter One)

Outdoor Activities: The lineup of choices can be found in Section II, Chapter One.

Pisgah National Forest: (Brevard) Plan a day trip and include stops at Looking Glass Falls, Sliding Rock, State Fish Hatchery and Cradle of Forestry. (*See* Section II, Chapter Eight, "Waterfalls and Trout!")

Tweetsie Railroad: (Blowing Rock) A child centered railroad adventure (*See* Section V, Chapter Two)

Waterfalls: (Brevard area) Great natural attractions. Looking Glass Falls is closest to Asheville. (*See* Section V, Chapter One)

Whitewater Rafting: Numerous places to do so. (*See* Section II, Chapter One)

Chapter Seven

Planning a Gourmet Picnic

A wonderful way to highlight a day trip into the surrounding mountains, no matter what your itinerary or destination, is to bring along a picnic lunch. This is particularly true if your exploring takes you for a ride on the Blue Ridge Parkway or deep into one of the national forests. Restaurants are few and far between there, and besides, what could be better than eating a picnic lunch beside a wilderness waterfall or on a rocky overlook perched high above the green valleys below? If this idea appeals to you, then you are in luck, because not only does Western North Carolina have an unlimited supply of really great picnic spots, but there are some stores in downtown Asheville within minutes of each other where you can purchase the ingredients for an unforgettable picnic lunch.

Asheville Wine Market: Extremely good selection of fine wines and quality beers. 65 Biltmore Ave., Asheville NC 28801; 828-253-0060.

French Broad Food Co-op: Just down the St. is an outstanding organic grocery, run by a local cooperative. Fresh vegetables, fruit, cheese, crackers and more. 90 Biltmore Ave., Asheville NC 28801; 828-255-7650.

The Chocolate Fetish: 36 Haywood St., Asheville NC 28801. Handmade truffles rated "America's best" by the Los Angeles Times.

Chapter Eight
Great Itineraries & Tours

For visitors new to an area, planning some day trips or itineraries can be a challenge, especially in an area as rich in interesting things to do as Asheville, Hendersonville and Flat Rock. Considering the size and scope of the whole Western North Carolina mountains, the task can seem overwhelming. In an attempt to make your visit easier, I have presented below a number of tours and itineraries, both local and farther afield, from which you can choose.

Guided Tours of Asheville

Asheville Brewery Tours

Tour Description: Daily walking, mobile and private tours of Asheville's microbrewery scene.
Days of Operation: Daily
Length of Tour: Vary depending upon tour
Ticket Locations: Visit website ashevillebrewerytours.com for tickets and schedules.
Telephone: 828-233-5006
Website: ashevillebrewerytours.com
Notes: Reservations required

Ghost & Haunt Tours

Tour Description: A leisurely, narrated walking tour taking approximately 90 minutes and covering less than a mile.
Days of Operation: Mar. 1–Oct. 31, 9pm, departure nightly, rain or shine. Nov. 1–Feb. 27 tour starts at 7pm.
Length of Tour: 90 minutes
Ticket Locations: Haywood Park Hotel, located on the corner of Haywood St. and Battery Park in downtown Asheville.
Boarding and Departure: Same
Telephone: 828-355-5855
Notes:. Reservations required

Gray Line Trolley Tours

Tour Description: Live narrated tours on replica antique "Red" Trolleys. Tours encompass all major points of interest, including the Montford Historic District, Grove Park Historic District, Omni Grove Park Inn Resort and Spa, downtown Asheville, the River Arts District and Biltmore Village. They also offer a haunted history and murder mystery Ghost Tour, as well.

Days of Operation: Tours operate daily, seven days a week, Mar. through Dec. except Easter, Thanksgiving, Christmas, Christmas Eve, New Year's Day and during the Bele Chere Festival.

Length of Tour: Tour lasts approximately 1.5 to 1.75 hours. There is an additional 15 minute stop at the Asheville Visitor Center.

Ticket Locations: Tickets available at the Asheville Visitor Center. You may also board the trolley at any one of the 8 stops and purchase your ticket on-board during the tour.

Boarding and Departure: You can board the trolley at any of their convenient trolley stops. See website for departure times. Main departure at Asheville Visitor Center, 36 Montford Ave., Asheville NC 28801.

Telephone: 828-251-8687, 866-592-8687.

Notes: Unlimited hop-on and hop-off privileges. 2nd day free.

LaZoom City Comedy Tours

Tour Description: Rolling Comedy or Haunted Comedy bus tours, all on LaZoom's famous purple bus.

Days of Operation: Apr.–Oct. Tue–Sat 6pm

Length of Tour: 90 minutes

Ticket Locations: Reserve seating online, by phone or arrive 15 minutes prior to departure and get on bus if seating remains available.

Boarding and Departure: Tours depart from the French Broad Food Co-op at 90 Biltmore Ave., in downtown Asheville.

Telephone: 828-225-6932

Moving Sidewalk Tours

Tour Description: Guided Segway tours of downtown Asheville, including the Grove Arcade, Urban Trail and historic architecture.

Days of Operation: 9am, 1pm and 5pm daily.

Length of Tour: Required 20–45 minutes of training followed by 2 to 2.5 hour tour.

Ticket Locations: Asheville Visitor Information Center, 36 Montford Ave., Asheville NC 28801.

Boarding and Departure: Asheville Visitor Center, 36 Montford Ave., Asheville NC 28801.

Telephone: 828-776-8687

Website: movingsidewalktours.com

Notes: Riders must weigh between 100 and 260 lbs.

Self-Guided Tours & Itineraries

Urban Trail

One of the best ways to experience downtown Asheville is by walking the Urban Trail. This self-guided tour takes a few hours and follows thematic markers (*See* Section III, Chapter Five).

Historic Asheville

If you are interested in history and especially architecture, then there are a number of self-guided tours by car that you might be interested in doing. These tours visit four of Asheville's eleven Historic Districts and highlight all of the interesting and really important buildings and sites. The four are Montford, Chestnut Hill, Grove Park and Biltmore Village. (*See* Section III, Chapter Four)

Historic Hendersonville

A self-guided walking tour by car of historic Main St. in downtown Hendersonville. (*See* Section IV, Chapter Three)

Biltmore Estate

A visit to Biltmore Estate is one of the high points of any visit to Asheville and is highly recommended. You will want to allow a minimum of half a day to see the grounds and estate as well as allowing time to eat at one of the Estate's three fine restaurants. Afterwards, be sure to take some time to visit the historic Biltmore Village just outside the estate entrance. (*See* Section III, Chapter Three)

High Country Adventure

For this tour, allow a whole day or more. Start off by packing a gourmet picnic (*See* Section II, Chapter Seven) and heading east on the Blue Ridge Parkway. Your first stop will be the Folk Art Center (*See* Section III, Chapter Two) just east of Asheville at milepost 382; then continue north to Craggy Gardens at milepost 364. Here you will find nature trails, native rhododendron and magnificent views. Continue on to Mount Mitchell State Park at milepost 355 (*See* Section V, Chapter One) and hike the short distance to the tower on the summit. Mount Mitchell will be a great place to picnic. After lunch continue up the parkway to Grandfather Mountain at milepost 305. (*See* Section V, Chapter One) After visiting Grandfather, if you have time, there are a couple of excellent options. You can visit Linville Caverns (*See* Section V, Chapter One) or take in Tweetsie Railroad. (*See* Section V, Chapter 2) Return to Asheville by Hwy. 19 East through Burnsville.

The Land of the Cherokee

Allow one full day for this outing that will take you two hours west to Cherokee Indian Reservation. (*See* Section V, Chapter Two) Take I-40 west from Asheville and get off at Exit 27. Follow 19/23 & 74 to Cherokee. At Cherokee you will want to also visit the Oconaluftee Indian Village and the Cherokee Indian Museum. During the afternoon you may wish to drive south on U.S. 441 about 14 miles to Dillsboro and take a ride on the Great Smoky Mountains Railway. (*See* Section V, Chapter Two)

View of Craggy Gardens off the Blue Ridge Parkway at milepost 364

Waterfalls & Trout!

This day trip is a great one for kids. Be sure and bring a picnic lunch. You will be visiting the Pisgah District of the Pisgah National Forest and seeing some spectacular waterfalls. Take the Blue Ridge Parkway south and stop at the Pisgah Inn for some wonderful views of the mountains. Just beyond, get on 276 south and follow this into the forest. Stop at the Cradle of Forestry and visit the Forest Discovery Center. (*See* Section V, Chapter Two) Continue on and turn right on Forest Rd. 445 to the Fish Hatchery. The kids will really love this. They can hand-feed monster trout! After the fish hatchery, continue on to Sliding Rock, where they can put on their bathing suits and slide down a wonderful natural waterslide. After Sliding Rock, the nearby Looking Glass Falls is the perfect place for a picnic lunch. If you have time, you may wish to see other waterfalls in the area (*See* Section V, Chapter One) or return to Asheville by way of Hwy. 280.

Last of the Mohicans

This day trip is also a great one for kids. It will take you from an historic site in Asheville to the exact spot where the famous trail scene in "The Last of the Mohicans" was filmed. Begin your tour in Asheville by taking Charlotte St. to #265, The Manor. This impressive historic building (*See* Section III, Chapter Four) was where the headquarters scene in the movie "Last of the Mohicans" was filmed. Cast members of an earlier movie, "The Swan," including Grace Kelly, also stayed here while filming. After visiting the Manor, return by way of Charlotte St. and get on I-240 east. Get off at exit 9 (Bat Cave, Lake Lure) and take Scenic Byway 74A through beautiful Fairview to Hickory Nut Gap. While passing through Hickory Nut Gap, you will see the historic Sherrill's Inn. (*See* Section III, Chapter Four) Continue on 74A through Bat Cave (so named for the numerous bat caves in the area) and down into Chimney Rock. This will be your major destination (*See* Section V, Chapter One) and at Chimney Rock you will be able to hike the wonderful trails with their unbelievable views.

After Chimney Rock, which will take you two-three hours, return to your car and journey on 74A to Lake Lure. At the beginning of the lake is a public beach where the kids can swim. Finish out the day with a wonderful boat tour of Lake Lure. (*See* Section V, Chapter One) Lake Lure is one of the most beautiful man-made lakes in the world and this boat ride is a real treat. The boats are operated by Lake Lure Tours and are located at the Lake Lure Marina on Hwy. 64/74A.

Chimney Rock Park

Return to Asheville by taking 74A west from Lake Lure through Chimney Rock and then turning left on Hwy. 64 toward Hendersonville. This will take you through some lovely apple growing sections (*See* Section IV, Chapter Seven) and to I-26, which you will take north to Asheville.

Famous Authors

If the lives of famous writers interest you, this is the day trip for you. Begin by visiting the Thomas Wolfe Memorial (*See* Section III, Chapter Two) in the morning. After touring the historic boyhood home of Thomas Wolfe, travel to nearby Riverside Cemetery in the Montford Historic District, where Wolfe and author O.Henry (William Sidney Porter) are buried. (*See* Section III, Chapter Four) From the Wolfe memorial get on I-240 heading west and get off at the next exit, Montford. Take Montford Ave. north into the Montford area and turn left onto Cullowee St. Turn right onto Pearson Dr. and then left onto Birch St. to the cemetery.

Connemara, former home of poet Carl Sandburg, located in Flat Rock

After visiting the grave sites (refer to cemetery map in Riverside Cemetery section), drive to the famous Omni Grove Park Inn (*See* Section III, Chapter Four) for lunch by retracing your steps to I-240 and going east to the Charlotte St. exit. Take Charlotte St. to Macon Ave. and then to the hotel. Many famous authors, including F. Scott Fitzgerald and his wife, Zelda, have stayed at this historic resort. After lunch, travel to Hendersonville via I-240 west and I-26 south. Take exit 18 off I-26 onto 64 west. Follow 64 west to just beyond Hendersonville. Look for Oakdale Cemetery on your left and the State Historic Hwy. Marker indicating the Thomas Wolfe Angel. (*See* Section IV, Chapter Four) You may park your car and get out and visit this lovely statue which Wolfe immortalized in his famous novel *Look Homeward Angel.* After viewing the statue, return to Hendersonville by way of 64 east. Turn right on Main St. (Highway 25 south) and follow this through Hendersonville to Flat Rock, a few miles south. In Flat Rock, you will pass by the famous Flat Rock Playhouse (*See* Section IV, Chapter Two), where the dramatic works of legendary authors are performed every summer. Turn right onto Little River Rd. just beyond the playhouse and visit the home of poet Carl Sandburg, "Connemara." After touring the home and seeing the grounds, return to Asheville by Hwy. 25 north through Hendersonville and then on I-26.

Chapter Nine
Historic Churches

The greater Asheville and Hendersonville area has over 350 religious institutions with the Baptist Church (150+ churches) and Methodist Church (60+ churches) being the two largest denominations. Of special interest to visitors and residents alike are the beautiful historic churches. Some of the more noteworthy and historic are presented below. For a complete listing of all of the historic churches, visit my guidebook website at ashevilleguidebook.com .

Basilica of St. Lawrence

To the north of the Grove Arcade area in downtown Asheville is the remarkable Basilica of Saint Lawrence, Deacon and Martyr, built in 1909. A Spanish Baroque Revival Roman Catholic Church built of red brick with polychrome glazed terracotta inserts and limestone trim, it was designed by world-famous architect/engineer Raphael Guastavino. The church employs his "cohesive construction" techniques in its large oval tile dome and Catalan-style vaulting in its two towers. The massive stone foundations and the solid brick superstructure give silent testimony to the architect's desire to build an edifice that would endure for generations. There are no beams of wood or steel in the entire structure; all walls, floors, ceilings and pillars are of tile or other masonry materials. The dome is entirely self supporting, has a clear span of 58 x 82 feet and is reputed to be the largest unsupported dome in North America. The Crucifixion tableaux of the Basilica altar feature a rare example of seventeenth century Spanish woodcarving. The windows are of German origin, and the Basilica has two chapels. Attached by an arcade is the 1929 Neo-Tuscan Renaissance brick rectory designed by Father Michael of Belmont Abbey. Self-guided tour brochures are available at the church, and guided tours are given after Sun masses.

Denomination: Roman Catholic
Address: 97 Haywood St., Asheville NC 28801
Telephone: 828-252-6042
Directions: From Pack Square take Patton Ave. west to Pritchard Park. Turn right onto Haywood St.

Cathedral of All Souls

Originally known as All Souls Church, this edifice was designated an Episcopal Cathedral in January 1995. The largest structure in Biltmore Village, it is an exquisite, lovely building of fine Romanesque style. Designed by Richard Morris Hunt, this complex building combines pebble dash wall surfaces, brick and wood trim, and expansive tiles roofs. In spite of the complexity, however, the church is a simple cruciform with a tall tower rising in the center which contains most of the interior space. The Parish House features the same materials but is considerably different in design. The interior is relatively simple but no less elegant and features wonderful stained glass windows created for the Vanderbilts by Maitland Armstrong and his daughter Helen. They illuminate a variety of scenes from the Old and New Testaments. George Vanderbilt was one of the organizers of the congregation in 1896. He financed the construction of the church and parish house and selected the furnishings. The church was consecrated on Nov. 8, 1896.

Denomination: Episcopal
Address: 9 Swan St., Biltmore Village, Asheville NC 28803
Telephone: 828-274-2681
Directions: From Pack Square, take Biltmore Ave. south to Biltmore Village. The Cathedral of All Souls will be on your left as you pass through the village.

First Baptist Church

Built in 1927, the First Baptist Church of Asheville was designed by noted architect Douglas Ellington from his sketches of a cathedral in Florence, Italy. Two major additions have been made to the building. The Children's Wing was added in 1968, and the Sherman Family Center in 1980. This wonderfully elegant building is an unusual combination of an Early Italian Renaissance form and color scheme arranged in a beaux arts plan with Art Deco detailing. Of particular interest is the Art Deco copper lantern atop the dome and the subtle gradation of color in the roofing tiles. The walls are an effective combination of orange bricks, terracotta moldings and pink marble.

Denomination: Baptist
Address: 5 Oak St., Asheville NC 28801
Telephone: 828-252-4781
Directions: From Pack Square go east on Broadway and turn right onto Woodfin St. to Oak St. The First Baptist Church will be on your left.

St. James Episcopal Church

St. James Episcopal Church, located on Main St. in downtown Hendersonville, is one of the area's most picturesque churches. Consecrated in 1861, the first rector was Rev. N. Collin Hughes. From 1970 to 1980, Henderson County experienced an unprecedented population growth. New economic developments, the discovery of Hendersonville as an outstanding retirement area, and growth in tourism marked this period. Consequently, St. James Church flourished and became the largest parish in the Episcopal Diocese of Western North Carolina during that time.

Denomination: Episcopal
Address: 766 North Main St., Hendersonville NC 28792
Telephone: 828-693-7458
Directions: North side of downtown on Main St.

St. John in the Wilderness Church

A unique spot of southern history in a setting of idyllic beauty, St. John in the Wilderness Episcopal Church in Flat Rock is a gable roof brick church that has at its southeast corner a three-story square tower with pyramidal roof. In 1833, Charles and Susan Baring built the church as a private chapel, and at the formation of the Episcopal Diocese of Western North Carolina in 1836, the Baring family gave up their rights to the church as a private chapel, turning the deed over to the bishop of the newly-formed diocese. Among the family plots in the graveyard are the graves of Christopher Memminger, first secretary of the Confederate treasury; Rev. John Grimke Dr.ayton, developer of the world famous Magnolia Gardens; members of families of three signers of the Declaration of Independence; and Edward P. King, the World War II general who led the infamous Bataan death march.

Denomination: Episcopal
Address: 1895 Greenville Hwy., Flat Rock NC
Telephone: 828-693-7458
Hours: The church and graveyard are open daily 9am–4pm for visitation.
Directions: From downtown Hendersonville take Hwy. 25 south toward Flat Rock. St. John in the Wilderness Church will be on your right.

St. Mary's Church in Grove Park

Described in the year of her founding in 1914 as a "Wayside Shrine in the Mountains of Western North Carolina," beautiful little St. Mary's Church has attracted countless visitors over the years. Designed by Richard Sharp Smith and built in 1914, the church is English Gothic in style and cruciform in plan. Constructed out of red brick with steeply pitched gable roofs, the building is like those dotting the hilly landscape of Counties Durham, Northumberland and Cumbria in northern England. The English cottage-style Rectory, also designed by Smith, was built and set in beautiful landscaped grounds. The landscape architect was Frederick Law Olmsted, architect for Biltmore Estate and designer of New York's Central Park. International attention was brought to St. Mary's by the writer Gail Godwin when she immortalized the church in her novel *"Father Melancholy's Daughter"*.

Denomination: Episcopal
Address: 337 Charlotte St., Asheville NC 28801
Telephone: 828-254-5836
Directions: From Pack Square, go south on College St. and turn left onto Charlotte St. east to 337 on your right.

Chapter Ten
Art Galleries

Asheville

Resources and art districts.

Mountain Xpress: A free weekly independent news, arts, and events newspaper for Western North Carolina. Excellent entertainment coverage, local commentary. PO Box 144, Asheville NC 28802; 828-251-1333.

Asheville Area Arts Council: Located in Asheville, the Asheville Area Arts Council is a nonprofit umbrella service organization that represents the interests of more than 100 cultural and arts related groups. 207 Coxe Avenue, Asheville NC 28801; 828-258-0710.

River Arts District: While most of the galleries exist in the downtown Asheville area (visit ashevilledowntowngalleries.org for current lineup of downtown galleries), the River Arts District, located on the French Broad River, is the newest artist hotspot. This former industrial and warehouse district now is home to a growing number of artists and crafts persons, many of whom open their studios to the public. The River Arts District is defined clearly by small "River District" signs along the roads and St. and is easy to find. To get to the River Arts District from Pack Square, go west on Patton Ave. and turn left on Clingman Ave. Clingman Ave. takes you directly to the River Arts District. Website: riverartsdistrict.com

Art Galleries

American Folk: Contemporary Southern folk art, North Carolina wood-fired pottery, custom picture frames and a generous helping of whimsy, exuberance and inspiration. 64 Biltmore Ave., Asheville NC 28801; 828-281-2134.

Asheville Art Museum: Ongoing exhibits of local and nationally known artists. The museum's permanent collection features 100 years worth of images, including those of America's acclaimed impressionists, regionalists and abstract artists. 2 South Pack Sq., Asheville NC 28801; 828-253-3227.

Asheville Gallery of Art: Top quality original paintings by local artists. Cooperative artist-run gallery. 16 College St., Asheville NC 28801; 828-251-5796.

Black Mountain College Museum + Arts Center: The Black Mountain College Museum + Arts Center is an exhibition space and resource center dedicated to exploring the history and legacy of the world's most acclaimed experimental educational community. 56 Broadway, Asheville NC 28801; 828-350-8484.

Blue Spiral 1: Features changing shows of sculptures and paintings. Oils, pastels, mixed media and watercolor. More than 11,000 square feet of gallery space. World-class gallery. 38 Biltmore Ave., Asheville NC 28801; 828-251-0202.

Cherry Orchard Studio: Pen and ink drawings of Asheville and Western North Carolina. 828-779-1569. cherryorchardstudio.com.

Flood Gallery Fine Arts Center: The Flood Gallery Fine Art Center is a non-profit arts organization dedicated to promoting the arts in Asheville through the exhibition of established and emerging artists from all over the world. 109 Roberts St., Asheville NC 28801; 828-254-2166.

Grand Bohemian Gallery: Located in the Grand Bohemian Hotel in Biltmore Village and other luxury Kessler Collection Hotels throughout the country. Contemporary painting, art glass, ceramics, jewelry and sculpture. 11 Boston Way, Asheville NC 28803; 828-274-1242.

Kress Emporium: Original crafts and art by local artists and crafters as well as home furnishings and decorative accessories. 19 Patton Ave., Asheville NC 28801; 828-281-2252.

Momentum Art Gallery: Contemporary and modern art in 4000 sq. ft gallery space. 24 N Lexington Avenue, Asheville, NC 28801; 828-505-8550

The Bender Gallery: One of Asheville's premier studio art glass galleries and its largest on two sun filled levels. 12 S. Lexington Ave., Asheville NC 28801; 828-505-8341.

The Complete Naturalist: Biltmore Village gallery representing local as well as internationally-known nature artists that include Carl Brenders, Robert Bateman, Bev Doolittle, Charles Frace, Charley Harper, Terry Isaac, Roger Tory Peterson, and John James Audubon. 2 Brook St., Asheville NC 28803; 828-274-5430.

The Haen Gallery: The Haen Gallery is committed to providing access to stunning and unique artwork for discerning collectors and the local community in general. 52 Biltmore Ave., Asheville NC 28801; 828-254-8577.

University of North Carolina at Asheville Gallery: The University has two galleries located in Owen Hall, Second Floor Gallery and University Gallery, that have monthly exhibitions. UNCA, Owen Hall, One University Heights, Asheville NC 28804; 828-251-6559.

Hendersonville

For a complete listing of all current exhibitions and ongoing art-related events, pick up a free local entertainment guide at the Hendersonville/Flat Rock Visitors Information Center. The *Hendersonville Times-News* also has current listings in the "Preview Page" of the Fri edition

Arts Council of Henderson County: The Arts Council of Henderson County is a community organization that advocates for the arts and provides opportunities to enrich the lives of Henderson County's children and adults through the arts by offering exhibits and art education programs. 401 N Main St., Hendersonville NC 28972; 828-693-8504. Website: acofhc.org

Art League of Henderson County: The purpose of the Art League of Henderson County is the promotion, development, and enjoyment of the visual arts. The Art League has more than 200 members. PO Box 514, Hendersonville NC 28793. Website: artleague.net

Art Galleries

Arts Council of Henderson County Gallery: Ongoing exhibits of national and regional artists. 401 North Main St., Hendersonville NC 28792; 828-693-8504.

Art League of Henderson County Gallery: Monthly ongoing exhibits of original work by local guest artists. Located at Opportunity House, 1411 Asheville Hwy., Hendersonville NC 28791; 828-692-0575.

Art Mob Studios and Marketplace: Wonderful, eclectic mix of over 90 renowned local artists and crafters conveniently located downtown Hendersonville. 124 4th Street East, Hendersonville NC 28792, 828-693-4545.

Chapter Eleven
Craft Galleries

Asheville

Resources:

For a complete listing of all current exhibitions and ongoing art-related events, pick up a copy of the free weekly publication "Mountain Express".

Mountain Xpress: A free weekly independent news, arts, and events newspaper for Western North Carolina. Excellent entertainment coverage, local commentary. PO Box 144, Asheville NC 28802; 828-251-1333.

Odyssey Center for Ceramic Arts: Studio school located in the River Arts District whose mission is to promote understanding, appreciation and development in the ceramic arts. Classes, workshops and gallery. 236 Clingman Ave., Asheville NC 28801; 828-285-0210. Website: highwaterclays.com

Craft Galleries

Allanstand Craft Shop at the Folk Art Center: One of Appalachia's oldest and best-known craft shops. Sells the work of more than 200 members of the Southern Highland Craft Guild. Milepost 382, Blue Ridge Parkway in Asheville, 298-7928.

American Folk: Contemporary Southern folk art, North Carolina wood-fired pottery, custom picture frames and a generous helping of whimsy, exuberance and inspiration. 64 Biltmore Ave., Asheville NC 28801; 828-281-2134.

Appalachian Crafts: Traditional hand-made Appalachian crafts, including pottery, heirloom quality quilts, hand blown glass and wood carvings. Two locations: 10 North Spruce St., Asheville NC 28801 and in the Renaissance Asheville Hotel, 1 Thomas Wolfe Plaza, Asheville NC 28801; 828-253-8499.

Ariel Gallery: A cooperative gallery featuring local artists working within a range of fine crafts, offering original works in pottery, sculpture, glass, furniture, jewelry, fiber wearables, decorative fiber and mixed media. 19 Biltmore Ave., Asheville NC 28801; 828-236-2660.

Bellagio: Biltmore Village gallery that features exquisitely handcrafted jewelry and clothing. One of top craft galleries in the Asheville area. 5 Biltmore Plaza, Asheville NC 28803; 828-277-8100.

Blue: Biltmore Village gallery offering jewelry designs in four colors of gold, plus sterling. Also works by local artists in raku, pottery, photography and glass. 1 Swan St., Asheville NC 28803; 828-277-2583.

Gallery of the Mountains: Extensive selection of fine mountain crafts by regional and national artisans. Hand-dyed and hand-painted silk vests, hand-woven coats, wraps and scarves, pottery, woodwork and jewelry. Located in the Omni Grove Park Inn Resort and Spa. 290 Macon Ave., Asheville NC 28804; 828-254-2068.

Grovewood Gallery: A spacious shop displaying the work of some of the Southeast's finest craftspeople. Highest quality innovative work on display. A must-see gallery located in the Homespun Shops next to the Omni Grove Park Inn Resort and Spa. 111 Grovewood Rd., Asheville NC 28804; 828-253-7651.

Guild Crafts: Features the work of regional artists who are members of the Southern Highland Handicraft Guild. 930 Tunnel Rd., Asheville NC 28805; 828-298-7903.

Kress Emporium: Original crafts and art by local artists and crafters as well as home furnishings and decorative accessories. 19 Patton Ave., Asheville NC 28801; 828-281-2252.

Lexington Glassworks: Original high-quality art glass studio, showroom and bar. 81 S Lexington Ave, Asheville, NC 28801; 828-348-8427

Mountain Made: Regional crafts, including jewelry, pottery, glass, wood, and metal. Local books and music. Owned by nonprofit Mountain BizWorks, located in the Grove Arcade Public Market. 1 Page Ave., Ste 123, Grove Arcade Asheville NC 28801, 828-350-0307.

New Morning Gallery: Located in Biltmore Village, New Morning Gallery is one of Asheville's premier craft galleries. Functional and sculptural pottery, fine art glass, furniture, jewelry and other handmade objects. 7 Boston Way, Biltmore Gallery, Asheville NC 28803; 828-274-2831.

Odyssey Gallery: Located in the River District, the Odyssey Gallery features pottery and works of art in clay and ceramics by Odyssey Center for Ceramic Arts instructors and artist. 236 Clingman Ave., Asheville NC 28801; 828-285-0210.

Stuart Nye Jewelry: Hand wrought jewelry since 1933. Originator of the Dogwood Jewelry. 940 Tunnel Rd., Asheville NC 28805, 828-298-7988.

Woolworth Walk: Over 150 artists and crafts persons selling and making jewelry, fine art, decorative art and crafts in a nearly 20,000 square foot air-conditioned display and studio space. 25 Haywood St., Asheville NC 28801; 828-254-9234.

Hendersonville

Resources:

For a complete listing of all current exhibitions and ongoing art-related events, pick up a free local entertainment guide at the Hendersonville/Flat Rock Visitors Information Center. *The Hendersonville Times-News* also has current listings in the "Preview Page" of the Fri edition.

Arts Council of Henderson County: The Arts Council of Henderson County is a community organization that advocates for the arts and provides opportunities to enrich the lives of Henderson County's children and adults through the arts by offering exhibits and art education programs. 401 N. Main St., #3, Hendersonville NC 28972, 828-693-8504. Website: acofhc.org.

Art League of Henderson County: The purpose of the Art League of Henderson County is the promotion, development, and enjoyment of the visual arts. The Art League has more than 200 members. PO Box 514, Hendersonville NC 28793. Website: artleague.net.

Craft Galleries

Art Mob Studios and Marketplace: Wonderful, eclectic mix of over 90 renowned local artists and crafters conveniently located downtown Hendersonville. 124 4th Street East, Hendersonville NC 28792, 828-693-4545.

Carolina Mountain Artists: Arts and crafts by regional artists. Fine art and traditional crafts 444 N. Main St., Hendersonville NC 28792; 828-696-0707.

Narnia Studios: Established in 1982, Narnia Studios features affordable original art by Hendersonville artists, including local pottery and art glass. Narnia is the creator of "Chalk It Up1" one of the country's oldest chalk art contests. 315 N. Main St., Hendersonville NC 28972; 828-697-6393.

Silver Fox Gallery: Contemporary American art, craft and furniture. 508 N. Main St., Hendersonville, 28801; 828-698-0601.

Chapter Twelve
Shopping

Asheville has a great range of shopping opportunities, from charming historic shopping districts to major malls. Downtown Asheville is a mix of art and craft galleries, specialty shops, bookstores and antique shops. Especially noteworthy is the historic Wall St. district, with its fascinating collection of shops, the recently restored Grove Arcade Public Market, and Biltmore Village, a historic district of specialty and gift shops.

Asheville Malls and Shopping Districts

Asheville Mall: Asheville's major mall located on Tunnel Rd. Take Exit 7 off I-240. 3 South Tunnel Rd., Asheville NC 28805, 828-298-0012.

Asheville Outlets: 325,000-sq.ft. open-air center that features 75 manufacturers and retail outlets. Located on the west side of Asheville off I-26. Take Exit 2 off I-26. 800 Brevard Rd., Asheville NC 28806.

Biltmore Village: Built in the late 1890s as a classic planned community at the entrance to George Vanderbilt's Biltmore Estate in Asheville NC.

Grove Arcade Public Market: Built by E.W. Grove, creator of the Omni Grove Park Inn Resort and Spa, the Grove Arcade opened in 1929 and thrived until World War II as one of the country's leading public markets. Restored and reopened to the public in 2002, the Grove Arcade is not only one of Asheville's architectural jewels, it is also home to a large number of unique shops and restaurants. The Arcade is located downtown just to the west of Haywood St.

Lexington Ave. District: The Lexington Ave. district is located in downtown Asheville, just north of Pack Square and is home to some of the city's most interesting and diverse stores. The lineup ranges from neo-hippy to contemporary chic and features shops known for funk, punk and creative gifts, as well as coffee shops and sidewalk cafes.

River Arts District: Located in a former industrial area of Asheville along the French Broad River, the River Arts District today is now one of the arts and crafts centers of Asheville.

Hendersonville Malls and Shopping Districts

Blue Ridge Mall: Located on the east side of Hendersonville on Hwy. 64.

Main St.: Downtown Hendersonville is the primary shopping district in Hendersonville. Specialty shops, gift stores, card stores, galleries, craft outlets, antiques and much more. This pleasant St. is unique not only for its rich collection of stores but also the beautiful flowers, benches, and shady trees.

Flea Markets

Smiley's Flea Market: Fri–Sun, 7am–5pm Located halfway between Asheville and Henderson. One of the largest outdoor flea markets in North Carolina. Every weekend. 5360 Hendersonville Rd., Fletcher NC 28732; 828-684-3532.

Auctions

Bagwell and Associates: Full-service auctions for businesses, estates and individuals and specialty auctions of entire collections. 29 Fanning Bridge Rd., Fletcher NC 28732; 828-651-9699.

Brunk Auctions: Asheville's version of Sotheby's. Elegant and respected, and includes world-class antiques that go up for sale. 117 Tunnel Rd., Asheville NC 28805; 828-254-6846.

Asheville Antique Stores

Asheville is a shopping mecca for antique lovers from all over the world. Here they can stroll through antique shops conveniently grouped in two different parts of town (Lexington Ave. District and Biltmore Village) or visit often larger antique "malls" sprinkled throughout the city.

Antique Market Gallery: Offering a large selection of functional antique items for the home including seating, beds and paintings. 52 Broadway, Asheville NC 28801; 828-259-9977.

Antique Tobacco Barn: The Antique Tobacco Barn is a 25-year-old, 77,000-square-foot antique store located in a historic tobacco barn that has the largest selection of antiques in North Carolina. Over 75 dealers offering antique furniture, collectibles, and fine art. 75 Swannanoa River Rd., Asheville NC 28805; 828-252-7291.

Chatsworth Art and Antiques: Antiques, oils, etchings, European collectibles and more. 54 N. Lexington Ave., Asheville NC 28801; 828-252-6004.

Fireside Antiques and Interiors: Twenty-five years experience importing English antiques. A premier source of antiques in Western North Carolina. Extensive selection of Oriental and European porcelain as well as reproduction gift items. 1 Village Lane, Asheville NC 28803; 828-274-7572.

L.O.F.T. Lost Objects Found Treasures: Unique furniture, handmade paper journals, ironwork, art, baskets, French soaps, scented candles, pottery and garden stuff... 53 Broadway St., Asheville NC 28801; 828-259-9303.

Oddfellows Antique Warehouse: Over 16,000 sq. ft of hand-picked European Antiques from England, France and much of Western Europe. They also have select dealers at our shop featuring antiques from the states and abroad giving an overall European flair to their warehouse. 124 Swannanoa River Rd., Asheville NC 28805; 828-350-7800.

The Regeneration Station: 36,000 sq. ft. of antiques, salvage materials, industrial items, home decor and consignment. 26 Glendale Avenue, Asheville NC 28803; 828-505-1108

ScreenDoor: 25,000 square feet of unique home and garden accessories from more than 100 vendors. 115 Fairview Road, Asheville NC 28803; 828-277-3667

Sweeten Creek Antiques and Collectibles: 31,000 Sq. Ft of antiques and collectibles of all types. 115 Sweeten Creek Rd., Asheville NC 28803; 828-277-6100.

Village Antiques: Since 1989, a destination shop for designers and collectors of fine antique furniture and art. Regularly imports from France, and their shop in offers over 25,000 square feet of antiques, fine art, and decorative arts, both European and American, as well as specialized collections of Southern Furniture, pottery, and folk art, and African art. 755 Biltmore Ave., Asheville NC 28803; 828-252-5090.

Hendersonville Antique Stores

Jane Asher Antiques and Fine Traditions: 344 N. Main St., Hendersonville NC 28792; 828-698-0018.

Mehri and Company: 501 N. Main St., Hendersonville NC 28792; 828-693-0887.

Nana's Antiques: 122 West Allen St., Hendersonville NC 28792; 828-697-8979.

Nancy Roth Antiques: 127 4th Ave. West, Hendersonville NC 28792; 828- 697-7555.

Piggy's and Harry's: 102 Duncan Hill Rd., Hendersonville NC 28792; 828-692-1995.

Scotties Jewelry and Fine Art: 314 N. Main St., Hendersonville NC 28792; 828-692-1350.

Village Green Antique Mall: 424 N. Main St., Hendersonville NC 28792; 828-692-9057.

Chapter Thirteen
Nightlife

Asheville has a vibrant downtown, and the combination of great historic architecture, fine restaurants, coffeehouses, specialty stores, art galleries and nightclubs, pubs and cafes all add to the mix that has made the city an exciting nighttime destination. Downtown Asheville is especially interesting and eclectic after dark, with street musicians and the popular long-running drum circle. The number one music venue in Asheville is The Orange Peel.

Listed below is a selection of the more established and popular venues and places to check out. The best way to get a handle on what is happening in Asheville is to pick up a copy of one of the mountain Xpress.

Mountain Xpress: A free weekly independent news, arts, and events newspaper for Western North Carolina. Excellent entertainment coverage, local commentary. PO Box 144, Asheville NC 28802; 828-251-1333.

Asheville

Asheville Pizza and Brewing: One screen, second-run Hollywood and independent films at discount prices. Pizza and microbrews available in theater or adjoining restaurant. Live entertainment and tons of dance floor. 675 Merrimon Ave., Asheville NC 28804; 828-254-5339.

Barley's Taproom and Pizzeria: One of Asheville's most popular watering holes. Great selection of beer, including microbrews, and wonderful pizzas. Entertainment Tue, Thu, Sat and Sun with a blend of jazz, blue-grass and more. Billiard tables and dart boards available upstairs. 42 Biltmore Ave., Asheville NC 28801; 828-255-0504.

Jack of The Wood: In addition to making their own unique beers and ales, Jack of the Wood offers a distinctively British-style pub atmosphere. They also feature fresh-baked breads and desserts to go along with the local performers. 95 Patton Ave., Asheville NC 28801; 828-252-5445.

LAB: Short for Lexington Ave. Brew, the LAB has emerged as a local favorite on the Asheville scene. Local microbrewery serving their own beer, music venue, great food and a full bar. 39 N. Lexington Ave., Asheville NC 28801; 828-252-0212

Malaprop's Bookstore and Café: Cafe located downtown in the Asheville's best privately owned bookstore. Live music (no cover charge) most Fri and Sat. 55 Haywood St., Asheville NC 28801; 828-254-6734.

Orange Peel Social Aid and Pleasure Club: Asheville's premier entertainment venue. Always a great lineup of big-name talent, huge concert hall with room enough for almost 1,000. Most shows start early, are standing only and non-smoking. Beer and wine. 101 Biltmore Ave., Asheville NC 28801; 828-225-5851.

Pack's Tavern: Located on the west side of Pack Square Park, Pack's Tavern offers an eclectic menu, over 30 beers on tap, and live music with no cover in a restored early 20th-century setting. 20 S. Spruce St., Asheville NC 28801; 828-225-6944.

Tressa's Downtown Jazz and Blues: Live jazz and blues every night in a unique setting. Old New Orleans elegance, great service and world-class jazz and blues performers. 28 Broadway, Asheville NC 28801; 828-254-7072.

The Garage at Biltmore: Live music venue sharing the same building with French Broad Brewery and Monte Vecchia Music and Arts Studio. 101 Fairfield Rd., Ste B, Asheville NC 28803; 828-505-2663.

The Grey Eagle: The Grey Eagle has become one of Asheville's premier music halls. Situated in Asheville's vibrant French Broad River district, the Grey Eagle is known for presenting local and nationally known artists, making it a cornerstone of the Asheville music scene. 185 Clingman Ave., Asheville NC 28801; 828-232-5800.

Westville Pub: Something happening seven evenings a week, including open mike nights. Non-smoking pub serving a light menu. 777 Haywood Rd., Asheville NC 28806; 821-225-9782.

Hendersonville

Eleanor's Sports Tavern and Grill: 12 drafts and full service bar, 10 H.D.TVs, 430 N. Main St., Hendersonville NC 28792; 828-692-3100.

Hannah Flanagan's Pub and Eatery: More than 30 beers on tap, pub food and Irish dishes. Live music. 300 N. Main St., Hendersonville NC 28739; 828-696-1665.

Chapter Fourteen

Theatre & Dance

Theatre is alive and well in Western North Carolina, especially in the Asheville, Hendersonville and Flat Rock area. Big-city ensembles regularly return each year. There is a strong local theatre, which ranges from innovative and cutting-edge performances by the Montford Park Players to the full-scale productions at the Diana Wortham Theatre (*See* Section III, Chapter Two, Pack Place Education, Arts & Science Center). You can even find Shakespeare in the summer from the Montford Park Players. Asheville also has an established theater in the Asheville Community Theatre (ACT), which regularly schedules award-winning shows. (*See* Section III, Chapter Two). Located in Flat Rock, the Flat Rock Playhouse has been rated one of the top ten summer theaters in the nation. Home to the Vagabond Players, this theater is a major attraction. (*See* Section IV, Chapter Two).

Theatre

For a complete listing of all current performances, pick up a copy of the free weekly publications Mountain Xpress.

Mountain Xpress: A free weekly independent news, arts, and events newspaper for Western North Carolina. Excellent entertainment coverage, local commentary. PO Box 144, Asheville NC 28802; 828-251-1333.

Asheville Area Theatres

(For a complete listing of all theatres in Western North Carolina, visit my guidebook website at ashevilleguidebook.com)

Asheville Community Theatre: Asheville's primary community theatre. 35 E. Walnut St., Asheville NC 28801; 828-254-1320.

Blue Ridge Performing Arts Center: Featuring a grand marble lobby, a cozy 100 seat theatre and a 20 seat digital screening room, the center is a venue for all types of musical entertainment, comedy, live theatre, host to various writers, speakers, community events, parties and children's events. 538 North Main St., Hendersonville NC 28702; 828-693-0087

Brevard Little Theatre: Official community theater of Transylvania County. American Legion Hall, 55 East Jordan St., Brevard NC 28712; 828-884-2587

Flat Rock Playhouse, home of the Vagabond Players

Diana Wortham Theatre: 500 seat theatre and performance venue located in Pack Place downtown Asheville. 2 South Pack Square, Asheville NC 28801; 828-257-4530.

Flat Rock Playhouse: State Theatre of North Carolina. Located in nearby Flat Rock (25 miles south of Asheville). 2661 Greenville Hwy., Flat Rock NC 28731; 828-693-0731.

Hendersonville Little Theatre: Since 1996, staging five shows annually. Located at the Barn, State St. between Kanuga and Willow, PO Box 66, Hendersonville NC 28793; 828-692-1082.

Southern Appalachian Repertory Theatre: 44 College St., Mars Hill NC 28754; 828-689-1384.

Performance Organizations & Concert Series

Asheville Lyric Opera: Opera at its best in Asheville. 39 S. Market St., Asheville NC 28801; 828-236-0670.

Asheville Symphony Orchestra: Asheville's major symphony orchestra. PO Box 2852, Asheville NC 28802; 828-254-7046.

Hendersonville Symphony: Hendersonville's symphony orchestra, performances at the Blue Ridge Conference Hall. PO Box 1811, Hendersonville NC 28793; 828-697-5884.

North Carolina Stage Company: Professional theatre in an intimate off-Broadway style in downtown Asheville. 15 Stage Lane, Asheville NC 28801; 828-239-0263.

Poetry Alive: Performance poetry like nothing else! 70 Woodfin Place, Ste WW4C, Asheville NC 28801, 800-476-8172.

Western North Carolina Jazz Society: Performances at Diana Wortham Theatre by acclaimed local and nationally recognized jazz artists. 828-257-4530.

W.C. Reid Center for the Creative Arts: The W.C. Reid Center, sponsored and supported by the City of Asheville, is the home to a variety of creative cultural art programs for all ages focusing on visual, performing and computer arts. 133 Livingston St., Asheville NC 28801; 828-350-2048.

Dance

For a complete listing of all current performances and ongoing dance-related events, pick up a copy of the free weekly publications Mountain Xpress.

Mountain Xpress: A free weekly independent news, arts, and events newspaper for Western North Carolina. Excellent entertainment coverage, local commentary. PO Box 144, Asheville NC 28802; 828-251-1333.

Suppliers

Dance Etc: Dancewear and dancer's supplies. 615 Greenville Hwy., Hendersonville NC 28792; 828-252-4761.

The Sock Basket: Providing quality dancewear and a professional staff to the dancers of the Upstate for more than 20 years. 99 Edgewood Rd. Suite A Asheville, North Carolina 28804, 828-251-7072

Dance Theaters and Venues

Asheville Contemporary Dance Theatre: The Asheville Contemporary Dance Theatre is a non-profit professional dance company created in 1979 that performs up to 80 times a year in Asheville and throughout the world. Repertory consists of both full-length modern dance ballets and children's shows. 20 Commerce St., Asheville NC 28801; 828-254-2621. acdt.org

Dance Troupes, Schools & Organizations

Asheville Academy of Ballet and Contemporary Dance: 4 Lynwood Rd., Asheville NC 28804; 828-252-4761 (ballet, contemporary)

Asheville Contemporary Dance Theatre: ACDT is a non-profit professional dance company created in 1979 that performs up to 80 times a year in Asheville and throughout the world. Repertory consists of both full-length modern dance ballets and children's shows. 20 Commerce St., Asheville NC 28801; 828-254-2621. acdt.org

Southside Dance Studio: Ages 3 through adult, professional training in ballet, tap, jazz, hip-hop and ballroom dancing. 4110 Hendersonville Rd., Ste 50, Fletcher NC 28732; 828-684-2118.

Terpsicorps Theatre of Dance: Professional contemporary ballet company, showcasing local talent as well as acclaimed dancers from nationally recognized dance companies in two summer concerts a year at Pack Place. 339 Old Lyman St., Building G, Asheville NC 28801; 828-231-8618.

Chapter Fifteen

Outdoor Recreation in Western North Carolina

Western North Carolina abounds with numerous outdoor recreational opportunities, many of them rare in other areas but plentiful here. Whitewater rafting, llama trekking, mountain biking and mountain climbing are prime examples.

Both Asheville and Hendersonville have excellent city parks (*See* Section III, Chapter Nine Asheville Parks; and Section IV, Chapter Seven Hendersonville Area Parks) that provide various outdoor sporting venues. The Buncombe County Parks and Recreation Department also manages a number of parks that are used for various outdoor and sporting activities. Their offices are at 205 College St., Asheville NC 28801; 828-255-5526.

Outdoor Stores & Outfitters

Asheville:

Black Dome: 140 Tunnel Rd., Asheville NC 28805; 828-251-2001.

Diamond Brand Outdoors Downtown: 53 Biltmore Ave, Asheville, NC 28801, 828-771-4761

Frugal Backbacker Outdoor Outlet: 2621 Hendersonville Rd., Arden NC 28704; 828-209-1530.

REI: 31 Schenck Parkway, Asheville NC 28803, 828-687-0918.

Ski Country Sports: 1000 Merrimon Ave., Asheville NC 28804; 828-254-2771.

Banner Elk:

High Mountain Expeditions: 3149 Tynecastle Hwy., Banner Elk NC 28604; 828-898-9786.

Blowing Rock:

Footsloggers of Blowing Rock: 921 Main St., Blowing Rock NC 28605; 828-295-4453.

Boone:

Footsloggers of Boone: 139 South Depot St., Boone NC 28607; 828-262-5111.

Bryson City:

Nantahala Outdoor Center: 13077 Hwy. 19W, Bryson City NC; 800-232-7238.

Cashiers:

Highland Hiker: 47 Hwy. 107 South, Cashiers NC 28717; 828-743-1668.

Cullowhee:

Adventure Depot: 200 Yellow Mountain Rd., Cullowhee NC 28723; 828-743-2052.

Fontana Dam:

Fontana Village Adventure Center: 300 Woods Rd., Fontana Dam NC 28733; 800-849-2258.

Hot Springs:

Bluff Mountain Outfitters: 152 Bridge St., Hot Springs NC 28743; 828-622-7162.

Murphy:

Appalachian Outfitters: 104A Tennessee St., Murphy NC 28906; 828-837-4165.

Pisgah Forest:

Looking Glass Outfitters: 69 Hendersonville Hwy., Pisgah Forest NC 28768; 866-351-2176.

Backcountry Outdoors: 49 Pisgah Hwy., Ste 6, Pisgah Forest NC 28768; 828-884-4262.

Valle Crucis:

Mast General Store: Hwy. 194, Valle Crucis NC 28691; 828-963-6511.

West Jefferson:

Mountain Outfitters: 102 South Jefferson Ave., West Jefferson NC 29694; 336-246-9133.

Airplane and Helicopter Tour Services

Shadowhawk Aviation: Based one hour from Asheville in Greenville South Carolina, Shadowhawk Aviation provides specialized helicopter tours over South Carolina and Western North Carolina; 864-884-4074

Bird Watching

The mountains of Western North Carolina are a bird watcher's paradise and since they cover regions of unspoiled territory, farmlands and woodlands, seeing birds is no problem. Still finding the best bird watching sites can be a bit tricky. The best resource to solve this dilemma is the NC Wildlife Resources Commission North Carolina Birding Trail. The trail is divided into three sections, including the mountains. From their website you may order trail guides which will help you in planning your outings. The trail physically links great bird watching sites and birders with communities, businesses and other local historical and educational attractions. Efforts to develop the North Carolina Birding Trail began in Oct. 2003. As of summer 2009, the Trail is now complete across the entire state—coastal plain, piedmont, and mountain regions.

In Asheville, the North Carolina Arboretum (a site on the North Carolina Birding Trail) offers great bird watching, as does the Blue Ridge Parkway which runs through Asheville. The Western North Carolina Nature Center, located in Asheville, is also a place of interest if you are a bird watcher. In north Asheville, off of Merrimon Ave., is the Beaver Lake Bird Sanctuary, known locally as a great bird watching site also. From downtown follow Merrimon Ave. north about two miles, and begin watching for the Beaver Lake Bird Sanctuary on your left. After you pass the North Asheville Public Library, look for stone pillars at a pair of driveways leading to the Sanctuary parking lot.

In Hendersonville, one of the best sites for bird watching is Jackson Park located at 801 Glover St., arguably one of the finest migration spots in North Carolina, with a wide range of habitats being represented in the park's 317 acres. In late Sep. it is possible to see over 70 bird species as they pass through the park on their way south.

Directions: From I-26 Eastbound from Asheville and take U.S. 64 West exit (Exit # 18B) toward downtown Hendersonville . Continue through the traffic light at end of exit ramp onto 4 Seasons Boulevard (U.S. 64) for 1.6 miles (passing 4 more traffic lights). After a wetland area on the left, turn left at the 5th traffic light (Harris St.). Go 0.2 mile to stop sign at end of street. Turn left onto E. 4th Ave., enter park and follow road to Administration Building (red-brick house on left) and parking.

Resources

Elisha Mitchell Audubon Society (Asheville Chapter): PO Box 18711, Asheville NC 28814; see website for local phone numbers (main.nc.us/emas/index.html)

North Carolina Birding Trail: North Carolina Wildlife Resources Commission, 1722 Mail Service Center, Raleigh NC 27699; 919-604-5183.

Mountains Region NC Birding Trail: List of 105 great birding sites in Western North Carolina. 919-604-5183.

Boating

Western North Carolina is an area blessed with many lakes, the vast majority of them man-made, with most having public boating access. The larger lakes generally are in the far western part of the state, with Lake Lure, southeast of Asheville, and Lake James, east of Asheville, exceptions. If whitewater rafting of interest to you, see Whitewater Rafting in this chapter for more on that popular mountain activity.

Boat Rides & Tours

Bryson City:

Paddlefish Kayaking, Inc: Calm water lake kayaking on Lake Fontana, PO Box 2696, Bryson City NC 28713; 828-488-8797.

Smoky Mountain Jet Boats: 12-passenger jet boat rides on Lake Fontana. 22 Needmore Rd., Bryson City NC 28713;, 828-488-0522.

Fontana Dam:

Fontana Village Marina: Pontoon boat trips on Fontana Lake. Hwy. 28 North, Fontana Dam NC 28733, 828-498-2211; 800-849-2258.

Lake Lure:

Lake Lure Tours: Covered pontoon boat trips on Lake Lure. 2930 Memorial Hwy., Lake Lure NC 28746; 828-625-1373.

Boating Associations, Clubs & Resources

Asheville Rowing Club: Non-profit athletic and social organization dedicated to promoting health, fitness and fun through the sport of rowing. Has boathouse on Lake Julian. Asheville Rowing Club, PO Box 861, Asheville NC 28802. ashevillerowing.org

Asheville Youth Rowing Association: Non-profit organization dedicated to promoting the sport of rowing among teenagers between the ages of 12 and 18. ashevilleyouth rowing.com

North Carolina Boating Law Basics: North Carolina Wildlife Resources Commission, 1701 Mail Services Center, Raleigh NC 27699. ncwildlife.org

North Carolina Online Boating Safety Course and Exam: North Carolina Wildlife Resources Commission, 1751 Varsity Dr., Raleigh NC 27606; 919-707-0010 ncwildlife.org

Western Carolina Paddlers: Asheville based canoe, kayak and rafting club. boatingbeta.com

Outfitters, Marinas & Boat Dealers

Asheville:

Boats Etc: 60 Dogwood Rd., Asheville NC 28806; 828-670-9595.

Diamond Brand Outdoors: 2623 Hendersonville Rd., Arden NC 28704; 828-684-6262.

Bryson City (Fontana Lake):

Alarka Boat Dock: 7230 Grassy Branch Rd., Bryson City NC 28713; 828-488-3841.

Fontana Village Marina: Hwy. 28 North, Fontana Dam NC 28733, 828-498-2211, 800-849-2258.

Hayesville (Lake Chatuge):

Chatuge Cove Marina: 2397 Hwy. 175, Hayesville NC 28904.

Hendersonville:

Todd's RV and Marine: 2918 North Rugby Rd., Hendersonville NC 28791; 828-651-0007.

Driftwood Marine LLC: 3400 Chimney Rock Rd., Hendersonville NC 28792; 828-685-1313.

Lake Lure (Lake Lure):

Lake Lure Town Marina: 2975 Memorial Hwy., Lake Lure NC 28746; 828-625-1373.

Murphy (Lake Hiwassee):

Mountain View Marina: 200 Dean Aldrich Dr., Murphy NC 28906; 828-644-5451.

Nebo (Lake James):

Bear Creek Marina: 608 Marina Dr., Nebo NC 28761; 828-655-1400.
Mountain Harbour Marina: 9066 Hwy. 126, Nebo NC 28761; 828-584-0666.

Robbinsville (Lake Santeetlah):

Santeetlah Marina: 1 Marina Dr., Robbinsville NC 28711; 828-479-8180.

West Jefferson:

Mountain Outfitters: 102 South Jefferson Ave., West Jefferson NC 28694; 336-246-9133.

Camping

Given the vast amount of wilderness area in the Western North Carolina mountains, one would expect to find a staggering array of campgrounds and camping facilities. Indeed this is exactly the case and it is beyond the scope of this guidebook to present all of the camping options available. Instead, this chapter presents some general resources and information about the most popular camping regions: the Blue Ridge Parkway, Pisgah National Forest, the Great Smoky Mountains National Park, the Appalachian Trail and three campgrounds close to Asheville: The Davidson River Campground, the North Mills River Recreation Area and the Lake Powhatan Recreational Area. It is highly recommended that you visit one of the outdoor stores or outfitters listed before heading out into the mountains. There you will not only get knowledgeable advice but can also pick up maps and specific guides to the area you plan to visit.

If you are looking for RV campgrounds, check out the Asheville Campgrounds or Hendersonville Campgrounds sections also in this chapter. Maps of the Pisgah National Forest and other wilderness areas can be ordered from the Cradle of Forestry in America Interpretive Association Forest Place Store. Their address is The Forest Place Store, 66 South Broad St., Brevard NC 28712. 800-660-0671.

Popular Asheville Area Campgrounds

Davidson River Campground

About: Located at the entrance to Pisgah National Forest in the Brevard area. The Davidson River is a premier trout stream. Located nearby is the Cradle of Forestry.
Address: 1 Davidson River Circle, Pisgah Forest NC 28768
Telephone: 828-862-5960, 877-457-4023
Reservations: 877-444-6777, or online at recreation.gov
Open: Year round
Fees: Yes, Federal Interagency Pass, Senior and Access discounts accepted.
Sites: 160 spacious shaded sites, singles and doubles. Sites with river access.
Facilities: Hot showers within walking distance of each site.
Directions: From I-26, take Exit 40 (US 280 to Brevard), right on US 276. Enter Pisgah National Forest, one mile on 276, turn left into Davidson River Campground.

North Mills River Recreation Area

About: The North Mills River runs through this recreation area and camping facility. Each campsite is only a short stroll from the river. Swimming, fishing and river tubing. Located between Asheville and Hendersonville.

Address: 5289 N. Mills River Rd., Mills River NC 28742

Telephone: 828-890-3284, 877-457-4023

Reservations: 877-444-6777, or online at recreation.gov

Open: Year round with limited service Nov. thru Mar.

Fees: Yes, Federal Interagency Pass, Senior and Access discounts accepted.

Sites: 32 primitive sites, including 9 double sites. No hooks up available.

Facilities: Restrooms close to sites.

Directions: From Exit 40 on Interstate 26, travel west on US 280 past the airport six miles to traffic light at North Mills River Rd. Turn right and travel five miles to the North Mills River Recreation Area.

Lake Powhatan Recreational Area

About: Located just minutes from Asheville, Lake Powhatan offers peace, quiet and solitude on the border of Bent Creek. Camping , swimming, fishing, hiking trails. Beach and fishing pier.

Address: 375 Wesley Branch Rd., Asheville NC 28806

Telephone: 828-670-5627, 877-457-4023

Reservations: 877-444-6777, or online at recreation.gov

Open: April through Oct.

Fees: Yes, Federal Interagency Pass, Senior and Access discounts accepted.

Sites: 98 sites, singles and doubles. Limited hook-ups available.

Facilities: Modern facilities with hot showers.

Directions: From I-26, take Exit 33 onto US 191. Travel south on US 191 approximately 2 miles to traffic light, turn right to the Lake Powhatan entrance.

Popular Camping Regions In The Mountains

Blue Ridge Parkway Campgrounds

There are six campgrounds open to the public on the Parkway in North Carolina from May 1 through Oct. or into early Nov., depending on weather conditions. Facilities are limited in winter. Fees are charged and length of stay may be limited. Camping is permitted only in designated campgrounds. Dr.inking water and comfort stations are provided; shower and laundry facilities are not. Sites in each campground are designated for trailers but none is equipped for utility connections. Campgrounds have sanitary dumping stations. Each campsite has a table and fireplace. Limited supplies may be purchased at most Parkway gasoline stations and camp stores. For further information, call the Blue Ridge Parkway headquarters at 828-298-0398. (*See* also Section V, Chapter One)

Milepost 241.1: Doughton Park
Milepost 297.1: Julian Price Memorial Park
Milepost 316.4: Linville Falls

Milepost 339.5: Crabtree Meadows
Milepost 408.6: Mount Pisgah
Milepost 418.8: Graveyard Fields

Pisgah National Forest Campgrounds

The Pisgah National Forest is a land of mile-high peaks, cascading waterfalls and heavily forested slopes. It is an ideal place, as are all of the national forests, for outdoor recreation. Located on two sides of Asheville, the forest is more than 490,000 acres and spreads over 12 Western North Carolina counties. The forest is more or less divided in half by the Blue Ridge Parkway, and the Appalachian Trail runs along its border with Tennessee. The Mountains-to-the-Sea Trail crosses through the forest. Pisgah National Forest contains three wilderness areas: Middle Prong, Linville Gorge and the Shining Rock section, and is divided into four districts: Pisgah District, French Broad District, Grandfather District and Tocane District. The Pisgah District of the forest borders the Asheville/Hendersonville area. This magnificent forest is easily accessible from many points and offers wonderful camping facilities. Keep in mind that there are some rules governing camping in national forests. You can pitch your tent just about anywhere providing you are 100 feet or more from all water sources, at least 1,000 feet from the road and there are no signs prohibiting camping. Pets must be under control and on a leash when you are near people or a campground. For more information about camping in the forest, call 828-257-4200. (*See* also Section V, Chapter One)

Great Smoky Mountains National Park Campgrounds

The Great Smoky Mountains, which lie along the common border of Tennessee and North Carolina, form a majestic climax to the Appalachian Highlands. With outlines softened by a forest mantle, the mountains stretch away to remote horizons in sweeping troughs that recede to evenness in the distance. Shrouding the peaks is a smoke-like mist that rises from the dense plant growth. The mountains get their name from this deep blue mist. The park's boundary wraps around 800 square miles of mountain wilderness, most of it virtually unspoiled. Many peaks rise above 6,000 feet. A great variety of trees, shrubs, herbs and other plants are nourished by the fertile land and heavy rainfall and rushing streams. The Great Smokey Park contains more than 700 miles of rivers and streams, over 200,000 acres of virgin forests, and over 850 miles of trails. It is the most visited national park with over 9,000,000 visitors a year. (*See* also Section V, Chapter One)

Appalachian Trail

The Appalachian Trail is a 2,167 mile footpath from Maine to Georgia which follows the ridge tops of the fourteen states through which it passes. Each day, as many as two hundred backpackers are in the process of hiking the full length of the trail. More than 250 backcountry shelters are located along the Appalachian Trail at varying intervals, as a service to all Appalachian Trail hikers. A typical shelter, sometimes called a "lean-to," has a shingled or metal roof, a wooden floor and three walls and is open to the elements on one side. Most are near a creek or spring, and many have a privy nearby. Hikers occupy them on a first-come, first-served basis until the shelter is full. They are intended for individual hikers, not big groups. (*See* also Section V, Chapter One)

Cycling & Mountain Biking

Biking is a very popular recreation in the mountains, with road cycling the main attraction followed closely by off-road and mountain biking. Scenic vistas winding country and mountain roads and a wide variety of terrain make for some of the best bicycle touring in the world. Because of this fact, Asheville was one of the stops in the Tour Dupont, which used the Omni Grove Park Inn Resort as race headquarters, and notable biking professionals regularly visit the mountains to ride. And as far as mountain and off-road biking goes, Western North Carolina is second to none in that category. Some of the world's greatest mountain biking trails can be found in Western North Carolina and thousands of enthusiasts flock here every year for just that reason.

Local bookstores and bicycle shops carry specialty guidebooks on biking in Western North Carolina that offer maps and trails advice, beyond the scope of what is presented here. One of the best for visitors who wish to find some road biking routes is *Rd. Bike Asheville*. This informative guide describes sixteen road-biking routes in and around Asheville that the Blue Ridge Bicycle Club of Asheville sees as tops. The bicycle shops listed below can give you personal advice as to mountain biking trails in the mountains as well as additional road routes.

Near Asheville, excellent off-road riding can be found in the nearby Pisgah District of the Pisgah National Forest. This section of the forest has more than 400 miles of trails. Check in at the Ranger Station Visitor Center, 1.5 miles west of NC 280 on U.S. 276 and pick up a copy of their trail map. The Bent Creek section of the forest near Asheville is an especially popular riding area, as is the nearby North Mills River Recreation Area and the Dupont State Forest near Hendersonville. An excellent online resource for mountain biking, including area maps and trail information can be found on the Mountain Biking in Western North Carolina website.

In addition to the many opportunities for road and mountain biking, Asheville also has its own racing oval located at 220 Amboy Rd. in the Asheville Parks and Recreation Carrier Park. Formerly the old Asheville Motor Speedway, this park is open to the public for multiple outdoor activities, including track racing. Cyclo-cross racing also has caught on in Western North Carolina as well. This discipline involves short off-road races in a circuit-race format with a one to two mile course, short, steep hills and a variety of surfaces from pavement to mud and sand.

Asheville Area Bicycle Clubs, Organizations & Training Centers

Asheville Bicycle Racing Club: Non-profit Asheville based organization established for the purpose of promoting amateur bicycle racing in Western North Carolina. abrc.net

Asheville Triathlon Club: Non-profit multisport club based in Asheville. ashevilletri.com

Asheville Women's Cycling Club: All-female cycling club. Rd. racing, mountain biking, cyclo-cross, track racing, triathlons and adventure racing. Also professional all-female racing team. ashevillewomenscycling.com

Blue Ridge Bicycle Club of Asheville: Premier Western North Carolina bicycle club includes both mountain and road cyclists. Blue Ridge Bicycle Club, PO Box 309, Asheville NC 28802. blueridgebicycleclub.org

Pisgah Area SORBA: Pisgah chapter of the Southeastern Off-Rd. Bike Association. PO Box 61, Skyland NC 28776. 770-654-3291. pisgahareasorba.org

Western North Carolina Unicyclists: wncunicycle.webs.com

Other Bicycle Clubs, Organizations & Training Centers

Bushy Mountain Cyclists Club: Club based in North Wilkesboro, North Carolina. PO Box 1281, North Wilkesboro NC 28659. bmcc.us

Great Smoky Mountains Triathlon Club: Non-profit multisport club based in Hayesville.828-389-6982. thebeastoftheeast.net/index1.htm

IMBA International Mountain Bicycling Association: IMBA works to keep trails open for mountain bikers by encouraging responsible riding and supporting volunteer trail work. 4888 Pearl East Circle Ste, Boulder CO 80302. 303-545-9011. imba.com/nmbp

Southern Appalachian Bicycling Association: PO Box 542, Hayesville NC 28804. sabacycling.com

USA Cycling: National cycling organization based in Colorado Springs, Colorado. 719-434-4200. usacycling.org/mtb

Bicycle Shops in the Asheville-Hendersonville Area

Bike Ways: 607 Greenville Hwy., Hendersonville NC 29792; 828-692-0613

Carolina Fatz Cycling Center: 1240 Brevard Rd., Ste #3, Asheville NC 28806; 828-665-7744.

Hearn's Cycling and Fitness: 28 Asheland Ave., Asheville NC 28801; 828-253-4800.

Liberty Bicycles: 1378 Hendersonville Hwy., Asheville NC 28803, 828-274-2453.

Motion Makers Bicycle Shop: 878 Brevard Rd., Asheville NC 28806; 828-633-2227.

Suspension Experts: (Bike repair, parts) 89 Thompson St., Unit K, Asheville NC 28803; 828-255-0205.

The Bicycle Company: 779 N. Church St., Hendersonville NC 28792; 828-696-1500.

Pro Bikes: 610-B Haywood Rd., Asheville NC 28806; 828-253-2800.

Ski Country Sports: 1000 Merrimon Ave., Asheville NC 28804; 828-254-2771.

Youngblood Bicycles: 233 Merrimon Ave., Asheville NC 28801; 828-251-4686.

Bicycle Shops in Western North Carolina

Boone: Boone Bike and Touring: 774 E. King St., Boone NC 28807; 828-262-5750.

Franklin: Smoky Mountain Bicycles: 31 E. Main St., Franklin NC 28734; 828-369-2881.

Pisgah Forest: Sycamore Cycles: 112 New Hendersonville Hwy., Pisgah Forest NC 28768; 828-877-5790.

Saluda: Keiths Triathlon Shop: 181 East Main St., Saluda NC 28773, 828-329-8806.

Sylva: Motion Makers Bicycle Shop: 552 West Main St., Sylva NC 28779; 828-586-6925.

Disc Golf & Ultimate Frisbee

Disc Golf and Ultimate Frisbee are two sports that are growing in popularity throughout Western North Carolina. There are a number of PDGA disc golf courses in the greater Asheville area, as well as others scattered throughout the mountains. If ultimate Frisbee is your game, your best resource is the Asheville-based Asheville Ultimate Club. They can be reached at 828-777-6115 for more information. The annual Mountain Sports Festival features competitions in both disc golf and ultimate Frisbee. The disc golf courses in the Asheville area are listed below. For a complete listing of all disc golf courses in Western North Carolina, visit my guidebook website at ashevilleguidebook.com .

Crookston Disc Golf Course: 9 holes, 4312 feet, occupies half of a 60- acre park with some open holes and several curving into the woods along a large creek.; 85 Howard Gap Rd., Fletcher NC 28732; 828-687-0751.

Richmond Hill Park Disc Golf Course: 18 holes, 4935 feet, hilly, wooded course.; 280 Richmond Hill Dr., Asheville NC 28806; 828-251-1122.

Buncombe County Sports Park: 6 holes; 58 Apac Circle, Candler NC 28715; 828-250-4260.

Golf in the Mountains

Golf is a major attraction in the mountains and the mild climate offers nearly four seasons on courses that range from wide river valleys and rolling terrains to fairways that pitch and roll to challenge even the most experienced golfer. The golf courses that allow public play in the greater Asheville area are listed below. For a complete listing of all golf courses in Western North Carolina, visit my guidebook website at ashevilleguidebook.com .

Asheville's standout courses are the prestigiousOmni Grove Park Inn Resort & Spa and the beautiful Reems Creek Golf Club course in Weaverville. Access to the Omni Grove Park Inn Resort & Spa course is generally limited to guests of the hotel while the Reems Creek Golf Club course is open to the public. Asheville has a number of driving ranges. These include Jake's Dr.iving Range, Hwy. 25 North, Naples NC 28760 (just south of Asheville), 828-684-8086, and the Practice Tee & Golf Shop at 161 Azalea Rd. East, Asheville NC 28805. 828-298-0123.

Asheville/Hendersonville Area Golf Courses That Allow Public Play

Asheville Municipal Golf Course: 226 Fairway Dr., Asheville NC 28805, 828-298-1867; Public; 18-holes.

Black Mountain Golf Club: 17 Ross Dr., Black Mountain NC 28711; 828-669-2710; Semi-Private; 18-holes; travel time from Asheville: 30 minutes east.

Broadmoor Golf Links: 101 French Broad Lane, Fletcher NC 28732; 828-687-1500; Public; 18-holes.

Connestee Falls Golf Course: 98 Overlook Clubhouse Rd., Brevard NC 28712; 828-885-2005; Semi-Private; 18-holes; travel time from Asheville: 1 hour west.

Crooked Creek Golf Course: 764 Crooked Creek Rd., Hendersonville NC 28739; 828-692-2011; Public; 18-holes; travel time from Asheville: 45 minutes south.

Migration of the Monarch Butterflies

A marvelous natural phenomenon that can be seen in the fall is the migration of the Monarch butterflies through the Western North Carolina mountain valleys as they make their way south on their long pilgrimage to Mexico, where they spend the winter in the Sierra Madre mountains. Monarchs that emerge in late summer and autumn in the Western North Carolina mountains are different than their cousins born earlier in the summer, as the shorter, cooler days of fall postpone the development of their reproductive organs. This, plus changes in light and temperature (perhaps along with other factors not yet understood) cues these butterflies to take to the skies, migrating hundreds and even thousands of miles across the continent to warmer wintering grounds. They are strong, fast fliers, reaching speeds of ten to thirty miles per hour. Along the way, they get nourishment from plants, fattening themselves for the coming winter. This migration usually takes place from Aug. to Oct., reaching a peak usually the third week in Sep. An excellent viewing site is the Cherry Cove Overlook on the Blue Ridge Parkway seven miles south of Pisgah Inn.

Crowne Plaza Asheville Golf Course: One Resort Dr., Asheville NC 28806; 828-253-5874; Resort/public; 18-holes.

Cummings Cove Golf and Country Club: 20 Cummings Cove Parkway, Hendersonville NC 28739; 828-891-5848; Semi-private; 18-holes; travel time from Asheville: 45 minutes south.

Glen Cannon Country Club: 337 Glen Cannon Rd., Brevard NC 28768; 828-883-8175; Semi-private; 18 holes; travel time from Asheville: 1 hour west.

High Vista Country Club: 88 Country Club Rd., Mills River NC 28759; 828-891-1986; Semi-private;18-holes.

Omni Grove Park Inn: 290 Macon Ave., Asheville NC 28804; 800-438-5800; Resort; 18-holes.

Orchard Trace Golf Club: 3389 Sugarloaf Rd., Hendersonville NC 28792; 828-685–1006; Public; 18-holes; travel time from Asheville: 1 hour south.

Reems Creek Golf Club: 36 Pink Fox Cove Rd., Weaverville NC 28787; 828-645-4393; Semi-Private; 18-holes.

Southern Tee Golf Course: 111 Howard Gap Rd., Fletcher NC 28732; 828-687-7273; Semi-Private; 18-holes.

Hiking & Backpacking

The mountains and valleys around Asheville and Hendersonville are a hiker's paradise. Hundreds of thousands of visitors come to this region every year just to hike and to experience the countless trails that range from short day hikes to the world famous Appalachian Trail.

The choice of possible hikes is too vast to be covered here. I strongly suggest that you first visit one of the outfitters mentioned at the start of this chapter. They will be able to help you make some good choices based on your preferences and skill level. These stores also have maps and books for sale about hiking in the mountains. There are also a number of hiking clubs in the mountains. For a complete list of these visit my guidebook website at ashevilleguidebook.com . The local office of the U.S. Forest Service is another valuable resource and can also answer questions you might have regarding hiking trails in the Pisgah and other national forests. Contact them at the U.S. Forest Service, PO Box 7148, Asheville NC 28802; 828-257-4200.

Because of the vast territory involved for possible hiking, some considerations should be made concerning planning and safety. For the most part, the Western North Carolina mountains are wilderness or semi-wilderness areas. That means there are a lot more trees and woods than people. Getting lost is a possibility if proper planning and cautions are not taken. In order to prevent any problems, you should always take the following precautions before venturing out into the woods on any hike that takes you away from civilization.

1. **Always check in at a ranger station or park headquarters** for the latest trail information before you leave. Trail conditions often change due to weather conditions, and knowing about any changes in advance can prevent much aggravation later. In addition, rangers know the trails and can best advise you regarding which trails to take, length of hikes and so on.
2. **Always leave word with someone about where you're going,** when you plan to leave and when you plan to return. In the worst case, this will insure that you will be searched for should you not return at the designated time.
3. **Always take a trail map on your hike,** unless it is a short self-guided nature trail or similar trail. Know how to read the map. Check with a local forest ranger if you have any questions about the map and the trail you intend to hike.
4. **If at all possible, never hike alone.** An injury alone in the woods can be life-threatening without someone else to assist or go for help.
5. **Lock valuables in the trunk of your car** or take them with you.
6. **Be prepared! Do your homework before you even start out.** Talk to professional outfitters to insure that you have the right hiking shoes, equipment, food, first aid supplies and maps. Take plenty of food and water, and cold weather gear in the fall or spring.
7. **Never leave the trail.** Even experienced hikers can get lost by taking off-the-trail shortcuts.
8. **Do not drink the water in streams or springs.** Bacterial diseases can be contracted by drinking untreated "wild waters."

Hiking Trails Accessible From the Blue Ridge Parkway

Listed below are the hiking trails in North Carolina that can be accessed from the Blue Ridge Parkway. Keep in mind that Asheville is located around milepost 380 and getting to milepost 260, for example, 100 miles on the parkway, will take a good three hours driving time.

Milepost	Trail	Mileage*	Difficulty
217.5	Cumberland Knob Trail (ideal lazy-day walk)	0.5	Easy
217.5	Gully Creek Trail (rewarding loop that meanders by stream)	2.0	Strenuous
218.6	Fox Hunters Paradise Trail (view)	0.2	Easy
230.1	Little Glade Millpond (easy loop stroll around pond)	0.4	Easy
238.5	Cedar Ridge Trail (great for day hike; vistas and forests)	4.2	Moderate
238.5	Bluff Mountain Trail (parallels Parkway to milepost 244.7)	7.5	Moderate
241.0	Fodder Stack Trail (great variety of plants)	1.0	Moderate
241.0	Bluff Ridge Trail (primitive trail with steep slopes)	2.8	Moderate
243.7	Grassy Gap Fire Rd. (wide enough for side-by-side hiking)	6.5	Moderate
243.7	Basin Creek Trail (access from back-country campground)	3.3	Moderate
244.7	Flat Rock Ridge Trail (forest path with vistas)	5.0	Moderate
260.3	Jumping Off Rocks Trail (forest path to vista)	1.0	Easy
264.4	The Lump Trail (to hilltop view)	0.3	Easy
271.9	Cascades Trail (self-guiding loop to view of falls)	0.5	Moderate
272.5	Tompkins Knob Trail (to Jesse Brown Cabin)	0.6	Easy
294.0	Rich Mountain Carriage, Horse & Hiking Trail	4.3	Moderate
294.0	Flat Top Mountain Carriage, Horse & Hiking Trail	3.0	Moderate
294.0	Watkins Carriage, Horse & Hiking Trail	3.3	Easy/Moderate
294.0	Black Bottom Carriage, Horse & Hiking Trail	0.5	Easy
294.0	Bass Lake Carriage, Horse & Hiking Trail	1.7	Easy
294.0	Deer Park Carriage, Horse & Hiking Trail	0.8	Moderate
294.0	Maze Carriage, Horse & Hiking Trail	2.3	Moderate
294.0	Duncan Carriage, Horse & Hiking Trail	2.5	Moderate
294.0	Rock Creek Bridge Carriage, Horse & Hiking Trail	1.0	Easy
294.1	Figure 8 Trail (short self-guiding loop around nature trail)	0.7	Easy
294.6	Trout Lake Hiking & Horse Trail (loop)	1.0	Easy
295.9	Green Knob Trail (to Green Knob)	2.3	Moderate/Strenuous
296.5	Boone Fork Trail (stream, forest and meadows)	5.5	Moderate/Strenuous
297.0	Price Lake Loop Trail (loop around Price Lake)	2.7	Moderate
304.4	Linn Cove Viaduct Access Trail	0.16	Easy
305.2	Beacon Heights Trail (10 minutes to view)	0.2	Moderate
305.5	Tanawha Trail (diverse features, parallels Parkway to Price Park)	13.5	Moderate/Strenuous
308.2	Flat Rock Trail (self-guiding loop)	0.6	Easy
315.5	Camp Creek Trail (leg stretcher through laurel and rhododendron)	0.1	Easy

* Mileage indicates length of trail one-way unless otherwise noted

Milepost	Trail	Mileage*	Difficulty
316.4	Linville Falls Trail (view of upper falls)	0.8	Moderate
316.4	Linville Gorge Trail (view of lower falls)	0.5	Strenuous
316.4	Duggers Creek Trail (loop to view of Duggers Falls)	0.25	Easy
316.5	Linville River Bridge Trail (leg stretcher to view of unusual bridge)	0.1	Easy
320.8	Chestoa View Trail (30–minute loop to vista)	0.6	Easy
339.5	Crabtree Falls Loop Trail (loop to view of falls)	2.5	Strenuous
344.1	Woods Mountain Trail (USES)	2.0	Moderate
350.4	Lost Cove Ridge Trail (USFS)	0.6	Moderate
351.9	Deep Gap Trail (USFS)	0.2	Easy
355.0	Bald Knob Ridge Trail (USFS)	0.1	Easy
359.8	Big Butt Trail (USFS) (trail continues on USFS lands)	0.2	Strenuous
361.2	Glassmine Falls (view of falls)	0.05	Moderate
364.2	Craggy Pinnacle Trail (to panoramic view)	0.7	Moderate
364.6	Craggy Gardens Trail (first portion is self-guiding nature trail)	0.8	Moderate
374.4	Rattlesnake Lodge Trail (woodland walk)	0.5	Moderate
382.0	Mountain-to-Sea Trail/MTS Trail (Folk Art Center to Mt. Mitchell; spring wildflowers & views, parallels Parkway; many accesses to trail segments)		Moderate/Strenuous
393.7	Shut-in Trail/MTS Trail (Bent Creek-Walnut Cove)	3.1	Strenuous
396.4	Shut-in Trail/MTS Trail (Walnut Cove-Sleepy Gap)	1.7	Moderate
397.3	Grassy Knob Trail (steep trail to USFS area)	0.9	Strenuous
397.3	Shut-in Trail/MTS Trail (Sleepy Gap-Chestnut Cove)	0.7	Moderate
398.3	Shut-in Trail/MTS Trail (Chestnut Cove-Bent Creek Gap)	2.8	Strenuous
400.3	Shut-in Trail/MTS Trail (Bent Creek Gap-Beaver Dam Gap)	1.9	Moderate
401.7	Shut-in Trail/MTS Trail (Beaver Dam Gap-Stoney Bald)	0.9	Moderate
402.6	Shut-in Trail/MTS Trail (Stoney Bald-Big Ridge)	1.2	Strenuous
403.6	Shut-in Trail/MTS Trail (Big Ridge-Mills River Valley)	1.1	Moderate/Strenuous
404.5	Shut-in Trail/MTS Trail (Elk Pasture Gap-Mt. Pisgah)	1.7	Strenuous
407.6	Mt. Pisgah Trail (summit view)	1.3	Moderate/Strenuous
407.6	Buck Springs Trail (Pisgah Lodge to view)	1.06	Easy/Moderate
408.5	Frying-Pan Mountain Trail	1.06	Moderate/Strenuous
417.0	East Fork Trail (USFS, access to Shining Rock Trail System)	0.1	Easy/Moderate
418.8	Graveyard Fields Loop Trail (loop by a stream)	2.3	Moderate
419.4	John Rock Trail (leg stretcher to view)	0.1	Easy
422.4	Devil's Courthouse Trail (panoramic summit view)	0.4	Moderate/Strenuous
427.6	Bear Pen Gap Trail (access to Mountains-to-Sea Trail)	0.2	Easy
431.0	Richland Balsam Trail (self-guiding loop through spruce-fir forest	1.5	Moderate
433.8	Roy Taylor Overlook Trail (paved trail to overlook)	0.1	Easy
451.2	Waterrock Knob Trail (summit view; .6 mile one way)	1.2	Moderate/Strenuous

* Mileage indicates length of trail one-way unless otherwise noted

Horseback Riding

Horseback riding and horse shows are very popular activities in the mountains. Many local horse stables provide not only traditional riding instruction and facilities but also can serve as outfitters for trail rides into the hills and mountains. Asheville area stables and riding facilities are presented below. For a complete listing of most of the horse facilities in the mountains, visit my guidebook website at ashevilleguidebook.com .

Of interest to horse lovers is the Western North Carolina Agricultural Center in Asheville which regularly schedules championship horse shows and related events. Another major equestrian facility fairly close to Asheville and Hendersonville is the Foothills Equestrian Nature Center (FENCE), located in Tryon, which is about an hour's drive south. They have world-class equestrian facilities, steeplechase and cross-country courses and regularly host horse shows of all types and classes. Asheville has a number of tack stores including Balsam Quarter Tack at 521 Long Shoals Rd., Arden NC 28704, 828-684-8445, and Jackson's Western Store at 641 Patton Ave., Asheville NC 28806, 828-254-1812.

Asheville/Hendersonville Area Riding Stables

Biltmore Estate Equestrian Center: Lessons, boarding, clinics and 80 miles of estate trails, the same paths used by the Vanderbilts and guests at the turn of the century; Biltmore Estate, Asheville NC 28803; 828-225-1454.

Cane Creek Farm: 65-acre equestrian center offering boarding and training programs for both horse and rider; 912 Cane Creek Rd., Fletcher NC 28732; 828-681-5975; travel time from downtown Asheville: 30 minutes.

Clear Creek Guest Ranch: Guided trail rides for non ranch guests depending on availability; 100 Clear Creek Dr., Burnsville NC 28714; 828-675-4510; travel time from Asheville: 45 minutes north.

Encore Stables: Dr.essage and Hunter/Jumper instruction, full board with daily turnout and pasture board; 338 Young Dr. Extension, Candler NC 28715; 828-665-0790; travel time from Asheville: 30 minutes west.

Foothills Equestrian Nature Center (FENCE): 380-acre non-profit nature and outdoor recreation center. FENCE's riding trails are normally open only to members of the Foothills Equestrian Trails Association; 3381 Hunting Country Rd., Tryon NC 28782; 828-859-9021; travel time from Asheville: 1 hour south.

Laurel Park Riding Stables: Trail rides on 36 acres of forest, lighted riding arena and boarding; 1790 Davis Mountain Rd., Hendersonville NC 28739; 828-692-0709: travel time from Asheville: 45 minutes south.

Pisgah Forest Riding Stables: 1–3 hour mountain top or waterfall trail rides in Pisgah National Forest; 476 Pisgah Circle, Brevard NC 28712; 828-883-8258; travel time from Asheville: 1 hour west.

Horseback riding is a popular pastime in WNC.

Pisgah View Ranch: Dude ranch and resort. Twice daily 1–3 hour trail rides; 70 Pisgah View Ranch Rd., Candler NC 28715; 828-667-9100; travel time from Asheville: 30 minutes west.

Randall Glen Stables: Horses outfitted with Australian saddles, trails at 3100 feet above sea level and higher; 96 Randall Cove Rd., Leicester NC 28748; 828-683-5758; travel time From downtown Asheville: 45 minutes.

Sandy Bottom Trail Rides: Trail rides for all ages accompanied by friendly, experienced guides; 1459 Caney Fork Rd., Marshall NC 28753; 828-649-3464; travel time from Asheville: 1 hour north.

Wolf Laurel Stables at The Preserve at Wolf Laurel: Established equestrian facility, offering trail rides in the mountains around Wolf Laurel; 5860 Bald Mountain Rd., Burnsville NC 28714; 828-678-9370; travel time from Asheville: 1 hour north.

Hot Air Balloon Rides

Are you interested in seeing the beautiful mountains and meadows of Western North Carolina from a unique perspective? Then a hot air balloon ride is for you! Flight times vary but a typical outing is from 45 minutes to an hour in the air and leave daily from April until January, weather permitting, at sunrise. The entire process from start to finish, including flight time, takes about 2.5 hours. The balloon floats in the direction of the wind and can rise from 500 to 2000 feet in the air. Flights offered by the Asheville Hot Air Balloon Company (in business since 1981 and the only hot air balloon outfit in WNC) are typically above the countryside west of Asheville and include parts of the Pisgah National Forest.

Asheville Hot Air Balloons: 909 Smokey Park Hwy., Candler NC 28715; 828-667-9943. ashevillehotairballoons.com

Llama Trekking

An unusual and popular way to experience the mountain trails is by llama trek. A couple of local companies offer guide service, camping gear, food and gentle llamas to carry the equipment. These friendly relatives of the camel are sure-footed and capable of carrying loads of up to 90 pounds. They are also kind to the trails and do much less damage than horses.

Hawkesdene House Llama Treks: Short treks for guests of the Hawkesdene House, April thru Oct.; 381 Phillips Creek Rd., Andrews NC 28901; 828-321-6027; travel time from Asheville: 2 hours west.

English Mountain Llama Treks: Llama treks from day (picnic) hikes to two day hiking trips or longer. English Mountain has special use permit for both Pisgah and Nantahala National Forest; 767 Little Creek Rd., Hot Springs NC 28743; 828-622-9686. travel time from Asheville: 45 minutes northwest.

Miniature Golf

Throughout Western North Carolina there are a number of cities and towns that have miniature or "putt-putt" golf courses. This is family fun that even non-golfers enjoy! The Asheville area courses are presented below. For a complete listing of all miniature golf courses in the mountains, visit my guidebook website at ashevilleguidebook.com .

Asheville's Fun Depot: 18-hole indoor mini golf course with waterfall, bridges and pond; 7 Roberts Rd. #B, Asheville NC 28803; 828-277-2386.

Boyd Park: Hendersonville city park that has a free miniature golf course; Located between N. Main and Church St. at 8th St., Hendersonville NC 28739; 828-697-3084 (City of Hendersonville Parks Department); travel time from Asheville: 45 minutes-1 hour south.

Outdoor Family Fun Center: 18-hole Harris designed mini golf course with waterfalls, ponds and spillways; 485 Brookside Camp Rd., Hendersonville NC 28792; 828-698-1234; travel time from Asheville: 45 minutes-1 hour south.

Tropical Gardens Mini Golf: Miniature golf course; 956 Patton Ave., Asheville NC 28806; 828-252-2207.

Rock & Mountain Climbing

The mountains of Western North Carolina offer a fabulous wealth of climbing opportunities if you are interested in rock, ice or mountain climbing. Rock cliffs, outcroppings, and slopes are to be found in endless abundance, and every year, thousands of professional and amateur climbers alike visit our area to test their skills. There are three outdoor stores in Asheville that can offer you professional and competent advice on local climbs: Black Dome, Diamond Brand Outdoors and REI. See the section at the start of this chapter for addresses of these stores.

Climbing Centers

Climbmax Climbing Center: A climbing center located in downtown Asheville offering instruction, guide services, apparel sales, and two on-site climbing walls-one 40-foot outdoor wall and an indoor climbing gym with a 20-foot wall geared to all skill levels, with staff on duty at all times to insure safety. 43 Wall St., Asheville NC 28801, 828-252-9996. climbmaxnc.com

Guide Services

Appalachian Mountain Institute: Guided rock and ice climbing near Asheville and Brevard North Carolina. AMGA certified guides. 21 Cherry Ridge Rd., Pisgah Forest NC 28768; 828-553-6323.

Climbmax Mountain Guides: Outdoor guided climbs range from local one-day climbs to multi-day Alpine-class climbs. AMGA certified guides. 43 Wall St., Asheville NC 288801; 828-252-9996. climbmaxnc.com

Fox Mountain Guides and Climbing School: Trips near Asheville, Boone, Chimney Rock and Charlotte. AMGA Certified guides. 951 Crab Creek Rd., Hendersonville NC 28739; 888-284-8433.

Granite Arches Climbing Guides: Rock, ice and mountain climbing in the American Southeast and South America. AMGA Certified guides. 423-413-1432.

Rock Dimensions: Guided rock climbing, rappelling and caving. Courses range from beginner to advanced. 131-B S. Depot St. Boone, North Carolina 28607; 828-265-3544.

Rockhounding & Gem Hunting

The mountains of Western North Carolina are one of the richest areas in the United States for gemstones and minerals. Two of the more popular gemstone areas in the mountains are centered around Franklin in the west and Spruce Pine in the east. There are close to 40 different minerals that rock hounds look for in the mountains. Corundum, beryl, moonstone, garnet, olivine, quartz, opal, amethyst, emerald, jasper, ruby, sapphire, spinel, turquoise, chrysoprase and zircon are among the most sought after. Gold also can still be found in some of the foothills streams.

Gemstone mines are very popular attractions open to the public, where you may sift through buckets of dirt to discover any treasure. Most mines sell "gem dirt" in a bucket or bag (few allow digging) and you may have to pay an admission fee for the day. You are provided with a screen for washing and there is a flume—a trough of running water—with a bench along its length. The dirt goes in the screen, the screen goes in the water and the mud is washed away. Depending on the mine, the buckets provided are either native ore, or enriched with ore from other countries. A list of those mines that use only native ore is presented in this chapter.

For serious rock hounds, the best resource available in planning your visit to the mountains is MAGMA (Mountain Area Gem and Mineral Association, wncrocks.com, 828-683-1048). There are privately owned mines in the mountains where you may collect for modest daily fees, but you need to plan in advance. Two of these are Crabtree Emerald Mine in Spruce Pine and Little Pine Garnet Mine in Madison County.

A great place to see gems in Asheville is the Colburn Hall of Minerals at the Asheville Museum of Science. Also fairly close to Asheville is the Museum of North Carolina Minerals at Milepost 331 on the Blue Ridge Parkway. In the Hendersonville area is the newly opened Mineral & Lapidary Museum of Henderson County. The Franklin Gem and Mineral Museum in Franklin also has interesting exhibits of regional minerals and gemstones.

Resources

Henderson County Gem and Mineral Society: PO Box 6391, Hendersonville NC 28793. hcgms.org

M.A.G.M.A-Mountain Area Gem and Mineral Association: PO Box 542, Leicester NC 28748; 828-683-1048. wncrocks.com/magma/magma.html

North Carolina Geological Survey: Division of Land Resources, 1620 Mail Center, Raleigh NC 27699; 919-733-7353. geology.enr.state.nc.us

Southern Appalachian Mineral Society: PO Box 15461, Asheville NC 28813; 828-670-1996. main.nc.us/sams

U.S. Geological Survey (USGS): 12201 Sunrise Valley Dr., Reston VA 20192; 888-275-8747. usgs.gov

Museums & Mineral Centers

(See also Section V, Chapter Two for more information on most of the centers listed below.)

Colburn Earth Science Museum: 2 South Pack Square, Asheville NC 28801; 828-254-7162

Emerald Village: 331 McKinney Mine Rd., Spruce Pine NC 28777; 828-765-6463

Franklin Gem and Mineral Museum: 25 Phillips St., Franklin NC 28734; 828-369-7831

Hiddenite Center: 316 Church St., Hiddenite NC 28636; 828-632-6966
Linville Caverns: Hwy. 19929 US Hwy. 221 North, Marion NC 28752; 828-756-4171
Mineral and Lapidary Museum of Henderson County: 400 N. Main St., Hendersonville NC 28792; 828-698-1977
Museum of North Carolina Minerals: Blue Ridge Parkway, Milepost 331, Spruce Pine; 828-765-2761
North Carolina Mining Museum: 331 McKinney Mine Rd., Spruce Pine NC 28777; 828-765-6463
Ruby City Gems Museum: 130 East Main St., Franklin NC 28734; 828-524-3967

Gem Mines & Stores

For a complete listing of all gem mines in the mountains, visit my guidebook website at ashevilleguidebook.com . The mines presented below are a selection of established facilities that do not "enhance" their ore with imported gemstones but use only native ore.

Cherokee Ruby and Sapphire Mine: Only native gemstone ore from the Cowee Valley; 41 Cherokee Mine Rd., Franklin NC 28734; 828-349-2941; travel time From Asheville: 2 hours west.
Cornerstone Minerals: Located in downtown Asheville. Premier gem and mineral store. Great resource for local gemstone information. 52 N. Lexington Ave., Asheville NC 28801; 828-225-3888.
Emerald Hollow Mine: Native gem ore, including emeralds, from their own mine;484 Emerald Hollow Mine Dr., Hiddenite NC 28636; 828-635-1126; travel time from Asheville: 1–1.5 hours east.
Emerald Village: Native gem ore from their mine and other area mines; 331 McKinney Mine Rd., Little Switzerland NC 28749; 828-765-6463, 828-765-0000; travel time from Asheville: 1–1.5 hours east.

The World's Largest Blue Star Sapphire

Located just a short drive west of Asheville in Canton is the Old Pressley Sapphire Mine. In 1986 and 1987, two blue sapphires were found there that were truly spectacular. Craig Peden and Steve Meyers, prospecting in the area of the mine, found one that was 1035 carats and was named the "Southern Star." At the time it was the world's largest. Around the same time, Bruce Caminiti found an even larger one. When it was cut in 1988, it was named the "Star of the Carolinas" and was an astounding 1445 carats! It is listed in the *Guinness Book of World Records,* and was cut by the master gem cutter, John Robinson.

Gem Mountain Gemstone Mine: Covered flumes. Gem ore brought in daily from mines; Hwy. 226, Spruce Pine NC 28777; 828-765-6130; travel time from Asheville: 1–1.5 hours east.
G3MStones: Asheville prospector Daniel Pantas who specializes in rare North Carolina rubies and sapphires. By appointment. 828-712-6461

Mason's Ruby and Sapphire Mine: Native gem ore where you dig your dirt from their own mine; 6961 Upper Burningtown Rd., Franklin NC 28734; 828-369-9742; travel time from Asheville: 2 hours west.

Old Pressley Sapphire Mine: World's largest blue star sapphires were found at this mine. Only native gemstone ore; 240 Old Pressley Mine Rd., Canton NC 28716; 828-648-6320; travel time from Asheville: 45 minutes west.

Mason Mountain Mine and Cowee Gift Shop: Native gem ore where you dig your dirt from their own mine. Also enriched buckets with imported ore; 5315 Bryson City Rd., Franklin NC 28734; 828-524-4570; travel time from Asheville: 2 hours west.

Rose Creek Mine: Native gem ore where you dig your own dirt from their own mine; 115 Terrace Ridge Dr., Franklin NC 28734; 828-349-3774; travel time from Asheville: 2 hours west.

Spruce Pine Gemstone Mine: Native gem ore from local gem mines; 15090 Hwy. 226 South, Spruce Pine NC 28777; 828-765-7981; travel time from Asheville: 1–1.5 hours east.

Running

Popular Asheville Area Races

January: Asheville Hot Chocolate 10K. kickitevents.com
Mar.: Dupont Forest 12K Trail Race. jusrunning.com
May: Mountain Sports Festival Mile Run: kickitevents.com
Jun.: Farm 2 Table 5K kickitevents.com
Oct.: Thomas Wolfe 8K. kickitevents.com
Nov.: Shut In Trail Run jusrunning.com

Running Stores in the Asheville-Hendersonville Area

Fleet Feet Sports: 8 Town Square Blvd, Asheville NC 28803, 828-676-3536
Foot RX Running: 1979 Hendersonville Rd., Asheville NC 28803; 828-687-2825.
Jus' Running: 523 Merrimon Ave., Asheville NC 28804; 828-252-7867.

Shuffleboard

Toms Park: Located on West Allen St. in Hendersonville, it is the site of state and national shuffleboard tournaments. 27 shuffleboard courts. For more information, call the Hendersonville Shuffleboard Club at 828-697-3016.

Skateboarding

Western North Carolina has a number of cities and towns that have public skate parks. The more popular ones are the City of Asheville Food Lion Skatepark, Zero Gravity Skate Park, the huge indoor facility in Brevard, and the City of Hendersonville Skate Park.

Asheville Food Lion Skatepark: 17,000 square feet, unique concrete park with three distinctive areas in the beginner bowl, intermediate street course and an advanced vertical bowl. Safe challenging skate park facility for all ages.; 50 North Cherry St., Asheville NC 28801; 828-225-7184.

Black Mountain Skatepark: Skate park maintained by the Black Mountain Recreation Department.; 101 Carver Ave., Carver Community Center, Black 28711; 828-669-2052; travel time from Asheville: 30 minutes east.

BP Skate Park: Indoor facility. Quarter and mini ramps, bank with 2 hubba ledges and hand rail, camel humps and vert walls.; 171A Muse Business Park, Waynesville NC 28786; 828-452-0011; travel time from Asheville: 1 hour west.

Hendersonville Skatepark: 20,000 square feet, skate park in Patton Park.; Asheville Hwy. and Clairmont Dr., Hendersonville NC 28792;828-551-3270; travel time from Asheville: 45 minutes south.

Zero Gravity Skatepark: 12,000 square feet indoor skating facility, largest in Western North Carolina Spine mini-ramp, fun boxes, mini three-quarter bowl, bank ramps, launch boxes, a pyramid, ledges and roll-ins.; 1800 Old Hendersonville Rd., Brevard NC 28712; 828-862-6700; travel time from Asheville: 1 hour west.

Skiing & Snowboarding

The slopes of the Western North Carolina mountains provide a wide variety of trails, from easy beginner to expert. The views are breathtaking and the facilities modern. Many of the resorts feature their own snow making equipment. Most people don't associate the south with skiing, but the Western North Carolina mountains, with their higher elevations and colder winters, do have excellent skiing and snowboarding. Wolf Ridge Ski Slopes, the closest to Asheville is a 30-minute drive north on Hwy. 19/23.

Skiing & Snowboarding Facilities

Appalachian Ski Mountain: Ten slopes, two quad chairlifts, one double chairlift, outdoor ice skating. Excellent ski school and a large number of family-oriented programs; 940 Ski Mountain Rd., Blowing Rock NC 28605; 828-295-7828, 800-322-2373; travel time from Asheville: 2 hours east

Beech Mountain Resort: Beech Mountain is the highest ski area in eastern North America at 5,506 feet. One high-speed quad lift, six doubles, one J-bar and one rope tow. Skiing, snowboarding and tubing; 1007 Beech Mountain Parkway, Beech Mountain NC 28604; 828-387-2011; travel time from Asheville: 2 hours east.

Cataloochee Ski Area: Fourteen slopes and trails. Full-service rental shop and PSIA ski school. Cataloochee is the oldest ski resort in North Carolina; 1080 Ski Lodge Rd., Maggie Valley NC 28751; 828-926-0285, 800-768-0285; travel time from Asheville: 2 hours east.

Hawksnest Tubing Park: Biggest snow tubing operation on the east coast. Four different areas to snow tube with over 20 lanes. Two moving carpet lifts. Located between Boone and Banner Elk; 2058 Skyland Dr., Seven Devils NC 28604; 800-822-4295; travel time from Asheville: 1.5–2 hours west.

Sapphire Valley Ski Area: Two runs, one each for beginner and intermediate skiing and snowboarding; 4350 Hwy. 64 West, Sapphire NC 28774; 828-743-1162; travel time from Asheville1.5–2 hours west.

Scaly Mountain Outdoor Center: Four slopes, snow tubing only. Also summer tubing on artificial turf slopes; 7420 Dillard Rd., Scaly Mountain NC 28775; 828-526-3737; travel time from Asheville: 2–2.5 hours west.

Sugar Mountain Resort: A full-service alpine snow ski and snowboard area. Features a 1,200-foot vertical drop, 18 slopes and trails, eight lifts, and a longest run of 1.5 miles. Tubing, ice skating and snowshoeing also; 1009 Sugar Mountain Dr., Banner Elk NC 28604; 828-898-4521, 800-784-2768; travel time from Asheville: 1.5 hours east.

Wolf Ridge Ski Slopes: 4 lifts/ and 4 magic carpet lifts: 2 full service Ski Lodges: 23 ski runs. 25 minutes north of Asheville NC and only 5 miles off the new I-26 Wolf Laurel Exit 3 Interchange. 578 Valley View Circle, Mars Hill NC 28754; 800-817-4111; travel time from Asheville: 30 minutes north.

Spelunking & Caving

Spelunking is the official name used for the recreational activity of exploring caves but it is more commonly referred to as "caving". Like skydiving and rock climbing, caving is about as adventurous as it gets, and while going out on your own is possible, the best advice is to hook up with a professional cave guide company and let them plan your outing and guide you. The Linville Caverns, located south of Boone, are open to the public and are a good place to experience caving in a safe and controlled environment without the need of hiring a guide.

Linville Caverns: Hwy. 221 North (PO Box 567), Marion NC 28752; 800-419-0540, 828-756-4171; travel time from Asheville: 1 hour east.

Caving Guides

Cripple Creek Adventures: 3555 Wheat Rd., Cosby TN 37720; 828-260-1111; travel time from Asheville: 1 hour west

High Mountain Expeditions: 3149 Tynecastle Hwy., Banner Elk 28604; 800-262-9036, 828-898-9786; travel time from Asheville: 2 hours east.

River and Earth Adventures, Inc: 1655 Hwy. 105, Boone NC 28607; 828-963-5491; travel time from Asheville: 2–2.5 hours west.

Rock Dimensions: 131-B South Depot St., Boone NC 28607; 828-265-3544; travel time from Asheville: 2 hours east.

USA Raft Caving: 2 Jones Branch Rd, Erwin TN 37650; 888-872-7238; travel time from Asheville: 1–2 hours west.

Swimming

In Asheville, the Buncombe County Parks, Greenways and Recreation Services offers five outdoor pools located in different areas of Buncombe County. The pools are open in Jun., Jul. and the early part of Aug. The water is heated in every pool and there is a small admission fee per person. The City of Asheville Parks, Recreation and Cultural Arts Department has three outdoor public swimming pools, with Recreation Park on Gashes Creek Rd. the nearest to downtown of any county or city pool. The city pools are open Jun. through Mid-Aug. and also charge a small fee for swimming.

If lake swimming is what you want, nearby Lake Lure has a public beach and is your best bet. While there, plan to check out the famous Chimney Rock attraction and also consider an evening boat ride on the lake. Tours leave from the town dock area.

An absolutely unique mountain water experience, especially on a hot summer day, is the extremely popular Sliding Rock located on the Davidson River in Pisgah National Forest, about an hour's drive west from Asheville in the Brevard area, Sliding Rock is a natural 60-foot long waterslide ending in a 7-foot deep pool that has been developed by the US Forest Service into a recreation area. From the intersection of US 276 and US 64 in Pisgah Forest NC (near Brevard), go about eight miles north into the National Forest on US 276 toward the Blue Ridge Parkway. You will pass Looking Glass Falls on the right after five miles. Look for signs directing you to the Sliding Rock recreation area parking lot on the left.

Selected City of Asheville and Buncombe County Pools

Cane Creek Pool: 590 Lower Brush Creek Rd., Fletcher NC 28732; 828-628-4494

Erwin Community Pool: 55 Lees Creek Rd., Asheville NC 28806; 828-251-4992

North Buncombe Park Pool: 892 Clarks Chapel Rd., Weaverville NC 28787; 828-645–1080

Owen Pool: 117 Stone Dr., Swannanoa NC 28778; 828-686-1629

Recreation Park: (Closest to downtown) 65 Gashes Creek Rd., Asheville NC 28805; 828-298-0880

Tennis

For tennis players, many mountain cities and towns have city parks that have tennis courts available for public play. In Asheville, the Asheville Parks and Recreation Department lists a total of 32 public tennis courts on their website. Information about these courts, as well as the annual city Open Tennis Tournament for Junior and Adult divisions held each Jul., can be obtained by calling the Asheville Parks and Recreation Department, 828-259-5800. Asheville area courts are presented below. For a complete listing of tennis facilities open to the public, visit my guidebook website at ashevilleguidebook.com .

Aston Park Tennis Center: City of Asheville Parks and Recreation public facility. Aston Park Tennis Center is one of the finest public clay court facilities in the United States. There are 12 lighted clay courts designed and constructed of the Har-Tru Fast Dry clay court material. Open April to Dec. Reservations & fees to play; 336 Hilliard Ave., Asheville NC 28801; 828-251-4074.

Jackson Park: Eight tennis courts in the best Hendersonville park; 801 Glover St., Hendersonville NC 28792; 828-697-4884.

Weaver Park: Very easy to find North Asheville park located on Merrimon Ave. Park and tennis courts will be on the right. No reservations needed—first come, first served basis; Merrimon Ave., Asheville NC 28801; 828-258-2453.

Whitewater Rafting, Canoeing & Kayaking

The rivers of Western North Carolina and the Tennessee border offer Class I through Class IV rapids for whitewater rafting. Major rafting rivers are the French Broad, Nolichucky, Nantahala, Ocoee, Chattooga and Green River. These six rivers mountains are considered the best whitewater in the Southeast. Of the many whitewater rafting companies in the mountains, none has a better reputation than the Nantahala Outdoor Center. Their center, located on the Nantahala River near Bryson City, is a sure bet if you are looking for a first class, professional whitewater experience.

The closest whitewater rafting companies to Asheville are USA Raft, Blue Heron Whitewater and French Broad Rafting Expeditions, all located on the French Broad River, 30 minutes north in Marshall. If you want to get on a river, and whitewater is not a must, check out the Asheville Outdoor Center located right in Asheville. They offer gentle tubing, rafting, kayaking and canoeing on the French Broad River.

There are few better ways to experience the excitement of the mountains than a whitewater rafting trip, and Western North Carolina has it all, from peaceful gentle streams to big tumbling rivers that roar through the deepest gorges. The most popular whitewater stream for professional and amateur alike is the Nantahala River in the Bryson City area. A class II and III stream, the Nantahala begins in the mountains of Macon County and flows northward through the beautiful Nantahala Gorge and on into Graham County where it joins the Little Tennessee River. The eight-mile run on the Nantahala takes about three hours. Be advised, though, on summer weekends the river can get very crowded.

Located north of Asheville in Woodfin on the French Broad River, the Ledges Whitewater Park is the closest whitewater section of the river for canoeing and kayaking without guided service. This is recommended for experienced canoeists and kayakers only. The Ledges play spots, of which there are several, begin to warm up at levels over 1,000 cfs, and rise to 3,500 cfs. The park is complete with movable holding "gates" that kayakers can paddle through to practice for slalom competition and to improve their dexterity and water skills. To get there from Asheville, take I-240 to 19-23 North (Exit 4) and continue six miles to the New Stock Rd. exit. Turn left off the exit ramp and drive 0.7 miles to left on Aiken Rd., then first right onto Goldview Rd. Follow Goldview Rd. to the river. Turn right onto NC 251. The Ledges Whitewater Park and Picnic Area will be on your right almost immediately. If you wish, you can continue north on NC 251 2.0 miles to the Alexander Bridge for put-in.

Stream Classifications

Class I: Easy. Moving water with a few riffles, small waves and few obstructions. Requires basic paddling know-ledge.

Class II: Moderate. Easy rapids with up to three-foot waves and few obstructions. Requires intermediate skill level.

Class III: Difficult. High rapids and narrow channels. Requires intermediate skill level.

Class IV: Very difficult. Long difficult rapids, constricted channels and turbulent water. Requires experienced skill level.

Class V: Exceedingly difficult. Extremely difficult, long and often violent rapids. Requires high skill level.

Class VI: Utmost difficulty. Very dangerous and for experts only.

Asheville Area (French Broad River)

Asheville Adventure Rentals: Full service outfitter offering shuttles, boat rentals, kayaking and float trips through the Asheville area. No whitewater rafting. 704 Riverside Dr., Asheville NC 28801; 828-505-7371; travel time from Asheville: 5 minutes.

Asheville Outdoor Center: Canoeing, Kayaking, Rafting and Tubing the French Broad River. No whitewater rafting; 521 Amboy Rd., Asheville NC 28806; 800-849-1970, 828-232-1970; travel time from Asheville: In Asheville.

Zen Tubing: Tube rentals on the French Broad River for 2–3 hours floats; 855-936-8823 zentubing.com

Western Mountains (From Murphy to Waynesville)

Adventurous Fast Rivers Rafting: Nantahala River; 14690 Hwy. 19 West, Bryson City NC 28713; 800-438-7238, 828-488-2386; travel time from Asheville: 1.5–2 hours west to Nantahala River location.

Appalachian Rivers Raft Company: Nantahala River; US Hwy. 19, Topton NC 28781; 800-330–1999; travel time from Asheville: 1.5–2 hours west to Nantahala River location.

Big Frog Expeditions: 1278 Welcome Valley Rd. Benton, TN 37307; 877-776-2633; travel time from Asheville: 3 hours west.

Carolina Outfitters: Nantahala River; 12121 Hwy. 19 West, Bryson City NC 28713; 800-572-3510, 828-488-6345; travel time from Asheville: 1.5–2 hours west.

Endless River Adventures: Nantahala, Cheoah and Ocoee Rivers; 14157 US Hwy. 19/74 West, Bryson City NC 28713; 800-224-7238, 828-488-6199; travel time from Asheville: 1.5–2 hours west to Nantahala River location.

Great Smokey Mountain Fish Camp and Safaris: Little Tennessee (Tubing and Canoe Rentals only); 81 Bennett Rd., Franklin NC 28734; 828-369-5295; travel time from Asheville: 2 hours west to Franklin.

Headwater Outfitters: Canoeing, kayaking and tubing on the French Broad River. No whitewater rafting; 25 Parkway Rd., Rosman NC 28772; 828-877-3106; travel time from Asheville: 1.5 hours west.

Nantahala Outdoor Center: Nantahala, Ocoee, Chattooga, Cheoah, Pigeon, French Broad, and Nolichucky Rivers; 13077 Hwy. 19 West, Bryson City NC 28713; 828-785-5082, 888-905-7238; travel time from Asheville: 1.5–2 hours west to Nantahala River location.

Ocoee Adventure Center: 4651 Hwy 64, Copperhill, TN 37317; 888-723-8622: travel time from Asheville: 2.5 hours west.

Paddle Inn Rafting Company: Nantahala River; 14611 US Hwy. 19 West, Bryson City NC 28713; 800-711-7238; travel time from Asheville: 1.5–2 hours west.

Rolling Thunder River Company: Nantahala River; 10160 Hwy. 19 West, Bryson City NC 28713; 800-408-7238; travel time from Asheville: 1.5–2 hours west.

Southeastern Expeditions: 7350 Hwy 76 E, Clayton, GA 30525; 800-868-7238; travel time from Asheville: 1.75 hours south west.

Triple Creek Adventures: 3555 Wheat Rd., Cosby TN 37720; 828-260-1111; travel time from Asheville: 1 hour west.

Tuckaseegee Outfitters: Tuckaseegee River; 4909 Hwy. 74, Whittier NC 28789; 828-586-5050; travel time from Asheville: 1.5–2 hours west.

USA Raft: Nantahala River; Bryson City NC 28713; 800-872-7238; travel time from Asheville: 1.5–2 hours west

Wildwater Ltd. Rafting: Pigeon, Nantahala, Chattooga, Ocoee and Cheoah Rivers; 10345 Hwy. 19, Bryson City NC 28713; 866-319-8870, 828-488-2384; travel time from Asheville: 1.5–2 hours west to Nantahala River location.

Central Mountains (From Waynesville through Asheville to Burnsville)

Asheville Adventure Rentals: Full service outfitter offering shuttles, boat rentals, kayaking and float trips through the Asheville area. No whitewater rafting. 704 Riverside Dr., Asheville NC 28801; 828-505-7371. In Asheville.

Asheville Outdoor Center: Canoeing, Kayaking, Rafting and Tubing the French Broad River. No whitewater rafting; 521 Amboy Rd., Asheville NC 28806; 800-849-1970, 828-232-1970; travel time from Asheville: In Asheville.

Big Creek Expeditions: Pigeon River; 3541 Hartford Rd., Hartford TN 37753; 877-642-7238, 423-487-0178; Travel time From Asheville: 1 hour northwest.

Blue Heron Whitewater: French Broad River; 35 Little Pine Rd., Marshall NC 28753; 888-426-7238; travel time from Asheville: 30–45 minutes north.

Cherokee Adventures Inc: Rivers: Nolichucky, Watauga and Holston Rivers; 2000 Jonesborough Rd., Erwin TN 37650; 800-445-7238, 423-743-7733; travel time from Asheville: 1 hour northwest to Nolichucky River location.

French Broad Rafting Expeditions: French Broad River; 9800 US Hwy. 25-70, Marshall NC 28753; 800-570-7238; travel time from Asheville: 30–45 minutes north.

Green River Adventures: 111 East Main St., Saluda NC 28773; 800-335-1530, 828-749-2800; travel time from Asheville: 45 minutes south.

Loafers Glory Rafting: Toe and French Broad Rivers; 2637 Hwy. 226 North, Bakersville NC 28705; 828-688-9290, 866-933-5628; travel time from Asheville: 1 hour west to Bakersville location.

Outdoor Rafting Adventures: Pigeon River; 3635 Trail Hollow Rd., Hartford TN 37753; 866-333-7238, 423-487-2085; travel time from Asheville: 1 hour northwest.

Rapid Descent River Co: Pigeon River; 3165 Hartford Rd., Hartford TN 37753; 800-455-8808; travel time from Asheville: 1 hour northwest.

Rafting in the Smokies: Pigeon River; 3595 Hartford Rd., Hartford TN 37753; 800-776-7238; travel time from Asheville: 1 hour northwest.

Rip Roaring Adventures: Pigeon River; 3375 Hartford Rd., Hartford TN 37753; 800-449-7238; travel time from Asheville: 1 hour northwest.

USA Raft: French Broad River; 13490 US Hwy. 25-70, Marshall NC 28753; 866-872-7238; travel time from Asheville: 30–45 minutes north to the French Broad River location.

Wahoo Adventures: Watauga and Nolichucky Rivers; 1201 Rock Creek Rd., Erwin TN 37650; 800-444-7238, 828-262-5774; travel time from Asheville:.45 minutes-1 hour northwest to Nolichucky River location.

White Water Rafting: Pigeon River; 453 Brookside Village Way, Gatlinburg TN 37738; 800-771-7238, 865-430–3838; travel time from Asheville: 1.5–2 hours northwest.

Zen Tubing: Tube rentals on the French Broad River for 2–3 hours floats. 855-936-8823. In Asheville.

Northern Mountains (From Burnsville to Sparta)

High Mountain Expeditions: Watauga and Nolichucky Rivers, Wilson's Creek; 3149 Tynecastle Hwy., Banner Elk NC 28604; 828-848-9786; travel time from Asheville: 1.5–2 hours east to Banner Elk location.

River and Earth Adventures, Inc : Watauga and Nolichucky Rivers; 1655 Hwy. 105, Boone NC 28607; 800-411-7238, 828-963-5491; travel time from Asheville: 2–2.5 hours east.

Riverside Canoe: South Fork of the New River (Tubing and canoeing only), 2966 Garvey Bridge Rd., Crumpler NC 28617; 336-982-9439; travel Time From Asheville: 3 hours east.

Zip Line Riding

Are you on the adventurous side, and interested in seeing the beautiful forests of Western North Carolina from a different perspective? Then a forest canopy zip line ride may be for you. This unique experience takes limited energy to participate in, and is not designed to scare but rather offers a gentle, self-controlled gliding experience. In 2009, Nantahala Gorge Canopy Tours became the first zip line facility in the mountains, and offers rides during the summer season. Their rides take you through multiple ecosystems in the Nantahala Gorge area. Navitat Canopy Adventures, located in the Asheville area, consistently get rave reviews for the design and function of their ziplines, as well as their concern for the environment.

Adventure Center of Asheville: Ziplines, treetop park, bike park. Located 5 minutes from downtown Asheville. 1 Resort Dr., Asheville NC 28806; 877-247-5539 advavl.com

Nantahala Gorge Canopy Tours: Nantahala Rafting Center, 10345 Hwy. 19 South, Bryson City NC 28713; 866-699-2402.

Navitat Canopy Adventures: 242 Poverty Branch Rd., Barnardsville NC 28709; 855-628-4828, 828-626-3700. Reservations required. navitat.com

The Beanstalk Journey at Catawba Meadows: 220 Catawba Meadows Dr., Morganton NC 28655; 828-430–3440

Zipline Wildwater: Five locations throughout the mountains, including Asheville and Bryson City. 800-647-9587 wildwaterziplines.com

Section III

Asheville, All-America City

Chapter One
About Asheville

Located at the hub of the Great Smoky and Blue Ridge mountains, 2,216 feet above sea level on the Asheville Plateau, Asheville is the largest city in Western North Carolina and the tenth largest municipality in the state, covering an area of 40.99 square miles. Asheville's population is estimated at over 92,000 and the city is located at the confluence of the French Broad and Swannanoa rivers in a river-formed valley that runs 18 miles north and south. Chartered in 1797 and named after Samuel Ashe, a former governor of North Carolina, Asheville attracts millions of visitors and tourists each year who come for the timeless natural beauty, the crisp highland air, the magnificent mountains and vibrant cosmopolitan hospitality the city offers. Every year publications of every type list Asheville and the Western North Carolina mountains as one of the best places in the world to live. Consistently ranked by major publications and organizations as one of the top cities in America to live or visit, and always on "Top 10 Lists," Asheville's recent accolades include "Top-10 Great Sunny Places to Retire (*AARP*), Top 10 River Towns (*Outside Magazine*), #10 Food and Wine Destination (TripAdvisor), #3 for Most Beautiful Places in the US (GMA), Top 25 Small Cities for Art (*AmericanStyle Magazine*), #4 Top College Small Towns (Best Place to Retire), America's #1 Quirkiest Town (*Travel and Leisure*), Most Beautiful Place In America to Live and More (Real Estate Scorecard) and The Biggest Little Culinary Capital in America (*Departures*). In 2017, Condé Nast Traveler named Asheville as one of the Best Small Cities in the U.S.

Surrounded by thousands of acres of majestic mountains, plateaus, rolling valleys and mystical coves, Asheville is a city not easily forgotten once visited. With its winding hilly streets graced by architectural gems from the past, Asheville has been called the "Paris of the South." Every section of this enchanting city is blessed with unique and irreplaceable buildings that few cities in America can match. From the awesomely majestic Biltmore House to the Art Deco masterpiece S&W Building to the stately rock-hewn beauty of the Omni Grove Park Inn, Asheville is overflowing with architectural treasures. More than 170 historic buildings have been preserved, some of which were designed by world-famous architects Richard S. Smith, Douglas Ellington, Richard M. Hunt and Rafael Guastavino. Couple this with all of the cultural, business and entertainment possibilities and you have an extraordinary city to experience.

A major tourist destination with more than 5,000,000 visitors annually, Asheville is also known for its varied and rich arts and crafts communities. Hundreds of galleries, craft shops, and artisans studios are to be found here. Asheville has become an important center for traditional Appalachian as well as contemporary crafts. The variety and quality of the craft galleries and the many craft exhibits and shows attest to this fact. Located only minutes from national forests and green valleys, outdoor recreation opportunities also abound. Whitewater rafting, golf, hiking, fishing, horseback riding, llama trekking, rock climbing, camping and ballooning are just a few of the choices. Asheville also has a number of wonderful public parks, including the small Pritchard Park, where street musicians and chess players are often found. The recently renovated 6.5-acre city showpiece, Pack Square Park, features a splash pad, restrooms, information center, sculptures, and a venue for major festivals and musical events throughout the year. Both of these parks are located downtown and easy to find.

As you would expect, Asheville is rich in museums, nature centers, historic sites and other attractions for the visitor. During your stay, you may wish to attend a performance of the Civic Ballet, the Asheville Symphony Orchestra or one of the many local theatre companies. A wonderful way to spend a summer evening is to take in a game at historic McCormick Field, where Babe Ruth once played baseball. Asheville is also a major medical center. Modern hospitals and numerous specialized medical facilities, as well as a large resident population of doctors and medical professionals combine to make Asheville the regional center for health care.

The largest city in Western North Carolina, Asheville is the regional center for manufacturing, transportation, banking and professional services and shopping. Asheville boasts a vibrant downtown, where nightclubs, cafes, galleries, theatres, coffeehouses, pubs and superb restaurants all add to the mix that now creates one of the most exciting and cosmopolitan downtown districts in the South. Voted an All-America City in 1997 by the National Civic League, Asheville was one of only ten U.S. cities to receive this prestigious award. An abundance of local microbreweries notably the Highland Brewery, French Broad Brewery and others, have also earned Asheville the title of "Beer City USA". Asheville is home to numerous venues, including many restaurants and most bars, where local handcrafted beers can be sampled. In Sep., the wildly popular Brewgrass Festival, a celebration of Asheville's many microbreweries and bluegrass music takes place.

Asheville has a number of unincorporated communities and distinct areas that are constellated in and around the city. These include Arden, Biltmore Forest, Candler, Enka, Fairview and Leicester. Of these, Biltmore Forest is the most historic. An incorporated town located right in the heart of Asheville, this residential community is immediately adjacent to the world famous Biltmore Estate and is known for its many elegant homes.

History

Surrounded by towering mountains, Asheville was a small crossroads town when it was founded by pioneer town planner John Burton in 1792. Known as Morristown during the early years, the city was also called Buncombe Courthouse until 1797, when it was incorporated and named Asheville in honor of North Carolina governor Samuel Ashe.

Buncombe County attained county status in 1792 and was named for Revolutionary War hero Col. Edward Buncombe. Growth was slow until 1880, when the first railroad system was constructed. This first steam train changed Asheville forever, bringing in the outside world. This small mountain settlement went from a population of 2,616 to 10,328 in just ten years. A trickle of summer visitors that had journeyed to Asheville for half a century turned into a

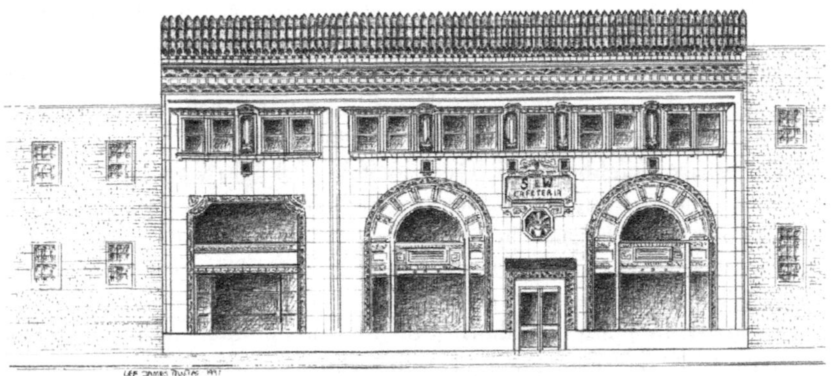

The S&W Cafeteria, 56 Patton Ave., Asheville

torrent. By 1886, an estimated 30,000 "summer people" visited the city annually. In 1885, the building of the first Battery Park Hotel was noted as the beginning of a great period of expansion for Asheville. Near the turn of the century, George Vanderbilt also began construction of the now world famous Biltmore House.

The greatest boom period in Asheville's history came during the 1920s with the construction of many new buildings throughout downtown, including the Grove Arcade, City Hall, Buncombe County Courthouse, Flat Iron Building and others. Many Art Deco buildings were also constructed in this period such as the S&W Cafeteria building.

Today, Asheville is experiencing another period of tremendous growth and revitalization. The downtown district, with its wealth of historic buildings, is one of the most vibrant city centers in the South. Major, ecologically sound riverfront development is also occurring along the French Broad River, with parks, greenways and cultural centers emerging. Asheville continues to attract people from around the world as an exciting vacation destination, and as a wonderful and beautiful place to live.

Downtown Neighborhoods

As a visitor to Asheville, it will be helpful to know that the downtown district is divided into a number of diverse neighborhoods, each with its own unique history and ambience. One of the very best ways to experience these neighborhoods is to walk the Asheville Urban Trail. This short self-guided walking tour visits all four of the neighborhoods discussed below, with stations and thematic markers along the way. For more information about this extraordinary way to trace the footsteps of Asheville's historic past, see Section III, Chapter Five, The Asheville Urban Trail.

For those interested in historic architecture, see Section III, Chapter Four, Historic Asheville. Each of Asheville's official historic districts are presented and the most important and historic buildings are highlighted. For some districts, self-guided tours are presented.

1. **Battery Hill Neighborhood:** This neighborhood is crowned by the magnificent Basilica of St. Lawrence, D.M., the former Battery Park Hotel and the historic Grove Arcade. This area contains some of Asheville's best shopping and dining. Be sure to take

a stroll down quaint Wall St. and visit some of its interesting and unusual stores. Farther down on Haywood St. is the Asheville Civic Center and the main library.

2. **Lexington Park Neighborhood:** This is Asheville's antique shop district. If you are at all interested in antiques, a visit to this district is a must. There you will also find trendy boutiques, neo-hippie stores, coffeehouses and nightclubs.
3. **Pack Square Neighborhood:** The heart of Asheville is Pack Square, a wonderful space surrounded by stunning architecture, from Art Deco to contemporary. This district overflows with nightlife from the many art galleries, pubs, coffeehouses, theatres and restaurants. Asheville's Pack Place and YMI Center for African-American Culture are also found here.
4. **Thomas Wolfe Plaza Neighborhood:** Crowned by the historic home of author Thomas Wolfe, the Thomas Wolfe Plaza area is home to the Asheville Community Theatre, historic churches, craft shops and art galleries.

In addition to the districts already mentioned, there are some others of special interest to visitors. You will want to be sure and visit Biltmore Village, located just outside the entrance to the Biltmore Estate. There you will find unique and enchanting gift shops, art and craft galleries, and specialty stores, including Chelsea's Village Cafe and Tea Room, where lunch begins at 11:30am and their quintessentially English afternoon tea begins at 3:30pm

Four other districts that have distinctive and historically important architecture in abundance are Montford, Chestnut Hill, Albermarle Park and the Grove Park areas. All of these neighborhoods, including Biltmore Village, are presented in depth in Section III, Chapter Four Historic Asheville.

Quick Facts

City Hall: 70 Court Plaza, PO Box 7148, Asheville NC 28802; 828-251-1122
Website: ashevillenc.gov
Elevation and Population: 2,216 feet, 73,000+
Visitor Center: 36 Montford St., Asheville NC 28801; 800-257-1300; exploreasheville.com
Directions To Visitor Center: From I-240, take exit 4C to Montford Ave.
Asheville Area Chamber of Commerce: 36 Montford Ave., Asheville NC 28801; 828-258-6101; ashevillechamber.org
County: Buncombe County: County Offices, 205 College St., Asheville NC 28801; 828-250-4000; buncombecounty.org

Biltmore Village Shops, Asheville

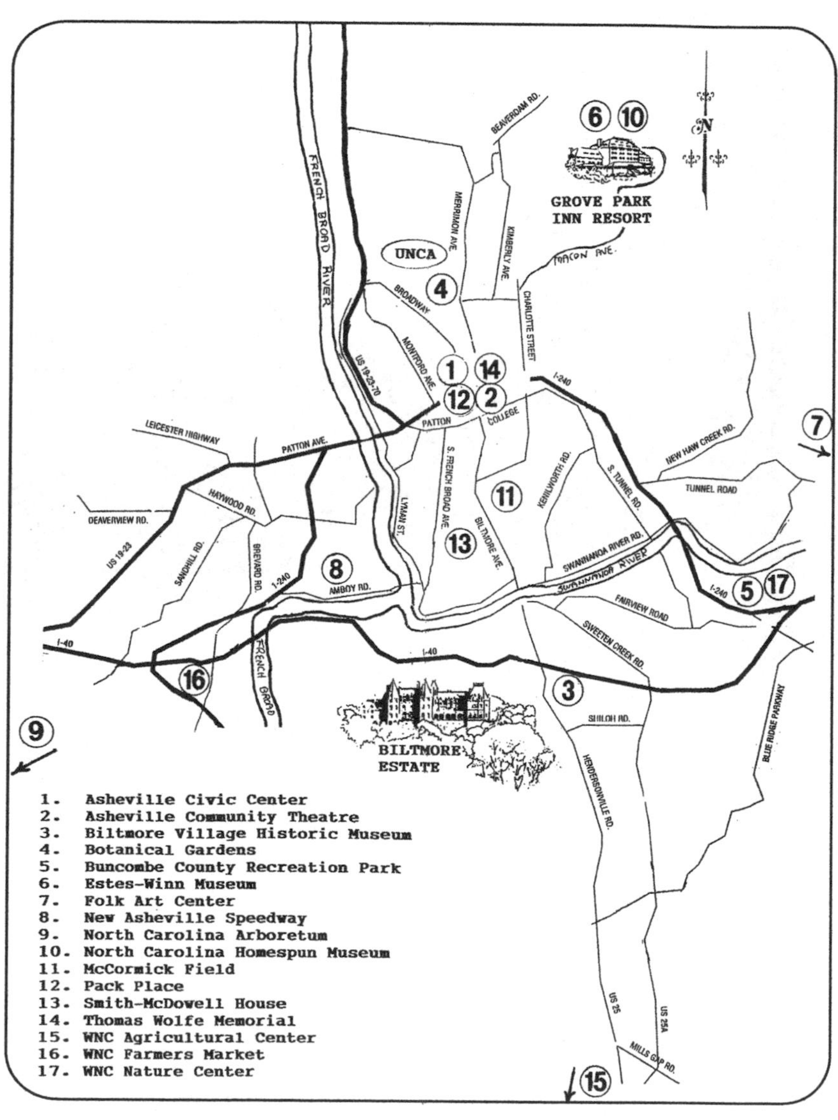

Asheville Museums, Cultural & Nature Centers

Chapter Two

Asheville Cultural Attractions

This chapter is devoted to the major cultural attractions and centers that Asheville has to offer. Those included here are very important to the life of Asheville as a city and each attracts thousands of visitors each year. The range of attractions is wide, from world-class crafts to baseball games at a park where Babe Ruth once swung a bat.

Asheville Art Museum

Located in the heart of downtown Asheville on Pack Square the Asheville Art Museum is set within the elegance of a restored 1926 structure of Italian Renaissance design. The museum's permanent collection features America's impressionists, as well as regionalist and contemporary abstract artists. In the spacious galleries above, traveling exhibitions spotlight a broad range of artistic talent in a full spectrum of media and highlight nationally renowned collections of sculpture, paintings, and traditional and contemporary crafts.

The Asheville Art Museum annually presents an exciting, inviting and active schedule of exhibitions and public programs based on its permanent collection of 20th and 21st century American art. Any visit will also include experiences with works of significance to Western North Carolina's cultural heritage including Studio Craft, Black Mountain College and Cherokee artists. Special exhibitions feature renowned regional and national artists and explore issues of enduring interest. The Museum also offers a wide array of innovative, inspiring and entertaining educational programs for people of all ages.

Location: Downtown Asheville
Address: 2 South Pack Square, Asheville NC 28801
Telephone: 828-253-3227
Hours: All Year: Daily 11am-6pm-Closed Tuesday
Fees: Adult, senior, student and child rates
Allow: 1–3 hours
Website: ashevilleart.org
Directions: From I-240 take exit 5A Merrimon Ave. and follow signs for Hwy. 25 south for three blocks to Pack Square.

Asheville Community Theatre (ACT), 35 Walnut St., Asheville

Asheville Community Theatre (ACT)

For more than 50 years, the Asheville Community Theatre has presented productions that have ranged from classics to contemporary comedies. The theater's Heston Auditorium (named after Charlton Heston and his wife, actress Lydia Clark, who served as artistic co-directors in 1947) is designed to provide an intimate theatre setting; the back row is only 55 feet from the stage edge. Air-conditioned and equipped with a Bose sound enhancement system, ACT is also home to youth acting classes, special student matinees and the Autumn Players outreach program produced by senior citizens.

Location: Downtown Asheville
Address: 35 Walnut St., Asheville NC 28801
Telephone: Box Office: 828-254-1320, Business Office: 828-254-2939
Hours: Business hours Tue–Fri 10am–4pm
Website: ashevilletheatre.org
Directions: From I-240 heading east, take exit 5A Merrimon Ave. Go straight up the hill through the light onto Market St. Make first left, in front of Magnolia's Grill and Bar. I-240 heading west, left off exit ramp. Left at light onto Woodfin St. Right on Market St. First left on Walnut St.

Asheville's Fun Depot

The Asheville Fun Depot is one of Asheville's most popular family-oriented attractions, designed with kids in mind. Facilities include a state-of-the-art arcade gallery, 18-hole indoor mini-golf, an outdoor go-kart track, multi-level laser tag, a soft play area, a climbing wall, batting cages and the Depot Diner.

Location: Southeast Asheville just off Interstate 1-40 at exit 5
Address: 7 Roberts Rd., Asheville NC 28803

Telephone: 828-277-2386, 866-303-4386
Hours: Mon–Thu 10am–9pm, Fri 10am–10pm, Sat 10am–11pm, Sun 1–8pm
Fees: Call for prices
Website: ashevillesfundepot.com
Directions: Take exit 51 off of Interstate 1-40, turn left at bottom of the ramp onto Sweeten Creek Rd. Turn left onto Roberts Rd.

Asheville Museum of Science

Located in the heart of downtown Asheville, The Asheville Museum of Science (AMOS) is Western North Carolina's home for experiential science learning, discovery, and exploration. Exhibits include the Colburn Hall of Minerals, the STEM lab, an interactive panorama screen, the AMOS Mars Rover, our Teratophoneus dinosaur skeleton and fossil dig, Southern Appalachian Forest, Toddler Nest, Hurricane Simulator, fun temporary exhibits, and gift shop. With fully interactive exhibits, street level access, and a variety of educational programs, AMOS is a must visit for the whole family! Be a geologist in our Colburn Hall of Minerals, dig for fossils and say hello to the Teratophoneus dinosaur skeleton, and climb into the tree canopy in their Southern Appalachian Forestry exhibit. One of the showcase features of AMOS is the Colburn Hall of Minerals, a wonderful place to explore the beauty of crystals, the magnificence of gemstones and the fantastic shapes and colors of minerals from around the world. The museum highlights the treasures that make North Carolina a geologic paradise, and regularly schedules exhibitions covering the full range of gem and mineral related subjects.

Location: Downtown Asheville
Address: 43 Patton Avenue, Asheville, NC 28801
Telephone: 828-254-7162
Hours: Monday-Saturday: 10am-5pm, Sunday: 1pm-5pm
Fees: Adult: $6, Children: $5.25, Military: $5.25, Senior: $5.25|, Student: $5.25, 2 & Under FREE
Website: ashevillescience.org
Directions: From I-240 take exit 5A Merrimon Avenue and follow signs for Highway 25 south for three blocks. The museum is located on Pack Square, directly in front of the Vance Monument.

Asheville and Appalachian Pinball Museums

Both Asheville and Hendersonville are homes to pinball museums run by the same company. At these two facilities the Asheville and Appalachian Pinball Museums, young and old can play pinball and classic video games. Once you pay admission, the machines are yours without the need for quarters or tokens. The Hendersonville museum is slightly smaller than the Asheville facility.

Location: Downtown Asheville and Hendersonville
Address: 1 Battle Square, Suite 1B. Asheville, NC 28801 and 538 North Main Street, Hendersonville, North Carolina 28792

Telephone: 828-776-5671 (Asheville) and 828-702-9277 (Hendersonville)
Hours: Visit website ashevillepinball.com for hours. Typically 1-6 or 1-9 depending on location and day
Fees: Adults $15, Children 10 and under $12 (Hendersonville slightly less)
Allow: 1–2 hours

Asheville Urban Trail

The Asheville Urban Trail, a 2-hour walking route through downtown that features 30 sculptural interpretive displays that commemorate people, places, and events of cultural, and architectural significance in the history of Asheville. On the Urban Trail you will encounter plaques and sculpture that bring to life major Asheville historical figures George Vanderbilt, E.W. Grove, Thomas Wolfe, F. Scott Fitzgerald, Douglas Ellington, and O. Henry, just to name a few. And of course, along the way there are plenty of opportunities for refreshment in Asheville's many cafes, pubs and coffeehouses. A good place to start is in front of Pack Place on Asheville's Pack Square where you can step up to Plaque #1, called "Walk Into History."

Location: Downtown Asheville
Hours: None, walk anytime
Website: exploreasheville.com/urban-trail

Basilica of St. Lawrence

To the north of the Grove Arcade area in downtown Asheville is the Basilica of Saint Lawrence, Deacon and Martyr, built in 1909. A Spanish Baroque Revival Roman Catholic Church built of red brick with polychrome glazed terracotta inserts and limestone trim, it was designed by world-famous architect/engineer Raphael Guastavino. The church employs his "cohesive construction" techniques in its large oval tile dome and Catalan-style vaulting in its two towers. The massive stone foundations and the solid brick superstructure give silent testimony to the architect's desire to build an edifice that would endure for generations. There are no beams of wood or steel in the entire structure; all walls, floors, ceilings and pillars are of tile or other masonry materials. The dome is entirely self-supporting, has a clear span of 58 x 82 feet, and is reputed to be the largest unsupported dome in North America. The Crucifixion tableaux of the Basilica altar feature a rare example of seventeenth century Spanish woodcarving. The windows are of German origin, and the Basilica has two chapels. Attached by an arcade is the 1929 Neo-Tuscan Renaissance brick rectory (now housing church offices) designed by Father Michael of Belmont Abbey. Self-guided tour brochures are available at the church, and guided tours are given after Sun masses.

Location: Asheville NC
Address: 97 Haywood St., Asheville NC 28801
Telephone: 828-252-6042
Hours: Open daily to the public. The Basilica is an active church, and note that masses may be in session.
Website: saintlawrencebasilica.org
Directions: From Pack Square go east on Broadway St. and turn left onto College St. Proceed to Pritchard Park and turn right onto Haywood St. The Basilica will be on your right.

Biltmore Estate

See Section III, Chapter Three (next chapter)

Biltmore Industries Homespun Museum

The Biltmore Industries Homespun Museum is located next to the Grove Park Inn and presents a historical overview of Biltmore Industries and its internationally renowned wool cloth. Inside the museum, photographs depict important events from Biltmore Industries history, including its founding in 1901 by Eleanor Vance and Charlotte Yale. The museum showcases memorabilia such as letters, photographs, and tailored suits made from homespun fabric.

Location: Asheville NC
Address: 111 Grovewood Rd., Asheville NC 28804
Telephone: 828-232-8353
Hours: Mon–Sat 10am–5pm, Sun 11am–5pm, closed Jan.–Mar.
Fees: None
Allow: One hour
Directions: From I-240 take Exit 5B. North on Charlotte Street. Right on Macon Avenue to Grove Park Inn. Museum is in the Grovewood Village area behind the inn, opposite the Vanderbilt wing garage.

Biltmore Village

When George W. Vanderbilt began building Biltmore Estate near Asheville in the late 1880s, he planned a picturesque manorial village to be built just outside the entrance to Biltmore Estate. Constructed in the early 1900s, the Village was primarily the work of Richard Hunt, Frederick Law Olmsted and Richard Smith. Today, Biltmore Village is a charming community of shops, restaurants and galleries offering world class shopping in an historic setting.

Be sure to take time to park your car and take a walking tour of the many shops housed in the original historic buildings. Buildings of special historical interest are the Cathedral of All Souls, the Administration Building at 1 Biltmore Plaza, the Depot, The Samuel Harrison Reed House at 119 Dodge St. and the cottages throughout the main section of the village. Buildings were added to the Village until about 1910, and shortly after Vanderbilt's death, the Village was sold. It was declared a National Historic District and a Local Historic District in 1989. (See Section III, Chapter Four, Historic Asheville for an in-depth look at the history and architecture of the Biltmore Village Historical District). Biltmore Village is also noted for its Christmas festival that surrounds the enacting of Charles Dickens' "A Christmas Carol." This enchanting festival includes concerts, lighting displays and arts and crafts exhibits.

Website: biltmorevillage.com
Directions: I-40 Exit 50 North on Hwy. 25/Biltmore Ave. Right immediately after All Souls Cathedral. From downtown Asheville, take Biltmore Ave. south from Pack Square through the hospital district

Black Mountain College Museum + Arts Center

The Black Mountain College Museum + Arts Center is an exhibition space and resource center dedicated to exploring the history and legacy of one of the world's most acclaimed experimental educational communities. The Center offers changing exhibitions, a video archive, research materials, and a selection of books and other materials for sale. The Center was founded in 1993 by Mary Holden to honor and pay tribute to the spirit and history of Black Mountain College and to acknowledge the College's role as a forerunner in progressive, interdisciplinary education with a focus on the arts.

Location: Downtown Asheville
Address: 120 College Street, Asheville NC 28801
Telephone: 828-350-8484
Hours: Wed thru Sat, 12pm-4pm
Fees: None
Allow: 1–2 hours
Website: blackmountaincollege.org
Directions: From I-240 take exit 5A Merrimon Ave. and go west on Broadway toward the center of town.

Blue Ridge Parkway Destination Center

A joint project of the National Park Service and the Blue Ridge National Heritage Area, the Blue Ridge Parkway Destination Center is a regional exhibit and education center focusing on the Blue Ridge Parkway. The center, housed in a LEED-certified "green" environmentally friendly building, features exhibits on the natural and cultural diversity and recreational opportunities found on the 469 mile length of the parkway. A key feature is the I-Wall, an oversized interactive, interpretive map of the parkway. The design, planning and construction of the 12,800 square foot center cost $9.8 million and was completed in 2007. There is also a gift shop and a 70-seat theatre showing a short movie about the parkway throughout the day.

Location: Milepost 384 on the Blue Ridge Parkway, two miles south of the Folk Art Center.
Address: 195 Hemphill Knob Rd., Asheville NC 28803
Telephone: 828-298-5330
Hours: 9am–5pm seven days a week except Christmas and New Year's Day.
Fees: None
Allow: Two hours
Website: blueridgeparkway.org
Directions: Located on the Blue Ridge Parkway just east of Asheville at Milepost 384. Access the highway at Hwy. 74A (I-240, Exit 9) and head east.

Botanical Gardens at Asheville

The Botanical Gardens at Asheville are located on a ten-acre site next to the campus of the University of North Carolina at Asheville. The Gardens were organized in 1960 by the Asheville Garden Club and were designed by Doan Ogden, a nationally known landscape architect. They were created to preserve and display the native plants and flowers of the

Botanical Gardens at Asheville, 151 W.T. Weaver Boulevard, Asheville

Southern Appalachian Mountains and are noted for their landscaping and as well as the great variety of plant life. The gardens are open year round and are intertwined with peaceful walking trails through varied habitats. There is a Botany Center, library and gift shop on the premises.

Location: North Asheville
Address: 151 W.T. Weaver Blvd., Asheville NC 28804
Telephone: 828-252-5190
Hours: Open year round, dawn to dusk
Fees: None
Allow: About two hours
Website: ashevillebotanicalgardens.org
Directions: From I-240 take Exit 5A Merrimon Ave. Go north to W.T. Weaver Blvd. and turn left.

The Wortham Center for the Performing Arts

The Wortham Center for the Performing Arts is located in the heart of downtown Asheville and includes three venues: the 500-seat Diana Wortham Theatre, the Tina McGuire Theatre, a multiuse black box theatre with seating for up to 100 people; and the Henry LaBrun Studio, a multiuse space and small performance venue. The main Diana Wortham Theatre offers live performances of music, theatre and dance by nationally touring artists, as well performances by regional arts groups

Location: Asheville NC
Address: 18 Biltmore Avenue, Asheville NC 28801
Telephone: 828-257-4530

Hours: See website
Website: worthamarts.org
Directions: From I-240 take exit 5A Merrimon Ave. and follow signs for Hwy. 25 south for three blocks to Pack Square.

Folk Art Center of the Southern Highland Craft Guild

Opened in 1980 on the 50th anniversary of the Southern Highland Craft Guild (SHCG), the Folk Art Center is home to Allanstand Craft Shop, one of Appalachia's oldest and best-known craft shops. Allanstand sells the work of more than 200 members of the SHCG. Both the finest in traditional mountain crafts of the region as well as the very best in contemporary American crafts are available for the discriminating visitor.

The center's upper level contains the museum space of the SHCG as well as the offices and the center's comprehensive craft library. The changing exhibition schedule showcases the works of SHCG members in addition to specially selected traveling exhibitions reflecting the traditions of the Southern Highlands. If crafts are of interest to you, a visit to the Folk Art Center is a must. Set in a forested glen just off the Blue Ridge Parkway, this special Asheville attraction is for young and old alike.

Location: Milepost 382 just east of Asheville on the Blue Ridge Parkway
Address: PO Box 9545, Asheville NC 28815
Telephone: 828-298-7928
Hours: Open daily 9am–6pm except Thanksgiving, Christmas, and New Year's Day
Fees: None
Allow: Two hours

The Folk Art Center, off the Blue Ridge Parkway at milepost 382

Website: southernhighlandguild.org
Directions: Located on the Blue Ridge Parkway just east of Asheville at milepost 382.

Grove Arcade Public Market

The Grove Arcade was the dream of E.W. Grove, a self-made millionaire who moved to Asheville in the early 1900s, where he conceived of the Arcade as "the most elegant building in America," and as a new type of retail center. When the Arcade opened in 1929, it quickly became home to a collection of local shops and services. For 13 years, the Arcade was the major commercial and civic center in Western North Carolina. The Federal Government took over the building in 1942, following America's entry into World War II, evicting all retail and office tenants. Following the war's end, the Arcade continued under Federal ownership. In 1997 the City of Asheville acquired title to the Grove Arcade under the National Monument Act, and the revitalized Grove Arcade now features over 50 specialty stores, restaurants, offices and apartments and is open to the public daily. The Arcade is located just west of Haywood St. and the Civic Center, an easy 10-minute walk from Pack Square.

Website: grovearcade.com
Directions: From Pack Square proceed east on Patton Ave., turn left onto Haywood St. and then left onto Battery Park. The Arcade will be ahead on your right.

Harrah's Cherokee Center Asheville

Located on Haywood St., Harrah's Cherokee Center Asheville is Western North Carolina's preeminent multi-purpose event facility. The facility first opened to the public in 1974 and has since hosted thousands of concerts, sporting events, trade and consumer shows, graduations, speeches, and other types of events. The Center primarily consists of four venues and has the ability to host a variety of events: Explore Asheville Arena, Thomas Wolfe Auditorium, the Exhibit Hall, and the Banquet Hall. It is home to the Asheville Symphony and contains historic elements from the previous Art Deco auditorium. The lobby of the current structure features Art Deco terrazzo floors, gilded plaster molding, and anthemia ornamented columns.

Location: Asheville NC
Address: 87 Haywood St., Asheville NC 28801
Telephone: 828-259-5736
Website: harrahscherokeecenterashevil le.com
Hours: Business office open Mon–Fri 8:30am–5pm; ticket office open Mon–Fri 10am–5:30pm, Sat 10am–1pm
Directions: Walking from Pack Square in downtown Asheville, take Patton Ave. to Pritchard Park. Turn right onto Haywood St.

McCormick Field & the Asheville Tourists

Opened in 1924, McCormick Field is one of the oldest operating minor-league baseball parks in North America. A 1992 remodeling replaced the field's rickety wooden grandstand with one of steel and brick and expanded the concession area. Despite the facelift, the field retained its signature short right field, a scant 300 feet down the line from home plate. As a result of remodeling, though, the wall is now an imposing 35 feet high. The entire outfield wall is surrounded by tall, verdant trees, and during the summer the smell of honeysuckle is heavy throughout the park. Scenes from the movie "Bull Durham" were filmed at the park. McCormick Field is home to the Asheville Tourists, a Class A farm team of the Colorado Rockies. Ty Cobb, Jackie Robinson and the immortal Babe Ruth all played at McCormick Field.

Historic McCormick Field, opened in 1924 and remodeled in 1992, can be seen in the film "Bull Durham."

Location: Asheville NC
Address: 30 Buchanan Pl., Asheville NC 28801
Telephone: 828-258-0428
Hours: Most games are played at night, starting at 7:05pm, Sun games begin at 5:05pm
Fees: Box seats start at around $10
Directions: Take I-240 to Exit 5B Charlotte St. Go south on Charlotte St. to McCormick Place.

North Carolina Arboretum

Established in 1986 as an inter-institutional facility of the University of North Carolina, the Arboretum is located within the 6,300-acre Bent Creek Experimental Forest and is surrounded by the 480,000-acre Pisgah National Forest. The 426-acre site is nestled in one of the most beautiful natural settings in the Southeast. The Arboretum has wonderful varied gardens, walking trails and natural habitats.

The Arboretum focuses on education, economic development, research, conservation, and garden demonstration with respect to landscape architecture and plant sciences. It is becoming the major state-supported attraction in Western North Carolina. A wide variety of classes and workshops are taught by the garden's staff and other plant experts. Educational programs target all ages and range from bonsai demonstrations to nature walks.

Location: Asheville NC
Address: 100 Frederick Law Olmsted Way, Asheville NC 28806
Telephone: 828-665-2492
Hours: Daily from 7am–9pm (daylight savings time) and 8am–9pm (Eastern Standard Time)
Fees: None
Allow: Three hours
Website: ncarboretum.org
Directions: From the Blue Ridge Parkway: N.C. 191 exit (Milepost 393.6). On the exit ramp, the entrance is on the left. From I-40: Exit 40 (Farmers Market). 191 south, follow signs.

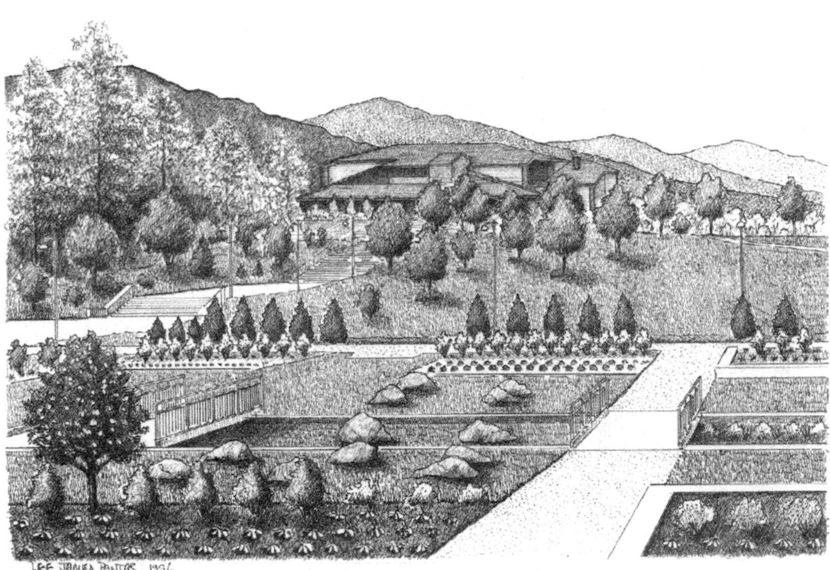

North Carolina Arboretum, 100 Frederick Law Olmsted Way, Asheville

Smith-McDowell House

Delve into mountain history and enjoy the Victorian splendor of Asheville's oldest brick residence by visiting the Smith-McDowell House. This elegant structure, circa 1840, is now open to the public as a local history museum. The house was built by James McConnell Smith as a private residence. A later owner, Charles Van Bergen, commissioned the famous Olmsted Brothers firm to landscape the property. In 1974, Asheville-Buncombe Technical College purchased the structure, and leased it to the Western North Carolina Historical Association. Five years later, after restoration, it was opened as a museum.

One of Asheville's architectural jewels, the Smith-McDowell House presents a wonderful opportunity to experience the past in a truly elegant restoration. It is especially delightful at Christmas time when all of the Victorian decorations are up. For an in-depth look at Smith-McDowell House's architecture and history, see Section III, Chapter Four Historic Asheville.

Location: Asheville NC
Address: 283 Victoria Rd., Asheville NC 28801
Telephone: 828-253-9231
Hours: Wed–Sat 10am–4pm, Sun 12–4pm
Fees: Adult and child rates
Allow: Two hours
Website: wnchistory.org
Directions: From Pack Square take Biltmore Ave. south toward hospitals. Just before Memorial Mission Hospital, make a right onto Victoria Rd.

Smith-McDowell House, 283 Victoria Rd., Asheville

Southern Appalachian Radio Museum

The Southern Appalachian Radio Museum has a wide range of radio memorabilia including exhibits of Atwater Kent, Philco, Silvertone, Edison phonographs, Crosley, Hammarlund, Harvey Wells, test instruments, spark gap transmitters, keys and ancient QSL cards. This is a museum where you can touch the radios and do things, and they also have an amateur radio station, W4AFM, on premises where you can take a turn at the mike!

Location: Campus of Asheville-Buncombe Technical Community College, Asheville NC
Address: Room 315 Elm Building, AB-Tech College, Asheville NC 28801
Telephone: 828-298-1847
Hours: Fri 1–3pm or call for a tour at other times
Fees: None
Allow: 1 hour
Website: saradiomuseum.org
Directions: From Pack Square proceed south on Biltmore Ave. As you pass the hospitals turn right onto Victoria Rd. for about .9 mile. When you see a pedestrian overpass, turn right (up the hill) at the electronic message board. Park in any of the spaces marked with white strips in several lots; and enter the nearby Elm Building. Take the elevator to the 3rd floor, room 315.

The Antique Car Museum at Grovewood Village

Located in Grovewood Village next to The Grove Park Inn is the The Antique Car Museum at Grovewood Village. More than twenty restored cars, including a 1926 Cadillac, a 1927 La Salle convertible and a 1922 La France fire engine now fill this building. Greeting you at the door is a 1913 Model T much like the ones Henry Ford and Thomas Edison traveled to Asheville in during their stays at the Omni Grove Park Inn.

The Antique Car Museum at Grovewood Village, 111 Grovewood Rd., Asheville

Location: Asheville NC
Address: 111 Grovewood Rd., Asheville NC 28804
Telephone: 828-253-7651
Hours: Saturday 10am–5:30pm and Sunday 11am–5pm
Fees: None
Allow: One hour
Directions: From I-240 take Exit 5B. North on Charlotte St. Right on Macon Ave. to Grove Park Inn. Museum is in Grovewood Village area behind the inn, opposite the Vanderbilt wing garage.

The Craggy Mountain Line

The Craggy Mountain Line offers old fashioned trolley rides on restored antique trolley cars that lasts about an hour and a half on approximately 3.45 miles of rail line known as the Asheville to Craggy Branch. This was part of the former Southern Railroad located in Woodfin, Buncombe County, NC just north of Asheville. The line has been preserved in an operable state and historic railroad equipment has been restored to its original condition for display on the premises. Your kids will love this attraction.

Location: Asheville NC
Address: 111 North Woodfin Avenue, Asheville, NC 28804
Telephone: 828-808-4877
Hours: Every Saturday, open car trolley rides take place at 4 o'clock
Fees: $12
Allow: Two hours
Nearby: The Antique Car Museum at Grovewood Village
Directions: Take I-26 north from Asheville. Take Exit 24 (Elk Mountain Road/Woodfin) and follow signs.

Thomas Wolfe Memorial

Thomas Wolfe left an indelible mark on American letters. His mother's boardinghouse in Asheville, now the Thomas Wolfe Memorial, has become one of literature's most famous landmarks. In his epic autobiographical novel, **Look Homeward Angel,** Wolfe immortalized the rambling Victorian structure, originally called "Old Kentucky Home," as "Dixieland." A classic of American literature, **Look Homeward Angel** has never gone out of print since its publication in 1929, keeping interest in Wolfe alive and attracting visitors to the setting of this great novel.

The Memorial is administered by the North Carolina Department of Cultural Resources and is open to the visiting public. For an in-depth look at the architecture and history of the Thomas Wolfe House, see Section III, Chapter Four Historic Asheville.

Location: Asheville NC
Address: 52 North Market St., Asheville NC 28801
Telephone: 828-253-8304
Hours: Tue–Sat 9am–5pm
Fees: Adult and student rates
Allow: Two hours
Website: wolfememorial.com
Directions: I-240 heading east: Take Exit 5A straight up hill through light onto North Market St. I-240 heading west: turn left off exit, then left onto Woodfin St. and right onto North Market St.

Thomas Wolfe Memorial, 52 North Market St., Asheville

U.S. Cellular Center (formerly The Asheville Civic Center), 87 Haywood St., Asheville

Western North Carolina Agricultural Center

One of the country's premier agricultural centers, the WNC Agricultural Center schedules over 50 events yearly, including 35 horse shows. The Center has a 65,000 square-foot fully enclosed show arena, with a 3,000-person seating capacity. There is also a 120′ x 240′ show ring, outdoor covered rings, and two outside, well-lighted warm-up rings. The Agricultural Center is host yearly to horse and livestock events, trade shows, RV and car shows, festivals, cat and dog shows, and many other events. This world-class multi-use facility is open year round. It is also home to the annual North Carolina Mountain State Fair.

Location: Fifteen minutes south of Asheville
Address: 1301 Fanning Bridge Rd., Fletcher NC 28732
Telephone: 828-687-1414
Website: wncagcenter.org
Directions: I-26 Exit 9. Follow airport signs off ramp. Continue past airport to make left onto Fanning Bridge Rd.

Western North Carolina Farmers Market

The Western North Carolina Farmers Market first opened for business in Sep. 1977. This model project, involving input from local, state and national leaders, is one of the most modern and best planned markets in the United States. Hundreds of thousands of visitors come to the market each year not only to shop, but to take in the wonderful country atmosphere. Fruits and vegetables can be purchased by the piece, pound, bushel or truckload. Former Commissioner of Agriculture James A. Graham stated it this way: "Think of shopping at a 36-acre roadside stand featuring farm-fresh fruits and vegetables, flowers and ornamental plants, mountain crafts and scores of gift items."

Retail vendors offer a year-round selection of farm fresh produce, canned goods, honey and handcrafted items. Five truck sheds provide space for farmers and dealers to display and sell their produce. Restaurants and a retail garden center are also located on Market grounds.

Location: Asheville NC
Address: 570 Brevard Rd., Asheville NC 28806
Telephone: 828-253-1691

At the Western North Carolina Farmers Market, 570 Brevard Rd., Asheville

Hours: Open year-round, 7 days a week.
Website: ncagr.gov/markets/facilities/markets/asheville
Directions: I-40 Exit 47. South on Hwy. 191/Brevard Rd. The market is on the left a short distance from Interstate.

Western North Carolina Nature Center

Owned and maintained by Buncombe County, the Western North Carolina Nature Center is open year-round with indoor and outdoor exhibits. This outstanding 42-acre center features indigenous wildlife and plant life of the Appalachian region. A great outing for kids and adults alike, the center has animals both large and small, from cougars and wolves to the tiniest insects. Special programs, demonstrations and "hands-on" activities are available for anyone who wishes to learn about the rich natural heritage of the Southern Appalachian mountains. Nowhere else in WNC will you find such diverse wildlife, gardens, trails, indoor exhibits, habitats and farm animals in one setting.

Location: Asheville NC
Address: 75 Gashes Creek Rd., Asheville NC 28805
Telephone: 828-259-8080
Hours: Open 7 days a week, 10am–5pm
Fees: Adult, senior, student, and child rates
Allow: 2–4 hours
Website: wildwnc.org
Directions: I-240 Exit 8 (74A West). East off ramp. Right onto Swannanoa River Rd. Right onto Gashes Creek Rd.

Cougars can be seen at WNC Nature Center

Vintage Mercury

YMI Cultural Center

The YMI Cultural Center, located in the Pack Place Education, Arts & Science Center, is an enduring asset for the city of Asheville. Housed in a local landmark building that is listed on the National Register of Historic Places, the YMICC runs programs in cultural arts, community education and economic development. Commissioned by George Vanderbilt in 1892, this beautiful pebble dash and brick building of Tudor design was built by and to serve several hundred African-American craftsmen who helped construct the Biltmore Estate. Today, the newly refurbished center continues its tradition of community service. Its galleries feature exhibits, programs, classes and performance that present African-American art, culture and history at their best. The YMI Cultural Center is located behind Pack Place at Eagle and Market St.

Location: Asheville NC
Address: 39 South Market St., Asheville NC 28801
Telephone: 828-257-4540
Hours: Tue–Fri 10am–5pm, Sat 1–5pm by appointment
Fees: Adult, student, and young child rates
Allow: Two hours
Website: ymicc.org
Directions: From I-240 take exit 5A Merrimon Ave. and follow signs for Hwy. 25 south for three blocks. Pack Place is located on Pack Square, directly in front of the Vance Monument.

The Red Wolf: A Nature Center Project

The Red Wolf, one of the lesser-known wolf species native to North America, once roamed throughout much of the Southeastern United States but have been eliminated from almost all of their natural range. The Nature Center located in Asheville is part of a breeding program to raise red wolves for eventual release into the wild.

Red Wolves average between 55 and 80 pounds, somewhat smaller than the better known gray wolf, but larger than the coyote which it resembles. Although many red wolves have a reddish cast to their fur, some do not. The usual coloration is a blend of cinnamon-brown, black and grayish-brown.

Western North Carolina Nature Center, 75 Gashes Creek Rd., Asheville

Not as much is known about the red wolf as it's more well-known cousin, and it is believed that they do not form large packs like gray wolves. Most of their food consists of smaller animals such as raccoons, rabbits, rodents and birds. Like other wolf species, the red wolf has been persecuted by man because of our hatred, fear and misconception of these large predators. Over the years, the red wolves were shot, trapped and poisoned as their habitat was cleared for use by man. Today, thanks to the efforts of organizations such as the Western North Carolina Nature Center, the red wolf is returning to the wild habitats of its ancestors.

Pack Place at Pack Square is many museums in one complex.

Chapter Three
Biltmore Estate

This chapter is devoted exclusively to Biltmore Estate. A national treasure, Biltmore Estate's importance to Asheville cannot be understated, and as one of the major attractions in Western North Carolina it warrants a chapter unto itself. A visit to Biltmore Estate, in the opinion of the author, is a must for anyone coming to Asheville.

Although it is not formally part of the present Biltmore Estate, Biltmore Village (**See** Section III, Chapter Two) was also originally conceived of by George Vanderbilt. The architecture of the original village buildings, especially the Cathedral of All Souls, clearly reflects the spirit of Vanderbilt's vision.

Biltmore Estate
Your Visit

A visit to Biltmore is an event, so you'll want to give yourself at least 4-6 hours to explore the house, grounds, and winery. You'll find numerous shops throughout the estate, all with an uncommon selection of special gifts, accessories, and mementos of your visit. Don't forget to allow time to browse through them all. Like the estate itself, Biltmore's restaurants offer a delicious blend of American and European flavors. Dining choices range from the distinctly American fare of the Stable Café to the seasonal buffets of the Deerpark Restaurant.

Every trip to Biltmore, no matter the time of year, is a new and exciting experience, whether you come for the breathtaking Festival of Flowers in the spring or the celebrated Candlelight Christmas Evenings. The beauty of Biltmore Estate is ever-changing, with new wonders and delights appearing every season. In the springtime, the gardens explode with brilliant color, calling for the celebration of the spring Festival of Flowers. Summertime brings lush greenery to the hillsides, deep shade in the cool, wooded groves, and Summer Evening Concerts performed on the South Terrace. Dec. brings the splendor of an elaborate 19th century Christmas to every corner of the decorated mansion. Finally, winter is a time when guests can enjoy the special presentations regarding many of the preservation projects taking place in the house.

George Vanderbilt's dream first began to take shape in 1887, when he visited Asheville on holiday. Enchanted by the remote majesty of the Blue Ridge Mountains, he decided to make Asheville the site of his country estate. Commissioning architect Richard Morris Hunt, he set out to create a mansion modeled after the châteaux of France's Loire Valley. They began to collect the finest building materials from all over the United States. It took an army of stonecutters and artisans six years to construct Biltmore House, which is today the largest private home in America, situated on more than eight thousand acres.

George Vanderbilt filled his 250-room mansion with treasures he had collected during his world travels. Works by Albrecht Dürer, John Singer Sargent, and Pierre Auguste Renoir cover the walls. Exquisite furniture and Oriental rugs fill each room. Minton china graces elaborate table settings. Guests of Mr. Vanderbilt had their choice of 32 guest rooms, and could pass the time in the Billiard Room, Winter Garden, Tapestry Gallery, or countless other sitting rooms, and be entertained in the Gymnasium, Bowling Alley, or indoor swimming pool. Ever mindful of his guest's comfort, Mr. Vanderbilt equipped his house with a centralized heating system, mechanical refrigeration, electric lights and appliances, and indoor bathrooms—all unheard of luxuries at the turn of the century.

Today, Biltmore House visitors can see the house virtually as it was in George Vanderbilt's day because its sculptures, paintings, furnishings, and household items have been carefully preserved.

Biltmore Estate Information

Location: South Asheville, adjacent to Biltmore Village
Address: Corporate Offices: Biltmore Estate, One North Pack Square, Asheville NC 28801
Telephone: General Information: 800-543-2961, 828-274-6333
Corporate Offices: 818-255-1776
Individual Ticket Sales: 800-411-3812
Group Ticket Sales: 828-274-6230
Inn on Biltmore Estate: 866-336-1245, 828-225-1600
Website: biltmore.com
Hours: Biltmore Estate is closed Thanksgiving and Christmas but open on New Year's Day. Biltmore Estate also has a number of special events including Summer Evenings Concerts and Candlelight Christmas Evenings (early Nov. through Christmas, taking place after normal hours.) Reservations are required.
Estate Entrance Hours (Subject to change without notice): 8:30am–7pm Admissions gate closes at 4 pm Biltmore House front door closes at 4:30pm
Admission Gate and Welcome Center: 8:30am–4pm
Biltmore House Hours: Jan.–Dec. daily 9am–4:30pm
Fees: Prices vary seasonally and depending on method of purchase (**Online or at gate**). 2011 prices are quoted. Adults $69.00, Youth 10-16 $34.50 Children nine and under free when accompanied by paying adult.
Admission Tickets Includes: Self-guided visit of Biltmore House, all-day access to gardens and Antler Hill Village, complimentary wine tasting and guided tour at the Winery, dining and shopping opportunities and free parking.
Outdoor Activities: Stop by the Outdoor Center in Antler Hill Village to check the many outdoor activities available at Biltmore Estate. These include Carriage Rides, Horseback Riding, River Float Trips, Biking, Hiking, Segway Tours, Sporting Clays, Flyfishing School and Land Rover Dr.iving School. Estate outdoor activities are available by

reservation to estate daytime guests, Biltmore Twelve-Month Passholders, and Inn on Biltmore Estate guests. Call 800-411-3812 for more information

Allow: Four to six hours minimum.

Directions: From I-40: Exit 50 or 50B. North on Hwy. 25. Left at fork. Entrance gate on left. From downtown Asheville: Biltmore Ave. south from Pack Square through hospital district. Left on Lodge St.

Antler Hill Village and Winery

Antler Hill Village is a casual place extending the Biltmore experience, from the fun and relaxing Winery to exhibits at The Biltmore Legacy to delectable pub fare and ale at Cedric's Tavern. You can also enjoy live entertainment on the Village Green, explore farm life in the early 1900s at the Farm, and get ready to explore the 8,000-acre backyard at the Outdoor Adventure Center. The village's name comes from Antler Hill, the "fine high ridge" where the Inn on Biltmore Estate is located. From the Civil War into the 1930s, the ridge was the site of Antler Hall, a residence and social center for many estate families. Main features at Antler Hill Village include:

Winery: Guests enter the Winery from Antler Hill Village where they walk underground through the old dairy's original tunnel, designed to immediately engage all of the senses into the winemaking process. As part of the tours offered at the Winery, guests can enjoy wines in the Tasting Rooms. On display also at the Winery is Edith Vanderbilt's 1913 Stevens-Duryea Model C-Six. This rare piece is the only car George Vanderbilt purchased that remains in the estate's collection.

The Biltmore Legacy: Discover the many sides of Edith Vanderbilt, George Vanderbilt's wife, or learn how the Cecils preserve Biltmore's legend of gracious hospitality. This facility includes exhibits filled with slices of estate life, including archival letters, photos, and drawings illustrating how the Vanderbilts lived. A small theater features a film narrated by Dini Cecil Pickering that shares the family story of the Vanderbilts.

Village Green and Bandstand: The centerpiece of Antler Hill Village, the Village Green has a gently sloping area perfect for people watching, listening to live music each afternoon, or relaxing with a snack or picnic.

Outdoor Adventure Center: Outdoor activities available at Biltmore Estate include Carriage Rides, Horseback Riding, River Float Trips, Biking, Hiking, Segway Tours, Sporting Clays, Fly-fishing School and Land Rover Dr.iving School. Tickets are available at the Outdoor Adventure Center, as well as outdoor gear and clothing.

Antler Hill Farm: The Farm offers a glimpse into the agricultural past of Biltmore Estate. Traditional farming demonstrations take place there, including authentic blacksmithing by local crafters. The Farmyard houses sheep, goats, chickens, cows and horses that children can see up close and personal. The Kitchen Gardens showcase fragrant herbs and vegetables used in Biltmore's restaurants.

Cedric's Tavern: Named after George Vanderbilt's beloved St. Bernard, Cedric, this warm, relaxing pub reflects the less formal side of Biltmore dining and entertaining. Specialties include shepherd's pie and fish and chips.

Tours & Seminars

Audio Guide to Biltmore House: Storytelling audio guide that leads you room-by-room sharing stories of occupants.

Biltmore House Architect's Tour: Guided 60-minute tour that offers a closer look at the design and construction of Biltmore House by going into areas not on regular house visit. The tour provides stunning photo opportunities from rooftop and balconies.

Biltmore House Butler's Tour: See how Biltmore House functioned, past and present, and learn about the work of the domestic servants during this 60-minute guided tour, which takes you into unrestored rooms and mechanical areas not open to the public on the regular house visit.

Vanderbilt Family and Friends Tour: This new guided tour spurs your imagination about staying at Biltmore with the Vanderbilts as your hosts. Tour bedrooms not on the regular house visit that are outfitted with clothing and accessories from the 1900s as your hear stories from your host about customs of the time and the fascinating people who visited Biltmore.

Premium Biltmore House Tour: Tour the house for two hours with a guide assigned to you exclusively. Includes areas seen in the Butler's Tour, Architect's Tour, and House Tours.

Legacy of the Land Tour: Take a motorcoach tour of the estate and learn about the history of the land, structures, and former residents. Visit areas not usually open to guests.

Winery Behind The Scenes Guided Walking Tour: Guests are guided on a walking tour of the Winery production areas. See and learn the difference between making red wine and white wine, as well as the bottling process. The tour ends in the Champagne finishing room where guests learn how true French style sparkling wines are made.

Farm Guided Walking Tour: Take a tour of what everyday life was like on the estate at the turn of the century. Meet friendly farmyard animals, a blacksmith, a woodworker, and try your hand at churning butter. Stroll through the stunning Kitchen Garden.

Farm Wagon Rides: Tours departs from the Farm's Kitchen Garden entrance in Antler Hill Village.

Red Wine and Chocolate Seminar at Winery: Discover why chocolate and red wine is a match made in heaven. Please register at the Winery Portal area in Antler Hill Village.

Biltmore Estate Lodging

Inn on Biltmore Estate: Superb is the one word to describe the Inn on Biltmore Estate. Opened in 2001, it is the newest addition to George Vanderbilt's turn-of-the-century retreat. The 213-room luxury accommodation provides guests with an opportunity to enjoy Vanderbilt-style hospitality firsthand. Located on the east side of the estate above the Winery, it affords spectacular views of Biltmore House. At 165,000 sq. ft., the Inn offers banquet meeting rooms, two executive boardrooms, 213 exquisitely appointed guest rooms and suites, a 150-seat dining room, library, lobby bar, exterior swimming pool and fitness center. Amenities offered to guests include walking and hiking trails, carriage rides, horseback riding, mountain hiking and river float trips. The design of this world-class facility is in keeping with gracious resorts of the turn-of-the-century, and elements and accents from the magnificent Biltmore House are everywhere. Many design materials and elements reflect other estate structures. Fieldstone stucco and a slate roof similar to that found on the house have been incorporated. The large lobby fireplace, the inn library and Indiana fieldstone reception desk all further reinforce the perception that one is truly in a creation inspired by the vision of George Vanderbilt. Landscaping reflects the style of landscape architect Frederick Law Olmstead and his overall plan for Biltmore Estate.

Address: One Antler Ridge Rd., Asheville NC 28801
Telephone: 866-336-1245, 828-225-1600.
Village Hotel on Biltmore Estate: An Estate hotel, this casual stay hotel is conveniently located in Antler village on the estate, only a stroll away from outdoor activities, the Winery, shopping and a number of distinctive restaurants.
Address: 207 Dairy Rd, Asheville, NC 28803
Telephone: 866-336-1245

Biltmore Estate Dining

Restaurants:

Arbor Grill: (Antler Hill Village) Savor al fresco dining beside the wintery. Delicious food, wine and the natural beauty of Biltmore come together at the Arbor Grill to give you an ultimate Biltmore experience. Live musicians entertain Fri through Sun. Open year round for lunch and dinner, 12–8pm, weather permitting.
Bistro: (Antler Hill Village) Open daily for lunch and dinner. The menu includes soups, salads, wood-fired pizza, homemade pasta, desserts, a children's menu, and entrées featuring estate-raised beef, lamb, and veal. Located at the Winery, the Bistro opens year-round from 12–8pm. 828-225-6230
Cedric's Tavern: (Antler Hill Village) Offering satisfying pub fare alongside robustly flavored American and global cuisine presented with Biltmore flair. Open daily for lunch, dinner, and late night entertainment.
Deerpark Restaurant: Originally part of the estate's farm operation, Deerpark is open late Mar.–Dec. 11am–3pm Deerpark offers delicious southern specialties served buffet-style in an outdoor atmosphere. 828-225-6260.
Stable Cafe: (Stable courtyard next to Biltmore House) Formerly the Biltmore Estate carriage house and stables, the Stable Café is open from 11am–5pm The menu includes rotisserie chicken, Biltmore beef, fresh salads, burgers, desserts, and a full selection of drinks including wine and beer. Open year-round from 11am–4pm 828-225-6370.
The Dining Room: (Inn on Biltmore Estate) The Dining Room at the Inn on Biltmore Estate with breakfast, lunch and dinner available to inn guests. The restaurant features estate-raised products and a regional cuisine paired with Biltmore Estate wines.

Light Bites:

Bake Shop: (Stable courtyard next to Biltmore House) Serves espresso, gourmet coffees, herbal teas, and freshly baked goods daily 9am–5pm
Conservatory Café: (Conservatory) Good news for garden lovers—you really can spend the whole day wandering the gardens and greenhouses, and when you're ready for refreshment, the Conservatory Café is right there in the open air with Biltmore wines, frozen daiquiris, light snacks and deli sandwiches.

Courtyard Market: (Stable courtyard next to Biltmore House) Specializing in Sicilian-style thin crust pizza, great hot dogs, snacks, beer, wine, and cold beverages.
Creamery: (Antler Hill Village) Ice cream, gourmet coffee, cupcakes, desserts, and drinks.
Ice Cream Parlor: (Stable courtyard next to Biltmore House) Located in the stable courtyard next to the house, the Ice Cream Parlor serves specialty ice cream, yogurt treats, beverages, and picnics for two. Open year-round 11am–5pm seasonally.
Smokehouse: (The Farm in Antler Hill Village) Carolina barbeque, quick sandwiches and light snacks at the Farm.
Wine Bar: (Winery in Antler Hill Village) Biltmore wines accompanied with light far.

Biltmore Estate Shopping

A Christmas Past: (Stable area near Biltmore House) Offers an assortment of Christmas ornaments and music.
A Gardener's Place: (Conservatory lower level) Features estate-grown plants, gardening accessories, books and gifts.
Bookbinder's: (Stable area near Biltmore House) Filled with books relating to the Vanderbilt family and the Gilded Age.
Carriage House: (Stable area near Biltmore House) Carries gifts, decorative accessories, and Biltmore Estate wines.
Confectionery: (Stable area near Biltmore House) Offers a delectable array of sweets.
Cottage Door: (The Inn on Biltmore Estate) Unique children's items, gourmet snacks, chocolates and amenities such as newspapers, magazine and toiletries.
Gate House: (Just outside main entrance to Biltmore Estate). Features Biltmore Estate reproductions, decorative accessories, and a full selection of fine estate wines. The only estate shop accessible without ticket purchase.
Marble Lion: (The Inn on Biltmore Estate) Sophisticated apparel and luxury items.
Mercantile: (The Barn at the Farm at Antler Hill Village) Appalachian crafts, dry goods and old-fashioned candy.
Outdoor Adventure Center: (Village Green in Antler Hill Village) Explore the many different outdoor activities offered at Biltmore Estate, plus purchase clothing and sundries.
Toymaker's: (Stable area near Biltmore House) Features old-fashioned toys and games.
Traditions: (Village Green in Antler Hill Village) Offers a graceful mix of products inspired by envisioning how Edith Vanderbilt would entertain her guests today—carrying forward her renowned hospitality and sense of style. Decorative home accents including tabletop accessories and home décor that blend perfectly in today's homes, plus pottery and jewelry crafted by local artisans.
Wine Shop: (Winery in Antler Hill Village) offering fine wines, gourmet foods, kitchen accessories, and other gifts.

The Gardens

George Vanderbilt commissioned Frederick Law Olmsted, designer of New York's Central Park, to create the stunning backdrop for his château. The resulting gardens and grounds are as spectacular as the house itself. A feast for the eyes, the ten acres of gardens also feature a remarkable array of flowers—many blooming through most of the year. From the orderly, manicured grounds framing the house to the lush forestland covering the mountains, the estate was carefully planned and designed by Olmsted's judicious hand. Today the grounds are still exquisitely maintained, and you are invited to explore them at your leisure.

The Lodge Gate at Biltmore Estate

Equestrian Center

Bring your own horse and explore more than 80 miles of estate trails—the same paths used by the Vanderbilts and their guests at the turn of the century. Enjoy wide, well-marked trails through pristine forests, green pastures, and along the banks of the French Broad River. Choose from five different 10–30 mile loops. Several trails include optional jumps and are suitable for carriages. Horseback riding is also offered for visitors who do not bring their own horses. For more information call the Estate Equestrian Center at 828-225-1454.

Lodge Gate

The entrance to Biltmore Estate is through the Lodge Gate opposite Biltmore Village. Both its bricks and roof tiles were made on the Estate. Beyond the Lodge Gate, the approach road winds for three miles through a deliberately controlled landscape. The road runs along the ravines instead of the ridges, creating a deep natural forest with pools, springs and streams. Around the last turn, the visitor passes through the iron gates and pillars that are topped by early 19th century stone sphinxes, and then into the expansive court of Biltmore House.

Statue of Diana

Statue of Diana

Located inside a small temple at the top of the hill, beyond the Rampe Douce at Biltmore Estate, is a statue which represents Diana. Diana was the daughter of Zeus and Leto, twin sister of Apollo and one of the twelve Olympians. As protector of wild animals, deer were especially sacred to her, which is particularly appropriate for Biltmore, with its large native deer population. Diana is usually portrayed with a bow and arrow and quiver, as she is here. The dog next to her in the statue could represent fidelity or chastity.

One of the Entrance Lions

The Entrance Lions

Guarding the main entrance at Biltmore House are two massive carved stone lions that survey visitors with magnificently serene countenances. Carved of Rosso di Verona marble that is from near San Ambrogio di Valpolicella in Italy, these lions are believed to date to the late nineteenth century and were not put in place until late 1899 or early 1900.

Biltmore House

George Vanderbilt commissioned two of America's most renowned designers to help plan his estate. His friend Richard Morris Hunt, the first American to receive an architectural degree from the Ecole des Beaux Arts in Paris, was the architect of Biltmore House, and Frederick Law Olmsted was chosen to lay out the gardens and parks surrounding the house.

For his house, Mr. Vanderbilt chose the period of the great 16th century châteaux, known as the Francis I style. In 1895, when the house was formally opened, it was named Biltmore from Bildt, the name of the Dutch town from which the family's ancestors came (van der Bildt), and "more," an old English word for rolling, upland country. Biltmore House became a favorite home for Mr. Vanderbilt and his wife, Edith Stuyvesant Dresser and their only child, Cornelia. Upon Cornelia's marriage to John Francis Amherst Cecil, it became the Cecils' residence.

To build Biltmore House, beginning in the summer of 1890, a thousand workers were steadily engaged for six years. A three-mile railway spur from the present Biltmore Station had to be built to carry materials to the site. Hundreds of workmen from the local area and artisans from all over the country and Europe came to carve and fit limestone that came from Indiana. So massive are some of these limestone blocks that one in the retaining wall weighs over three tons. So great was the project that a brick manufacturing facility was established on the estate grounds to satisfy the need for building materials. One of the greatest private houses in America, Biltmore House, once seen, will never be forgotten.

Biltmore House

The Building of a Legend

The following section was provided courtesy of The Biltmore Company for use in this chapter:

Biltmore House took six years and 1,000 men to build it; it opened its doors on Christmas Eve in 1895. With its 390-foot facade, the House has more than 11 million bricks, 250 rooms, 65 fireplaces, 43 bathrooms, 34 bedrooms, and three kitchens, all of which are contained in more than four acres of floor space. The massive stone spiral staircase rises four floors and has 102 steps. Through its center hangs an iron chandelier suspended from a single point containing 72 electric light bulbs.

At its completion, Biltmore House was one of the most innovative and technologically advanced homes in the world. Imagine having hot and cold running water, elevators, indoor heating, a fire alarm system, refrigeration, electric light bulbs and 10 Bell telephones—all of which were unheard of luxuries at the turn of the century.

Imagine what it must have been like to call this your home. Dozens of servants to meet your every need. A vast collection of art and furniture comprising more than 70,000 items, including approximately 23,000 books, furniture from 13 countries, over 1,600 art prints, and many paintings.

If you were lucky enough to be one of Vanderbilt's guests, your choice of inside activities included bowling, billiards, an exercise room, swimming, and games of all sorts. Outdoors, guests could ride horseback, swim, play croquet, hunt, camp, fish, and hike, The Vanderbilts could entertain as many as 64 guests at their dinner table in the massive Banquet Hall. The room spans 72 feet by 42 feet and is 70 feet high. Meals served in the Banquet Hall were usually seven courses and required as many as 15 utensils per person. Enough fresh fish to feed 50 people was often shipped daily from New York, and the sameamount of lobster was often shipped twice a week to feed the ever-changing guest list.

You'll experience a different kind of awe when you walk the Estate's grounds. Originally more than 125,000 acres of land, the Estate includes wooded parks, six pleasure gardens, a conservatory, and 30 miles of paved roadway. You will be overwhelmed every spring with the sight of tens of thousands of tulips in the Walled Garden. Or strollamong the carpets of mums that decorate the grounds each fall. The rest of the year the grounds willamaze you with their colors, shapes, aromas, and natural beauty.

The Tea House

The Tea House in the southwest corner of the South Terrace was an addition landscape-architect Frederick Law Olmsted advocated throughout the construction of Biltmore House. He viewed it as a much-needed focal point and an ideal spot from which to contemplate the mountains.

The Tea House

The Italian Garden

Designed by Olmsted, the Italian Garden is located to the east of the lower terrace adjacent to Biltmore House. Its three formal pools are part of a design concept that dates back to the 16th century. These gardens have an architectural purity in which the plantings are secondary to the design. Nature is completely controlled and the gardens serve as an extension of the house. The outline of the three pools, grass areas and the paths are all part of a symmetrical design. The nearest pool contains the sacred lotus of Egypt. In the second are aquatic plants and in the third, water lilies.

The Conservatory

The Conservatory was used to provide citrus fruit, flowers, and plants for Biltmore House during Vanderbilt's time. It is located at the far end of the four-acre Walled Garden, the lower half of which contains the Rose Garden featuring 159 of 161 All-American Rose selections as well as more than 2,300 other roses of the finest varieties. The Conservatory, restored in 1999, serves the same function today as it did in Vanderbilt's time: providing cut flowers and ornamental plants for the house and growing bedding plants for the estate's gardens.

Italian Garden at Biltmore House

The Winery Clock Tower

One of the highlights at Biltmore Estate's Winery is Richard Morris Hunt's European winery clock tower. Since the winery was previously a dairy, the central clock tower with its "candle-snuffer" roof originally had only three working faces; the side toward the pasture featured a painted-on clock, as the grazing cows did not need to know the time.

The Clock Tower at the Winery

The Winery

The Winery, opened in 1985, followed George Vanderbilt's original concept of a self-supporting European estate. The 96,500 square-foot facility is located in buildings designed by Richard Morris Hunt as part of the dairy operation on Biltmore

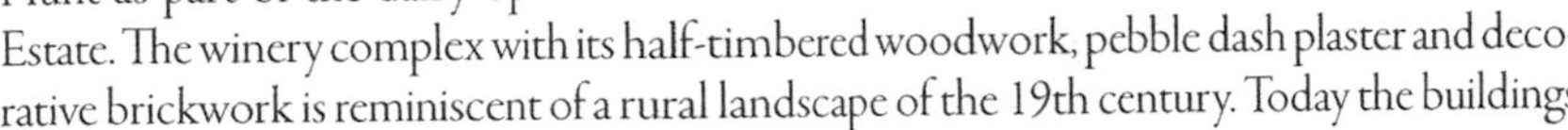

Estate. The winery complex with its half-timbered woodwork, pebble dash plaster and decorative brickwork is reminiscent of a rural landscape of the 19th century. Today the buildings house state-of-the-art wine making equipment, cellars for wine storage, an elaborately stenciled tasting room, and the spacious Wine Shop.

The Winery on Biltmore Estate

Deerpark Restaurant

Deerpark Restaurant is part of a series of handsome outbuildings designed by architect Richard Morris Hunt in the 1890s for George Vanderbilt's farm operations at Biltmore Estate. Originally a dairy barn, Deerpark has been renovated into a unique open-air restaurant in a beautiful pastoral setting. The historic architectural detailing includes pebble dash plaster, half-timbered woodwork, and decorative brickwork. The name Deerpark is taken from a nearby area of the estate which George Vanderbilt set aside as a deer preserve.

Deerpark Restaurant on Biltmore Estate

Vignette: George Washington Vanderbilt, III

William Henry Vanderbilt's youngest son, George, was born in the Vanderbilt farmhouse in New Dorp, Staten Island, New York on Nov. 18, 1862, the youngest of eight children. Little interested in his father's business affairs, Vanderbilt was influenced instead by the collection of art and antiques in his father's home.

A quite shy person, he began collecting books and art objects at a young age. After his mother died, George inherited the family home at 640 Fifth Ave. in New York City and all the art objects within it, including the large collection of paintings his father had assembled. He showed no interest in the social world of the Vanderbilt family, instead preferring the adventure of travel and the world of books.

After visiting Asheville in the 1880s, which was then a fashionable resort, he decided to create a home for himself away from the noise and pace of New York City. During the five years of the construction of Biltmore House, he was a bachelor. However, on a trip to Europe in 1896 he met Edith Stuyvesant Dr.esser and on Jun. 1, 1898, they were married in a civil ceremony in Paris, followed the next day by a religious ceremony at the American Church. Their only child, Cornelia, was born on Aug. 22, 1900.

While George Vanderbilt is well known for his creation of Biltmore Estate, he also accomplished a number of important good works in his lifetime. He established the first school of scientific forestry management practices in the United States and he also brought modern farming techniques to the relatively rural area surrounding his estate. Together, the Vanderbilts started Biltmore Estate Industries in 1901. In this apprenticeship program, young people were instructed in skills to produce furniture, baskets, needlework and woven fabric for resale.

George Vanderbilt died in 1914 and was buried in the family vault on Staten Island. In the memorial service held at All Souls Church in Biltmore Village, the following remarks were made:

"Courteous in manner, dignified in deportment, kind in heart and pure in morals, he was beloved by his friends, honored by his acquaintances and respected by everyone."

Chapter Four
Historic Asheville

One encounters Asheville today as a modern city, rapidly growing and expanding out into the surrounding Buncombe County. Today's Asheville does not look at all like the Asheville from before the turn of the century. Regrettably, much of the best of that time has vanished, including the elegant Queen Anne style Battery Park Hotel and the very hilltop on which it stood and dominated the city landscape. Only scattered buildings remain from that period.

Much of the city landscape does still remain from the early days of the century through to the present day, especially downtown, which retains a strong presence from the early third of the twentieth century. Asheville's slow recovery from the Great Depression did not allow it to demolish wholesale the early buildings as did so many American cities and, because of that, they have been preserved intact. Within the central downtown district, for example, one can find excellent examples of Neo-Gothic, Neo-Georgian, Commercial Classical, Art Deco, Romanesque Revival, and other style structures that make up the most extensive collection of early twentieth-century architecture in the state. They remain an open-air museum, reminders of the optimism and unbounded investment that characterized Asheville in its boom period. Asheville is the only city of its magnitude in which such an urban landscape survives almost intact.

Asheville, through the efforts of local preservation and historic resources organizations, as well as the North Carolina Department of Cultural Resources, has been divided into a number of historic districts. These districts form the basis for this chapter and also the framework for a series of mini-tours, should you wish to experience some of the wonderful and diverse architectural heritage of Asheville during your visit.

Historic Designations

Historic District

Historic District refers to a district of Asheville that has been so designated by the United States Department of the Interior. These districts serve as frameworks for further discussion of the historic buildings and sites of Asheville and in some cases as self-guided mini-tours. Some of these Historic Districts include whole neighborhoods while others are only a small cluster of buildings.

Local Historic Landmarks (LHL)

These are designated by the Asheville City Council or the Buncombe County Board of Commissioners.

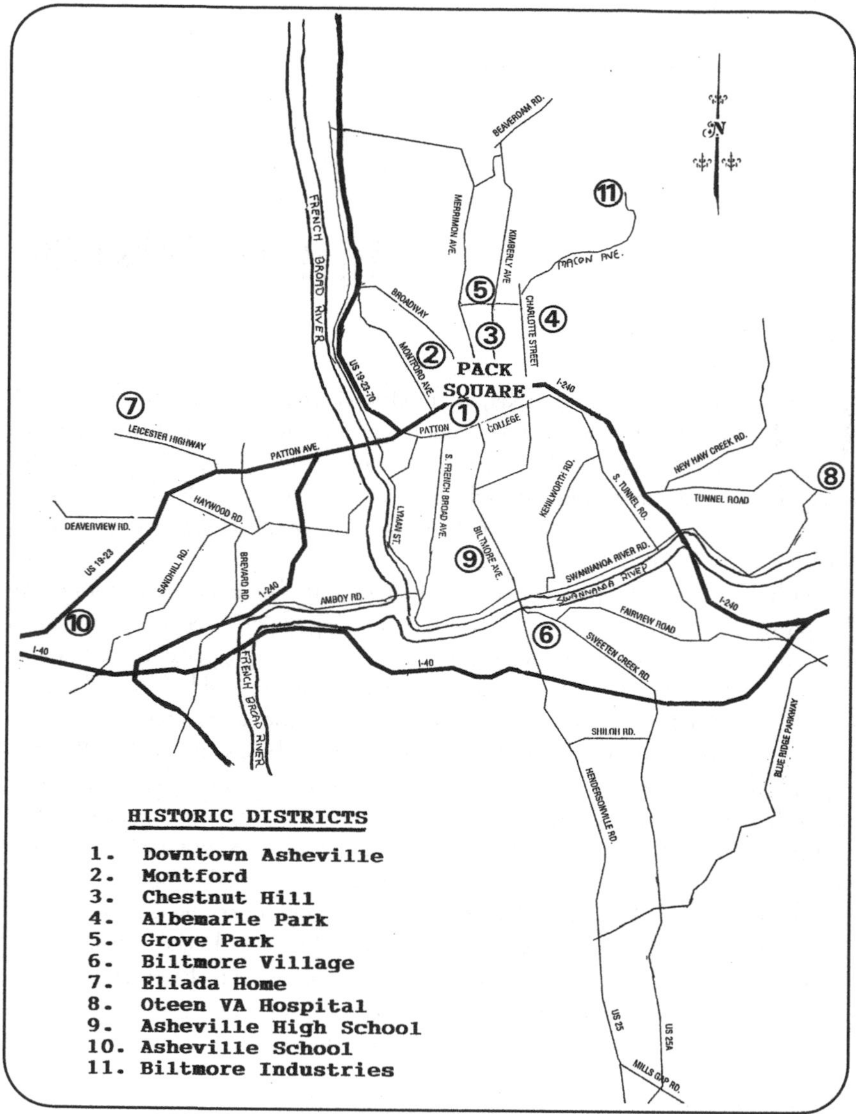

Historic Districts of Asheville

National Historic Landmarks (NHL)

National Historic Landmark are structures, buildings or sites which are of significance to all Americans. This designation is by the Secretary of the Interior and the listings are registered with the United States Department of the Interior National Park Service.

National Register of Historic Places (NRHP)

The National Register is the official list of the nation's cultural resources worthy of preservation. The National Register includes all historic areas in the National Park System, National Historic Landmarks, and properties significant to the nation, state or community which have been nominated by the states, federal agencies and others and have been approved by the National Park Service.

Downtown Asheville Historic District

Downtown Asheville itself has four distinct neighborhoods, each with their own distinctive qualities and ambience: **Battery Park**, the area that includes Haywood St., Wall St., and Battery Park Ave.; **Lexington Park**, spanning Lexington Ave. and Broadway; Pack Square, encompassing **Pack Square**, South Pack Square, Biltmore Ave., and Patton Ave.; and **Thomas Wolfe Plaza**, centered on Market St. and Spruce St.

One of the very best ways to experience these neighborhoods and most of the downtown Asheville historic buildings presented below is to walk the Asheville Urban Trail. This self-guided walking tour visits all four of the neighborhoods discussed here, with stations and thematic markers along the way. For more information about this extraordinary way to trace the footsteps of Asheville's historic past, see Section III, Chapter Five, The Asheville Urban Trail.

Pack Square (NRHP)

Pack Square, and the nearby South Pack Square, Biltmore Ave., and Patton Ave., is the heart of Asheville. Located at the intersection of Biltmore Ave., Broadway, and College St., it was once known as Public Square and was renamed in 1901 for city benefactor George Willis Pack when he moved the courthouse off the square and, in agreement with county commissioners, the square was designated a public park. This spacious square is surrounded by wonderful examples of Classical, Gothic, Art Deco, and Contemporary architecture.

Pack Square, the heart of downtown Asheville

Today, Pack Square and its surrounding streets are a vibrant and historic city center that not only boasts elegant architecture but superb museums, shops, music halls, art galleries and world class restaurants. A visit to Pack Square will show you immediately why Asheville has been called "Paris of the South."

Vance Monument (NRHP) — Pack Square

Located in the square's center is a 75-foot tall granite obelisk, the Vance Monument, erected in 1896 and named in honor of Zebulon B. Vance, an Asheville attorney who was twice governor of North Carolina and was also a U.S. Senator. Two-thirds of the $3,000 cost was paid by philanthropist George W. Pack, and the architect R.S. Smith donated his services. The granite obelisk was cut from the Pacolet quarries in Henderson County.

Pack Memorial Library Building (NRHP, LHL) — 2 South Pack Square

Located on the southern side of Pack Square is the Pack Memorial Library Building. Today this noble Second Renaissance Revival structure is home to the Asheville Art Museum, part of the Pack Place Education, Arts & Science Center. Built in 1925–26 and designed by New York Library architect Edward L. Tilton, the four-story building presents symmetrically arranged elevations faced with white Georgia marble and ornamented with a low-relief classical cornice.

Asheville City Hall

Jackson Building (NRHP)

22 South Pack Square

To the left of the Library Building is the wonderfully elegant Jackson Building. Built in 1923–24 by real estate developer L.B. Jackson and it was the first skyscraper in Western North Carolina. The architect was Ronald Greene and the building he designed rises 13 stories on a small 27 x 60 foot lot. Neo-Gothic in style, the building originally had a searchlight on top that illuminated the surrounding mountains.

Asheville City Hall (NRHP, LHL) — 70 Court Plaza

To the east of Pack Square is the Art Deco masterpiece designed by Douglas D. Ellington, and built in 1926–28. One of the crown jewels of Asheville it is set on a marble base and topped with a pink and green tiled octagonal ziggurat roof. A wonderful unity of appearance is achieved through the luxurious use of color and form. The main entrance is through a loggia of pink marble with multicolored groin vaults. One of the most striking and beautiful buildings in all of North Carolina, City Hall is a show-stopper in a city graced by many unusual and beautiful buildings.

Buncombe County Courthouse (NRHP) — 60 Court Plaza

To the left of City Hall is the Buncombe County Courthouse. Designed by Milburn and Heister of Washington DC, and built in 1927–28, this steel-frame seventeen-story courthouse has a brick and limestone classical surface. It has an opulent lobby ornamented with polychrome classical plaster work and marble balustrades. Polished granite columns at the entrance are echoed by similar columns above at the jail section. The large superior court room has a coffered plaster ceiling and elegant woodwork.

Young Men's Institute Building (NRHP, LHL) — Market and Eagle St.

Located behind the Pack Place Education, Arts, & Science Center on the corner of South Market and Eagle streets is the Young Men's Institute (YMI) Building, built by George Vanderbilt in 1892 to serve as a recreational and cultural center for black men and boys. It was sold to the Young Men's Institute in 1906 and became a center for social activity in the black community and contained professional offices and a black public library. Designed by R.S. Smith in a simplified English Cottage style with a pebble dash and brick surface, today it houses the YMI Cultural Center, part of Pack Place Education, Arts & Science Center.

Eagle and Market St. District (NRHP)

This district was the heart of the black community in Asheville in the early days and today contains many fine buildings of historic importance, including the YMI Building mentioned earlier. Of interest are the Campbell Building at 38 South Market St., originally an office building, and the former Black Masonic Temple Building at 44 South Market St.

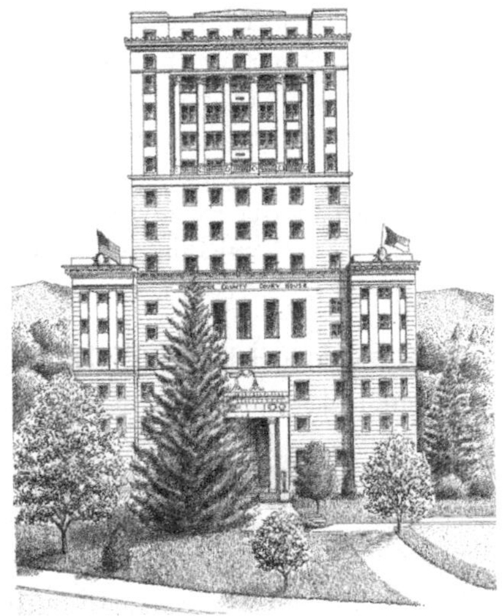

Buncombe County Courthouse

Mount Zion Missionary Baptist Church (NRHP) — 47 Eagle St.

Also in this historic area is the large and handsome Mount Zion Missionary Baptist Church. A three-tower red brick Late Victorian Gothic structure built in 1919, it has a tin-shingled roof that has ornamental sheet-metal finials. The large number of Art Glass windows that grace the church are another unusual feature. It was home to one of Asheville's largest black congregations, organized in 1880 by the noted Reverend Rumley.

Kress Building (NRHP, LHL) — 21 Patton Ave.

Just down from Pack Square on Patton Ave., you will encounter one of Asheville's finest commercial buildings, the Kress building. Housing today an antique and crafts emporium, this four-story building was built in 1926-27. Distinctive features are the cream colored glazed terracotta with orange and blue rosette borders that face the front three bays of the building. In addition the side elevations above the first level are tan brick with terracotta inserts. This classical design preceded the many Art Deco Kress stores built around the country in the late 1930s and is unique in that sense.

Drhumor Building (NRHP) 48 Patton Ave.

Farther west is the splendid Romanesque Revival Drhumor Building. Built in 1895, this structure is an imposing four stories of brick trimmed with rock-faced limestone and graced by a marvelous first floor frieze by sculptor Fred Miles. One of the bearded visages is supposedly of local merchant E.C. Deake, who watched Miles sculpt. Miles was also the sculptor who did the figures atop the Basilica of St. Lawrence. A complementary limestone frontispiece was added to the north side of the building in the 1920s and the original corner entrance was filled in.

Detail from Dr.humor Building

The building was designed by A.L. Melton for Will J. Cocke and his relatives, Mrs. Marie Johnson and Miss Mattie. The name Drhumor comes from the Johnson family's ancestral home in Ireland.

S&W Cafeteria Building (NRHP, LHL) 56 Patton Ave.

A little farther down Patton Ave. is another of the crown jewels of Asheville, and one of the finest examples of Art Deco architecture in North Carolina, the S&W Cafeteria Building. It was built in 1929 for the cafeteria chain which occupied the building until 1973. The building was designed by Douglas D. Ellington, and is two stories with a polychrome cream, green, blue, black and gilt glazed terracotta facade that employs geometrically-stylized Indian and classical motifs. The interior is divided into dining rooms and lobbies with Art Deco decorations of superb quality. The building today is used for catering of meetings, receptions and banquets. (See illustration Section III, Chapter One)

Public Service Building (NRHP, LHL) 89-93 Patton Ave.

Farther west is the Public Service Building built in 1929. This imposing eight-story Neo-Spanish Romanesque steel frame office building is one of North Carolina's most attractive 1920s skyscrapers. Built of red brick and glazed terracotta, its first two and upper floors are lavishly ornamented with polychrome terracotta, including such whimsical details as Leda-and-the-Swan spring blocks on the second-floor windows.

Flatiron Building (NRHP, LHL) 10-20 Battery Park Ave.

The Flatiron Building is an eight-story tan brick building that has classical detailing and a "flatiron" plan. Built in 1925–26, and designed by Albert C. Wirth, this elegant and unique building is faced with limestone ashlar and is perched at the entrance to the historic Wall St.

district. A large metal sculpture of a household iron sits outside on the Wall St. side of the building.

The Flatiron Building

Wall St. (NRHP)

This charming one-block street of small shops was named Wall St. after the retaining wall built behind the structures that face Pritchard Park. In 1926 Tench Coxe and Ed Ray remodeled and repainted the rear entrances to these building to create a boutique district, which they called "Greenwich Village." That name never caught on, and the district was simply called Wall St. Today it is a one of Asheville's most interesting shopping districts, with many top-quality gift and specialty shops. When there, notice the unusual gingko trees planted along the street.

Grove Arcade (NRHP, LHL) — 10-20 Battery Park Ave.

Located just north of Wall St., the grand Grove Arcade building occupies a full city block. This imposing building was begun in 1926 by E.W. Grove to be a commercial mall topped with an office skyscraper. Completed after Grove's death minus the skyscraper, the building is surfaced with cream glazed terracotta in a Neo-Tudor Gothic style. It is one of several major buildings for which the millionaire was responsible, with the most noteworthy among them being the Omni Grove Park Inn. The arcade was designed by Charles N. Parker. Among the most interesting details are a pair of winged Griffin statues guarding the Battle Square entrance of the building. After years of service as offices for the federal government, the Grove Arcade is now home to commercial shops and venues.

Griffin from Grove Arcade

Battery Park Hotel (NRHP, LHL) — 1 Battle Square

The hotel is a huge 14-story T-plan Neo-Georgian hotel erected by E.W. Grove in 1923-24. This extraordinary building was designed by hotel architect W.L. Stoddart of New York and replaced a previous Queen Anne style hotel of the same name. It is surfaced in brick with limestone and terracotta trim. The hotel building today houses apartments and is located just north of the Grove Arcade.

United States Post Office and Courthouse (NRHP) — 100 Otis St.

Located just west of the Grove Arcade is the former post office and courthouse building, one of the state's finest Depression-era Federal buildings. This Art-Deco influenced building was designed by the Federal Architect's Office under James A. Wetmore. The building has a majestically massed central entrance in which the Art Deco influence can be seen.

First Church of Christ Scientist

First Church of Christ Scientist (NRHP) — 64 North French Broad Ave.

The First Church of Christ Scientist is of a refined Jeffersonian, Neo-Classical Revival style, constructed of orange brick. Built between 1909 and 1912, it was designed by S.S. Beaman of Chicago.

Basilica of Saint Lawrence, D.M. (NRHP) — 97 Haywood St.

To the north of the Grove Arcade area is the Basilica of Saint Lawrence, Deacon and Martyr, built in 1909. A Spanish Baroque Revival Roman Catholic Church built of red brick with polychrome glazed terracotta inserts and limestone trim, it was designed by world-famous architect/engineer Raphael Guastavino. The church employs his "cohesive construction" techniques in its large oval tile dome and Catalan-style vaulting in its two towers. The massive stone foundations and the solid brick superstructure give silent testimony to the architect's desire to build an edifice that would endure for generations. There are no beams of wood or steel in the entire structure; all walls, floors, ceilings and pillars are of tile or other masonry materials. The dome is entirely self supporting, has a clear span of 58 x 82 feet and is reputed to be the largest unsupported dome in North America. The Crucifixion tableaux of the Basilica altar features a rare example of seventeenth century Spanish woodcarving. The windows are of German origin, and the Basilica has two chapels. Attached by an arcade is the 1929 Neo-Tuscan Renaissance brick rectory designed by Father Michael of Belmont Abbey.

Basilica of Saint Lawrence, D.M.

Loughran Building (NRHP, LHL) — 43 Haywood St.

The Loughran Building was in 1923 and is a six-story steel-frame commercial building that has a restrained white glazed terracotta classical facade. It was designed by Smith and Carrier for Frank Loughran and its first occupant was Denton's Department Store.

Central United Methodist Church (NRHP) — 27 Church St.

Located on Church St., south of Patton Ave., this Gothic limestone-faced church was designed by R.H. Hunt of Chattanooga, Tennessee. The church is noted for its fine stained and Art Glass windows and was built between 1902 and 1905.

First Presbyterian Church (NRHP) — 40 Church St.

This Gothic Revival church is home to one of Asheville's oldest congregations and is one of the oldest church buildings in the city. Located on the corner of Church and Aston streets, the brick nave and steeple were constructed in 1884-85 and have deep, corbelled cornices, hood-moulded windows and blind arcading at the eaves. The north chapel and the south building were added in 1968.

Trinity Episcopal Church (NRHP) — Church and Aston St.

Located on the opposite corner of Church and Aston St., Trinity Episcopal Church is the third of three churches in this Church St. neighborhood. Built in 1921, it is a Tudor Gothic Revival style brick with granite trim building and was designed by Bertram Goodhue of Cram, Goodhue and Ferguson, well-known church architects. This lovely building has a simple gable roofed sanctuary with transepts and a short gable-roofed blunt tower.

Ravenscroft School Building (NRHP, LHL) — 29 Ravenscroft Dr.

Ravenscroft School Building

Built in the 1840s, this two-and-a-half story brick Greek Revival house is probably the oldest structure in the downtown area and one of the oldest in Asheville. It housed the Ravenscroft Episcopal Boys' Classical and Theological School after 1856 until the Civil War. Thereafter it was used as a training school for the ministry. In 1886 it was used again as a boys' school. After the turn of the century, it was a rooming house, and today it is used for professional offices. Details of the house in Academic Greek Revival are of a type not common to Western North Carolina.

Mears House (NRHP) 137 Biltmore Ave.

Located on Biltmore Ave., the Mears House is a wonderful example of Queen Anne style architecture. Built around 1885, this brick residence has a slate-shingled mansard roof, gables and dormers. This is the most distinguished of the remaining late nineteenth century residences near downtown.

Scottish Rite Cathedral and Masonic Temple Building (NRHP) 80 Broadway

Built in 1913, this imposing four-story building is constructed of pressed brick and trimmed in limestone and grey brick. A two-story limestone portico with a pair of Ionic columns graces the Broadway entrance. The building was designed by Smith and Carrier.

Lexington Ave. (NRHP)

This once thriving market district was where farmers and others once came to water their horses and buy and sell local produce. Because natural springs kept it wet, Lexington Ave. was first called Water St. Double doorways accommodating farmers' wagons are still evident on renovated buildings. Lexington Ave. is Asheville's premier antique district and also home to Asheville's oldest store, T.S. Morrison (circa 1891). Many antique shops, specialty stores, galleries and nightclubs are found today in this interesting neighborhood.

Lexington Ave. is home to T.S. Morrison, Asheville's oldest store.

First Baptist Church of Asheville

First Baptist Church of Asheville (NRHP) 5 Oak St.

Built in 1927, the First Baptist Church of Asheville was designed by noted architect Douglas Ellington from his sketches of a cathedral in Florence, Italy. Three major additions have been made to the building. The Children's Wing was added in 1968, and the Sherman Family Center in 1980. This wonderfully elegant building is an unusual combination of an Early Italian Renaissance form and color scheme arranged in a beaux arts plan with Art Deco detailing. Of particular interest is the Art Deco copper lantern atop the dome and the subtle gradation of color in the roofing tiles. The walls are an effective combination of orange bricks, terracotta moldings and pink marble. This striking building is at the corner of Oak and Woodfin St.

First Christian Church (NRHP) 20 Oak St.

Right across the street is the First Christian Church, built between 1925 and 1926 in a traditional Late Gothic Style, and constructed of rock-faced grey granite masonry with smooth granite trim. Designed by the home office, it has an unusual feature in that the placement of the tower is at the intersection of the nave and transept.

Montford Historic District

The Montford Historic District is Asheville's oldest and largest with over 600 buildings reflecting a variety of late 19th and early 20th century styles. Montford is a culturally diverse and thriving community, and was the creation of Asheville's boomtimes, having its origins as an upper middle class suburb in 1889. Asheville's most famous son, writer Thomas Wolfe, describes Montford Ave. in **Look Homeward Angel** as "the most fashionable street in town."

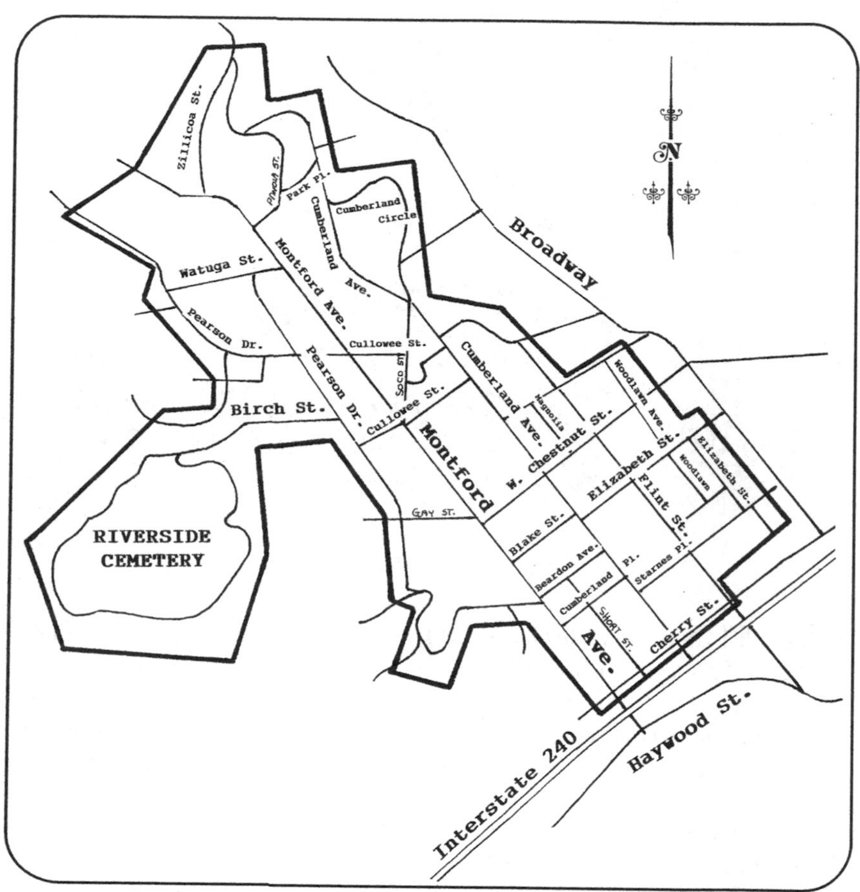

Montford Historic District

Montford's Riverside Cemetery is well worth a visit for scenic beauty alone; but is also notable as the final resting place for two of America's most important writers: O.Henry (William Sidney Porter) and Thomas Wolfe.

Located just across I-240 from downtown Asheville, a drive through Montford reveals a collection of architecture from the Queen Anne to Georgian Revival styles, with many variations in between. Quite a few of these majestic old homes have been converted to bed & breakfasts, making Montford one of Asheville's premier destinations for those seeking a pleasant stay in a historic setting. The best way to see Montford is by car and the historic sites in this section will be presented as a self guided tour. Plan at least an hour, perhaps more if you wish to get out and visit Riverside Cemetery on foot, for the tour.

From I-240, take Exit 4C Haywood St./Montford Ave. Begin at the top of Montford Ave. just on the north side of I-240. Montford Ave. turns off of Haywood St. just west of the Asheville Visitor Center. Continue down Montford to 276, The Lion and The Rose Bed & Breakfast on your left.

The Lion & The Rose Bed & Breakfast (NRHP) 276 Montford Ave.

This beautifully landscaped bed & breakfast is housed in a charming three-story Queen Anne/Georgian Revival style pebble dash building and is officially known as the Craig-Toms House. Interesting features are the double Doric posts on stone pedestals and the elaborate center gable. Built in 1898, this house has been faithfully restored to its original elegance, with all its rooms furnished with antiques, oriental rugs and period appointments. High embossed ceilings, golden oak, classic leaded and stained glass windows create a feeling of the Victorian era.

Right next door is The Black Walnut Bed & Breakfast Inn.

The Black Walnut Bed & Breakfast Inn (NRHP) 288 Montford Ave.

This large handsome residence, designed by Richard Sharp Smith was constructed around 1900. Known historically as the Otis Green House, after Otis Green who owned the residence for many years, it embodies the eclecticism characteristic of Smith's work, combining flourishes of the Shingle style, Queen Anne and Colonial Revival styles of architecture. Beautifully landscaped also, this striking building is faithfully restored and decorated throughout with antiques and fine traditional furniture.

The third of three bed & breakfasts located on this side of the street is The Inn on Montford, next door to The Black Walnut.

The Inn on Montford (NRHP) 296 Montford Ave.

Originally known as the Dr. Charles S. Jordan House, this "Old English" style house at 296 Montford Ave. was designed by Richard Sharp Smith. The house is typical of architect Smith's interpretation of the "Old English" style. Two major gables with splayed eaves are presented to the street at attic level, and a combination of shingles and pebble dash are employed. Construction of the house dates back to around 1900. This lovely bed & breakfast has period landscaping with rows of neatly trimmed boxwoods and other plantings. Queen-sized poster beds, English and American antiques and fine paintings all add to the atmosphere of an "English Cottage." After viewing these three inns, turn left on Watauga St. and proceed to Pearson Dr. Turn left on Pearson. On your left will be the romantic Wright Inn.

The Wright Inn and Carriage House (NRHP) 235 Pearson Dr.

The Wright Inn is one of the finest examples of Queen Anne architecture in the Montford District and in all of Western North Carolina. With stylized Doric porch posts on paneled pedestals, multiple gables and slate roof, this wonderfully restored building is a delight to behold. Elegantly appointed inside with antiques and family heirlooms, the 1899-1900 Victorian masterpiece was designed by George Barber.

Right across the street is the Colby House, another bed & breakfast.

The Colby House (NRHP) 230 Pearson Dr.

This bed & breakfast was built in 1924, and is a Dutch Colonial Revival-style dwelling with Gambrel roof. Interesting features include the elliptical leaded fanlight at the entrance door and the exterior of North Carolina blue granite with beaded mortar joints. Originally called the Dr. Charles Hartwell Cocke House, the Colby House today welcomes guests to a relaxing refined environment.

Continue down Pearson Dr. and turn right onto Birch St. to the historic Riverside Cemetery.

Riverside Cemetery (NRHP) 53 Birch St.

Historic Riverside Cemetery at the end of Birch St. and is operated under the direction of the City of Asheville Parks, Recreation and Public Facilities Department. It is the burial site of Thomas Wolfe, O.Henry (William Sidney Porter), Zebulon Vance (N.C. Governor and U.S. Senator), three Civil War Confederate Generals, Thomas L. Clingman and Robert R. Reynolds (U.S. Senators), and many of Asheville's founding families. Group tours are welcomed at this 87-acre cemetery. A walk through Riverside Cemetery is a walk through

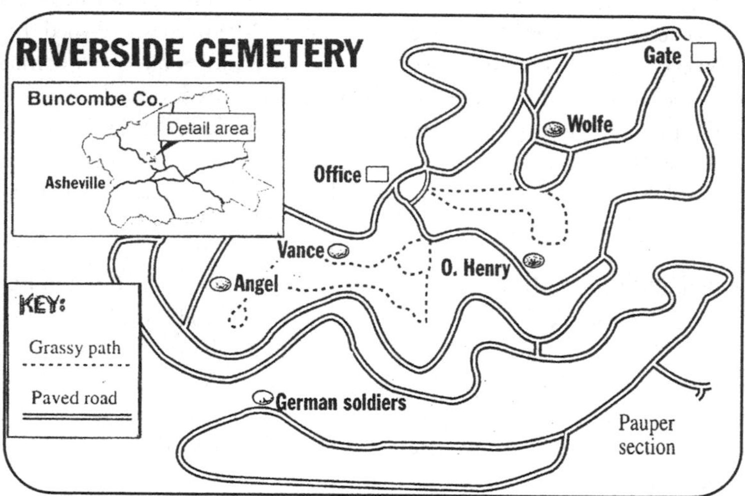

a rich source of area history. More than 13,000 people lie in marked graves, many with grave sites marked with angels and lambs crafted of Italian Carrera marble. The cemetery is open around the clock, but office hours are Mon–Fri, 8am–4:30pm. The office phone number is 258-8480. Website: ci.asheville.nc.us/parksrec/riversid.htm

Leaving the cemetery, return by way of Birch St. back to Pearson Dr. and turn right. Continue down Pearson to West Chestnut St. and turn left. On West Chestnut you will cross Montford Ave. and continue on to Cumberland Ave. Turn left at Cumberland and look for another lovely Victorian bed & breakfast, A Bed of Roses, immediately on your right.

A Bed of Roses (NRHP) 135 Cumberland Ave.

This splendidly restored house dates back to around 1897 and is a playful variant of the Queen Anne style, with the dominant feature being the large second store polygonal corner projection with a broad ogee roof. The front porch also has stylized Doric type posts on stone pedestals. It was built by O.D. Revell and is officially named after the first long-term occupant Marvin B. Wilkinson who purchased it in 1904. Today, the house welcomes guests to its rooms furnished with antiques, handmade quilts and fresh flowers. (See illustration Section II, Chapter One)

Thomas Wolfe's gravestone at Riverside Cemetery in historic Montford

Continuing on down Cumberland Ave. you will see the Maria T. Brown House on your right at 177, restored as the Carolina Bed & Breakfast.

The Carolina Bed & Breakfast (NRHP) 177 Cumberland Ave.

This 2.5-story stucco dwelling was designed by Richard Sharp Smith and built before 1901. The porch has unusual brackets, shed dormers and a high hipped roof. The pebble dash stucco is typical of that period of architecture. The Carolina Bed & Breakfast has been graciously restored and features warm heart-pine floors, spacious rooms and seven working fireplaces.

Farther down Cumberland on your left is The Arbor Rose Inn at 254 Cumberland Ave.

Cumberland Falls Bed & Breakfast (NRHP) 254 Cumberland Ave.

This early 20th century house is a 2.5-story vernacular shingle dwelling which features shingles over weatherboards, bay windows and porch. Charming rooms with antique furnishings, ornamental fireplaces and ceiling fans await the visitors to this graciously restored dwelling.

At this point you will want to take the right fork onto Cumberland Circle. Ahead on the left will be the Wythe Peyton House at 46 Cumberland Circle, known today as Abbington Green Bed & Breakfast Inn.

Abbington Green Bed & Breakfast Inn (NRHP) 46 & 48 Cumberland Cir.

This stunning Colonial Revival home was built in 1908 for businessman David Latourette Jackson and was officially named the Wythe Peyton House for another prominent resident who lived here during the 1950s. It was designed by Richard Sharp Smith and has been lovingly restored to all of its former glory. It features shingles over weatherboards, Doric porch posts, molded trim and a central gable. Inside, each of the eight stylishly appointed guest rooms is named after parks and gardens in London.

Continuing on Cumberland Circle you will see the red Applewood Manor Inn on your left.

Applewood Manor Inn

Applewood Manor Inn (NRHP) — 62 Cumberland Cir.

Built before 1917, this shingle-sided Colonial Revival building features a pedimented entrance supported on Doric columns and flanking porches. Located on an acre and a half this finely restored bed & breakfast is a touch of country in the city!

Continue on Cumberland Circle until it rejoins Cumberland Ave. and turn right. Take Cumberland Ave. until you reach Panola St. Turn left and go to Montford Ave. Turn right on Montford and then right again on Zillicoa St. Directly ahead on your left is the Homewood School Building and just beyond it is the magnificent Rumbough House.

Homewood (NRHP) — 19 Zillicoa St.

Constructed in 1934 and designed by Dr. Robert S. Carroll, founder of Highland Hospital, Homewood was for many years the home to Dr. Carroll and his second wife Grace Potter Carroll. The castle-like Homewood was constructed of uncoursed stone masonry, with an asymmetrical facade and entrance deeply recessed beneath a basket arch. A crenellated polygonal tower at the building's southeast corner and additional crenellation atop a projecting bay at the north end give the former residence the romantic image of a fortified castle.

Rumbough House (NRHP) — 49 Zillicoa St.

Built in 1892 by James H. Rumbough, this elegant building, featuring a combination of Queen Anne, Colonial Revival and Neoclassical elements, is generally considered to be the most impressive residence in the Montford area. It features weatherboarding, wide porches and pairs of tapered and molded porch posts on stone pedestals. It is also known for its elaborately finished rooms. The house was owned by James Edwin Rumbough (1861-1941) who became the first and only mayor of the autonomous village of Montford when it was incorporated in 1893. Among his various other distinctions he is credited with being the first person to drive an automobile across the Appalachian Mountains, a feat that he accomplished in 1911. The house was purchased in 1952 by Duke University to become the administration building for the former Highland Hospital. It now houses the Carolina Center for Metabolic Medicine.

Turn around here and return on Zillicoa St. to Montford Ave. and turn left. Continue down Montford for 3 blocks to Blake St. and turn left on Blake to the stop sign. Turn right onto Cumberland Ave. and you'll find The Redwood House immediately on your right.

Redwood House (NRHP) — 90 Cumberland Ave.

This early 20th century house is officially known as Redwood House and is a fine example of Colonial Revival architecture. It features shingles over stucco, Doric porch posts and a high pitched roof.

Turn left in front of Redwood House onto Elizabeth St. and continue to Flint St. Turn right on Flint. Just ahead on your right you'll see the Flint St. Inns.

Flint St. Inns (NRHP) — 100 & 116 Flint St.

The Flint St. Inns are two, side by side, distinguished old family homes that date back to the turn of the century. The structure at 100 Flint St. is a half-timbered stucco gable end dwelling. 116 Flint St. is thought to be one of Richard Sharp Smith's designs and features shingle over weatherboard, bracketed eaves, Montford brackets and a large dormer. Rooms in the Inns are furnished in turn-of-the-century style.

Your tour of Historic Montford is now over. Continue straight ahead up Flint St. to Haywood St. and downtown Asheville.

Vignette:
Richard Sharp Smith

Few persons have left their mark upon the face of a city as British-born Richard Sharp Smith has upon Asheville. Employed in his younger years by the prestigious architectural firm of Hunt and Hunt, he was sent to Asheville to supervise the construction of Biltmore House, which had been designed by Richard Morris Hunt. Smith stayed in Asheville, married here and raised two sons and two daughters. He became an American citizen and opened a private practice. During his life, he designed scores of private homes and dozens of commercial buildings in downtown Asheville. His distinctive architectural style has a British accent and Smith is remembered today as one of the most prominent of the many architects who helped shape Asheville.

Chestnut Hill Historic District

The Chestnut Hill Historic District is centered around Chestnut Hill, the apex of a knoll running west from Patton Mountain just 500 yards north of the center of Asheville. The neighborhood surrounding the hill was once an extension of the nineteenth-century residential streets that began a block off the city's Public Square. This district is a relatively compact late-nineteenth and early-twentieth-century residential neighborhood whose architectural styles and landscaping form a well-defined place. Tree-lined streets, brick-paved sidewalks and granite curbing are all unique features.

Practically all of the more than 200 buildings in the district were originally dwellings. Architecturally they range from the local in-town vernacular of the period to sophisticated versions of the nationally popular Queen Anne, Colonial Revival and Shingle styles.

The district dates from Asheville's post-railroad (post-1880) boom period and its finer homes reflect the relative sophistication of the city's more substantial citizens of that time. Besides a continuous growth in permanent residents, Asheville experienced an annual influx of thousands of summer and winter tourists and a number of Chestnut Hill "cottages" were built as high quality rental properties.

In this section, some of the more important houses will be presented as a self-guided driving tour. This is a very convenient way to see the Chestnut Hill district. Allow about an hour for the tour, and slightly more if you wish to park occasionally to get out and examine some of the buildings closer. As a note, Chestnut Hill District and the following two districts, Albermarle Park and Grove Park are very close together. It is possible to see all three of these important neighborhoods in a few hours.

Begin your tour by taking Merrimon Ave. north to Hillside St. Turn right onto Hillside and go to second right North Liberty St. Turn right onto North Liberty. A short distance on the left you'll see a classic Victorian House.

North Liberty Victorian House — 76 North Liberty St.

A wonderful example of Victorian architecture, the elegant house is intricate in its detail and styling. It is a multi-gabled structure with flaring eaves and standing-seam tin roof, and has a square tower with a mansard-like shingled cap dominating the house adjacent to two projecting bays. The house's elaborate porch features turned posts, a scroll-bracketed cornice above a ladder frieze and a Chinese-Chippendale-like balustrade. Currently the building is undergoing restoration.

Continuing on North Liberty you will come upon the historic Beaufort House Bed & Breakfast on your left.

Beaufort House — 61 North Liberty St.

This Victorian bed & breakfast is a grand 2.5-story pink Queen Anne style house built in 1895 by former State Attorney general and prominent Asheville resident Theodore Davidson. This elegant building features a roofline that sweeps down upon an ample veranda accented at its southern end by a fanciful pergola. Elaborate interior woodwork includes paneled wainscoting and a closed-stringer stairway with intricately carved newel post and balusters. The building has been wonderfully restored as Beaufort House Bed & Breakfast and is furnished with antiques and period furniture.

Chestnut St. Inn

From this unique house continue down North Liberty and turn left on East Chestnut St. Located just one block down are two wonderfully restored bed & breakfasts. Chestnut St. is noted for its many fine examples of Colonial Revival, Queen Anne-influenced and bracketed Victorian homes.

White Gate Inn & Cottage — 173 East Chestnut St.

Known officially as the Kent House, it was built circa 1889 and is a tall 2.5-story Shingle style house. The building features tall exterior chimneys centered on minor gables. Mr. Kent who owned the house reportedly ran the Asheville Ice Company. Today it houses the White Gate Inn that is beautifully furnished with period antiques, fine furniture and collectibles.

Directly across the street is the newly restored Chestnut St. Inn.

Chestnut St. Inn — 176 East Chestnut St.

Officially known as the William R. Whitson house, this Grand Colonial Revival House was built circa 1905. The house is constructed out of pressed brick and is two and a half stories with hip-on-hip roof with central Palladian dormer. The house, constructed for Whitson by J. M. Westall, has some of the finest woodwork in Asheville, including a graceful closed stringer stairway, beautiful arts & crafts wainscoting, and elaborate mirrored mantles. Today, Chestnut St. Inn welcomes visitors to its gracious and exquisite interior impeccably furnished with antiques and period decorations.

Just down the street on the right is the Annie West House.

Annie West House — 189 East Chestnut St.

Built around 1900, this picturesque half-timbered cottage was designed by Richard Sharp Smith. Standing 1.5 stories, it features a "veranda" across facade beneath a large central gable and smaller flanking dormers. This detail links it stylistically to early Biltmore Village architecture. Continue down East Chestnut to the Jeter Pritchard House.

Jeter Pritchard House — 223 East Chestnut St.

This imposing two-story frame house was built by architect and builder James A. Tennent, who sold it to Senator Jeter Conly Pritchard in 1904. Construction dates back to around 1895. The building is a boxy weatherboard form under a multi-gabled roof. The interior of the house features exceptional woodworking.

Continue down East Chestnut to Charlotte St. and turn left. Take a right onto Baird St. and take your second left onto Albemarle Place to find The Carl Von Ruck House on your left.

Carl Von Ruck House (NRHP, LHL) — 52 Albemarle Pl.

This rambling three-story house was built in three distinct stages by Dr. Carl Von Ruck, famed tuberculosis specialist who founded the Winyah Sanitorium on Sunset Mountain. In 1904 he bought twenty acres, including two houses that were on the property. One of the houses is incorporated into the north end of the present structure. In 1912 he built a separate house for his resident MDs just to the south and in 1915 he built between these two buildings, connecting them with a grand two-story music room with twin elliptic conservatories to either side. The music room features Viennese-crafted mahogany woodwork and houses Dr. Ruck's sixty-seven rank Aeolian Organ, with 4800 handmade wooden pipes rising two stories behind a curved mahogany screen.

At this point, turn around and return down Albemarle Place to Baird St. At Baird turn left and look on the left for the Edward I. Holmes House.

Edward I. Holmes House — 60 Baird St.

Built around 1883, this wonderfully restored house is an elaborated frame two-story double-pile plan design. There is a hip roof with internal brick chimneys and gabled projecting bays on each elevation. Other unique features are chamfered posts on opaque shoulder

Edward I. Holmes House

brackets and an elaborate scrollwork balustrade. No other 20th-century building in Asheville, especially of the finer structures, is as little altered as this house.

Turn right onto Furman Ave. across from the Holmes House and continue down to East Chestnut St. Turn right onto East Chestnut and just before you reach Charlotte St. you will see the white Thomas Patton House on your left. The main entrance is off Charlotte St. but virtually impossible to see from that direction because of the trees and landscaping. Turn left onto Charlotte St. and continue south to downtown Asheville.

Thomas Patton House — 95 Charlotte St.

Built in 1869, the Thomas Patton House is a two-story frame house formally organized around central and traverse hallways. It has very interesting external features in chevron-latticed bargeboards. Tradition maintains that the house was built by black carpenters working from the plans of Thomas Patton. Patton was the grandson of James Patton, mayor of Asheville and active public servant.

Albemarle Park Historic District

Albemarle Park, located off Charlotte St., is a planned residential community that is composed of 45 residences reflecting diverse and very attractive architectural styles that were built on a 32.42-acre tract of land acquired by William Green Raoul in 1886. Raoul, who served as president of both Georgian and Mexican railroads, was the visionary who conceived of Albemarle Park and who purchased the land from a local farmer named Deaver. It was his third son, Thomas Wadley Raoul, however who was to be the foreman of the project and the one who made the vision a reality. For almost twenty-five years he devoted his energies to overseeing the construction and management of The Manor and cottages.

The main building, The Manor, was built in 1898 by Thomas. He conceived the idea of a twenty-five room English style country inn to be used as a boarding house. He later modified his plan to include several individually designed cottages to complement the main house. From these beginnings the Albemarle Park neighborhood began to take shape, with Raoul insisting upon only the finest materials and workmanship to be used in the construction.

This neighborhood has very narrow curving streets that preserve much of the wooded landscape of the area. It is situated on the western slope of Sunset Mountain and is crowned by The Manor that graces a knoll that slopes down to Charlotte St. This district is evocative of Asheville's dramatic turn-of-the century resort town boom era, and its rich craftsmanship and informal quaintness is related to Biltmore Village.

The original site plan was designed by Samuel Parsons Jr., the landscape architect of New York's Central Park. The design catered to wealthy lowlanders from Georgia and North and South Carolina who saw the mountains as a summer refuge. The crown jewel of this marvelous complex is The Manor, one of the last intact grand hotels from the late 19th century resort era. It was used for the filming of one of the scenes for the recent movie "The Last of the Mohicans." This historic building also hosted the film crews for the movie, "The Swan," and Grace Kelly, who starred in the film was a guest at the inn. Her former rooms are now known as the Princess Ste. Alec Guiness, Agnes Morehead and Louis Jordan also stayed at The Manor during that time.

The Manor was converted to a retirement hotel in 1961 by Charles Lavin. By 1976 The Manor had changed owners again and at this time it became a residential hotel, and in 1984, after severe winter damage, it was closed. The Preservation Society bought The Manor in 1989 when it was threatened with demolition, and in 1991, it was sold and restored in an historically sensitive way as an apartment complex. Without the efforts of this important local organization, this historical treasure would have been lost forever.

Each building in the neighborhood was intended to have a distinctive architectural style. A walk through the neighborhood reveals cottages that show Italian, French and Swiss influences as well as Georgian Revival, Appalachian and Adirondack styles of architecture. The primary architect of Albemarle Park was Bradford Lee Gilbert, who also designed the Virginia Beach Hotel (1888) in Virginia Beach, Virginia, and the Berkeley Arms Hotel (1883) in Berkeley, New Jersey.

To reach Albemarle Park take Charlotte St. north till you come to the original Gatehouse on your right at 265. Turn right onto Cherokee Rd. The Manor will be on your left. Park your car if you wish in the small parking lot on Cherokee Rd.

The Manor (NRHP, LHL) — 265 Charlotte St.

Constructed in 1889, The Manor is a rambling group of interconnecting wings which combine elements of Shingle, Tudoresque and Dutch Colonial Revival architecture. The main portion of The Manor was built soon after the property, originally part of the Deaver Farm, was purchased in 1886 by the elder Raoul. This main portion of the inn is a twenty-five room five-part structure of rough field rock above which is a stucco and timber level.

A second wing, built in 1903, angles out from the main body of the inn toward the road. The main level of this wing is Tudoresque and has cross timbering beneath the windows that is painted a deep red color.

A third wing projects in the opposite direction and is composed of rough stone below green shingles. This wing was added in 1913-1914.

The interior of The Manor is wonderfully executed craftsmanship that is believed to have been done by Italian workmen from Biltmore Estate. An immense brick fireplace, a long,

The Manor

curved glass-enclosed sun corridor and Tiffany-type stained glass windows are among the notable features.

Just below The Manor are the Gatehouse and the Clubhouse.

The Gatehouse (NRHP)

Also referred to as the Lodge, this building was the first structure built in Albemarle Park, erected by James A. Tennent in 1898. It was designed by Gilbert in the Tudoresque Shingle style with pebble dash stucco at the first floor and granite foundation. The Lodge arched over the entrance drive leading from Charlotte St. into The Park. During the early years of the development, the offices of the Albemarle Park Company were on the ground floor of the two-story shingle and stone turret. Today the Gatehouse is used for commercial office space.

The Club House (NRHP)

Built around 1903, it originally contained the tennis courts, bowling alleys, pool and billiard rooms and a reading lounge. It is an L-shaped building of stone and timber that has a long gallery on the second floor. Three small hexagonal offices now dot the area between the old tennis court and the Gatehouse, and though modern, are in character with the round and polygonal forms found on several of the earlier buildings. The Club House today is used for commercial office space.

After viewing these main buildings, you may wish to venture on foot to see some of the lovely cottages throughout Albemarle Park. Dogwood Cottage, Foxhall and Rose Bank are all within walking distance.

Dogwood Cottage Inn (NRHP) — 40 Canterbury Rd.

This large 1.5-story rustic shingle cottage is now operated as a bed & breakfast, the Dogwood Cottage Inn. Main features are a continuous shed dormer across the main facade, casement windows and a bracketed hood over the entrance. It was built as a home

Dogwood Cottage Inn

for William Green and Mary Raoul in 1910 and sits on a commanding mountainside site offering views of the mountains to the west. The rustic style of the Dogwood Cottage relates to the traditional architecture of the Appalachians.

Foxhall and Fox Den (NRHP) — 60 Terrace Rd.

Foxhall is the larger of the two and was built in 1914 by E.A. Fordtran, who was the owner of the New Orleans Times/Picayune newspaper. It is a 2.5-story building, originally stucco and shingle, which has been refaced with brick veneer and siding. The building has graceful roof lines and fenestration and is beautifully landscaped. Fox Den is a two-story gambrel roofed garage apartment of stucco and timber that adjoins Foxhall.

Rose Bank (NRHP) — 106 Orchard Rd.

Rose Bank is a two-story shingle cottage with a projecting Dutch gambrel wing and double porches, designed in the Dutch Colonial Revival Style. Built around 1905, Rose Bank has distinctive windows that have diamond-paned upper sashes playfully arranged. Windows of various sizes and shapes are tied together with simple trim.

Grove Park Historic District

The Grove Park Historic District is located in an area that adjoins the Grove Park Country Club golf course and extends on either side of Charlotte St. This district also includes part of Kimberly Ave. that runs along side the golf course in a northerly direction.

The Grove Park neighborhood was designed and developed by St. Louis entrepreneur Edwin Wiley Grove with the help of Chauncey Beadle, landscape designer and later superintendent of Biltmore Estate and is a superb example of early twentieth century planned residential development. Grove wanted his development, like every other real estate venture he engaged in, to be exciting and innovative. Some of his ventures, such as the Grove Arcade and the Battery Park Hotel, were on the cutting edge of design and planning and hisOmni Grove Park Inn stands today as a monument to Grove's vision and genius.

The early phases of Grove Park were laid out by Chauncey Beadle and have curvilinear streets, large tree canopies, stone retaining walls and a grand entry park. There are many architectural styles represented and these include Shingle, Neo-Classical, American Foursquare, Colonial Revival, Tudor Revival, Georgian Revival, Bungalow, Italian Renaissance, Queen Anne and Chateauesque. Many nationally known and historically important architects worked within the Grove Park neighborhood. These included Richard Sharp Smith, Ronald Greene, Henry I. Gaines and James Gamble Rogers. Local Asheville developers E.A. Jackson and W.H. Westall also contributed to Grove Park's growth, buying and developing many lots in the 1920s.

Especially notable in this lovely neighborhood are the large number of deciduous and evergreen trees. Stonework in retaining walls and stairs are found throughout and many of the houses are on terraced grounds.

Like the Montford and Chestnut Hill historic districts, Grove Park is easily seen by car, and a self-guided tour is presented below.

To reach Grove Park take Charlotte St. north to 324 Charlotte St. where you will see Mr. Grove's Real Estate Office on the left.

E.W. Grove's Office (NRHP) — 324 Charlotte St.

This building is a small one-story rubble rock structure with rough-faced ashlar covering. It features a tile-on-gable roof. It was constructed around 1909 and is said to have been used by Grove when he was building the Omni Grove Park Inn and developing the Grove Park neighborhood. The building was designed by Richard Sharp Smith and is the only structure of its type in the area. Grove left the building and the adjacent park to the City of Asheville. Note also the handsome stone gates to the right, entrances into the park.

Continue on Charlotte St. to 337 where you will see the beautiful St. Mary's Parish Church just ahead on your right.

St. Mary's Parish, Grove Park (NRHP) — 337 Charlotte St.

Described in the year of her founding in 1914 as a "Wayside Shrine in the Mountains of Western North Carolina," beautiful little St. Mary's Church has attracted countless visitors over the years. Designed by Richard Sharp Smith and built in 1914, the church is English Gothic in style and cruciform in plan. Constructed out of red brick with steeply pitched gable roofs, the building is like those dotting the hilly landscape of County Durham, Northumberland and Cumbria in northern England. The English cottage-style Rectory, also designed by Smith, was built and set in beautiful landscaped grounds. The landscape architect was the famous Frederick Law Olmsted, architect for Biltmore Estate and designer of New York's Central Park. International attention was brought to St. Mary's by the writer Gail Godwin when she immortalized the church in her novel Father Melancholy's Daughter.

From St. Mary's Parish, return down Charlotte St. and turn left onto Sunset Parkway. Continue on Sunset to the end where you will turn left onto Glendale Rd. Look for 50 on your right, the Edgar Fordtran House. It is up on a hill at the intersection of Ridgewood St., behind ivy covered stone walls.

St. Mary's Parish at Grove Park

Edgar Fordtran House

Edgar Fordtran House (NRHP) — 50 Glendale Rd.

This Tudor Revival style house was built in 1936 for Edgar Fordtran for $30,000. It is constructed of cut ashlar stone with stucco infill as part of the half-timbering in the front gable. This lovely building features outstanding chimneys and a decorative wrought iron front door. The landscaping is especially noteworthy and includes a winding drive, stone retaining wall and large wrought iron gates. This residence was the ASID Designer House for 1994.

Continue on Glendale Rd. to the stop sign and turn left onto Macon Ave. Look for the Ralph Worthington House on your left.

Ralph Worthington House (NRHP) — 41 Macon Ave.

This handsome house was built in 1920 by Ralph Worthington and is a wonderful example of the quality of the houses that abound in the Grove Park District. The ASID Designer House for 1992, it is an excellent blend of Colonial Revival and Spanish Revival styles of architecture. It was operated as a boarding house from 1942 to 1959 but is now a private residence.

Continue on Macon to Charlotte St. and at the stop sign take a right onto Charlotte St. Turn left onto Evelyn Place just beyond the park. Immediately on your left, just past the intersection of Gertrude Place, is the J.R. Oates House.

Ralph Worthington House

J.R. Oates House (NRHP) — 90 Gertrude Pl.

Built in 1913 for J.R. Oates, a local banker, the house was designed by the architectural firm of Smith and Carrier. It is an excellent example of the Prairie style of architecture. A striking two-story house with smooth stucco and a cross gable roof with wide overhanging eaves. According to the portfolio of Richard Sharp Smith, the building was designated as "fireproof." It is noteworthy also for the superb craftsmanship of the interior as well as the exterior spaces, including the beautifully landscaped grounds.

Directly across the street on Evelyn Place is the Reuben Robertson House.

Reuben Robertson House (NRHP) — 1 Evelyn Pl.

This elegant house was built for Reuben Robertson in 1922 and was designed by New York architect James Gamble Rogers. This is an excellent example of the Colonial Revival style of architecture.

Continue on Evelyn Place to 107, The William Bryan Jennings House, which will be on your right.

Reuben Robertson House

William Jennings Bryan House (NRHP) — 107 Evelyn Pl.

William Jennings Bryan, famous orator, statesman, politician and presidential candidate spent many summers in this house. Built in 1917, it was designed also by Richard Sharp Smith, and is a refined example of a Colonial Revival style house. Exceptional details include paired columns and pilasters on front stoop and dentil molding beneath the roof lines.

After viewing the Jennings House, turn right onto Kimberly Ave. and continue on up Kimberly.

Kimberly Ave.

Kimberly Ave. is one of the finer residential streets in all of Asheville, bordered on one side by the Omni Grove Park Inn golf course and one the other by grand houses from the 1920s. The Ave. is a favorite for local walkers and joggers and the views of the Omni Grove Park Inn and nearby mountains from the tree-lined street are outstanding.

Residence on Kimberly Ave.

This concludes your tour of the historic Grove Park District. To return to downtown Asheville, retrace your path down Kimberly Ave. and Edwin Place to Charlotte St. While you are in the vicinity, you may wish to visit the Omni Grove Park Inn and The Biltmore Industries Buildings which are close by. Both of these are presented later in this chapter.

Biltmore Village Historic District

Biltmore Village was built by George W. Vanderbilt on the south bank of the Swannanoa River at the edge of his vast estate. Much has changed over the years by the flood tide of urban sprawl, Biltmore Village nonetheless has some remaining buildings from that early period. Many of these form a small neighborhood which evokes the village's original ambience. The landscaping, the quaintness of the cottages, the presence of other remaining buildings and the street pattern all form an important historic district.

The symmetrical, fan-shaped street plan is the least changed element of the original design. At the north end, Brook and Lodge streets join at an obtuse angle at the railway station and plaza. All Souls Crescent swings south from these streets to form the boundaries of the village, and within the village itself a network of streets forms the fan pattern.

Vanderbilt planned Biltmore Village as a picturesque manorial village, to complement his estate and grounds and as a practical solution to solving the housing problem of estate workers and servants. This model village, English in flavor with its Tudor buildings, was primarily the work of three men: Richard Morris Hunt (1827–1895), the nationally prominent architect who designed Biltmore House itself, the village church of All Souls, the railway station and the estate office; Frederick Law Olmsted (1822–1903), the renowned landscape architect who designed the grounds of the estate and the village plan; and Richard Sharp Smith (1852–1924), an architect employed by Hunt who designed the cottages, school, post office, infirmary and other village buildings.

The site along the Swannanoa River, a small crossroads known as Asheville Junction or Best (for William J. Best, an owner of the Western North Carolina Railroad) was chosen

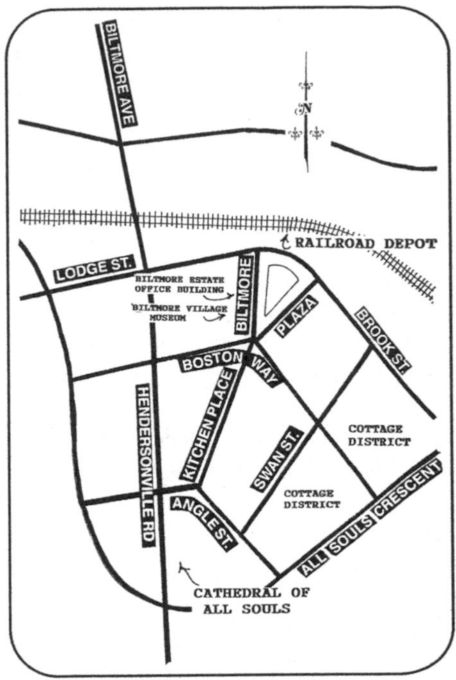

Biltmore Village

for Biltmore Village, planning for which began in 1889. Vanderbilt bought the village, relocated the residents and constructed an entirely new town. Construction was largely complete by 1910. Shortly after Vanderbilt's death, the village was sold and over the years, many changes were made, not all compatible with the original concept and design of Vanderbilt and his architects. Recently however, through the efforts of the Historic Resources Commission of Asheville and Buncombe County, the Preservation Society and the Biltmore Village Merchants Association, much restoration has been accomplished and an enlightened program of adaptive use instituted. At the heart of Biltmore Village's recent revival has been the conversion of former cottages into commercial spaces that include gift shops, restaurants, art and craft galleries and clothing stores. The Village is a Local as well as a National Historic District which will insure its preservation and continued restoration.

Biltmore Village is an ideal setting for a walking self-guided tour and the historic buildings highlighted in this section will be presented in that fashion. I suggest also that you visit the Biltmore Village Historic Museum at 7 Biltmore Plaza, one building to the left of the Biltmore Estate Office Building on the plaza. (*See* Section III, Chapter Two)

Begin your walking tour by parking near the plaza, across from the old railroad depot, which will be your first stop.

Biltmore Village Railway Depot Building (NRHP) — 1 Biltmore Plaza

This Southern Railway passenger depot was designed by Richard Morris Hunt and is a symmetrical one-story structure with half-timbered pebble dash walls. It is significant as one of the four structures that were designed by Hunt for the Village and it serves as one of the major functional and architectural landmarks of the community. It was built in 1896.

Walk across the Plaza and you will see the Biltmore Estate Office on your right.

Biltmore Estate Office Building (NRHP) — 10 Biltmore Plaza

Another of the four structures designed by Hunt it is a combination of the design motifs and materials utilized in other structures in the village. It is a 1.5-story building that features pebble dash walls, half-timbering, brick trim, chamfered and bracketed porch posts and stylized classical ornament. This building served as the office for the operations of Biltmore Estate and was constructed also in 1896. It is still in use today by the Biltmore Company for offices.

After viewing the Biltmore Estate Office Building, you will see the Biltmore Village Historic Museum, also on the plaza. If they are open, stop in for a visit. After leaving the museum, continue on your way from the plaza area and walk south on Kitchen Place toward The Cathedral of All Souls directly ahead.

The Cathedral of All Souls (NRHP) 9 Swan St.

Originally known as All Souls Church, it was designated an Episcopal Cathedral in Jan. 1995. The largest structure in Biltmore Village, it is an exquisite, lovely building of fine Romanesque style. Designed by Richard Morris Hunt, this complex building combines pebble dash wall surfaces, brick and wood trim, and expansive tiles roofs. In spite of the complexity however, the church is a simple cruciform with a tall tower rising in the center which contains most of the interior space. The Parish House features the same materials but is considerably different in design.

The interior is relatively simple but no less elegant and features wonderful stained glass windows created for the Vanderbilts by Maitland Armstrong and his daughter Helen. They illuminate a variety of scenes from the Old and New Testaments.

George Vanderbilt was one of the organizers of the congregation in 1896, financed the construction of the church and parish house and selected the furnishings. The church was consecrated on Nov. 8, 1896.

From this lovely building, you may now begin to explore the Cottage District which is found on Swan St., All Souls Crescent, and Boston Way. There are fourteen cottages in this district, which will be on your left and behind you as you face the front of the church and the Parish House.

The Cathedral of All Souls

Biltmore Cottage District

Biltmore Village Cottage District (NRHP)

The English Tudor cottages on the east side of Biltmore Village were designed by architect Richard Sharp Smith. All are one-and-one-half to two-story pebble dash cottages with recessed porches, multiple gables and steeply pitched roofs. No two cottages are alike although they are closely similar and in some cases mirror images. They are located at 1 and 3 Swan St., 2, 4, 6, 7, 10 and 11 All Souls Crescent and 5 and 6 Boston Way. Besides being architecturally interesting, these cottages now house specialty shops and restaurants.

This concludes the walking tour of Biltmore Village. Another structure of historical importance, The Reed House, is in the district and can be visited by car. From the plaza area take Lodge St. to Hendersonville Rd. (Highway 25) and turn left. Go south on Hendersonville Rd. to Irwin St. and turn left. Turn left at the end onto Dodge St. and look for 119, The Samuel Harrison Reed House.

Samuel Harrison Reed House (NRHP) — 119 Dodge St.

Built in 1892, this house is one of the most important Queen Anne style residences in Asheville. The frame structure features a prominent corner turret with an ogee dome and a wraparound porch. It is historically significant for its associations with Mr. Reed, who sold to George Vanderbilt and his land agents the property on which Biltmore Village was constructed.

Eliada Home Historic District

The Eliada Home is a youth home complex located in the Leicester neighborhood of Asheville. This historic district includes the early administrative, residential and agricultural buildings of the home as well as associated sites that include a residence, a tabernacle site, a log guest cabin and cemetery. Eliada Home is in a parklike setting with concrete walks and shade trees, and is situated on a hilltop.

Eliada Home was founded by Lucius B. Compton as a refuge for unwed mothers in 1903. The first facility was "Faith Cottage" on Atkinson St. in Asheville. The children's home was established in 1906, with buildings on the property dating back to 1907, and is still in operation today.

To reach Eliada Home, take Patton Ave. west from Asheville and turn right onto Leicester Hwy. Turn right again onto Compton Dr. Eliada Home is at the end of Compton Dr. eliada.org

Main Building (NRHP) — 2 Compton Dr.

The main building is a two-and-a half story, five-course American-bond brick structure that originally served as a dormitory and was used also for administration, food processing (canning) and as an outlet store for excess clothing and as a chapel. The exterior style is Colonial Revival and Foursquare-inspired, and was designed by architect Thomas E. Davis.

Located behind the Main Building and accessible down a short gravel drive is the most impressive of the structures at Eliada Home, the Dairy Barn.

Dairy Barn (NRHP)

This magnificent barn was built between 1930 and 1931 and is a two-level, six course American-bond brick building with room for forty dairy cows on the fireproof first level and machinery and tools on the second level. The barn was used for milk production and the motto "Eliada Dairy, Pure Bred Guernseys" was originally painted on the west side of the roof. This has been replaced with the motto "Eliada Home Outlet Barn," indicating its use as a retail outlet since the late 1970s.

Oteen Veterans Administration Hospital Historic District

Located in the Oteen district of Asheville on US Hwy. 70 just beyond the intersection of Hwy. 70 and Riceville Rd., the Oteen Veterans Administration Hospital District is a striking collection of massive yellow stucco Georgian Revival and white frame Colonial Revival buildings. As Riceville Rd. leaves Hwy. 70 at the foot of the hospital's lawn it runs north through the district and divides employees' dormitories and other residential structures to its west from the facility's main campus.

The structures included in the Historic District were built between 1924 and 1940 to replace a large collection of frame buildings which had served as U.S. Army General Hospital No. 19 in the late teens and early twenties. The work accomplished at the Oteen location turned out to be one of the nation's best and most beautiful permanent military hospitals. The focus of care at the hospital was tubercular and respiratory treatment. Today the hospital still functions as a major care center, although some of the outlying buildings have been converted to apartment use. For more information about the current medical programs at the VA Hospital, see Section III, Chapter Eight Asheville VA Medical Center.

Asheville High School Historic District (NRHP)

To reach the Asheville High School Historic District, take Patton Ave. west from Pritchard Park. Turn left onto Asheland Ave. until you reach McDowell St. Continue on McDowell until you reach the high school at 419.

Asheville High School is an Italian Renaissance and Art Deco pink granite building that was a state-of-the-art facility when it opened Feb. 5, 1929. It cost $1,362,601 when it was built by general contractor Palmer-Spivey Construction Co. of Charlotte, using the plans of architect Douglas D. Ellington. The main school building is visible from McDowell St. and is a large Art Deco/Italian Renaissance style structure that features a tile roof. The landscaping in front is extraordinary and the formal stairs, drives and walkways of Ellington's plan serve as a graceful setting for the magnificent building. The whole school complex is contained within this district. Originally named Asheville High School, it was renamed Lee H. Edwards High School but was changed back to Asheville High School in 1969 when the city schools were integrated.

Asheville School Historic District (NRHP)

To reach the Asheville School Historic District, take Patton Ave. west from Pritchard Park. Continue on Patton Ave. (19-23 South); 3.4 miles after you cross over the French Broad River, look for Asheville School Rd. on your left just beyond Goodwill Industries.

The Asheville School and its attendant buildings compose the Asheville School Historic District. This lovely parklike campus is approximately 276 acres, with a winding entrance road lined with native evergreens. These were planted by Chauncey Beadle, landscape gardener for Biltmore Estate, who donated his design services to the school. Asheville School is still in operation today, many years after its founding in 1900, and still provides excellent secondary education as a private boarding school. It was founded by Newton Anderson and Charles Mitchell. Over the years, they commissioned many prominent architects to design the campus buildings, including John Milton Dyer, Thomas Hibben, and Anthony Lord. The result was a collection of wonderful and architecturally impressive buildings. asheville-school.org

Following the entrance road you will pass in front of the three main administration buildings and then around to the larger structures, Anderson Hall, Mitchell Hall and Lawrence Hall, all on your right.

Asheville High School

Mitchell Hall, Asheville School Historic District

Anderson Hall (NRHP) — Asheville School Rd.

This building was built as the main academic building in 1900 and is the oldest one on the campus. It was designed by John Milton Dyer of Cleveland and is Tudor Revival in style. Constructed primarily of brick with limestone lintels and sills on the first and second floor windows, it is three stories tall.

Mitchell Hall (NRHP) — Asheville School Rd.

Built in 1903, this building was also designed by Dyer and is a long, linear plan with porches on the front and rear of the building. Walls on the lower floors are brick, with half-timbering on the uppermost floors. The exterior and interior design of this superb building is Art Deco with Tudor Revival detailing.

Lawrence Hall (NRHP) — Asheville School Rd.

Lawrence Hall is the third of the main campus buildings and was constructed in 1907. It is likely that Dyer also designed this building. The building was originally used as a dormitory, which it remains today along with administrative use. Three stories high, it is Tudor Revival in style.

Biltmore Industries Historic District (NRHP)

Directions: Take Charlotte St. to Macon Ave. Turn right on Macon and go toOmni Grove Park Inn Resort, 290 Macon Ave. Turn left into the inn's parking area and bear right to go down the hill and left at the stop sign to Grovewood Rd. and Grovewood Shops area.

The Biltmore Industries complex of buildings is situated on an eleven and one-half acre tract adjacent to the Omni Grove Park Inn Resort. The seven buildings of the grouping, which vary in size and form, lie in a row along the top of a ridge. These cottages were constructed in 1917 under the supervision of Fred Seely, designer and owner of the Omni Grove Park Inn. The purpose was to provide workshops for the production of high-quality crafts

Biltmore Industries buildings include Estes-Winn Automobile Museum. The buildings are adjacent to the Omni Grove Park Inn.

and fine hand-woven cloth that would be pleasing to the workers, and to provide a special to visitors at the Grove Park by offering the opportunity to observe the manufacturing process and to purchase completed items.

Today the Biltmore Industries Buildings house the Grovewood Gallery, the Estes-Winn Automobile Museum, the North Carolina Homespun Museum and the Grovewood Cafe.

Other Historic Asheville Sites & Buildings

This section of Historic Asheville is devoted to those sites and buildings of architectural or historic importance that have not been covered in the previous section.

Albemarle Inn Bed & Breakfast (NRHP, LHL) 86 Edgemont Rd.

Officially known as the Dr. Carl V. Reynolds House, this large frame Neo-Classical Greek Revival building is today the Albemarle Inn Bed & Breakfast. It is distinguished by a gable roof and a two-story portico with twin pairs of Corinthian columns and half-round pilasters. The interior features oak paneling and an exquisite carved oak stairway with a unique circular landing and balcony. Dr. Carl Reynolds built this house in 1909 and occupied it until 1920. Thereafter it was leased to the Grove Park School and then to the Plonk sisters, who operated an arts school there until it became the Albemarle Inn in 1941. Hungarian composer Bela Bartok stayed at the Inn during 1943 and while there completed his Third Piano Concerto, also known as the Asheville Concerto or Concerto of Birds. (See also Section II, Chapter One)

Directions: From Pack Square, take College St. east to Charlotte St. Turn left and go 0.9 miles. Turn right onto Edgemont Rd.

Albemarle Inn Bed & Breakfast

Beaucatcher Tunnel (NRHP) — College St.

This two-lane tunnel was originally built in 1930 to replace a winding road that went over Beaucatcher Mountain. The tunnel was blasted out of solid granite and has served Asheville for these many years. In 1997 it was refurbished and modernized and new granite stonework installed over the entrances.

Directions: From Pack Square take College St. east to the nearby tunnel entrance.

Biltmore Estate (NRHP, NHL) — Entrance opposite Biltmore Village

This magnificent estate built by George Vanderbilt is a national treasure. Biltmore House, the largest privately owned house in America, is visited by hundreds of thousands of visitors each year. For architectural and historical information see Section III, Chapter Three Biltmore Estate.

Biltmore Forest

Biltmore Forest is an area of fine residential homes that adjoins part of Biltmore Estate. Dr.iving through this lovely parklike neighborhood you will see many architecturally interesting and historic buildings. Notice also the street lamps, antique ornamental fixtures still in use throughout that combine lighting and signage functions. The high quality copper and bronze swan-neck lamp posts are thought to have been manufactured in California and bought by a Judge Adams before 1928. Of special interest are the Biltmore Forest Municipal Buildings (circa 1927) at Vanderbilt Place, the Silver Shop Building (circa 1930) at 365 Vanderbilt Rd. and the Biltmore Forest Country Club (circa 1922) at Country Club Rd. Although Biltmore Forest is not a Historic District, many of the buildings are individually listed in the National Register of Historic Places.

Directions: Biltmore Forest can be entered at many places along Hendersonville Rd. going south from Biltmore Village. An easy-to-find entrance is Vanderbilt Rd. that enters the Forest just to the right of the Quality Inn Biltmore.

Residence in Biltmore Forest

Cedar Crest (NRHP, LHL) 674 Biltmore Ave.

Officially known as the William E. Breese, Sr. House, this is one of the largest and most opulent residences surviving from Asheville's 1890s boom period. A wonderful Queen Anne-style dwelling, it was constructed by contractor Charles B. Leonard in 1891. It features a prominent turret, expansive side and rear porches and interior woodwork of extraordinary beauty. It was opened as a tourist home with the present name "Cedar Crest" in the 1930s. Today, it is a Victorian bed & breakfast. (**See** also Section II, Chapter One)

Directions: From Pack Square take Biltmore Ave. south.

Church of the Redeemer (NRHP) 1201 Riverside Dr.

This small, coursed-ashlar church was reportedly built in 1886 by a Dr. Willis, an immigrant from England. It features a cruciform plan, patterned slate roof and round arched windows with beautiful stained glass. An Episcopal Church, it still is in operation and visitors are welcome.

Directions: From Pack Square take Broadway north to Riverside Dr. Turn right onto Riverside Dr.

Omni Grove Park Inn (NRHP, NHL) 290 Macon St.

The Omni Grove Park Inn is one of the largest resort and conference centers in the Carolinas. Built in 1913 by Edwin Wiley Grove of native granite boulders, the main block of the inn is four double bays wide and four stories deep with a deep hip roof pierced by two rows of eyelid dormers, thus making six floors in all. The granite for the inn was quarried locally from nearby Sunset Mountain.

A magnificent building, it has many noteworthy architectural features including more than 600 handmade solid copper lighting fixtures still in use, the main lobby with the huge fireplaces at each end and the striking red clay tile roof. Recently wings were added to each side of the hotel, thus providing over 500 rooms. (**See** Section III, Chapter Six for more about the history of the Omni Grove Park Inn)

Directions: Take exit 5B onto Charlotte St. off I-240. Go one-half mile north on Charlotte St. to Macon Ave. Turn right. The Inn is one-half mile up Macon Ave.

Omni Grove Park Inn Country Club Building (NRHP) Country Club Rd.

Formerly the Asheville Country Club, this rambling stucco-on-masonry structure was designed in a chateauesque style by English architect H.T. Linderberg in 1925. Distinctive features include a diminutive round tower with tall conical cap and weathervane adjacent to the archway drive and a grand Flemish bond chimney on the west side of the north-south section of the building. The Country Club building is owned today by the Omni Grove Park Inn and houses the Golf Pro Shop, swimming pool facilities and is also used to host meetings and weddings.

Directions: Take exit 5B onto Charlotte St. off I-240. Go one-half mile north on Charlotte St. to Macon Ave. Turn right. Inn is one-half mile up Macon. Enter into main driveway and in front of the hotel bear right. Go down hill to stop sign and turn left and then left again at stop sign onto access road. Country Club building in on your left.

Longchamps Apartments (NRHP) 185 Macon Ave.

This imposing six-story structure was designed by Ronald Greene and built around 1925. Chateauesque and Tudor elements are combined in the unusual facade. The body of the building is a combination of half-timbers, rectilinear and half-round towers and brick and slate. A controversial building because of the unusual combination of elements, the building is nevertheless pleasing and has a majestic presence.

Directions: From I-240 take the Charlotte St. exit 5B. Take Charlotte St. north and turn right onto Macon Ave.

The Old Reynolds Mansion (NRHP) 100 Reynolds Heights.

Officially known as the Reynolds-Reynolds House, this two-story American bond brick structure is supposed to have been built around 1846. During the 1920s the house was completely remodeled at which time a third floor within a mansard roof with dormers as well as other rooms were added giving the house a Second-Empire look. Today the house is known as The Old Reynolds Mansion and is operated as a bed breakfast.

Directions: From Pack Square, take Broadway to the juncture of Merrimon Ave. Follow Merrimon Ave. north past Beaver Lake and turn right just past next stop light onto Beaver Dr. Turn left up gravel lane.

Sherrill's Inn (NRHP) Hwy. 74A, Fairview

This large weatherboarded house was operated as an inn that served travelers passing through Hickory Nut Gap during the 19th century. Bedford Sherrill began operating the inn in 1834. It is a two-story saddlebag-plan structure that probably dates back to around 1801. Also located on the property is a very old smokehouse and tradition maintains that this building served as a frontier "fort" in the 1790s. More than likely this small rectangular building is the area's oldest structure. The inn, which is a private residence today, is visible on

St. Matthias Church

the right as you drive up the winding Hickory Nut Gap Rd. from Fairview going toward the Lake Lure area. As a note, if you happen to be in Asheville or Hendersonville in the fall during apple harvest the owners of the house sell excellent homemade cider and fresh apples grown in the property's orchards.

Directions: From Asheville take I-240 east to exit 9 (Bat Cave, Lake Lure and Hwy. 74A east). Take Hwy. 74A east through Fairview to the very end of the valley. As you climb up the winding road to Hickory Nut Gap, look for the State Historic Sign and Sherrill's Inn on your right up on a hill.

St. Luke's Episcopal Church (NRHP) — 219 Chunns Cove Rd.

St. Luke's is a tiny historic country frame church located in the Chunns Cove section of Asheville. The building was consecrated on Jul. 9th, 1898 and features triangular arched windows with simple geometric stained glass. The building is noteworthy for its simple, honest beauty.

Directions: From I-240 take Exit 6 Chunns Cove Rd. Look for the church on your right.

St. Matthias Church (NRHP) — One Dundee St.

Saint Matthias began as Trinity Chapel in 1867 on land donated by Captain Thomas Patton. It has the distinction of being Asheville's first black congregation. In addition, a strong Sun School and Day School flourished on the site and offered the only formal education at that time for the children of the black community. However, they soon outgrew the smaller structure and the present building was begun in 1894. It was completed two years later under the supervision of James Vester Miller, whose crew then went to begin work on Biltmore House. At this time it was renamed Saint Matthias to honor the 13th apostle and the first missionary to Africa. A handsome Gothic-brick structure, the building features elaborate interior woodwork.

Directions: Located in downtown Asheville. Take exit 5B off I-240 onto Charlotte St. heading south. Take a left on Carver St., then a quick right on Grail St., and then turn right onto Dundee St.

Smith-McDowell House (NRHP, LHL) 283 Victoria Rd.

The Smith-McDowell House is one of Asheville's major historic structures. Built around 1848, the house is an impressive two-story double-pile plan Flemish-bond brick house with a graceful two-tier porch. It is one of the oldest buildings surviving in Asheville and definitely the oldest brick structure in Buncombe County. The house was constructed for James M. Smith, one of the wealthiest and most influential men in antebellum Asheville. It is open today as a museum. See Section III, Chapter Two, Smith-McDowell House for more information about the museum and the programs offered.

The Smith-McDowell House as it appeared in 1848

Directions: From Pack Square take Biltmore Ave. south. Just past St. Joseph Hospital and just before Memorial Mission Hospital turn right onto Victoria Rd.

Thomas Wolfe House (NHL, NRHP, LHL) 48 Spruce St.

This historic two-story Queen Anne style house was the childhood home of North Carolina's most famous writer, Thomas Wolfe. The building was built around 1883 and features a decoratively-shingled slate roof, colored glass windows and bracketed cornice. In 1906 it was purchased by Wolfe's mother, Julia, who operated it as a boarding house that she called Dixieland. Wolfe immortalized it in his novel **Look Homeward Angel.** Almost destroyed by fire in 1998, the house was authentically restored in 2004. It is operated today as the Thomas Wolfe Memorial and is open to the public. For more information about this important house, *see* Section III, Chapter Two, Thomas Wolfe Memorial.

Thomas Wolfe House, "Dixieland"

Directions: From Pack Square take Broadway north and turn right onto Woodfin St. Take first right onto Market St. Memorial parking lot is ahead on the left (Spruce St., the official address for the house no longer exists as a operational city St.)

Chapter Five

The Omni Grove Park Inn

The Omni Grove Park Inn was the dream of Edwin Wiley Grove and his son-in-law, Fred Loring Seely, who envisioned the building of a resort hotel in the beautiful and restful mountains of the Southern Appalachians. Mr. Grove, who was the owner of a pharmaceutical company in St. Louis, Missouri, had come to Asheville for health reasons and liked the area so much he bought land here, including acreage on the western slope of Sunset Mountain. It was on this land that he eventually built a unique resort, the Omni Grove Park Inn, patterned after the Old Faithful Inn in Yellowstone National Park, but built of native stone instead of logs.

Over the years, this grand hotel has had many distinguished guests. President Franklin D. Roosevelt and his wife, Eleanor, President Woodrow Wilson, F. Scott Fitzgerald, William Jennings Bryan and Will Rogers all journeyed to E.W. Grove's luxurious mountainside inn. The attraction of the inn was compelling and guests came in great numbers from all over the world. Other noteworthy visitors were John D. Rockefeller, General Pershing, Chief Justice Taft and Thomas Edison.

The hotel was designed by Mr. Seely and was constructed of granite boulders which were brought from nearby Sunset Mountain or from land owned by Mr. Grove. Hundreds of North Carolina laborers helped in the construction was well as Italian stone masons. Each rock was used only if it fit perfectly where it was needed, and the great fireplaces, which are thirty-six feet wide required one hundred and twenty tons of boulders to build. The hotel was completed in just over a year and was opened on July 1, 1913.

Originally a guard house protected the main entrance to the hotel grounds. The roads leading up the hill along Macon Ave. were also originally paved in smooth brick and converged on a circular parking area in front of the east porch, now the main entrance. Seven hundred pieces of furniture and over six hundred lighting fixtures were handmade by Roycrofters of East Aurora, New York, and the bedroom furniture was made by the White Furniture Company of Mebane, North Carolina. The rugs were woven in Aubusson, France, and lasted until 1955, when Charles and Elaine Sammons of Dallas came to the resort and refurnished the entire property. In the early years, entertainment at the hotel included bowling, swimming and billiards, and in the Great Hall there were concerts, organ recitals and movies, after which each guest received an apple wrapped in gray paper for depositing the core. Another hotel practice which amazed visitors was the presenting of change at the cashier's window in washed and polished silver and crisp new paper money.

Grove Park Inn on Sunset Mountain

The rocking chairs on the porches and terraces were very popular as guests would sit for hours enjoying the mountain views and refreshing air. Walking paths on the grounds were also provided for the guests. During the years of the Second World War, the U.S. State Department leased the property for an internment center for Axis diplomats. Later, the Navy Department took over the hotel as a rest and rehabilitation center for soldiers returning from the war, and the Philippine Government in exile functioned from the Presidential Cottage on the hotel grounds. For a decade after the war, the hotel was operated as such by the owner, Ike Hall.

The complete restoration and modernization, begun in 1955, included private baths in every room, electric and water lines replaced, American fabrics and rugs installed and furniture cleaned, restored and reupholstered. A beautiful swimming pool was added, tennis courts were resurfaced and a putting green constructed. In later years, wings were added to the original stone hotel body to provide needed guest accommodations.

In 1917, the Biltmore Industries, a cottage craft industry started by Mrs. George Vanderbilt, was sold to Mr. Seely who installed it in the Old English type shops at the edge of the Omni Grove Park Inn grounds. Visitors to the Omni Grove Park Inn could watch the spinning and carding of wool and the looming of cloth. These cottages still operate in much the same spirit and are home to the Grovewood Gallery, the Estes-Winn Memorial Automobile Museum and the North Carolina Homespun Museum.

In the early 1980s the famous resort hotel was converted from a seasonal enterprise into a year-round resort and convention center. Refurbishing of all the guest rooms, public areas, dining rooms and meeting rooms was undertaken, and the electric and plumbing system fully modernized. New wings included complete meeting and conference facilities.

Today, The Omni Grove Park Inn is the epitome of a world-class resort. This great hotel has it all—superb facilities, a rich history, overwhelmingly beautiful mountain setting, a Four Diamond Restaurant, and championship golf course. Recent renovations and additions to the resort include an updated Sports Center with indoor pool, the restoration of the historic main Inn's roof, new outdoor tennis courts and an extraordinary 40,000 sq. ft. spa complex that is one of the finest in the world (See review of the spa below).

Location: Asheville NC
Address: 290 Macon Ave., Asheville NC 28804
Telephone: 800-438-5800, 828-252-2711
Website: omnihotels.com/hotels/asheville-grove-park
Directions: From I-40 or I-26, take I-240 into Asheville. Take exit 5B, Charlotte St. Proceed north on Charlotte St. for .5 miles, then turn right on Macon Ave. After .5 mile, takeOmni Grove Park Inn entrance on left.

The Spa at The Omni Grove Park Inn

Completed in 2001, the 40,000 square foot spa is one of the finest in the world and features stone and timber construction, cascading waterfalls, waterscaped gardens and harmonious landscaping. Built into the face of Sunset Mountain and largely underground, the spa reflects the strong mountain arts and crafts traditions with a palette of soft greens, rust and ochre. Arts and crafts decorations abound, including torchieres that illuminate the main spa pool. The pool area, with its ocean themes, is absolutely spectacular. In addition to a relaxation pool and a lap pool, the area also boasts plunge pools and whirlpools. Saunas, steam rooms, inhalation rooms, treatment rooms and outdoor sun decks are only steps away. There are a wide range of services and treatments offered and these can be reviewed at the spa's website (groveparkinn.com). The following personal account of her own experience by writer Liza Schillo will give you an insider's view of just how wonderful the Spa at the Omni Grove Park Inn really is.

Vignette: Stone Poems

One of the many surprises that await guests of the Omni Grove Park Inn are the two magnificent fireplaces that grace both ends of the great entrance hall. Made out of massive boulders and large enough for a bunch of kids to camp out in, these transcendently massive stone structures also have a delicate literary side, and if you look closely, you will find written here and there on some of the stones poems and quotations. The one below is from the north fireplace:

"This old world we're living inis
mighty hard to beat
We get a thorn with every rose
but ain't the roses sweet?

In order to get to The Spa at the Omni Grove Park Inn, you must walk through the resort's grand lobby, which is breathtaking enough—all stone, vast ceiling and a fireplace at each end large enough to fit a handful of people. But stepping out onto the Sunset Terrace overlooking Asheville, and descending the stone steps winding through the garden and around a lit waterfall, pennies scattered over every rock the water touches, a feeling quite overwhelming wells inside me. The anticipation and excitement of spending an entire day of pampering, inside one of the world's best spas! The feeling augments the closer I get to the entrance, where I can catch the fragrant scent of herbs, and that warm, spicy smell that saunas give when they are warm.

Upon stepping inside I was amazed at the interior design. The theme I was told is "Rock, Water, Fire, and Light," and this is apparent as the lighting resembles torches in increments along the walls, which are all of rock. The ambience is one of an ancient library, or a revered museum. I am immediately greeted with the fine manners of one of their receptionists, who takes my name and hands me a black notebook in which is an itinerary and a question sheet. He courteously explains to me what I will be doing, and I take a seat. Not a minute later another spa employee comes out to give me and the other waiting ladies a tour before our treatments! We are lead through the back and I learn that only paying customers over the age of 18 are allowed here, to ensure maximum comfort and quiet to The Spa's clients. I also learned that no matter what treatment you are undergoing, you are permitted to remain at the spa, using the full facilities, for the entirety of the day, coming and going as you please! The spa divides into men and women's halves, and we are all taken to a very classy locker room where we change into robes and flip flops. The robes I was pleased to learn may be found in the spa store, as well as most of the products used during massages. A hall leading to the ladies' fireside lounge stems from it a shower room (with large showers, all of tile in a teal color, the "water" portion of their decorating theme I'd assume), bathroom and vanity room. Let me speak some on the vanity room: it was built for two Marilyn Monroes. The Hollywood lights that run above the wrap-around mirror highlight every amenity you could possibly need during your stay at The Spa. Mouthwash, hair gel, razors, deodorant, you name it and it is there at your fingertips! Tiny windows throughout the interior allow peeks at things to come, some looking over the huge pool room that I will come to momentarily. In the lounge fancy snacks and cucumber water are provided, as well as a spot by the fireplace, but if you'd rather, the ladies' sundeck, complete with a hammock, is right outside. I was soon led to my massage, but I do not want to ruin this surprise for you! Let me just say that after I came out, my skin was literally glowing and my head was huge from so much attention given just to me for a solid 80 minutes! I can't remember the last time my body felt so good, so cool and relaxed, yet strengthened. It is a feeling that can only be created when you allow yourself enough time to drop everything you are currently worrying with and simply focus on the now, on how your body feels and what can ease that stress that so many of us today are under too often. You can be assured that every masseuse at the Omni Grove Park Inn is an absolute expert. I myself have applied for various positions at the resort with an above-average resume, and I know from experience that there is quite an extensive and selective application process. They know exactly what they are looking for, and at the Grove Park, they get it. My masseuse was one of the younger ones; he told me that a lot of the staff is around 50 years of age. He also described to me some of the other massage rooms, and all are different; mine was The Dome Room: waterproof, containing a bathtub and a water massager, as well as other special treats.

After my treatment, I am taken to another lounge and provided with a neck warmer until I am guided through another tour. This one leads me to the pool that I've seen so many pictures of. However there is much more to it than just the simple lap pool. There are of course more king-size showers, and an unlimited stock of towels. Then the women rejoin the men in this cavernous space containing several pools and whirlpools. There is a sauna, what I caught a waft of outside. To get to the sauna however you enter a room I'd never heard of, an Inhalation Room. This room remains at room temperature but inside is burning essential oils to breathe in! There is a double whirlpool next to it titled the Contrast Pools. One pool of 103 degrees and an adjoining one of 65. After minutes in the hot one, you are to plunge into the icy one! This is good for circulation and detoxification of the bloodstream, especially good after massages or strenuous workouts. Needless to say I did not spend much time here but my body certainly tingled with a refreshing cleanliness afterwards. I decide to try the large pools next. There is one in the back of the "cave," where the lights are dimmer. This pool is unique because in the ceiling there are tiny, twinkling fiber optic cable stars, just beautiful. A waterfall cuts through between this pool and the front one, which is a mineral salts pool. This was my favorite, at 86 degrees (several degrees above the latter), I could open my eyes without the burning of strong chlorine! Both pools are no deeper than 4 feet, and have speakers underwater so that their soft, soothing music may still be heard while you are swimming. Massage waterfall whirlpools bank this pool on either side, and I test them out. These are like hot tubs but with two streams of water that are just strong enough to sit beneath for a good, hard massage on the shoulders. For the remainder of the day I rotate between these varying pools of water, and spend a good deal of time on their large patio with comfy lounge chairs and another large fireplace. Here I order lunch, and it is brought to me on a silver platter! The spa café is not just hot dogs; I enjoyed the vegetarian BLT—their menu is clearly health conscious, though if you're not counting calories I recommend their fruit creams, made with real fruit! Though menu items may seem a little pricey, believe me you get more than what you pay for. That is probably the most remarkable thing I found during my visit. I noticed two outdoor gazebos while on the patio, and learned that these are available if you wish to upgrade a massage to the outdoors, with a view of our Blue Ridge Mountains. I shared the patio with a good number of people, though I was astounded at how vacant and spacious it seemed for such a renowned spa. Upon questioning I found that there is usually a constant 30 to 40 people at The Spa during busy summer months, yet even in the winter they stay pretty full. This is because they have found that now spouses and other acquaintances of people arriving at the Grove Park for business have discovered The Spa! These otherwise stay-at-homes now tag along for treatment while their significant other is in meetings (a good idea, I think). Though 30 to 40 people may sound like a lot, spread throughout The Spa it is a tiny number for the size of the building, which I greatly appreciated. For most of the day I had the pools to myself! It is good to make reservations several weeks in advance, especially on weekends and summer days.

After inspection of the spa's store in the front (in which I was very happy to find that my robe is carried there!), I exit the building sometime around dusk, sorry to be returning to what I'd left behind that morning. But as I stare into the wishing well of the waterfall as I climb the steps, I feel no need to toss a penny in, because tonight, I can't wish for anything else.

Chapter Six

Asheville Parks

Surrounded on all sides by majestic mountains, with a major river, the French Broad, flowing through its center, Asheville is blessed with nearby outdoor recreation opportunities and natural attractions for visitors. Excellent golf courses, parks, lakes and the river itself are within a few minutes' drive from downtown.

Asheville Parks

Woven throughout the Asheville community are 11 neighborhood recreation centers, two pools, over 35 parks and play areas, 20 tennis courts, and a stadium complex supervised and maintained by the Asheville Parks and Recreation Department (828-259-5800).

Asheville parks are full of activity in the summer.

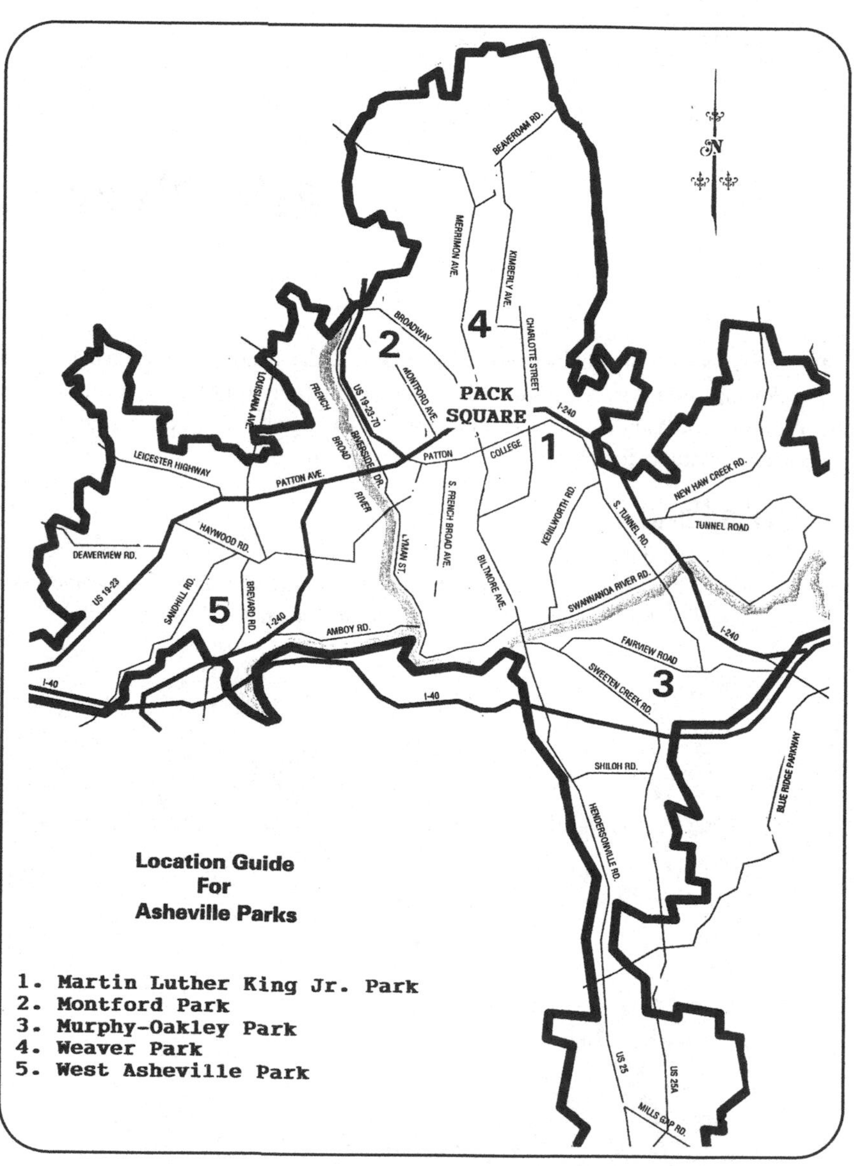

Asheville Parks

Recommended Parks

The following listing of Asheville Parks were recommended to the author by the Asheville Parks and Recreation Department for first-time Asheville visitors. They are easy to find, and offer outstanding facilities.

French Broad River Park: One of the most popular parks in Asheville, it is located on Amboy Rd. along the French Broad River. Also one of Asheville's most beautiful parks, this 14-acre park meanders alongside the tranquil French Broad River. The property features a vast area of open green space with gracious old trees, a wildflower garden, a paved half-mile walking path, a large gazebo, picnic tables and grills, a fishing/observation deck, and a small playground. The natural beauty of this park makes it a popular spot for warm weather weddings and romantic picnics in the meadow. The newest addition of the property is the Dog Park, which features a large fenced-in area made just for exercising and socializing your pooch! Off-St. parking and restrooms are also available.

Martin Luther King Jr. Park: (Martin Luther King Jr. Dr., 828-259-5800) Ball field, concession stand, fitness course, soccer field, picnic tables, playground, restrooms, open shelters.

Montford Park: (Montford Ave., 828-253-3714) Outdoor basketball court, playground, restrooms, open shelters, tennis.

The French Broad River runs through 117 miles of Western North Carolina.

Lake Julian District Park

Lake Julian, off Long Shoals Rd. in South Asheville

Lake Julian is an ideal family recreational facility and an excellent spot for the fishing enthusiast. Located near Skyland, N.C., the park offers opportunities for picnicking, canoeing, sailing and outdoor games. The park is open year-round for all county residents and visitors to enjoy. Lake Julian was named in honor of Julian Byrd Stepp.

Location: South Asheville
Address: Entrance is off Long Shoals Rd. (Hwy 146)
Telephone: 828-684-0376
Hours: Open year-round except Thanksgiving, Christmas, and New Year's Day. Oct.–Mar. 8am–6pm, April 8am–8pm, May–Sep. 8am–9pm
Fees: Fees for fishing boat and canoe rentals, and picnic area rentals
Directions: Take Hendersonville Hwy. south from Biltmore Village. Turn left onto Long Shoals Rd. in south Asheville. The entrance to the park is a few miles on the left opposite Overlook Rd.

Jewel of the Appalachians

Visitors to the mountains are often surprised by how often during the summer months they encounter the ruby-throated hummingbird. This tiny creature belongs to a family that numbers more than 300 tropical species, but the ruby-throated is the only one found in the mountains. It is a great migratory flier and strong enough to make the 500-mile flight across the Gulf of Mexico each spring and fall. During the summers it can be found in the mountains sipping nectar from flowers garden variety and wildflower alike. They are very good flyers and posses incredible stamina and endurance. In fact, they can hover in mid-air and even go backwards when necessary.

Section IV
Hendersonville

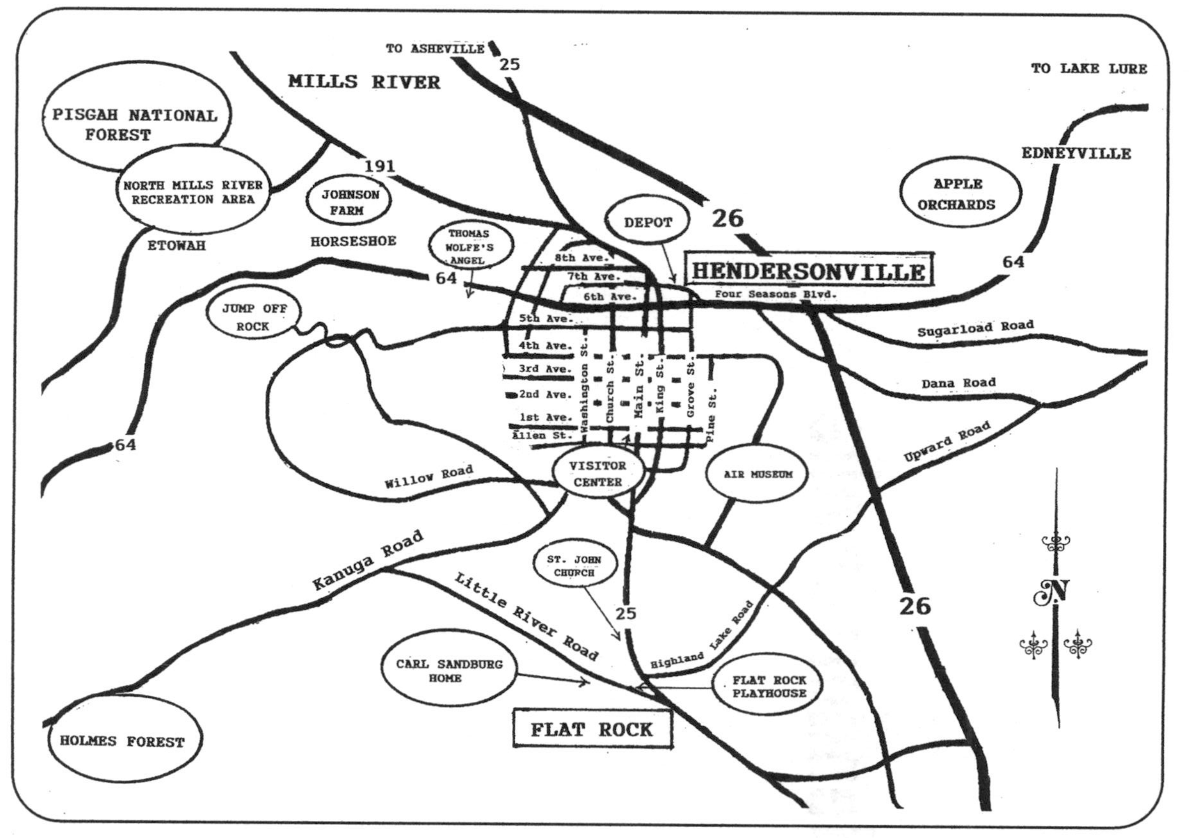

Hendersonville & Flat Rock

Chapter One

Hendersonville

Located amidst the majestic mountains of the Southern Appalachians, Hendersonville has come to be known as the "City of Four Seasons," and as an ideal retirement community. Since the early 1900s, Hendersonville has attracted visitors and families seeking a gentle climate, lovely mountain scenery, and great recreational resources. It is located in Henderson County, which has a population of over 104,000, and is by far the largest city in the county. The other two primary communities in Henderson County are the incorporated villages of Flat Rock and Fletcher, both which are covered in Section V, Chapter Four of this book (Western North Carolina Cities and Towns).

Situated 2,200 feet above sea level, on a mountain plateau between the Blue Ridge and the Great Smoky Mountains, Hendersonville is blessed with a moderate and mild climate, yet the area still experiences the four seasons. With a mean summer temperature of around 70 degrees and 40 degrees in the winter, the climate is conducive to year-round outdoor recreation.

Tourism is a major industry in Hendersonville, with agriculture and industry also strong economic forces. Noted for its scenic beauty and tranquility, Hendersonville has industrial development restrictions that encourage small industries that will not disturb the peaceful quality of Henderson County life. Retirement development is also a major economic force in Hendersonville as retirees continue to flock to the area. Hendersonville also has a vibrant and modern visitor center located at 201 South Main St. downtown, and should be your first stop before exploring the area.

Two popular downtown events in the summer are Music on Main St. on Fri evenings (during Jun. and Aug.), and Dancing in the St. on Mon nights (Jul. through Aug.). Both events usually last from 7 to 9 in the evenings, with parking lot seating beginning at 5:30pm. It is recommended to bring a chair, and also note that both alcohol and pets are prohibited.

Blessed with an abundance of cultural opportunities, Hendersonville offers something for all ages. A symphony orchestra, theatres, libraries, and festivals throughout the year enrich the life of Hendersonville residents. Henderson County is also rich in parks, picnic areas, hiking trails and other outdoor attractions.

Over the years, Hendersonville has preserved its traditional downtown Main St. area from the decline which has happened in so many other cities. Main St. has been transformed into a beautiful tree-lined avenue complete with flower-filled brick planters. A stroll down

Downtown Hendersonville

this lovely thoroughfare will surround you with sounds of classical music, sights of exquisite seasonal plantings in a hometown setting of boutiques, numerous antique and clothing shops and an old fashioned pharmacy, plus benches on which to sit and people-watch. Few hometowns have remained as beautiful, vital, and alive as historic downtown Hendersonville. The streets bring history to life and bring the best of yesteryear into the excitement of today.

Hendersonville was a largely uninhabited Cherokee hunting ground before Revolutionary War soldier William Mills moved to the area in the late 1780s. He received one of the first land grants west of the Blue Ridge and established the first community. By right of discovery, Mills christened some of Henderson County's picturesque regions: Mills River and Mills Gap are names that are still in use today.

The county was named for Chief Justice of the State Supreme Court Judge Leonard Henderson and has five incorporated areas: the city of Hendersonville, the village of Flat Rock, the town of Fletcher, Mills River, and the town of Laurel Park. Agriculture was the sole industry for early Hendersonville citizens. Tourism came later as visitors from the lowlands in South Carolina and Georgia discovered the scenic beauty and cooler climate. Industrial development grew after World War II, with the founding of the Chamber of Commerce program. Henderson County has long been known for its superior apples, and apple production still continues to be a major industry. Hendersonville celebrates this fact every summer with its famous "Apple Festival."

Location: Central Mountains. 22 miles south of Asheville

Elevation and Population: 2,200 feet, 13,000+

Henderson County Visitor Information Center: (Henderson County Tourism Development Authority), 201 South Main St., Hendersonville NC 28792; 828-693-9708, 800-828-4244, historichendersonville.org

Directions to Visitor Center: Take exit 49B off I-26. Travel west on Hwy. 64 (Four Seasons Blvd.) for about 2 miles. Turn left onto Main St. and continue eight blocks to 201 South Main St.

City Hall: 145 5th Ave. East, Hendersonville NC 28792; 828-697-3000, cityofhendersonville.org

Henderson County: County Offices, 1 Historic Courthouse Square, Hendersonville NC 28792; 828-697-4809 hendersoncountync.org

Henderson County Chamber of Commerce: 204 Kanuga Rd., Hendersonville NC 28739; 828-692-1413, hendersonvillechamber.org

Newspaper: Hendersonville Times-News 1717 Four Seasons Blvd, Hendersonville NC 28792; 828-692-0505.

Movie Theatres:

Epic Theatres of Hendersonville, 200 Thompson St., Hendersonville NC 28792; 828-693-1146

Henderson County High Schools:

Hendersonville High School (City), 1 Bearcat Blvd, Hendersonville NC 28791; 828-697-4802

East Henderson High School (County), 150 Eagle Pride Dr., East Flat Rock NC 28726; 828-697-4768

North Henderson High School (County), 35 Fruitland Rd., Hendersonville NC 28792; 828-697-4500

West Henderson High School (County), 3600 Haywood Rd., Hendersonville NC 28791; 828-891-6571

Colleges and Universities:

Blue Ridge Community College, 180 West Campus Dr., Flat Rock NC 28731; 828-694-1700

Wingate University (Hendersonville Campus), 220 Fifth Ave. East, Hendersonville NC 28792; 828-697-0105

Hospitals:

Pardee Hospital, 800 North Justice St., Hendersonville NC 28791; 828-696-1000

Park Ridge Hospital, 100 Hospital Dr., Fletcher NC 28972; 828-684-8501

Other Henderson County Communities: Bat Cave, Dana, Edneyville, East Flat Rock, Etowah, Flat Rock (*See* Section V, Chapter Four), Fletcher (*See* Section V, Chapter Four), Gerton, Horse Shoe, Laurel Park, Mills River, Mountain Home, Naples, Tuxedo, and Zirconia

Hendersonville Major Festivals: Garden Jubilee Festival (May), North Carolina Apple Festival (Sep.)

Area Natural Attractions: Apple Orchards in Henderson County, Dupont State Forest, Holmes Educational State Forest, Pisgah National Forest

Recommended Places to Stay: *See* Section II, Chapter One "Author's Choice Accommodations/Hendersonville"

Recommended Restaurants: *See* Section II, Chapter Two "Author's Choice Dining/ Hendersonville"

Chapter Two

Hendersonville Cultural Attractions

Bullington Gardens

Once the nursery of former NY City policeman Bob Bullington, Bullilngton Gardens is a public botanical garden and horticultural education center on 12 acres of rolling land in Henderson County providing hands-on education in horticulture and other sciences to students, youth clubs and adults. These gardens incorporate some of the many unusual mature trees that Mr. Bullington collected and introduced to the area. Visitors are welcome to visit and enjoy the gardens and facilities. Themed gardens include Perennial Borders, Dahlia Garden, Shade Garden, Reflection Garden, Herb Garden, Native Woodland Garden, Sally's Garden, Pollinator Garden, Rain Garden and Therapy Garden

Location: Hendersonville NC
Address: 95 Upper Red Oak Trail, Hendersonville NC 28792
Telephone: 828-698-6104
Hours: Monday through Saturday, 8 am–4:40 pm
Fees: None
Allow: Two hours
Directions: Directions from I-26 & Hwy. 64 East: I-26, Exit 49-A onto Hwy 64 E, 2.5 Mi. Left on Howard Gap Rd., 1 Mi Right onto Zeb Corn Rd, .6 Mi. Right onto Upper Red Oak Trail, Left into Bullington Gardens Entrance

Carl Sandburg Home

A very popular attraction, Pulitzer Prize-winning writer Carl Sandburg's farm, "Connemara," is a National Park Service Historic Site open to the public for visitation. The farm includes 264 acres of rolling hills, forests, lakes, pastures, goat barn, and buildings. Located in Flat Rock, three miles south of Hendersonville, the grounds are open for self-guided tours. Guided tours of the home are also scheduled daily. The barn and the many delightful goats are a hit with the kids!

Location: Flat Rock NC
Address: 1928 Little River Rd., Flat Rock NC 28731

Carl Sandburg Home

Telephone: 828-693-4178
Hours: Open-year round 9am–5pm, Closed Christmas Day.
Fees: Adults and senior rates, children under 15 free
Allow: Two hours
Website: nps.gov/carl
Directions: Connemara is located 3 miles south of Hendersonville in Flat Rock. Take Hwy. 25 south from Hendersonville and turn right just beyond the Flat Rock Playhouse onto Little River Rd.

Flat Rock Playhouse

The State Theatre of North Carolina, Flat Rock Playhouse, is one of the top ten summer theatres in the nation. Broadway-mountain style is the best way to describe this professional equity theatre found in a lovely forested setting in Flat Rock. Actors at the Playhouse come from across the nation and have acting credits including Broadway, feature films, national tours, television, off-Broadway and regional theatres. Sets are designed by the resident scenic designer and in the scenic studio adjacent to the theatre by Playhouse carpenters.

Flat Rock Playhouse (The Vagabond School of the Drama, Inc.) was established in 1952. In 1961, the playhouse was given special status with the honorary title of The State Theatre of North Carolina by the N.C. State Legislation in recognition of its high production standards. As the State Theatre, the Playhouse strives to offer a variety of fare each year with an emphasis on diversity.

Location: Flat Rock NC
Address: 2661 Greenville Hwy., Flat Rock NC 28731
Telephone: Box Office: 828-693-0731, Business Office: 828-693-0403

Flat Rock Playhouse, home of the Vagabond Players

Allow: Performances last from two to three hours.
Website: flatrockplayhouse.org
Directions: From downtown Hendersonville take Hwy. 25 south to Flat Rock. The Playhouse is on the right at the intersection of Hwy. 25 and Little River Rd.

Hands On! A Child's Gallery

Hands On! A Child's Gallery offers an affordable, educational and fun way to spend the day with your children, grandchildren, and students ages 1–10. This is a safe gathering place where kids can be kids while learning is nurtured. Field trips, special events, and birthday parties are welcome.

Location: Hendersonville NC
Distance: 40 minutes from Asheville
Address: 318 N. Main St., Hendersonville NC 28792
Telephone: 828-697-8333
Admission: Adult and child rates
Hours: Sat 10am–5pm
Website: handsonwnc.org
Directions: From Asheville take I-26 South. Get off at exit 49B onto US 64. Turn left onto Main St.

Henderson County Curb Market

The Curb Market, in continuous operation in Hendersonville since 1924, offers home-grown fresh vegetables and fruits, baked goods, home-made jams and jellies as well as gifts and handicrafts of all kinds. It was started on Main St. in 1924 with eight sellers using umbrellas and has grown to the present number of 137 selling spaces, with many sellers being third and fourth generation. The sellers are required to be residents of Henderson County and to make or grow all items sold.

Henderson County Curb Market

Location: Hendersonville NC
Address: 221 N. Church St., Hendersonville NC 28792
Telephone: 828-692-8012
Website: curbmarket.com
Hours: Tue, Thu and Sat 8am–2pm
Fees: None
Directions: From Asheville take I-26 South. Get off at exit 49B onto US 64. Turn left onto Main St. Heading south on Main St. in Hendersonville, take any right turn to take you to Church St. It parallels Main St. The market is behind the historic old Courthouse.

Henderson County Heritage Museum

The Henderson County Heritage Museum opened on April 11th, 2008, and uses displays and multimedia technology to tell the story of the people of Henderson County, from the Cherokee and pioneers who carved homes out of the wilderness to today's residents and events. The displays include rare artifacts, artwork, photographs, maps, video tours, oral histories, re-enactments, music, stories and legends. The museum is housed in the Historic Courthouse with rooms portraying periods in Henderson County's history: Wilderness to 1860, 1860–1920, 1920 to the Present, and the "Window on Main St.".

Location: Hendersonville, in the Historic Henderson County Courthouse building.
Distance: 30 minutes from Asheville
Address: One Historic Courthouse Square, Ste 4, Hendersonville NC 28792.
Telephone: 828-694-1619
Hours: Wed–Sat 10am–5pm, Sun 1–5pm
Fees: None
Allow: 1 hour
Website: hendersoncountymuseum.org
Directions: From Asheville take I-26 South. Get off at exit 49B onto US 64. Turn left onto Main St. and proceed down Main St. The Historic Courthouse building will be on your right.

Henderson County History Center

Located on Main St. in downtown Hendersonville, the Henderson County Historical Center consists of four separate entities under one roof: 1) Henderson County Historical Museum, 2) Henderson County Archives, 3) Henderson County Genealogical and

Historical Society, and 4) Mineral and Lapidary Museum of Henderson County. The Henderson County Historical Center has grown over the years under the direction of Dr. Jack Jones, noted local historian, into one of the area's most prestigious attractions.

Location: Hendersonville NC
Distance: 30 minutes from Asheville
Address: 400 North Main St., Hendersonville NC 28792
Telephone: 828-693-1531, County Archives: 828-693-1531; County Historical Museum: 828-693-1531; Mineral and Lapidary Museum: 828-693-1531
Hours: Mon–Fri 10am–4pm
Fees: None
Allow: 1–2 hours
Website: hcghs.com
Directions: From Asheville take I-26 South. Get off at exit 49B onto US 64. Turn left onto Main St. and proceed down Main St.

Hendersonville Railroad Depot

The Hendersonville Railroad Depot was the second station to be built by Southern Railway in the city and was built between 1902 and 1904. A frame structure with characteristics of the Craftsman style of architecture, it originally was 87 feet long and consisted of two waiting rooms, an agent's office and had indoor plumbing. In 1906, 15 more feet were added to each end of the station to provide a ladie's waiting room and more baggage space. A few years later, an open pavilion area was added to the north end, and in 1916 another 50 feet were added to the roofed-over, open pavilion area.

Recently the depot has been restored to its original color, and a Southern Railway caboose is located at the south end. The depot currently houses an operating model railroad, maintained by the Apple Valley Model Railroad Club, in the former baggage room.

Location: Hendersonville NC
Distance: 30 minutes from Asheville
Address: 650 Maple St., Hendersonville NC 28792.
Telephone: Apple Valley Model Railroad Club, 828-698-5465
Hours: Sat 10am–2pm
Fees: None
Allow: 1 hour
Directions: From Asheville take I-26 South. Get off at exit 49B onto US 64. Turn right at North Grove St., take the 1st right onto 7 Ave. East and then the 1st right onto Maple St.

Historic Johnson Farm

The Johnson Farm originally was the home of a wealthy tobacco farmer, Oliver Moss. Construction began in 1876 and was completed by 1880. It is handmade entirely of bricks fired on site from French Broad River mud. Over the years various outbuildings were added, including a tool shed and blacksmith shop, barn, boarding house and cottage. In 1913 Sallie Leverett Johnson inherited the farm and a new era began. The farm was now operated as a farm and summer boarding home for tourists. Historic Johnson Farm is a non-profit education center and

Historic Johnson Farm, just northwest of Hendersonville

farm museum for area school children and the community. It features an 1880's home, a barn loft museum, 10 historic buildings, animals, nature trails, and 15 acres of fields, forest and streams. It is owned and administered by the Henderson County Board of Education and operates today as a community museum and heritage center, with guided tours available for visitors.

Location: Hendersonville NC
Address: 3346 Haywood Rd., (Route 191), Hendersonville NC 28791
Telephone: 828-891-6585
Hours: Weekdays 8am–2:30pm.
Fees: Adult, student, and child rates
Allow: Two hours
Directions: From Hendersonville take Haywood Rd. (Rt. 191) north four miles. From Asheville take Hwy. 280 West past the airport and turn left onto Hwy. 191 in Mills River

Mineral & Lapidary Museum of Henderson County

Founded by Larry Hauser, the Mineral & Lapidary Museum of Henderson County, is a small institution with exhibits that include fossils, Cherokee Indian artifacts, and gems and minerals found in North Carolina. The purpose of the museum is to support the education of the children of Henderson and neighboring counties in the Earth Science areas of Mineralogy, Geology, Paleontology and the associated Lapidary Arts. The museum has ongoing exhibits of regional minerals and gemstones of interest to the general public, a workshop where gem-cutting and polishing demonstrations are held, and a gift shop.

Location: Hendersonville NC
Address: 400 N. Main St., Hendersonville NC 28792

Telephone: 828-698-1977
Hours: Mon–Fri 11am–5pm, Sat 10–5
Fees: Free
Allow: One hour
Website: mineralmuseum.org
Directions: From Asheville take I-26 South. Get off at exit 49B onto US 64. Turn left onto Main St. and proceed down Main St.

Mountain Farm & Home Museum

The Mountain Farm & Home Museum has displays of agricultural and domestic equipment, buildings, implements, utensils, methods and literature typical of rural life in 19th century Western North Carolina. Noteworthy also is the museum's outstanding collection of over 40 unique restored tractors.

Location: Hendersonville NC
Address: 10 Brookside Camp Rd., Hendersonville NC 28792
Telephone: 828-697-8846
Hours: Mon–Fri 9am–3pm, by special appointment at other times
Fees: None
Allow: 1–2 hours
Website: mfhmuseum.homestead.com
Directions: From Asheville take I-26 South, take exit 44 for US/25 toward Fletcher/ Mountain Home. Turn right off exit onto Hwy. 25 south toward Naples. After approximately 3 miles turn left onto Brookside Camp Rd.

Team ECCO Aquarium & Shark Lab

Team ECCO Center for Ocean Awareness is a children's educational center for ocean awareness, with exhibits and small aquariums focusing on marine life. The mission of Team ECCO is to promote scientific discovery through interactive learning encounters that develop understanding and respect for water-based ecosystems. This mission is designed to foster stewardship, develop leadership, and build friendship—all skills critical to team work.

Location: Hendersonville NC
Distance: 40 minutes from Asheville
Address: 511 N. Main St., Hendersonville NC 28792
Telephone: 828-692-8386
Admission: $4.00–$5.00
Website: teamecco.org
Hours: Wednesday thru Saturday 1:00–5:00 pm, Closed on Sunday and Monday
Nearby: Hendersonville Antique Toy Museum, Hands On! A Child's Gallery
Directions: From Asheville take I-26 South. Get off at exit 49B onto US 64. Turn left onto Main St.

Thomas Wolfe Angel

The marble angel statue immortalized by Thomas Wolfe in his novel Look Homeward Angel now stands at Oakdale Cemetery in Hendersonville. The completed statue was imported from Carrara, Italy by Wolfe's father, and was bought by members of the Johnson family after the death of Mrs. Johnson in 1905. The gravesite belongs to Reverend and Mrs. H.F. Johnson and their son. In 1975, when the statue was accidentally knocked from its stand, the Henderson County Commissioners had the graves enclosed with a six-foot tall iron picket fence set on a stone wall. This still allows visitors to view the statue and reduces the possibility of damage to the monument.

Location: Hendersonville NC
Distance: 40 minutes from Asheville
Address: Oakdale Cemetery, Hwy. 64 West, Hendersonville NC 28972
Directions: From downtown Hendersonville, take Hwy. 64 west. Look for Oakdale Cemetery on your left. The Angel Statue is visible from the road, and the location is indicated by a State Hwy. Marker.

Western North Carolina Air Museum

The Western North Carolina Air Museum, founded in 1989, is dedicated to preserving and promoting the flying heritage of the Western North Carolina Mountains region. They have over 15 vintage aircraft on display. In addition to the historic aircraft, the Western North Carolina Air Museum has exhibits of flight manuals and engines from historic aircraft as well as more modern reciprocating and jet engines, photographs of historic airplanes and pilots, and models of historic airplanes.

Location: Hendersonville NC
Address: 1340 Gilbert St., Hendersonville NC 28793

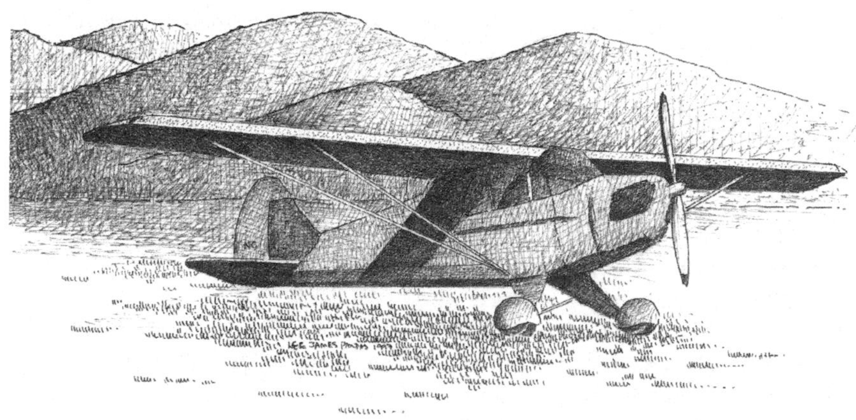

Impromptu rides sometimes happen at the N.C. Air Museum

Telephone: 828-698-2482
Hours: Apr.–Oct.: Sat 10am–5pm, Sun & Wed 12–5pm; Nov.–Mar.: 12–5pm
Fees: None
Allow: 1–2 hours
Website: wncairmuseum.com
Directions: From I-26 south take exit 22 Upward Rd. Take right onto Spartanburg Hwy. (US 176) and then another right onto Shepherd St. Museum is on Gilbert St.

Chapter Three

Historic Hendersonville

Hendersonville, while in existence as early as 1841, did not reach its peak of development until the late 19th and early 20th centuries. The boom started in 1879 when the railroad arrived and commercial development expanded greatly, both in the downtown Main St. area and in the district around the railroad depot. The influx of tourists at that time greatly increased and this in turn spurred the building of resort hotels and boarding houses, as well as fine residential homes for those tourists who decided to stay in Hendersonville. This building and development continued into the early 20th century but stopped abruptly in 1929 with the advent of the Great Depression.

During the early years of development, two individuals, W.F. Edwards and Erle G. Stilwell had major influence on the shape and character of Hendersonville. Edwards was a builder, and was responsible for the construction of many important commercial and residential buildings, including the early Town Hall and Opera House which stood on Main from 1893 to the 1920s, the Neo-Classical People's Bank at 225–231 North Main St. and the historic Henderson County Courthouse. Stilwell was an architect who had considerable influence on the shape of municipal, religious and commercial architecture in Hendersonville by bringing a new level of sophistication and competence to the local architecture. Among his important works were the Hendersonville High School, City Hall and the Citizens National Bank.

The face of domestic architecture was changed significantly with the arrival of the railroad. The industrial growth that the railroads brought also resulted in fine homes being built in the Queen Anne, Eastlake, Colonial Revival and Neo-Classical styles to house the wealthy industrialists. Today, in modern Hendersonville, many of these remaining significant residential properties in downtown have survived and continue to grace the city with their historic presence.

In this chapter, a selection of important historic buildings and structures will be presented, both as part of the two major downtown historic districts; Main St. and the 7th Ave. Depot area, and as separate structures not part of any designated historic district.

As in the chapter on Historic Asheville, certain abbreviations will be used to signify buildings of historical importance. NRHP indicates the structure is listed in the National Register of Historic Places, NHL indicates a National Historic Landmark property and LHL means the building is a Local Historic Landmark. Discussion of these designations is given in depth in the Historic Asheville chapter (*See* Section III, Chapter Four).

The Hendersonville Historic Preservation Society is instrumental in the preservation and restoration of historic properties. They are a valuable resource for anyone interested in historic Hendersonville. The Preservation Society may be reached by calling the Henderson County Genealogical & Historical Society offices at 828-693-1531, also an excellent historical resource. They are located at 400 North Main St., Hendersonville NC 28792.

Historic Districts of Hendersonville

Main St. Historic District

This district will be presented in the form of a self-guided walking tour. The best place to start is to park at the Hendersonville and Flat Rock Area Visitors Information Center located at 201 South Main St. From there your tour will take you up and back on Main St. Allow about an hour for the stroll.

Leaving the Visitors Center proceed north up Main St. One block up on your left will be the Historic Henderson County Courthouse.

Historic Henderson County Courthouse (NRHP) 113 North Main St.

Built in 1905, the historic Henderson County Courthouse overlooks Main St. Graced with a gold dome and a statue of Lady Justice, this imposing building was constructed by W.F. Edwards, father of A.V. Edwards, who served as Hendersonville's mayor for 36 years. Neo-Classical Revival in style, this building replaced an earlier two-story stuccoed brick structure. The architect was Richard Sharp Smith and is Smith's only structure in Hendersonville. The most notable feature of the courthouse is the gold domed three-stage cupola, which consists of a columned drum and domical roof, crowned by a statue of Lady Justice. This Lady Justice is thought to be the only one in the United States that does not wear a blindfold.

Although its main function was as a courthouse, the graceful building served other purposes over the years. The main courtroom was used in the early 1900s for various purposes,

The Historic Henderson County Courthouse

including speeches by governors, and as a gathering place for church congregations. Although it no longer is Henderson County's courthouse, it remains a dignified and majestic reminder of the past. The sophistication and grandeur reflect the past aspirations of a small county seat at a time when the economy was booming and whose population was beginning to soar.

Farther up Main St. in the next block you will see the People's National Bank Building on your left.

People's National Bank Building (NRHP) — 227–231 North Main St.

This building, dating back to around 1910, is a two story Neo-Classical structure of cream colored brick and was built by W.F. Edwards. It has a recessed central entrance beneath entablature supported by Ionic columns, and storefronts to either side. The bank building was the earliest use of Neo-Classical style and reinforced concrete construction for a commercial building in Hendersonville.

Continuing on up North Main St. to the end, look for the Maxwell Store Building on your left, which is now home to Mast General Store.

Maxwell Store Building (NRHP) — 529 North Main St.

This building once housed a fancy grocery business run by Maxwell Brown, a longtime proprietor. It was built around 1910 and is a two-story pressed brick structure. Highlights are round and segmentally arched windows with fanlights.

Turn around at this point and continue south on North Main. Turn left at 5th Ave. and look for the Hendersonville City Hall on your left.

Hendersonville City Hall Building (NRHP) — 145 5th Ave. East

Built between 1926 and 1928, this Neo-Classical Revival building was designed by Erle Stilwell. A flight of stairs leads up to the main entrance which is under a tetrastyle portico, on

People's National Bank Building

which is inscribed '"Erected by the People, Dedicated to the Perpetuation of Civic Progress, Liberty and the Security of Public Honor." This building reflects the prosperity of Hendersonville during the 1920s and the architectural refinement that Stilwell brought to the city.

After viewing the City Hall, return to Main St., and turn left. Proceed south on Main. The Ripley-Shepherd Building will be three blocks down on your left.

Ripley-Shepherd Building (NRHP) 218 North Main St.

This building is believed to be the second-oldest building on Main St., one of several buildings built by Colonel Valentine Ripley and once known as the "Ripley Brick Store House." It is said to have served as a district commissary under a Major Noe during the Civil War. Later it was also a post office for Hendersonville. Later still it was the home of Shepherd and Hart's furniture store and undertaking business. Notable features are the high hip roof and bracketed eaves.

7th Ave. Depot Historic District

This district is located two blocks northeast of Main St. and separated from Main St. by new commercial development. The district still shows a cohesive grouping of commercial, residential and transportation-related structures typical of the early development of Hendersonville, especially the period after the arrival of the railroad.

Seventh Ave. East developed as a commercial district during the late 19th and early 20th centuries and was centered around the first depot built in 1879. The majority of buildings are one and two story brick commercial and warehouse structures located along 7th Ave. Only minor alterations to the commercial buildings have occurred and these are mainly at the storefront level. Very little construction took place after the Great Depression. This district, with its frame depot, approximately 28 brick commercial buildings and the Station Hotel is one of the best surviving examples of a railroad district in western North Carolina. The buildings in the district are primarily commercial in function and provided services that were associated with a shipping point for locally grown cash crops.

Directions: Take North Main St. north to 6th Ave. Turn right and go 2 blocks. Turn left onto North Grove St. Proceed on North Grove across Four Seasons Boulevard. Take a right onto East 7th Ave. The Depot is just ahead on your right.

Hendersonville Depot (NRHP) SE Corner of 7th Ave. and Maple St.

This depot was the second station to be built by Southern Railway in the city and was built between 1902 and 1904. A frame structure with characteristics of the Craftsman style of architecture, it originally was 87 feet long and consisted of two waiting rooms, an agent's office and had indoor plumbing. In 1906, 15 more feet were added to each end of the station to provide a ladies waiting room and more baggage space. A few years later, an open pavilion area was added to the north end, and in 1916 another 50 feet were added to the roofed over, open pavilion area.

The railroad line was opened from Spartanburg, S.C. to Hendersonville in 1879, a year before Asheville was to receive a line from the east. The railroad brought large numbers of visitors to Hendersonville and allowed the county's produce to reach a wider market in other cities. The last passenger service ended in 1968. Since then the depot has been restored to

Hendersonville Depot, built between 1902 and 1904

its original color, and a Southern Railway caboose located at the south end. Restoration is ongoing, and the depot currently houses an operating model railroad in the baggage room. Visitors are invited to visit this historic station. The Depot is open for visitors year-round, Sat 10am–2pm Free.

Just north of the Depot, on the same side of the railroad tracks is the Station Hotel Building.

Station Hotel (NRHP) — 729 Maple St.

Built between 1912–1922, the Station Hotel is a two story brick building that features a low tripped roof and a two tiered, full facade frame porch. This relatively plain hotel was built near the tracks to serve the visitors who came to Hendersonville by the railroad. The building is still operated today as a hotel, although without its former polish and poise.

Other Historic Sites & Buildings

This section of Historic Hendersonville is devoted to those sites and buildings of architectural or historic importance that have not been covered in the previous section.

Aloah Hotel Building (NRHP) — 201 3rd Ave. West

The Aloah Hotel, called the Hendersonville Inn since the 1930s, is a large three-story brick building built in the early years of the 20th century. The building has a modest Classical Revival porch and entrance and is remarkably unaltered on its exterior and very well preserved on the interior. One of the few hotels in Hendersonville still operated as such, it was also known as the Carson House and then the Hendersonville Inn. Its plain sturdy brick design and great wraparound porch reflect comfort and integrity, and is a good example of the type of hotel built to handle the influx of visitors and tourists to Hendersonville in the early years. This sector of town was originally filled with other hotels catering to the tourist boom.

Directions: From Main St. take 3rd Ave. heading west. The Aloah Hotel, known today as the Hendersonville Inn, is on your right just beyond Church St.

The Cedars (NRHP)

227 7th Ave.

The Cedars is a large 3.5-story brick veneer hotel built in a Neo-Classical Revival style. It derives its name from the large ancient cedars on the lot in which it stands. The building is highlighted by a monumental Ionic portico that has a deck with railing. The Cedars is the largest and one of the most important of the historic tourist accommodations in Hendersonville. It was built in 1914 for Jennie Bailey, wife of a local Southern Railroad executive. Mrs. Bailey and, later, her daughter operated the hotel until 1976. Today it is privately owned and used for weddings, receptions, parties and club meetings.

The Cedars

Directions: Take 7th Ave. west off of Main St.

Chewning House (NRHP)

755 North Main St.

Located on the same shady street as the Waverly Inn, Chewning House is also one of Hendersonville's treasures. Built sometime between 1888 and 1906 by W.A. Smith, the inn's original name was "The Smith-Green House." The house underwent a complete transformation between 1912 and 1922 when it was enlarged from a two-story building to the present three-story structure. It is a prime example of the simpler domestic architectural styles of the 1920s. Chewning House, like the Waverly next door, still serves its original purpose and today is known as the Claddagh Inn.

Directions: Located on Main St. in downtown Hendersonville.

Clarke-Hobbs-Davidson House (NRHP)

229 5th Ave. West

Built about 1907, the Clarke-Hobbs-Davidson House is one of the most imposing historic residences remaining near downtown Hendersonville. Purchased by the Masons in 1958, it is a 2.5-story brick Queen Anne-Colonial Revival style house that has had a rear brick wing added, nearly doubling the size of the building. The house was probably built by Charles S. Clarke and his wife Louise, and in 1907 it was sold to Alfred J. Hobbs, and thereafter to Charles A. Hobbs and his wife Harriet. In 1911 it was again sold to a Mrs. Davidson who left the property to her brother Edgar Sutton and his wife Eleanor. Since that time it has had a number of other owners, including the Masons, who now operate it as a Masonic Lodge. It is a rare example of a large brick house in Hendersonville at the time of the tourism boom during the early part of the 20th century.

Directions: From Main St., take 5th Ave. heading west. The Clarke-Hobbs-Davidson House will be on your right.

Connemara (NRHP, NHL) — Little River Rd., Flat Rock

Designated a National Historic site because of its association with Carl Sandburg, who lived there from 1945 until his death in 1967. It was built in 1838–1839 by Christopher Gustavus Memminger, later secretary of the treasury of the Confederacy, on land purchased from Charles Baring. Memminger named the house Rock Hill and after his death, the new owner Captain Ellison Adder Smyth, a textile executive, changed the name to Connemara. The farm today includes 264 acres of rolling hills, forests, lakes, goat barn and buildings. The grounds and farm are open for self-guided tours, and guided tours (admission charged) of the home are scheduled daily. (*See* Section IV, Chapter Two Carl Sandburg Home)

Directions: Take Hwy. 225 (Greenville Hwy.) south from Hendersonville. Turn right on Little River Rd. in Flat Rock

Henderson County Courthouse — 200 North Grove St.

Dedicated on April 29, 1995, the Henderson County Courthouse occupies approximately 99,100 square feet on a 13-acre site. Designed by Grier-Fripp Architects of Charlotte NC, and built by M.B. Kahn Construction Company of Greenville, SC, this imposing structure replaced the historic old courthouse on Main St.

The ceilings in the lobby and court waiting areas are painted to resemble the sky with clouds. The clock over the main steps is over five feet in diameter, and the grounds are planted with Japanese Yoshino cherry trees, Japanese Zelkova, and Sugar Maples.

Directions: Located in downtown Hendersonville on North Grove St. North Grove St. parallels North Main St. and is two blocks to the east.

King-Waldrop House (NRHP) — 103 South Washington St.

The King-Waldrop House was built around 1881 and shows features of both the Queen Anne and the Italianate building styles. Its main feature is a square three-stage cupola with a concave pyramidal roof. The general condition of the house is excellent and both the inside, with its dark woodwork and Victorian detailing, and the outside are little altered. The house is an excellent example of the large spacious residences built for the wealthy in Hendersonville in the 1880s. It is one of the few surviving 19th century dwellings in downtown

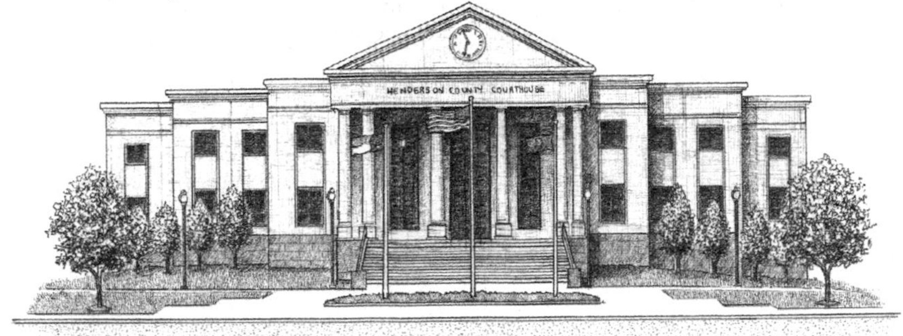

The Henderson County Courthouse, dedicated in 1995

Hendersonville. It was built for Laura V. King, the daughter of Colonel Valentine Ripley, one of Hendersonville's earliest businessmen and entrepreneurs. In 1897, Laura King and Dr. J.G. Waldrop traded houses, and the residence was then titled "Maple Grove" by Dr. Waldrop, who occupied the home with his wife, Nancy, and their eight children.

Directions: Take First Ave. west from Main St. and turn left onto Washington St. The King-Waldrop House is on your right at 103.

Mary Mills Coxe House (NRHP) 1210 Greenville Hwy.

The Mary Mills Coxe House is located south of Hendersonville on the Greenville Hwy., formerly known as Flat Rock Rd. Built around 1911 as a single family residence, it is notable as one of only a handful of pebble dash houses remaining in Henderson County. A Colonial-Revival style dwelling, it is two-and-a-half stories and has as distinctive features a large porch formed by fifteen columns and a roof of pressed metal shingles. The house was built by Mary Mills Coxe, widow of Colonel Franklin Coxe, one of the more influential and wealthy men in Henderson and Buncombe counties. The building is significant historically since it is a very well-preserved pebble dash house that is a rare, unchanged structure that has not been modernized stylistically. The pebble dash stucco walls reflect the influence of noted Asheville architect Richard Sharp Smith.

Directions: Take Main St. heading south. This street turns into Greenville Hwy. The Mary Mills Coxe House is on your left heading toward Flat Rock.

Reese House (NRHP) 202 South Washington St.

The Reese House, built in 1885 by Harriet Louise and William Reese is one of the best preserved Queen Anne style houses in Hendersonville. Wonderfully restored, the house boasts rich, red heart of pine floors, seven fireplaces and hand-carved gingerbread mouldings. On the front lawn is a buckeye tree that was one of the original plantings.

Directions: Just down the street to the south of the King-Waldrop House on South Washington St.

St. James Episcopal Church 766 North Main St.

St. James Episcopal Church, located on Main St. in downtown Hendersonville, is one of the area's most picturesque churches. Consecrated in 1861, the first rector was Rev. N. Collin Hughes. From 1970 to 1980, Henderson County experienced an unprecedented population growth. New economic developments, discovery of Hendersonville as an outstanding retirement area, and growth in tourism marked this period. Consequently, St. James Church flourished and became the largest parish in the Episcopal Diocese of Western North Carolina during that time.

Directions: Located on North Main St.

St. James Episcopal Church

St. John in the Wilderness Church (NRHP) 1895 Greenville Hwy., Flat Rock

A unique spot of southern history in a setting of idyllic beauty, St. John in the Wilderness Episcopal Church in Flat Rock is a gable roof brick church that has at its southeast corner a three-story square tower with pyramidal roof.

In 1833, Charles and Susan Baring built the church as a private chapel, and at the formation of the Episcopal Diocese of Western North Carolina in 1836, the Baring family gave up their rights to the church as a private chapel, turning the deed to the bishop of the newly-formed diocese. The church and graveyard are open daily 9am–4pm for visitation.

Directions: Take Hwy. 225 (Greenville Hwy.) south from Hendersonville.

Thomas Wolfe's Angel Oakdale Cemetery

Highway 64 West

The marble angel statue immortalized by Thomas Wolfe in his novel Look Homeward Angel now stands at Oakdale Cemetery in Hendersonville. The statue was imported from Carrara, Italy by Wolfe's father, and was bought by members of the Johnson family after the death of Mrs. Johnson in 1905. The gravesite belongs to

Thomas Wolf's Angel in Oakdale Cemetery

Reverend and Mrs. H.F. Johnson and their son. In 1975, when the statue was accidentally knocked from its stand, the Henderson County Commissioners had the graves enclosed with a six-foot tall iron picket fence set on a stone wall. This still allows visitors to view the statue and reduces the possibility of damage to the monument.

Directions: From downtown Hendersonville, take Hwy. 64 west. Look for Oakdale Cemetery on your left. The Angel Statue is visible from the road, and the location is indicated by a State Hwy. Marker.

The Waverly Inn (NRHP) 783 North Main St.

Built just after 1898, the Waverly Inn is a three-story Queen Anne style inn. The third story was added in 1910 after a fire did extensive roof damage. With the exception of minor changes, the Waverly has undergone relatively little change and is in remarkably pristine condition. The interior boasts a magnificent Eastlake style stair and twenty-one guest rooms, with seventeen bathrooms. Today the Waverly is still operated as an inn.

Directions: Located on North Main St. in downtown Hendersonville.

Chapter Four

Hendersonville Parks

Natural beauty abounds in the Hendersonville and Flat Rock areas, from enchanting apple orchards to lush green valleys and rugged mountains. Visitors to the area are only minutes away from a wide variety of natural attractions and opportunities for outdoor recreation. Chimney Rock Park, Lake Lure, and area waterfalls are covered separately in Section V, Chapter One.

Hendersonville City Parks

Hendersonville maintains seven city parks, listed below, that are easily accessible. The most popular is the 20-acre Patton Park located on Patton Ave. Hendersonville City Parks, Public Works Department, 415 8th Ave. East, Hendersonville NC 28792, 828-697-3084.

Patton Park: Hwy. 25 north to Patton Ave.
Boyd Park: 840 Church St.
Edwards Park: North Main St. and Locust St.
Green Meadows Park: Ash St. and Park View Dr.
King Memorial Park: 7th Ave. and Robinson Terrace
Toms Park: Allen St. and Lily Pond Rd., shuffleboard
Lennox Park: Park Dr. off Whitted St.

Henderson County Parks

Maintained by the Henderson County Parks and Recreation Department, there are seven parks total over 259 acres of playing fields, recreation facilities, woodland and playgrounds. The major park is Jackson Park on Glover St. Henderson County Parks & Recreation Department, 801 Glover St., Hendersonville NC 28792. 828-697-4884.

Jackson Park: 801 Glover St., Hendersonville NC 28792. 828-697-4888.

Established in 1974, is located conveniently near downtown Hendersonville, and covers 212 acres in Henderson County. The parks' facilities include 4 picnic shelters, 9 baseball fields, cross country courses for local middle and high schools, soccer fields, 8 tennis courts, a BMX track, playgrounds, and many walking trails, providing a central location for many community sports and activities. The park is home to several species of birds, wildlife, and plants, making the park a great place to observe nature. Jackson Park is noted for its great bird watching also.

Black Bears: Spirit of the Mountains

If any animal personifies the spirit of the Western North Carolina mountains, it is the black bear. They inhabited these mountains long before the Cherokees arrived and it is estimated that the entire population numbers around 4,000 for the Southern Appalachians, with the heart of bear country located in the Great Smoky Mountains National Park. With over 500,000 acres, it is the largest protected bear habitat east of the Mississippi. Over 1,000 bears are estimated to live in the park, one of the highest densities anywhere.

Although only one human death has ever been recorded in the Great Smokies, bears are to be respected. Each year there are an average of seven bear incidents reported that involve human injury, and over 150 incidents each year of property damage—coolers destroyed, backpacks ripped open, cars scratched and tents torn down. Most of these incidents involved violation of a primary rule—don't feed the bears!

The black bear has long been held as a symbol of power by the Cherokee Indians, both on the land and in the psyche. And to visitors, the bear is the one animal that is hoped to be seen, perhaps for similar reasons. More than any other animal, it is an embodiment of the wilderness and represents the mystery and power of the mountains.

Section V
Western North Carolina

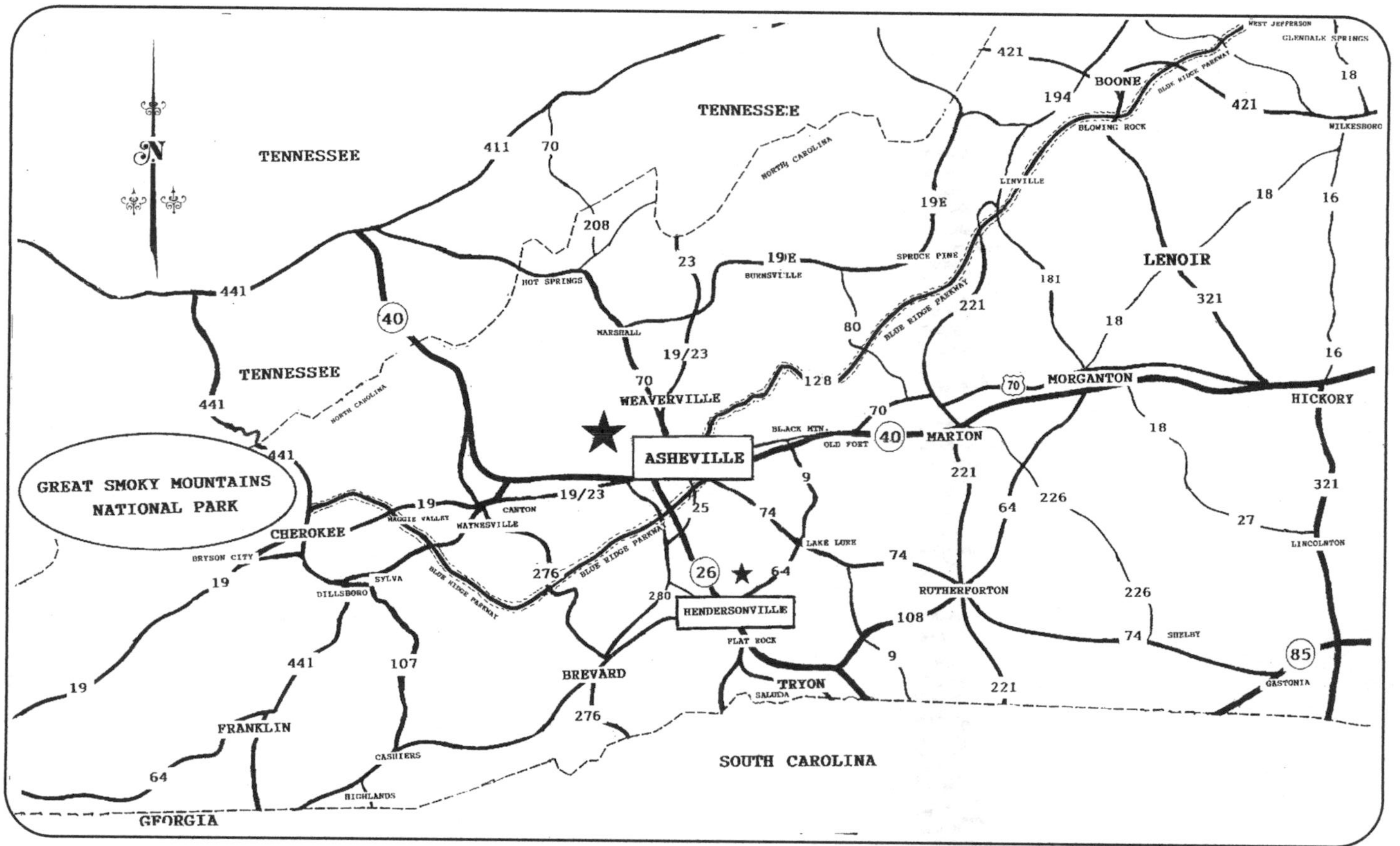

Western North Carolina

Chapter One

Natural Attractions

Waterfalls in Western North Carolina

In Transylvania County, within an hour's drive of Asheville, are a number of truly spectacular waterfalls. These Brevard area waterfalls are a national treasure and worth a visit at any time of the year. In fact Transylvania County is known as "The Land of Waterfalls." There are hundreds to choose from, many of which are easy to get to, and some even visible from the highway. The most popular and easily accessible is Looking Glass Falls in the Pisgah National Forest. To plan a great day trip to the falls, first check in at the Brevard Chamber of Commerce Visitor Center and pick up a copy of their "Land of the Waterfalls" guide and map. Be sure to take a picnic lunch. Besides the Brevard area waterfalls, there are others worth mentioning and are listed below. A cautionary note: when visiting waterfalls, keep in mind that while they are beautiful, they can also be treacherous. Death or injury may be only seconds away if one misjudges the force of moving water or height of the cascades. Rocks are slippery when wet. Do not attempt to climb the rocks beside the falls or venture near the top. Viewing the falls is safe, family fun only if you stay on the designated trails and viewing areas.

Looking Glass Falls in the Brevard Area

Location: Pisgah National Forest
Distance: 1 hour from Asheville
Address: Highway 276, Pisgah National Forest
Telephone: Pisgah District Office: 828-877-3350, 828-257-4203
Website: s.usda.gov/detail/nfsnc/specialplaces/?cid=stelprdb5188439
Fees: None
About: A short drive into Pisgah Forest, these popular waterfalls are visible from, and located right beside, the paved road.
Directions: From Asheville, take NC 280 South. NC 280 begins as Airport Rd. after you leave Hendersonville Hwy. (US 25). Take a right into Pisgah National Forest at Hwy. 276 in Pisgah Forest just before you reach Brevard. Follow 276 for 6 miles.

Lower Falls at Graveyard Fields on Blue Ridge Parkway

Location: Pisgah National Forest, Blue Ridge Parkway
Distance: 1 hour from Asheville
Address: Milepost 418, Blue Ridge Parkway
Telephone: Pisgah District Office: 828-877-3350, 828-257-4203
Fees: None
About: One of the most popular recreational stops on the parkway, Graveyard Fields has wonderful hiking trails. The trail to the Lower Falls is a short 20 minute hike and worth every step. Restrooms located in parking lot.
Directions: From Asheville, take Blue Ridge Parkway south to Milepost 418.

Other Notable Waterfalls

Brevard Area west of Asheville

Bird Rock Falls: Take Hwy. 64 West from Brevard 8.5 miles and turn right on NC 215. Continue approximately 9 miles. Falls are on the left just below the confluence of Shoal-Creek and the North Fork of the French Broad River in the Balsam Grove Community.

Bridal View Falls: Bridal Veil Falls is unique because you can drive your car right underneath it! The water falls 120 feet from above, right over the highway. From Brevard take Hwy. 64 West, and look for the sign 2.5 miles west of Highlands in the Cullasaja Gorge.

Cullasaja Falls: The lower portion of Cullasaja Falls is a cascade of water which flows about 250 feet down. It is located on the Cullasaja River, 9 miles west of Highlands off Hwy. 64 in the Cullasaja Gorge. Cullasaja Falls is only visible from your car as there is no adequate pull-off spot from the road.

Rainbow Falls: Follow Hwy. 64 West from Brevard 18 miles to Whitewater Rd. (NC 281) and turn left 2.5 miles. A trail begins at a turn in the road and continues downstream past Dr.ift Falls a half-mile to the 200 foot high Rainbow Falls.

Silver Run Falls: Silver Run Falls has a drop of 30 feet into a quiet pool below, and is located off NC 197, 4.1 miles south of Cashiers. Park in the pull-off on the left.

Toxaway Falls: Take Hwy. 64 West from Brevard 15.5 miles. The highway crosses the top of the falls 123 feet just below Toxaway Dam. The area was named Toxaway (Red Bird) by the Cherokee Indians. Easily visible from the road.

Whitewater Falls: A spectacular plunge of 411 feet makes this the tallest waterfall east of the Mississippi. A park with parking and restrooms provides easy access. Take US 64 West from Brevard, go 18 miles to Whitewater Rd. (NC 281), turn left 8 miles to park entrance on left. Falls can be viewed from the end of a paved road 100 yards from the parking area.

Chimney Rock Area south of Asheville

Hickory Nut Falls: Located in Chimney Rock Park, this waterfall is 404 feet high, making it one of the tallest in the eastern United States. The park has an short hiking trail, which leads to the base of this magnificent falls. To see this waterfall, you must purchase a ticket to enter Chimney Rock Park. While you are there visit the famous Chimney Rock Attraction. (*See* Section V, Chapter One)

Franklin Area west of Asheville

Dry Falls: Dry Falls is located on Hwy. 64 between Franklin and Highlands, and you can find the falls with a short, easy walk. Once there you can walk right behind them without getting wet! A well-marked path and handrail to guide you behind and around the 75-foot curtain of rushing water.

Blue Ridge Parkway north of Asheville

Linville Falls: Linville Falls is located on the Blue Ridge Parkway at milepost 316.3. Two main hiking trails lead to great views of the falls which drop into the spectacular Linville Gorge. It is probably the most photographed in the state, and is considered one of the most beautiful. Both begin at the Linville Falls Visitor Center, which is operated by the National Park Service (open only in the late spring to fall). The trails range in difficulty from moderate to strenuous. Access is from the Blue Ridge Parkway (closed in winter) or by taking a slightly faster route using I-40 east to Marion, getting off at the US Hwy 221 exit in Marion and heading north. Take 221 all the way to the Blue Ridge Parkway, go north on the Parkway about a mile to Linville Falls.

Morganton Area east of Asheville

Upper Creek Falls: A steep, 0.8-mile trail leads to this popular cascading waterfall. Upper Creek Falls is located in the Jonas Ridge Area of Burke County, and is only accessible by hiking in. The Falls are located 13.5 miles from Morganton. Take NC 181 North from Morganton. The parking area is on the right about 6 miles north of the Pisgah National Forest boundary.

Natural Attractions North of Asheville

Appalachian National Scenic Trail

The Appalachian Trail is a 2,167-mile footpath from Maine to Georgia that follows the ridge tops of the fourteen states through which it passes. Each day, as many as two hundred backpackers are in the process of hiking the full length of the trail. On average, it takes about four to five months to hike the entire length. More than 250 backcountry shelters are located along the Appalachian Trail at varying intervals, as a service to all Appalachian Trail hikers. A typical shelter, sometimes called a "lean-to," has a shingled or metal roof, a wooden floor and three walls, and is open to the elements on one side. Most are near a creek or spring, and many have a privy nearby. Hikers occupy them on a first-come, first-served basis until the shelter is full. They are intended for individual hikers, not big groups.

The Appalachian Trail Conservancy website has more complete information for hikers who intend to camp on the trail. The Trail, which passes through North Carolina, was conceived by Benton MacKaye in the 1920s. With the support of local hiking clubs and interested individuals, MacKaye's dream eventually became a reality. By 1937 the trail was completed

Swallowtail butterfly

by opening a two-mile stretch in a densely wooded area between Spaulding and Sugarloaf Mountains in Maine. It may be entered at many points as it passes through North Carolina for over 300 miles.

Location: The trail passes to the north of Asheville
Address: Appalachian Trail Conference Southern Regional Offices: 160-A Zillicoa St., Asheville NC 28801
Telephone: Appalachian Trail Conservancy 828-254-3708
Website: appalachiantrail.org
Distance: From Asheville, approximately 30 miles (a 45-minute drive)
Resources: Appalachian National Scenic Trail, (National Park Service) Appalachian National Scenic Trail, PO Box 50, Harpers Ferry WV 25425; 304-535-6278
Directions: Closest access is at Sams Gap, on the North Carolina/Tennessee line. Take US 19/23 north to the state line. Look for the parking on the west side. Just before the parking lot at the crest of the ridge is a trail sign. The parking lot is just before 19/23 becomes a four-lane road. After parking, walk back along 19/23 about 100 meters to access the trail.

Max Patch

Max Patch is one of Western North Carolina's best kept secrets, and it is located about 40 miles north of Asheville in the Hot Springs area. It is 300 acres of a grassy bald that is 4,629 feet at its highest point, and from which, on clear days, one can see Mount Mitchell to the east and the Great Smokies far off in the west! Some balds are naturally occurring areas in the mountains where trees do not grow and only flowers and grasses have taken hold. In Max's case, evidently it was cleared by sheep and cattle in the 1800s and has remained as such, with a little mowing help from the U.S. Forest Service. Max Patch is a premier example of a southern mountain bald, and if you have a half-day free, it is well worth the trip. Great panoramic views and a hundreds of places to picnic or camp await those making the trip.

The area is closed to motor vehicles however, although there is road access and parking near the summit, which requires about a 1/4 mile uphill walk. Visitors are encouraged to travel the area by foot and enjoy the fresh mountain air and clear views of open country. Many visitors come to Max Patch to camp, fly kites and walk the Appalachian Trail.

Location: Madison County NC
Distance: 1 hour from Asheville
Directions: From Asheville take Leicester Hwy. North 30 miles to NC 209. Follow 209 about 7 miles to Meadow Fork Rd. (State Rd. 1175). Follow this road south 5.3 miles to State Rd. 1181. Follow 1181 for 2 miles (will turn into gravel). At the top of the mountain, the road intersects with State Rd. 1182. Turn right and drive about 3 miles to the Max Patch parking area, which will be on your right. From the parking area, it is a short 1.4 miles to the top.

Natural Attractions South of Asheville

Apple Orchards in Henderson County

Henderson County, North Carolina, is the seventh largest apple producing county in the United States and is one of the leading producer of apples in the Southeast, producing over 85% of the apples grown in North Carolina. Its main city, Hendersonville, is home to the famous North Carolina Apple Festival, held every summer. Apple orchards in the county range in size from small family backyard plantings to some with over 600 acres. The most popular varieties are Rome, Red Delicious, Golden Delicious, Gala, Fuji, and Jonagold. An average of one million mature apple trees are growing on nine thousand acres producing approximately 5 million bushels of apples per year. A drive in the country out Route 64 heading east through Edneyville toward Chimney Rock will take you past some very scenic apple orchards as well as past roadside stands that sell fresh apples and cider. There are also a number of orchards where you may pick you own apples. The Blue Ridge Farm Direct Market Association website, ncapples.com, has more information about specific apple orchards and roadside stands, as well as maps to these locations.

Location: South of Asheville in Henderson County

Telephone: Blue Ridge Farm Direct Market Association (Hendersonville NC Apple Growers) 828-697-4891

Website: ncapples.com

Directions: From Asheville take I-26 south toward Hendersonville. Take Exit 49 and proceed east on NC Hwy. 64 toward Edneyville. The apple orchards begin a few miles down Hwy. 64.

Chimney Rock State Park

Chimney Rock Park is a natural scenic attraction nestled in the foothills of the Blue Ridge Mountains just above Lake Lure. Southeast of Asheville and only a short drive from Hendersonville, this 1,000-acre park provides breathtaking views from its many trails and from the top of the 315-foot monolithic "Chimney Rock." Towering 315 feet over the village of Chimney Rock, the park, which was privately owned, in 2007 became Chimney Rock State Park, one of the newest North Carolina state parks. With an elevation range from about 1,100 feet to 2,800 feet, the park is expanding to include some 5,000 acres.

Chimney Rock Park

The park features three hiking trails that lead to the 404-foot Hickory Nut Falls, one of the highest waterfalls in the eastern United

States. At 2,280 feet above sea level, Chimney Rock is a 535-million-year-old remnant of igneous rock. You can climb a trail to its top, or take the 26-story elevator carved out of solid rock if you wish. The movie "Last of the Mohicans" was filmed at Chimney Rock, and you may recognize part of the Cliff Trail from scenes in the film. Picnic tables and grills are located along the roadway to the Chimney Rock, and a less strenuous trail leads to the base of Hickory Nut Falls. There is also a nature center on the access road where you may learn about the flora, fauna and geology of the park.

Location: Southeast of Asheville
Address: Box 39, Chimney Rock NC 28740
Distance: From Asheville, approximately 25 miles
Telephone: 828-625-9611, 800-277-9611
Website: chimneyrockpark.com
Hours: Open year-round except Thanksgiving, Christmas and New Year's Day; 8:30am–4:30pm
Fees: Adult and child rates
Allow: 2–3 hours
Directions: From Asheville, take I-240 East to Exit 9 (Bat Cave, Blue Ridge Parkway) and continue on Hwy. 74A through Fairview and Hickory Nut Gap to Chimney Rock. From Hendersonville, take Hwy. 64 East. Turn right on Hwy. 74 to Chimney Rock.

Holmes Educational State Forest

North Carolina has six Educational State Forests that have been developed as living environmental education centers. These forests are designed to promote a better understanding of the value of forests in our lives. Holmes Forest, located in the Blue Ridge Mountains, offers a rich mixture of mountain hardwoods, rhododendron, flame azaleas and a variety of wildflowers. These features are accessible to the visiting public by a series of well-marked trails accented by exhibits and displays depicting the ecology of the managed forest. Picnic sites with tables and grills are provided, and ranger-conducted programs are available to groups visiting the 235-acre forest.

Location: Just west of Hendersonville
Address: 1299 Crab Creek Rd., Hendersonville NC 28739
Telephone: 828-692-0100
Website: ncesf.org/hesf/home.htm
Hours: Mid-Mar. to the day Fri before Thanksgiving. Closed Mon, Tue–Fri 9am–5pm, Sat and Sun 11am–8pm DST/11am–5pm ST.
Fees: None
Allow: Two hours
Directions: From Hendersonville take Kanuga Rd. west 8 miles. Forest is on the left.

Jump Off Rock

Legend has it that more than 300 years ago a young Indian maiden leapt from this rock to her death when she learned that her lover, a Cherokee chief, had been killed in battle. Indian lore to this day maintains that on some moonlit nights the ghost of the heartbroken maiden can be seen on the rock. Views from the rock are breathtaking of the valleys below during daylight hours and are also especially noteworthy at sunset. The rock itself is surrounded by landscaped grounds.

Location: South of Asheville in the Laurel Park section of Hendersonville.
Fees: None
Directions: From Asheville take I-26 south toward Hendersonville. Get off at Exit 49 and take NC Hwy. 64 west toward Hendersonville. After it passes North Main St., it becomes 7th Ave. West. Continue on this road a short distance and turn left on Buncombe St. Proceed down Buncombe St. two blocks and turn right onto 5th Ave. West. Continue on 5th Ave. West as it turns into Laurel Park Hwy. Follow Laurel Park Hwy. to the very end to find Jump Off Rock.

Lake Lure

Located southeast of Hendersonville just below Chimney Rock is sparkling Lake Lure, selected by National Geographic as one of the ten most spectacular and beautiful man-made lakes in the world. Over 1,500 acres of crystal clear water and 27 miles of inviting shoreline await the visitor to this majestic body of water. A marina and sandy beaches are open to the public and boat tours of the lake, offered by Lake Lure Tours, are a popular attraction. The boat tour dock is located at Lake Lure Marina, off of highway 64/74A.

Location: Southeast of Asheville
Distance: From Asheville, approximately 30 miles, a 45-minute drive
Address: Lake Lure Boat Tours, 2930 Memorial Hwy., Lake Lure NC 28746 (located at Lake Lure Marina)
Telephone: Lake Lure Tours: 828-625-1373, 877-386-4255
Website: lakelure.com
Hours: Lake Lure Tours: Mar.–Nov. Daily cruises on the hour from 10am–5 p.m
Fees: Lake Lure Tours: Adult and child rates, Swimming at beach, no fee.
Allow: Cruises take one hour
Directions: From Hendersonville, take Hwy. 64 West. Turn right on Hwy. 74. Go through Chimney Rock to Lake Lure. From Asheville, take I-240 East to Exit 9 (Bat Cave, Blue Ridge Parkway) and continue on Hwy. 74A through Hickory Nut Gap and Chimney Rock. Lake Lure is one mile past Chimney Rock.

North Mills River Recreation Area

The North Mills River Recreation Area and Campground is part of the Pisgah District of the Pisgah National Forest and is a great place to take kids on a picnic. Bring inner tubes and rubber rafts. A gentle yet bold stream provides the perfect place for summer fun. The section of the stream where the kids tube even has a natural beach area. There are over 39 picnic units with grills along the river for cookouts, and large ball playing fields and walking trails along the river. For campers there are 32 excellent primitive campsites which can accommodate tents and some sites that can accommodate RVs up to 22 feet in length. No hookups available.

Location: 20 minutes west of Hendersonville
Address: 5289 North Mills River Rd. Mills River NC 28742
Telephone: 828-890-3284, 877-457-4023, Reservations: 877-444-6777
Hours: Open year round with limited service Nov.–Mar.
Fees: Yes, Federal Interagency Pass, Senior and Access discount accepted.
Directions: From downtown Hendersonville take Hwy. 191 north toward the community of Mills River. Go approximately 13 miles. Turn left onto North Mills Rd. to the recreation area.

Pearson's Falls

This botanical preserve, owned and maintained by the Tryon Garden Club, is comprised of 268 acres of native forest, granite, spring-fed streams and a moderate ¼ mile trail to a 90 ft. waterfall. There are over 200 species of rare wildflowers, as well as plants. Mosses, lichens and trees are in the glen which is classified as a deciduous climax forest.

Location: Between Tryon and Saluda NC
Distance: 1 hour from Asheville
Address: 2748 Pearson Falls Rd., Saluda NC 28773
Telephone: 828-749-3031
Website: pearsonsfalls.org
Hours: Mar.–Oct.: Mon–Sat 10am–5:15pm, Sun 12–5:15pm; Nov.–Feb.: Mon–Sat 10am–4:15pm, Sun 12–4:15pm
Fees: Adult and child rates. Under Six: Free
Directions: From Asheville take I-26 south toward Hendersonville. Take exit 59 toward Saluda and turn right at State Rd 1142 . Take 3rd left onto Thompson Rd. for 2 miles and turn left at US 176E. Turn right at Old Melrose Rd./Pearson Falls Rd.

Natural Attractions East of Asheville

Blue Ridge Parkway

The Blue Ridge Parkway is ranked "America's most scenic drive" by leading travel writers. Following mountain crests from the Shenandoah National Park in Virginia to the Great Smoky Mountains National Park in North Carolina and Tennessee, the Parkway is the gateway to a wondrous mountain empire. The Parkway's 469 toll-free miles of awesome natural beauty, combined with the pioneer history of gristmills, weathered cabins and split-rail fences, create one of the most popular areas in the national park system. This extraordinary region encompasses a world of mountain forest, wildlife and wildflowers thousands of feet above a patchwork of villages, fields and farms.

Passing right through Asheville, the Parkway is easily accessible to visitors. Located at Milepost 384 just southeast of Asheville is the newly constructed Blue Ridge Parkway Destination Center. A unique feature about the Parkway is that there are no tolls. Speed limits are set at a leisurely 45 miles per hour, and stops are frequent with more than 250 overlooks on the parkway that offer magnificent uninterrupted views. More than 600 million visitors have traveled the Parkway over the years since it opened in the 1930s.

A free Parkway trip planning information packet is available by writing to the Blue Ridge Parkway Association, PO Box 2136, Asheville NC 28802. This packet contains maps, the official Park Service Trip map, guides, and other useful information. Much of this information is also available at the parkway website (blueridgeparkway.org). A complete list of hiking trails that can be accessed from the Blue Ridge Parkway is presented in Section II, Chapter One6.

A nonprofit organization, Friends of the Blue Ridge Parkway, continues to work toward the preservation of the environmental heritage of the Parkway. This grassroots organization welcomes memberships in its work to preserve and protect the Parkway. Information about Friends of the Blue Ridge Parkway can be obtained by calling, 800-228-7275 or by writing them at PO Box 20986, Roanoke, VA 24108. Another organization dedicated to preserving the Blue Ridge Parkway is the Blue Ridge Parkway Foundation (brpfoundation.org). They fund specific programs and projects that further the parkway's preservations, protection, and enhancement. For further information, call 336-721-0260 or write 717 South Marshall St., Ste 105B, Winston-Salem NC 27101.

Camping is allowed along the parkway May.–Oct. at designated sites, many requiring a small fee that covers the use of a fireplace and table. Winter camping is allowed, weather permitting. Facilities are limited and you will need to check in advance. Copies of campground regulations are available at Parkway Visitor Centers, and are posted at all campgrounds. Campgrounds near Asheville are at Linville Falls (Milepost 316.3; 50 tent, 20 RV sites), Crabtree Meadows (Milepost 339.5; 71 tent, 22 RV sites) and Mount Pisgah (Milepost 408.6; 70 tent, 70 RV sites).

Location: The Parkway begins at Fort Royal, Virginia, and ends in Cherokee, North Carolina. It goes right through the east side of Asheville, running north to south overall.

Address: 195 Hemphill Knob Rd., Asheville NC 28803

Telephone: Parkway Information: 828-298-0398, 828-259-0701, 828-271-4779, Emergency Parkway Telephone: 800-727-5928, Parkway Headquarters: 828-271-4779, Visitor Information: 828-271-4779

Website: blueridgeheritage.com

Fees: None

Directions: From Asheville, take I-240 East and get off at Exit 9 (Bat Cave, Blue Ridge Parkway). Take Hwy. 74A East to parkway entrance roads. It is also accessible off of Tunnel Rd. (US 70) near the V.A. Hospital in East Asheville and Brevard Rd. (Hwy. 191) in South Asheville past the Biltmore Square Mall.

Tips: The Parkway is closed intermittently during the winter due to ice and snow. Peak traffic is during the summer months and especially the autumn leaf season. With a 45-mph speed limit on a windingtwo-lane road, be prepared for a leisurely trip.

Lodging on the Parkway within one hour of Asheville

The Pisgah Inn: Located at 5,000 feet, and less than an hour's drive from Asheville south on the Parkway at Milepost 408, the historic Pisgah Inn provides breath-taking views, fine dining in a casual atmosphere, comfortable accommodations, unique area crafts and gifts and an incomparable escape into the mountains of Western North Carolina. PO Box 749, Waynesville NC 28786; 828-235-8228. pisgahinn.com

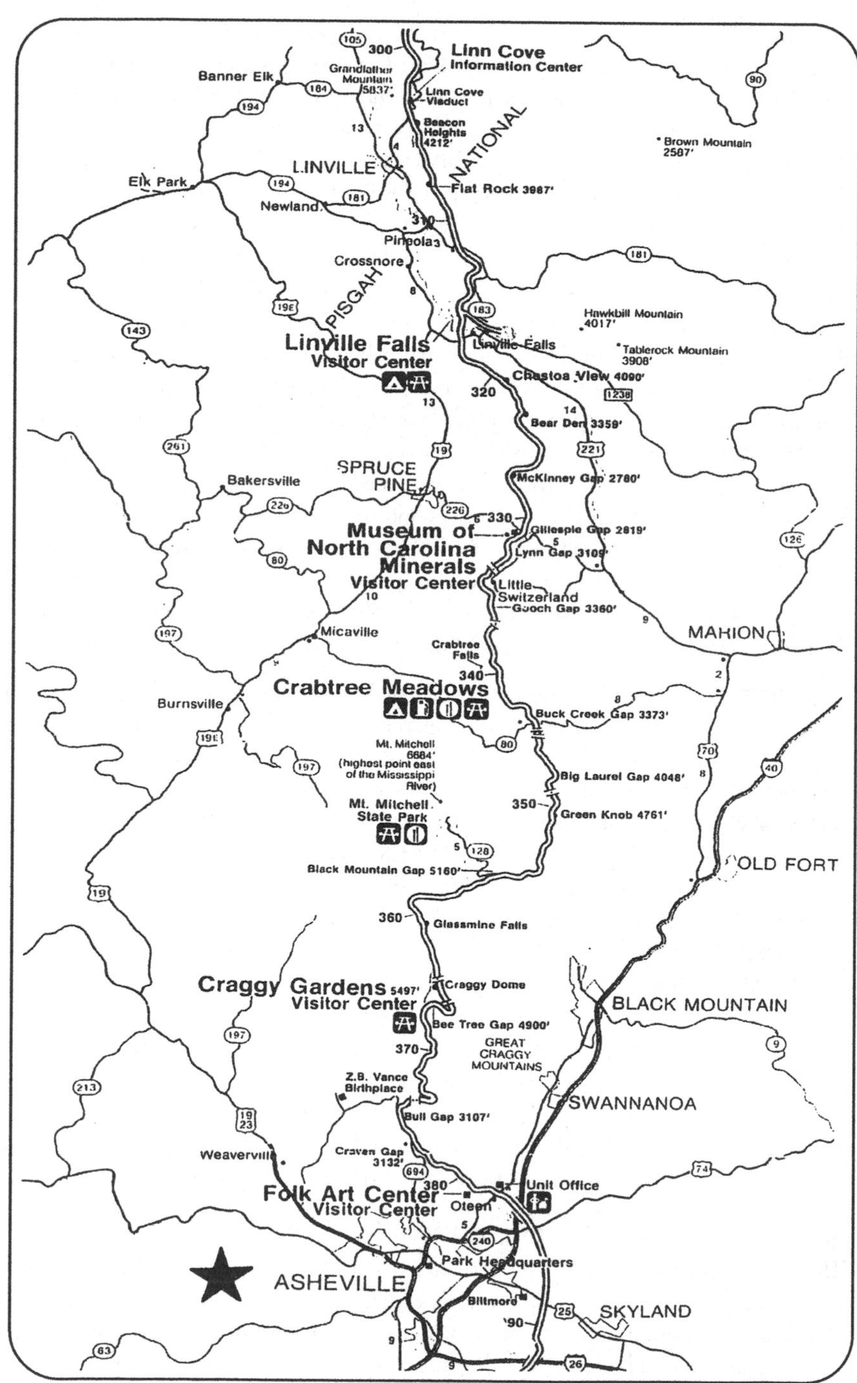

Blue Ridge Parkway North of Asheville

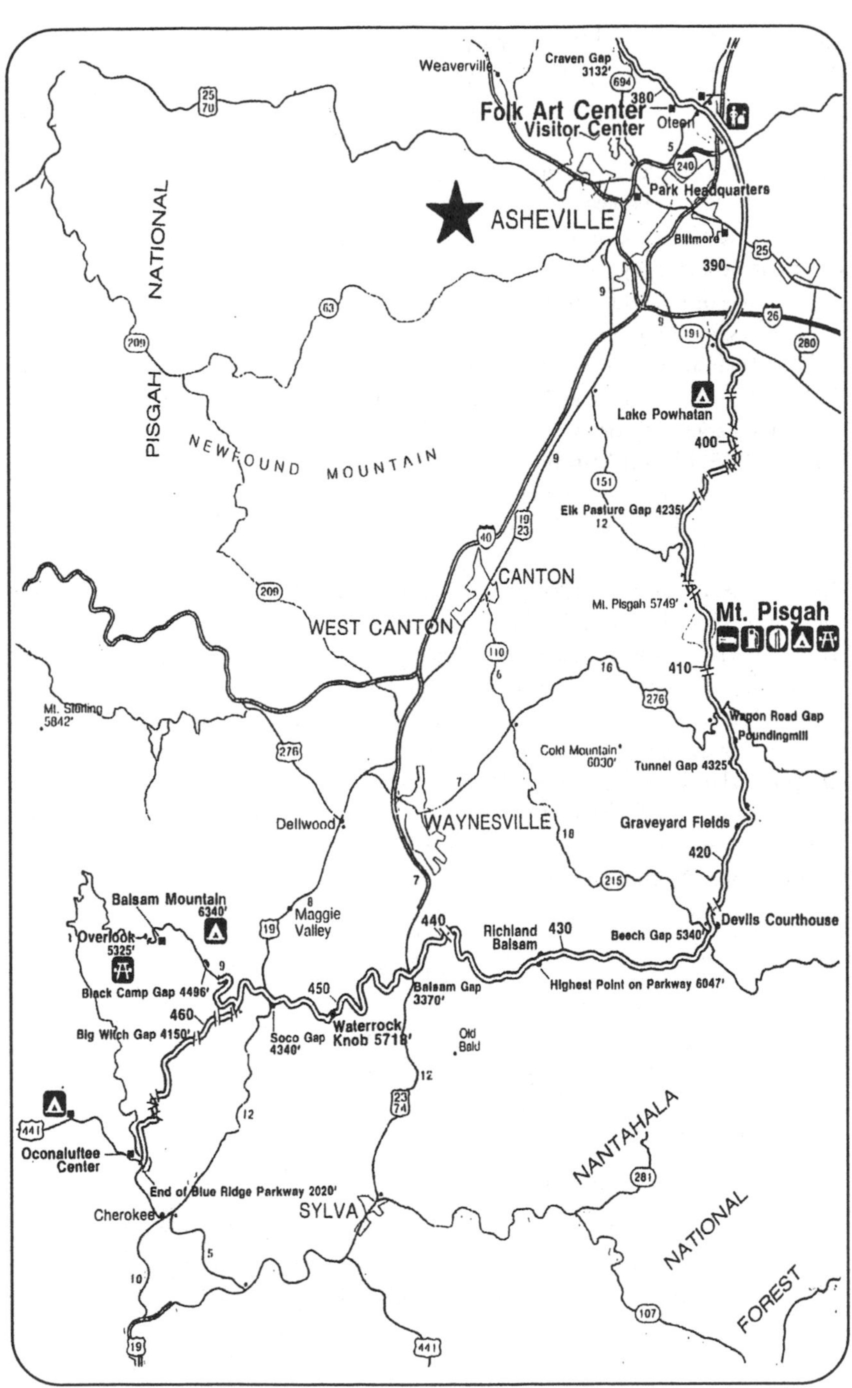

Blue Ridge Parkway South of Asheville

Parkway Attractions Near Asheville Heading North

Milepost 384, Blue Ridge Parkway Destination Center: The Blue Ridge Parkway Destination Center is the major exhibit and education center on the parkway. (*See* Section III, Chapter Two)

Milepost 382, Folk Art Center: Located just east of Asheville, the Folk Art Center offers a look at traditional and contemporary crafts of the Appalachian region through interpretive programs, a museum and library. (*See* Section III, Chapter Two)

Milepost 364, Craggy Gardens: Craggy Gardens is an area of exposed rocks and high peaks that provides breathtaking views. Large expanses of native rhododendron cover its slopes and summits. In mid-Jun., pink and purple blooms of these Catawba rhododendrons are at their peak. This popular stop has restrooms, nature exhibits, and is open May.–Oct. Well-marked trails lead through the rhododendron thickets to Craggy Dome's awe-inspiring views.

Milepost 355, Mount Mitchell: Mount Mitchell State Park offers tent camping, trails, nature study, picnic area, natural history museum and restaurant. At 6,684 feet above sea level, it is the highest peak in the eastern United States. 828-675-4611. (*See* other listing on Mount Mitchell in this chapter for complete information)

Milepost 331, Museum of North Carolina Minerals: Displays of over 300 varieties of minerals found in North Carolina. Open 9–5 daily. (*See* Section V, Chapter Two)

Milepost 317, Linville Caverns: North Carolina's only caverns open year-round. Smooth paths takes visitors deep into the innermost recesses of this beautiful underground fairyland. Located on route 221, between Linville and Marion NC. (*See* main Linville Caverns listing later in this chapter for complete information)

Milepost 316, Linville Gorge: Located off NC 105 in the Pisgah National Forest. Excellent hiking trails that lead to superb views of Linville Falls. Linville Gorge is one of the most spectacular sites in North Carolina. (*See* main Linville Gorge listing later in this chapter for complete information)

Craggy Gardens

Milepost 305, Grandfather Mountain: One of North Carolina's top scenic attractions. Extraordinary views, wildlife habitats, famous Mile High Swinging Bridge, trails, picnic areas, nature museum, restaurant and theatre. (*See* main Grandfather Mountain listing in this chapter for complete information)

Milepost 304, Linn Cove Viaduct: Linn Cove Viaduct is a spectacular bridge that offers outstanding views and is noteworthy for its elegant and unique construction. Opened in 1987, this engineering marvel represents the final link in the construction of the Blue Ridge Parkway. The Viaduct is the most complicated concrete bridge ever built, snaking around boulder-strewn Linn Cove in a sweeping "S" curve.

Milepost 294, Moses H. Cone Memorial Park: This great mountain park has hiking and horseback riding trails, and Flat Top Manor houses the Parkway Craft Center. No fees, and the Craft Center is open from Mid-Mar. to Nov., 9am–5pm Ranger-guided activities are also available throughout the summer.

Parkway Attractions Near Asheville Heading South:

Milepost 408, Pisgah Inn at Mount Pisgah: Mount Pisgah was part of the original 145,000 acre parcel bought in the 1800's by George Vanderbilt to build his estate. The area is now the Pisgah National Forest. Located on the parkway is the historic Pisgah Inn, a great place to stop for a meal. A moderately strenuous hiking trail leads from the inn to the Mount Pisgah Overlook.

Milepost 412, Cradle of Forestry: Four miles south of the parkway on US 276 is the Cradle of Forestry, a National Historic Site located in the Pisgah National Forest. The Cradle of Forestry was the birthplace of American forestry. Visitors will find forestry

Linn Cove Viaduct

The old Pisgah Inn

exhibits, guided tours, restored historic buildings, craft exhibits and more. 1002 Pisgah Hwy. (*See* Section V, Chapter Two)

Milepost 418, Graveyard Fields: An unusual flat area that takes its name from the mounds dotting the site, which are remains of fallen trees, victims of a 1925 Thanksgiving Eve fire. One of the most popular recreational sites on the parkway. Wonderful easy hiking trails, river crossings, waterfalls, camping and swimming in the summer.

Milepost 469, Mountain Farm Museum: Located at the southern end of the Parkway on US Hwy. 441, the Mountain Farm Museum is a National Park Service reconstruction of early pioneer farm buildings that show a past lifestyle. 497–1900. Located nearby also is Oconaluftee Visitors Center, which has restrooms, exhibits and park information.

Brown Mountain Lights

To the east of Asheville, near Morganton in Burke County, lies Brown Mountain. Rising to an elevation of only 2,600 feet, this foothills mountain has been at the center of a mystery since the earliest days of recorded history. For hundreds of years, lights have been seen on the mountain to the astonishment of all that have seen them. Cherokee Indians were familiar with the lights as far back as the year 1200, and their legends claim the lights are the spirits of Indian maidens searching for their fallen husbands and sweethearts. Early scientists, including German engineer Gerard William de Brahm, Dr. W.J. Humphreys of the Weather Bureau, and members of the U.S. Geological Survey, studied the lights and offered various explanations, none of which has stood the test of time. In fact, there has been no satisfactory explanation to date, making the lights one of North Carolina's most enduring mysteries as well as one of its most famous legends. Possible explanations that have been rejected by the scientific community include nitrous vapor emissions, locomotive or automobile reflections,

"Andes Light" manifestations, marsh gas spontaneous combustion, moonshine still reflections, electrical phenomenon such as St. Elmo's Fire, mirages, UFOs, radioactive uranium ore emissions, and atmospheric reflections from nearby Hickory, Lenoir, or other area towns.

The lights are visible from several locations, the most popular being Brown Mountain Overlook, located 20 miles north of Morganton on NC Hwy.181 one mile south of the Barkhouse Picnic area; Wiseman's View Overlook, located five miles south of the village of Linville Falls on Kistler Memorial Hwy. (Old NC 105/SR 1238); and Lost Cove Cliffs Overlook, located on the Blue Ridge Parkway at Milepost 310, two miles north of the NC 181 junction.

Brown Mountain lights have been seen as far away as Blowing Rock and the old Yonahlossee Trail over Grandfather Mountain twelve miles away. The lights are an irregular and somewhat rare occurrence and are not always visible. Your best chance of seeing them is on a night with clear weather conditions, good visibility, and little to no moonlight. Witnesses have reported seeing them at all hours of the night between sundown and sunrise. The lights vary widely in appearance, at times seeming like large balls of fire from a Roman candle, sometimes rising to various heights and fading, at other times expanding as they rise to finally burst without a sound.

It is best to keep your expectations low since there is absolutely no certainty that the lights will be visible. In this case, the journey is just as important as the destination. The adventure of looking, not finding, should be your focus. In any event, you will be participating in a North Carolina mystery that has baffled plenty of smart people over the years!

Location: Near Morganton, North Carolina (*See* viewing locations above)
Distance: 1.5–2 hours from Asheville
Telephone: 828-433-6793 (Morganton Visitor Information Center)
Directions: To Lost Cove Cliffs Overlook on Blue Ridge Parkway: From Asheville, take I-40 East to Morganton and NC 181 North. The Blue Ridge Parkway is a more scenic though slower alternative (allow three hours). Follow the parkway north from the Tunnel Rd. (US 70) entrance to Milepost 310.

Grandfather Mountain and Grandfather Mountain State Park

Grandfather Mountain's pristine wildlife and sweeping vistas are perfect for rejuvenation, excitement, and creating family memories. With amazing panoramic views from the Mile High Swinging Bridge, Grandfather Mountain is a place where you can stand eye-to-eye with native wildlife in natural habitats and learn more about the wonders around you from their museum, trails, and friendly naturalists.

One third of the Mountain is operated as a scenic travel destination by the Grandfather Mountain Stewardship Foundation. All proceeds from sales of tickets and souvenirs go toward preserving Grandfather Mountain and sharing its wonders in ways that deepen visitors' appreciation of nature and inspire good stewardship of the earth. The other two thirds of the wild and undeveloped sections of Grandfather Mountain is owned by the state of North Carolina. Accessible only on foot, visitors to Grandfather Mountain State Park can hike several miles of rugged alpine trails that lead across or around rock walls and pinnacles (often with the aid of cables and ladders) through high-elevation terrain unlike any other in the Southeast.

Location: Linville N.C.
Distance: 2 hours from Asheville
Address: 2050 Blowing Rock Hwy., Linville NC 28846
Telephone: 800-468-7325, 828-733-4337
Website: grandfather.com
Hours: 8am–5pm year-round (weather permitting in winter).
Fees: Adults $20, children 4–12 $9, under 4 free
Directions: Just two miles from the Linn Cove Viaduct. Take Linville exit, Milepost 305 off of Blue Ridge Parkway to US 221 or take I-40 from Asheville. Get off in Marion and take Hwy. 221 North 35 miles to Linville. Look for Grandfather Mountain signs.

Lake James State Park

Tucked away in rolling hills at the base of Linville Gorge is Lake James, a 6,510-acre lake with more than 150 miles of shoreline. This impressive waterway is the centerpiece of Lake James State Park. The park offers a variety of activities, including swimming, boating and fishing. The park has a well-maintained campground for public use, with twenty backpack campsites, each with fire pit, picnic table and tent space. Water and a washhouse with showers are also nearby. Campsites are available Mar. through Nov. for a modest fee on a first-come basis.

Location: Nebo NC.
Distance: About an hour's drive
Address: 2785 NC Hwy. 126, Nebo NC 28761
Telephone: 828-584-7728
Website: ncparks.gov/Visit/parks/laja/main.php
Hours: 8am–9pm in summer, check website for hours in other seasons.
Directions: Traveling east on I-40: From I-40, take the Nebo/Lake James exit (Exit 90) and head north. After a half-mile, turn right onto Harmony Grove Rd., and follow it for 2 miles to a stoplight. Proceed straight across the intersection and past Nebo Elementary School to a stop sign. Turn right onto NC 126, and follow the signs to the park entrance 2.3 miles on the left.

Linville Caverns

At the head of beautiful Linville Valley, Linville Caverns lie deep under Humpback Mountain. The caverns entrance is in a beautiful glade and they are open year-round. In the winter many of the skiers from various popular ski slopes in the Banner Elk, Boone and Blowing Rock areas add a visit to Linville Caverns, "Inside the Mountain" as a delightful contrast to their skiing on the slopes above. The wondrous splendors deep inside Humpback Mountain were unknown to the white man until they were explored by H.E. Colton, an eastern Carolinian, and his local guide, Dave Franklin, more than one hundred years ago. The mysterious appearance of fish swimming out of the mountains led the explorers to probe deep into the mountain, following the underground stream through passageways and rooms whose ceilings, when lit by torches," looked like the arch of some grand cathedral." Linville Caverns have lighted smooth paths that take visitors deep into the innermost recesses. Courteous and experienced guides accompany each party through the caverns, pointing out the most interesting features and answering all questions.

Location: Marion NC
Distance: 1 hour from Asheville
Address: 19929 Us Hwy. 221 North, Marion NC 28752
Telephone: 800-419-0540, 828-756-4171
Website: linvillecaverns.com
Hours: Open year-round, closed Thanksgiving and Christmas. Jun. 1-Labor Day: 9am–6pm; April, May, Sep., Oct.: 9am–5pm; Nov.–Mar.: weekends only 9am–4:30pm
Fees: Adult, senior, and child rates, under 5 free
Directions: Take Linville Falls exit on Blue Ridge Parkway and turn left on US 221. Caverns are 4 miles south of Linville on US 221 north of Marion. A faster route is I-40 from Asheville. Exit in Marion and take Hwy. 221 North.

Linville Gorge

Linville Gorge is a rugged wilderness area in Pisgah National Forest. Excellent hiking trails lead to superb views of Linville Falls. Linville Gorge, carved by the Linville River forming Jonas Ridge on the east and Wiseman's View on the western rim, is one of the most spectacular sites in North Carolina. The Linville Gorge area was originally donated to the Parkway by John D. Rockefeller. Linville Falls is perhaps the best-known waterfall in the entire Appalachian Mountains, and certainly it is one of the most scenic. The waterfall marks the beginning of the gorge, one of the deepest canyons in the east, with walls rising to almost 2,000 feet in places. Peregrine falcons and numerous other rare animals and plants are found in the gorge. One species of plant, the mountain golden heather (Hudsonia montana) is found nowhere else in the world.

Location: Linville NC
Distance: Two hours from Asheville
Address: Linville Falls Visitor Center, spur road off of Blue Ridge Parkway at Milepost 316.4.
Telephone: Grandfather District Ranger Station: 828-652-2144, Linville Falls Visitor Center: 828-765-1045, U.S. Forest Service: 828-768-6062
Website: fs.usda.gov/recarea/nfsnc/null/recarea/?recid=48974&actid=37
Hours: The Linville Falls Visitor Center is open 9am–5:30pm
Fees: None, but permit must be obtained at Information Cabin along top of Gorge in order to enter Gorge area. This cabin is open 8*a*m–4:30pm
Directions: Turn off of the Blue Ridge Parkway at Milepost 316.3, and follow the paved road 1.4 miles to Linville Falls Visitor Center. Faster route is I-40 East from Asheville. Get off in Marion and take Hwy. 221 North for 26 miles to Linville Falls Community. At intersection of Hwy. 183, take right and go east .25 miles to entrance.

Mount Jefferson State Natural Area

Mount Jefferson in the Mount Jefferson State Natural Area is a National Natural Landmark. Two short trails give hikers spectacular views of the New River and the surrounding mountains. One of the more interesting features of the area is Luther's Rock Overlook. No bicycles or camping are allowed. There are picnic areas, and canoeing can be done at the nearby New River State Park. Mount Jefferson has a self-guided nature trail for hikers who wish to take their time and learn about the natural history of the area. By special request, park naturalists lead guided walks explaining the area's natural history and legends. The Park Service also offers a program history that advertises upcoming hikes and events.

Location: Ashe County NC
Distance: 2.5–3 hours from Asheville
Address: State Rd. 1152, Jefferson NC 28604
Telephone: 336-246-9653 (park office)
Website: ncparks.gov/Visit/parks/moje/main.php
Hours: Jun.–Aug. 9am–8pm; call for hours other times of the year.
Fees: None
Directions: From Asheville, take I-40 East to Hickory. Use 321 North through Blowing Rock and West Jefferson to US 221 North. Mount Jefferson State Natural Area is located a half-mile south of Jefferson. From NC 163, take SR 1149 to the park entrance on SR 1152.

Mount Mitchell State Park

Mount Mitchell State Park is in the Black Mountain range, which reaches higher than the Blue Ridge or Smoky Mountains. At 6,684 feet, its dominant mountain, Mount Mitchell, is the highest peak in the eastern United States. A cool climate, unique flora and fauna and easy access from the Blue Ridge Parkway make this a very popular vacation spot. Mount Mitchell State Park offers tent camping, six trails of varying difficulty, nature study, picnic areas, Natural History Museum and restaurant. The Park is 1,727 acres in size, and the summit of Mount Mitchell is famous for its spectacular views. On a clear day it is possible to see for more than 70 miles. The Natural History Museum located on the way to the Stone Observation Tower at the summit has dioramas, exhibits and recordings that present some of the unusual higher elevation plants and wildlife.

These high elevations give Mount Mitchell a cooler climate than the surrounding lowlands, a climate more typical of the boreal forests that dominate Canada and Alaska. Flora and fauna associated with the mountain's ecosystem are atypical of the southern Appalachians. Rare and uncommon plant and animal species live in the spruce-fir forest that covers the summit. This spruce-fir forest is among the rarest of forest environments in North Carolina, and one of the most endangered. The Park was created in 1916 by individuals concerned with the destruction of virgin forests by logging, and the mountain was named for Dr. Elisha Mitchell, the first person to take measurements of the Black Mountains, which include Mt. Mitchell. Dr. Mitchell is buried on the summit of Mount Mitchell at the base of the observation tower.

Location: Northeast of Asheville.
Distance: 1.5 hours from Asheville
Address: Milepost 355 on the Blue Ridge Parkway
Telephone: 828-675-4611, Park Office
Website: ncparks.gov/Visit/parks/momi/main.php
Hours: Jun.–Aug.: 8am–9pm; call for hours in other times of the year.
Fees: None; campsites $8 per night
Directions: Take the Blue Ridge Parkway north from Asheville. The entrance to the park is at Milepost 355.

New River State Park

One of the oldest rivers in the world, the New River is designated as a National Wild and Scenic River and an American Heritage River. At the New River State Park, it is possible to canoe the more than 26 miles of the river's South Fork, embarking for your journey from any of three access points. A trip down the gentle New River promises excellent canoeing and picnicking as well as inspiring mountain scenery. The park itself encompasses 1,580 acres and is located in Ashe and Alleghany counties.

The park has a number of hiking trails, picnic areas including a 12-table covered picnic shelter with fireplace and grill, and a community building which includes a large meeting room, kitchen facilities, and restrooms. The community building is available for rent per day and is often used for family reunions and other groups' meetings. Canoe camping is very popular on the New River and the three access areas provide over 30 canoe-in or walk-in primitive campgrounds with tables and grills. Pit toilets and drinking water are located nearby. Campers must first register with the park staff or at registration boxes. Campsites require a small fee.

Easy paddling and beautiful scenery make canoeing the New River a spectacular and rewarding trip. Gentle waters with some rapids make it fun for both beginning and advanced paddlers. Canoes may be launched at the three access sites as well as from several bridges and roadways that cross the river.

Location: Jefferson NC
Distance: 2.5–3 hours from Asheville
Address: 1477 Wagoner Access Rd., Jefferson NC 28640-
Telephone: Park Office: 336-982-2587
Website: ncparks.gov/Visit/parks/neri/main
Hours: Nov.–Feb. 8am–6pm; Mar. & Oct. 8am–7pm; April, May, & Sep. 8am–8pm; Jun.–Aug. 8am–9pm; Closed Christmas. Gates remain locked after hours.
Fees: Small fees for camping only
Directions: From Asheville, take I-40 East to Hickory. From there, take US 321 North through Blowing Rock and West Jefferson to US 221 to Jefferson. Wagoner Access Rd. off NC 88 can reach the Wagoner Rd. Access Area, which is eight miles southeast of Jefferson, 1.2 miles east of the intersection of NC 16 and NC 88. The US 221 Access Area, at river mile 15, is located eight miles northeast of Jefferson.

Rendezvous Mountain Educational State Forest

North Carolina has six Educational State Forests that have been developed as living environmental education centers. These forests are designed to promote a better understanding of the value of forests in our lives. Rendezvous Mountain Educational State Forest, located near Purlear, offers a rich mixture of mountain hardwoods, rhododendron, flame azaleas and a variety of wildflowers. These features are accessible to the visiting public by a series of well-marked trails accented by exhibits and displays depicting the ecology of the managed forest. The Talking Tree Trail features" talking trees," each with a recorded message about itself, its site, and the forest history. Also, actual forestry practices are explained on the Forest Demonstration Trail. Close to the start of the trail, a natural amphitheater is available for special sessions or groups.

Location: 2.5 hours west of Asheville
Address: 1956 Rendezvous Mountain Rd., Purlear NC 28651
Telephone: 336-667-5072
Website: ncesf.org/RMESF/rmesf_about.htm
Hours: Third season in Mar. to the day after Thanksgiving. Call office for hours.
Fees: None
Allow: Two hours
Directions: From Asheville take 1–40 East toward Statesville. Take Exit 123 to Hwy. 321 North to Boone. In Boone take US 421 East. Take the exit toward Blue Ridge Parkway, turn left at Parkway and stay right on Parkway. Take the 1st right onto Phillips Gap Rd. and then turn left at State Rd. 1300/Summit Rd. Turn right and the Forest will be on the right.

South Mountains State Park

Nestled deep in the woods, rugged South Mountains State Park is a phenomenal place to enjoy nature. The 132,747-acre park includes elevations that range from 1000 feet in the rolling piedmont to majestic mountain ranges towering over 3,000 feet. Other highlights are the beautiful High Shoals Falls that drops 80 feet, and more than 40 miles of trails including a 17-mile mountain bike loop. From equestrian camping to trout fishing, mountain biking to picnicking, a number of activities are available at the park.

Location: Connelly Springs NC. .
Distance: 1 hour and 30 minutes east of Asheville
Address: 3001 South Mountain State Park, Connelly Springs NC 28612
Telephone: 828-433-4772
Website: ncparks.gov/Visit/parks/somo/main.php
Hours: May.–Aug.: 8am–9pm, call for hours other times of the year.
Directions: Traveling east on I-40: From I-40, turn south on NC 18, travel 11.1 miles and make a right turn onto SR 1913 (Sugarloaf Rd.). Take SR 1913 to Old NC 18 4.3 miles and turn left. Travel 2.7 miles and make a right turn onto SR 1901 (Ward's Gap Rd.). The park is 1.4 miles off SR 1901 on SR 1904 (South Mountains Park Ave.). Travel one mile from the beginning of South Mountain Park Ave. to the South Mountains State Park gate.

Stone Mountain State Park

Stone Mountain is not immediately visible upon entering the park that bears its name, but this magnificent 600-foot granite dome is well worth the wait. The 132,747-acre park offers 17 miles of designated trout waters and more than 16 miles of hiking trails. Designated as a National Natural Landmark in 1975, Stone Mountain is bounded on the north by the Blue Ridge Parkway and on the west by the Thurmond Chatham Game Lands.

Location: Roaring Gap NC
Distance: 3 hours
Address: 3042 Frank Parkway, Roaring Gap NC 28668
Telephone: 336-957-8185
Website: ncparks.gov/Visit/main.php
Hours: Jun.–Aug.: 8am–9pm, call for hours other times of the year.
Directions: Stone Mountain State Park is located in Wilkes and Alleghany counties, seven miles southwest of Roaring Gap. From I-77, turn west onto US 21. Veer left onto Traphill Rd. (SR 1002), and follow it to the John P. Frank Parkway. Turn right and follow the parkway to the park. From the west, take NC 18 North and turn right onto Traphill Rd. (SR 1002). Follow the road to the John P. Frank Parkway and turn left, following the parkway to the park.

The Blowing Rock

The Blowing Rock, located near Boone, is an immense cliff rising about 1,000 feet above the Johns River Gorge below. The rock is named Blowing Rock because the cliff walls of the gorge form a flume through which the northwest wind sweeps with such force that it returns light objects cast over the cliff. This phenomena prompted the Ripley's "Believe It or Not" cartoon about "the only place in the world where snow falls upside down."

The Blowing Rock

Location: Blowing Rock NC
Distance: 2 hours from Asheville
Address: Hwy. 321 South, Blowing Rock NC 28645
Telephone: 828-295-7111
Website: theblowingrock.com
Hours: Mar., April, May and Nov.: 9am–6pm; Jun.–Oct.: 8am–8pm; Closed Dec.–Feb.
Fees: Adult, senior, and child rates, under 5 free
Directions: From Blue Ridge Parkway take Boone exit to 321 South to Blowing Rock. A faster route from Asheville is to take I-40 East to Marion and take Hwy. 221 North to Blowing Rock

Tuttle Educational State Forest

North Carolina has six Educational State Forests that have been developed as living environmental education centers. These forests are designed to promote a better understanding of the value of forests in our lives. Tuttle Educational State Forest, located near Lenoir, offers a rich mixture of mountain hardwoods and pines, rhododendron, flame azaleas and a variety of wildflowers. These features are accessible to the visiting public by a series of well-marked trails accented by exhibits and displays depicting the ecology of the managed forest. Tuttle boasts a wide variety of pines and hardwoods plus rolling terrain and clear streams. These features are accessible by a series of well-marked trails accented by exhibits and displays which explain the ecology of the managed forest.

Location: 1.5 hours east of Asheville
Address: 3420 Playmore Beach Rd., Lenoir NC 28655
Telephone: 828-757-5608
Website: ncesf.org/TESF/home.htm
Hours: Mid-Mar. to Mid-Nov. Closed Mon, Call office for hours.
Fees: None
Allow: Two hours
Directions: From Asheville take Exit 103 Burkemont Ave. to Hwy. 18–64 north toward Lenoir. Turn left onto SR 1311. The forest will be on your right.

W. Scott Kerr Dam & Reservoir

W. Scott Kerr Dam and Reservoir are named in honor of William Kerr Scott, 1896–1958, former Governor of North Carolina and U.S. Senator. The project was included in the general plan for the improvement of the Yadkin-Pee Dee River for the purpose of reducing flood damage such as was caused by the devastating floods of 1899, 1916, and 1940.

User Fees are required in some park areas for day use activities and boat launching. The remaining parks, access areas, fringe shorelines and all water areas are open to the public without charge for public and recreational use. Public use facilities have been provided by the Corps of Engineers in the recreational areas, including seven boat launching ramps, four swimming areas, paved access roads, picnic areas and campsites with potable water and sanitary facilities. Flush type toilets, laundry trays, and shower facilities are available in Bandit's Roost and Warrior Creek Parks. Public service facilities consisting of a marina, snack bar, and fueling and bait supplies are available at the Skyline Marina. Anyone visiting the reservoir for the first time should check in at the Visitor Assistance Center on Reservoir Rd.

Location: Wilkesboro
Distance: 2.5 hours from Asheville
Address: Visitor Assistance Center, 499 Reservoir Rd., Wilkesboro NC 28697
Telephone: 336-921-3390
Directions: (To the Visitor Assistance Center) From Asheville take I-40 East and get off at Exit 100 toward Jamestown Rd. Turn left at Jamestown Rd. and go 2 miles to right at Carbon City Rd. In one mile turn left at the US 64 Bypass and go 2.7 miles to NC18. Follow NC18 over 30 miles to the Wilkesboro area, and

turn left at Boomer Rd. Turn right onto Hwy. 268, go 3 miles, turn right onto Reservoir Rd. at the W. Kerr Scott Dam and Reservoir sign, go ¼ mile, then turn left beside Shady Grove Baptist Church

Natural Attractions West of Asheville

Bent Creek Experimental Forest

Bent Creek Experimental Forest (SRS-4101), located just outside Asheville, is one of the oldest research areas maintained by the USDA Forest Service. Since 1925, scientists at Bent Creek have been developing and practicing sound forestry practices. The fruits of their research on fire, insects, wildlife, water, diseases, and recreational uses are being applied today in forests all around the world and in particular the Southern Appalachians. Open to visitors, Bent Creek is popular with area hikers and runners.

Location: Just west of Asheville
Distance: 30 minutes west of Asheville
Address: 1577 Brevard Rd., Asheville NC 28806
Telephone: 828-667-5261
Website: srs.fs.usda.gov/bentcreek
Hours: 8am–4:30pm Mon–Fri
Fees: None
Directions: I-26 Exit 2 (Biltmore Square Mall exit). Follow Hwy. 191 South 1.5–2 miles. Turn right onto Bent Creek Ranch Rd. and follow signs to Lake Powhatan and the Experimental Forest.

Cades Cove

Cades Cove is a broad, verdant 6,800-acre valley near Townsend, Tennessee in the Great Smoky Mountains National Park. It is surrounded by mountains and is one of the most popular destinations in the park. It offers some of the best opportunities for wildlife viewing in the park. Large numbers of white-tailed deer are frequently seen, and sightings of black bear, coyote, ground hog, turkey, raccoon, skunk, and other animals are also possible.

For hundreds of years Cherokee Indians hunted in Cades Cove, but archeologists have found no evidence of major settlements. The first Europeans settled in the cove sometime between 1818 and 1821. By 1830 the population of the area had already swelled to 271. Cades Cove offers the widest variety of historic buildings of any area in the national park. Scattered along the loop road are three churches, a working grist mill, barns, log houses, and many other faithfully restored eighteenth and nineteenth century structures. An inexpensive self-guiding tour booklet available at the entrance to the road provides in-depth information about the buildings and the people who built and used them.

An 11-mile, one-way loop road circles the cove, offering motorists the opportunity to sightsee at a leisurely pace. Allow at least two to four hours to tour Cades Cove, longer if you walk some of the area's trails. Traffic is heavy during the tourist season in summer and fall and on weekends year-round. While driving the loop road, please be courteous to other visitors and use pull-offs when stopping to enjoy the scenery or view wildlife. A visitor center (open daily), restrooms, and the Cable Mill historic area are located half-way around the loop road.

Numerous trails originate in the cove, including the five-mile roundtrip trail to Abrams Falls and the short Cades Cove Nature Trail. Longer hikes to Thunderhead Mountain and Rocky Top (made famous by the popular song) also begin in the cove. Several designated backcountry campsites (camping by permit only) are located along trails. A campground with 159 sites is open year round in Cades Cove. Tents and RVs up to 35 feet can be accommodated in the campground.

Only bicycle and foot traffic are allowed on the loop road until 10am every Sat and Wed morning from early May until late Sep. Otherwise the road is open to motor vehicles from sunrise until sunset daily, weather permitting.

Location: Great Smoky Mountains National Park, West of Asheville near Townsend TN
Distance: 3–4 hours from Asheville
Address: The Cades Cove Visitor Center is near the western entrance of the park in Tennessee
Telephone: General Information 423-436-1200, Cades Cove Campground: 877-444-6777
Website: nps.gov/grsm/planyourvisit/cadescove.htm
Directions: From Asheville take I-40 west toward Tennessee. After you reach Tennessee take Exit 443 onto Foothills Parkway toward Gatlinburg and Great Smoky Mountains National Park. Go 6.3 miles and turn left at TN 73/US 321 heading west to Gatlinburg. In Gatlinburg take 441 toward the National Park and turn at the Sugarlands Visitor Center. From here you will take Little River Rd. to Laurel Creek Rd which runs straight into Cades Cove.

Chatuge Lake

Chatuge Lake was created in 1942 when the Tennessee Valley Authority constructed a dam across the Hiwassee River. The lake has over 133 miles of shoreline, is over 7,200 acres in size and is in both North Carolina and Georgia. Chatuge Dam is 144 feet high and stretches 2,850 feet across the Hiwassee River. Chatuge was originally built to store water to help prevent flooding downstream. A single hydropower generating unit was added in 1954. The Weir, just north of the dam, offers picnic tables and a launch for canoes and tubes for a trip on the Hiawassee River to a takeout area near Fires Creek Wildlife Management Area. Call the Tennessee Valley Authority for information regarding water conditions and release schedules at 828-837-7395.

There are three public boat ramps accessible from North Carolina: Jackrabbit Mountain Campground off Hwy. 175, Ledford Chapel Wildlife Access Ramp on Hwy. 64, and Gibson Cove Campground, on Myers Chapel Rd. Contact the Clay County Chamber of Commerce office at 828-389-3704 for more information. Clay County operates two campgrounds on the lake with spaces available for tents and campers. Call 828-389-3532 evenings. Both have: public swimming areas with a sandy beach, BBQ grills, and picnic tables. Other amenities include a boat launch, playground, ball park, pavilions, and showers.

Location: Near Hayesville NC
Distance: From Asheville allow 2–2.5 hours
Resources: Clay County Chamber of Commerce 388 Business Hwy. 64, Hayesville NC 28904; 828-389-3704 and Tennessee Valley Authority/Lake Hiwassee, 221 Old Ranger Rd., Murphy NC 28906; 828-837-7395

Directions: From Asheville take I-40 West toward Knoxville. Take Exit 27 to merge into US Hwy. 74/19 West toward Waynesville/Murphy. In approximately 25 miles take Exit 81 to merge onto US 23/441 toward Franklin/Dillsboro. Continue on Murphy Hwy./US 64 and after approximately 28 miles take sharp left onto Hwy. 175. This will take you to the lake in the Hayesville area.

Cherohala Skyway

The Cherohala Skyway was completed and dedicated in 1996 and cost over $100,000,000 to construct. Spectacular to say the least, the road has been designated a National Scenic Byway. The Skyway crosses through the Cherokee National Forest in Tennessee and the Nantahala National Forest in North Carolina. The Skyway connects Tellico Plains, Tennessee, with Robbinsville, North Carolina, and is about 50 miles long. It is a wide, paved 2-lane road maintained by the Tennessee Department of Transportation and the North Carolina Department of Transportation, and the elevations range from 900 feet above sea level at the Tellico River in Tennessee to over 5400 feet above sea level at the Tennessee-North Carolina state line at Haw Knob (mile marker 11).

The name "Cherohala" comes from the names of the two National Forests: "Cher" from the Cherokee and "ahala" from the Nantahala. The Cherohala Skyway is located in southeast Tennessee and southwest North Carolina. Keep in mind that the skyway can be desolate at night and dangerous driving in the winter months. Also, keep in mind that there are no gas stations also for the entire 50 miles.

Location: West of Asheville
Address: Graham County Visitor Center: 12 North Main St., Robbinsville NC 28711
Distance: From Asheville, approximately 2.5 hours driving time.
Telephone: 423-253-8010
Website: cherohala.org
Directions: From Asheville take 1–40 West. Take Exit 27 to merge onto US Hwy. 74 West toward Waynesville/Murphy/US 19. Turn right at Hwy. 19 West/74 and continue to follow US 19/74. Turn right at US 129/Tallulah Rd. Continue to follow US 129 into Robbinsville. Turn left at Massey Branch Rd./NC 1116/ NC 143. Turn right at NC 1127/NC 143/Snowbird Rd. Turn right at NC 143/Santeetlah road and continue to follow 143 to the Skyway.

Dupont State Forest

The Dupont State Forest is located between Hendersonville and Brevard and its 10,400 acres of forest feature four major waterfalls on the Little River and several on the Grassy Creek. Originally 7,600 acres and established in 1996 through a donation from the Dupont Corporation, the forest was expanded in 2000 by two property additions, including the spectacular 2,200-acre tract in the center of the forest. It lies in the upland plateau of the Little River valley with elevation between 2,300 and 3,600 feet. Key waterfalls, all of which are easily accessed by short trails, include Triple Falls (a series of three waterfalls), High Falls, Hooker Falls (an 11-foot drop into Cascade Lake), Bridal Veil Falls (the most unique falls in the State Forest, with a long, shallow veil-like whitewater incline along the lower section), Wintergreen

Falls (20-foot cascade on Grassy Creek) and Grassy Creek Falls. Cedar Rock Mountain in the forest has hundreds of acres of exposed granite, making it a very popular destination for cyclists and hikers, and Stone Mountain is the forest's high point at 3,600 feet. It offers a 180-degree view during the summer and a full 360 degrees during the winter months.

Location: Between Hendersonville and Brevard
Distance: Approximately 45 minutes to 1 hour from Asheville
Telephone: 828-877-6527
Website: dupontforest.com
Address: Division of Forest Resources, 14 Gaston Mountain Rd., Asheville NC 28806
Fees: None
Directions: From Asheville, take I-26 West to Exit 9, and then take Hwy. 280 to Pisgah Forest. Turn left on US 64 in Pisgah Forest and travel 3.7 miles to the Texaco station in Penrose. Turn right on Crab Creek Rd. and continue 4.3 miles and turn right onto Dupont Rd. As the road climbs the hill, turn left at Sky Valley Rd. and continue about a mile past the farmhouse to the parking lot on the right.

French Broad River

The third oldest river in the world, trailing only the Nile in Africa and the New in West Virginia, the French Broad River flows north through 117 miles of Western North Carolina from its headwaters in Rosman to Tennessee. In Tennessee it joins the Holston to form the Tennessee River and eventually reaches the Mississippi. It is a great recreational resource offering splendid scenery, perfect picnic spots, Class I through IV whitewater, and good fishing. It flows right through Asheville on its journey north. One of the river's Cherokee names was Tahkeeostee, "racing waters." Others, frequently used for only a part of the river, were Poelico, Ariqua, and Zillicoah. By 1776 the present name French Broad River was in use. The name French Broad comes from the fact that this river used to flow into French Indian territory in Tennessee during colonial days.

On its way through Asheville, the river is accessible at a number of places. These access sites are maintained by the Buncombe County Department of Parks, Recreation & Greenways and are listed below. The City of Asheville Parks, Recreation & Cultural Arts Department also maintains a number of river parks on the French Broad River in the Asheville area. One of these, the Jean Webb Park is located on Riverside Dr. which parallels the river. This small park is convenient from downtown and a good spot for a picnic lunch. The major river park in the Asheville area is the French Broad River Park, also maintained by the city of Asheville. One of Asheville's most beautiful parks, it features a vast area of open green space with old trees, a wildflower garden, a paved trail, a gazebo, picnic tables and grills, an observation deck, and a small playground. Riverlink, an important non-profit river preservation organization, was instrumental in helping to develop this park, the Jean Webb Park and others. Riverlink's website (riverlink.org) has an extensive "River Guide" which has maps and directions to all of the access points on the river.

If you are interested in whitewater rafting, the French Broad River north of Asheville is home to a number of whitewater rafting companies. In Asheville, the Asheville Outdoor Center is conveniently located minutes from downtown. They offer gentle tubing, rafting, kayaking and canoeing trips, including ones that go through lands owned by Biltmore Estate.

Location: West of downtown Asheville
Resources: Riverlink: PO Box 15488, Asheville NC 28813; 828-252-8474; riverlink.org; Buncombe County Department Parks, Recreation & Greenways: 828-250-4260; City of Asheville Parks, Recreation & Cultural Arts Department: 828-251-1122
Directions: The French Broad River is accessible from many points in Asheville. To reach the Riverlink French Broad River Park, take Meadow Rd. west from Biltmore Village. This road eventually begins to parallel the river. Turn left at Amboy Rd. to access the park.

Buncombe County River Access Sites & River Parks

Bent Creek: 1592 Brevard Rd., Asheville NC 28806; From Asheville take 26 East and take Exit 2–go left at light on to Brevard Rd. and travel 2.4 mile–see the park on the left.

Jean Webb Park: 30 Riverside Dr., Asheville NC 28801; From downtown Asheville head west on Patton Ave. and turn left at South French Broad Ave. Turn right at Hilliard Ave., turn left at Clingman Ave. and then turn right on Lyman St. Turn right at Riverside Dr. and park will be on your left.

French Broad River Park: 508 Riverview Dr., Asheville NC 28806; From downtown Asheville head west on Patton Ave. and turn left at South French Broad Ave. Turn right at Hilliard Ave., turn left at Clingman Ave. and then turn left on Lyman St. Turn right on Amboy Rd. and the immediate right on Riverview Dr.

Corcoran Paige: 9 Pinners Rd., Arden NC 28704; From Asheville take 26 East and take Exit 6–turn left on to Long Shoals Rd. and travel 1.8 miles–turn right on to Hendersonville Rd. and travel 1.4 miles–turn right on to Glenn Bridge Rd. and travel 1.0 mile; turn left on to Pinner Rd.–see park on right.

Glen Bridge: 77 Pinners Rd., Arden NC 28704; From Asheville take 26 East and take Exit 6–turn left on to Long Shoals Rd. and travel 1.8 miles–turn right on to Hendersonville Rd. and travel 1.4 miles–turn right on to Glen Bridge Rd. and travel 1.0 mile–turn left on to Pinner Rd. and travel .5 mile–see park on right.

Hominy Creek: 194 Hominy Creek Rd., Asheville NC 28806; From Asheville take I-240 West. Take exit 1B. At the end of the ramp, turn right. After about .1 mile, turn left onto Shelburne then left onto Hominy Creek Rd. and travel .7 mile–see park on left.

Ledges Whitewater: 1080 Old Marshall Hwy, Alexander NC 28701; From Asheville take 19/23 North and immediately take the Hill St. Exit–go left and travel .1 mile–turn right on to Riverside Dr. and travel 8.1 miles–see park on left.

Walnut Island: 3042 Old Marshall Hwy, Alexander NC 28701; From Asheville take 19/23 North and immediately take the Hill St. Exit–go left and travel .1 mile–turn right on to Riverside Dr. and travel 13.3 miles–see park on left.

Fontana Lake

Fontana Lake, located in Swain and Graham counties, is surrounded on the north side by the Great Smoky Mountains National Forest, and by national forest on the remainder of the shoreline. At 10,230 acres, Fontana Lake is the largest in the Western North Carolina mountains and offers visitors an abundance of recreational opportunities. There are over 39 miles of hiking trails along its shores, and the Appalachian Trail actually passes over the top of

Fontana Dam. The hot showers available at the trail shelter maintained by TVA have led grateful hikers to dub it the Fontana Hilton. There are over 238 miles of shoreline, and most of it is protected from development, since 90% is owned by the National Park and U.S. Forest Service.

Fontana Dam, which forms the lake, is the highest dam east of the Rockies is a Tennessee Valley Authority project. It towers an amazing 480 feet in height and stretches 2,365 feet across the Little Tennessee River. The dam itself is a major tourist attraction, with thousands of visitors each year. The construction of the dam began in 1942 to provide electric power for the war effort and was completed in 1944. The lake is fed by Chambers Creek, Eagle Creek, Forney Creek, Hazel Creek, Lands Creek, Nolands Creek, and Pilkey Creek, and reaches depths of over 440 feet. The Fontana Dam Visitor Center is open to the public from 9am–7pm daily from May through Nov.

Tsali Recreational Area, located on the southeastern shore of Fontana Lake, has a well-deserved reputation as a great spot for hiking, mountain biking, bird watching and horseback riding. Fontana Village Resort in Fontana Dam is a good place to begin when you arrive in the Fontana Lake area. From there the dam is a short drive, and the village offers restaurants and resources for more lake information.

Location: Swain and Graham Counties NC
Distance: From Asheville allow 2–2.5 hours
Resources: Tennessee Valley Authority/Lake Hiwassee, 221 Old Ranger Rd., Murphy NC 28906;
Telephone: 828-837-7395
Directions: (To Fontana Village) take I-40 west. Take the exit for Hwy 74 (Great Smoky Mountain Expressway). Stay on Hwy 74 (four lane) you will pass Clyde, Sylva, and 8 miles past Bryson City (last chance for groceries, restaurants) turn right on Hwy 28. Continue on Hwy 28 for 25 miles.

Joyce Kilmer Memorial Forest

The 526,798-acre Nantahala National Forest located to the west of Asheville is home to the Joyce Kilmer Memorial Forest, one of the nation's most impressive preserves of old-growth forest. Here you may view magnificent examples of over 100 species of trees, including hemlocks and tulip-poplars over 20 feet in circumference and 100 feet high. Some of these trees are over 450 years old. Explored in 1540 by Spanish Conquistador Hernando DeSoto and established in 1920 under the 1911 Weeks Act, this 3,800-acre forest was set aside in 1936 as a memorial to Joyce Kilmer, the soldier/poet who wrote the famous poem "Trees."

The only way to see the impressive memorial forest is on foot. The figure-eight Joyce Kilmer National Recreation Trail covers 2 miles and has two loops: the 1.25-mile lower loop passes the Joyce Kilmer Memorial plaque, and the upper 0.75-mile loop swings through Poplar Cove—a grove of the forest's largest trees. The trailhead parking area has a flush toilet and picnic tables. No camping or overnight parking is allowed.

Location: West of Asheville
Distance: 2–3 hours from Asheville
Address: Cheoah District Ranger Office, 1070 Massey Branch Rd., Robbinsville NC 28771

Telephone: Nantahala National Forest Cheoah District Ranger 828-479-6431
Hours: Daily 8am–4:30pm (Ranger Office hours)
Fees: None
Directions: Take I-40W to Exit 27. Exit right onto U.S. 19/74 toward Waynesville. Go about 47 miles, and bear right on NC 28N. Go 5 miles, and turn left on NC 143 to Robbinsville. From Robbinsville take NC 143W. After about 12 miles, turn right on Joyce Kilmer Rd. (SR1134). Go 2 miles and turn left to memorial forest.

Gorges State Park

Located near Sapphire, Gorges State Park contains spectacular waterfalls, sheer rock walls, rugged river gorges, and one of the greatest concentrations of rare and unusual plant species in the Eastern United States. An elevation that rises over 2,000 feet in only three to five miles and an annual rainfall in excess of 80 inches creates a unique temperate rain forest. Gorges' 7,484 acres were designated a state park in April of 1999 to protect these nationally significant natural resources, and it is the newest state park in North Carolina. Park highlights are Horsepasture River (a National Wild and Scenic River), Toxaway River, Bearwallow Creek, Thompson River, Bearcamp Creek, Windy Falls, Lower Bearwallow Falls, Toxaway Creek Falls, Chestnut Mountain, Grindstone Mountain, Misery Mountain, many major trout streams, and numerous wildflowers including rare species.

Location: Sapphire, North Carolina
Distance: Approximately 2 hours from Asheville
Address: NC Hwy. 281 South, Sapphire NC 28774
Telephone: 828-966-9099
Website: ncparks.gov/Visit/parks/gorg/main
Hours: Jun.–Aug. 8am–9pm; call for hours during other times of the year.
Fees: None
Directions: From Asheville, take the I-26 Airport Rd. Exit (US 280 South) past the airport to Brevard where it will turn into US 64. Continue on Hwy. 64 to Sapphire. Gorges State Park is located in Transylvania County and overlaps the North Carolina/South Carolina state lines. It is approximately 45 miles west of Asheville.

Great Smoky Mountains National Park

The Great Smoky Mountains National Park, which lies along the common border of Tennessee and North Carolina, forms a majestic climax to the Appalachian Highlands. With outlines softened by a forest mantle, the mountains stretch away to remote horizons in sweeping troughs that recede to evenness in the distance. Shrouding the peaks is a smoke-like mist that rises from the dense plant growth. The mountains get their name from this deep blue mist.

The park's boundary wraps around 800 square miles of mountain wilderness, most of it virtually unspoiled. Many peaks rise above 6,000 feet. A great variety of trees, shrubs, herbs and other plants are nourished by the fertile land and heavy rainfall and rushing streams. The Great Smokey Park contains more than 700 miles of rivers and streams, over 200,000 acres of virgin forests, and over 850 miles of trails. It is the most visited national park with over 9,000,000 visitors a year.

When you get to the border of the park coming from the Asheville direction you will want to check in at the Oconaluftee Visitor Center in Cherokee. Although there are many opportunities to drive through the park, the most rewarding experiences are found along the trails. More than 650 miles of horse and foot trails wind along the crystal clear streams and waterfalls, past forest giants that have been living for hundreds of years, through the wild beauty of flower-filled coves and into high mountain meadows. One of the most popular attractions in the park is Cades Cove, a lush beautiful valley complete with historic buildings (*See* Cades Cove, earlier in this same section).

The park offers guided nature walks as well as self-guided tours. Copies of maps and schedules are available at Visitors Centers and at all ranger stations. Not to be missed during your visit is the Mountain Farm Museum, located at the Oconaluftee Visitor Center. It is part of an effort to preserve some of the cultural heritage of the Smokies and is a collection of buildings that were moved from their original locations to form an open-air museum. Highly recommended auto tours include the Roaring Fork Auto Tour, the Newfound Gap Rd. Auto Tour, the Cades Cove Auto Tour and the Cataloochee Auto Tour. Self-guided tour books are available and will enrich your stops at the many historical sites and natural wonders along the way.

The famed Appalachian Trail (*See* Appalachian Trail, earlier in this same section), which stretches from Maine to Georgia, enters the park near the eastern boundary. Straddling the boundary line of two states, it zigzags a course for 71 miles along the crest of some of the highest peaks and ultimately leaves the park again at Fontana Dam. If you wish to hike the full distance in the park, you can cover the 71 miles in 6 to 8 days. Trailside shelters and campsites are spaced about a day's journey apart. Many other horse and foot trails are scattered throughout the park. There are short, self-guiding trails that are perfect for beginners. Just pick up a leaflet at the start of each trail. A backcountry-use permit, required for all overnight hiking parties, can be obtained free at ranger stations or visitors centers (except Cades Cove Visitors Center).

There are ten developed campgrounds in the park; fees are charged at each. Reservations are recommended at Cades Cove, Elkmont and Smokemont from May 15 to Oct. 31; they can be made by calling 800-365-2267. Sites may be reserved up to three months in advance. All other campgrounds are first-come, first-served. Cosby and Look Rock campgrounds rarely fill up. Campgrounds have tent sites, limited trailer space, water, fireplaces, tables and restrooms. There are no showers or hookups for trailers. No more than six people may occupy a campsite. Two tents or one RV and one tent are allowed per site. The camping limit is seven days between May 15 and Oct. 31, and 14 days between Nov. 1 and May 14. Some campgrounds close in winter. Sewage disposal stations are located at Smokemont, Cades Cove, Deep Creek and Cosby campgrounds, and across from the Sugarlands Visitor Center. They are not available for use in the winter.

Saddle horses are available from April 1 to Oct. 31 at Cades Cove, Smokemont, Deep Creek (near Greenbrier on U.S. 321), and near park headquarters. Bicycles are permitted on park roads but prohibited on all trails except Gatlinburg, Oconaluftee River, and lower Deep Creek. Bicycles may be rented from the Cades Cove Store, near the Cades Cove Campground.

One of the most biologically diverse regions in all of North America, the Park has been designated an International Biosphere Reserve under the UNESCO "Man in the Biosphere" program. Within its boundaries there are over 1500 species of flowering plants; 100 different types of trees; 600 mosses, lichens and liverworts; 50 species of mammals including black bears, whitetail deer, raccoons, foxes, bobcats, opossums, coyotes, and possibly cougars; more than 80 types of snakes and amphibians; and 70 kinds of fish from small colorful darters to brook, brown and rainbow trout. And over 200 kinds of birds have been observed within the park borders. Bring along your bird book and binoculars; the Great Smokies are a bird watcher's paradise.

The Great Smoky Mountains National Park was formally dedicated on Feb. 6, 1930 by both Tennessee and North Carolina governors. Its mission continues today; to preserve and protect the wild beauty and natural charm of the Great Smoky Mountains for all time. LeConte Lodge (accessible by trail only) provides the only lodging in the park. Call 423-429-5704 for more information on this secluded retreat.

Location: West of Asheville

Distance: 2–3 hours from Asheville

Address: Headquarters: Great Smoky Mountains National Park, 107 Park Headquarters Rd., Gatlinburg, TN 37738. There are three visitor centers that provide maps and information: Sugarlands (Tennessee side), Cades Cove (Near the western entrance of the park), and Oconaluftee (in North Carolina). Oconaluftee is the nearest entrance to Asheville. Oconaluftee Visitor Center: 150 Hwy. 441 N., Cherokee NC 28719.

Telephone: General Information: 423-436-1200, Communications Center: 423-436-1230, Back Country Information: 423-436-1297, Oconaluftee Visitor Center: 423-497-1900, 423-497-1904, Park Headquarters: 423-436-1294, Campground Reservations: 800-365-2267, National Park Service: (Washington DC) 202-208-6843, Friends of the Smokies: 828-452-0720

Website: nps.gov/grsm

Hours: Visitor Centers open daily except Christmas. Winter: 9am–5pm, Summer: 8am–7pm Hours vary depending on time of year.

Fees: None to enter park. Fees are charged at developed campgrounds and for certain special programs.

Camping: There are ten developed campgrounds in the park including Cades Cove in Tennessee and Smokemont in North Carolina, which are open year-round. The other developed campgrounds are generally open from late Mar. or April to early Nov. Fees range from $10-$15 per night. Backcountry camping, on the other hand, is free but requires a permit. Most campsites use self-registration at visitor centers or ranger stations, but shelters and rationed sites require reservations. Reservations can be made 30 days in advance by calling 423-436-1231 or 800-365-2267 between 8am and 6pm any day of the week.

Lodging: LeConte Lodge, which is accessible only by foot or horseback, sits atop 6,593-foot tall Mt. LeConte. This is the Park's third highest peak. Reservations are required and can be made by calling 423-429-5704. The lodge is open mid-Mar. to mid-Nov. A variety of lodging facilities are available in the outlying communities.

Directions: From Asheville, take I-40 West to Exit 27. Follow Hwy. 19 South to Cherokee. In Cherokee, take 441 North and follow signs to the park entrance.

Of Note: The most visited National Park in America. Hosts the International Biosphere Reserve and the World Heritage Site. Elevations in the park range from 800–6643 feet and topography affects local weather. Temperatures are 10–20 degrees cooler on the mountaintops. Annual precipitation averages 65 inches in lowlands to 88 inches in high country. Spring often brings unpredictable weather, particularly in higher elevations. Summer is hot and humid, but more pleasant in higher elevations. Fall has warm days and cool nights and is the driest period. Frosts occur starting in late Sep. and continue into April. Winter is generally moderate, but extreme conditions become more likely as elevation increases.

Tips: In summertime the park is heavily visited. Expect long lines during this season. Late spring is a great time to visit because of the wildflowers, pleasant weather, and absence of crowds. The Great Smoky Mountains are vast. Plan your trip carefully. Write or call ahead for information to help in planning. During the summer and fall, the park provides regularly scheduled ranger-led interpretive walks and talks, slide presentations, and campfire programs at campgrounds and visitor centers.

Hiwassee Lake

Lake Hiwassee was formed in 1940 with the construction of the Tennessee Valley Authority dam, which currently has the highest dam overspill in the world at 307 feet. The dam was created for flood control and hydroelectric power generation, with the resulting 6090 acre Lake Hiwassee, which has almost 180 miles of shoreline, measures 22 miles long, and is more than 200 feet deep in places. Hiwassee Dam stretches 1,376 feet across the Hiwassee River.

Lake Hiwassee is surrounded by the Nantahala National Forest and offers extraordinary scenery, boating and lake activities. Easy access for boaters and kayakers can be found at the Hanging Dog Recreation Area, which also offers a campground, picnic area and hiking trails as well as a boat launching ramp. To get to the Hanging Dog Recreation Area from Murphy, go 4.4 miles northwest on Peachtree Rd. which turns into Joe Brown Hwy. Entrance to the lake is on the left.

Location: Near Murphy NC
Distance: From Asheville allow 2–2.5 hours
Telephone: 828-837-7395
Resources: Tennessee Valley Authority/Lake Hiwassee, 221 Old Ranger Rd., Murphy NC 28906;
Directions: From Asheville take I-40 West toward Knoxville. Take Exit 27 to merge onto US Hwy. 74/19 West toward to Murphy.

Nantahala National Forest

This 526,798-acre National Forest located to the west of Asheville offers family camping, boating, fishing, horse trails and miles of hiking trails. Nantahala is home to the Joyce Kilmer Memorial Forest, one of the nation's most impressive preserves of old-growth forest. Here you may view magnificent examples of over 100 species of trees, some over 20 feet in circumference and 100 feet high. Explored in 1540 by Spanish Conquistador Hernando DeSoto and established in 1920 under the 1911 Weeks Act, this 3,800-acre forest was set aside in 1936 as a memorial to Joyce Kilmer, the soldier/poet who wrote the famous poem Trees. Scenic drives, excellent fishing and rafting the white waters of the Nantahala River are among the forest's biggest attractions. Nantahala is also renowned for waterfalls and its beautiful chain of pristine lakes. Black bears, bobcats, white-tailed deer and other animals indigenous to the Appalachians abound in the Forest.

"Trees" by Joyce Kilmer
(1886–1918)

I think I shall never see
A poem lovely as a tree.
A tree whose hungry mouth is pressed
Against the earth's sweet flowing breast;
A tree that looks at God all day
And lifts her leafy arms to pray;
A tree that may in summer wear
A nest of robins in her hair;
Upon whose bosom snow has lain;
Who intimately lives with rain.
Poems are made by fools like me,
But only God can make a tree.

Location: West of Asheville
Distance: 2–3 hours from Asheville
Address: Cheoah District Ranger Office, Massey Branch Rd., Rt. 1 (PO Box 16A), Robbinsville NC 28771, Highlands Ranger District: 2010 Flat Mountain Rd., Highlands NC 28741; 828-526-3765
Telephone: Nantahala National Forest Cheoah District Ranger 828-524-6441 Highlands Ranger District 828-526-3765
Website: fs.usda.gov/recarea/nfsnc/null/recarea/?recid=48634&actid=30
Hours: Ranger Office: Apr.–Nov. Daily 8am–4:30pm; Dec.–Mar. Mon–Fri 8am–4:30pm
Fees: None to enter park
Camping: Tsali campground, Cheoah, Horse Cove, and Cable Cove campgrounds.
Directions: From Asheville take I-40 West. Take Exit 27 to 74 West, then to NC 19. Follow NC 19 to Nantahala.

Pisgah National Forest

Pisgah National Forest is a land of mile-high peaks, cascading waterfalls and heavily forested slopes. It is an ideal place, as are all of the national forests, for outdoor recreation. The forest gets its name from Mount Pisgah, a prominent peak in the area. In the 1700s a Scotch-Irish minister saw the peak and named it for the Biblical mountain from which

Moses saw the promised land after 40 years of wandering in the wilderness. Located on two sides of Asheville, the forest has more than 490,000 acres and spreads over 12 western North Carolina counties. The forest is more or less divided in half by the Blue Ridge Parkway, and the Appalachian Trail runs along its border with Tennessee. The Mountains-to-the-Sea Trail crosses through the forest. Pisgah National Forest contains three wilderness areas. Middle Prong, Linville Gorge and the Shining Rock section and is divided into four districts: Pisgah District, French Broad District, Grandfather District and Tocane District.

A short drive from downtown Asheville, the Pisgah District of the National Forest has a number of outstanding features and points of interest. This district is the most popular of all four, and receives over five million visitors a year. Over 156,000 acres in size, it encompasses parts of Buncombe, Haywood, Henderson, and Transylvania counties. There are over 275 miles of trails for hiking, horseback riding, and mountain biking. Two of the three wilderness areas, Shining Rock and Middle Prong, are in this district. There is a Ranger Station and Visitor Center located on US 276 a few miles into the forest from Hwy. 280 in Brevard. I recommend you visit the center before continuing on into the forest.

Location: The Pisgah District of the Pisgah National Forest is located to the west of Asheville

Distance: 45 minutes-1 hour from Asheville

Address: Pisgah District Office, 1001 Pisgah Hwy., Pisgah Forest NC 28768

Telephone: Pisgah District Office: 828-877-3350, 828-257-4203, Appalachian Ranger District, French Broad Station: 828-622-3202, Appalachian Ranger District, Toecane Ranger Station: 828-682-6146, Grandfather Ranger District: 828–652-2144

Website: fs.usda.gov/recarea/nfsnc/recarea/?recid=48114

Hours: Pisgah District Ranger Station Visitor Center: Mon–Fri 8am–5pm; holidays and Sat 9am–5pm; Sun noon-5pm

Fees: None to enter park

Camping: Davidson River, Lake Powhatan, North Mills River, Sunburst

Directions: From Asheville: Take Airport Rd. (Hwy. 280) off of Hendersonville Hwy. in Arden. Continue on 280 past Asheville airport to Wal-Mart Shopping Plaza just before Brevard. Turn right onto US 276 into Pisgah Forest. The Ranger Visitor Center will be located on the right a few miles in. From Hendersonville: Take US 64 West from downtown to the intersection of Hwy. 280 and Hwy. 276 at the Wal-Mart Shopping Plaza. Continue straight through light to US 276 and into the Forest. Look for the Ranger Visitor Center on your right.

Tips: Obtain maps and information at Visitor Center. You may order maps through the mail by calling 828-884-4734.

Major Points of Interest:

Andy Cove Nature Trail: A self-guided trail located behind Pisgah Ranger Station (0.7 miles), that goes through several forest habitats. The trail takes about 30 minutes to walk.

Forest Heritage National Scenic Byway: A 79-mile highway loop (US 276, US 64 NC 215 and FS 475) provides numerous opportunities to view the outstanding scenery of the forest, in an area rich in forest history.

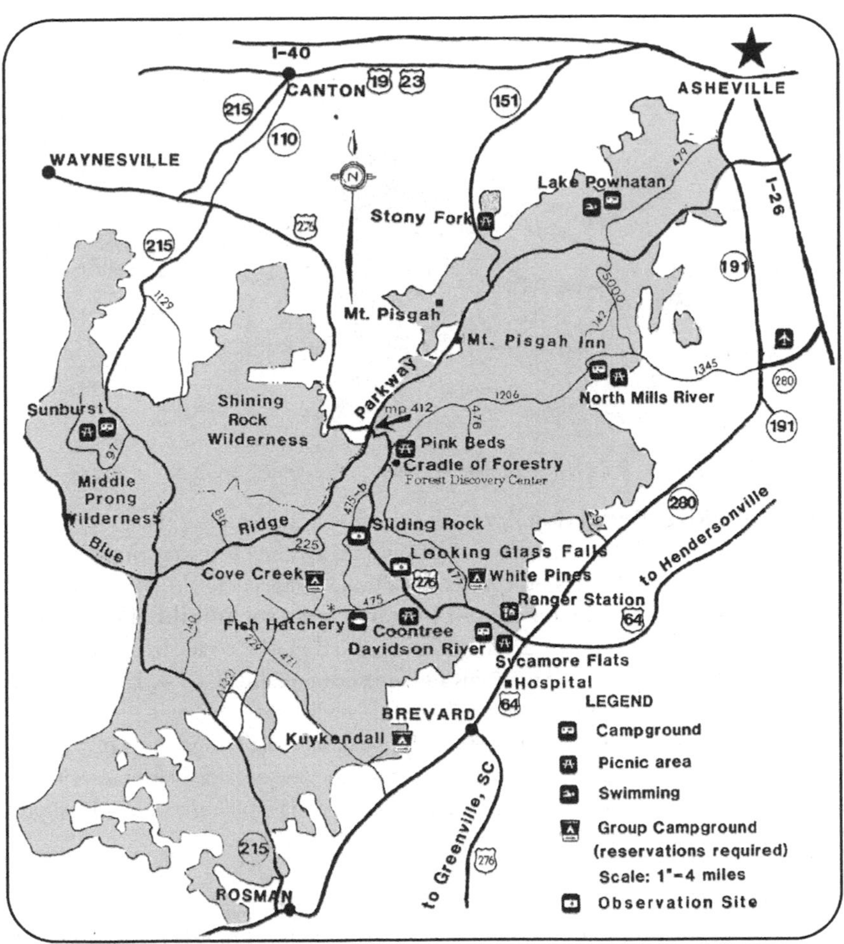

Pisgah District, Pisgah National Forest

The Forest Discovery Center at The Cradle of Forestry in America: This National Historic Site commemorates the birthplace of American forestry and forest education. The Forest Discovery Center features two interpretive exhibits and a gift shop, guided tours on two trails featuring eight historic buildings, restored stationary logging locomotive and living history interpretation by local crafters. cradleofforestry.com. Open 9am–5pm Apr.–Oct. 828-877-3130. (*See* Section V, Chapter Two "Cradle of Forestry")

Lake Powhatan: A family recreation area in Asheville's backyard, Lake Powhatan is located off NC 191 at the end of Bent Creek Rd. The park provides picnic tables with grills and water sources, fishing, swimming beach and hiking trails.

Looking Glass Falls: A beautiful 30–foot wide waterfall that drops more than 60 feet down to a rock cliff. A trail with steps leads to an overlook and to the bottom of the falls. Located along Hwy. 276. Parking is provided.

The Pisgah View Ranch in Candler, showing Mount Pisgah in the distance

North Mills River Recreation Area: This popular area offers picnic tables with grills along the beautiful North Mills River. A popular activity here is tubing on the river, as well as trout fishing. 13 miles north of Hendersonville. (*See* Section IV, Chapter Seven)

Pisgah Forest State Fish Hatchery and Pisgah Center for Wildlife Education: Different species and size of trout can be observed in the raceways and fish food is available to feed the fish. For group programs and information call 828-877-4423. ncwildlife.org. Located off Hwy. 276 on Davidson River Rd. (FS Rd. 475).

Sliding Rock Recreation Area: This very popular observation and water play area is a natural waterslide located on Hwy. 276. Visitors can slide down a 60-foot rock into a 7-foot deep pool; restrooms, changing areas, large parking lot, observation deck, site attendant on duty Memorial Day through mid-Aug. Small fee.

Santeetlah Lake

Santeetlah Lake, located in Graham County, has 76 miles of mostly natural forested shoreline, is over 3,000 acres in size and is surrounded by the Cheoah District of the Nantahala National Forest. Almost 80% of the shoreline is public land which is managed by the North Carolina Forest Service. Boating, kayaking and canoeing are popular activities and Cheoah Point on the east side of the Santeetlah Lake offers swimming at a lakeside beach, picnic areas, over 26 campsites and hiking trails. Cheoah Point is the only campground with facilities on Santeetlah Lake. Since most of the surrounding land is public access, there are many primitive campsites scattered along the shoreline. These free sites however have no facilities, no toilets or grills.

Nearby Forest Service Campgrounds are Horse Cove, located on Big Santeetlah Creek with 17 campsites, toilets, and no showers (Modest fee per day/open winter with no fees/first come first served), and the group camp at Rattler Ford which has four sites (up to 50 people each site), showers, and toilets (Fee per site by reservation). For more information contact the Cheoah District Office at 828-479-6431.

The lake was created in 1928 by the damming of the Cheoah River to create hydroelectric power as it flows northward to join the Little Tennessee River. During the last decades of the twentieth century non-public lands were developed as scenic residences and vacation homes, most notably in the area now incorporated as the town of Lake Santeetlah. Cheoah Dam was also one site of the film "The Fugitive" starring Harrison Ford.

Location: Along US Hwy. 129 in Graham County NC.
Distance: From Asheville 2–2.5 hours
Website: grahamcountytravel.com/santeetlahlaketrail
Resources: Graham County NC Travel and Tourism Authority, 12 Main St., Robbinsville NC,28711; 828-479-3790
Directions: From Asheville take I-40 West toward Knoxville. Take Exit 27 to merge into US Hwy. 74/19 West toward Waynesville/Murphy. Approximately 20 miles past Bryson City take right into Hwy. 129 to Robbinsville. Santeetlah Lake is six miles north of Robbinsville on Hwy. 129.

Chapter Two

Cultural Attractions

Asheville

For information about the attractions listed below, see Section III, Chapter Two, Asheville Cultural Attractions.

Asheville & Appalachian Pinball Museums
Asheville Art Museum
Asheville Community Theatre (ACT)
Asheville's Fun Depot
Asheville Museum of Science
Asheville Urban Trail
Basilica of St. Lawrence
Biltmore Estate (*See* Section III, Chapter Three, Biltmore Estate)
Biltmore Industries Homespun Museum
Biltmore Village
Black Mountain College Museum + Art Center
Blue Ridge Parkway Destination Center
Botanical Gardens at Asheville
Estes-Winn Memorial Automobile Museum
Folk Art Center of the Southern Highland Craft Guild
Grove Arcade Public Market
Harrah's Cherokee Casino Asheville
McCormick Field & the Asheville Tourists
North Carolina Arboretum
North Carolina Homespun Museum
Omni Grove Park Inn (*See* Section III, Chapter Five, Omni Grove Park Inn)
Pack Place Education, Arts & Science Center
Smith-McDowell House
Southern Appalachian Radio Museum
The Antique Car Museum at Grovewood Village
The Wortham Center for the Performing Arts
Thomas Wolfe Memorial
Western North Carolina Agricultural Center

Western North Carolina Farmers Market
Western North Carolina Nature Center
YMI Cultural Center

Cultural Attractions North of Asheville

Dry Ridge Historical Museum

The Dry Ridge Historical Museum, housed in the Weaverville Public Library, documents the life of the area's first settlers dating back to 1787, especially residents of the Reems Creek and Flat Creek Townships. The museum displays a collection of artifacts that include furniture, tools, clothing, letters, ledgers, books, photographs, and portraits.

Location: Weaverville NC
Distance: 30 minutes from downtown Asheville
Address: Weaverville Public Library, Lower Level, 41 N. Main St. Weaverville NC 28787
Telephone: 828-250-6482
Hours: Mar.–Nov.: Sat only from 10am–4pm
Fees: None

Allow: 1 hour minimum
Directions: From I-240, take the Weaverville Exit 4A onto 19/23 North. Go seven miles and take the New Stock Rd. Exit. Turn right off the ramp and left onto US 25/70 North. Make a left onto Main St.

Penland Gallery & School of Crafts

The Penland Gallery, located at the Penland School of Crafts, features work by artists affiliated with the school. The Penland School of Crafts is a national center for craft education dedicated to helping people live creative lives. The school offers one-, two-, and eight-week workshops in books & paper, clay, drawing, glass, iron, metals, photography, printmaking and letterpress, textiles, and wood. Tours of the Penland School are available on Tue at 10:30am and Thu at 1:30pm Reservations are required.

Location: Penland NC
Distance: 1 hour from Asheville
Address: 3135 Conley Ridge Rd., Penland NC 28765
Telephone: Gallery: 828-765-6211, School: 828-765-2359
Website: penland.org
Admission: Free
Hours: Early Mar. through mid-Dec. Tue–Sat 10am–5pm, Sun 12–5pm, Closed Mon
Directions: From Asheville take 19/23 North and get off at exit 9 toward Burnsville/ Spruce Pine. Continue on US 19 for approximately 16 miles. Turn left at NC 1160 Rabbit Hop Rd. then take first right onto NC 1162 Penland Rd. Turn left at Bailey's Peak Rd.

Rural Heritage Museum

This small museum is housed in the Montague building on the campus of Mars Hill College and is dedicated to preserving mountain farm and craft culture. It focuses on Pre-Industrial Appalachia as well as the Industrial period that followed, with depictions of hearth and home, exhibits of farm and craft implements, and historic photographic murals. An exhibit honoring the Hooked-Rug Industry, which existed in Madison County and other parts of Western North Carolina, is one of the museum's most fascinating displays.

Location: Mars Hill College, Mars Hill NC
Distance: 30 minutes from Asheville
Address: NC 213, Montague Building, Mars Hill College, Mars Hill NC 28754
Telephone: 828-684-1400
Hours: Tue–Sun 1–5pm and by appointment
Fees: None
Allow: 1 hour
Directions: From I-240, take Weaverville Exit 4A (19/23N) to the Mars Hill Exit. Follow Hwy. 213 to the first light. Just ahead will be the college campus. The museum is housed in the native stone Montague building just inside the gate on the right.

Rush Wray Museum of Yancey County History

Located within the historic McElroy House, this museum focuses on Yancey County's local history and Appalachian mountain heritage. One of their permanent exhibits is "Our people, our heritage, our pride," which features the settlement of Yancey County and Burnsville NC. The Revolving Exhibit Room hosts changing exhibits including "The Pisgah Village," "Cane River Archeological Site," "The Civil War and the Home Guard," and "The McElroy House."

Location: Burnsville NC
Distance: 45 minutes to 1 hour from Asheville
Address: 11 Academy St., Burnsville NC 28714
Telephone: 828-682-3671
Hours: April 10–Oct. 10, Sat 1–7pm Call for weekday hours.
Fees: None
Allow: 1 hour
Directions: From Asheville, take 19/23 North to Mars Hill/Burnsville Exit. Follow 19E to Burnsville. The museum is located behind the visitor center.

Zebulon B. Vance Birthplace

The birthplace of the "War Governor of the South," Zebulon B. Vance, is located in Weaverville, just a few miles north of Asheville. Administered by the N.C. Department of Cultural Resources, the Vance birthplace is one of North Carolina's Historic Sites and is open to the public year-round. The homestead, a large two-story structure of hewn yellow pine

Zebulon B. Vance Birthplace

logs, has been reconstructed around the original chimney with its two enormous fireplaces. The furnishings and household items on display today are representative of the period from 1790 to 1840 and include a few pieces original to the home. Clustered about the grounds of the house are six log outbuildings, loom house, slave house, and tool house. Nearby the Visitor Center/Museum houses exhibits portraying the life of Governor Vance.

Each spring and again in the fall, visitors to the Vance home have the opportunity to experience Pioneer Living Days; the grounds come alive with history as costumed staff members and volunteers demonstrate the skills and cherished occupations of settlers in the early days.

Location: Weaverville NC
Distance: 30 minutes from Asheville
Address: 911 Reems Creek Rd., Weaverville NC 28787
Telephone: 828-645-6706
Website: nchistoricsites.org/vance/vance
Hours: Tue–Sat 9am–5pm
Fees: None; donations accepted.
Allow: 1–2 hours
Directions: From Asheville take the I-240 Weaverville Exit 4A off of I-240 (US 19/23N) to New Stock Rd. Turn right off the ramp, left onto US 25/70 North, and follow to Reems Creek Rd. where you will turn right.

Cultural Attractions South of Asheville

Hendersonville

For information about the attractions listed below, *See* Section IV, Chapter Two Hendersonville Cultural Attractions

Bullington Gardens
Carl Sandburg Home
Flat Rock Playhouse
Flat Rock Playhouse
Henderson County Curb Market
Henderson County Heritage Center
Henderson County History Center
Hendersonville Railroad Depot
Historic Johnson Farm
Holmes Educational State Forest
Mountain Farm & Home Museum
Team ECCO Aquarium & Shark Lab
Thomas Wolfe Angel
Western North Carolina Air Museum

Bennett Classics Antique Auto Museum

Located in Forest City, the Bennett Classics Antique Auto Museum has a collection of over 50 antique and completely restored automobiles. They also have a show room with resorted cars for sale, and well as displays of automotive memorabilia.

Location: Forest City NC
Distance: 1 hour from Asheville
Address: 241 Vance St., Forest City NC 28043
Telephone: 828-247-1767
Website: bennettclassics.com
Hours: Mon–Fri 10am–5pm, Sat 10am–3pm
Fees: Adult and child rates
Allow: 1–2 hours
Directions: From Asheville take I-26 south past Hendersonville to exit for US 74 toward Columbus/Rutherfordton, Shelby. Hwy. Take exit 181 off of MC 74 and travel north. Turn right on Church St., and then left on Main St. Go two stop lights and turn right onto Vance St.

Foothills Equestrian Nature Center (FENCE)

The Foothills Equestrian Nature Center, also known as FENCE, provides the South Carolina Upstate and Western North Carolina with a nature preserve of 380 acres, open to the public year-round. FENCE has an award-winning equestrian facility that hosts local, regional and national events, offers birding activities and programs, and is a learning center for children. FENCE also hosts youth cross-country meets. The are over five miles of trails for walking, riding and carriage use, a wildlife pond, quiet meadows and sweeping panoramas. FENCE also hosts steeplechases, horse trails, dressage shows, pleasure driving and cross-country races. Stabling is available for over 180 horses, and there are lighted show rings, and cross-country and steeplechase courses.

Location: Tryon NC
Distance: 1 hour from Asheville
Address: 3381 Hunting Country Rd. Tryon NC 28782
Telephone: 828-859-9021
Website: fence.org
Hour: Dawn to dusk daily; Office Hours: 9am–4pm
Fees: None for hiking and nature trails. Equestrian fees charged for Bed and Barn Program (Bring your own horse, rental stalls and apartment are available. Call the Equestrian Director)
Directions: Take I-26 East from Asheville or Hendersonville. Take S.C. Exit 1. Turn right toward Landrum. Go 1.5 miles and take a right onto Bomar Rd. Go one short block and turn right onto Prince Rd. After 1.7 miles, turn left onto Hunting Country Rd., just before the I-26 overpass. Go slightly over .5 mile to FENCE's entrance on the right.

Green River Plantation

The Green River Plantation, located in Rutherfordton, is a 42-room antebellum mansion built circa 1804–1807 on 356 acres. It is open to the public for tours by reservation only. The Plantation also hosts: weddings, receptions, rehearsal dinners, parties, picnics & other special events. The Green River Plantation is listed in the National Register of Historic Places. If you are interested in seeing a classic example of a southern plantation home, then a visit to Green River will be worth the trip.

Location: Rutherfordton NC
Distance: 1 hour, 30 minutes from Asheville
Address: 6333 Coxe Rd., Rutherfordton NC 28139
Telephone: 828-286-1461.
Website: green-river.net/Green_River_Plantation/Home
Fees: Tours by reservation only: Adult, senior, and child rates
Allow: Tours last approximately one hour.
Directions: From Asheville take 1–26 south past Hendersonville and take the exit for US 74 toward Columbus and Rutherfordton. Take exit 173 off of 74 and turn right at Union Rd. Turn left at Coxe Rd.

House of Flags

The House of Flags is an educational museum, opened on Sep. 8, 2001, that houses over 300 different flags. The collection includes U.S. military service and Veteran's flags, religious flags, pre-Colonial and Colonial flags as well as flags of the Revolutionary and Civil War eras to the birth of the "Stars and Stripes" of the U.S. The centerpiece of the collection is the display of all 27 official flags of America from 13 to 50 stars. Each state's and territory's flags are also on display along with a number of unique flags associated with historical events.

Location: Columbus NC
Distance: 45 minutes from Asheville
Address: 33 Gibson St., Columbus NC 28722
Telephone: 828-894-5640
Hours: Tue–Thu 10am–1pm; Sat 10am–4pm
Fees: None; donations accepted.
Allow: 1 hour
Directions: From Asheville take I-26 south approximately 38 miles to the exit for Hwy. 74 E and Columbus. Take Exit 163 off of 74 to 108 West to Columbus. Turn left onto Gibson St. in downtown Columbus.

KidSenses Children's InterACTIVE Museum

KidSenses Children's InterACTIVE Museum is located in Rutherfordton, and has exhibits and special workshops to stimulate the imagination and educate the minds of young children. Discovery Garden, Virtual Reality Ride and Lights! Camera! Action! are a few of the many themed interactive exhibits.

Location: Rutherfordton NC
Address: 172 North Main St., Rutherfordton NC 28139
Distance: 1 hour from Asheville
Telephone: 828-286-2120
Website: kidsenses.com
Hours: Mon–Thu 9am–5pm, Fri 9am–8pm, Sat 9am–5pm
Fees: Adult and child rates
Directions: From Asheville Take I-40 east to NC 221 and get off at exit 85. Go right toward Rutherfordton.

Polk County Historical Museum

Located in the Feagan Building at 60 Walker St. in Columbus the Polk County Historical Museum contains a large collection that includes artifacts from the Cherokee Indians, early settlers, the Revolutionary War, the Civil War, and World War II. Museum items include tools and clothing of the settlers, various railroad treasures, photos and paintings of historic sites in Polk County, and memorabilia from local residents. They also have a large collection of early maps, records, and pictures including important items in American history. The Polk County History Museum is within walking distance of the Polk County Courthouse which was built in 1859, and historical markers and points of interest such as the Howard Monument, the Dough Boy statue and Stearns Park.

Location: Columbus NC
Distance: 45 minutes from Asheville
Address: Feagan Building, 60 Walker St., Columbus NC 28722
Telephone: 828-894-3351, 828-859-6655
Hours: Tue–Thu 10am–1pm Sat 10am–4pm and by appointment
Fees: None
Allow: 1 hour
Directions: From Asheville, take I-26 East to US-74E (signs for Columbus, Rutherfordton NC Hwy. 108). Take exit 163 for NC Hwy. 108 West toward Columbus. Turn left onto Walker St. in Columbus.

Rutherford County Farm Museum

The Rutherford County Farm Museum has exhibits of antique farm equipment and items dating back to the earliest days of the nineteenth century. Two large murals, depicting the cycle of growing cotton and the early textile mills of the county, are outstanding features of the museum.

Location: Forest City NC
Distance: 45 minutes from Asheville
Address: 240 Depot St., Forest City NC 28043
Telephone: 828-248-1248
Hours: Wed–Sat: 10am–4pm
Fees: Adult rate, children free
Allow: 1 hour

Directions: From Asheville take I-26 South to Exit 35. Take Hwy. 74 East to Columbus/ Rutherfordton. Take exit 182 to US 221 to Forest City. In Forest City turn left at South Broadway, then turn left at Florence St. and continue to Depot St.

Tryon Arts & Crafts Heritage Gallery

The Tryon Arts & Crafts Heritage Gallery, run by Tryon Arts & Crafts, has permanent exhibitions of over 200 artifacts native to Western North Carolina, and specifically the Tryon Area, some dating back as far as 1775. On display are animals, dolls and tiny pieces of furniture from the original Tryon Toy-Makers and Wood Carvers, including a small version of Morris, made by Eleanor Vance, an original founder of the Tryon Toy-Makers.

Cherokee artifacts include a large collection of pottery and several collections of arrowheads, tomahawks, dolls and baskets. The Pisgah Forest pottery collection includes a pitcher featuring a fine cameo or pate sure embellishment. Other exhibits include original forged work and kitchen tools, quilts, furniture, musical instruments and paintings by local artists.

The mission of Tryon Arts & Crafts is to preserve, enhance and promote native mountain arts & crafts by providing education, instruction and opportunity to express, develop and showcase creative talent. The organization has its home in the former Tryon Middle School, a building of over 10,000 square feet. Classes and instruction in arts and crafts are offered at the center on a regular basis, and there is a gift shop on the premises as well.

Location: Tryon NC
Distance: 45 minutes from Asheville
Address: 373 Harmon Field Rd., Tryon NC 28782
Telephone: 828-859-8323
Website: ryonartsandcrafts.org
Hours: Mon–Fri 10am–4pm, Sat 10am–1pm
Fees: None
Allow: 1–2 hours
Directions: From Asheville, take Interstate 26 South to Exit 67 (Columbus NC). Turn right onto Hwy 108 and West Mills St. and continue straight to 373 Harmon Field Rd.

Tryon Fine Arts Center

The Tryon Fine Arts Center has a 315-seat auditorium, a Mural Room for gatherings, an Exhibition Gallery, work rooms, an outdoor garden and is home to the Tryon Little Theater, with more than 900 members It also houses Tryon Crafts, whose classes include weaving, silver making, enameling on copper, rug hooking, crewel and needlepoint, macramé, wood carving, knitting, stained glass and lampshades. The center is home to the Carolina Camera Club, and the Tryon Painters & Sculptors, whose members, both professional and amateur, regularly exhibit in the gallery and other public areas. The center has a retail shop which is open to the public.

Location: Tryon NC
Distance: 45 minutes from Asheville
Address: 34 Melrose Ave., Tryon NC 28782
Telephone: 828-859-8322

Website: tryonarts.org
Hours: Weekdays 10am–4pm
Fees: None
Allow: 1–2 hours
Directions: From Asheville, take Interstate 26 South to Exit 67 (Columbus, North Carolina). Turn right onto Hwy 108. Head toward Tryon approximately 6.5 miles. Hwy 108 joins Hwy 176 at traffic light (Texaco at corner). Count this as first traffic light and continue on Hwy 176 east until you reach fourth traffic light. (Big wooden horse across and right of intersection.) At fourth traffic light turn right onto Pacolet St., up over railroad tracks, then make second left onto Chestnut St. (before the Bank of America Building). Dr. to top of hill and turn right onto Melrose Ave.

Tryon International Equestrian Center

The Tryon International Equestrian Center (TIEC) is a year-round venue located in Mill Spring, NC and is the world's premier Equestrian Lifestyle Destination showcasing some of the top riders in the Hunter/Jumper, Dressage, and Eventing disciplines. This world-class equestrian center welcomes guests 365 days a year to watch, dine, shop, and experience one of the premier riding facilities in the world built for the love of horses and the sport of horseback riding. Riders and horses from all over the world compete at TIEC from the comfort of our elevated viewing areas around each ring with ample shade and seating. Admission to all horse shows is free and open to the public with complimentary parking. On-site lodging is also available as well as the best in equine stabling and services. During non-competition weeks, TIEC hosts other events including festivals and concerts and boasts a diverse range of dining options, with numerous on-site restaurants and event vendors selling sushi, fresh-roasted coffee, wood-fired pizza, lemonade, ice cream and a variety of candy and carnival snacks are on-site during horse show weeks. The center also features a range of stores offering the top equestrian brands of tack and riding apparel to jewelry, antique and clothing boutiques as well as local performers and bands on various weeknights throughout the year.

Location: Tryon NC
Distance: One hour from Asheville
Address: 25 International Blvd. Mill Spring, NC 28756
Telephone: 828-863-1000
Website: tryon.coth.com
Hours: Varies depending upon venue and event. Check Center website.
Directions: From Asheville get on I-26 E / US 74 E, then take exit 67, US 74 E to Columbus. Drive 8 miles, then take exit 170.

Cultural Attractions East of Asheville

Alleghany County Courthouse

Built in 1933–34 following the destruction by fire of the first courthouse, this two-story brick County Courthouse with white columns is an example of Classical Revival architecture of the period. The architect was Harry Barton. Alleghany County is nestled in the Blue Ridge Mountains of Northwestern North Carolina. Alleghany County was formed out of Ashe

County by an act of the 1858–1859 session of the North Carolina legislature. The Courthouse is listed on the National Register of Historic Places and continues to the present day as a functioning courthouse.

Location: Sparta NC
Distance: 3 hours from Asheville
Address: 12 North Main St., Sparta NC 28675
Telephone: 336-372-8949
Admission: Free
Directions: From Asheville, take I-40 East to Marion and take Hwy. 221 North to through Boone to Sparta.

Appalachian Heritage Museum

The Appalachian Heritage Museum is a living history museum in the same complex as Mystery Hill in Blowing Rock NC. It is housed in the historic Dougherty House, which was the home of the Dougherty Brothers, D.D. and B.B., founders of Appalachian State University. The purpose of the museum is to show visitors how middle class mountain families lived at the turn of the century.

Location: Mystery Hill complex between Boone and Blowing Rock NC
Distance: 2 hours, longer if using the Blue Ridge Parkway
Address: 129 Mystery Hill Lane, Blowing Rock NC 28605
Telephone: 828-264-2792
Hours: Jun.–Aug. 8am–8pm; Sep.–May 9am–5pm
Fees: Rates vary. Call for current rate schedule. Senior, military, group, and AAA discounts are available.
Allow: 1 hour
Directions: From Asheville, take I-40 East to Marion. Take Hwy. 221 North to Blowing Rock. Then, take 321 North four miles to the Mystery Hill complex. Alternately, take the Blue Ridge Parkway north to exit at mile marker 291 and take Hwy. 321 North for 1.5 miles.

Ashe County Arts Council Gallery

Located in the Ashe Arts Center, The Ashe County Arts Council Gallery consists of changing exhibits of local artists and performances of music, poetry, literature and more. The spectrum of work shown ranges from traditional to contemporary, from quilts to pottery to abstract fine art.

Location: West Jefferson NC
Address: 303 School Ave., West Jefferson 28694
Telephone: 336-847-2787
Website: ashecountyarts.org/gallery
Hours: Mon–Fri 9am–5pm, Sat 10am–4pm (Apr.–Dec.)
Fees: None
Allow: 1–2 hours

Directions: From Asheville take I-40 west to exit 72 and merge onto US 70 toward Old Fort. After 11 miles turn left at US 221 and follow US 221 through Boone to West Jefferson.

Avery County Historical Museum

The Avery County Historical Museum is housed in the historic (circa 1912) Avery County Jail and has displays of early Avery County life. The jailhouse is one of the last intact old jails in North Carolina. The museum was formed in 1976 to collect, preserve and display vital information, photographs and artifacts about people, events and places that make up the history of Avery County and this area.

Location: Newland NC
Distance: 2 hours from Asheville
Address: 1829 Schultz Circle, Newland NC 28657
Telephone: 828-733-7311
Website: averymuseum.com/avery_county_museum%20guide.htm
Admission: Free
Hours: 10 am–4 pm Fri, 11 am–3 pm Sat
Directions: From Asheville, take I-40 East to Morganton and take Hwy. 181 North to Pineola, just past the Blue Ridge Parkway. Turn left on Hwy. 221 and then right onto 194 North to Newland.

Banner House Museum

The Banner House Museum presents a glimpse of 19th century life in Banner Elk and the High Country in the home of Samuel Henry Banner, one of Banner Elk's original settlers. The restored household dates back to the 1870-80s and is an authentic window into that period of history.

Location: Banner Elk NC
Distance: 2 hours from Asheville
Address: 7990 Hickory Nut Gap Rd., Banner Elk NC 28604
Telephone: 828-898-3634
Website: bannerhousemuseum.org
Hours: Jun. 20th–Oct. 17th, Tue–Sat: 11am–4pm Private tours available
Fees: Adult and child rates
Directions: From Asheville take i-40 West. Get off at exit 72 and merge onto US 70 toward Old Fort. Turn left at NC 226/US 221 and take 221 north. In Linville take 105 north and turn left at NC 184. Tynecastle Hwy. to Banner Elk. Turn right on Hickory Nut Gap Rd. After you cross the bridge, you will see the museum on your left.

Ben Long Frescoes

Western North Carolina is home to four churches that are graced by Ben Long's frescoes. Fresco painting is an ancient art form based on the immediate application of pigment to wet plaster, and Western North Carolina artist Ben Long is considered one of the few American masters of the art. The marvelous luminous beauty of his frescoes in these churches attract over 80,000 visitors annually from around the world. The closest of Long's frescoes to Asheville is located in the Black Mountain area, in Montreat College's Chapel of the Prodigal Son. Farther east, the Holy Trinity Church in Glendale Springs features his fresco of the Lord's Supper and other assorted artworks. St. Mary's Church in nearby West Jefferson is home to frescoes of the Mystery of Faith, Mary Great with Child, and John the Baptist. The fourth church, St. Paul's Episcopal Church in Wilkesboro is home to Long's fresco depicting the story of St. Paul.

Locations: Montreat, Glendale Springs, West Jefferson and Wilkesboro NC
Distance: Glendale Springs, West Jefferson and Wilkesboro (2–3 hours from Asheville); Montreat (30 minutes from Asheville)
Address: Montreat–Lookout Rd., Montreat NC 28757
Address: Glendale Springs–Holy Trinity Church, 195 J.W. Luke Rd., Glendale Springs NC 28629
Telephone: 336-982-3076
Address: West Jefferson–St. Mary's Church, 400 Beaver Creek School Rd., West Jefferson NC 28694
Telephone: 336-246-3552
Address: Wilkesboro–St. Paul's Episcopal Church, 200 West Cowles St., Wilkesboro NC 28697
Hours: Please call and ask about hours for viewing.
Fees: None
Allow: .5 to 1 hour each church
Directions to Montreat: From Asheville take I-240 East to I-40. Take I-40 to Exit 64 (Black Mountain/Montreat). Turn left onto NC 9/Broadway. Stay in the left-hand lane. Dr. over the railroad tracks and through the traffic light. At the second traffic light, continue through. At the third traffic light, continue through; the street changes to Montreat Rd. At the stone Montreat Gate, the road changes to Assembly Dr. Turn right on Lookout Rd. to Chapel on the right.
Directions to Wilkesboro, Glendale Springs, and West Jefferson: From Asheville, take I-40 East to Hickory. Take Exit 131 to NC 16 North to Wilkesboro to St. Paul's Church. To see the other two churches, take 421 North toward Watauga. Turn left onto NC 16 North again to Glendale Springs and Holy Trinity Church. From Glendale Springs take NC 16 North to NC 221. Turn left onto NC 221 to West Jefferson and St. Mary's Church.

Bunker Hill Covered Bridge

Designated as a National Civil Engineering Landmark in 2001, the Bunker Hill Covered Bridge is the only remaining example in wood of the Improved Lattice Truss patented by General Herman Haupt. It joins the Cape Hatteras Lighthouse, the Blue Ridge Parkway, and Dorton Arena in representing North Carolina on this prestigious list.

One of only two original remaining covered bridges in North Carolina, the other being Mt. Pisgah in Randolph County. The bridge was built in 1895 by Andy L. Ramsour. In 1894 Catawba County Commissioners had called on nearby owners of Bunker Hill Farm to build and maintain a bridge that would cross Lyle's Creek on the old Island Ford Rd., a former Native American trail. The landowners hired Ramsour, keeper of the Horseford covered bridge that spanned the Catawba River north of Hickory. He likely found Haupt's design in a popular book on bridge building. Originally constructed as an open span, the Bunker Hill Covered Bridge, whose roof is ninety-one feet long, was covered in 1900. In 1921 its wooden shingles were replaced with a tin roof.

Location: Claremont NC
Distance: 1 hour and 30 minutes from Asheville
Address: Highway 70, Claremont NC 28610
Telephone: 828-465-0383
Website: catawbahistory.org/bunker_hill_covered_bridge.php
Hours: Open 24/7 365 days a year
Fees: None
Allow: .5 hour
Directions: From Asheville take I-40 East toward Statesville. Take Exit 135 toward Claremont. Turn right at North Oxford St. and then then left at West Main St./US Hwy. 70. Follow Hwy. 70 two miles east of town.

Burke Arts Council Jailhouse Gallery

The Jailhouse Gallery is a public gallery dedicated to promoting the art and crafts of Burke County artists and craftsmen as well as out of state artists, and is run by the Burke Arts Council. The Council was founded in 1975 and is a non-profit, tax-exempt corporation funded by individual membership and corporate donors. It hosts three galleries which provide space for both local and out of state artists.

Location: Morganton NC
Address: 115 Meeting St., Morganton NC 28655
Telephone: 828-433-7282
Website: burkearts.org
Hours: Mon–Fri 10am–4pm
Fees: None
Allow: 1–2 hours
Directions: Take I-40 East from Asheville, take the US 64 exit-Exit 103 toward Morganton and Rutherfordton, turn left onto US 64, turn right onto West Union St./US 64 /US 70, Continue to follow US 64 E/ S 70, end at 115 E Meeting St.

Caldwell Heritage Museum

The Caldwell Heritage Museum was opened in 1991 and is dedicated to preserving and presenting the history of Caldwell County, North Carolina, through about two dozen permanent exhibits and rotating special exhibits. The museum is housed in the last remaining building of Davenport College, a prestigious institution of higher learning for women that was supported by the Methodist Church from 1855 to 1933.

Over 35,000 square feet of vertical, horizontal, and floor space have been utilized in the Caldwell Heritage Museum to show Caldwell Country's history and culture from pre-colonial, pioneer, Revolutionary, and Civil War eras to the present day. Specialized collections and exhibits also include antique furniture and farm implements; Native American artifacts; World War I and II memorabilia; the Caldwell County Music Preservation collection; an antique phonograph, radio, and TV exhibit; and Plains and Western Indian exhibits.

Location: Lenoir NC
Distance: 1 hour from Asheville
Address: 112 Vaiden St. SE (PO Box 2165), Lenoir NC 28645
Telephone: 828-758-4004
Website: caldwellheritagemuseum.org
Hours: Tue through Fri from 10am–4:30pm, and on Sat from 10am–3pm.
Fees: None, donations accepted
Allow: 1–2 hours
Directions: From Asheville, take I-40 East to Rte. 321 in Hickory. Follow 321 North to Lenoir. In Lenoir, you will come to a major intersection (Burger King and Eckerd's Drugstore). Take a left and after 100 yards, bear again to your left. The road turns into Harper Ave. Stay on Harper and bear to the right in front of the Fire Department and Post Office. Turn right after the Police Department and then left onto Willow. Left again at the stop sign will take you onto Harper. Make a right at the first light and then left at the stop light at the top of the hill. The first street on your right will be Vaiden St. The museum is on Vaiden at the top of the hill.

Catawba County Museum of History

The Catawba County Museum of History offers testimony to the hardy settlers of the Catawba River Valley and their resourceful descendants who carved a world-renowned furniture and textile empire out of the backwoods. The story is artfully displayed in the unique setting of the former Catawba County Courthouse, an imposing National Register Renaissance Revival structure built in 1924, on the square in downtown Newton.

Museum collections include agricultural tools and implements forged from hand-dug iron ore, as well as handcrafted household cupboards, wagon benches, beds, tables, chests, cradles, plantation desks, a firkin, and miniature furniture samples shown by "drummers" or early salesmen. There are treasured military uniforms, including a British Red Coat from the Revolutionary War era (one of the few such coats in existence) and a major repository of Civil War objects.

Two full-scale, original antebellum parlors have been reconstructed and preserved in the museum: the Shuford-Jarett from 1830, featuring deft molding-plane embellishments and pegged muntins, and the Munday Parlor from 1840, with trompe l'oeil dentils, marbleized wooden baseboards, and a dazzling hand-painted central medallion. Visitors can also walk through Dr. Hambrick's 1920's medical office, containing his ice-cold stainless steel examination table and an extensive variety of instruments from the period. Also on permanent exhibit at the museum is a 1930's racecar which roared around the county fairgrounds, complemented with a photograph gallery of the first race at the Hickory Motor Speedway, in 1951.

Location: Newton NC
Distance: 1 hour and 15 minutes from Asheville
Address: 30 North College St., Newton NC 28658

Telephone: 828-465-0383
Website: catawbahistory.org/catawba_county_museum_of_history.php
Hours: Wed–Sat 9am–4pm, Sun 1:30–4:30pm
Fees: None
Allow: 1–2 hours
Directions: From Asheville take I-40 East toward Statesville. Take Exit 130 toward Old US 70. Turn left at West 1st St., take the 2nd right onto 1st Ave. South. Continue onto North Main Ave., and turn left at East 1st St. Take the 1st right onto North College Ave. in Newton.

Catawba Science Center

The Catawba Science Center has permanent exhibit areas that explore the physical, natural and earth sciences, and interactive traveling exhibits that rotate throughout the years. CSC also has some outstanding freshwater and saltwater aquarium exhibits, featuring North Carolina's only marine touch pool with live sharks and stingrays.

One of the main highlights of the Science Center is the Millholland Planetarium, a state of the art theater, featuring 30–ft full dome illuminated by digital technology-MEDIAGLOBE 3-D, created by Konica Minolta of Japan-and a powerful surround sound system. In addition to traditional planetarium shows, the Millholland Planetarium also has an AVI Skylase full-dome laser system, enabling visitors to experience dynamic laser light shows accompanied by modern pop, alternative, holiday and classic rock presentations.

CSC also offers many and varied educational programs to the general public on an on-going basis, and also maintains two science-oriented gift shops as well as a climbing wall in the courtyard. One of the more popular features of the center is the Naturalist Center where exhibits of live reptiles, amphibians, insects and arachnids are presented.

Location: Hickory NC
Distance: 1 hour and 15 minutes from Asheville
Address: 243 3rd Ave., Hickory NC 28603
Telephone: 828-322-8169
Website: catawbascience.org
Hours: Tue–Fri 10am–5pm, Sat 10am–4pm, Sun 1–4pm
Fees: Adults $6, Seniors $4, Youth (2–18) $4, Children under 3-Free; Planetarium-$3
Allow: 1–2 hours
Directions: From Asheville take I-40 East toward Statesville. Take Exit 123A-123B for US 321 toward Hickory. Continue on US 321 North. Turn right at 2nd Ave. NW, turn left at 3rd St. NE and take the 1st left onto 3rd Ave.

Catherine Smith Gallery

The Catherine Smith Gallery is a program of Appalachian State University and is located within Farthing Auditorium at the University. The gallery is a non-profit institution, in the service of society and its development and open to the public. The gallery is committed to researching, exhibiting and interpreting, for the purpose of study, education, and enjoyment of objects, activities and documents which are part of the focus of visual arts. The mission of the gallery is to become a center for the presentation of the visual arts in Northwestern North Carolina by establishing a regionally significant exhibition and research program in support of the educational mission of Appalachian State University.

Location: Boone NC
Address: Farthing Auditorium, 731 Rivers St., ASU, Boone NC 28608
Telephone: 828-262-7338
Website: art.appstate.edu/cjs
Hours: Mon–Fri 10am–5pm
Fees: None
Allow: 1–2 hours
Directions: From Asheville take I-40 east. At exit 72 merge onto US 70 E toward Old Fort. Turn left onto US 221 N. Continue on US-221 N to Linville. Turn left onto NC 105 N. Follow NC 105 N to Boone. To go Directly to Farthing Auditorium: Turn left onto US 321 N. Turn left onto Rivers St. Holmes Convocation Center and Appalachian welcome sign will be on the left. Farthing Auditorium is on the left at the 3rd stoplight. Parking for evening events is on the right at the 3rd stoplight in the Raley Parking Lot.

Chapel of Rest

The Chapel of Rest Preservation Society was created in 1984 to preserve the historical integrity of the Chapel of Rest and to maintain the building and grounds. The Chapel, built in 1887, is in the heart of Happy Valley and situated on a knoll, is reminiscent of a more simple life when locals lined the pews in their Sun best clothing. Travelers who stop in for a rest along the Scenic Byway will find the chapel as peaceful today as those did who visited many years ago.

Location: Lenoir NC (nine miles north of Lenoir, adjacent to the Patterson School)
Distance: 1 hour and 30 minutes east of Asheville
Address: NC Hwy. 268, Lenoir NC 28645
Telephone: 828-758-8619, 828-758-0906
Website: chapelofrest.org
Admission: Free
Hours: Open daily during daylight hours
Directions: From Asheville, take I-40 East to Exit 100 toward Jamestown Rd. Turn left at Jamestown Rd. and after 2 miles right at Carbon City Rd. Go 1 mile and turn left at US 64 Bypass West. After 2.7 miles turn left at NC Hwy. 18 and continue for 14.5 miles. Turn right at Harper Ave. NW and then a quick left at US 321 North. Turn right at NC Hwy. 268 to the Chapel.

Crossnore Fine Arts Gallery

The Crossnore Fine Arts Gallery is located at the Crossnore School in Crossnore, which has been providing residential child care for disadvantaged children since 1913. A significant portion of the proceeds from the sale of artwork in the gallery goes toward helping children through Crossnore's social outreach programs. Artwork displayed ranges from traditional to contemporary in all mediums.

Location: Crossnore NC
Distance: 1 hour from Asheville
Address: 205 Johnson Lane, Crossnore NC 28816
Telephone: 828-733-3144
Website: crossnoregallery.org
Hours: 9am–5pm Apr.–Dec. (Mon–Sat); Dec.–Mar. (Thur-Sat)
Fees: None
Allow: 1 hour
Directions: From I-40, Exit 105 Morganton on Hwy. 181, travel north about 30 miles to Pineola to the intersection of Hwy. 181 and US Hwy. 221. At Pineola, turn left on 221 S. for 1.5 miles, turn right onto Crossnore Dr. .6 miles, turn right onto Johnson Lane at The Blair Fraley Sales Store. Gallery is third building on the left.

Davidson's Fort

Davidson's Fort is located on eighteen acres inside the Old Fort city limits, and is a replica of the original historic fort that existed in the area during colonial days. It is a living history site dedicated to telling the true story of the families of Western North Carolina during the 18th Century and the American Revolution. Facilities include a welcome center/museum area as well as the replicated fort. The fort interprets living conditions and daily life during the late 18th and 19th centuries, and also includes a replica Cherokee village where other reenactments and interpretations are performed.

Location: Old Fort NC
Distance: 30 minutes east of Asheville
Address: Lackey Town Rd., Old Fort NC 28762
Telephone: 828-668-4831
Website: davidsonsfort.com
Admission: Free, donations accepted
Hours: April 1st until end of Nov. Sat from 8am–5pm, or by appointment
Allow: 1–3 hours
Directions: From Asheville take I-40 west to exit 72 and follow Hwy 70. At the stop light turn right, cross the RR and make a left at water street and the Mountain Gateway Museum. Take the next left, then the next right and follow the road to the fort on your left. From the East on I-40—Take exit 73, turn right at the bottom of the ramp turn right on Water St make your next left, then right and follow the road to the fort on your left.

Emerald Village

Emerald Village features the North Carolina Mining Museum, a historic tour, gem-cutting shops with resident goldsmith, gem mining with stone identification, and gem cutters at work. In this famous historic mining area, over 45 different rocks, minerals and gems have been found including aquamarine, beryl, emerald, garnet and smoky quartz. The North Carolina Mining Museum is located underground in a real mine. Authentic mining equipment and displays bring to life the early days of North Carolina mining.

Location: Little Switzerland NC
Distance: 1–2 hours from Asheville
Address: 331 McKinney Mine Rd., Little Switzerland NC 28749.
Telephone: 828-765-6463, 828-765-0000
Website: emeraldvillage.com
Hours: 9am–5pm, seven days a week, May through Oct. Museum is open Apr.–Nov.
Fees: Museum and Displays free. Underground Mine Tour: $6 adults, $5 students (1–12), $5.50 seniors.
Allow: 2 hours
Directions: From Asheville, take I-40 East to Marion. Take NC 221 North to NC 226. Left on NC 226 and go 9 miles to the Blue Ridge Parkway. Go south on parkway and get off at next exit, Little Switzerland, Milepost 334. Take right under parkway onto Chestnut Grove Rd. Turn left onto McKinney Mine Rd.

Fort Defiance

The home of Revolutionary War hero, General William Lenoir, is open to the public. Original clothing and furnishings of this1792 house are on display. General Lenoir was a member of the Council of State, served in both houses of the Legislature and was President of the NC Senate. The history of this house is the history of the opening of the Western North Carolina frontier. Furnishings include more than 300 original pieces, from teacups to bedsteads.

Location: Lenoir NC
Distance: 1.5–2 hours from Asheville
Address: Highway 268, Lenoir NC 28645
Telephone: 828-758-1671
Website: fortdefiancenc.org
Hours: Apr.–Oct., Thu–Sat 10am–5pm, Sun 1–5pm; Nov.–Mar.: Weekends.
Allow: 1 hour
Directions: Take I-40 East from Asheville to Rte. 321 in Hickory. North on Rte. 321 to Patterson. Take 268 East 5.5 miles.

From This Day Forward

Held in the Old Colony amphitheater, From This Day Forward is a seasonal outdoor drama produced by the Old Colony Players that portrays the compelling story of the Waldensian struggle for religious freedom in the 17th century and their eventual migration to Valdese in 1893.

Location: Valdese NC
Distance: 1 hour from Asheville
Address: 400 N. Main St., Valdese NC 28690
Telephone: 828-879-2126
Website: oldcolonyplayers.com/ftdf.html
Hours: 16 evening performances held on Fri, Sat, & Sun at 8:15pm in Jul. and Aug.

Fees: Adult, senior and student rates
Allow: 2.5 hours
Directions: From Asheville, take I-40 East to Exit 111. Take Carolina St. and turn left onto Main St. Turn right on Church St. You will see signs at every intersection.

Granite Falls History & Transportation Museum

The Granite Falls History & Transportation Museum, located in the restored former home of Andrew Baird, showcases local history for Granite Falls, with a special emphasis on history as it relates to transportation in the Granite Falls area. The museum opened to the public in 2006. Exhibits include photographs, furniture and memorabilia dating back over 100 years.

Location: Granite Falls NC
Distance: 1 hour from Asheville
Address: 107 Falls Ave., Granite Falls NC 28630
Telephone: 828-396-2792
Website: granitefallsnc.com/transportationmuseum.html
Hours: Sat 10am–4pm, Sun 2–4pm
Fees: None
Directions: From Asheville take I-40 west to exit 123B for US 321 toward Hickory & Lenoir. Take the Falls Ave. exit.

Happy Valley

From Patterson east to the Wilkesboro Reservoir, this rural route follows NC 268 along the upper Yadkin River from the mountains to the gently rolling foothills of the Piedmont. Historically a farming region, today travelers can see acres of horticultural nurseries and turf farms alongside more traditional crops. This road twists and turns through a river valley dotted with historic homes and old barns. Around Happy Valley, visitors can stop at the Chapel of Rest, a restored Episcopal Church that served The Patterson School in the early 1900s; and Fort Defiance, the 18th century home of Revolutionary War hero William Lenoir. Dr.iving toward Wilkesboro, history buffs will find Whippoorwill Academy and Village where a replica log-cabin village has been reconstructed, or they can find Kerr Scott Dam and Reservoir, a 3,754-acre recreational area for camping, fishing, swimming, boating, hiking, or camping. Frontiersman Daniel Boone also lived here in the mid-18th century with his wife and six children before settling in Kentucky.

As you drive along this scenic 28-mile stretch of road, listen as valley residents describe the area's musical traditions, stories, legends, and traditional farming practices. They're captured in the world-famous ballad, Hang Down Your Head, Tom Dooley, and brought to life by Charles Frazier's award-winning book, Cold Mountain.

Location: Just north of Lenoir-NC Hwy. 268 between Patterson NC and the Wilkesboro Reservoir
Distance: 1 hour and 45 minutes from Asheville to start of Happy Valley in Patterson
Website: happyvalleync.org

Directions: From Asheville take I-40 East to Exit 100 toward Jamestown Rd. Turn left at Jamestown Rd. for 2 miles and then right at Carbon City Rd. Go 1 mile and turn left at US-64 Bypass W. Go 2.7 miles and turn left at NC 18N/US 64. Continue 14.5 miles and turn right at Harper Ave. and then quick left at US 321. Continue for 5.8 miles and turn right at NC 268. Follow 268 North to Happy Valley.

Harper House/Hickory History Center

Considered by the North Carolina Department of Archives and History to possess "the finest Queen Anne interior styling in the entire state," the Harper House and the accompanying Craftsman style Bonniwell-Lyerly House, another of Hickory's finest structures, serve a broad spectrum of visitors and local residents as the Harper House & Hickory History Center. Through a momentous preservation project, with the Catawba County Historical Association having raised $2,000,000 for restorations, the Harper House today welcomes visitors as a house museum, interpreting both Hickory history, through the numerous significant families who lived in the house, and Victorian life in the South, circa 1887, the date of the house's construction.

On the same lot, the Lyerly House, rescued and moved for preservation on Jun. 24, 2004, is devoted to the further interpretation of Hickory's rich past, serving as the Betty Allen Education Center and Margaret Huggins Gallery, as well as a conference facility. Current exhibits include quilts from the CCHA's extensive collection, historical photographs of Hickory, and "Panoramic Catawba," the CCHA's collection of Benjamin Porter panoramic photographs of significant Catawba County sites, events, and groups. The Harper House/ Hickory History Center is maintained by the Catawba County Historical Association.

Location: Hickory NC
Distance: 1 hour and 15 minutes from Asheville
Address: 310 North Center St., Hickory NC 28601
Telephone: 828-324-7294
Website: catawbahistory.org/harper_house_hickory_history_center.php
Hours: Thu–Sat 9am–4pm, Sun 1:30–4:30pm Open Tue & Wed by appointment for groups of ten or more.
Fees: Harper Hours tours: adult, senior, and student rates. Exhibits in the Bonniwell-Lyerly House are free.
Allow: 1–2 hours
Directions: From Asheville take I-40 East toward Statesville. Take Exit 123A-123B for US 321 toward Hickory. Continue on US 321 North. Turn right at 2nd Ave. NW and turn left at North Center St.

Hickory Furniture Mart

The Hickory Furniture Mart is a unique mix of nearly 100 furniture outlet stores, shops and galleries and has long been well-known as one of North Carolina's most popular travel and tourism destinations among furniture shopper enthusiasts nationwide. Within the four-story complex, you'll find home furnishings, accessories, lighting, art, fine rugs, fabrics, and more, all with discounts up to 80% off retail. Over 500,000 visitors travel to the Mart every year to visit these renowned discounted furniture destination. The mart also offers valuable amenities and an exceptional array of furniture-related services including guest, shipping, decorating, design, and upholstery services, a gourmet Café, coffee bar, and group tours. This extraordinary shopping complex has over a million square feet of furniture. The lineup of manufacturers include, Baker, Bassett, Broyhill, Century Furniture, Dr.exel Heritage, Ekornes, Flexsteel, Hancock & Moore, Henredon, Hickory Chair, Hickory White, Hooker Furniture, Kincaid, La-Z-Boy, Maitland-Smith, Mitchell Gold + Bob Williams, Schonbek, Sherrill Furniture, Stanley, and Thomasville, among many others.

Location: Hickory NC
Distance: 1 hour and 15 minutes from Asheville
Address: 2220 Hwy 70 SE, Hickory NC 28602
Telephone: 828-322-3510, 888-640-0025
Website: hickoryfurniture.com
Hours: Mon–Sat 9am–6pm
Directions: Take I-40 East to Hickory, leaving the highway at Exit 126. Turn right at the off-ramp, then right onto Hwy 70 West. Hickory Furniture Mart is on the left.

Hickory Motor Speedway

The Hickory Motor Speedway has been in operation for over 50 years and is the oldest professional sporting venue in Catawba County. Hickory Motor Speedway also stands as the oldest continually operated motor speedway in the country and is known as the "Birthplace of the NASCAR Stars" and "The World's Most Famous Short-Track" (the oval is .363 miles in length). The Speedway has three fully equipped concession stands, a souvenir stand, six large restrooms areas, and three enclosed air-conditioned hospitality suites. There is also a game room and kid's fenced-in area with a climbing gym and swings. RV parking is also available.

Location: Newton NC
Distance: 1 hour and 30 minutes from Asheville
Address: 3130 Hwy. 70 SE, Newton NC 28658
Telephone: 828-464-3655
Website: hickorymotorspeedway.com
Hours: Call for hours
Fees: Adults $10, Teens/Seniors $7.00, Ages 7–12 $4.00, 6 and under Free
Directions: From Asheville take I-40 East toward Statesville. Take Exit 126 for US 70 toward Newton. Turn right at McDonald Parkway and turn left at Conover Boulevard to Speedway.

Hickory Museum of Art

The Hickory Museum of Art is located in a 3-story brick building on the SALT block in the right wing of the Arts and Science Center of Catawba Valley. The museum has permanent and rotating exhibits and feature their Permanent Collection of American Art and works borrowed from private collectors and other institutions. The museum operates the HMA Galleria, a shop that sells unique gifts and collectibles. The shop is open during regular museum hours. The Museum also offers many learning opportunities and regularly holds classes for youth, high school students and adults.

Location: Hickory NC
Distance: 1 hour and 15 minutes from Asheville
Address: 243 Third Ave. NE, Hickory NC 28601
Telephone: 828-327-8576
Website: hickoryart.org/home.php
Hours: Tue–Sat 10am–4pm, Sun 1–4pm
Fees: None
Allow: 1–2 hours
Directions: From Asheville take I-40 East toward Statesville. Take Exit 123A-123B for Hickory. Take US 321 North and turn right at 2nd Ave. NW, turn left at 3rd St. NE, and take the 1st left onto Third Ave. NE.

Hickory Ridge Homestead

Hickory Ridge Homestead is an eighteenth-century living history museum that highlights the daily lives of the early settlers of the Appalachian Mountains. Early furniture, period clothing, utensils, farm implements, and many other early artifacts, as well as displays and exhibits, contribute to the experience of Hickory Ridge. This is a great place to take the kids.

Location: Located at Horn in the West, Boone NC
Distance: 2 hours from Asheville
Address: 591 Horn in the West Rd., Boone NC 28607
Telephone: 828-264-2120
Website: horninthewest.com/museum
Hours: May.–Jun. Sat 9am–8pm, Sun noon-8pm; Jul-Oct 9am–8pm daily; Nov.–Apr. by appointment
Fees: Donations accepted
Allow: 1 hour minimum
Directions: From Asheville, take I-40 East to Marion. In Marion, take NC 221 North to Boone. Located just past the intersection of NC 321.

Historic Carson House

Built in 1793 by Colonel John Carson, the Carson House today is a privately owned history museum that is open to the public. This plantation home is filled with furnishings typical of the upper-class of that period. Exhibits and artifacts describe not only the influential Carson family, but the culture and history of the region and state.

Location: Marion NC
Distance: 45 minutes from Asheville
Address: 1805 Hwy. 70 West, Marion NC 28752
Telephone: 828-724-4948
Website: historiccarsonhouse.com
Hours: Apr.–Nov, Wed–Sat 10am–4pm, Sun 2–5pm
Fees: None
Allow: 1 hour

Directions: From Asheville, take I-40 East to Old Fort. Take NC 70 North through Pleasant Gardens to the House. It is located on the right just beyond the intersection of NC 80.

Historic Murray's Mill

Maintained by the Catawba County Historical Association, the Historic Murray's Mill is a complex of historic building preserved intact. Included are the 1913 mill (the centerpiece of the complex), the 1890's Murray & Minges General Store, the 1880's Wheathouse, used as an exhibit gallery, the 1913 John Murray House, furnished to the period, and numerous outbuildings. Run by three generations of the Murray Family, who abandoned operations in 1967, the picturesque structures and surrounding land form the last milling complex in the county, meticulously preserved and interpreted by the Catawba County Historical Association.

Location: Hickory NC
Distance: 1 hour and 30 minutes from Asheville
Address: 1489 Murray's Mill Rd., Catawba NC 28609
Telephone: 828-241-4299
Website: catawbahistory.org/historic_murrays_mill.php
Hours: Closed Jan.–Mar. In season, Thu–Sat 9am–5pm, Sun 1–5pm
Fees: Adult and child rates
Allow: 1–2 hours
Directions: From Asheville take I-40 East toward Statesville. Take Exit 138 at Wike Rd., and take the first right onto Oxford School Rd. (NC 10). Turn right at 2nd Ave. SW and then left at Murray's Mill Rd.

Historic Newton NC Depot

The Historic Newton NC Depot is open to visitors on Sat, and features displays and exhibits of local railroad history. The building, built in 1924, served both the Southern Railway and the Carolina & North-Western lines which traversed Catawba County. Railroad service into the area started in 1860 when rails of the Western North Carolina Railroad reached the county. In 1881, tracks of the Chester & Lenoir Narrow Gauge railroad also reached Newton and joined the rails of the WNCRR.

The renovated depot, which was built an all-brick structure by the Elliott Building Company, opened to the public in Sep., 2006, and houses a railroad museum, model railroad club, and a banquet room. The banquet room of the depot can seat up to 80 people at one time and is available for rent for family, church, business or civic events. Currently, the Depot Authority is exploring the feasibility of creating the North Carolina Narrow Gauge Museum, with displays of North Carolina railroad equipment that is smaller than the typical standard gauge railroad. Preliminary plans call for a covered car-barn with three storage tracks on land adjacent to the depot.

Location: Newton NC
Distance: 1 hour and 15 minutes from Asheville
Address: 1123 North Main Ave., Newton NC 28658
Telephone: 828-695-4317

Wildflowers on the Road Sides

As you drive along some of the major roads and interstates in North Carolina in the spring, summer and fall, you can't help but notice the spectacular plantings of wildflowers. In 1985, the North Carolina Department of Transportation (NCDOT) began planting wildflower beds as an integral part of the highway beautification. The program has been a great success and visitors and residents alike are treated to wonderful colorful displays as they travel throughout the state. If you are planning a trip to North Carolina, I suggest you write to the North Carolina Department of Transportation offices for a copy of their wildflower identification booklet. This guide will allow you to identify and learn about each type of wildflower planting you encounter on your travels. The cost is $6. Checks should be made payable to the NC Wildflower Program. Their address is Road Side Environmental Unit, PO Box 25201, Raleigh NC 27611.

Website: Historic Newton NC Depot
Hours: Sat 1–3pm, other times by appointment only.
Fees: None
Allow: 1–2 hours
Directions: From Asheville take I-40 East toward Statesville. Take Exit 130 toward Old US 70. Turn left at West 1st St., take the 2nd right onto 1st Ave. South. Continue onto Hwy. 16 Business/Main St. to depot.

History Museum of Burke County

The History Museum of Burke County seeks to promote the collection, preservation, educational interpretation and display of those artifacts, documents, and events most representative of Burke County–its prehistory and history, its cultural and economic development, its people and institutions. The museum is housed in the Old City Hall, and has 22 rooms, each with its own theme, devoted to various aspects of local history.

Location: Morganton NC
Distance: 1 hour from Asheville
Address: 201 West Meeting St., Morganton NC 28655
Telephone: 828-437-1777
Website: thehistorymuseumofburke.org
Hours: Tue–Fri: 10am–4pm; Sat 10am–2pm
Fees: None
Allow: 1 hour
Directions: From Asheville take I-40 west to exit 103 toward Morganton. Turn left at Burkemont Ave. (US Hwy. 64) and then right at West Union St. Continue on West Meeting St.

Horn in the West

One of North Carolina's best known outdoor dramas, Horn in the West, is a re-creation of North Carolina's early pioneers, including Daniel Boone, and their struggle for independence from Britain. The production takes place in pre-Revolutionary days and lasts two hours. Horn in the West first premiered in 1952.

Location: Boone NC
Distance: 2 hour from Asheville
Address: 591 Horn in the West Rd., Boone NC 28607
Telephone: 828-264-2120
Website: hornin thewest.com
Hours: Season is mid-Jun to mid-Aug. Performances begin at 8pm No show on Mon
Fees: Adult, senior, and child rates
Allow: Performances last about two hours
Directions: From Asheville, take I-40 East to Marion. In Marion take NC 221 to Boone. Just past intersection of NC 321 look for the Horn in the West sign.

Hudson Depot Railroad Museum

The Hudson Depot Railroad Museum is housed in a former train depot built around the turn of the 20th century and chronicles the history of the town of Hudson and the local railroad industry through photographs and artifacts. The depot was in operation until the 1970's. A highlight of the museum is its collection of several restored cabooses including a restored 1912 wood-sided Rear Cupola Caboose furnished with railroad artifacts, and a Delaware & Hudson.

Location: Hudson NC
Distance: 1.5 hours east of Asheville
Address: 550 Central St., Hudson NC 28638
Telephone: 828-728-8272
Website: explorecaldwell.com/historic
Hours: Open by appointment and during special events
Fees: Free
Allow: 1 hour
Directions: From Asheville, take I-40 East to Exit 113 toward Rutherford College Rd./ NC 1001, turn right at Cajah Mountain Rd./NC 1130 and then right at Elm Ave. in Hudson. Take the 1st left onto Central Ave.

J. Summie Propst House Museum

The J. Summie Propst house, built between 1881 and 1883, is the only remaining example of the Second Empire Style of architecture in Hickory. J. Summie Propst (1853–1940) was the son of Absalom Propst and was born in the Propst Crossroads section of Catawba County. A carpenter and cabinetmaker by trade, he built this house soon after his marriage to Nancy Jane Abernathy. Still in their twenties, they represented the new generation. Amenable to change, they accepted the new styles of architecture printed in the latest pattern books and erected an asymmetrical, spacious, modest house. This house remained in the family until it was vacated for a short period prior to its acquisition by the Hickory Landmarks Society in 1968.

The Society moved the house to the present site in the Shuford Memorial Gardens, from its original location on Tenth Ave. (now Main Ave. SW). An early twentieth-century kitchen wing was not moved to the new site. Since its relocation to Shuford Park, the house has been rehabilitated and is used as a museum. Trained docents serve as guides at the museum.

Location: Hickory NC
Distance: 1 hour and 15 minutes from Asheville
Address: 332 Sixth St. NW, Hickory NC 28601
Telephone: 828-322-4731
Website: hickorync.gov/eGov/apps/document/center.egov?view=item;id=2062
Hours: Mar. 15-Dec. 15; Thu and Sun, 1:30–4:30pm
Fees: None
Allow: 1–2 hours
Directions: From Asheville take I-40 East toward Statesville. Take Exit 123A-123B for US 321 toward Hickory. Continue on US 321 North. Turn right at 2nd Ave. NW and turn right at 2nd Ave. NW, then turn left at 6th St. NW.

Maple Grove Historical Museum

Built in 1883 and listed on the National Register of Historic Places, this restored Italianate style house features authentic Victorian furnishings and was the home of Adolphus Lafayette Shuford and his family, and is one of the oldest remaining houses in Hickory. It is a simple but handsome representation of the Italianate style. A.L. Shuford was a prominent early citizen of Hickory. He was one of the six founding commissioners when the first attempt to incorporate the village of Hickory Tavern was made in 1863. He was also the first agent in Hickory of the Western North Carolina Railroad, and he played an important role in the founding of Claremont College. Shuford is credited with having imported the first Jersey cattle to Catawba County.

Maple Grove is a two-story frame house with weather-board siding, a pedimented-gable roof, gable-end brick chimneys, a three-bay facade, and a two-story rear ell. One of the most distinctive features of the house is its two-tier front porch with paired chamfered posts, bracketed cornices, and decorative sawn-work balustrades. The main body of the house has a center-hall plan with simple detailing. One of the most striking interior features is the closed-string stairs with its heavy chamfered and moulded newel and unusual sawn work balustrade reminiscent of the front porch balustrades. In 1973, it was listed on the National Register of Historic Places.

Location: Hickory NC
Distance: 1 hour and 15 minutes from Asheville
Address: 542 2nd St. NE, Hickory NC 28601
Telephone: 828-322-4731
Website: hickorylandmarks.org/MapleGrove.asp
Hours: Mon–Fri 9am–5pm
Fees: None
Allow: 1 hour
Directions: From Asheville take I-40 East toward Statesville. Take Exit 123A-123B for US 321 toward Hickory. Continue on US 321 North. Turn right at 2nd Ave. NW and turn left at 2nd St. NE.

Mariam & Robert Hayes Performing Arts Center

The Blowing Rock Community Arts Center Foundation, Inc. was formed in Dec. 2000 by community members to promote the advancement of cultural arts and humanities in Blowing Rock and the North Carolina High Country through a regional Arts Center, The Mariam & Robert Hayes Performing Arts Center. Home to the Blowing Rock Stage Company, the Arts Center benefits residents and visitors by providing a permanent home for a multitude of arts groups and a facility in which to host live theatre, dance groups, a variety of musical performances, visual arts displays, classic films, and children's theatre workshops.

Location: Blowing Rock NC
Distance: 2 hours from Asheville
Address: 152 Jamie Fort Rd., Blowing Rock NC 28605
Telephone: 828-295-9627
Website: brcac.org/blog
Directions: From Blue Ridge Parkway take Boone exit to 321 South to Blowing Rock. A faster route from Asheville is to take I-40 East to Marion and take Hwy. 221 North to Blowing Rock.

McDowell Arts Council Association Gallery

Located in the McDowell Arts Council Association building, this art gallery features local and regional artists and craft persons working in a variety of media. It is known locally for their annual Holiday Show showcasing the work of McDowell County artisans exhibiting pottery, woodworking, basketry, jewelry, textile arts and other fine crafts.

Location: Marion NC
Distance: 1 hour from Asheville
Address: 50 South Main St., Marion NC 28752
Telephone: 828-652-8610
Website: mcdowellarts.net/taxonomy/term/1
Hours: Mon–Sat, 10am–6pm
Fees: None
Allow: 1 hour
Directions: From Asheville take I-40 east toward Statesville. Take exit 81 toward Marion, turn left at Sugar Hill road. Continue for 2 miles onto West Henderson St. and turn left onto South Main St.

Mast General Store

The century-old Mast General Store is one of the best remaining examples of old country stores in America. It has featured traditional clothing and quality goods since 1883. There are four other Mast General Stores: Asheville, Boone, Hendersonville, and Waynesville. However, the store in Valle Crucis is the original and as such, is a landmark.

Location: Valle Crucis NC
Distance: 2 hours from Asheville
Address: Hwy. 194, Valle Crucis NC 28691

Telephone: 828-963-6511
Website: mastgeneralstore.com
Hours: 7am–6:30pm Mon through Sat; 12-6pm Sun
Directions: From Asheville take I-40 East to Marion. Take Hwy. 221 North to Hwy. 105. Take 105 North and turn left on Hwy. 194 into Valle Crucis.

20 Miles of Furniture

Thousands of people visit Lenoir and Hickory each year with one thing on their minds-furniture! With 20 miles of furniture stores located along or near a stretch of U.S. Hwy. 321 between Lenoir and Hickory, North Carolina, the area is a required destination for any serious shopper looking for discount furniture. Nearly all manufacturers including Bernhardt, Broyhill, Fairfield Chair, Hammary, Kincaid and Thomasville can be found here along with an abundance of smaller, perhaps lesser known companies that also produce top-quality furnishings. Hwy. 321 passes through the towns of Granite Falls, Sawmills and Hudson.

Location: Highway 321 Between Hickory and Lenoir NC
Distance: 1 hour and 15 minutes from Asheville
Telephone: 800-737-0782
Website: 20milesoffurniture.com
Directions: From Asheville take I-40 East toward Statesville. Take Exit 123A-123B for Hickory. Take US 321 North toward Lenoir.

Morganton 1916 Railroad Depot

The Morganton 1916 Railroad Depot was built in 1886, and restored to its 1916 appearance in 2004. The Depot is open to the public on Sat and features exhibits of original station master and railroad equipment memorabilia and photos from the 19th and 20th centuries. The Depot is maintained by the History Museum of Burke County.

Location: Morganton NC
Distance: 1 hours from Asheville
Address: 624 South Green St., Morganton NC 28655
Telephone: 828-437-1777
Website: thehistorymuseumofburke.org/depot
Hours: Sat 2–4pm, other times by appointment
Allow: 30 minutes–1 hour
Directions: From Asheville take I-40 East to Morganton. Get off at exit 103 onto US 64 toward Morganton. Within one mile turn left at Burkemont Ave., turn right at West Fleming Dr. and then slight left at South Sterling St. Continue onto South Green St.

Mountain Gateway Museum

The Mountain Gateway Museum offers visitors an opportunity to learn about North Carolina's mountain region. Exhibits, programs, and living history demonstrations depict area history from the earliest original inhabitants through the settlement period and into the twentieth century. The museum site includes a picnic area, amphitheater, two pioneer-era log cabins and the museum itself, all located on the banks of historic Mill Creek, a Catawba River tributary.

Location: Old Fort NC
Distance: 45 minutes from Asheville
Address: 102 Water St., Old Fort NC 28762
Telephone: 828-668-9259
Website: mountaingatewaymuseum.org
Hours: Mon: 12–5pm, Tue–Sat: 9am–5pm, Sun: 2–5pm
Fees: None
Allow: 1 hour
Directions: From Asheville take I-40 East to Old Fort and get off at Exit 73 onto Catawba Ave. Go left 2 blocks to Water St.

Museum of Ashe County History

The Museum of Ashe County History is located in the historic 1904 Ashe County Courthouse building and has exhibits pertaining to the history of Ashe County and its people. The major permanent exhibit presents the story of the "Virginia Creeper" Railroad.

Location: Jefferson NC
Distance: 3 hours from Asheville
Address: 301 East Main St., Jefferson NC 28640
Telephone: 336-846-1904
Website: ashehistory.org
Hours: April–Oct.: Mon–Sat 10am–4pm
Fees: None
Allow: 1–2 hours
Directions: From Asheville take I-40 west to exit 72 and merge onto US 70 toward Old Fort. After 11 miles turn left at US 221 and follow US 221 through Boone to Jefferson.

Museum of North Carolina Minerals

The Museum of North Carolina Minerals opened in 1956 as a joint project of the National Park Service and the North Carolina Department of Conservation and Development and displays more than 300 varieties of minerals found in North Carolina. Renovated in 2002, the museum also has numerous interpretative exhibits and a gift shop.

Location: Milepost 331 Blue Ridge Parkway, Spruce Pine area
Distance: 1–1.5 hours
Address: Blue Ridge Parkway, Milepost 331
Telephone: 828-765-2761
Website: blueridgeheritage.com/attractions-destinations/museum-of-north-carolina-minerals
Hours: 9am–5pm Mon–Sun, early May through Oct.
Fees: None

Allow: 1–2 hours
Directions: Take Blue Ridge Parkway north out of Asheville to Milepost 331

Mystery Hill

Mystery Hill is a hands-on entertainment center for kids and grown-ups alike that has been around for over 50 years. The self-guided tour includes the famous Mystery House where you stand at a 45-degree angle and experience unusual gravitational effects. Other venues include the Hall of Mystery with over 40 puzzles and science-based experiments, the Bubble-Rama with bubble experiments including human-sized bubbles the kids can enter, the Native American Artifacts Museum with over 50,000 relics on display, and the Appalachian Heritage Museum.

Location: Between Boone and Blowing Rock NC
Distance: 2 hours from Asheville
Address: 129 Mystery Hill Lane, Blowing Rock NC 28605
Telephone: 828-264-2792
Website: mysteryhill-nc.com
Hours: Jun.–Aug. 8am–8pm; Sep.–May 9am–5pm
Fees: Rates vary. Call for current prices. Senior, military, group, and AAA discounts are available.
Allow: 1–2 hours
Directions: From Asheville, take I-40 East to Marion, take Hwy. 221 North to Blowing Rock, and then take 321 North four miles to Mystery Hill. From the Blue Ridge Parkway north out of Asheville, get off at mile marker 291. Take Hwy. 321 North 1.5 miles.

Native American Artifacts Museum

The Native American Artifacts Museum is part of the Mystery Hill complex and houses over 50,000 pieces of authentic Native American artifacts. Almost every time period of American Indian history is represented in the collection that took over 70 years to collect. From arrowheads and effigy pipes to bowls, celts and awls, this is one of the largest collections of its kind in North Carolina.

Location: Blowing Rock NC
Distance: 2 hours from Asheville
Address: 129 Mystery Hill Lane, Blowing Rock NC 28605
Telephone: 828-264-2792
Website: mysteryhill-nc.com
Hours: Jun.–Aug. 8am–8pm; Sept-May 9am–5pm
Fees: Rates vary. Call for current prices. Senior, military, group, and AAA discounts are available
Allow: 1 hour
Directions: From Asheville, take I-40 East to Marion, take Hwy. 221 North to Blowing Rock, and then take 321 North four miles to Mystery Hill. From the Blue Ridge Parkway north out of Asheville, get off at mile marker 291. Take Hwy. 321 North 1.5 miles.

North Carolina Mining Museum

The large North Carolina Mining Museum is part of Emerald Village and is located adjacent to and inside the historic Bon Ami Mine and features a general mining history exhibit, information on the minerals extracted and their uses, authentic mining equipment, and fascinating information on the Bon Ami Mine and Bon Ami Company.

Location: Little Switzerland NC
Distance: 1–2 hours from Asheville
Address: 331 McKinney Mine Rd., Little Switzerland NC 28749
Telephone: 828-765-6463, 828-765-0000
Website: emeraldvillage.com
Hours: 9am–5pm, seven days a week, May through Oct. Museum is open Apr.–Nov.
Fees: None
Allow: 1 hour
Directions: From Asheville, take I-40 East to Marion. Take NC 221 North to NC 226. Left on NC 226 and go 9 miles to the Blue Ridge Parkway. Go south on parkway and get off at next exit, Little Switzerland, Milepost 334. Take right under parkway onto Chestnut Grove Rd. Turn left onto McKinney Mine Rd.

North Carolina School for the Deaf Museum

The North Carolina School for the Deaf Historical Museum is located in Morganton, and is a museum run by the Historic Rusmisell Museum Society. The museum contains yearbooks, scrapbooks, histories, photographs and other artifacts documenting the school and its community since its founding in 1894.

Location: Morganton NC
Distance: 1 hour from Asheville
Address: 517 West Fleming Dr., Morganton NC 28655
Telephone: 828-433-2971
Website: ncsdmuseum.net
Hours: Call for hours
Fees: None
Allow: 1 hour
Directions: From Asheville take I-40 west to exit 103. Take Hwy. 64 toward Morganton and turn left at Burkemont Ave. Turn right onto West Fleming Dr. to the museum.

Old Burke County Courthouse & Heritage Museum

The Old Burke County Courthouse & Heritage Museum features a restored 19th-century courthouse with displays and exhibits about the building, the early court system, and local history. Exhibits include a restored turn-of-the-century lawyer's office, including information on the North Carolina Supreme Court justices who held summer sessions of the Supreme Court in the Old Courthouse from 1847 to 1862. The museum also has changing exhibits on selected aspects of early Burke County life and culture as well as a 20-minute slide presentation on Burke County heritage.

Location: Morganton NC
Distance: 1 hour from Asheville
Address: 102 East Union St. Morganton NC 28655
Telephone: 828-437-4104
Website: historicburke.org/museum
Hours: Mon–Fri 9am–4pm, Sat 10am–1pm
Fees: None
Allow: 1 hour
Directions: From Asheville, take I-40 East to Exit 105. Turn left off the exit and continue straight into Morganton to Courthouse Square.

Old Depot & Caboose Museum

The Old Depot Gallery & Caboose Museum are located in Black Mountain, and are operated by the Old Depot Association. The Gallery, located in the historic restored railroad depot, sells only original and juried crafts of local Western North Carolina Artists. Separate from the depot building is the Caboose Museum housed in an authentic railroad caboose. The little museum display features a photographic history of the depot, train memorabilia, and period music.

Location: Black Mountain NC
Distance: 20 minutes from Asheville
Address: 207 Sutton Ave., Black Mountain NC 28711
Telephone: 828-669-5483
Website: olddepot.org/galleryindex.html
Hours: Tue–Sat 10am–5pm
Fees: None
Allow: 1 hour
Directions: From Asheville take I-40 west to exit 64. Turn left at exit ramp onto Hwy. 9 toward Black Mountain. Turn left at Sutton Ave.

Old Fort Railroad Museum

The Old Fort Railroad Museum presents the impact of the railroads in the mountains of North Carolina. Train exhibits, original tools and signal lights, furniture and signs are housed in the historic 1890s vintage Old Fort Depot. There is also an original caboose on display.

Location: Old Fort NC
Distance: 45 minutes from Asheville
Address: 25 West Main St., Old Fort NC 28762
Telephone: 828-668-4282
Website: mcdowellnc.org/links/144
Admission: None
Hours: Mon–Sat 9am–5pm
Directions: Take I-40 East to Old Fort exit 72. Take US70 West toward Old Fort and Main Street.

Old Wilkes Jail Museum

Built in 1859, the Old Wilkes Jail was in continuous use as a jail until 1915. The first jail had four cells and included a residence for the jailer and his family. It is now restored as a history museum. One famous inmate, Tom Dula (of the famous ballad "Hang Down Your Head Tom Dooley") was incarcerated here until a change of venue was obtained by his defense attorney, former NC Governor Zebulon Vance. The building was restored to its original state using as many of the original building materials as possible. Access to the cells are through the original iron and wood doors. The old Wilkes County jail is one of the best preserved examples of nineteenth century penal architecture in North Carolina.

Location: Wilkesboro NC
Distance: 2 hours from Asheville
Address: 203 North Bridge St., Wilkesboro NC 28697
Telephone: 336-667-3712
Website: wilkesheritagemuseum.com
Hours: Mon–Fri 9am–4pm; weekends by appointment
Fees: None
Allow: 45 minutes
Directions: From Asheville take I-40 East to Hickory. Exit at Hickory and take Hwy. 16 North to downtown Wilkesboro. Turn right at the light and go through town past the courthouse. Take first left onto to Broad St. to behind the courthouse. Turn left onto North St. and then right onto North Bridge St.

Orchard at Altapass

The Orchard at Altapass is a unique Blue Ridge experience. This is a great place to take the kids and enjoy an afternoon of Appalachian culture, music, and fun. In addition to the splendid apple orchards, activities include hayrides, storytelling, clogging, performances by local mountain musicians, cider and apple butter making, picnic lunches and craft exhibits.

Located on land right next to the Blue Ridge Parkway, the Orchard has always been an important economic base for the local folks. In the 1930s, the Orchard was split in two by the building of the parkway. Because of that proximity, it is the only private business with direct access to the parkway. Nearby railroad lines bring up to thirty trains a day to the area and train whistles are part of the Orchard experience. The trees grown at Altapass are heritage varieties including the much-prized Virginia Beauty, King Luscious, and Stayman Winesap apples.

Location: Milepost 328.3 at Orchard Rd. near Spruce Pine NC
Distance: 2 hours by way of the Blue Ridge Parkway
Address: 1025 Orchard Rd., Spruce Pine NC 28777
Telephone: 888-765-9531, 828-765-9531
Website: altapassorchard.com
Hours: May 1–Nov. 1, Mon, Wed–Sat: 10am–6pm Sun: 12–6pm, Closed Tue
Fees: Orchard: Free; Various fees for other activities
Allow: 2–3 hours

Directions: Take the Blue Ridge Parkway! Hard to find, even with directions by any other route. Get off 3 miles north of the Spruce Pine exit at Milepost 328.3 onto Orchard Rd. Look for little brown Orchard at Altapass signs.

Presbyterian Historical Society Museum

The Presbyterian Historical Society Museum is located at the Montreat Conference Center in Black Mountain, and is maintained by the Presbyterian Historical Society. The museum contains collections of items related to the history of the Presbyterian Church, USA and its missions.

Location: Montreat NC
Distance: 30 minutes from Asheville
Address: 318 Georgia Terrace, Montreat NC 28757
Telephone: 828-669-6556
Hours: Mon–Fri 8:30am–4:30pm Closed all major holidays.
Fees: Fee for any research done by the Society. Otherwise free.
Allow: .5–1 hour
Directions: From Asheville, take I-40 East to Exit 64. Take Rte. 9 North through Black Mountain and the Montreat Gate. Continue on Assembly drive one mile and turn left onto Georgia Terrace.

Quaker Meadows Plantation

Quaker Meadows Plantation is the restored 1812 Catawba Valley Plantation House of Captain Charles McDowell, Jr. It was the site of the 1780 gathering of the Overmountain Men, patriots that marched to Kings Mountain and helped defeat the British in the Revolutionary War. This authentically furnished house museum interprets antebellum culture in Burke County from that era.

Location: Morganton NC
Distance: 1 hour from Asheville
Address: 119 St. Mary Church Rd., Morganton NC 28655
Telephone: 828-437-4104
Hours: Sun 2–4pm or by appointment
Fees: Small admission fee for adults
Allow: 1 hour
Directions: From Asheville, take I-40 East to Exit 100. Turn left onto Hwy. 181 and go two blocks to St. Mary's Church Rd. Turn right and the plantation will be on the left.

Rutherford County Farm Museum

The Rutherford County Farm Museum has exhibits of antique farm equipment and items dating back to the earliest days of the nineteenth century. Two large murals, depicting the cycle of growing cotton and the early textile mills of the county, are outstanding features of the museum.

Location: Forest City NC
Distance: 45 minutes from Asheville
Address: 240 Depot St., Forest City NC 28043
Telephone: 828-248-1248
Hours: Wed–Sat: 10am–4pm
Fees: $2 adults, children free
Allow: 1 hour
Directions: From Asheville take I-26 South to Exit 35. Take Hwy. 74 East to Columbus/Rutherfordton. Take exit 182 to US221 to Forest City. In Forest City turn left at South Broadway, then turn left at Florence St. and continue to Depot Street.

Rutherford Hospital Museum

The Rutherford Hospital Museum opened in Oct. of 2005 and was created because the Hospital played an important role in Rutherford County history. The design of the museum features vignettes that showcase several areas of hospital life. It is a treasure trove of artifacts including many pieces of medical equipment and furniture from earlier years at the hospital. Other items were used privately by physicians in Rutherford County who were once associated with the hospital.

Among the prized pieces of the collection are a massive roll-top desk used by Dr. Henry Norris, one of the three founders of Rutherford Hospital located in the Founders' Corners. He used the roll-top desk in the 1906 hospital and later in the 1911 building.

Location: Rutherfordton NC
Distance: 1 hour from Asheville
Address: 288 South Ridgecrest Ave., Rutherfordton NC 28139
Telephone: 828-286-5000
Hours: Mon–Fri 6am–5pm
Fees: Free
Allow: 1 hour
Directions: From Asheville Take I-40 east to Exit 85 (NC 221). Go north toward Rutherfordton on NC 221. In Rutherfordton turn left onto Maple St. to hospital on South Ridgecrest Ave.

Senator Sam J. Ervin Jr. Library

The Senator Sam J. Ervin Jr. Library is located on the campus of Western Piedmont Community College in the Phifer Learning Resources Center, and is a replica of the late Senator Ervin's home library, as it existed at 515 Lenoir St. in Morganton. A 7,500-item collection of Ervin's books and professional and family memorabilia is housed in the library. Senator Ervin is best known for serving as the Chairman of the Senate Watergate Committee in the 1970s.

Location: Morganton NC
Distance: 1 hour from Asheville
Address: Western Piedmont Community College, 1001 Burkemont Ave., Morganton NC 28655

Telephone: 828-448-6195
Website: samervinlibrary.org
Hours: Mon–Fri 8am–5pm
Fees: None
Allow: 1 hour
Directions: Driving east on I-40 from Asheville, take Exit #103 and turn left onto Burkemont Ave. Cross the bridge over I-40. Western Piedmont Community College is on the right, 1 block up.

Swannanoa Valley Museum

The Swannanoa Valley Museum resides in what was formerly the Black Mountain Fire Department and was founded in 1989 by the Swannanoa Valley Historical and Preservation Association. Exhibits focus on Swannanoa Valley history and culture and include Native American exhibits, artifacts and early tools, plants indigenous to the region and photographic displays.

Location: Black Mountain NC
Distance: 20 minutes from Asheville
Address: 223 West State St., Black Mountain NC 28711
Telephone: 828-669-9566
Website: swannanoavalleymuseum.org
Hours: April Apr.–Oct.: Tue–Fri 10am–5pm; Sat 12–4pm, Sun 2–5pm
Fees: None
Allow: 1 hour
Directions: From Asheville, take I-40 East to Black Mountain. Get off at Exit 64 and turn left onto Hwy. 9. Proceed to State St. and turn left. The museum is two blocks on the left.

Town of Catawba Historical Museum

Catawba is one of the oldest towns between Salisbury and Asheville, having been selected as an early railroad station. Trains ran to the town before the War Between the States, beginning about 1859. The museum opened to the public in 2003 to present the history of the region, including the impact of the railroad.

The museum is housed in the oldest brick building in Catawba, the Dr. Q. M. Little House built around 1873. This Federal-style building, which contains five rooms of unique local history, and a room dedicated to the National Little Family Archives, features a two-tier porch, exterior stairway, six front doors and vintage handmade brick construction. The museum is maintained by the Town of Catawba Historical Society. Nearby is the Catawba Historic District, where visitor may enjoy a walking tour that features brick-detailed commercial buildings, homes and churches dating from the 1860's.

Location: Catawba NC
Distance: 1 hour and 30 minutes from Asheville
Address: 101 First St. S.W., Catawba NC 28609

Telephone: 828-241-4077
Website: townofcatawbanc.org
Hours: Call for hours
Fees: None
Allow: 1 hour
Directions: From Asheville take 1–40 East to Exit 138. Take NC10, Oxford School Rd. south to Catawba.

Trail of Faith

The Trail of Faith is a walk-through outdoor trail showing the terrible religious persecution of the Waldensians in Northern Italy and their eventual settling in Valdese. There are over nine life-sized exhibits are on the trail with more being added yearly. Summer evening dramas reenact the historic struggles of Waldensians (*See* "From This Day Forward," earlier in this section).

Location: Valdese NC
Distance: 1 hour from Asheville
Address: 401 Church St., Valdese NC 28690
Telephone: 800-635-4778, 828-874-1893
Website: waldensiantrailoffaith.org
Hours: Sat–Sun 2–5pm
Fees: Small admission fee
Allow: 1–2 hours for the trail
Directions: From Asheville, take I-40 East to Exit 111. Take Carolina St. and turn left at traffic light and travel Main St. to Church St. Turn right onto Church St. The Trail of Faith is located on top of the hill to the right.

Turchin Center for the Visual Arts

The Turchin Center for the Visual Arts presents exhibition, education, and collection programs that support Appalachian State University's role as a key regional educational, cultural, and economic resource. The center has exhibits that focus on a blend of new and historically important artworks, and features the work of regional, national and international artists.

Location: Boone NC
Distance: 2 hours from Asheville
Address: 423 West King St., Appalachian State University, Boone NC 28608
Telephone: 828-262-3017
Website: tcva.org
Admission: Free
Directions: From Asheville, take I-40 East to Marion and take Hwy. 221 North to Blowing Rock. Then take US 321 North to Boone. In Boone turn left on US 421 and then left onto West King St.

Tweetsie Railroad

Tweetsie Railroad is an exciting Western theme park. An authentic early American, full-size coal-fired steam locomotive takes you on a 3-mile trip over a scenic route with an enacted Indian raid. There is a complete old-time western town that features live entertainment at the Palace Variety Show. A petting zoo, gift shops, and rides for the kids make for great family entertainment.

Location: Highway 321 between Boone and Blowing Rock NC
Distance: 2 hours from Asheville
Address: 300 Tweetsie Lane, Blowing Rock NC 28605
Telephone: 800-526-5740
Website: tweetsie.com
Hours: May 22-Aug. 23: Open seven days a week, 9am–6pm; May 1–May 17, Aug. 28–Nov. 1: Open Fri, Sat & Sun, 9am–6pm
Fees: Adult and child rates
Directions: Exit at Milepost 291, Boone Exit, off Blue Ridge Parkway. Tweetsie Railroad is located on US 321 between Boone and Blowing Rock. Faster route: Take I-40 from Asheville and take Hwy. 221 North at Marion. Proceed to Linville and take Hwy. 105 North into Boone. In Boone take 321 South 5 miles.

Waldensian Heritage Museum

The Waldensian Heritage Museum is dedicated to preserving the rich heritage and culture of the Waldensian settlers. It features several rooms and thousands of items that date back to the earliest immigrants, including: clothing, tools, books, pictures, and household items.

Location: Valdese NC
Distance: 1 hour from Asheville
Address: 208 Rodoret St. South, Valdese NC 28690
Telephone: 828-874-1111
Website: waldensianpresbyterian.org/13-museum
Fees: None
Allow: 1 hour
Directions: From Asheville, take I-40 East to Valdese, Exit 111. Turn right at Millstone Ave. toward Valdese. In approximately one mile take the 1st right onto Carolina St. Then left at Massel Ave. and take the 2nd right onto Rodoret St.

Whippoorwill Academy and Village

The Whippoorwill Academy and Village was created by Mrs. Edith Ferguson Carter by moving historical buildings to the family farm many years ago. The complex today features historical museums, including: Tom Dooley Museum, Daniel Boone Replica Cabin, Smokehouse Art Gallery, Matt's Store, Indian Teepee, Jail, School House, Chapel, Tavern, Blacksmith shop and Weaving room.

Location: Ferguson NC
Distance: 2 hours from Asheville
Address: 11929 Hwy 268 West, Ferguson NC 28624

Telephone: 336-973-3237
Website: ncagr.gov/ncproducts/ShowSite.asp?ID=100673
Hours: Apr.–Dec.: Sat–Sun 3–5pm and during the week by appointment
Fees: None
Allow: 1 hour
Directions: From Asheville take I-40 east. Take exit 103 and follow US 64 north to US 321 in Lenoir. Take US 321 north and turn right onto NC 268 to Whippoorwill Academy and Village.

Wilkes Art Gallery

The Wilkes Art Gallery is a 10,000 square foot facility which includes over 3,500 square feet of exhibition space, an education center with a complete ceramics studio, painting and drawing studios, two multi-purpose classrooms, and a Gallery Gift Shop. The art gallery that has changing monthly exhibitions of local, regional, student, and nationally known artists.

Location: North Wilkesboro NC
Distance: 2 hours from Asheville
Address: 913 C St., North Wilkesboro NC 28659
Telephone: 336-667-2841
Website: wilkesartgallery.org/
Hours: Tue 10am–8pm; Wed–Fri 10am–5pm; Sat 10am–2pm
Fees: None
Allow: 1–2 hours
Directions: From Asheville, take I-40 East to Exit 131 just beyond Hickory. Take NC 16 North to Wilkesboro. At the juncture of East Main St., turn right and then left Wilkesboro Boulevard toward North Wilkesboro. At NC 421 turn right and then right at 10th St. Take the 1st left onto C St.

Wilkes Heritage Museum & Blue Ridge Music Hall of Fame

The Wilkes Heritage Museum, located in the restored historic Wilkes County Courthouse, opened in Nov. of 2005 and celebrates the unique heritage of Wilkes County. Through a collection of artifacts and images, stories of all facets of life in Wilkes County are told. Self-guided tours feature exhibits that include early settlement, medicine, military history, moonshine, and early stock-car racing. The Blue Ridge Music Hall of Fame is also located at the museum and showcases the rich musical heritage of the greater Blue Ridge Mountains area from northern Georgia to northern Virginia. The Hall of Fame educates, defines and interprets the history of music in the Blue Ridge area and musicians in all genres from the region with exhibits and an annual celebration of inductees.

Location: Wilkesboro NC
Distance: 2 hours from Asheville
Address: 100 East Main St., Wilkesboro NC 28697
Telephone: 336-667-3171
Website: wilkesheritagemuseum.com

Hours: Tue–Sat 10am–4pm
Fees: Adult, senior and student rates, under four free
Allow: 1–2 hours
Directions: From Asheville, take I-40 East to Exit 131 just beyond Hickory. Take NC 16 North to Wilkesboro.

Cultural Attractions West of Asheville

Allison-Deaver House

The Allison-Deaver house is one of Western North Carolina's finest surviving examples of early 19th-century architecture. Located in Transylvania County in Brevard NC, the superbly restored house and farmstead are open to the public. The main house, a two story, wood timber structure with a full two-tiered porch, sits on a steep hill overlooking an old Indian trail which later became a main road for settlers into the Davidson River region of what was Old Buncombe County. The house, built by Benjamin Allison in 1815, was added onto by William Deaver in 1840.

Location: Brevard NC
Distance: 45 minutes from Asheville
Address: 200 Hwy. 280, Brevard NC 28712
Telephone: 828-884-5137, Transylvania Historical Society
Website: tchistoricalsociety.com/?page_id=9
Hours: Apr.–Oct.: Fri–Sat 10am–4pm, Sun 1–5pm
Fees: Donations accepted
Allow: 1 hour
Directions: From Asheville, take I-26 East or US 25 South to Airport Rd. Follow Airport Rd. south toward Brevard. The Allison-Deaver House is on a hill just before you reach the intersection of NC 64. From Hendersonville, take Hwy. 64 West to the intersection of NC 280. Turn right. The Allison-Deaver House will be a short distance on your left.

Andrews Art Museum

The Andrews Art Museum is housed on the mezzanine floor of the Cultural Arts Center in Andrews and is run by the Valleytown Cultural Arts and Historical Society. The museum hosts regularly scheduled exhibitions of local and regional artists in the museum's gallery spaces. The historic building that is home to the Andrews Art Museum was originally the First Baptist Church of Andrews.

Location: Andrews NC
Distance: 2 hours from Asheville
Address: Corner of Chestnut and Third St., Andrews NC 28901
Telephone: 828-360-5071
Website: andrewsvalleyarts.com/the-museum.asp
Hours: Sat and Sun, call for hours
Fees: None

Allow: 1–2 hours
Directions: From Asheville take I-40 West to Exit 27. Proceed on US 74 West, by-passing the towns of Waynesville, Cherokee, Sylva and Bryson City. The four lane then becomes two lane US 19/74 West as you approach the Nantahala Gorge. You will travel about 15 miles before entering Cherokee County at Topton. In Andrews turn left at the first red light. Make a right onto Main St. followed by a left onto Chestnut St. to the second building on the left.

Brevard Music Center

In operation for more than 60 years, the Brevard Music Center is known for its premiere festivals, pleasant setting and the highest standards in music education. With more than fifty concert events scheduled each year, the Music Center provides not only wonderful entertainment but a unique training environment for over 400 gifted students from across the nation.

Location: Brevard NC
Distance: 45 minutes from Asheville
Address: 349 Andante Lane, Brevard NC 28712
Telephone: 828-862-2100
Website: brevardmusic.org/index.php
Hours: Box Office: Mon–Wed noon-4:30pm Other days noon-show intermission. Performances Jun. 26-Aug. 10.
Fees: Vary with performances
Allow: Performances average two hours.
Directions: From Asheville, take NC 280 South to Brevard. From downtown Brevard follow Probart St. to the Brevard Music Center. St. signs mark the way.

Canton Area Historical Museum

The Canton Area Historical Museum is a history heritage museum focusing on the culture and history of Canton and Haywood County. The museum has extensive photo archives, exhibits, as well as coverage of Champion Paper Mill and the area's early logging railroads.

Location: Canton NC
Distance: 30 minutes from Asheville
Address: 36 Park St., Canton NC 28716
Telephone: 828-646-3412
Hours: Mon–Fri 8am–5pm, weekends by appointment only
Fees: None
Allow: 1 hour
Directions: From Asheville, take I-40 West to East Canton, Exit 37. Take 19/23 South to Park St. in Canton.

Cherokee County History and Arts Museum

Housed in the old Carnegie Library in downtown Murphy, the Cherokee County History and Arts Museum has a collection of more than two thousand artifacts from the time of the infamous Trail of Tears. Many of the artifacts were collected in Cherokee County, excavated from Indian mounds, or purchased from area citizens over the past seventy years. For the most part, the museum reflects the lifestyle of the Cherokee Indians, although some exhibits also focus on the early white settlers as well as the 16th century Spanish explorers who passed through the area in search of gold and other precious metals. The museum also has an exhibit of over 700 antique dolls, the oldest dating back to around 1865.

The museum serves as an interpretive center for the Trail of Tears National Historic Trail. Murphy was once the site of Fort Butler, one of the main holding areas for Cherokees who were being removed from North Carolina in the 1830's. Other sites in and around Murphy play a prominent role in Cherokee history, mythology, and culture.

The museum houses a replica of the log cabin dwellings used by the Cherokee residents of the area at the time of their removal. This type of dwelling was also typical of that used by pioneer settlers, many of whom moved into the vacated Cherokee cabins.

Location: Murphy NC
Distance: 2 hours from Asheville
Address: 87 Peachtree St., Murphy NC 28906
Telephone: 828-837-6792
Hours: Mon–Fri 9am–5pm; Closed national holidays.
Fees: Adult and child rates
Allow: 1–2 hours
Directions: From Asheville, take I-40 West. Take Exit 27 to 74 West. Follow 74 West to NC 19. Follow 19 into Murphy. The Museum is right behind the courthouse in the center of town.

Cherokee Indian Reservation

The 56,000-acre Cherokee Indian Reservation is home to more than 10,000 members of Eastern Band of the Cherokee Indians. Each year, thousands of visitors from across the country come to discover this enchanted land and to share the natural mountain beauty the Cherokee have treasured for centuries.

A visit to Cherokee is like stepping into the past. You'll find a nation still linked to ancient customs and traditions that enable them to live in harmony with nature as their ancestors did. The Reservation, known as the Qualla Boundary, has a number of outstanding attractions. Among them is the Museum of the Cherokee Indian, Qualla Arts & Crafts Mutual, "Unto These Hills" Outdoor Drama, Oconaluftee Indian Village, and Harrah's Cherokee Casino & Hotel. There are 28 campgrounds on the Reservation, and many motels and cabins. Be sure to visit the Cherokee Welcome Center at 489 Tsali Boulevard in downtown Cherokee. Be prepared, however, to be turned off by the somewhat glitzy atmosphere on Main St., which overflows with tourist stores selling "Indian" souvenirs made in China, and street performers wearing non-Cherokee Plains Indian costumes.

Location: Cherokee NC
Distance: 1–1.5 hours from Asheville
Address: Cherokee Welcome Center, 498 Tsali Boulevard, Cherokee NC 28719
Telephone: 800-438-1601
Website: cherokee-nc.com/index.php

Allow: Plan to spend the whole day
Directions: From Asheville take I-40 west to exit 27 (Great Smoky Mountains Expressway). Continue west on U.S. 74 past Waynesville, Sylva, and Dillsboro to Exit 74, Cherokee. U.S. Hwy. 441 will take you into Cherokee.

Clay County Historical & Arts Council Museum

The Clay County Historical & Arts Council Museum is housed in the Old County Jail which was constructed in 1912 and used as a jail until 1972. The Museum displays items pertinent to the history of the area through changing exhibits. Displays include school house artifacts, a collection of farm equipment, Indian artifacts from a local excavation and a replica of the office of Dr. Paul Killian, along with many of his medical implements. Ongoing exhibitions are also regularly scheduled for local and regional artists and crafters.

Location: Hayesville NC
Distance: 1.5 hours from Asheville
Address: 21 Davis Loop, Hayesville NC 28904
Telephone: 828-389-6814
Website: clayhistoryarts.org
Hours: May through Labor Day: Tue–Sat 10am–4pm; Sep.–Oct. Fri-Sat 10am–4pm
Fees: None
Allow: 1–2 hours
Directions: From Asheville take I-40 west to exit 27. Take 19/23 Hwy. 74 West to the Dillsboro area. Take exit 81 for US 441 toward Franklin. In Franklin area take Hwy. 64 to Hayesville and in Hayesville turn left at Davis Loop.

Cradle of Forestry

The Cradle of Forestry, a National Historic Site, is located in Pisgah National Forest. It is the site where scientific forestry was first practiced in America over 85 years ago. In 1889, George Vanderbilt began buying land southwest of Asheville to build a country estate. His plans included a palatial home surrounded by a large game preserve. To manage the forest property, Vanderbilt hired Gifford Pinchot, father of American forestry. Pinchot's management proved profitable through the sale of wood products, so Vanderbilt purchased an additional 100,000 acres in the mountains surrounding Mt. Pisgah. Pisgah Forest, as it became known, was the first large tract of managed forest land in America. It later became the nucleus of the Pisgah National Forest.

In 1895, a German forester, Dr. Carl Schenck, succeeded Pinchot as manager of Pisgah Forest. Schenck intensified forest operations and three years later launched the first forestry school in America, the Biltmore Forest School. The school lasted until 1914. In 1968, Congress passed the Cradle of Forestry in America Act, establishing 6,400 acres of the Pisgah National Forest to preserve and make available to the public the birthplace of forestry and forestry education in America.

Public facilities at the Cradle of Forestry provide visitors with exciting programs and displays on the rich history of American forestry. The Forest Discovery Center, two paved interpretive trails, and living history exhibits are major attractions at the historic site. A 1900 portable steam powered sawmill and a restored 1915 Climax locomotive are also on exhibit.

Location: Pisgah District of the Pisgah National Forest
Distance: 1 hour from Asheville
Address: Cradle of Forestry, Pisgah National Forest, 1001 Pisgah Hwy., Pisgah Forest NC 28768
Telephone: 828-877-3130
Website: cradleofforestry.com
Hours: Open April to Oct., 9am–5pm
Fees: Adult and student rates, ages 15 and younger free
Allow: 3 hours
Directions: From Asheville: Take Airport Rd. (NC 280) off Hendersonville Hwy. in Arden. Continue on 280 past Asheville Airport to Wal-Mart Shopping Plaza just before Brevard. Turn right onto US 276 into Pisgah Forest to Cradle of Forestry. From Hendersonville: Take US 64 West from Hendersonville to intersection of Hwy. 280 and US 276 at the Wal-Mart Shopping Plaza. Continue straight through light to US 276 into Pisgah Forest and Cradle of Forestry.

Fine and Performing Arts Center at Western Carolina University

The $30 million Fine and Performing Arts Center at Western Carolina University is an exciting cultural arts and art education destination and combines state-of-the-art educational opportunities for students and instructors with a fresh and inspiring venue for world-class performers and artists. Major features include an elegant 1,000 seat concert hall, fine arts academic wing, and a Fine Art Museum with nearly 10,000 feet of exhibit space and a growing permanent collection.

Location: Cullowhee NC
Distance: 45 minutes from Asheville
Address: Centennial Dr., Western Carolina University, Cullowhee NC 28723
Telephone: 828-227-2479
Website: wcu.edu/fapac/index
Hours: Fine Art Museum: Tue–Fri 10am–4pm, Sat 1–4pm
Fees: Museum: None, Performances & Theatre: vary with performances
Allow: 1–2 hours
Directions: From Asheville follow I-40 West to exit 27 (Highway 74 West). Follow Hwy. 74 West to exit 85 in Sylva. At third light turn left onto Hwy. 107 South. Follow Hwy. 107 South to campus.

Franklin Gem & Mineral Museum

Housed in the historic old jail (circa 1850) of Macon County, the Franklin Gem and Mineral Museum has many fascinating exhibits concerning North Carolina gems and minerals. The "Jail House Museum" now imprisons thousands of specimens on display in eight rooms. The museum displays not only specimens of local minerals and Cowee Valley gem stones but gems, minerals and artifacts from around the world, among these a 2¼ pound ruby.

Location: Franklin NC
Distance: 1.5 to 2 hours from Asheville

Address: 25 Phillips St., Franklin NC 28734
Telephone: 828-369-7831
Website: fgmm.org
Hours: May 1-Oct. 31 Mon–Fri: 10am–4pm; Sat: 11am–3pm, 6-9pm; Nov 1–April 30: Sat only 11am–3pm
Fees: None
Allow: .5–1 hour
Directions: From Asheville, take I-40 West to Exit 27. Take Hwy. 74 West to Hwy. 441 South (Exit 81). Follow 441 South to Franklin.

Graham County Museum of Prehistoric Relics

The Graham County Museum of Prehistoric Relics is housed in The Hike Inn, and is a collection of thousands of prehistoric artifacts from North, South and Central America. They also have a rock bed in front of the museum from which kids can take home samples.

Location: The Hike Inn at Fontana Dam NC
Distance: 2 hours from Asheville
Address: 3204 Fontana Rd., Fontana Dam NC 28733
Telephone: 828-479-3677
Hours: 9am–6pm (Please call ahead from Dec. 1 through Feb. 15)
Fees: None
Allow: 1 hour
Directions: From Asheville take I-40 west. Take the exit for Hwy 74 (Great Smoky Mountain Expressway). Stay on Hwy 74 (four lane) you will pass Clyde, Sylva, and 8 miles past Bryson City (last chance for groceries, restaurants), turn right on Hwy 28 to #3204, The Hike Inn.

Great Smoky Mountains Railroad

The Great Smoky Mountains Railroad gives passengers a chance to recapture the thrills and romance of early trains with its excursions through the mountain countryside. Steam and diesel locomotives pull authentic passenger cars on half-day excursions through the mountains and valleys of Western North Carolina. With 53 miles of track, two tunnels and 25 bridges, the Great Smoky Mountains Railroad offers a variety of excursions that explore the amazing landscape of the mountains.

There are open cars, coaches and club cars to choose from, as well as a popular weekly dinner train. Excursions leave from a number of sites: Dillsboro, Bryson City and Andrews. The trains run on passenger schedules for half-day round trips. Passengers ride in comfortable, reconditioned coaches, crown coaches, club cars, cabooses and even open cars. The club cars and dining cars have historic pasts and have been lovingly restored, as have the cabooses. A full excursion schedule is offered, including summer season "Raft and Rail" trips that combine a train ride and whitewater rafting experience into one package, Gourmet Dinner Trains, and many other special events.

Location: Departures from Dillsboro, Bryson City, and Andrews NC
Distance: 1–3 hours depending upon departure point

Address: Great Smoky Mountains Railroad, 1 Front St., Dillsboro NC 28752
Telephone: 800-872-4681, 828-586-8811
Website: gsmr.com
Hours: Mar.–Dec., times vary.
Fees: Adult and child rates. Prices vary depending on season and excursion.
Allow: 3.5 to 4.5 hours round trip.
Directions: From Asheville to Dillsboro (closest departure point), take I-40 West to Exit 27. Take 19/23 Hwy. 74 West to Exit 81 (Dillsboro). Go to first red light and turn left on Haywood St. Proceed to post office and turn right onto Depot St.

Harrah's Cherokee Casino Resort

Located on a site known as the "Magic Waters" in Cherokee NC is the visually stunning complex of Harrah's Cherokee Casino Resort. Superbly designed to blend in with the breathtaking natural surroundings beside a sparkling trout stream, the huge 175,000 square-foot casino building is barely visible from Hwy. 19. The approach drive features landscaping highlighting native plants and trees and nearing the casino, one is greeted by massive stone columns and a waterfall. The overall effect upon first seeing the building in its natural setting is that of a remote mountain lodge nestled deep in some immense wilderness.

The casino cost $85 million to build and is situated on 37 acres, tucked tightly between two mountains that reflect the bluish haze that gives the Great Smoky Mountains their name, featuring virgin forest and a stunning panoramic backdrop. Harrah's Cherokee Casino is owned by the Eastern Band of Cherokee Indians and was designed by one of the nation's leading casino and destination resort design firms, the Minneapolis-based Cunningham Group. Harrah's Cherokee Casino is an architectural triumph. Inside, the mountain lodge theme is continued, with colorful Native American art and artifacts, the use of natural materials indigenous to the area and a truly spectacular display of neon lightning in the ceiling that comes to life, complete with rolling bursts of thunder whenever a jackpot is won at one of the 1,800 video gaming machines.

In the 150,000 square-foot gaming area, guests can play at a staggering array of video gaming machines, as well as live table games like Blackjack, Roulette, and Craps. Guests can also take in a variety of shows and performances highlighting nationally famous entertainers at the 20,000 square-foot entertainment area complete with a 1,500-seat concert hall, with space for special events and festivals. Or, select from in-house restaurants.

Located adjacent to the casino is the luxurious 21-story Harrah's Cherokee Hotel that provides an upscale experience with over 1,100 rooms with breathtaking views. Amenities include 24/7 fitness room, an indoor pool and an outdoor pool featuring a zero entry door, cabanas and bar area

Location: Cherokee NC
Distance: 1.5 to 2 hours from Asheville
Address: Intersection of Hwy. 19 and Business Rte. 441, Cherokee NC 28719
Telephone: 800-342-7724, 828-497-7777
Website: harrahscherokee.com
Hours: Casino: 24 hours a day, seven days a week, all year.;

Hotel: Harrah's Cherokee Hotel, 777 Casino Dr., Cherokee NC 28719; 828-497-7777, 800-342-7724
Fees: None to enter casino, parking is free. Fees for childcare facilities.
Directions: From Asheville take I-40 West to Exit 27. Follow US-74 West through Waynesville. Take Hwy. 441 North to Cherokee. Take right at first light. Harrah's is at the next intersection.

Highlands Biological Station

Founded in 1927, the Highlands Biological Station acquired its first laboratory for scientific research in 1931. Since that time, scientists based at the Station have made significant contributions in a number of fields, particularly in the study of salamander biology, plant ecology, mycology, and aquatic ecology. The mission of the Station is to foster education and research focused on the rich natural heritage of the Highlands Plateau, while preserving and celebrating the integrity of the "biological crown of the southern Appalachian Mountains." The Highlands Biological Station offers courses and tours, and also has an onsite botanical garden open to the public.

Location: Highlands NC
Distance: 1–1.5 hours from Asheville
Address: 265 North Sixth St., Highlands NC 28741
Telephone: 828-526-2602
Website: highlandsbiological.org
Fees: None
Hours: Botanical Gardens are open year-round, sunrise to sunset.
Allow: 1–2 hours
Directions: From Asheville, take NC 280 West to Brevard (280 begins as Airport Rd., accessible from US 25 or I-26). NC 280 joins NC 64 just before reaching Brevard. Follow 64 West to Highlands. In Highlands, turn left at the first light onto Main St. Proceed to left onto Sixth St. and make a right turn into the Station driveway.

Highlands Museum & Historical Village

The Highlands Museum & Historical Village is composed of a number of restored buildings which make up the Historical Village. These include the House-Trapier-Wright Home, the Highlands Historical Museum, and Bug Hill Cottage. The House-Trapier-Wright Home is the oldest existing house in Highlands and was built in 1877. The museum house exhibits consist of artifacts, photographs and memorabilia relating to the history of the Highlands area.

Location: Highlands NC
Distance: 1 hour from Asheville
Address: 524 N. 4th St., Highlands NC 28741
Telephone: 828-787-1050
Website: highlandshistory.com
Hours: May 23–Oct. 31, Fri & Sat, 10am–4pm, or by appointment

Fees: None
Allow: 1–2 hours
Directions: From Asheville, take NC 280 West to Brevard (280 begins as Airport Rd., accessible from US 25 or I-26). NC 280 joins NC 64 just before reaching Brevard. Follow 64 West to Highlands. In Highlands, turn left at the first light onto Main St.

Highlands Nature Center

Live animal exhibits, garden tours, and children's programs are all facets of this excellent nature center. Their emphasis is on Southern Appalachian biodiversity and geology. They also have exhibitions of Native American artifacts and culture, and exhibits of native wildflowers that are currently in bloom in their Botanical Garden.

Location: Highlands NC
Distance: 1–1.5 hour from Asheville
Address: 930 Horse Cove Rd., Highlands NC 28741
Telephone: 828-526-2623
Website: highlandsbiological.org
Hours: Mar.–Oct.: Mon–Sat 1–5pm
Fees: None
Allow: 1–2 hours
Directions: From Asheville, take NC 280 West to Brevard (280 begins as Airport Rd., accessible from US 25 or I-26). NC 280 joins NC 64 just before reaching Brevard. Follow 64 West to Highlands. In Highlands, turn left at the first light onto Main St. Proceed through the next light (Main St. turns into Horse Cove Rd.) and look for the Nature Center on your left.

John C. Campbell Folk School

Established in 1925, the John C. Campbell Folk School is one of America's premier folk art schools. Listed on the National Register of Historic Places, the school offers a wide range of instruction in traditional and contemporary art, crafts, music, dance, nature studies, gardening and cooking. The Folk School's Craft Shop represents more than 300 juried craftspeople and features an impressive collection of traditional and contemporary Appalachian craft, including jewelry, pottery, wood, fiber, ironwork, basketry and other disciplines. The school's fascinating 82-year background is captured in their History Center, where you'll find interesting examples of 20th-century Appalachia on display, including visual art, fine and folk craft, music, historic film footage, photographs and written panels.

Location: Brasstow NC
Distance: 2 hours from Asheville
Address: One Folk School Rd., Brasstown NC 28902
Telephone: 800-365-5724, 828-837-2775
Website: folkschool.org
Hours: Craft Shop and History Center: Mon–Sat 8am–5pm; Sun 1–5pm
Admission: Free

Directions: I-40 West to Exit 27, US 19/23/74. Take 23/74 to Waynesville/Sylva. At Exit 81 take US 23/441 South to Franklin. In Franklin, the US 441 bypass merges with US 64 West. Follow 64 West from Franklin toward Hayesville. Eight miles west of Hayesville, turn left on Settawig Rd. Follow the signs to the Folk School.

John W. Bardo Fine and Performing Arts Center

The $30 million John W. Bardo Fine and Performing Arts Center at Western Carolina University is an exciting cultural arts and art education destination and combines state-of-the-art educational opportunities for students and instructors with a fresh and inspiring venue for world-class performers and artists. Major features include an elegant 1,000- seat concert hall, fine arts academic wing, and a Fine Art Museum with nearly 10,000 feet of exhibit space and a growing permanent collection.

Location: Cullowhee NC
Distance: 45 minutes from Asheville
Address: Centennial Dr.ive, Western Carolina University, Cullowhee NC 28723
Telephone: 828-227-2479
Website: wcu.edu/bardoartscenter/www.wcu.edu/fapac/index
Hours: Fine Art Museum: Tue–Fri 10am.-4pm, Sat 1–4pm.
Fees: Museum: None, Performances & Theatre: vary with performances
Allow: 1–2 hours
Directions: From Asheville follow I-40 West to exit 27 (Highway 74 West). Follow Hwy. 74 West to exit 85 in Sylva. At third light turn left onto Hwy. 107 South. Follow Hwy. 107 South to campus.

Junaluska Memorial & Museum

The Junaluska Memorial & Museum, located at the burial site of Cherokee Warrior Junaluska in the Great Smoky Mountains near the Nantahala River, is dedicated to preserving Cherokee history and culture. Displays include: arrowheads, spear points and other artifacts found here in the Cheoah Valley, artwork and crafts by Snowbird Indian community members, and information about this valley, its people and its place in American history as the starting point of the Trail of Tears.

Location: Robbinsville NC
Distance: 2 hours from Asheville
Address: 1 Junaluska Dr., Robbinsville NC 28771
Telephone: 828-479-4727
Website: junaluska.com
Hours: Mon–Sat, 8am–4pm
Fees: None
Allow: 1–2 hours
Directions: From Asheville, take I-40 West to Exit 27. Take Hwy. 74 South through Sylva and Nantahala. Turn right on NC 129 to Robbinsville. Turn left at East Main St. in Robbinsville and take the 1st left onto South Main St. Junaluska Dr. will be on the left.

Macon County Historical Society & Museum

Housed in the historic Pendergrass Building (circa 1904), the Macon County Museum collection including clothing, antiques, photographs, textiles, documents, and other artifacts pertaining to the history and culture of Macon County and other areas of Western North Carolina. They also have extensive genealogy files and archives relating to local history.

Location: Franklin NC
Distance: 1.5–2 hours from Asheville
Address: 36 West Main St., Franklin NC 28734
Telephone: 828-524-9758
Website: maconnchistorical.org/museum
Hours: Nov.–April: Mon–Fri 10am–4pm; Sat 1–4pm; May.–Oct.: Mon–Fri 10am–5pm; Sat 1–5pm
Fees: None
Allow: 1 hour
Directions: From Asheville, take I-40 West to Exit 27. Take Hwy. 74 West to Hwy. 441 South (Exit 81). Follow 441 South to Franklin.

Mountain Farm Museum

The Mountain Farm Museum is located in the Great Smoky Mountains National Park and is a collection of historic log buildings gathered from throughout the Smoky Mountains and preserved on a single site. Buildings include a house, barns, springhouse, and smokehouse.

Location: Great Smoky Mountains National Park
Distance: 2–3 hours from Asheville
Address: Great Smoky Mountains National Park. Oconaluftee Visitor Center (Closest to Mountain Farm Museum), 150 Hwy. 441 N., Cherokee NC 28719.
Telephone: General Information: 423-436-1200 Oconaluftee Visitor Center: 423-497–1900
Website: nps.gov/grsm/planyourvisit/mfm.htm
Fees: None to enter park.
Allow: 2–4 hours
Directions: From Asheville, take I-40 West to Exit 27. Follow Hwy. 19 South to Cherokee. In Cherokee, take 441 North and follow signs to the park entrance.

Mountain Heritage Center

This museum highlights Southern Appalachian history through exhibitions, publications, educational programs and demonstrations and promotes the rich mountain traditions. The "Migration of the Scotch Irish People" is the center's permanent exhibit. The center also produces temporary exhibits highlighting blacksmithing, mountain trout, the southern handicraft movement, the enduring popularity of handwoven coverlets and other subjects. The Center maintains three major galleries. Gallery A houses the Center's only permanent exhibit, while Galleries B and C house traveling or temporary exhibits.

Location: Campus of Western Carolina University in Cullowhee NC
Distance: 1 hours from Asheville
Address: H.F. Robinson Building, Western Carolina University, Cullowhee NC 28723
Telephone: 828-227-7129
Website: wcu.edu/about-wcu/centers-institutes-affiliates/mountain-heritage-center
Hours: 8am–5pm Mon through Fri; 10am–5pm Sat Jun. through Oct. only.
Fees: None
Allow: 1–2 hours
Directions: From Asheville, take I-40 West to Exit 27 and follow Hwy. 19/23, Hwy. 74 to Exit 85 for Western Carolina University.

Museum of American Cut and Engraved Glass

The Museum of American Cut and Engraved Glass, in Highlands, is considered one of the finest collections of its kind in the world. The museum exhibits cut and engraved glass primarily from the American Brilliant Period, 1876–1916. The museum seeks to educate people about glass from this period and increase awareness of and appreciation for this American art form. Housed in a rustic log cabin, the collection's brilliance is a direct contradiction to its humble setting.

Location: Highlands NC
Distance: 1.5 hours from Asheville
Address: 472 Chestnut St., Highlands NC 28741
Telephone: 828-526-3415, 828-521-3427
Hours: May–Oct.: Tue, Thu & Sat 1–4pm, Nov.–April: Sat 1–4pm
Fees: None
Directions: From Asheville take NC 280 South to Brevard. Continue on through Brevard on NC 64 to Highlands.

Museum of North Carolina Handicrafts

Located in the historic 1875 Shelton House, the Museum of North Carolina Handicrafts features a unique collection of the works of some of the state's most renowned artisans. Special collections of pottery are exhibited in nearly every room of the Shelton House including examples from Seagrove and rare pieces from Jugtown Potteries and Pisgah Potteries. There is also an extensive collection of Native American artifacts as well. Other rooms house collections of coverlets, quilts, china painting, jewelry, period furniture and musical instruments.

Location: Waynesville NC
Distance: 1 hour from Asheville
Address: 49 Shelton St., Waynesville NC 28786
Telephone: 828-452-1551
Hours: May.–Oct.: 10am–4pm Tue–Sat. Call for winter hours.
Fees: Adult, senior, and child rates, under five free
Allow: 1 hour

Directions: From Asheville take I-40 West to Exit 27 and follow NC 19/23 South to Waynesville onto Hwy. 276. This road turns into Main St. Past the First Baptist Church, bear left 2 blocks to intersection of 276 and Shelton St. Museum is on corner.

Museum of the Cherokee Indian

The mission of the Museum of the Cherokee Indian is "to perpetuate the history, culture, and stories of the Cherokee people". To accomplish this mission, the museum maintains a permanent exhibit, extensive artifact collection, archives, education programs, artist series and a gift shop. The Museum of the Cherokee Indian opened in 1948 and moved to its present facility in 1976. Its exhibit was totally renovated in 1998, when a new 12,000-square-foot exhibit was installed. The museum has helped to revitalize the stamped pottery tradition by creating and working with the Cherokee Potters Guild as well as traditional dance by sponsoring the Warriors of AniKituhwa, who wear traditional 18th century Cherokee dress; feather capes; and language. There are a number of permanent exhibits in the museum, including some that combine state-of-the-art computer-generated imagery, special effects and audio with an extensive artifact collection.

Location: Cherokee NC
Distance: 1–1.5 hours from Asheville
Address: 589 Tsali Boulevard, Cherokee NC 28719
Telephone: 828-497-3481
Website: cherokeemuseum.org
Hours: Daily 9am–5pm year round except for Thanksgiving Day, Christmas Day, and New Year's Day.
Allow: 2–3 hours
Fees: Adult and child rates
Directions: From Asheville take Interstate 40 west to exit 27 (Hwy. 74), and travel west on Hwy. 74 to Exit 74 (the Cherokee/Great Smoky Mountains National Park exit). Bear right on Exit 74 and proceed approximately five miles on Hwy. 441 N to the fourth traffic light. Turn right and proceed about a half mile to the next traffic light. Turn left onto Hwy. 441 N/Tsali Boulevard. Proceed .6 mile to the next traffic light (intersection of Hwy. 441/Tsali Boulevard and Drama Rd.). Turn left and the museum will be on your left at 589 Tsali Boulevard.

Oconaluftee Indian Village

The Oconaluftee Indian Village, located on the Cherokee Indian Reservation, is an authentic replica of an 18th-century Cherokee village and offers guided and self-guided tours to explore the village with dwellings, residents, and artisans right out of the 1750's. Visitors can experience traditional medicine and interact with villagers as they hull canoes, make pottery and masks, weave baskets and beadwork, and participate in their daily activities. The Village also hosts live reenactments, interactive demonstrations, "Hands-On Cherokee" arts and crafts classes, villager outfit rentals for children, and evening storytelling performances.

Location: Cherokee NC
Distance: 1–1.5 hours from Asheville
Address: Drama Rd., Cherokee NC 28719
Telephone: 828-497-2111
Hours: Daily 9am–5pm, May 1–Oct 24
Allow: 2–3 hours
Fees: Adult and child rates
Directions: From Asheville take Interstate 40 west to exit 27 (Hwy. 74), and travel west on Hwy. 74 to Exit 74 (the Cherokee/Great Smoky Mountains National Park exit). Bear right on Exit 74 and proceed approximately five miles on Hwy. 441 N to the fourth traffic light. Turn right and proceed about a half mile to the next traffic light. Turn left onto Hwy. 441 N/Tsali Boulevard. Proceed .6 mile to the next traffic light (intersection of Hwy. 441/Tsali Boulevard and Drama Rd.). Turn onto Drama Rd.

Perry's Water Garden

Located in Franklin and established in 1980, Perry's Water Gardens is a wholesale-retail aquatic plant nursery by Perry D. Slocum and is known for shipping high quality mature plants. Perry's Water Garden also has the country's largest collection of aquatic gardens and is a major tourist attraction. Perry Slocum created over 147 ponds on 13 acres featuring exotic sunken gardens highlighted with old fashioned antique rose beds and other above-ground flowers. Naturalized grass and dirt paths meander throughout. In addition to the multitude of iris, water lilies, and lotus, the gardens are home to thousands of brightly colored koi and goldfish. If you love flowers and gardens, this center is a must!

Location: Franklin NC
Distance: 2 hours from Asheville
Address: 136 Gibson Aquatic Farm Rd., Franklin NC 28734
Telephone: 828-524-3264
Website: perryswatergarden.net
Hours: April 1 through Labor Day. Mon–Sat 9am–5pm, Closed Sun
Fees: None
Allow: 2 hours
Directions: From Asheville, take I-40 West to Exit 27. Take Hwy. 74 West to Hwy. 441 South (Exit 81). Follow 441 for 14 miles and turn right on Sanderstown Rd., then right on Bryson City Rd. for 2 miles. Turn right on Cowee Creek for 1 mile, then left on Leatherman Gap Rd. ¼ mile. Turn right onto Gibson Aquatic Farm Rd.

Pisgah Center for Wildlife Education

Located in the Pisgah National Forest at the site of the Bobby N. Setzer Fish Hatchery, the Pisgah Center for Wildlife Education features a reception and orientation area that includes aquarium exhibits, the NC Wild Store gift shop, and wildlife exhibits. Run by the NC Wildlife Resources Commission, this facility is a wonderful place to become acquainted with the diverse wildlife and habitats of the Blue Ridge and Appalachian mountains.

Besides the fascinating fish hatchery, with thousands of trout both large and small, informative exhibits strung along an interpretive trail are another of the Center's popular aspects. The outdoor exhibits on the trail include stations that focus on wildlife conservation, the geology of the Blue Ridge Mountains, unique NC habitats, preservation of streams and wetlands, responsibility and safety in the woods, the science of wildlife management, NC Wild Education Sites, the ecology of wetlands, and ways to get involved in wildlife conservation.

Location: Pisgah District of the Pisgah National Forest
Distance: 1 hour from Asheville
Address: 1401 Fish Hatchery Rd., Pisgah Forest NC 28768
Telephone: 828-877-4423
Website: ncwildlife.org/Education_Workshops/Pisgah_Center.htm
Hours: Open Mon–Sat 8am–4:45pm, closed on Sun. Closed on Easter weekend and other state holidays except for Good Fri, Memorial Day, Independence Day and Labor Day.
Fees: None
Allow: 2–3 hours
Directions: From Asheville: Take I-26 East or US 25 South to Airport Rd. (NC 280). Follow 280 past the airport to the Wal-Mart Shopping Plaza just before Brevard. Turn right onto US 276 into Pisgah Forest. Turn left onto Forest Service Rd. 475. From Hendersonville: Take US 64 West to the intersection of Hwy. 280 and US 276 at the Wal-Mart. Take US 276 into Pisgah Forest. Turn left onto Forest Service Rd. 475.

Qualla Arts & Crafts Mutual

The Qualla Arts & Crafts Mutual located in Cherokee is considered to be one of the premier such organizations in any Indian community in America. The store offers a wide range of traditional and contemporary Cherokee arts and crafts. Groups are welcome to experience Qualla "Hands-On" and learn a specific art from one of Qualla's artists.

Location: Cherokee NC
Distance: 1–1.5 hours from Asheville
Address: 645 Tsali Boulevard, Cherokee NC 28719
Telephone: 828-497-3103
Hours: Mon–Sat: 8am–7pm, Sun: 9am–5pm year round except for Thanksgiving Day, Christmas Day and New Year's Day. Winter hours (Sep.–May) 8am–5pm
Fees: None
Allow: 2–3 hours
Directions: From Asheville take Interstate 40 west to exit 27 (Hwy. 74), and travel west on Hwy. 74 to Exit 74 (the Cherokee/Great Smoky Mountains National Park exit). Bear right on Exit 74 and proceed approximately five miles on Hwy. 441 N to the fourth traffic light. Turn right and proceed about a half mile to the next traffic light. Turn left onto Hwy. 441 N/Tsali Boulevard. Proceed .6 mile to the next traffic light (intersection of Hwy. 441/Tsali Boulevard and Drama Rd.). Turn left and the museum will be at 645 Tsali Boulevard.

Red Barn Mountain Museum

The Red Barn Mountain Museum presents the history of rural mountain life in the Haywood County area from mountain men to the 1920's through exhibits and interpretation of artifacts, photographs, and memorabilia from the local region and from local families. On display are horse-drawn farming equipment, quilts, area photographs, tools, Civil War artifacts and mountain lore.

Location: Waynesville NC
Distance: 1 hour from Asheville
Address: 1856 Dellwood Rd., Waynesville NC 28786
Telephone: 828-926-1901
Hours: 10am–5pm Mon–Sat. Call to confirm hours as they can vary seasonally.
Admission: None
Allow: 1 hour
Directions: From Asheville take I-40 West and take exit 27 to US 74W toward Waynesville. Take exit 102 and merge onto Russ Ave. Turn right at Dellwood Rd.

Ruby City Gems Museum

The Ruby City Gems Museum has on display thousands of gem and mineral specimens, including fluorescent (glow-in-the-dark) pieces, fossils dating to millions of years old, petrified wood from all over the world, an expansive Native American collection of pipes, tools, and other daily artifacts, and one of the largest, private pre-Columbian collections in the world.

Location: Franklin NC
Distance: 2 hours from Asheville
Address: 131 East Main St., Franklin NC 28734
Telephone: 828-524-3967
Website: rubycity.com
Hours: Mon–Fri 9am–5pm, Sat 9am–5pm
Fees: None
Allow: 1 hour
Directions: From Asheville, take I-40 West to Exit 27. Take Hwy. 74 West toward Waynesville/Franklin. After approximately 16 miles take exit 81 to US 23/US 441. Continue straight onto East Main St. in Franklin.

Scottish Tartans Museum

Located in Franklin NC, the Scottish Tartans Museum focuses on the history of Scottish Tartans—how they were woven and used in dress over the centuries since 325 A.D. Cultural programs of weaving, music, and dance are also provided at the Center throughout the year by Friends of the Museum and volunteers. Ongoing educational programs and exhibits interpret Scottish history and culture, including migrations of the Scots, concentrating on the Scots who settled in Western North Carolina. The museum is over 2,200 square feet and contains the official registry of all publicly known tartans and is the only American extension of the Scottish Tartans Society. Visitors are invited to view their family tartan on computer and trace their Scottish heritage in the tartan research library. The Center also has a gift shop offering a large selection of Scottish and Celtic treasures.

Location: Franklin NC
Distance: 1.5–2 hours from Asheville
Address: 86 East Main St., Franklin NC 28734
Telephone: 828-524-7472
Website: scottishtartans.org
Hours: Mon–Sat 11am–4pm, Closed Sun and major holidays.
Fees: Adult and child rates
Allow: 1–2 hours
Directions: From Asheville, take I-40 West to Exit 27. Hwy. 74 West to Hwy. 441 South (Exit 81). Take the first Franklin exit at the Days Inn, and go straight into town to Main St.

SEJ Heritage Center at Lake Junaluska

The mission of the SEJ Heritage Center at Lake Junaluska is to preserve and keep alive the stories of the remarkable persons and events that make up the unique history of United Methodists in the Southeast. The museum features exhibits depicting the history of the United Methodist Church and its antecedents with special emphasis on the Southeastern Jurisdiction. The archives contain records of SEJAC, journals and newspapers of the SEJ Annual Conferences, some local church histories and clergy biographical information and books on a variety of subjects related to Methodism and its people in the Southeastern Jurisdiction. A special portion of the archives is dedicated to the correspondence and other personal papers of Harry Denman.

Location: Lake Junaluska NC
Distance: 1 hour from Asheville
Address: Harrell Center, 710 North Lakeshore Dr., Lake Junaluska NC 28745
Telephone: 828-454-6781
Website: akejunaluska.com/activities/museums/heritage_center
Hours: Mon–Fri 9am–4:30pm, Sat 9:30am–1:30pm, other times by appointment
Fees: None
Allow: 1–2 hours
Directions: From Asheville, take I-40 West to Exit 27. Take Hwy. 19/23 South to Lake-shore Dr.

Shook Museum

The Shook Museum is housed in the historic Shook-Smathers house in Clyde NC. The original "Shook" portion of the house dates back to between 1810 and 1820. It is the oldest frame structure still standing in Haywood County. Outstanding in its architectural detail, the Shook-Smathers house offers a fascinating glimpse into life in North Carolina years ago. The museum docents give regularly scheduled tours.

Location: Clyde NC
Address: 178 Morgan St., Clyde NC 28721
Distance: 45 minutes from Asheville
Telephone: 828-620-2300
Website: shookmuseum.org
Hours: Sat 10am–2pm Tours at other times by appointment only
Fees: $5 adults, $3 students.
Allow: 2 hours
Directions: From Asheville take I-40 west and take exit 27 and US 74 toward Waynesville/Murphy. Take exit 106 to merge onto Great Smoky Mountain Expressway/US 19 toward Clyde. Turn left at Morgan St. in Clyde.

Smoky Mountain Trains

Smoky Mountain Trains is an outstanding train museum with a collection of 7,000 Lionel engines, cars and accessories, impressive operating layout, children's activity center, and gift & toy shop. The extensive collection dates back to 1918 and features such classics as the 1934 Blue Comet Passenger set and the more recent Joshua Lionel Cowen Challenger Steam Locomotives.

Location: Bryson City NC
Distance: 1 hour from Asheville
Address: 100 Greenlee St., Bryson City NC 28713
Telephone: 828-488-5200, 800-872-4681
Website: smokymountaintrains.com
Hours: 9am–5pm 7 days a week.
Fees: Adult and child rates
Directions: From Asheville take I-40 west. Take exit # 27 US 74 West toward Waynesville and Sylva. Take US 74 West to Bryson City. Take the second Bryson City exit # 67, turn right at the bottom of the exit ramp, turn right onto Main St. and then turn left onto Everett St. Turn right onto Frye St. and you will see Smoky Mountain Trains straight ahead.

Stecoah Valley Cultural Arts Center

The Stecoah Valley Cultural Arts Center has its roots in the Stecoah Union School in Robbinsville, which first opened its doors in 1916. The historic school property is now the heart of the center, and consists of the restored original main school building, and adjacent gymnasium building and grounds. The Center now offers over 20 programs each year to approximately 10,000 people, and brings music to the mountains through the summer performing arts series An Appalachian Evening, as well as the annual Mountain Music Championship, Folkmoot USA, Harvest Festival and other events. Additionally, the new Stecoah Artisans Gallery & Guild provides sales promotion and support for over 100 local and regional artists.

Location: Robbinsville NC
Distance: 1.5–2 hours from Asheville

Address: 121 Schoolhouse Rd., Robbinsville NC 28711
Telephone: 828-479-3364, Gallery 828-479-3098
Website: stecoahvalleycenter.com
Hours: Gallery: Mon–Fri 10am–5pm
Fees: None
Allow: 1–2 hours
Directions: From Asheville take I-40 west. Take the exit for Hwy 74 (Great Smoky Mountain Expressway). Stay on Hwy 74 (four lane) you will pass Clyde, Sylva, and 8 miles past Bryson City (last chance for groceries, restaurants) turn right on Hwy 28. Turn left on Stecoah Rd. in Robbinsville and then sharp left at Schoolhouse Rd.

The Bascom

The Bascom, a nonprofit center for the visual arts in Highlands, has a six-acre, "green," architect-designed pastoral campus where it serves people through high-quality rotating exhibitions, classes and educational presentations. The campus features historic buildings, a covered bridge, a nature trail, a 27,500 square foot main building for two-dimensional adult and children's art, a separate reconstructed Studio Barn for three-dimensional art, a café, a shop, a terrace for venue rentals, and much more. The Bascom complex and landscape, evocative of the former horse stable and agrarian landscape that once thrived there, inspires audiences of all ages and backgrounds. Individuals come together, participate in studio art classes and public programs, share cultural experiences, and enjoy the synergy of art and nature.

Location: Highlands NC
Distance: 1.5 hours from Asheville
Address: 323 Franklin Rd., Highlands NC 28741
Telephone: 828-526-4949
Website: thebascom.org
Hours: Mon–Sat 10am–5pm, Sun 12–5pm
Fees: None
Allow: 1–2 hours
Directions: From Asheville, take NC 280 West to Brevard (280 begins as Airport Rd., accessible from US 25 or I-26). NC 280 joins NC 64 just before reaching Brevard. Follow 64 West to Highlands. In Highlands, turn right onto Main St. and continue to Franklin St.

Transylvania Heritage Museum

The Transylvania Heritage Museum presents the historical heritage of Transylvania County and its families through exhibits, educational programs, collections of artifacts, and heritage-related cultural activities. Temporary and permanent exhibits include displays of heirlooms, artifacts, genealogical exhibits, vintage photographs, and other memorabilia reflective of the history and heritage of the county.

Location: Brevard NC
Distance: 45 minutes from Asheville

Address: 189 West Main St., Brevard NC 28712
Telephone: 828-884-2347
Website: transylvaniaheritage.org
Hours: Wed–Sat 10am–5pm, Mar. to mid-Dec.
Fees: None
Allow: 1 hour
Directions: From Asheville take I-26 south and get off at exit 40. Take left onto NC280 past the Asheville Airport to Brevard. In Brevard continue on 280 to Main St. in downtown.

Unto These Hills

One of America's most popular outdoor dramas, "Unto These Hills," is presented at the Cherokee Indian Reservation, and is the tragic and triumphant story of the Cherokee Indians. Set against the backdrop of the Great Smoky Mountains, the drama is performed under the stars on three stages in the beautiful Mountainside Theatre. Since opening in 1950, "Unto These Hills" has been seen by over five million people (*See* Section V, Chapter Two "Cherokee Indian Reservation").

Location: Cherokee NC
Distance: 2 hours from Asheville
Address: Mountainside Theatre, Drama Rd., Cherokee NC 28719
Telephone: 866-554-4557, 800-438-1601
Hours: Shows nightly except Sun (Jun.–Aug.).
Fees: Adult and child rates
Allow: Drama takes about 2 hours. Pre-show entertainment begins 40 minutes before show times.
Directions: From Asheville, take I-40 West to Exit 27. Take Hwy. 19/23, Hwy. 74 West to Cherokee. In Cherokee turn right at Hospital Rd. which turns into Drama Rd.

Wheels Through Time Museum

The Wheels Through Time Museum is a vintage motorcycle and automobile museum in Maggie Valley that houses a collection of over 250 rare antique motorcycles and automobiles, accompanied by an outstanding collection of memorabilia.

Location: Maggie Valley NC
Distance: 1.5 hours from Asheville
Address: 62 Vintage Lane, Maggie Valley NC 28751
Telephone: 828-926-6626
Website: wheelsthroughtime.com
Hours: 9am–5pm
Fees: Adult, senior, and child rates
Directions: From Asheville take I-40 West to exit 27 onto US 74 W toward Clyde/Waynesville (1.3 Miles). Merge onto Great Smoky Mountain Expressway US 19/74. Exit on to US 19 South to Maggie Valley (6.7 Miles). Wheels Through Time is located on the right, three miles past junction of 276 N.

World Methodist Museum

Located at beautiful Lake Junaluska, the World Methodist Museum includes the largest collection in America of artifacts and memorabilia of John Wesley and the Wesley family. The collection includes displays of antique Wedgwood pottery and oil portraits of John Wesley and other Methodist church founders.

Location: Lake Junaluska NC
Distance: 1 hour from Asheville
Address: 575 Lakeshore Dr., Lake Junaluska NC 28745
Telephone: 456–9432
Hours: Mon–Fri 9am–5pm
Fees: None
Allow: 1–2 hours
Directions: From Asheville, take I-40 West to Exit 27. Take Hwy 19/23 South to Lakeshore Dr., which circles the lake.

Zachary-Tolbert House Museum

Built by Mordecai Zachary in 1842, the Greek Revival Zachary-Tolbert House remains in its original state along with the world's largest collection of plain style furniture made by one craftsman where the craftsman's identity is known.

Location: Cashiers NC
Distance: 1.5 hours from Asheville
Address: 1940 Hwy. 107 Cashiers NC 28771
Telephone: 828-743-7710
Website: cashiershistoricalsociety.org/zacharytolberthouse.htm
Hours: 11am–3pm Fri & Sat, Grounds: open daily
Fees: None
Directions: From Asheville take NC 280 South to Brevard. Continue on through Brevard on NC 64 to Cashiers.

Chapter Three

Retreat & Conference Centers

Western North Carolina, due in part to its overwhelming natural beauty, is home to a number of religious retreat and conference centers. These are included in this book since you may be interested in visiting one or more during your stay. As would be expected, all are in breathtaking settings and immaculately maintained. The administration at each center has indicated that they welcome all visitors.

Billy Graham Training Center at The Cove

Located in a lovely mountain cove just east of Asheville, the Billy Graham Training Center holds year-round seminars and retreats for those seeking in-depth Bible studies, and a deeper experience of God's love. The Cove features two inns: Shepherd's Inn and Pilgrim's Inn. The facilities and grounds at the Cove are especially beautiful in design and landscaping.

Telephone: 828-298-2092, 800-950-2092

Directions: From Asheville take I-40 East. Get off at Exit 55 Porters Cove Rd. Center entrance is on immediate right.

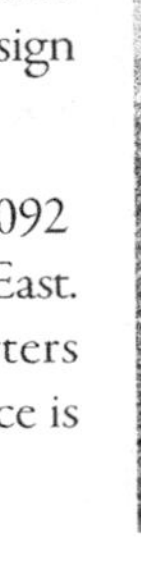

Chatlos Chapel at The Cove

Bonclarken

Located in historic Flat Rock in the Blue Ridge Mountains of Western North Carolina, Bonclarken is nestled among acres of tall white pines, hemlocks, spruce and rhododendron. Bonclarken is owned by the Associate Reformed Presbyterian Church and is available for use year-round by any groups desiring to rent the facilities and agreeing to live within the rules and regulations governing its use. Rich in history and tradition, Bonclarken has served the Associate Reformed Presbyterian Church and others since 1922. The beautiful hotel on the grounds was built in 1886 as a private home. Dr. Arthur Rose Guerard, a Charlestonian, came to Flat Rock to build a home for his German bride. He used only the finest materials in the parquet floors and the wainscoting, and the mantels were carved in Germany of rosewood, ebony and cherry. Bonclarken today offers a variety of facilities to individuals and groups. Complete dining, meeting, recreational and camping facilities round out the total service offering.

Telephone: 828-692-2223
Directions: From Main St. in Hendersonville go south on Hwy. 25 four miles to Pine Dr. Look for Bonclarken sign on left.

Bonclarken, a haven for birds and others

Christmount

Christmount, an agency of the Christian Church (Disciples of Christ), is located one mile south of Black Mountain. The Christmount conference center occupies one square mile of mountain land, cooled by numerous springs and creeks, at an elevation of just under 3,000 feet. Christmount is open year-round with a variety of accommodations including the Gaines M. Cook Guest House, the Guest House East, Davis Hall, Holly Park, and camp cabins. Most camps and conferences are related to the Christian Church (Disciples of Christ).

Telephone: 828-669-8977
Directions: Exit from I-40 in Black Mountain onto Hwy. 9 (Exit 54). Go south one mile to gate on left.

Prayer garden at Christmount

Kanuga

Kanuga is a year-round conference facility, closely affiliated with the Episcopal Church. Kanuga maintains the following programs: Kanuga-sponsored conferences, two summer camps for young people, parish family weekends, guest accommodations, Mountain Trail Outdoor School, retreats, national and regional programs sponsored by the Episcopal Church, and a special camp session for homeless, abused, and disadvantaged children.

Located near Hendersonville, Kanuga's extensive conference center and camp facilities are situated on 1,400 acres of woodland, crisscrossed by streams, ridges and valleys. There is a 30–acre lake, ponds, and complete outdoor recreational facilities and accommodations that range from rustic cottages to the spacious and modern Kanuga Inn.

Kanuga Lake

Telephone: 828-692-9136

Directions: From I-26, take Exit 18 onto US 64 West into Hendersonville. Turn left on Hwy. 25 South (Church St.) and drive 9 blocks. Turn right onto Kanuga St., go 4 miles to Kanuga triangular sign. Turn right, drive 1.5 miles to Kanuga Entrance Park. Turn right and go .5 mile.

Lake Junaluska Assembly

Nestled in the mountains of Western North Carolina west of Asheville, Lake Junaluska Assembly is the conference and retreat center for the Southeastern Jurisdiction of the United Methodist Church, and home of the SEJ Administrative Council. The Assembly provides a wide variety of accommodations and conference facilities which will comfortably support groups ranging in size from 5 to 2,000. The Assembly welcomes individuals, families, church groups, educational organizations and many other groups. The 200-acre Lake Junaluska is surrounded by 1,200 acres of beautiful rolling hills and valleys. Located on the lake is the Cokesbury Gift Shop, which carries gifts, books and crafts.

Telephone: 828-452-2881, 800-222-4930

Directions: From Asheville, take I-40 West to Exit 27 to 19/23. Lake Junaluska is a few miles on the right.

Lake Junaluska

Lifeway Ridgecrest Conference Center

Lifeway Ridgecrest Conference Center began in 1907 as a summer retreat for Southern Baptists. Today Ridgecrest thrives as a year-round conference center, attracting over 60,000 guests a year. While the Sun School Board of the Southern Baptist Convention owns and operates the conference center, Ridgecrest attracts Christian groups from diverse backgrounds, as well as nonprofit organizations, school groups, and government groups. Ridgecrest offers over 52,000 square feet of conference space, eighty-one conference rooms, and three auditoriums of various sizes. Outstanding dining and recreational facilities are also available to guests.

Telephone: 828-669-8022, 800-588-7222
Directions: From Asheville, take I-40 East and get off at Exit 66. At top of ramp, turn left. At the first junction, turn right onto Old US 70 and continue a short distance to Ridgecrest

Lutheridge Conference Center & Camp

Lutheridge is a 160-acre conference center and camp atop scenic Crescent Hill just south of Asheville. The Center offers an intimate setting that boasts a mix of comfortable adult lodging and rustic cabins for youth, modern conveniences, and beautiful

Ridgecrest Confernece Center

year-round scenery. Lutheridge is owned and operated by the North Carolina, South Carolina, Southeastern and Florida-Bahamas synods of the Evangelical Lutheran Church in America (ELCA).

Telephone: 828-684-2361
Directions: Take Exit 9 Airport Rd. off I-26 South. Proceed to Rt. 25, Hendersonville Rd. Lutheridge is located south on Hendersonville Rd.

Entrance gate at Lutheridge

Montreat Conference Center

Montreat Conference Center, a conference center of the Presbyterian Church (U.S.A.) is located 15 miles east of Asheville, just outside Black Mountain. Montreat is a special place to meet and enjoy the refreshing sights and sounds of the Blue Ridge Mountains. With 29 meeting facilities, Montreat offers a comfortable environment for conferences, retreats seminars or other special gatherings. Year-round facilities include a number of options available for housing, dining, classrooms, and recreation. Montreat's beautiful setting makes it the perfect place for all types of outdoor recreation. Hiking on marked trails in the surrounding mountains, swimming in the outdoor Olympic-size pool, and boating and canoeing on Lake Susan are among the many options. Montreat also has superb guest accommodations including Assembly Inn, and the Winnsborough.

Left Bank Building on Lake Susan at Montreat Conference Center

Telephone: 828-669-2911, 800-572-2257
Directions: Take I-40 West from Asheville. Get off at Exit 64, Black Mountain. Go north on Route 9 through Black Mountain, two miles to the Montreat Gate.

YMCA Blue Ridge Assembly

Located in Black Mountain, 15 miles east of Asheville, is the YMCA Blue Ridge Assembly. Founded in 1906 as a YMCA student conference center, the Assembly has hosted over half a million people in its rich history. Blue Ridge serves a diverse mix of not-for-profit religious, social, educational and family groups. Nestled on over 1,200 acres of woodlands, YMCA Blue Ridge Assembly provides restful surroundings for groups large and small and a variety of comfortable accommodations that range from hotel-style to cottages. Blue Ridge also offers a diverse range of meeting facilities, and numerous recreational options. In the summer, Blue Ridge is known for its plentiful and delicious food served family style.

Robert E. Lee Hall at YMCA Blue Ridge Assembly

Telephone: 828-669-8422

Directions: From Asheville take I-40 East. Get off at Exit 64 and go south on Hwy. 9. Proceed less than .5 mile and bear right on Blue Ridge Rd. Turn left at the small Blue Ridge Assembly sign.

Valle Crucis Conference Center

Secluded in an area of spectacular beauty near Boone, the Valle Crucis Conference Center overlooks a peaceful, rural valley in the Blue Ridge Mountains. An outreach of the Episcopal Diocese of Western North Carolina, the Conference Center is located on 448 acres of lush wooded mountain and open valley land, with bold rushing streams and waterfalls. Groups come to Valle Crucis for spiritual and personal renewal, including family reunions, and the Center offers a ministry of hospitality to a diverse range of church and nonprofit groups from around the Southeast. The Center is also right up the road from the original Mast General Store. Grandfather Mountain is close by, and Blowing Rock and Boone are nearby for shopping, etc.

Telephone: 828-963-4453; e-mail: vccc@highsouth.com; web site: highsouth.com/vallecrucis

Directions: From Asheville take take I-40 East to US 70 exit (Old Fort exit). Exit onto US 70 East toward Old Fort and Marion. Dr. approximately eleven (11) miles to intersection with US 221 in Marion. Turn left onto US 221 North. Dr. approximately 35 miles to the intersection with NC 105 in Linville. Turn left onto NC 105 North. Dr. approximately twelve (12) miles to the traffic light at Broadstone Rd. (State Rd. 1112, just before the Watauga River Bridge). Turn left onto Broadstone Rd. Dr. approximately three (3) miles to the intersection with NC 194 (in front of Valle Crucis Elementary School). Turn left onto NC 194 South. Dr. approximately 1.3 miles, past the Valle Crucis Conference Center.

Chapter Four

Western North Carolina Cities & Towns

Andrews

Andrews is a beautiful small town located within the heart of the Western North Carolina Mountains that is largely untouched by large city influences. In today's hectic, modern world, Andrews remains a place that enjoy a more leisurely pace of life. The city has a thriving downtown with restaurants, retail shops, bed and breakfast inns, and artists' galleries and is a great jumping off point for outdoor adventures in the surrounding mountains.

The highest elevation near Andrews in Cherokee County is 5,149 feet, near Tusquitee Bald in the Fires Creek area, and the 466 square mile county encompasses 300,000 acres, with over 90,000 of those owned by the US Forest Service. Andrews is also home to the Andrews Art Museum run by the Valleytown Cultural Arts and Historical Society. The museum has rotating exhibits of local and regional artists. A unique activity in Andrews is the annual Western North Carolina Wagon Train, where wagon train enthusiasts annually make the trek from Andrews to Walhalla, South Carolina in covered wagons and on horseback.

Location: Western Mountains, 2 hours west of Asheville
Town Hall: 1101 Main St., Andrews NC 28901; 828-321-3113
Website: andrewsnc.com
County: Cherokee County: County Offices, 75 Peachtree St., Murphy NC 28906; 828-837-5527
Elevation and Population: 2,350 feet, 1,600+
Visitor/Welcome Center: Cherokee County Welcome Center, 805 West Hwy. 64, Murphy NC 28906, 828-837-2242
City Chamber of Commerce: Andrews Chamber of Commerce, 345 1st St., Andrews NC 28901, 828-321-3584
County Chamber of Commerce: Cherokee County Chamber of Commerce, 805 West Hwy. 64, Murphy NC 28906, 828-837-2242
Newspaper: Andrews Journal, PO Box 250, Chestnut St., Andrews NC 28901; 828-321-4271

Movie Theatres: Andrews Twin Cinema, 125 Main St., Andrews NC 28901, 828-321-3333
High School: Andrews High School, 50 High School Dr., Andrews NC 28901; 828-321-5415
Area Major Festivals: Andrews Valley Music Festival (Jun.)
Area Natural Attractions: Chatuge Lake, Joyce Kilmer Memorial Forest, Lake Santeetlah, Nantahala Lake, Nantahala National Forest, Nantahala River
Area Cultural Attractions: Andrews Art Museum, Cherokee County History and Arts Museum, Great Smoky Mountains Railroad
Recommended Restaurants: (For a complete list of all restaurants visit ashevilleguide book.com
Granieri's Italian Restaurant: 983 Main St, Andrews, NC 28901; 828-321-5555
Recommended Places To Stay: (For a complete list of all accommodations visit ashe villeguidebook.com
Hawkesdene House Mountain Retreat: (Country Lodge) 381 Phillips Creek Rd., Andrews NC 28901; 800-447-9549
Quality Inn: (Motel) 138 Upper Valley River Lane, Andrews NC 28901; 828-321-2176

Bakersville

Bakersville, founded in the mid 1800's and incorporated in 1870, is the home of the famous North Carolina Rhododendron Festival held every spring during the height of the blooming season. The county seat of Mitchell County, Bakersville still retains the charm of a small mountain community, and is a convenient jumping-off point to explore the surrounding mountains. Every spring the Bakersville Creek Walk Arts Festival is held along the banks of Cane Creek, with over 50 artists and crafters displaying their work. Bakersville also has two farmer's markets open every Sat morning-the Bakersville Farmers Market and the Community Market held at the Creek Walk pavilion.

Location: Central Mountains, 1 hour northeast of Asheville
Town Hall: 26 South Mitchell Ave., Bakersville NC 28705; 828-688-2113
Website: bakersville.com
County: Mitchell County: County Administration Building, 26 Crimson Laurel Circle, Bakersville NC 28705; 828-688-2139
Elevation and Population: 2,460 feet, 350+
County Visitor Center: Mitchell County Visitor Center; Located in the Museum of NC Minerals, Milepost 331, Blue Ridge Parkway; Spruce Pine NC 28777; 800-227-3912
County Chamber of Commerce: Mitchell County Chamber of Commerce: 11 Crystal St., Spruce Pine NC 28777; 828-765-9033
Newspaper: Mitchell News-Journal 261 Locust Ave., Spruce Pine 28777; 828-765-2071
Movie Theatres: None
High School: Mitchell High School, 416 Ledger School Rd., Bakersville NC 28705; 828-688-2101
Area Major Festivals: North Carolina Rhododendron Festival (Jun.)
Area Natural Attractions: Mount Mitchell State Park

Area Cultural Attractions: Penland Gallery and School of Crafts

Recommended Restaurants: (For a complete list of all restaurants visit ashevilleguide book.com

- **Helen's Restaurant:** (Country-American) 99 N 226 Hwy, Bakersville NC 28705; 828-688-9999
- **Mammie's Kitchen:** (County-American) 624 Hwy 226, Bakersville NC 28705; 828-688-7272

Recommended Places To Stay: (For a complete list of all accommodations visit ashe villeguidebook.com

- **Bakersville Bed & Breakfast:** (B&B) 71 N. Mitchell Ave., Bakersville NC 28705; 828-688-6012

Banner Elk

Banner's Elk, as the village was once called, was settled around 1850, and is located in the northeast section of the mountains in Avery County, Banner Elk is a quaint mountain community that offers tourist activities including skiing and snowboarding at the world famous Sugar Mountain Resort. Golf, hiking & backpacking, horseback riding and whitewater rafting are also available. Surrounded by high peaks and rugged ridges, Banner Elk has strong historic and cultural ties with the neighboring mountainous regions of Tennessee and Virginia as well as Western North Carolina. Lees-McRae College has been located in the area for over 100 years and the College Drama Department presents theatrical productions during the summer months. Banner Elk is also host every Oct. to the famous Woolly Worm Festival.

Location: Northern Mountains, 2 hours east of Asheville

Town Offices: 200 Park Ave., Banner Elk NC 28604; 828-898-5398

Website: townofbannerelk.org

County: Avery County: County Administrative Building, 175 Linville St., Newland NC 28657; 828-733-8202

Elevation and Population: 3,739 feet, 950+

City Chamber of Commerce: Banner Elk Chamber of Commerce: 100 West Main St., Banner Elk NC 28604; 828-898-8395

County Chamber of Commerce: Avery County Chamber of Commerce: 4501 Tynecastle Hwy., Unit #2, Banner Elk NC 28604; 800-972-2183

Newspaper: The Mountain Times PO Box 1815, Boone NC 28607; 828–264-6397

High School: Avery County High School, 401 High School Rd., Newland NC 28657; 828-733-0151

Colleges and Universities: Lees-McRae College, 191 Main St., Banner Elk NC 28604; 828-898-5241

Area Major Festivals: Woolly Worm Festival (Oct.)

Area Natural Attractions: Blue Ridge Parkway, Grandfather Mountain, Linville Caverns, Linville Gorge.

Area Cultural Attractions: Avery County Historical Museum, Banner House Museum, Crossnore Fine Arts Gallery, Horn in the West, Mast General Store, Mystery Hill, Orchard at Altapass, Tweetsie Railroad

Recommended Restaurants: (For a complete list of all restaurants visit ashevilleguide book.com

Artisanal: (Contemporary-American) 1200 Dobbins Road, Banner Elk NC 28604; 828-898-5395

Louisana Purchase Food and Spirits: (Cajun) 397 Shawneehaw Ave., Banner Elk NC 28694; 866-734-4124

Sorrentos Bistro: (Italian) 140 Azalea Circle, Banner Elk NC 28604; 828–898-5214

The Mast Farm Inn: (American) 2543 Broadstone Rd., Banner Elk NC 28604; 828-963-5857

Recommended Places To Stay: (For a complete list of all accommodations visit ashe villeguidebook.com

Banner Elk Inn B&B and Cottages: (B&B) 407 E. Main St., Banner Elk NC 28604; 888-487-8263

Little Main St. Inn & Suites: (Village Inn) 607 Main St. East, Banner Elk NC 28604; 800-851-4397

The Mast Farm Inn: (B&B) 2543 Broadstone Rd., Banner Elk NC 28604; 888-963-5857

Beech Mountain

The town of Beech Mountain, originally begun as a private resort development in the mid 1960's and incorporated in 1981, is today known for its world-famous ski resort, Beech Mountain Resort, as well as its cool summer weather where temperatures rarely get above 72 degrees. Located in the northeast section of the Western North Carolina mountains, upscale Beech Mountain is the highest in elevation of all towns in the northeastern United States at 5,506 feet above sea level. Offering a nice selection of stores and restaurants, as well as a large choice of outdoor sports, Beech Mountain is a year-round destination. When Oct. rolls around, Beech Mountain magically transforms into the Land of Oz in their annual Autumn at Oz Festival, complete with all your favorite people and places from Frank Baum's silver screen classic.

Location: Northern Mountains, 2 hours east of Asheville

Town Offices: 403 Beech Mountain Parkway, Beech Mountain NC 28604; 828-387-4862

Website: townofbeechmountain.com

County: Avery County: County Administrative Building, 175 Linville St., Newland NC 28657; 828-733-8202

Elevation and Population: 5,506 feet, 300+

City Chamber of Commerce: Beech Mountain Chamber of Commerce 403-A Beech Mountain Parkway, Beech Mountain NC 28604; 800-468-5506

County Chamber of Commerce: Avery County Chamber of Commerce: 4501 Tynecastle Hwy., Unit #2, Banner Elk NC 28604; 800-972-2183

Newspaper: The Mountain Times PO Box 1815, Boone NC 28607; 828–264-6397

High School: Avery County High School, 401 High School Rd., Newland NC 28657; 828-733-0151

Area Major Festivals: Autumn at Oz Festival (Oct.), Annual Roasting of the Hog and Fireworks Display (Jul.)

Area Natural Attractions: Blue Ridge Parkway, Grandfather Mountain, Linville Caverns, Linville Gorge.

Area Cultural Attractions: Avery County Historical Museum Banner House Museum, Crossnore Fine Arts Gallery, Horn in the West, Mast General Store, Mystery Hill, Orchard at Altapass, Tweetsie Railroad

Recommended Restaurants: (For a complete list of all restaurants visit ashevilleguide book.com

Alpen Restaurant & Bar: (American) 700 Beech Mountain Parkway, Beech Mountain NC 28604; 828-387-2252

Famous Brick Oven Pizzeria: (Pizza) 402 Beech Mountain Parkway,Beech Mountain, NC 28604; 828) 387-4000

Recommended Places To Stay: (For a complete list of all accommodations visit ashe villeguidebook.com

Beech Alpen Inn: (Country Inn) 700 Beech Mountain Parkway, Beech Mountain NC 28604; 866-284-2770

Black Mountain

Located just ten miles east of Asheville on Interstate 40 is the charming mountain city of Black Mountain, known as "The Little Town That Rocks". One of the hallmarks of Black Mountain is the magnificent view of the nearby Black Mountains, including Mount Mitchell, the highest peak east of the Mississippi River and the famous Seven Sisters range. Known for its arts & crafts and antiques, Black Mountain has many top quality galleries, antique and specialty shops, bookstores, and furniture stores. The epicenter of this eclectic mix of stores is the historic Cherry St. district. The community also offers a diverse program of outdoor recreation with golf at the Black Mountain Golf Club, public tennis, ball-fields, croquet, and walking paths, including a spectacular one at Lake Tomahawk.

In the Swannanoa Valley, where Black Mountain is located, is the largest concentration of religious conference centers in the world, including Montreat Conference Center, Lifeway Ridgecrest Conference Center, Christmount Retreat, Camp & Conference Center, Cragmont Assembly, The Cove: Billy Graham Training Center, United Research/Light Center, and the YMCA Blue Ridge Assembly. Famous residents include Evangelist Billy Graham and former NBA star Brad Dougherty. In the late summer, Black Mountain is also host to the famous Sourwood Festival and the bi-annual Lake Eden Arts Festival, also known as LEAF.

The Swannanoa Valley, home to the unincorporated community of Swannanoa, has been a coveted spot for hundreds of years. The Cherokee Indians guarded the mountainous ridges while would-be settlers from what is now Old Fort looked westward toward the game-filled forests. The Cherokee boundary was moved farther west in the late 1780s and settlers rapidly rushed through the Swannanoa Gap into the coves to establish homesteads along the many creeks and rivers. By 1850, there was a turnpike up the mountains from the east, but one so steep that wheels on the wagons had to be larger on one side to make the journey up and then switched to the other side to make the journey down. In 1879, the railroad arrived and changed things forever. Black Mountain has been known as a tourist destination and a wonderful place to vacation and live ever since.

Montreat is a small residential community adjacent to Black Mountain, located in a secluded mountain cove at the foot of Greybeard Mountain. Montreat is home to the Montreat Conference Center which currently hosts religious conferences throughout the year, and Montreat College, a four-year Christian liberal arts college affiliated with the Presbyterian Church (USA).

Location: Central Mountains,10 minutes east of Asheville
Town Offices: 160 Midland Ave., Black Mountain NC 28711; 828-419-9300
Website: townofblackmountain.org
County: Buncombe County: County Offices, 205 College St., Asheville NC 28801; 828-250-4100
Elevation and Population: 2405 feet, 7500+
Visitor/Welcome Center: Black Mountain-Swannanoa Visitor Center 201 East State St., Black Mountain NC 28711; 800-669-2301 exploreblackmountain.com
City Chamber of Commerce: Black Mountain-Swannanoa Chamber of Commerce 201 East State St., Black Mountain NC 28711; 800-669-2301 exploreblackmountain.com
County Chamber of Commerce: Buncombe County Chamber of Commerce 205 College St., Asheville NC 28801; 828-250-4100
Newspaper: Black Mountain News 111S. Richardson Blvd., Black Mountain NC 28711; 828-669-8727
High School: Owen High School, 99 Lake Eden Rd., Black Mountain NC 28711; 828-686-3852
Colleges and Universities: Montreat College, 310 Gaither Circle, Montreat NC 28757; 800-622-6968; Warren Wilson College, 701 Warren Wilson College Rd., Swannanoa NC 28778; 828-298-3325
Area Major Festivals: Lake Eden Arts Festival (LEAF) (May and Oct.) Sourwood Festival (Aug.).
Area Natural Attractions: Lake Tomahawk, Blue Ridge Parkway, Mount Mitchell State Park, Pisgah National Forest
Area Cultural Attractions: Black Mountain Center for the Arts, Old Depot Gallery and Caboose Museum, Sourwood Gallery, Swannanoa Valley Fine Arts League–Red House Gallery, Swannanoa Valley Museum
Recommended Restaurants: (For a complete list of all restaurants visit ashevilleguidebook.com

Berliner Kindl German Restaurant & Deli: (German) 121 Broadway, Black Mountain NC 28711; 828-669-5255
Que Sera Restaurant: (American) 400 East State St., Black Mountain NC 28711; 828-664-9472
Red Rocker Inn & Restaurant: (American) 136 N. Dougherty St., Black Mountain NC 28711; 828-669-5991
Black Mountain Bistro: (American) 203 E. State St., Black Mountain NC 28711; 828-669-5041

My Father's Pizza: (Italian) 110 Cherry St., Black Mountain NC; 828-669-4944

Okie Dokies Smokehouse: (BBQ) 2375 US Hwy. 70, Swannanoa NC 28778; 828-686-0050

Ole's Guacamoles: (Mexican) 401 E. State St., Black Mountain NC 28711; 828-669-0550

Sake-Sushi: (Japanese) 6 E. Market St., Black Mountain NC 28711; 828-669-8833

Veranda Café: (Café) 119 Cherry St., Black Mountain NC 28711; 828–669-8864

Recommended Places To Stay: (For a complete list of all accommodations visit ashe villeguidebook.com

Arbor House of Black Mountain: (B&B) 207 Rhododendron Ave., Black Mountain NC 28711; 828-669-9302

Inn Around the Corner: (B&B) 109 church St., Black Mountain NC 28711; 800-393-6005

Red Rocker Inn & Restaurant: (Hotel-Village Inn) 136 N. Dougherty St., Black Mountain NC 28711; 828-669-5991

The Monte Vista Hotel: (Hotel-Village Inn) 308 W. State St., Black Mountain NC 28711; 828-669-8870

Blowing Rock

The quaint upscale resort village of Blowing Rock sits aside the Eastern Continental Divide in the Northern Mountains of Western North Carolina and is centrally located to most of the major area attractions. There is a professional summer stock theatre (the Blowing Rock Stage Company), wonderful festivals, Art in the Park and the Blue Ridge Wine and Food Festival, and abundant outdoor recreational opportunities, including skiing at Appalachian Ski Mountain. Its rich history stretches back to the 1500s, when the famous explorer Desoto supposedly looked for gold in the area. The town is named after its main attraction, The Blowing Rock, cliff walls that form a flume through which the north-west wind sweeps with such force that it returns light objects cast over the cliff. Another of Blowing Rock's main attractions is the Moses H. Cone Memorial Park. The park, once a 3,500 acre estate, was donated by Moses H. Cone and now includes 26 miles of horse and carriage trails, which are also used for hiking and cross-country skiing, and a deer park.

Location: Northern Mountains, 2 hours west of Asheville

Town Offices: 1036 Main St., Blowing Rock NC 28605; 828–95–5200

Website: townofblowingrock.com

County: Watauga County: County Offices, 814 West King St., Ste 205, Boone NC 28607; 828-265-8000

Elevation and Population: 4,000 feet, 1,500+

Visitor/Welcome Center: Blowing Rock Visitor Center, 7738 Valley Blvd., Blowing Rock NC 28605; 877-750-4636

City Chamber of Commerce: Blowing Rock Chamber of Commerce, 7738 Valley Blvd., Blowing Rock NC 28605; 828-295-7851

Newspaper: The Blowing Rocket, 452–1 Sunset Dr., Blowing Rock NC 28605; 828-295-7522

High School: Watauga High School, 300 Go Pioneers Dr., Boone NC 28607; 828-264-2407

Hospitals: Blowing Rock Hospital, 418 Chestnut Dr., Blowing Rock NC 28605; 828-295-3136

Area Major Festivals: Art in the Park (Monthly: May.–Oct.) Blue Ridge Wine and Food Festival (April)

Area Natural Attractions: Blue Ridge Parkway, Grandfather Mountain, Linville Caverns, Linville Gorge, Moses H Cone Memorial Park, Pisgah National Forest, The Blowing Rock

Area Cultural Attractions: Appalachian Heritage Museum, Appalachian Ski Mountain, Mariam and Robert Hayes Performing Arts Center, Mystery Hill, Orchard at Altapass, Tweetsie Railroad

Recommended Restaurants: (For a complete list of all restaurants visit ashevilleguide book.com

Best Cellar: (American) The Inn at Ragged Garden, 203 Sunset Dr., Blowing Rock NC 28605; 828-295-3466

Bistro Roca: (American Bistro) 143 Wonderland Trail, Blowing Rock NC 28605; 828-295-4008

Speckled Trout: (American) 922 Main St., Blowing Rock NC 28605; 828-295-9819

Twigs Restaurant: (Continental) 7956 Valley Boulevard, Blowing Rock NC 28605; 828-295-5050

Recommended Places To Stay: (For a complete list of all accommodations visit ashe villeguidebook.com

Azalea Garden Inn: (Village Inn) 793 North Main St., Blowing Rock NC 28605; 828-295-3272

Chetola Resort at Blowing Rock: (Resort Inn) 500 Main St., Blowing Rock NC 28605; 828-295-5500

Gideon Ridge Inn: (County Inn) 202 Gideon Ridge Rd., Blowing Rock NC 28605; 828-295-3644

Meadowbrook Inn: (Hotel) 711 Main St., Blowing Rock NC 28605; 828-295-4300

Victorian Inn: (B&B) 242 Ransom St., Blowing Rock NC 28605; 828-295-0034

Westglow Resort & Spa: (Resort) 224 Westglow Circle, Blowing Rock NC 28605; 800-562-0807

Boone

Located just off the Blue Ridge Parkway in the northeast section of the mountains, Boone, incorporated in 1872, is a destination in very much the same way Asheville is. Consistently ranked as one of the "Best Small Towns in America," Boone is a bustling town and the center of tourism and commerce for Watauga County and the region. With a population of over 17,000, the city is home to Appalachian State University, which adds a distinctive college atmosphere to the already vibrant, outdoors oriented mountain city. Boone is located in the "Heart of the High Country" and has a wide array of stores, restaurants, galleries and things to do. It is even known as the "Firefly Capital of America!" Named for Daniel Boone, the frontiersman who hunted in the area from 1760 to 1769, this tourist-oriented mountain city has much to offer the visitor.

Boone also has the highest elevation of any town of its size east of the Mississippi River and because of that, on average, the city receives over 34" of snowfall a year, far more than most other cities in North Carolina. In 2005, Boone was recognized by travel journalists as the ultimate outdoor adventure destination in the Southeast. Along with Durango, Colorado, Bend, Oregon and North Vancouver, British Columbia, Boone was selected as one of four multi-sport vacation destinations in North America, featured in an article in the May 2005 issue of Adventure Sports Magazine. In the winter, one of the major draws to Boone is the many ski and snowboarding resorts in the area. These include Appalachian Ski Mountain, Sugar Mountain Resort, Beech Mountain Resort and Hawksnest Tubing Park.

Boone also has one of North Carolina's most progressive public school systems. All eight K-8 schools are ranked as Schools of Excellence, a claim to fame no other public school district in the state can match.

Location: Northern Mountains, 2 hours east of Asheville
Town Offices: 567 West King St., Boone NC 28607; 828-268-6200
Website: townofboone.net
County: Watauga County: County Offices, 842 West King St., Boone NC 28607; 828-265-8000
Elevation and Population: 3,500 feet, 15,000+
Visitor/Welcome Center: North Carolina High Country Host and Visitor Information Center, 1700 Blowing Rock Rd., Boone NC 28607; 828-264-1299 highcountryhost.com
City Chamber of Commerce: Boone Area Chamber of Commerce, 870 West King St., Ste A, Boone NC 28607; 828-264-2225
County Chamber of Commerce: Boone Area Chamber of Commerce 870 West King St., Ste A, Boone NC 28607; 828-264-2225
Newspaper: The Watauga Democrat 474 Industrial Park Dr., Boone NC 28607; 828-264-3612 and The Mountain Times PO Box 1815, Boone NC 28607; 828-262-0282
Movie Theatres: Regal Boone Cinema 7 210 New Market St. Center, Boone NC 28607; 828-262-3330
High School: Watauga High School, 300 Go Pioneers Dr., Boone NC 28607; 828-264-2407
Colleges and Universities: Appalachian State University, ASU Box 32004, Boone NC 28608; 828-262-2000, Caldwell Community College and Technical Institute, 372 Community College Dr., Boone NC 28607; 828-263-5370.
Hospitals: Watauga Medical Center, 336 Deerfield Rd., Boone NC 28607; 828-262-4100
Area Major Festivals: Boone Heritage Festival (Oct), MusicFest 'n Sugar Grove (Jul.), Appalachian Summer Festival (Jul.)
Area Natural Attractions: Blue Ridge Parkway, Grandfather Mountain, Pisgah National Forest
Area Cultural Attractions: Hickory Ridge Homestead, Horn in the West, Mast General Store, Turchin Center for Visual Arts, Tweetsie Railroad

Recommended Restaurants: (For a complete list of all restaurants visit ashevilleguide book.com

Café Portofino: (Eclectic-Thai, Eurasian, Italian) 970 Rivers St., Boone NC 28607; 828-264-7772

Casa Rustica: (Italian-American) 1348 Hwy. 105 South, Boone NC 28607; 828-262-5128

Dan'l Boone Inn: (American Family Style) 130 Hardin St., Boone NC 28607; 828-264-8657

Makoto's: (Japanese) 2124 Blowing Rock Rd., Boone NC 28607; 828–264-7770

Pepper's Restaurant: (American) 240 Shadowline Dr. #4, Boone NC 28607; 828-262-1250

Red Onion Café: (Café-Eclectic) 227 Hardin St., Boone NC 28607; 828-264-5470

Stick Boy Kitchen: (Café) 211 Boone Heights Dr., Boone NC 28607; 828-265-4141

The Gamekeeper Restaurant: (Southern-Gourmet) 3005 Shulls Mill Rd., Boone NC 28607; 828-963-7400

Vidalia: (Eclectic American) 831 West King Street, Boone NC 28607; 828-263-9176

Recommended Places To Stay: (For a complete list of all accommodations visit ashe villeguidebook.com

Highland Hills Motel & Cabins: (Cabins) 2748 Hwy. 105 South, Boone NC 28607; 800-948-5276.

Lovill House Inn: (B&B) 404 Old Bristol Rd., Boone NC 28607; 800-849-9466

Parkway Cabins: (Cabins) 749 Turkey Knob, Boone NC 28607; 866–679-3002

The Inn at Crestwood: (Resort, Spa) 3236 Shulls Mill Rd., Boone NC 28607; 877-836-5046

Willow Valley Resort: (Resort) 354 Bairds Creek Rd., Boone NC 28607; 828-963-6551

Brevard

Located in the heart of Transylvania County, Brevard is a wonderful small town that is not only a great place to live but also a renowned tourist destination. In downtown Brevard you'll find all of the familiar touchstones of a classic American small town-an old-fashioned soda shop, a 1930s-era movie theater, even a locally-owned hardware store. And surrounding the city are hundreds of thousands of acres of pristine wilderness, protected forever in the Dupont State Forest, Gorges State Park, and Pisgah National Forests. Brevard is also right at the center of one of the most famous waterfall regions in America. In fact Transylvania County is known as "The Land of Waterfalls." Over 250 are located within a short drive of downtown.

Brevard is also home to a colony of white squirrels that even have their own festival, the White Squirrel Festival, and to the Brevard Music Festival, one of the best music festivals in America. Brevard College, a small, private, United Methodist liberal arts college, is the educational centerpiece of Brevard, and its lovely campus is located just east of downtown.

Location: Central Mountains, 45 minutes west of Asheville
Municipal Building: 151 West Main St., Brevard NC 28712; 828-885-5601

Website: cityofbrevard.com

County: Transylvania County: County Offices, 21 East Main St., Brevard NC 28712; 828-884-3100

Elevation and Population: 2,200 feet, 7,000+

Visitor/Welcome Center: Transylvania County Tourism Development Authority, 175 East Main St., Brevard NC 28712; 800-648-4523

Resource Website: Heart of Brevard 175 East Main St., Ste 200, Brevard NC 28712; 828-884-3278

City Chamber of Commerce: Brevard Transylvania Chamber of Commerce, 175 East Main St., Brevard NC 28712; 828-883-3700

Newspaper: The Transylvania Times 37 North Broad St., Brevard NC 28712; 828-883-8156

Movie Theatres: Falls Co-Ed Cinema, 79 W. Main St., Brevard NC 28712; 828-883-2200

High School: Brevard High School, 609 N. Country Club Rd., Brevard NC 28712; 828-884-4103

Colleges and Universities: Brevard College, One Brevard College Dr., Brevard NC 28712; 828-883-8292

Hospitals: Transylvania County Hospital, 260 Hospital Dr., Brevard NC 28712; 828-884-9111

Area Major Festivals: Brevard Music Festival (Jun.–Aug.), White Squirrel Festival (May), Mountain Song Festival (Sep.)

Area Natural Attractions: Dupont State Forest, Gorges State Park, Pisgah National Forest, Waterfalls in Western North Carolina.

Area Cultural Attractions: Allison-Deaver House, Brevard Little Theatre, Brevard Music Center, Cradle of Forestry, Pisgah Center for Wildlife Education, Transylvania Heritage Museum

Recommended Restaurants: (For a complete list of all restaurants visit ashevilleguide book.com

- **Dugan's Pub:** (Irish) 29 West French Broad St., Ste 101, Brevard NC 28712; 828-862-6527
- **Marco Trattoria:** (Italian) 204 West Main St., Brevard NC 28712; 828–883-4841
- **Sora Japanese Restaurant:** (Japanese) 91 Forest Gate Dr., Pisgah Forest NC 28768; 828-483-4539
- **The Falls Landing Restaurant:** (Seafood) 18 East Main St., Brevard NC 28712; 828-884-2835
- **The Square Root:** (American) 33 Times Arcade Alley, Brevard NC 28712; 828-884-6171

Recommended Places To Stay: (For a complete list of all accommodations visit ashe villeguidebook.com

- **Ash Grove Resort Cabins & Camping:** (Cabins) 749 East Fork Rd., Brevard NC 28712; 828-885-7216
- **Red House Inn:** (B&B) 266 West Probart St.; Brevard NC 28712; 828–884-9349
- **The Inn at Brevard:** (Village Inn) 315 East Main St., Brevard NC 28712; 828-884-2105

Bryson City

Unique among mountain communities, Bryson City, the county seat of Swain County, is located right next to the Great Smoky Mountains National Park. Over 40 percent of this great national park is located in Swain County, and the park sets the tone for this lovely mountain city, with outdoor recreation as one of the major highlights. There are a large number of accommodations for such a small city, largely because of the number of visitors who wish to visit the park.

Bryson City, because of its central location in the mountains, is also a great jumping off point to many of Western North Carolina's natural and cultural attractions as well, including the popular Great Smoky Mountains Railroad, which has departures from downtown, and the nearby Cherokee Indian Reservation. The train depot at Bryson City is also the venue for "Music in the Mountains," live performances that take place every Sat evening from Jun. through Oct. Motorcycle and sports car enthusiasts also make Bryson City their base camp for riding the "Tail of the Dragon" at nearby Deal's Gap, a section of Hwy. 129 that has 318 curves in only 11 miles. A number of great mountain rivers flow through Swain County, the most popular of which are the Nantahala and the Tuckaseegee. Both offer great whitewater rafting and other recreational opportunities. A famous and long established outdoor center is also located near Bryson City on the Nantahala, the Nantahala Outdoor Center, offers everything from great dining on the river to world-class whitewater rafting.

Location: Western Mountains, 45 minutes west of Asheville
Town Offices: 45 Everett St., Bryson City NC 28713; 828-488-3335
County: Swain County: County Administration Building, 101 Mitchell St., Bryson City NC 28713; 828-488-9273
Elevation and Population: 2,000 feet, 1,400+
Visitor/Welcome Center: Bryson City-Swain County Chamber of Commerce and Visitor Center 210 Main St., Bryson City NC 28713; 800-867-9246
City and County Chamber of Commerce: Bryson City-Swain County Chamber of Commerce and Visitor Center 210 Main St., Bryson City NC 28713; 800-867-9246
Newspaper: Smoky Mountain Times 114 Everett St., Bryson City NC 28713; 828-488-2189
Movie Theatres: Cherokee Phoenix Theatre, 91 Sequoyah Trail, Cherokee NC 28719; 828-487-7384
High School: Swain County High School, 1415 Fontana Rd., Bryson City NC 28713; 828-488-2152
Colleges and Universities: Southwestern Community College, 60 Almond School Rd., Bryson City NC 28713; 828-488-6413
Hospitals: Swain County Hospital, 45 Plateau St., Bryson City NC 28713; 828-488-2155
Area Major Festivals: Music in the Mountains 800-867-9246 (Sat evenings Jun.–Oct.), Smoky Mountains Bluegrass Festival (May)
Area Natural Attractions: Blue Ridge Parkway, Fontana Lake, Great Smoky Mountains National Park, Whitewater Rafting
Area Cultural Attractions: Cherokee Indian Reservation, Great Smoky Mountains Railroad, Harrah's Cherokee Casino and Hotel, Mountain Farm Museum, Museum of

the Cherokee Indian, Oconaluftee Indian Village, Qualla Arts and Crafts Mutual, Smoky Mountains Train Museum, Smoky Mountain Community Theatre, Smoky Mountain Trains, Unto These Hills

Recommended Restaurants: (For a complete list of all restaurants visit ashevilleguide book.com

Hemlock Inn: (American-Family Style) Galbraith Creek Rd., Bryson City NC 28713; 828-488-2885

Mountain Perks Espresso Bar & Café: (Café) 9 Depot St., Bryson City NC 28713; 828-488-9561

Pasqualino's Italian Restaurant: (Italian) 25 Everett St., Bryson City NC 28713; 828-488-9555

Recommended Places To Stay: (For a complete list of all accommodations visit ashe villeguidebook.com

Folkestone Inn: (B&B) 101 Folkestone Rd., Bryson City NC 28713; 888-812-3385

Hemlock Inn: (B&B) 911 Galbraith Creek Rd., Bryson City NC 28713; 828-488-2885

Lloyd's on the River Country Inn: (Country Inn) 5370 Ela Rd., Bryson City NC 28713; 888-611-6872

The Fryemont Inn: (Country Inn) 245 Fryemont St., Bryson City NC 28713; 800-845-4879

The Historic Calhoun House Hotel: (Hotel) 135 Everett St., Bryson City NC 28713; 828-488-1234

Burnsville

Located about halfway between Asheville and Boone, Burnsville is nestled among nineteen of the highest mountains in the east. Nearby Mount Mitchell, at 6,684 feet, is the highest peak east of the Mississippi River, and it is accompanied by 18 other peaks over 6,300 feet. The county seat of Yancey County, Burnsville was established in 1833, and has as many artisans and crafts persons per capita as any town in the United States, with nearly 400 full-time and 200 part-time residing in Yancey County. Burnsville is also home to the Yancey County Farmers' Market, one of the oldest and largest tailgate markets in western North Carolina, held on Sat mornings behind the Burnsville Town Center.

The major festival is the Mount Mitchell Craft Fair, held every Aug. on the beautiful town square of Burnsville. This great arts and crafts festival is one of the longest running in the mountains and has been held for over 50 years. Burnsville is also home to the historic Nu Wray Inn, also located on the town square.

Location: Central Mountains, 45 minutes north of Asheville

Town Offices: 2 Town Square, Burnsville NC 28714; 828-682-2420

Website: townofburnsville.org

County: Yancey County: County Offices, Yancey County Courthouse, 110 Town Square, Burnsville NC 28714; 828-682-3971

Elevation and Population: 2,815 feet, 7,000+

Visitor Center: Yancey County/Burnsville Chamber of Commerce 106 West Main St., Burnsville NC 28714; 828-682-7413

City and County Chamber of Commerce: Yancey County/Burnsville Chamber of Commerce 106 West Main St., Burnsville NC 28714; 800-948-1632

Newspaper: Yancey Common Times Journal (Weekly), 22 North Main St., Burnsville NC 28714; 828-682-2120

Movie Theatres: Yancey Theatre, 119 West Main St., Burnsville NC 28714; 828-678-3322

High School: Mountain Heritage High School, 333 Mountain Heritage High School Rd., Burnsville NC 28714; 828-682-6103

Colleges and Universities: Mayland Community College, Yancey Campus, 107 Wheeler Hills Rd., Burnsville NC 28714; 828-682-7315

Area Major Festivals: Mount Mitchell Craft Fair (Aug.), Music in the Mountains Festival (Oct.)

Area Natural Attractions: Blue Ridge Parkway, Mount Mitchell State Park

Area Cultural Attractions: Parkway Playhouse, Rush Wray Museum

Recommended Restaurants: (For a complete list of all restaurants visit ashevilleguide book.com

- **Garden Deli:** (Deli) 107 Town Square, Burnsville NC 28714; 828-682-3946
- **In The Garden:** (American) 117 West Main St., Burnsville NC 28714; 828-682-1680
- **Nu Wray Inn:** (American) 105 Town Square, Burnsville NC 28714; 800–368-9729

Recommended Places To Stay: (For a complete list of all accommodations visit ashe villeguidebook.com

- **Celo Inn:** (Country Inn) 45 Seven Mile Ridge Rd., Burnsville NC 28714; 828-675-5132
- **Nu Wray Inn:** (Village Inn) 105 Town Square, Burnsville NC 28714; 828-682-2329
- **Terrell House Bed & Breakfast:** (B&B) 109 Robertson St., Burnsville NC 28714; 888-682-4505

Canton

Canton is a small town nestled among five hills along the banks of the Pigeon River in the mountains of Western North Carolina, near major highways and within easy driving distance of the regional airport in Asheville. Canton's beautiful residential communities lie along tree-lined streets in this quaint town. Canton is also the home of Blue Ridge Papers, Haywood County's largest industry. The mill produces paper and allied products and has made great strides in reducing the amount of air and water pollution spewed with devastating effects into the environment, especially the Pigeon River, by the former owner, the Champion Paper Company. Blue Ridge Papers today is a partner with the community in not only providing jobs for local residents, but also in reducing the environmental impact of the company's manufacturing operation.

Canton has a recreation program as part of its services to its citizens and guests. The Recreation Park has a large, modern swimming pool, playground, picnic tables, lighted tennis courts, and ball fields adjacent to the park. The community was named for Canton, OH, the source of the steel used in construction of the bridge over the Pigeon River.

One of the largest mountains in Haywood County, the now famous Cold Mountain lies in the Bethel Community near Canton. Popularized by the novel which was turned into a major motion picture, Cold Mountain was written by Charles Frazier, who was born in Haywood County and spent weekends and summers in the area. While here, he explored the mountains and decided to immortalize Cold Mountain in his memorable novel. Another of Canton's claims to fame are the Star of the Carolinas (1445 carats), and the Southern Star (1035 carats), two of the world's largest star sapphires, both found in Canton's Old Pressley Sapphire Mine, now open to the public.

Location: Central Mountains, 20 minutes west of Asheville
Town Hall: 58 Park St., Canton NC 28716; 828-646-3412
Website: cantonnc.com
County: Haywood County: County Offices, 215 North Main St., Waynesville NC 28786; 828-452-6625
Elevation and Population: 2,589 feet, 2,500+
Visitor/Welcome Center: Haywood County Tourism Development Authority Visitor Center, (Exit 31 off I-40) 761 Champion Dr., Canton NC 28716; 828-235-9238
County Chamber of Commerce: Greater Haywood County Chamber of Commerce: 28 Walnut St., Waynesville NC 28786; 828-456-3021
Newspaper: The Mountaineer, 220 North Main St., Waynesville NC 28786; 828-452-0661
Movie Theatres: Colonial Theatre 53 Park St., Canton NC 28716; 828–235-2760
High School: Pisgah High School, 1 Black Bear Dr., Canton NC 28716; 828-646-3440
Area Major Festivals: Christmas Parade (Dec.), Folkmoot USA (Jul.)
Area Natural Attractions: Blue Ridge Parkway, Old Pressley Sapphire Mine, Pisgah National Forest
Area Cultural Attractions: Canton Area Historical Museum, Shook Museum
Recommended Restaurants: (For a complete list of all restaurants visit ashevilleguide book.com

Sagebrush Steakhouse: (American) 1941 Champion Dr., Canton NC 28716; 828-646-3750

Recommended Places To Stay: (For a complete list of all accommodations visit ashe villeguidebook.com

See Waynesville Accommodations

Cashiers

Nestled in the southwestern section of the mountains, Cashiers is a beautiful, upscale little resort town that has welcomed visitors for over 150 years. Nineteen easily accessible pristine waterfalls in the immediate area are one of the main attractions as well as the numerous restaurants and gift, antique and craft shops that line the streets coming into town.

Cashiers has long had a reputation as a mountain retreat, and as early as 1850, people from nearby South Carolina flocked to this region during the summer to escape the hot and humid lowland weather. Eventually, investment in second and vacation homes started and this transformed the Cashiers area into the affluent resort destination it is today. No one knows for sure the origin of the name Cashiers but one good guess is that it was a crossroads where miners (this part of the mountain is known for its mines and gemstones) cashed out after success in the field.

Near Cashiers itself are a number of beautiful mountain lakes, including Lake Toxaway, Lake Glenville, and Sapphire Lake, and the surrounding communities of Lake Toxaway, Glenville and Sapphire. The Sapphire Valley Ski Area is also located in Sapphire and has two runs open to the public during the ski season.

Cashiers is also known for a bizarre annual phenomenon called "Shadow of the Bear" that occurs on the side of the 4,930 ft. Whiteside Mountain. Each day from late Oct. through early Nov., and then again from mid-Feb. through early Mar., the shadow of an enormous "bear," caused by the configuration of nearby mountain ridge tops, casts its shadow for 30 minutes (starting at 5:30pm). A major tourist sight, the best place to view the shadow is off Hwy. 64 at Rhodes Big View Overlook.

Location: Western Mountains, 1.5 hours west of Asheville
County: Jackson County: County Offices, 401 Grindstaff Cove Rd., Ste A-207, Sylva NC 28779; 828-631-2207
Elevation and Population: 3,486 feet, 1,500 full-time, 10,000 part-time residents
Visitor/Welcome Center: Cashiers Area Chamber of Commerce Visitor Center, 202 Hwy. 64 West, Cashiers NC 28717; 828-743-5191
City Chamber of Commerce: Cashiers Area Chamber of Commerce, 202 Hwy. 64 West, Cashiers NC 28717; 828-743-5191
County Chamber of Commerce: Jackson County Chamber of Commerce, 773 West Main St., Sylva NC 28779; 800-962-1911
Newspaper: Crossroads Chronicle, PO Box 1040, Cashiers NC 28717; 828–743-5101
High School: Blue Ridge School, 95 Bobcat Dr., Cashiers NC 28717; 828-743-2646
Area Major Festivals: Cashiers Mountain Music Festival (Jul.), Highlands-Cashiers Chamber Music Festival (Jul.–Aug.), Leaf Festival of Cashiers Valley (Oct.)
Area Natural Attractions: Pisgah National Forest, Waterfalls in Western North Carolina
Area Cultural Attractions: Mountain Heritage Center, Zachary-Tolbert House Museum
Recommended Restaurants: (For a complete list of all restaurants visit ashevilleguide book.com

Canyon Kitchen at Lonesome Valley: (American) 94 Lonesome Valley Road Sapphire, North Carolina 28774: 828-743-7696

The Dining Room at the High Hampton Inn: (American) 1525 Highway 107 South, Cashiers NC 28717; 800-334-2551

The Orchard: (American with Southern flavor) 905 Hwy. 107 South, Cashiers NC 28717; 828-743-7614

Recommended Places To Stay: (For a complete list of all accommodations visit ashe villeguidebook.com

Earthshine Lodge: (Resort) 1600 Golden Rd., Lake Toxaway NC 28747; 828-862-4207

High Hampton Inn : (Resort) 1525 Hwy. 107 South, Cashiers NC 28717; 800-334-2551

Innisfree Boutique Inn By-The-Lake: (Country Inn) 8 Innisfree Dr., Cashiers NC 28736; 828-743-2946

Laurelwood Inn: (Village Inn) 58 Hwy. 107 North, Cashiers NC 28717; 800-346-6846

The Cabins at Seven Foxes: (Cabins) Seven Foxes Lane, Lake Toxaway NC 28747: 828-877-6333

The Greystone Inn: (Resort) Greystone Lane, Lake Toxaway NC 28747; 800-824-5766

Catawba

Catawba is a small town in the heart of the beautiful Catawba Valley in the foothills, and is one of only two municipalities in Catawba County that borders the Catawba River. The name "Catawba" recalls the tribe of Native Americans which once inhabited the area. Catawba is one of the oldest towns between Salisbury and Asheville as a result of having been selected to be the site of an early railroad station. Trains ran to the town before the Civil War, as early as 1859, and continue to do so today.

The Town of Catawba Historical Association maintains a museum in the oldest brick building in town, the former residence of Dr. Q.M. Little, circa 1873, to showcase local history. The museum is located at 101 First St. SW downtown and contains five rooms. Visitors to the museum should call 828-241-4077 for scheduling and information. Catawba has an annual Catawba Festival and Parade held each Nov., which features vendors offering everything from crafts and toys to festival food.

Location: Foothills, 1 hour and 15 minutes east of Asheville

Town Hall: 102 First St. NW, Catawba NC 28609; 828-241-2215

Website: townofcatawbanc.org

County: Catawba County: County Offices, 100-A South West Blvd., Newton NC 28658; 828-465-8201

Elevation and Population: 886 feet, 700+

County Visitor/Welcome Center: Catawba County Visitor Information Center, 1055 Southgate Corporate Park SW, Hickory NC 28602; 828-328-6111

County Chamber of Commerce: Catawba County Chamber of Commerce, 1055 Southgate Corporate Park SW, Hickory NC 28602; 828-328-6111

Newspapers: The Claremont Courier, 3283 White Oak Court, Claremont NC 28610; 828-320-8450 and the Hickory Daily Record, 1100 Park Place, Hickory NC 28603; 828-322-4510

High Schools: Bandys High School, 5040 East Bandys Rd., Catawba NC 28609; 828-241-3171

Area Major Festivals: Catawba Festival and Parade (Nov.), Catawba Valley Pottery Festival (Mar.)

Area Natural Attractions: Pisgah National Forest, South Mountains State Park

Area Cultural Attractions: Bunker Hill Covered Bridge, Catawba County Museum of History, Catawba Science Center, Town of Catawba Historical Association Museum,

Harper House/Hickory History Center, Hickory Furniture Mart, Hickory Motor Speedway, Hickory Museum of Art, Hiddenite Center, Historic Murray's Mill

Recommended Restaurants: (For a complete list of all restaurants visit ashevilleguide book.com

Sasha's On The Lake: (American) 7774 Hudson Chapel Rd, Catawba, NC 28609; 828-241-1385

Recommended Places To Stay: (For a complete list of all accommodations visit ashe villeguidebook.com

There are no accommodations in Catawba

Cherokee

Located in the heart of the 56,000-acre Cherokee Indian Reservation, the village of Cherokee is a major destination. Offering a wide range of accommodations, restaurants and things to do, Cherokee is host to a great number of visitors each year. Cherokee is home to more than 10,000 Eastern Band of the Cherokee members. Each year, thousands of visitors from across the country come to discover this enchanted land and to share the natural mountain beauty the Cherokee people have treasured for centuries.

A visit to Cherokee is like stepping into the past. You'll find a nation still linked to ancient customs and traditions that enable them to live in harmony with nature as their ancestors did. The Reservation, known as the Qualla Boundary, has a number of outstanding attractions. The main attraction in the area is Harrah's Cherokee Casino, but other more historical and cultural attractions are also very popular, especially the 12,000 square-foot. Museum of the Cherokee Indian, Oconaluftee Indian Village, Qualla Arts & Crafts Mutual and Unto These Hills outdoor drama.

Surrounded by the vast forests of the Cherokee Indian Reservation and adjacent to the Great Smoky Mountains National Park, a visit to Cherokee affords countless outdoor recreational opportunities, and one of the most accessible is the popular Oconaluftee Islands Park, a beautiful multi-faceted family-oriented park in the middle of the Oconaluftee River right in town.

Location: Western Mountains, 1.5 hours west of Asheville

Website: cherokee-nc.com

County: Jackson County: County Offices, 401 Grindstaff Cove Rd., Ste A-207, Sylva NC 28779; 828-631-2207

Elevation and Population: 3,000 feet, 13,000+

Visitor/Welcome Center: Cherokee Welcome Center, 498 Tsali Blvd., Cherokee NC 28719; 800-438-1601

City Chamber of Commerce: Cherokee Chamber of Commerce, 1148 Tsali Blvd., Cherokee NC 28719; 828-497-6700

County Chamber of Commerce: Jackson County Chamber of Commerce, 773 West Main St., Sylva NC 28779; 828-586-2155

Newspaper: The Cherokee One Feather, 828-554-6264

Movie Theatres: Cherokee Phoenix Theatres, 91 Sequoyah Trail, Cherokee NC 28719; 828-497-7384

High School: Cherokee Central School, 1582 Ravensford Dr., Cherokee NC 28719; 828-554-5000

Hospitals: Cherokee Indian Hospital, 188 Hospital Rd., Cherokee NC 28719; 828-497-9163

Area Major Festivals: North Carolina State Bluegrass Festival (Jun.) Festival of Native Peoples (Jul.) Cherokee Indian Fair (Oct.)

Area Natural Attractions: Blue Ridge Parkway, Great Smoky Mountains National Park

Area Cultural Attractions: Cherokee Indian Reservation, Harrah's Cherokee Casino and Hotel, Mountain Farm Museum, Museum of the Cherokee Indian, Oconaluftee Indian Village, Qualla Arts and Crafts Mutual, Unto These Hills

Recommended Restaurants: (For a complete list of all restaurants visit ashevilleguide book.com

Brio Tuscan Grill: (Italian) 777 Casino Drive, Harrah's Casino, Cherokee NC 28719: 828-497-8233

Granny's Kitchen: (County) 1098 Painttown Rd., Cherokee NC 28719; 828-497-5010

Ruth's Chris Steak House: (American) 777 Casino Drive, Cherokee NC 28719: 828- 497-8577

Recommended Places To Stay: (For a complete list of all accommodations visit ashe villeguidebook.com

Cherokee/Great Smokies KOA: (Campground) 92 KOA Campground Rd., Cherokee NC 28719; 828-497-9711

Fairfield Inn & Suites Cherokee: (Motel) 568 Painttown Rd., Cherokee NC 28719; 828-497-0400

Hampton Inn: (Motel) 185 Tsalagi Rd., Cherokee NC 28719; 828-497-3115

Harrah's Cherokee Casino & Hotel: (Hotel) 777 Casino Dr., Cherokee NC 28719; 800-342-7724

Chimney Rock

Located just south of Asheville, the Village of Chimney Rock, incorporated in 1921, sits at the base of the famous Chimney Rock and along the Rocky Broad River. Primarily catering to tourists who are visiting the Rock and nearby Lake Lure, the Village is a convenient stopping spot for lunch or some souvenir shopping. A number of restaurants are also located right on the bold Rocky Broad River, which flows right through the Village on its way to nearby Lake Lure. Most buildings downtown, just outside Chimney Rock Park, date to the 1920s. The Village became a resort town around Chimney Rock Park, which began to be developed in 1902.

Towering over the Village, Chimney Rock Park, which was privately owned, recently became Chimney Rock State Park, one of the newest North Carolina state parks. With an elevation range from about 1,100 feet to 2,800 feet, the park ultimately will include over 5,000 acres. The nearby 404-foot Hickory Nut Falls is among the most dramatic waterfalls in Western North Carolina, and movie fans should be aware that parts of "The Last of the Mohicans" were filmed at the park.

Location: Central Mountains, 45 minutes south of Asheville

Website: chimneyrock.org

County: Rutherford County: County Offices, 289 North Main St., Rutherfordton NC 28139; 828-287-6060

Elevation and Population: 1,000 Feet, 200+

Visitor/Welcome Center: Hickory Nut Gorge Visitor Center, 2926 Memorial Hwy., Lake Lure NC 28746; 877-625-2725

City Chamber of Commerce: Hickory Nut Gorge Chamber of Commerce, PO Box 32, Chimney Rock NC 28720; 877-625-2725

County Chamber of Commerce: Rutherford County Chamber of Commerce, 162 North Main St., Rutherfordton NC 28139; 828-287-3090

County Tourism Development: Lake Lure and the Blue Ridge Foothills, 1990 US Hwy. 221 South, Forest City NC 28043; 828-245-1492

Newspaper: The Digital Courier, PO Box 1149, Forest City NC 28043; 828-245-6431

Area Natural Attractions: Apple Orchards in Henderson County, Chimney Rock Park, Lake Lure

Recommended Restaurants: (For a complete list of all restaurants visit ashevilleguide book.com

- **Medina's Village Bistro:** (American) 430 Main Street, Chimney Rock NC 28720: 828-989-4529
- **Old Rock Café:** (Café) 431 Main St., Chimney Rock NC 28720; 828–625-2329
- **Riverwatch Bar & Grill:** (American) 379 Main Street Chimney Rock NC 28720; 828-625-1030
- **The Esmeralda Inn:** (American) 910 Main Street, Chimney Rock NC 28720; 888-897-2999

Recommended Places To Stay: (For a complete list of all accommodations visit ashe villeguidebook.com

- **Chimney Rock Inn:** (Village Inn) 126 Main St., Chimney Rock NC 28720; 828-625-1429
- **Evening Shade River Lodge & Cabins:** (Lodge) 745 Main St., Chimney Rock NC 28720; 828-625-4774
- **The Esmeralda Inn:** (Village Inn) 910 Main St., Chimney Rock NC 28720; 888-897-2999

Claremont

Claremont is a small town located in the foothills of Western North Carolina in Catawba County, and has roots that date back to the early 1800's when the area around present day Claremont was first referred to as "Charlotte Crossing." Later, the name was changed again to "Setzer's Depot" but ultimately the name was changed in 1892 to Claremont, after an early settler, Clare Sigmon. The town has seen strong economic growth over the years and is blessed with large and small businesses that provide a good tax base. These include high quality furniture industries and two fiber optical and coaxial cable manufacturing plants within the city limits. The Norfolk-Southern Railroad also passes through the city limits.

An attraction in the Claremont area is the Bunker Hill Covered Bridge located on Hwy. 70, a few miles east of town. The bridge spans Lyles Creek as part of a road that originally followed a Native American trail and is one of only two covered bridges left in the state. Claremont also has a lovely downtown park, Claremont Park, located on East Main St., next to Claremont Elementary School. This park is 21 acres, and has tennis courts, horseshoe pits, sheltered picnic areas, a pavilion and an amphitheater, and a paved quarter mile walking trail.

Location: Foothills, 1 hour and 15 minutes east of Asheville
City Hall: 3288 East Main St., Claremont NC 28610; 828-459-7009
Website: cityofclaremont.org
County: Catawba County: County Offices, 100-A South West Blvd., Newton NC 28658; 828-465-8201
Elevation and Population: 981 feet, 1,050+
County Visitor/Welcome Center: Catawba County Visitor Information Center, 1055 Southgate Corporate Park SW, Hickory NC 28602; 828-328-6111
County Chamber of Commerce: Catawba County Chamber of Commerce, 1055 Southgate Corporate Park SW, Hickory NC 28602; 828-328-6111
Newspapers: The Claremont Courier, 3283 White Oak Court, Claremont NC 28610; 828-320-8450 and the Hickory Daily Record, 1100 Park Place, Hickory NC 28603; 828-322-4510
High Schools: Bunker Hill High School, 4675 Oxford School Rd., Claremont NC 28610; 828-241-3355
Area Major Festivals: Catawba Valley Pottery Festival (Mar.)
Area Natural Attractions: Pisgah National Forest, South Mountains State Park
Area Cultural Attractions: Bunker Hill Covered Bridge, Catawba County Museum of History, Catawba Science Center, Harper House/Hickory History Center, Hickory Furniture Mart, Hickory Motor Speedway, Hickory Museum of Art, Hiddenite Center, Historic Murray's Mill
Recommended Restaurants: (For a complete list of all restaurants visit ashevilleguide book.com

Boxcar Grill: (American) 3140 N Oxford St, Claremont, NC 28610 ; 828) 459-9287

Recommended Places To Stay: (For a complete list of all accommodations visit ashe villeguidebook.com

Claremont Inn & Suites: 3054 North Oxford Street, Claremont, NC 28610; 828-615-7551

Clyde

Clyde is a small town located just west of Asheville and has the distinction of being "away from it all" but without the isolation usually associated with mountain living. Long associated with neighboring Canton, Clyde is also home to Haywood Community College and the Haywood Regional Medical Center. Recently two industrial parks have been developed just north of Clyde. Clyde Township was formed in 1877 from Pigeon, Beaverdam and Waynesville. At first it was called Lower Pigeon, with the name later changed to Clyde.

Clyde is surrounded by mountains and valleys which afford numerous outdoor recreational opportunities to the visitors and residents. Clyde is also the home of the Shook

Museum, housed in one of the oldest buildings still standing in Haywood County. Build circa 1795 by Jacob Shook for his son Peter, this historic house is known and associated with the founding of Methodism in Haywood County.

Location: Central Mountains, 30 minutes west of Asheville
Town Hall: 8437 Carolina Blvd., Clyde NC 28721; 828-627-2566
Website: townofclyde.com
County: Haywood County: County Offices, 215 North Main St., Waynesville NC 28786; 828-452-6625
Elevation and Population: 2,543 feet, 1,300+
County Visitor/Welcome Center: Visitor/Welcome Center: Haywood County Tourism Development Authority Visitor Center, (Exit 31 off I-40) 761 Champion Dr., Canton NC 28716; 828-235-9238
County Chamber of Commerce: Haywood County Chamber of Commerce: 28 Walnut St., Waynesville NC 28786; 828-456-3021
Newspaper: The Mountaineer, 220 North Main St., Waynesville NC 28786; 828-452-0661
High School: Pisgah High School, 1 Black Bear Dr., Canton NC 28716; 828-646-3440
Colleges and Universities: Haywood Community College, 185 Freelander Dr., Clyde NC 28721; 828-627-2821
Hospitals: Haywood Regional Medical Center, 262 Leroy George Dr., Clyde NC 28721; 800-834-1729
Area Major Festivals: Folkmoot USA (Jul.)
Area Natural Attractions: Blue Ridge Parkway, Pisgah National Forest
Recommended Restaurants: (For a complete list of all restaurants visit ashevilleguide book.com

Sherrill's Pioneer Restaurant: (American) 8363 Carolina Boulevard, Clyde NC 28721; 828-626-9880

Recommended Places To Stay: (For a complete list of all accommodations visit ashe villeguidebook.com
No accommodations currently available in Clyde. *See* Canton and Waynesville

Columbus

Columbus is the Polk County seat where the government offices and the historic 1857 Polk County Courthouse are located. The beautiful courthouse building is one of the oldest still in use in North Carolina and has been fully restored to its original grandeur. Of historical interest is the ancient slave block that still remains on the courthouse lawn as a daily reminder of that terrible period of American history.

Dr. Columbus Mills, for whom the town was named, has been called the "Father of Polk County." It was largely through his efforts as a state senator that Polk County was established by sectioning off parts of Rutherford and Henderson Counties, deliberately carved from 100 acres of wilderness on what was then known as Foster Race path in the shadow of Foster's Mountain, known today as Chocolate Dr.op.

Columbus has all the charm of a small mountain city, and has two major festivals, the Fabulous 4th in Jul. and the Columbus Day Farm Festival in Oct. It is also home to the

Howard Monument, a landmark in the County for over 100 years, and the famous Doughboy statue. Originally laid out with a church at each corner of the main streets, only two of these are in their original locations today, the Columbus Baptist Church and the Columbus Presbyterian Church.

Location: Foothills, 45 minutes south of Asheville
Town Hall: 95 Walker St., Columbus NC 28722; 828-894-8236
Website: columbusnc.com
County: Polk County: County Offices, 40 Courthouse St., Columbus NC 28722; 828-894-3301
Elevation and Population: 1,131 feet, 1,000+
Visitor/Welcome Center: Polk County Travel and Tourism 20 East Mills St., Columbus NC 28722; 800-440-7848
County Chamber of Commerce: Carolina Foothills Chamber of Commerce 2753 Lynn Rd., Ste A, Tryon NC 28782; 828-859-6236
Newspaper: Tryon Daily Bulletin 16 North Trade St., Tryon NC 28782; 828-859-9151 and Polk County News Journal PO Box 576, Columbus NC 28722; 864-457-3337
High School: Polk County High School, 1681 East NC Hwy. 108, Columbus NC 28722; 828-894-2525
Hospitals: St. Luke's Hospital, 101 Hospital Dr., Columbus NC 28722; 828-894-3311
Area Major Festivals: Fabulous 4th (Jul.), Columbus Day Farm Festival (Oct.)
Area Natural Attractions: Pisgah National Forest
Area Cultural Attractions: Foothills Equestrian Nature Center (FENCE), Polk County Courthouse, Polk County Historical Museum, Tryon Fine Arts Center
Recommended Restaurants: (For a complete list of all restaurants visit ashevilleguide book.com

Giardini Trattoria: (Italian) 2411 Hwy. 108 East, Columbus NC 28722; 828-894-0234

Recommended Places To Stay: (For a complete list of all accommodations visit ashe villeguidebook.com

Butterfly Creek Inn Tryon: (B&B) 780 Smith Dairy Rd., Columbus NC 28722; 828-894-6393

Connelly Springs

Connelly Springs is located in eastern Burke County between Hickory and Morganton, and was originally named Happy Home. The first settler in the area was William Lewis Connelly and in the 1880s the town's name was changed to Connelly Springs after the discovery of mineral springs by Mrs. Elmira Connelly. The town, because of the popularity of the springs for natural healing, soon became a resort destination with a number of large hotels constructed for visitors. These former hotels included The Connelly Mineral Springs Hotel, The Sides Boarding House, The Connelly Springs Inn and The Haliburton Hotel.

Connelly Springs was incorporated in 1920, and later again in 1989, and eventually became a bedroom community with residents employed in the textile and furniture manufacturing facilities in neighboring towns. Recently Connelly Springs has seen considerable growth: a new town hall was opened in 2002 and numerous community projects undertaken as well as a revitalization of the business sector along NC Hwy. 70. Connelly Springs is also home to the Raintree Cellars winery, and adjacent to the community is the beautiful South Mountains State Park.

Location: Foothills, one hour and fifteen minutes east of Asheville
Town Hall: 1030 US Hwy. 70, Connelly Springs NC 28612; 828-879-2321
County: Burke County: Burke County Government Center, 200 Avery Ave., Morganton NC 28680; 828-439-4340
Elevation and Population: 1236 feet, 1,900+
County Visitor/Welcome Center: 110 East Meeting St., Morganton NC 28655; 828-433-6793
County Chamber of Commerce: Burke County Chamber of Commerce, 110 East Meeting St., Morganton NC 28655; 828-437-3021
Newspaper: The News Herald, 301 Collett St., Morganton NC 28655; 828-437-2161
High Schools: East Burke High School, 3695 East Burke Blvd., Connelly Springs NC 28612; 828-397-5541 and Jimmy C. Dr.aughn High School, 709 Lovelady Rd. NE, Valdese NC 28690, 828-879-4200
Area Major Festivals: Connelly Springs Fall Festival (Oct.)
Area Natural Attractions: Brown Mountain Lights, Lake James State Park, South Mountains State Park
Area Cultural Attractions: History Museum of Burke County, North Carolina School For The Deaf Museum, Old Burke County Courthouse Heritage Museum, Quaker Meadows Plantation, Senator Sam J. Ervin Jr. Museum
Recommended Restaurants: (For a complete list of all restaurants visit ashevilleguide book.com

Granny's Country Kitchen: (Country) 3448 Miller Bridge Rd., Icard NC 28666; 828-397-3588

Recommended Places To Stay: (For a complete list of all accommodations visit ashe villeguidebook.com
No accommodations currently available in Connelly Springs. *See* Morganton.

Conover

Conover is located in the foothills of Western North Carolina, in Catawba County, and is a small town that offers historic charm, access to excellent recreational opportunities, entertainment and shopping, especially if you are in the market for furniture. Historically, Conover was home to a number of important furniture manufacturers, including the former Conover Furniture Company. The origin of the name Conover is uncertain but it is known the city was chartered in 1876 and incorporated in 1877. Conover was also home at one time to Concordia College, an institution of higher education that trained Lutheran ministers. The college closed in 1935 after the college buildings were destroyed by fire. Today the city has several large industrial parks which make Conover one of the main employment bases in Catawba County, and daytime residency, because of this, is over 20,000.

Conover has eight neighborhood parks; the most centrally located is the Downtown Park located on 2nd Ave. NE just across from both the city hall and the police department. This great little park is the geographical and cultural heart of Conover, and is home to a large gazebo that has become the unofficial symbol of the town. Along with the gazebo, the park also contains walking trails, benches, picnic tables and play equipment for children. Another of the town's outstanding parks is Hunsucker Park. This 1.13 acre park has playground equipment, including a slide, merry-go-round and other recreational equipment.

Location: Foothills, 1 hour and 15 minutes east of Asheville
City Hall: 101 First St. East, Conover NC 28613; 828-464-1191
Website: conovernc.gov
County: Catawba County: County Offices, 100-A South West Blvd., Newton NC 28658; 828-465-8201
Elevation and Population: 1,060 feet, 7,500+
County Visitor/Welcome Center: Catawba County Visitor Information Center, 1055 Southgate Corporate Park SW, Hickory NC 28602; 828-328-6111
County Chamber of Commerce: Catawba County Chamber of Commerce, 1055 Southgate Corporate Park SW, Hickory NC 28602; 828-328-6111
Newspapers: The Claremont Courier, 3283 White Oak Court, Claremont NC 28610; 828-320-8450 and the Hickory Daily Record, 1100 Park Place, Hickory NC 28603; 828-322-4510
High Schools: Newton-Conover High School 338 West 15th St., Newton NC 28658; 828-465-0920 and Newton-Conover Science High School, 605 North Ashe Ave., Newton NC 28658; 828-464-3191
Area Major Festivals: Catawba Valley Pottery Festival (Mar.)
Area Natural Attractions: Pisgah National Forest, South Mountains State Park
Area Cultural Attractions: Bunker Hill Covered Bridge, Catawba County Museum of History, Catawba Science Center, Harper House/Hickory History Center, Hickory Furniture Mart, Hickory Motor Speedway, Hickory Museum of Art, Hiddenite Center, Historic Murray's Mill
Recommended Restaurants: (For a complete list of all restaurants visit ashevilleguidebook.com

Dos Amigos: (Mexican) 1222 Conover Boulevard W, Conover NC 28613; 828-466-1920

Recommended Places To Stay: (For a complete list of all accommodations visit ashevilleguidebook.com

La Quinta Inn & Suites: (Motel) 1607 Fairgrove Church Rd., Conover NC 28613; 828-465-1100

Lake Hickory RV Resort: (RV Campground) 6641 Monford Dr., Conover NC 28613; 828-256-4303

Rock Barn Golf & Spa: (Resort) 3791 Clubhouse Dr., Conover NC 28613; 828-459-1125

Cullowhee

The community of Cullowhee is home to Western Carolina University, a member of the University of North Carolina system, and is located in a scenic valley in Jackson County about 45 minutes west of Asheville. A college town with the median resident age of 20.7 (the university has over 10,000 students), Cullowhee is also a stopping point for the millions of visitors who are drawn to this mid-mountain region for its spectacular landscapes and vast array of outdoor recreational opportunities, including world-class mountain biking, backpacking and whitewater rafting. The beautiful Tuckasegee River flows through the Cullowhee area and passes right by the Western North Carolina campus.

Cullowhee is also home to the Jackson County Recreational Complex, a public-use park located on Cullowhee Mountain Rd. that includes a 24,000 square-foot facility complete with full size gym, state of the art fitness room and multipurpose meeting rooms. The park has softball and soccer fields, a basketball court, picnic shelters, playgrounds and 10,000 feet of running trails.

Location: Western Mountains, 1 hour west of Asheville

County Visitor/Welcome Center Website: mountainlovers.com

County: Jackson County: County Offices, 401 Grindstaff Cove Rd., Ste A-20: , Sylva NC 28: 828–631–220:

Elevation and Population: 2,400 ft, 4,000+

County Chamber of Commerce: Jackson County Chamber of Commerce: 773 West Main St., Sylva NC 28779; 828-586-2155

Newspaper: The Sylva Herald 539 West Main St., Sylva NC 28779; 800-849-3193

High School: Smoky Mountain High, 100 Smoky Mountain Dr., Sylva NC 28779; 828-586-2177

Colleges and Universities: Western Carolina University, University Way, Cullowhee NC 28723; 828-227-7211

Area Major Festivals: Mountain Heritage Day (Sep.), Mountain Artisans Arts and Crafts Shows (Jul. and Nov.)

Area Natural Attractions: Pisgah National Forest, Waterfalls in Western North Carolina, Great Smoky Mountains National Park

Area Cultural Attractions: Cherokee Indian Reservation, Fine and Performing Arts Center at WCU, Great Smoky Mountains Railroad, Mountain Heritage Center, Western Carolina University

Recommended Restaurants: (For a complete list of all restaurants visit ashevilleguide book.com

Recommended Places To Stay: (For a complete list of all accommodations visit ashe villeguidebook.com

The University Inn: (Motel) 563 North County Club Dr., Cullowhee NC 28723; 828-293-5442

Dillsboro

Founded by Williams Dills in 1884 just after the coming of the Western North Carolina Railroad, Dillsboro was incorporated in 1889. An early destination stop not only because of its scenic mountain location and railroad, this quaint mountain village had many popular restaurants and tourist hotels, one of which, the historic Jarrett House, is still serving meals. Today Dillsboro is well-known as one of the best places to board the Great Smoky Mountains Railroad, a very popular tourist excursion train.

Dillsboro is also going to be the future home to the Southern Appalachian Women's Museum located in the Monteith Community Park. This local history museum will be open to the public in the near future, and will honor and recognize generations of Appalachian women for their work both in and out of the home. Plans include permanent displays of historical artifacts, traveling exhibits and educational shows, and a restored landscape plan that will showcase local heritage and heirloom gardening.

Location: Western Mountains, 1 hour west of Asheville
Website: visitdillsboro.org/index.html
County: Jackson County: County Offices, 401 Grindstaff Cove Rd., Ste A-207, Sylva NC 28779; 828-586-4055
Elevation and Population: 1,800 ft, 200+
County Chamber of Commerce: Jackson County Chamber of Commerce 773 West Main St., Sylva NC 28779; 828-586-2155
Newspaper: The Sylva Herald 539 West Main St., Sylva NC 28779; 800-849-3193
High School: Smoky Mountain High, 100 Smoky Mountain Dr., Sylva NC 28779; 828-227-7211
Area Major Festivals: Dillsboro Arts and Music Festival (Jun.), Dillsboro Lights and Luminaries (Dec.)
Area Natural Attractions: Pisgah National Forest, Waterfalls in Western North Carolina, Great Smoky Mountains National Park
Area Cultural Attractions: Appalachian Women's Museum, Cherokee Indian Reservation, Fine and Performing Arts Center at WCU, Great Smoky Mountains Railroad, Mountain Heritage Center
Recommended Restaurants: (For a complete list of all restaurants visit ashevilleguide book.com

Dillsboro Smokehouse: (BBQ) 403 Haywood Rd., Dillsboro NC 28725; 828-586-9556
Jarrett House: (American Family-Style) 100 Haywood Rd., Dillsboro NC 28725; 828-586-0265

Recommended Places To Stay: (For a complete list of all accommodations visit ashe villeguidebook.com

Dillsboro Inn: (Village Inn) 146 North River Rd., Dillsboro NC 28725; 866-586-3898
Jarrett House: (B&B) 100 Haywood Rd., Dillsboro NC 28725; 828-586-0265

Drexel

Drexel was named after Anthony Joseph Drexel, a Philadelphia financier and philanthropist who served on the board of directors of the Norfolk Southern Railroad, which ran through the middle of this small community. On Feb. 5, 1913, the North Carolina General Assembly granted a charter to incorporate the Town of Drexel. Drexel's corporate limits were determined by using the railroad depot as a central point and establishing the town limits one-half mile in all direction, thus the town was round. In the early 1900's the Drexel Knitting Mills Company and Drexel Furniture Factory were established and the city prospered. These important textile and furniture industries were at the heart of Drexel's existence for the rest of the 20th century and now into the 21st. Both companies made significant contributions to the Town of Drexel and are an important part of its heritage.

Location: Foothills, one hour and fifteen minutes east of Asheville
Town Offices: 202 Church St., Drexel NC 28619; 828-437-7421
Website: ci.drexel.nc.us
County: Burke County: Burke County Government Center, 200 Avery Ave., Morganton NC 28680; 828-439-4340
Elevation and Population: 1,194 feet, 1,900+
County Visitor/Welcome Center: Burke County Visitor Center, 102 East Union St., Morganton NC 28655; 888-462-2921
County Chamber of Commerce: Burke County Chamber of Commerce, 110 East Meeting St., Morganton NC 28655; 828-437-3021
Newspaper: The News Herald, 301 Collett St., Morganton NC 28655; 828-437-2161
High School: Jimmy C Draughn High School, 709 Lovelady Rd. NE, Valdese NC 28690, 828-879-4200
Area Major Festivals: Waldensian Festival (Aug.)
Area Natural Attractions: Brown Mountain Lights, Lake James State Park
Area Cultural Attractions: History Museum of Burke County, North Carolina School For The Deaf Museum, Old Burke County Courthouse Heritage Museum, Quaker Meadows Plantation, Senator Sam J. Ervin Jr. Museum
Recommended Restaurants: (For a complete list of all restaurants visit ashevilleguidebook.com

No recommended restaurants currently available in Drexel. *See* Morganton.

Recommended Places To Stay: (For a complete list of all accommodations visit ashevilleguidebook.com

No accommodations currently available in Drexel. *See* Morganton.

Flat Rock

Flat Rock began about a century and a half ago with large summer estates being built in the English manner by the affluent Charlestonians, Europeans and prominent plantation owners of the South's low country. The first great estate was built in 1827 by Charles Baring of Baring Brothers Banking firm of London, consisting of 3,000 acres, which he named Mountain Lodge. Baring also built a private chapel on his estate which is now St. John in the

Wilderness Episcopal Church. The second large estate was built by Judge Mitchell King of Charleston, South Carolina, and was named Argyle. He later donated the land on which Hendersonville was built and directed the laying out of Main St.

Many other coastal families soon followed, until the settlement grew to about fifty estates. They came to Flat Rock to escape the sweltering heat, yellow fever and malaria, which were running rampant. Summers in Flat Rock became a round of southern gaiety in antebellum days. South Carolina's low country gentry called Flat Rock "The Little Charleston of the Mountains." A few of these old estate homes still stand, surrounded by wide lawns, gardens, towering trees and virtually all graced by white pillar porches. A few of these gracious homes remain in the possession of the families of the original owners, although many of these grand estates are now centerpieces of planned residential communities.

Flat Rock was built around a tremendous outcropping of granite which is said to have been the site of Cherokee gatherings, most of which has been blasted away and used for highway material. The main "rock" can be found on the grounds of the Flat Rock Playhouse. Besides the Flat Rock Playhouse, the other main attraction in Flat Rock is Connemara, the Carl Sandburg Home, now a National Park Service Historic Site open to the public.

Location: Central Mountains. 45 minutes south of Asheville

Town Offices: 2685 Greenville Hwy., Flat Rock NC 28731; 828-697-8100

County: Henderson County: County Offices, 1 Historic Courthouse Square, Hendersonville NC 28792; 828-697-4809

Elevation and Population: 2,205 feet, 2,500+

Visitor/Welcome Center: Hendersonville/ Flat Rock Visitors Information Center 201 South Main St., Hendersonville NC 28792; 800-828-4244

County Chamber of Commerce: Henderson County Chamber of Commerce 204 Kanuga Rd., Hendersonville NC 28739; 828-692-1413

Newspaper: Hendersonville Times-News 1717 Four Seasons Blvd, Hendersonville NC 28792; 828-692-0505.

Movie Theatres: Flat Rock Cinema First-run foreign, independent and classic films. 2700 Greenville Hwy., Flat Rock NC 28731; 828-697-2463

High School: East Henderson High School, 110 Upward Rd., East Flat Rock NC 28726; 828-697-4768

Colleges and Universities: Blue Ridge Community College, 180 West Campus Dr., Flat Rock NC 28731; 828-694-1700

Area Major Festivals: North Carolina Apple Festival (Sep.)

Area Natural Attractions: Apple Orchards in Henderson County, Dupont State Forest, Holmes Educational State Forest, Pisgah National Forest

Area Cultural Attractions: Carl Sandburg Home, Flat Rock Playhouse

Recommended Restaurants: (For a complete list of all restaurants visit ashevilleguidebook.com

Hubba Hubba Smokehouse: (BBQ) 2724 Greenville Hwy., Flat Rock NC 28731; 828-694-3551

Season's at Highland Lake: (American) Highland Lake Inn, 86 Lily Pad Lane, Flat Rock NC 28731; 800-758-8130

Recommended Places To Stay: (For a complete list of all accommodations visit ashevilleguidebook.com

Highland Lake Inn: (Resort) 86 Lily Pad Lane, Flat Rock NC 28731; 800-758-8130

Mansuri Mansion: (County Inn) 2905 Greenville Hwy., Flat Rock NC 28731; 828-693-6016

Fletcher

The Town of Fletcher, which was incorporated in 1989, is located in Henderson County, North Carolina. The town contains 6.1 square miles of land area and measures six miles in an east-west direction and less than four miles from north to south. Fletcher was incorporated in 1989 by way of an activist movement spearheaded by local politician Sara Waechter, who then became the first interim mayor of Fletcher.

Fletcher consists of primarily level and at times hilly terrain, which is dominated by Cane Creek and the French Broad River and their tributaries. Several major roadways provide easy access to Fletcher. US Hwy. 25 runs north-south through the center of the Town and is the main thoroughfare for residents. Interstate 26 is located to the west and travels through North Carolina to Tennessee and South Carolina. Fletcher is also home to a number of great parks, including the extensive Fletcher Community Park, which has youth and adult baseball and softball fields, multiple soccer fields, a playground, disc golf course, arboretum gardens and walking trails.

Location: Central Mountains, approximately 13 miles south of downtown Asheville

Town Offices: 4005 Hendersonville Rd., Fletcher NC 28732; 828-687-3985

County: Henderson County: County Offices, 1 Historic Courthouse Square, Hendersonville NC 28792; 828-697-4809

Elevation and Population: 2,123 feet, 4,200+

County Chamber of Commerce: Henderson County Chamber of Commerce 204 Kanuga Rd., Hendersonville NC 28739; 828-692-1413

Newspaper: Hendersonville Times-News 1717 Four Seasons Blvd, Hendersonville NC 28792; 828-692-0505 or Asheville Citizen-Times,14 OHenry Ave., Asheville NC 28801; 828-252-5611, 800-800-4204.

High School: North Henderson High School, 35 Fruitland Rd., Hendersonville NC 28792; 828-697-4500 and West Henderson High School, 3600 Haywood Rd., Hendersonville NC 28791; 828-891-6571

Hospitals: Park Ridge Hospital: 100 Hospital Dr., Fletcher NC 28792, 828-684-8501

Area Major Festivals: North Carolina Mountain State Fair (Asheville-Sep.)

Area Natural Attractions: North Mills River Recreation Area, Pisgah National Forest, French Broad River

Area Cultural Attractions: Historic Johnson Farm

Recommended Restaurants: (For a complete list of all restaurants visit ashevilleguidebook.com

Blue Sky Café: (American) 3987 Hendersonville Rd., Fletcher NC 28732, 828-684-1247

Recommended Places To Stay: (For a complete list of all accommodations visit ashevilleguidebook.com

Hampton Inn & Suites I-26: (Motel) 18 Rockwood Rd., Fletcher NC 28732; 828-687-0806

Forest City

Located on the far eastern edge of the mountains, Forest City began as a crossroads on the Shelby-Rutherfordton and Spartanburg-Lincolnton Rd. and was incorporated in 1877 as Burnt Chimney, with the name changed to Forest City in 1887 after a prominent citizen, Forest Davis. This small city in the foothills, once a bustling mill town, still has much to offer visitors, including a large selection of stores and restaurants. In 1914, the Forest City Betterment Club embarked on a project to beautify the town's Main St. and today the original landscaped medians and fountain still exist. In 1927, the town was selected as one of the ten most beautiful and best planned towns in the United States by the US Department of Agriculture.

Forest City is famous for the great display of Christmas lights that brighten the city every holiday season; over half a million lights sparkle in the downtown area alone at Christmastime. Forest City is also home to the Bennett Classics Antique Auto Museum, the Rutherford County Farm Museum, and McNair Field, the home of the semi-professional baseball team the Forest City Owls.

Location: Foothills, 1 hour southeast of Asheville
Town Hall: 128 North Powell St., Forest City NC 28403; 828-248-5202
County: Rutherford County: County Offices, 229 North Main St., Rutherfordton NC 28139; 828-287-6045
Elevation and Population: 860 feet, 7500+
County Visitor/Welcome Center: Rutherford County Tourism 1990 US Hwy. 221 South, Forest City NC 28043; 800-849-5998
County Chamber of Commerce: Rutherford County Chamber of Commerce 162 North Main St., Rutherfordton NC 28139; 828-287-3090
Newspaper: The Daily Courier 601 Oak St., Forest City NC 28043; 828-245-6431
Movie Theatres: Retro Cinema 4 2270 US 221 South, Forest City NC 28043; 828-248-1670
High School: Chase High School, 1603 Chase High Rd., Forest City NC 28043; 828-245-7668
Area Major Festivals: Christmas Festivities and Lights (Dec.)
Area Natural Attractions: Chimney Rock Park, Lake Lure
Area Cultural Attractions: Bennett Classics Antique Auto Museum, KidSenses Children's InterACTIVE Museum, McNair Field/Forest City Owls, Rutherford County Farm Museum, Rutherford County Museum
Recommended Restaurants: (For a complete list of all restaurants visit ashevilleguidebook.com

Big Dave's Family Seafood: (Seafood) 123 Commercial Dr., Forest City NC 28043; 828-245-9844

Scott's on Broadway: (American) 753 South Broadway, Forest City NC 28043; 828-245-9811

Recommended Places To Stay: (For a complete list of all accommodations visit ashevilleguidebook.com

Baymont by Wyndham Forest City (Motel): 164 Jameson Inn Dr, Forest City, NC 28043; 828-351-6192

Hampton Inn & Suites Forest City (Motel): 227 Sparks Dr, Forest City, NC 28043; 828-382-1001

Franklin

Known as the "Gem of the Smokies," Franklin is the county seat of Macon County and is next to the Little Tennessee River. Settled in the early 1800's, much of the land around Franklin is still wilderness, making the town an excellent stopping-off point if your destination is the outdoors. In fact, nearly half of Macon County lies within the Nantahala National Forest which is comprised of over a half-million acres of unspoiled natural beauty. Franklin is also situated between two popular scenic gorges, the Cullasaja and the Nantahala. In its rush downhill, the Cullasaja River takes some spectacular spills, creating lower Cullasaja Falls with a drop of 250 feet. Dry Falls is a favorite with visitors, who can actually walk behind the roaring 75 foot wall of water.

The Franklin area is also famous for its many gem mines, with rubies, sapphires and garnets the major gemstones found. The area is so important as a gem hunting region that it has earned the name "Gem Capital of the World." In Sep., the Macon County Fair, the state's only true agricultural fair, is held here and in Oct., Scottish Heritage Week brings to life traditional concerts, lectures and highland games. Franklin is also home to the regional Macon County Airport, one of the few airports in the mountains.

Location: Western Mountains, 2 hours west of Asheville

Town Hall: 188 West Main St., Franklin NC 28744, 828-524-2516

Website: franklinnc.com

County: Macon County: County Offices, 5 West Main St., Franklin NC 28734; 828-349-2025

Elevation and Population: 1,900 feet, 3,000+

Visitor/Welcome Center: Franklin Chamber of Commerce 425 Porter St., Franklin NC 28734; 828-524-3161

City Chamber of Commerce: Franklin Chamber of Commerce, 425 Porter St., Franklin NC 28734; 828-524-3161

Newspaper: The Franklin Press 40 Depot St., Franklin NC 28744; 828–524-2010

Movie Theatres: Ruby Cinemas, 2097 Georgia Rd., Franklin NC 28734; 828-524-2076

High School: Franklin High School, 100 Panther Dr., Franklin NC 28734; 828-524-6467

Colleges and Universities: Southwestern Community College, 44 Siler Farm Rd., Franklin NC 28734; 800-447-4091

Hospitals: Angel Medical Center, 120 Riverview St., Franklin NC 28734; 828-524-8411

Area Major Festivals: Macon County Fair (Sep.), Macon County Gemboree (Jul.), Pumpkinfest (Oct.), Window Wonderland (Dec.)

Area Natural Attractions: Appalachian Scenic National Trail, Fontana Lake, Great Smoky Mountains National Park, Joyce Kilmer Memorial Forest, Nantahala National Forest, Waterfalls in Western North Carolina

Area Cultural Attractions: Franklin Gem and Mineral Museum, Macon County Historical Society and Museum, Perry's Water Gardens, Ruby City Gems Museum, Scottish Tartans Museum, Smoky Mountain Center for the Performing Arts

Recommended Restaurants: (For a complete list of all restaurants visit ashevilleguide book.com

Lucio's Italian Restaurant: (Italian) 313 Highlands Rd., Franklin NC 28734; 828-369-6670

Root + Barrel Kitchen: (American) 77 E Main St, Franklin, NC 28734; 828-369-3663

Recommended Places To Stay: (For a complete list of all accommodations visit ashe villeguidebook.com

Carolina Motel: (Motel) 2601 Georgia Rd., Franklin NC 28734; 828-524-3380

Hampton Inn: (Motel) 244 Cunningham Rd., Franklin NC 28734; 800-426-7866

Oak Grove Cabins: (Cabins) 9835 Bryson City Rd., Franklin NC 28734; 828-369-0166

Oak Hill Country Inn Bed & Breakfast: (B&B) 1689 Old Murphy Rd., Franklin NC 28734; 800-587-6374

Glen Alpine

With roots that date back to the mid 1800's, Glen Alpine began with the arrival of the Southern Railroad. Originally called Turkey Tail by railroad workers, Glen Alpine also was named Sigmundsburg, after Edmund Sigmund, a mill founder, and then later Glen Alpine Station. In the early 1870's the town was home to one of the then largest wooden structures in North Carolina, the Glen Alpine Springs Hotel, which was said to have had as many as 100 guests at a time. After the hotel closed in 1890's, the town's name was finally changed to just Glen Alpine. Glen Alpine today is primarily a residential community, and is also home to the Lake James Cellars winery.

Location: Foothills, 1 hour east of Asheville

Town Hall: 103 Pitts St., Glen Alpine NC 28628; 828-584-2622

Website: townofglenalpinenc.org

County: Burke County: Burke County Government Center, 200 Avery Ave., Morganton NC 28680; 828-439-4340

Elevation and Population: 1,201 feet, 1,100+

County Visitor/Welcome Center: Burke County Visitor Center, 110 East Meeting St., Morganton NC 28655; 828-726-0616

County Chamber of Commerce: Burke County Chamber of Commerce, 110 East Meeting St., Morganton NC 28655; 828-437-3021

Newspaper: The News Herald, 301 Collett St., Morganton NC 28655; 828-437-2161

High School: Freedom High School, 511 Independence Blvd., Morganton NC 28655; 828-433-1310

Area Major Festivals: Glen Alpine Fall Festival (Oct.), Glen Alpine Christmas Parade (Dec.), Glen Alpine 4th of Jul. Parade (Jul.)

Area Natural Attractions: Brown Mountain Lights, Lake James State Park

Area Cultural Attractions: History Museum of Burke County, North Carolina School For The Deaf Museum, Old Burke County Courthouse Heritage Museum, Quaker Meadows Plantation, Senator Sam J. Ervin Jr. Museum

Recommended Restaurants: (For a complete list of all restaurants visit ashevilleguidebook.com

Doogies Pizza & Subs: (Pizza) 500 West Main St., Glen Alpine NC 28628; 828-584-1111

Recommended Places To Stay: (For a complete list of all accommodations visit ashevilleguidebook.com

The Inn at Glen Alpine: (B&B) 105 Davis St., Glen Alpine NC 28628; 828-584-9264

Granite Falls

Granite Falls, established in 1899, is located in southern Caldwell County just north of Hickory on U. S. Hwy. 321. Its history dates back before the Revolutionary War and its roots can be traced to land grants as early as 1754. Granite Falls was incorporated on May 1, 1899 and was named after the Falls at Gunpowder Creek, where a solid formation of granite spans the creek.

Home to the nationally recognized Bank of Granite, the Town of Granite Falls' economy has been centered on manufacturing, with tourism and the retirement industry also diversifying the economic base. Granite Falls is also home to one of the world's largest collection of soda pop memorabilia housed in the Antique Vending Company showroom. Recreational opportunities for visitors include the nearby Pisgah National Forest and the town's Lakeside Park on scenic Lake Rhodhiss. The Granite Falls History & Transportation Museum is also located in Granite Falls and is housed in the historic home of Andrew Baird, one of the town's original founders.

Rhodhiss is a small, quaint community near Granite Falls with a unique claim to fame. The town is known for a sign that proudly proclaims that the flags planted on the moon by the United States were woven in Rhodhiss. Located in both Caldwell and Burke counties, Rhodhiss is situated alongside the Catawba River just below Duke Energy's Rhodhiss Dam.

Location: Foothills, 1.5 hours east of Asheville

Town Hall: 30 Park Square, Granite Falls NC 28630; 828-396-3131

Website: granitefallsnc.com

County: Caldwell County: County Offices, 905 West Ave. NW, Lenoir NC 28645; 828-757-1300

Elevation and Population: 1,191 feet, 4,600+

County Visitor/Welcome Center: Caldwell County Chamber of Commerce Visitor Center,1909 Hickory Blvd. SE, Lenoir NC 28645; 828-726-0616

County Chamber of Commerce: Caldwell County Chamber of Commerce, 1909 Hickory Blvd. SE, Lenoir NC 28645; 828-726-0616

Newspaper: News-Topic, 123 Pennton Ave., Lenoir NC 28645; 828–758-7381

Movie Theatres: Carmike Westgate Twin, 1966 Morgantown Blvd. SW, Lenoir NC 28645; 828-758-9902

High School: South Caldwell High School, 7035 Spartan Dr., Hudson NC 28638; 828-396-2188

Area Major Festivals: Granite Falls Art in the Park (Jun.), Christmas Parade (Dec.)

Area Natural Attractions: Pisgah National Forest, Tuttle Educational State Forest, Wilson Creek

Area Cultural Attractions: Caldwell Heritage Museum, Chapel of Rest, Fort Defiance, Granite Falls History and Transportation Museum, Happy Valley, 20 Miles of Furniture

Recommended Restaurants: (For a complete list of all restaurants visit ashevilleguide book.com

Huffy's Soup, Sandwiches & Creamery: (Café) 23–3 Falls Ave., Granite Falls NC 28630; 828-396-6111

New City BBQ: (BBQ) 108 South Main Street, Granite Falls NC 28630; 828-396-1413

Recommended Places To Stay: (For a complete list of all accommodations visit ashe villeguidebook.com

Hayesville

Hayesville, incorporated in 1913, is the county seat of Clay County and is located at the far western edge of the North Carolina Mountains. The focal point of the town is the historic county seat court house, built in 1888, where many of the county's festivities are held. Hayesville is also home to the Clay County Historical & Arts Council Museum and the Peacock Playhouse where performances by the local theatrical group, The Licklog Players, can be seen. The museum is housed in the Old County Jail, which was constructed in 1912 and used until 1972. Another doorway to history is The People's Store (68 Church St.), a general store in operation since 1946 and now open as a small museum. Hours by appointment only by calling 828-557-0759.

Nearby Chatuge Lake, a TVA lake, has over 130 miles of shoreline, much of which can never be developed, and provides wonderful recreational opportunities for residents and visitors alike. This beautiful lake sets the tone for Hayesville. Few mountain cities can boast of such a great natural resource right in their own backyard.

Location: Western Mountains, 2 hours west of Asheville

County: Clay County: County Offices, 33 Main St., Hayesville NC 28904; 828-389-0089

Elevation and Population: 2,200 feet, 300

County Visitor/Welcome Center: Clay County Chamber of Commerce, 388 Hwy. Business 64, Hayesville NC 28904; 828-389-3704

County Chamber of Commerce: Clay County Chamber of Commerce, 388 Hwy. Business 64, Hayesville NC 28904; 828-389-3704

Newspaper: Clay County Progress 43 Main St., Hayesville NC 28904; 828-389-8431 and Smoky Mountain Sentinel 116 Sanderson St., Hayesville NC 28904; 828-389-8338

Movie Theatres: Fieldstone Cinemas Six 1159 Jack Dayton, Young Harris GA 30582; 706-898-6843

High School: Hayesville High School, 205 Yellow Jacket Dr., Hayesville NC 28904; 828-389-6532

Area Major Festivals: Hayesville Festival on the Square (Jul.)

Area Natural Attractions: Chatuge Lake, Joyce Kilmer Memorial Forest, Nantahala National Forest

Area Cultural Attractions: Clay County Historical and Arts Council Museum, John C. Campbell Folk School, Peacock Playhouse, The People's Store

Recommended Restaurants: (For a complete list of all restaurants visit ashevilleguidebook.com

The Copper Door: (American) 2 Sullivan Street, Hayesville NC 28904; 828-237-4030

Recommended Places To Stay: (For a complete list of all accommodations visit ashevilleguidebook.com

Chatuge Mountain Inn: (Country Inn) 4238 Hwy. 64 East, Hayesville NC 28904; 828-389-3000

Deerfield Inn: (Country Inn) 40 Chatuge Lane, Hwy. 64 East, Hayesville NC 28904; 828-389-8272

Hickory

Located in the foothills of Western North Carolina, Hickory is the second largest city in the mountains and a great destination for furniture shopping as well as for cultural activities and outdoor recreation. Hickory and surrounding Catawba County uniquely enjoy a world-wide reputation as one of the premier destinations for shoppers looking for fine furniture and home furnishings. A large percentage of America's furniture is produced within a 200-mile radius of Hickory, and virtually every major furniture manufacturer has a presence here. There are a number of malls featuring furniture stores and manufacturer's outlets in the greater Hickory area. These include the Catawba Furniture Mall and the prestigious Hickory Furniture Mart, both located on Hwy. 70. The Hickory Furniture Mart is the largest of its kind in the country and houses over 100 factory outlets, stores and galleries, representing over 1000 manufacturers. The Mart has been well-known for years as one of North Carolina's most popular travel and tourism destinations for furniture shoppers and enthusiasts nationwide. The mall also is home to the Catawba Valley Furniture Museum, which includes in its collections some of the area's first pieces of furniture ever produced. It is estimated that this mall receives over 500,000 visitors every year. Hickory is also one end of the "20 Miles of Furniture," a stretch of US Hwy. 321 between Lenoir and Hickory where numerous furniture outlets and stores also offer deep discounts. Think of this as a 20-mile-long furniture mall!

Hickory started in the 1850s when Henry Robinson built a tavern of logs under a huge Hickory tree. The city of "Hickory Tavern" was established shortly afterwards in 1863, and in 1873, the name was changed to Hickory. Hickory was known in the years after World War II for the "Miracle of Hickory." In 1944 the area around Hickory became the center of one of the worst outbreaks of polio ever recorded. Since local facilities were inadequate to treat the victims, the citizens of Hickory and the Mar. of Dimes decided to build a hospital to care for the children of the region. From the time the decision was made until equipment, doctors, and patients were in a new facility, took less than 54 hours.

The cultural hub of Hickory is the famous SALT Block (an acronym that stands for Science, Art and Literature Together), where on one block downtown clustered together are the Catawba Science Center, the Hickory Museum of Art, the Hickory Public Library, the Western Piedmont Symphony, the United Arts Council of Catawba County and the Hickory Choral Society. A unique concentration of science and art, the SALT block is a major tourist destination in Hickory, with over 200,000 visitors a year. The block's anchor is the iconic former Claremont Central High School, built in 1925 and transformed 60 years later into the 74, 923 square-foot Arts and Science Center of Catawba Valley that houses many of the SALT Block organizations and institutions.

Hickory is also home to the Hickory Community Theatre and other important cultural institutions. These include the Harper House/Hickory History Center, located in the historic and stunningly beautiful Harper House, one of the finest examples of Queen Anne architecture and interior design to be found in North Carolina, and two historical houses that also are local cultural history museums, the Maple Grove Historical Museum and the J. Summie Propst House Museum.

Hickory has a Class A minor league baseball team, the Hickory Crawdads, that play at L.P. Frans Stadium, located at 2500 Clement Boulevard NW, and also the Hickory Motor Speedway, a racing facility that has presented competitions for over 50 years and is hailed as the birthplace of NASCAR stars Dale Earnhardt, Junior Johnson, Ned and Dale Jarrett and Harry Gant.

Recreational opportunities abound in the area, with more than 10 public golf courses in the Hickory metro area, and numerous parks and recreational facilities. One of the most convenient is the city park, Glenn C. Hilton, Jr. Memorial Park, located at 2000 6th St. NW, which features five picnic shelters, gazebo, lighted and paved walking trails, disc golf course, and fitness and nature trails. Other popular parks in Hickory include Bakers Mountain Park, at 6680 Bakers Mountain Rd., the Ivey Arboretum in Carolina Park located at 1441 9th Ave. NE, and St. Stephens Park at 2247 36th Ave. NE. Bakers Mountain Park is located at the highest point in Catawba County (1,780 feet) and features 189 acres of mature Chestnut Oak forest with nearly six miles of trails. The Ivey Arboretum in Carolina Park contains a collection of over 400 labeled species of native and rare trees and shrubs within a three-acre park and St. Stephens Park, a 9.1 acre park that features walking trails, a playground, educationally-themed landscaping and a dog park. Kiwanis Park located at 805 6th St. SE now includes Zahra Baker All Children's Playground. It is a playground where children of different abilities can meet and play together.

Hickory has been named an "All-America City" three times, the last time in 2007. This prestigious award is given annually to only ten cities in the United States. The Hickory Metro area has also been named the 10th best place to live and raise a family in America by Readers Digest. Higher educational institutions include Lenoir-Rhyne University and Catawba Valley Community College. Hickory, as one would expect for a city of 40,000 residents, has a strong lineup of festivals and cultural events. One of the major festivals is the famous Catawba Valley Pottery Festival held every Mar. in the Hickory Metro Convention Center. Another popular annual event is the Hickory Alive program, featuring free concerts held every Fri evening in Jun. and Jul. in downtown Hickory. Oktoberfest, held in downtown Hickory, is one of the anticipated events in the greater Hickory area. This festival offers a weekend of family entertainment, with five performance stages for musical entertainment. The festival also has a popular Kidsfest area featuring amusement rides and games, an arts and crafts section, and numerous commercial and food vendors.

Hickory is conveniently located off I-40, and also has a small regional airport, the Hickory Regional Airport, for non-commercial aircraft.

Location: Foothills, 1 hour and 15 minutes east of Asheville
Town Hall: 76 North Center St., Hickory NC 28601; 828-323-7400
Website: hickorygov.com
County: Catawba County: County Offices, 100-A South West Blvd., Newton NC 28658; 828-465-8201
Elevation and Population: 910 feet, 40,000+
Regional Visitors Center: Hickory Metro Convention Center and Visitors Bureau, 1960-A 13th Ave. Dr. SE, Hickory NC 28602; 800-509-2444
County Visitor/Welcome Center: Catawba County Visitor Information Center, 1055 Southgate Corporate Park SW, Hickory NC 28602; 828-328-6111
County Chamber of Commerce: 1055 Southgate Corporate Park SW, Hickory NC 28602; 828-328-6111
Newspaper: Hickory Daily Record, 1100 Park Place, Hickory NC 28603; 828-322-4510
Movie Theatres: Carmike 14, 2000 SE Catawba Valley Blvd., Hickory NC 28603; 828-298-4885 and Carolina Theater, 221 1st Ave. NW, Hickory NC 28601; 828-322-7210
High Schools: St. Stephens High School, 3205 34th St. Dr. NE, Hickory NC 28601; 828-256-9841 and Challenger High School, 2550 Hwy. 70 SE, Hickory NC 28602; 828-485-2980
Colleges and Universities: Lenoir-Rhyne University, 625 7th Ave. NE, Hickory NC 28601; 828-328-1741 and Catawba Valley Community College, 2550 US Hwy. 70 SE, Hickory NC 28602; 828-327-7000
Hospitals: Frye Regional Medical Center, 420 North Center St., Hickory NC 28601; 828-315-5000 and Catawba Valley Medical Center, 810 Fairgrove Church Rd. SE, Hickory NC 28602; 828-326-3000
Parks: Bakers Mountain Park, Glenn C. Hilton, Jr. Memorial Park, Ivey Arboretum in Carolina Park, St. Stephens Park, Kiwanis Park
Area Major Festivals: Apple Festival (Oct.), Art Crawl (May and Sep.), Catawba Valley Pottery Festival (Mar.), Hickory Alive (Fri evenings Jun. and Jul.), Hickory American Legion Fair (Sep.), Hickory Hops (April), Oktoberfest (Oct.), Old Soldier Reunion (Aug.), and Swinging under the Stars (May)
Area Natural Attractions: Pisgah National Forest, South Mountains State Park
Area Cultural Attractions: Bunker Hill Covered Bridge, Catawba County Museum of History, Catawba Science Center, Harper House/Hickory History Center, Hickory Community Theatre, Hickory Crawdads, Hickory Furniture Mart, Hickory Motor Speedway, Hickory Museum of Art, Hiddenite Center, Historic Murray's Mill, J. Summie Propst House Museum, Maple Grove Historical Museum
Recommended Restaurants: (For a complete list of all 100+ Hickory restaurants visit ashevilleguidebook.com

Backstreets Bar & Grill: (American) 246 14th Ave. NE, Hickory NC 28601; 828-328-6479

Café Gouda: (Café) Belle Hollow, 2960 North Center St., Hickory NC 28601; 828-267-1300

Dickey's BBQ Pit: (BBQ) 1036 Lenoir Rhyne Blvd. SE, Hickory NC 28602; 828-855-9390

Hannah's BBQ: (BBQ) 3198 Hwy. 127 South, Hickory NC 28602; 828-294-4227

Kobe Japanese House of Steak & Seafood: (Japanese) 1103 13th Ave. Dr. SE, Hickory NC 28602; 828-328-5688

Vintage House: (Continental) 271 3rd Avenue NW, Hickory NC 28601; 828-324-1210

Wild Wok Hickory Asian Bistro: (Asian) 2403 Catawba Valley Boulevard SE, Hickory NC 28602; 828-328-1688 and 303 N. Center St., Hickory NC 28602; 828-322-1115

Recommended Places To Stay: (For a complete list of all accommodations visit ashevilleguidebook.com

Courtyard by Marriott: (Motel) 1946 13th Ave. Dr. SE, Hickory NC 28602; 828-267-2100

Crowne Plaza Hotel: (Hotel) 1385 Lenoir-Rhyne Boulevard SE; Hickory NC 28602; 828-323-1000

Days Inn & Suites: (Motel) 1725 13th Ave. Dr. NW, Hickory NC 28601; 828-431-2100

Fairfield Inn & Suites by Marriott: (Motel) 1950 13th Ave. Dr. SE, Hickory NC 28602; 828-431-3000

Hampton Inn: (Motel) 1520 13th Ave. Dr. SE, Hickory NC 28602; 828-624-3000

Holiday Inn Express: (Motel) 2250 US Hwy. 70 SE, Hickory NC 28602; 828-328-2081

Indian Springs Campground: (RV Campground) 4361 Whitener Dr., Hickory NC 28602; 828-397-5700

Red Roof Inn: (Motel) 1184 Lenoir-Rhyne Boulevard SE, Hickory NC 28602; 828-323-1500

The Pecan Tree Inn of Hickory: (B&B) 2303 Ewing Dr., Hickory NC 28602; 704-462-0822

Highlands

Highlands, incorporated in 1883, is located in the heart of the beautiful Nantahala National Forest. An affluent and quaint resort town with a large annual influx of families that own second homes, Highlands has an abundance of fine restaurants, shops, accommodations and upscale stores. Outdoor recreational opportunities abound, including hiking, fishing, boating, horseback riding and rock climbing. Highlands is also home to the Highlands Playhouse, which for over 50 years has provided summer stock theatre. Other great local resources in this culturaly rich mountain town are the Highlands Nature Center, the Highlands Biological Station, The Bascom Center for the Visual Arts, the Martin-Lipscomb

Performing Arts Center (Home to the Highlands Cashiers Players) and the Hudson Library located at 554 Main St.

The Scaly Mountain Outdoor Center in nearby Scaly Mountain offers snow tubing in the winter and summer tubing on artificial turf slopes. Also, only two miles from Highlands is the Dry Falls waterfall in the Nantahala National Forest, easily accessible and worth the trip.

Location: Western Mountains, 1.5 hour west of Asheville
Town Hall: 210 South 4th St., Highlands NC 28741; 828-526-2118
Website: highlandsnc.org
County: Macon County: County Offices, 5 West Main St., Franklin NC 28734; 828-349-2025
Elevation and Population: 4,118 feet,1,000+
Visitor/Welcome Center: Highlands Chamber of Commerce Visitor Center 269 Main St., Highlands NC 28741; 828-526-5841
City Chamber of Commerce: Highlands Chamber of Commerce 269 Main St., Highlands NC 28741; 828-526-5841
Newspaper: The Highlander 134 North 5th St., Highlands NC 28741; 828-526-4114
High School: Highlands School, 545 Pierson Dr., Highlands NC 28741; 828-526-2147
Hospitals: Highlands-Cashiers Hospital, 190 Hospital Dr., Highlands NC 28741; 828-526-1200
Area Major Festivals: Highlands-Cashiers Chamber Music Festival (Jul.–Aug.)
Area Natural Attractions: Joyce Kilmer Memorial Forest, Nantahala National Forest, Waterfalls in Western North Carolina
Area Cultural Attractions: Highlands Biological Station, Highlands Museum and Historical Village, Highlands Nature Center, Macon County Historical Society and Museum, Museum of American Cut and Engraved Glass, The Bascom
Recommended Restaurants: (For a complete list of all restaurants visit ashevilleguide book.com

- **Madison's Restaurant:** (American-Fine Dining) Old Edwards Inn and Spa, 445 Main St., Highlands NC 28741; 828-526-5477
- **On The Verandah:** (American/International-Fine Dining) 1536 Franklin Rd., Highlands NC 28741; 828-526-2338
- **Wild Thyme Gourmet:** (Café) 343 Main St., Highlands NC 28741; 828-526-4035
- **Wolfgang's Restaurant and Wine Bistro:** (Eclectic Contemporary American-Fine Dining) 474 Main St., Highlands NC 28741; 828-526-3807

Recommended Places To Stay: (For a complete list of all accommodations visit ashe villeguidebook.com

- **Colonial Pines Inn Bed & Breakfast:** (B&B) 541 Hickory St., Highlands NC 28741; 866-526-2060
- **Half Mile Farm:** (Country Inn) 214 Half Mile Dr., Highlands NC 28741; 800-946-6822
- **Main St. Inn:** (Village Inn) Main St. Inn, 270 Main St., Highlands NC 28741; 800-213-9142

Mitchell's Lodge & Cottages: (Country Lodge) 264 Dillard Rd., Highlands NC 28741; 800-522-9874

Old Edwards Inn and Spa: (Hotel and Spa) 445 Main St., Highlands NC 28741; 866-526-8008

Hildebran

Hildebran, incorporated in 1910, was originally known as Switch but was later changed to Hildebran after J. A. Hildebran, a local lumber dealer. Today, the town has nearly 1,800 residents. Each Christmas, this small community stages an annual Christmas parade and is working to build its business and industrial base. Hildebran is home also to the Hildebran Farmer's Market, held every Thu May through Oct. in the Town Hall parking lot.

Location: Foothills, 1.5 hours east of Asheville

Town Hall: 202 South Center St., Hildebran NC 28637; 828-397-5801

County: Burke County: Burke County Government Center, 200 Avery Ave., Morganton NC 28680; 828-439-4340

Elevation and Population: 1,188 feet, 1,800+

County Visitor/Welcome Center: Burke County Visitor Center, 110 East Meeting St., Morganton NC 28655; 828-433-6793

County Chamber of Commerce: Burke County Chamber of Commerce, 110 East Meeting St., Morganton NC 28655; 828-437-3021

Newspaper: The News Herald, 301 Collett St., Morganton NC 28655; 828-437-2161

High School: East Burke High School, 3695 East Burke Blvd., Connelly Springs NC 28612; 828-397-5541

Area Major Festivals: Hildebran Heritage Festival (Oct.), Hildebran Christmas Parade (Dec.), Hildebran Festival of Lights (Dec.)

Area Natural Attractions: Brown Mountain Lights, Lake James State Park

Area Cultural Attractions: History Museum of Burke County, North Carolina School For The Deaf Museum, Old Burke County Courthouse and Heritage Museum, Quaker Meadows Plantation, Senator Sam J. Ervin Jr. Museum

Recommended Restaurants: (For a complete list of all restaurants visit ashevilleguide book.com

Chubby's: (Café) 511 US Hwy. 70, HIldebran NC 28637; 828–397-3911

Recommended Places To Stay: (For a complete list of all accommodations visit ashe villeguidebook.com

No accommodations currently available in Hildebran. *See* Morganton.

Hot Springs

Hot Springs, located on the French Broad River about 40 minutes north of Asheville, was started when hot mineral springs were discovered in 1792. It is reported that people were visiting the springs by 1778 for the waters' reported healing properties. In 1828 a major road, the Buncombe Turnpike, was constructed through the current town making the area more accessible and Hot Springs became a famous resort town that catered to folks looking for relaxation in the mountains as well as healing in the mineral springs. Today Hot Springs still welcomes visitors who wish to explore and play in the surrounding mountains, and the naturally occurring hot springs are still an attraction. The major center, if you are interested in trying the hot springs, is the Hot Springs Resort & Spa located on Bridge St.

The Appalachian Trail runs along downtown's Bridge St. and climbs the mountains on either side of the river and Whitewater Rafting and kayaking are popular on the French Broad River itself. There are numerous other hiking, mountain biking, backpacking, and sightseeing opportunities in the nearby Pisgah National Forest.

Location: Central Mountains, 1 hour northwest of Asheville
City Hall: 186 Bridge St., Hot Springs NC 28743; 828-622-7591
Website: townofhotsprings.org
County: Madison County: County Offices, 2 North Main St., Marshall NC 28753; 828-649-2854
Elevation and Population: 1,330 feet, 700+
City Visitor/Welcome Center: Hot Springs Visitors Center Hwy. 25–70, Hot Springs NC 28743; 828-622-7611
County Visitor/Welcome Center: Madison County Visitors Center 635–4 Carl Eller Rd., Mars Hill NC 28754; 877-262-3476, 828-680-9031
County Chamber of Commerce: Madison County Chamber of Commerce 635-4 Carl Eller Rd., Mars Hill NC 28754; 828-689-9351
Newspaper: News-Record and Sentinel 58 Back St., Marshall NC 28753; 828-649-1075
High School: Madison High School, 5740 US Hwy. 25/70, Marshall NC 28753; 828-649-2876
Area Major Festivals: French Broad River Festival (May), Bluff Mountain Music Festival (Jun.), Civil War Warm Springs Skirmish (Jun.)
Area Natural Attractions: Appalachian Scenic National Trail, French Broad River, Pisgah National Forest, Max Patch
Area Cultural Attractions: Rural Life Museum, Zebulon B. Vance Birthplace
Recommended Restaurants: (For a complete list of all restaurants visit ashevilleguide book.com

Iron Horse Station: (American) 24 South Andrew Ave., Hot Springs NC 28743; 866-402-9377

Mountain Magnolia Inn: (American-Fine Dining) 204 Lawson St., Hot Springs NC 28743; 800-622-9553

Recommended Places To Stay: (For a complete list of all accommodations visit ashe villeguidebook.com

Mountain Magnolia Inn, Suites & Restaurant: (Country Inn) 204 Lawson St., Hot Springs NC 28743; 800-622-9553

Iron Horse Station: (Village Inn) 24 South Andrew Ave., Hot Springs NC 28743; 866-402-9377

Treehouse Cabins: (Cabins) High Mountain Rd., Hot Springs NC 28743; 828-622-7296

Hudson

The Town of Hudson, incorporated in 1905, is located in Caldwell County approximately 15 miles north of Interstate 40 and was named after the Hudson brothers, Monroe and Johnnie, who were among the first lumber men in the area and became leaders of what was then known as Hudsonville. Hudson started as a sawmill camp and as the city grew textile and furniture industries played prominent roles in the economy. Hudson today has a vibrant economy based on small business and tourism, and there are approximately 150 businesses currently established. Hudson is home to many of the country's industrial leaders, including Kincaid Furniture, Shurtape Technologies, Shuford Mills and Sealed Air Corporation.

The town has two parks: Redwood Park, which features a beautiful playground with children's slides and activities, a swimming pool and several ball fields; and the Hickman Windmill Park which features the Hudson Railroad Depot Museum as well as a 100-year-old windmill. Hudson is also home to South Caldwell High School and Caldwell Community College, which has a campus in Hudson with an enrollment of 4,000 students.

Caldwell County, known as the Furniture Capital of the South, is home to the "20 Miles of Furniture" where numerous outlets and stores offer deep discounts. Located along or near a stretch of U.S. Hwy. 321 between Lenoir and Hickory, the area, which passes through Hudson, is a required destination for any serious shopper looking for furniture. Hudson's downtown features a mix of mom-and-pop businesses and is a short drive to the Hudson Uptown Building, known locally as the HUB. This former renovated school building has become a favorite for community gatherings and Hudson's acclaimed annual dinner theatres.

Cajah's Mountain, founded in 1983, is one of Caldwell County's most popular residential communities. The town is located near Hudson and has seen recent expansion in residential growth along with commercial and industrial development.

Location: Foothills, 1.5 hours east of Asheville
Town Hall: 550 Central St., Hudson N C 28638; 828-728-8272
Website: ci.hudson.nc.us
County: Caldwell County: County Offices, 905 West Ave. NW, Lenoir NC 28645; 828-757-1300
Elevation and Population: 1,263 feet, 3,000+
County Visitor/Welcome Center: Caldwell County Chamber of Commerce Visitor Center,1909 Hickory Blvd. SE, Lenoir NC 28645; 828-726-0616
County Chamber of Commerce: Caldwell County Chamber of Commerce, 1909 Hickory Blvd. SE, Lenoir NC 28645; 828-726-0616
Newspaper: News-Topic, 123 Pennton Ave., Lenoir NC 28645; 828–758-7381
Movie Theatres: Carmike Westgate Twin, 1966 Morganton Blvd. SW, Lenoir NC 28645; 828-758-9902
High School: South Caldwell High School, 7035 Spartan Dr., Hudson NC 28638; 828-396-2188
Colleges and Universities: Caldwell Community College, 2855 Hickory Blvd., Hudson NC 28638; 828-726-2200
Area Major Festivals: Butterfly Festival, (May), Foothills Pottery Festival (Oct.), 4th of Jul. Kiddie Kar Parade (Jul.)

Area Natural Attractions: Pisgah National Forest, Tuttle Educational State Forest, Wilson Creek

Area Cultural Attractions: Caldwell Heritage Museum, Chapel of Rest, Fort Defiance, Granite Falls History and Transportation Museum, Happy Valley, 20 Miles of Furniture

Recommended Restaurants: (For a complete list of all restaurants visit ashevilleguide book.com

Vintage Café & Bakery: (Café) 540 Central St., Hudson NC 28638; 828-728-3043

Recommended Places To Stay: (For a complete list of all accommodations visit ashe villeguidebook.com

No accommodations currently available in Hudson. *See* Lenoir and Granite Falls.

Jefferson

Jefferson, the county seat of Ashe County, was established in 1800 and was one of the first towns in the United States to be named after President Thomas Jefferson, who at the time was Vice-President. Originally called Jeffersonton, the name was later changed to Jefferson. The ancient New River, one of the oldest rivers in the world, flows through the town. The Museum of Ashe County History is located in the historic 1904 Ashe County Courthouse building and has exhibits pertaining to the history of Ashe County and its people. The largest hospital in Ashe County is located also in Jefferson, Ashe Memorial Hospital, as well as the Ashe campus of Wilkes Community College.

Nearby Lansing is home to the famous Ola Belle Reed Homecoming Festival, a celebration of mountain music. Lansing's classic small town setting is enhanced by the surrounding hills and Phoenix Mountain (elevation 4,170 feet) in the background as well as the homes dotting the narrow, tree lined streets.

Location: Northern Mountains, 2.5 hours east of Asheville

Lansing Town Hall: 173 B St., Lansing NC 28643; 336-384-3938

County: Ashe County: County Offices, 150 Government Circle, Ste 2500, Jefferson NC 28640; 336-846-5501

Elevation and Population: 3,000 feet, 1400+

County Chamber of Commerce: Ashe County Chamber of Commerce 01 North Jefferson St., Ste C, West Jefferson NC 28694: 336-846-9550

Newspaper: Jefferson Post, 203 South Second St., West Jefferson NC 28694; 336-846-7164

High School: Ashe County High School, 184 Campus Dr., West Jefferson NC 28694; 336-846-2400

Colleges and Universities: Wilkes Community College, 363 Campus Dr., Jefferson NC 28640; 336-846-3900

Hospitals: Ashe Memorial Hospital, 200 Hospital Ave., Jefferson NC 28640; 336-846-7101

Area Major Festivals: Ola Belle Reed Homecoming Festival (Aug.)

Area Natural Attractions: Blue Ridge Parkway; Mount Jefferson State Natural Area, New River State Park

Area Cultural Attractions: Ashe County Arts Council Gallery, Ben Long Frescoes, Museum of Ashe County History

Recommended Restaurants: (For a complete list of all restaurants visit ashevilleguide book.com

Shatley Springs Inn: (Family Style-American) 407 Shatley Springs Rd., Crumpler NC 28617; 336-982-2236

Recommended Places To Stay: (For a complete list of all accommodations visit ashe villeguidebook.com

Days Inn Jefferson: (Motel) 829 East Main Street, Jefferson NC 28640; 336-313-2115

Holiday Inn Express West Jefferson: (Motel) 203 Hampton Place Court, West Jefferson, NC 28694; 336-846-4000

Lake Lure

Located on the beautiful northern end of 720-acre man-made Lake Lure, the town of Lake Lure offers an eclectic and tourist-oriented selection of shops, restaurants and accommodations. The town also has a boating facility, the Lake Lure Marina where boats can be rented, a public beach for swimming and a lovely lakeside park at the Morse Park peninsula that is open to residents and visitors. The lake was created in 1927 by the creation of a hydroelectric dam on the Rocky Broad River and is considered one of the most beautiful man-made lakes in America by National Geographic. Covered, pontoon boat tours of Lake Lure are offered at the Marina and are a wonderful way to see this extraordinary lake. In recent years, the Lake Lure area has served as the filming location for several major motion pictures including Last of the Mohicans with Daniel Day-Lewis; My Fellow Americans, a 1996 comedy starring Jack Lemmon and James Garner; and Dirty Dancing starring Patrick Swayze. Lake Lure, for a town of its small size, is fortunate to have an outstanding library, the Mountain Branch Library, located at 150 Bill's Creek Rd.

Location: Central Mountains, 45 minutes south of Asheville

Town Hall: 2948 Memorial Hwy., Lake Lure NC 28746; 828-625-9983

Website: townoflakelure.com

County: Rutherford County: County Tourism Development Authority Offices, 1990 Hwy. 221 South, Forest City NC 28043; 828-245-1492

Elevation and Population: 1,000 Feet, 1,000+

Visitor/Welcome Centers: (Two) Hickory Nut Gorge Visitor Center, 2926 Memorial Hwy., Lake Lure NC 28746; 877-625-2725 and Rutherford Tourism Development Authority Center, 1990 Hwy. 221 South, Forest City NC 28043; 828-245-1492

City Chamber of Commerce: Hickory Nut Gorge Chamber of Commerce, PO Box 32, Chimney Rock NC 28720; 877-625-2725

County Chamber of Commerce: Rutherford County Chamber of Commerce, 162 North Main St., Rutherfordton NC 28139; 828-287-3090

County Tourism Development: Lake Lure and the Blue Ridge Foothills, 1990 US Hwy. 221 South, Forest City NC 28043; 828-245-1492

Newspaper: The Mountain Breeze, 828-625-9330

High School: R.S. Central High School, 641 US Hwy. 221 North, Rutherfordton NC 28139; 828-287-3304

Area Major Festivals: Lure of the Dr.agons (May)

Area Natural Attractions: Apple Orchards in Henderson County, Chimney Rock Park, Lake Lure, Pisgah National Forest

Recommended Restaurants: (For a complete list of all restaurants visit ashevilleguide book.com

- **La Strada at Lake Lure:** (Italian) 2693 Memorial Hwy., Lake Lure NC 28746; 828-625-1118
- **LakeHouse Restaurant Bar & Grill:** (American) 1020 Memorial Hwy., Lake Lure NC 28746; 828-625-4075
- **The Veranda Restaurant:** (American) 1927 Lake Lure Inn & Spa, 2771 Memorial Hwy., Lake Lure NC 28746; 828-625-2525

Recommended Places To Stay: (For a complete list of all accommodations visit ashe villeguidebook.com

- **Gaestehaus Salzburg Bed & Breakfast:** (B&B) 1491 Memorial Hwy., Lake Lure NC 28746; 877-694-4029
- **1927 Lake Lure Inn & Spa:** (Resort) 2771 Memorial Hwy., Lake Lure NC 28746; 828-625-2525
- **Lodge on Lake Lure:** (B&B) 361 Charlotte Dr., Lake Lure NC 28746; 800-733-2785
- **Rumbling Bald Resort on Lake Lure:** (Resort) 112 Mountains Boulevard, Lake Lure NC 28746; 800-419-3854

Lenoir

Lenoir, the county seat of Caldwell County, is a foothills city rich in history, diverse recreational and cultural opportunities, local attractions and a rich quality of life. The largest city in Caldwell County, Lenoir is also home to the Caldwell County Historical Society Heritage Museum and Tuttle Educational State Forest. The first settlement in Lenoir was known as Tucker's Barn, named for the family who settled in the area around the 1760s. The settlement became a large meeting place for many gatherings and became so popular a fiddle tune was composed and written titled "Tucker's Barn." Doc Watson eventually recorded this tune in 1964 on an album titled, The Watson Family Tradition.

Caldwell County, known as the Furniture Capital of the South, is home to the "20 Miles of Furniture" where numerous outlets and stores offer deep discounts. Located along or near a stretch of U.S. Hwy. 321 between Lenoir and Hickory, the area is a required destination for any serious shopper looking for furniture. The County also contains more than 50,000 acres of recreational land, much of it part of the Pisgah National Forest. Two of the outstanding local attractions in the county near Lenoir are the Wilson Creek Gorge area and the beautiful T.H. Broyhill Park, on Lakewood St., which has a half-mile nature loop circling a man-made lake. A joint project of the Broyhill Family Foundation and the city of Lenoir, Oriental gardens on the park set the tone of elegance and serenity where walkers and joggers can enjoy a lovely nature sanctuary.

Stretching from Lenoir toward Wilkesboro along Hwy. 268 is historic "Happy Valley." Located on the banks of the Yadkin River, Happy Valley was so named by the early settlers who described the valley as "a place of beauty, peace and tranquility" and the name aptly remains. A number of attractions are in the valley, including Fort Defiance, the Chapel of Rest and Whippoorwill Academy and Village.

The Village of Cedar Rock is the smallest and the youngest of Caldwell County's municipalities. Built around Cedar Rock Country Club, the town is nestled at the foot of the Brushy Mountains. Gamewell, incorporated in 1981, is situated midway between Lenoir and Morganton along NC Hwy. 18 and is primarily residential.

Location: Foothills, 1.5 hours east of Asheville
Town Hall: 801 West Ave., Lenoir NC 28645; 828-757-2200
Website: cityoflenoir.com
County: Caldwell County: County Offices, 1909 Hickory Blvd., Lenoir NC 28645; 828-726-0323
Elevation and Population: 1,182 feet, 17,000+
County Visitor/Welcome Center: Caldwell County Chamber of Commerce Visitor Center,1909 Hickory Blvd. SE, Lenoir NC 28645; 828-726-0323
County Chamber of Commerce: Caldwell County Chamber of Commerce, 1909 Hickory Blvd. SE, Lenoir NC 28645; 828-726-0323
Newspaper: News-Topic, 123 Pennton Ave., Lenoir NC 28645; 828–758-7381
Movie Theatres: Carmike Westgate Twin, 1966 Morgantown Blvd. SW, Lenoir NC 28645; 828-758-9902
High School: West Caldwell High School, 300 West Caldwell Dr., Lenoir NC 28645; 828-758-5583 and Hibriten High School, 1350 Panther Trail, Lenoir NC 28645; 828-758-7376
Hospitals: Caldwell Memorial Hospital, 321 Mulberry St. SW, Lenoir NC 28645; 828-757-5100
Area Major Festivals: Blackberry Festival (Jul.), Historic Happy Valley Heritage Old-time Fiddler's Convention (Sep.)
Area Natural Attractions: Pisgah National Forest, Tuttle Educational State Forest, Wilson Creek
Area Cultural Attractions: Caldwell Heritage Museum, Chapel of Rest, Fort Defiance, Granite Falls History and Transportation Museum, Happy Valley, 20 Miles of Furniture
Recommended Restaurants: (For a complete list of all restaurants visit ashevilleguide book.com

1841 Cafe: (American) 117 Main Street NW, Lenoir 28645; 828-572-4145

Recommended Places To Stay: (For a complete list of all accommodations visit ashe villeguidebook.com

Brown Mountain Beach Resort: (Cabins) 6785 Brown Mountain Beach Road, Lenoir NC 28645; 828-758-4257
Comfort Inn & Suites: (Motel) 970 Blowing Rock Boulevard NE, Lenoir NC 28645; 828-754-2090
Days Inn: (Motel) 206 Blowing Rock Boulevard, Lenoir NC 28645; 828-754-0731
Irish Rose Bed & Breakfast: (B&B) 1344 Harper Ave. NW, Lenoir NC 28645; 828-758-2323

Little Switzerland

Little Switzerland is an unincorporated community in Mitchell County, and was formed in 1909 on eleven hundred acres surveyed from the top of Grassy Mountain by the "Switzerland Company." It began as a private resort on the Blue Ridge Parkway and continues today as a primarily summer vacation destination.

The elevations in the Little Switzerland area range from 3200 feet in the village to 4000 feet at the top of Grassy Mountain, offer incredible views of Mt. Mitchell to the west, Table Rock, Hawksbill and Grandfather Mountain to the east, and the valleys of the South Toe, Turkey Cove and the bustling Catawba. Little Switzerland was named because of its sweeping panoramas of deep valleys and distant ranges resembling those of the foothills of the Swiss Alps.

Location: Northern Mountains, 2 hours east of Asheville

County: McDowell and Mitchell Counties: 26 Crimson Laurel Circle, Bakersville NC 28705; 828-688-3295

Elevation and Population: 3,500 feet, 200+

County Visitor/Welcome Center Website: Mitchell County Visitor Center In Museum of North Carolina Minerals, Milepost 331, Blue Ridge Parkway, Spruce Pine NC 28777; 800-227-3912

County Chamber of Commerce: Mitchell County Chamber of Commerce 11 Crystal St., Spruce Pine NC 28777; 828-765-9033

Newspaper: Mitchell News-Journal 291 Locust Ave., Spruce Pine 28777; 828-765-2071

High School: Mitchell High School, 416 Ledger School Rd., Bakersville NC 28705; 8280-688-2101

Area Natural Attractions: Blue Ridge Parkway, Pisgah National Forest

Area Cultural Attractions: Emerald Village, Museum of North Carolina Minerals, North Carolina Mining Museum, Orchard at Altapass

Recommended Restaurants: (For a complete list of all restaurants visit ashevilleguide book.com

- **Cavern Tavern at the Skyline Village Inn:** (American) Skyline Village Inn, 12255 Hwy. 226A, Little Switzerland NC 28749; 828-994-0027
- **Switzerland Café:** (American) 9440 Hwy. 226A, Little Switzerland NC 28749; 828-765-5289

Recommended Places To Stay: (For a complete list of all accommodations visit ashe villeguidebook.com

- **Alpine Inn:** (Country Inn) 8576 Hwy. 226A, Little Switzerland NC 28749; 877-765-5380
- **Big Lynn Lodge:** (Country Lodge) Hwy. 226A, Little Switzerland NC 28749; 800-654-5232
- **Skyline Village Inn:** (Village Inn) 12255 Hwy. 226A, Little Switzerland NC 28749; 828-994-0027
- **Switzerland Inn:** (Country Inn) 86 High Ridge Rd., Little Switzerland NC 28749; 800-654-4026

Long View

Long View is a small city located primarily in Catawba County in the foothills of Western North Carolina and adjacent to the much larger city of Hickory. Long View was incorporated in 1907, and part of it also extends into nearby Burke County. Long View is primarily a residential community and is continuous with Hickory, where most Long View residents work. It has an outstanding Recreation Center for public use which is located on 2nd Ave., with nearby facilities that include a playground for children, walking track, tennis courts and a ball field. Long View also is home to a number of businesses of note, including the industrial service Maple Springs Laundry, and furniture companies Dr.exel Heritage and Century Furniture. The Hickory Regional Airport is located in the Long View area and the city is also close to the home field of the Hickory Crawdads, a Class A minor league baseball team.

Location: Foothills, 1 hour and 15 minutes east of Asheville
City Government Center: 2404 1st Ave. SW, Long View NC 28602; 828-322-3921
County: Catawba County: County Offices, 100-A South West Blvd., Newton NC 28658; 828-465-8200
Elevation and Population: 1,155 feet, 4,700+
County Visitor/Welcome Center: Catawba County Visitor Information Center, 1055 Southgate Corporate Park SW, Hickory NC 28602; 828-328-6111
County Chamber of Commerce: Catawba County Chamber of Commerce, 1055 Southgate Corporate Park SW, Hickory NC 28602; 828-328-6111
Newspapers: The Claremont Courier, 3283 White Oak Court, Claremont NC 28610; 828-320-8450 and the Hickory Daily Record, 1100 Park Place, Hickory NC 28603; 828-322-4510
High Schools: Hickory High School, 1234 3rd St. NE, Hickory NC 28601; 828-322-5860 and East Burke High School, 3695 East Burke Blvd., Connelly Springs NC 28612; 828-397-5541
Area Major Festivals: Catawba Valley Pottery Festival (Mar.)
Area Natural Attractions: Pisgah National Forest, South Mountains State Park
Area Cultural Attractions: Bunker Hill Covered Bridge, Catawba County Museum of History, Catawba Science Center, Harper House/Hickory History Center, Hickory Furniture Mart, Hickory Motor Speedway, Hickory Museum of Art, Hiddenite Center, Historic Murray's Mill
Recommended Restaurants: (For a complete list of all restaurants visit ashevilleguide book.com

No restaurants currently available in Long View. *See* Hickory

Recommended Places To Stay: (For a complete list of all accommodations visit ashe villeguidebook.com

No accommodations currently available in Long View. *See* Hickory

Maggie Valley

Maggie Valley is a well-known tourist-oriented village that occupies a lush green valley in Haywood County and gets its name from Maggie Mae Setzer. Her father, John "Jack" Sidney

Setzer, founded the area's first post office and named it after Maggie, one of his daughters. The main street through town is lined with craft, antique and gift shops, campgrounds, motels and restaurants. Some of the more popular outdoor activities in Maggie Valley are whitewater rafting, horseback riding, and skiing and snowboarding in the winter. Maggie Valley, with its central location in the mountains, has a lot to offer visitors. The Great Smoky Mountains National Park and the Blue Ridge Parkway are both nearby and the surrounding Pisgah National Forest also offers many choices for exploring the surrounding mountains. The oldest ski resort in North Carolina, the Cataloochee Ski Area, is also located in Maggie Valley.

Maggie Valley is home to Eaglenest Entertainment, a music venue featuring regional and national performers. For automotive buffs, the Wheels Thru Time Museum is an obligatory stop on your itinerary. Maggie Valley hosts a number of festivals, the best known are the Great Smoky Mountain Trout Festival and the Maggie Valley Summer Arts & Craft Show.

Location: Western Mountains, 45 minutes west of Asheville
Town Hall: 3987 Soco Rd., Maggie Valley NC 28751; 828-926-0866
Website: townofmaggievalley.com
County: Haywood County: County Offices, 215 North Main St., Waynesville NC 28786; 828-452-6625
Elevation and Population: 3,020 feet, 600+
Visitor/Welcome Center: Maggie Valley Visitors Bureau and Visitor Center, 2511 Soco Rd., Maggie Valley NC 28751; 800-624-4431
City Chamber of Commerce: Maggie Valley Visitors Bureau, 2511 Soco Rd., Maggie Valley NC 28751; 800-624-4431
County Chamber of Commerce: Greater Haywood County Chamber of Commerce: 591 North Main St., Waynesville NC 28786; 828-456-3021
Newspaper: The Mountaineer, 220 North Main St., Waynesville NC 28786; 828-452-0661
High School: Tuscola High School, 564 Tuscola School Rd., Waynesville NC 28786; 828-456-2408
Area Major Festivals: Great Smoky Mountain Trout Festival (May), Maggie Valley Summer Arts and Craft Show (Jul.)
Area Natural Attractions: Blue Ridge Parkway, Great Smoky Mountains National Park, Pisgah National Forest
Area Cultural Attractions: Cherokee Indian Reservation, HART-Haywood Arts Regional Theatre, Harrah's Cherokee Casino and Hotel, Wheels Thru Time Museum
Recommended Restaurants: (For a complete list of all restaurants visit ashevilleguidebook.com

Guayabitos: (Mexican) 3422 Soco Rd., Maggie Valley NC 28751; 828-926-7777
J. Arthur's Restaurant: (American-Fine Dining) 2843 Soco Rd., Maggie Valley NC 28751; 828-926-1817
Joey's Pancake House: (Breakfast) 4309 Soco Rd., Maggie Valley NC 28751; 828-926-0212
Rendezvous Restaurant: (American) Maggie Valley Inn, 70 Soco Rd., Maggie Valley NC 28751; 828-926-0201

Snappy's Italian Restaurant: (Italian) 2769 Soco Rd., Maggie Valley NC 28751; 828-926-6126

Recommended Places To Stay: (For a complete list of all accommodations visit asheville guidebook.com

Best Western-Mountainbrook Inn: (Motel) 3811 Soco Rd., Maggie Valley NC 28751; 800-213-1914

Brooksong B&B: (B&B) 252 Living Waters Lane, Maggie Valley NC 28751; 866-926-5409

Cataloochee Ranch: (Resort-Guest Ranch) 119 Ranch Rd., Maggie Valley NC 28751; 828-926-1401

Comfort Inn: (Motel) 3282 Soco Rd., Maggie Valley NC 28751; 866-926-9106

Jonathan Creek Inn and Creekside Villas: (Motel, Villas) 4324 Soco Rd., Maggie Valley NC 28751; 800-577-7812

Maggie Valley Creekside Lodge: (Country Lodge) 2716 Soco Rd., Maggie Valley NC 28751; 800-621-1260

Maggie Valley Inn & Conference Center: (Hotel) 70 Soco Rd., Maggie Valley NC 28751; 866-926-0201

Ramada by Wyndam: (Motel) 4048 Soco Rd., Maggie Valley NC 28751; 800-305-6703

Timberwolf Creek Bed & Breakfast: (B&B) 391 Johnson Branch Rd., Maggie Valley NC 28751; 888-525-4218

Maiden

Maiden, incorporated in 1883, is a small town located primarily in Catawba County in the foothills of Western North Carolina. Part of the township extends also into adjacent Lincoln County. Local historians agree that Maiden was named after Maiden Creek, and in the early days the township was the site of a cotton mill and also became a trading center for the region. Maiden is noted for its enthusiastic support of the local Maiden High School Blue Devils football team, and is known as "The Biggest Little Football Town in the World." While that may not be completely true, it is a true reflection of the great vitality and home-town spirit of the residents of Maiden. Over the years the city has enjoyed a large industrial base, and continues to do so today. A number of textile and furniture manufacturing companies, typical of the greater Hickory area, call Maiden home. Maiden has a number of parks and recreational facilities. These include the superb Recreation Center located on East Klutz St. that is open to the general public, and the Maiden Municipal Park. The Recreation Center facilities include a gym, banquet room, classrooms, softball complex, playgrounds, picnic shelters and a walking trail. Maiden has an annual Christmas Parade held the Sat after Thanksgiving and a spring festival, Springfest, held every May.

Location: Foothills, 1 hour and 15 minutes east of Asheville
Town Hall: 113 West Main St., Maiden NC 28650; 828-428-5010
Website: maidennc.com
County: Catawba County: County Offices, 100-A South West Blvd., Newton NC 28658; 828-465-8201

Elevation and Population: 899 feet, 3,300+

County Visitor/Welcome Center: Catawba County Visitor Information Center, 1055 Southgate Corporate Park SW, Hickory NC 28602; 828-328-6111

County Chamber of Commerce: Catawba County Chamber of Commerce, 1055 Southgate Corporate Park SW, Hickory NC 28602; 828-328-6111

Newspapers: The Claremont Courier, 3283 White Oak Court, Claremont NC 28610; 828-320-8450 and the Hickory Daily Record, 1100 Park Place, Hickory NC 28603; 828-322-4510

High Schools: Maiden High School, 600 West Main St., Maiden NC 28650; 828-428-8197

Area Major Festivals: Christmas Parade (Nov.), Catawba Valley Pottery Festival (Mar.), Springfest (May)

Area Natural Attractions: Pisgah National Forest, South Mountains State Park

Area Cultural Attractions: Bunker Hill Covered Bridge, Catawba County Museum of History, Catawba Science Center, Harper House/Hickory History Center, Hickory Furniture Mart, Hickory Motor Speedway, Hickory Museum of Art, Hiddenite Center, Historic Murray's Mill

Recommended Restaurants: (For a complete list of all restaurants visit ashevilleguide book.com

Brookwood Café & Catering: (American) 202 Providence Mill Rd., Maiden NC 28650; 828-428-8944

Recommended Places To Stay: (For a complete list of all accommodations visit ashe villeguidebook.com

No accommodations currently available in Maiden. *See* **Hickory**

Marion

Marion is the county seat of McDowell County and has as its motto "where Main St. meets the mountains". The motto is reinforced by Mount Ida, the dominant feature of the landscape in downtown. Marion is a thriving small city located on the eastern edge of the mountains along the Catawba River Basin and is home to many small industries including those that manufacture medical supplies, lumber and paper products, electronics and transportation equipment, tools, apparel, textiles and furniture.

Marion was planned and built on land selected by the first McDowell County Commissioners on Mar. 14, 1844 at the Historic Carson House on Buck Creek. It was not until 1845, however, that the official name of Marion was sanctioned as the county seat by the state legislature. The name of Marion came from Francis Marion, the American Revolutionary War hero, known as the "Swamp Fox" and the man upon whom the movie "The Patriot" was based.

The city is home to a number of historic buildings open to the public, including the Historic Carson House, the Joseph McDowell House built in 1787, and the Marion Depot, the oldest surviving depot on the Western Rail Line. Nearby Lake James State Park is only minutes away and is a popular recreational attraction for both residents and visitors alike. Between 1804 and 1827, McDowell County contributed to North Carolina's gold legacy as the nation's leader in gold production. There are still opportunities for visitors to pan for gold in the Marion area.

Location: Foothills, 45 minutes east of Asheville
Town Hall: 194 North Main St., Marion NC 28752; 828-652-3551
Website: marionnc.org
County: McDowell County: County Offices, 21 South Main St., Marion NC 28752; 828-652-7121
Elevation and Population: 1,395 feet, 8000+
County Tourism Development: McDowell Tourism Development, Historic Depot, 25 Hwy. 70 West, Old Fort NC 28762; 888-233-6111
County Visitor/Welcome Center: McDowell County Visitor Center, 1170 West Tate St., Marion NC 28752; 828-652-4240
County Chamber of Commerce: McDowell Chamber of Commerce, 1170 West Tate St., Marion NC 28752; 828-652-4240
Newspaper: The McDowell News, 136 Logan St., Marion NC 28752; 828-652-3313
Movie Theatres: McDowell Twin Cinemas, 1240 North Main St., Marion NC 28752; 828-652-8368
High School: McDowell High School, 600 McDowell High Dr., Marion NC 28752; 828-652-7920
Colleges and Universities: McDowell Technical Community College, 54 College Dr., Marion NC 28752; 828-652-6021
Hospitals: McDowell Hospital, 430 Rankin Dr., Marion NC 28752; 828–659-5000
Area Major Festivals: Mountain Glory Festival (Oct.), North Carolina Gold Festival (May)
Area Natural Attractions: Lake James State Park, Linville Caverns
Area Cultural Attractions: Historic Carson House, Joseph McDowell House, McDowell Arts Council Association Gallery, Mountain Gateway Museum and Heritage Center
Recommended Restaurants: (For a complete list of all restaurants visit ashevilleguidebook.com

- **Bruce's Fabulous Foods:** (Café) 63 South Main St., Marion NC 28752; 828-659-8023
- **Countryside Barbeque:** (BBQ) 2070 Rutherford Rd., Marion NC 28752; 828-652-4885
- **Eddie's Pizza & Pasta:** (Pizza-Italian) 1284 Rutherford Rd., Marion NC 28752; 828-652-4777
- **Jalapeno's Fresh Grill:** (Mexican) 1582 Rutherford Rd., Marion NC 28752; 828-652-5154

Recommended Places To Stay: (For a complete list of all accommodations visit ashevilleguidebook.com

- **Comfort Inn:** (Motel) 178 Hwy. 70 West, Marion NC 28752; 877–424-6423
- **Hampton Inn:** (Motel) 3560 US 221 South, Marion NC 28752; 800–426-7866
- **The Cottages at Spring Farm House:** (Cottages-Eco Retreat) 219 Haynes Rd., Marion NC 28752; 877-738-9798

Mars Hill

Mars Hill is a small college town perched on a hill a few miles north of Asheville. Dominated by the Mars Hill College campus, this quaint village is surrounded by picturesque rolling mountains and valleys. The college, a Christian liberal arts school, is the oldest educational institution in North Carolina and attracts students from all across America. Wolf Ridge Ski Slopes, the closest ski resort to Asheville, is also found on the outskirts of Mars Hill. Mars Hill is also known for its rich music and crafts heritage. Renowned musicologist Bascom Lamar Lunsford, founder of the Mountain Dance and Folk Festival, grew up here and brought international recognition to the region's traditional mountain music. Every autumn the Heritage Festival celebrates mountain crafts, arts, and music, and highlights the town's role as the historic center of the clogging dance tradition.

Location: Central Mountains, 30 minutes northwest of Asheville
Town Hall: 280 North Main St., Mars Hill NC 28754; 828-689-2301
Website: townofmarshill.org
County: Madison County: County Offices, 2 North Main St., Marshall NC 28753; 828-649-2854
Elevation and Population: 2,325 feet, 2,000+
County Visitor/Welcome Center: Madison County Visitors Center, 56 South Main St., Mars Hill NC 28754; 877-262-3476, 828-680-9031
County Chamber of Commerce: Madison County Chamber of Commerce, 56 South Main St., Mars Hill NC 28754; 828-689-9351
Newspaper: News-Record and Sentinel 58 Back St., Marshall NC 28753; 828-649-1075
High School: Madison High School, 5740 US Hwy. 25/70, Marshall NC 28753; 828-649-2876
Colleges and Universities: Mars Hill College, 100 Athletic St., Mars Hill NC 28754; 866-642-4968
Area Major Festivals: Bascom Lamar Lunsford Music Festival (Oct.), Madison County Heritage Festival (Oct.)
Area Natural Attractions: Appalachian Scenic National Trail, French Broad River, Pisgah National Forest, Max Patch
Area Cultural Attractions: Southern Appalachian Repertory Theatre, Rural Life Museum
Recommended Restaurants: (For a complete list of all restaurants visit ashevilleguidebook.com

The Original Papa Nicks: (Pizza) 15 College St., Mars Hill NC 28754; 828-689-8566

Recommended Places To Stay: (For a complete list of all accommodations visit ashevilleguidebook.com

Comfort Inn North of Asheville: (Motel) 167 J. F. Robinson Lane, Mars Hill NC 28754; 828-689-9000

The Bald Mountain House at the Wolf Laurel Resort: (Country Inn) 85 Woodfern Lane, Mars Hill NC 28754; 866-680-9329

Marshall

Located right on the beautiful French Broad River, Marshall, the county seat of Madison County, is one of the most picturesque villages in all of Western North Carolina. The village has a rich history, with the Buncombe County Turnpike passing through it in colonial days, as the location of notorious Civil War events, and as the hub of Madison County commerce for many years. A fun place to visit, Marshall, like other true mountain towns, retains much of its past and is like stepping back into time. There is a good selection of stores and restaurants, and an historic 1906 Neo-Classical Revival courthouse. Marshall's location along the river is a great jumping-off place to further adventures, including whitewater rafting on the river.

Location: Central Mountains, 45 minutes northwest of Asheville
Town Hall: 180 South Main St., Marshall NC 28753; 828-649-3031
Website: townofmarshall.org
County: Madison County: County Offices, 2 North Main St., Marshall NC 28753; 828-649-2854
Elevation and Population: 1,920 feet, 900+
County Visitor/Welcome Center: Madison County Visitors Center, 56 South Main St., Mars Hill NC 28754; 877-262-3476, 828-680-9031
County Chamber of Commerce: Madison County Chamber of Commerce, 56 South Main St., Mars Hill NC 28754; 828-689-9351
Newspaper: News-Record and Sentinel 58 Back St., Marshall NC 28753; 828-649-1075
High School: Madison High School, 5740 US Hwy. 25/70, Marshall NC 28753; 828-649-2876
Area Major Festivals: Hot Doggett 100 Cycling Tour (Jul.), Madison County Fair (Aug.)
Area Natural Attractions: Appalachian Scenic National Trail, French Broad River, Pisgah National Forest, Max Patch
Recommended Restaurants: (For a complete list of all restaurants visit ashevilleguidebook.com

Zuma Coffee: (Coffee House) 10 South Main Street, Marshall NC 28753; 828-649-1617

Recommended Places To Stay: (For a complete list of all accommodations visit ashevilleguidebook.com

Bend of Ivy Lodge: (Country Lodge) 3717 Bend of Ivy Rd., Marshall NC 28753; 888-658-0505
Marshall House Inn: (B&B) 100 Hill St., Marshall NC 28753; 828-649-9205
RiverDance: (B&B) 179 Deer Leap, Marshall NC 28753; 847-809-3098

Morganton

Morganton, the county seat, is the largest city in Burke County and encompasses an area of over nineteen square miles. It was named after Revolutionary War General Daniel Morgan. The community is located on Interstate 40 and is bisected by US 70 and 64 and North Carolina Hwy. 181, 18, and 126.

Morganton offers big city services wrapped in small town charm while embracing technology, new development and progressive thinking. The heart of Morganton is its vibrant downtown filled with restaurants, galleries, clothiers and specialty shops. One of the must-see art galleries downtown is the Burke Arts Council Jailhouse Gallery, located at 115 E. Meeting St. The City of Morganton's 1,058-seat CoMMA Municipal Auditorium at 401 South College St. also showcases a wide variety of ever changing entertainment ranging from Broadway performances to the best in Celtic music and dance. One of the artistic highlights of the Auditorium is the Ben Long Fresco of the Nine Muses on the ceiling of the atrium.

Major festivals include The Red, White and Bluegrass Festival that brings the best in bluegrass to Morganton's Catawba Meadows Park every summer. Residents also enjoy great music and the family-friendly atmosphere of Morganton's TGIF Free Fri night concerts during the summer. Each Sep. the annual two-day Historic Morganton Festival attracts upwards of 40,000 people. Craft and food booths line the downtown streets and well known musical entertainers offer free concerts. Another unique event in Morganton is the Festival of Lights in Nov., when the city kicks off the Christmas season.

The city is also home to the Morganton Farmer's Market, located at 300 Beach St., open Sat mornings from May to Oct., and a number of outstanding local cultural attractions. These include the History Museum of Burke County, the North Carolina School For The Deaf Museum, the Old Burke County Courthouse Heritage Museum, Quaker Meadows Plantation, the Morganton 1916 Railroad Depot and the Senator Sam J. Ervin Jr. Museum.

Near Morganton lies Brown Mountain, home to a mysterious phenomenon referred to as the Brown Mountain Lights. Rising to an elevation of only 2,600 feet, Brown Mountain has been at the center of a mystery since the earliest days of recorded history. For hundreds of years, unexplained lights have been seen on the mountain to the astonishment of all that have seen them.

Morganton has a superb greenway system. The Catawba River Greenway Park offers year-round biking, jogging and strolling, canoeing and picnicking, and features children's playgrounds, fishing piers, a 1200-foot multilevel observation deck and a 170-foot bridge that crosses Silver Creek.

Location: Blue Ridge Foothills, 1 hour east of Asheville
Town Offices: 305 East Union St., Ste A100, Morganton NC 28655; 828-437-8863
Website: ci.morganton.nc.us
County: Burke County: Burke County Government Center, 200 Avery Ave., Morganton NC 28680; 828-439-4340
Elevation and Population: 1,182 feet, 17,000+
County Visitor/Welcome Center: Burke County Visitor Center, 110 East Meeting St., Morganton NC 28655; 828-433-6793
County Chamber of Commerce: Burke County Chamber of Commerce, 110 East Meeting St., Morganton NC 28655; 828-437-3021
Newspaper: The News Herald, 301 Collett St., Morganton NC 28655; 828-437-2161

Movie Theatres: Marquee Cinemas Mimosa 7, 103 South Green St., Morganton NC 28655; 828-437-8084

High School: Freedom High School, 511 Independence Blvd., Morganton NC 28655; 828-433-1310 and Robert L. Patton High School, 701 Enola Rd., Morganton NC 28655; 828-433-3000

Colleges and Universities: Western Piedmont Community College, 1001 Burkemont Ave., Morganton NC 28655; 828-438-6000

Hospitals: Grace Hospital, 2201 South Sterling St., Morganton NC 28655; 828-580-5000

Area Major Festivals: Red, White and Bluegrass Festival (Jun.–Jul.), Historic Morganton Festival (Sep.), Festival of Lights (Nov.)

Area Natural Attractions: Brown Mountain Lights, Lake James State Park, South Mountains State Park

Area Cultural Attractions: Burke Arts Council Jailhouse Gallery, History Museum of Burke County, North Carolina School For The Deaf Museum, Old Burke County Courthouse Heritage Museum, Quaker Meadows Plantation, Morganton 1916 Railroad Depot, Senator Sam J. Ervin Jr. Museum

Recommended Restaurants: (For a complete list of all restaurants visit ashevilleguidebook.com

Abele's: (Southern) 2156 South Sterling St., Morganton NC 28655; 828-433-5400

Butch's BBQ & Breakfast: (BBQ) 1234 Burkemont Ave., Morganton NC 28655; 828-432-5040

Friday Friends: (American) 315 Sanford Dr., Morganton NC 28655; 828-430–3024

Grind Café: (Coffeehouse-Café) 141 West Union St., Morganton NC 28655; 828-430–4343

Judge's Riverside Restaurant: (American) 128 Greenlee Ford Rd., Morganton NC 28680; 828-433-5798

Limbertwig Café: (Café) 120 North Sterling St., Morganton NC 28655; 828-438-4634

Pat's Snack Bar: (American) 124 Sterling St., Morganton NC 28655; 828-437-5744

Timberwoods Family Restaurant: (American) 1301 Bethel Rd., Morganton NC 28655; 828-433-1767

Recommended Places To Stay: (For a complete list of all accommodations visit ashevilleguidebook.com

Fairway Oaks Bed & Breakfast: (B&B) 4640 Plantation Dr., Morganton NC 28655; 828-584-7677

Comfort Inn and Suites: (Motel) 1273 Burkemont Ave., Morganton NC 28655; 828-430–4000

Days Inn & Suites by Wyndham: (Motel) 1100 Burkemont Ave., Morganton NC 28655; 828-430–8778

Hampton Inn: (Motel) 115 Bush Dr., Morganton NC 28655; 828–434-2000

Quality Inn: (Motel) 2400 South Sterling St., Morganton NC 28655; 828-437-0171

The Inn at Glen Alpine: (B&B) 105 Davis St., Glen Alpine NC 28628; 828-584-9264

Murphy

Murphy, founded in 1835, is the county seat of Cherokee County and is the westernmost county seat in North Carolina. It is closer to the capitals of six other states (Georgia, Alabama, Tennessee, South Carolina, Kentucky, and West Virginia) than to Raleigh, the capital of North Carolina, and occupies a serene corner of the mountains highlighted by hundreds of creeks, waterfalls and deep lush forests. This delightful mountain city offers to visitors a quaint downtown for shopping, the historic Murphy County Courthouse, a public library and an historical museum, the Cherokee County Historical Museum. Originally named Huntington, the town later became Murphy, named after Archibald D. Murphy, state senator and advocate of education in Western North Carolina. In 1851 Murphy became the county seat.

Murphy is also home to an historic movie theater, the Henn Theater, built in 1934 and still showing movies. This little single screen, 174-seat theater combines modern cinema technology with a classic setting. Another historic highlight of the village is the L&N Depot (circa 1887), a remnant of the Southern and Louisville & Nashville railroad, which ran through Murphy prior to 1974. The Murphy Pyramid (circa 1930) is also of interest, and is a wooden pyramid erected by Hitchcock Coit in honor of her grandfather, ARS Hunter, who was the first white settler in the area.

Cherokee County has several unique communities sprinkled throughout its mountains and valleys, the best known is the nearby crafts-oriented community of Brasstown which is home to the famous John C. Campbell Folk School.

Location: Western Mountains, 2.5 hours west of Asheville
City Offices: 5 Wofford St., Murphy NC 28906, 828-837-2510
Website: townofmurphync.com
County: Cherokee County,75 Peach St., Murphy NC 28906; 828-837-5527
Elevation and Population: 1,604 feet, 1,600+
County Visitor/Welcome Center: Cherokee County Welcome Center, 805 West Hwy. 64, Murphy NC 28906; 828-837-2242
County Chamber of Commerce: Cherokee County Chamber of Commerce, 805 West Hwy. 64, Murphy NC 28906; 828-837-2242
Newspaper: Cherokee Scout, 89 Sycamore St., Murphy NC 28906; 828-837-5122
Movie Theatres: Henn Theater, 110 Tennessee St., Murphy NC 28906; 828-837-2618
High School: Murphy High School, 234 High School Circle, Murphy NC 28906; 828-837-2426 and Hiwassee Dam High School, 267 Blue Eagle Circle, Murphy NC 28906; 828-644-5916
Colleges and Universities: Tri-County Community College, 21 Campus Circle, Murphy NC 28906; 828-837-6810
Hospitals: Murphy Medical Center: 3990 East Hwy. 64 Alternate, Murphy NC 28906; 828-837-8161
Area Major Festivals: Spring Festival (Jun.), Heritage Walk and Festival (Jul.), Hometown Christmas Celebration Parade and Christmas Festival (Dec.)
Area Natural Attractions: Chatuge Lake, Joyce Kilmer Memorial Forest, Lake Santeetlah, Nantahala National Forest, Nantahala River

Area Cultural Attractions: Cherokee County Historical Museum, Great Smoky Mountains Railroad, John C. Campbell Folk School, LandN Depot, Murphy Pyramid

Recommended Restaurants: (For a complete list of all restaurants visit ashevilleguide book.com

- **Brother's Restaurant:** (American) 1466 Andrews Rd., Murphy NC 28906; 828-835-9100
- **Chevelles 66:** (Grill) 66 Hiwassee St., Murphy NC 28906; 828-835-7001
- **Herb's Pit Bar-B-Que:** (BBQ) 15735 Hwy. 64 West , Murphy NC 28906; 828-494-5397
- **Murphy's Chophouse:** (American-Fine Dining) 130 Valley River Ave., Murphy NC 28906; 828-835-3287
- **ShoeBooties Café:** (Café) 25 Peachtree St., Murphy NC 28906; 828-837-4589
- **The Daily Grind & Wine:** (Café-Coffeehouse) 46 Andrews Rd., Murphy NC 28906; 828-837-3400

Recommended Places To Stay: (For a complete list of all accommodations visit ashe villeguidebook.com

- **Alpaca Ranch at Cobb Creek Cabins:** (Cabins) 106 Cobb Circle, Murphy NC 28906; 828-837-0270
- **Angels Landing Inn Bed & Breakfast:** (B&B) 94 Campbell St., Murphy NC 28906; 828-835-8877
- **Hampton Inn:** (Motel) 1550 Andrews Rd., Murphy NC 28906; 828–837-1628

Newland

Newland, incorporated in 1913, is the county seat of Avery County and has the distinction of being the highest county seat east of the Mississippi. A recently remodeled classical courthouse overlooks a quaint town square, bordered by shops and churches and a memorial to Avery County veterans. Newland is also home to the Avery County Historical Museum. Historically, Newland's original name was "Old Fields of Toe" because it is located in a broad flat valley and is at the headwaters of the Toe River. It was also a mustering place for Civil War troops. Newland today is also known for the many Christmas tree farms which thrive in the surrounding mountains.

The nearby little community of Linville, located at the foot of Grandfather Mountain, takes its name from the Linville River. Linville was originally developed as a summer resort where families from the North Carolina Piedmont could escape the heat and mosquitoes that characterize summers in the south. Nestled at the confluence of Hwy. 221 and 183, Linville Falls is a convenient stopping point for travelers from all directions. Linville Falls is named after a beautiful two-tiered waterfall located nearby in Linville Gorge.

Location: Northern Mountains, 2 hours east of Asheville

Town Offices: 301 Cranberry St., Newland NC 28657; 828-733-2023

Website: newlandgov.com

County: Avery County: County Administrative Building, 175 Linville St., Newland NC 28657; 828-733-8202

Elevation and Population: 3,621 feet, 700+

County Chamber of Commerce: Avery County Chamber of Commerce: 4501 Tynecastle Hwy., Unit #2, Banner Elk NC 28604; 800-972-2183

Newspaper: The Mountain Times PO Box 1815, Boone NC 28607; 828–264-6397

High School: Avery County High School, 401 High School Rd., Newland NC 28657; 828-733-0151

Colleges and Universities: Mayland Community College, Avery Campus, 785 Cranberry St., Newland NC 28657; 828-733-5883

Area Major Festivals: Avery County Christmas Parade (Dec.)

Area Natural Attractions: Blue Ridge Parkway, Grandfather Mountain, Linville Caverns, Linville Gorge.

Area Cultural Attractions: Avery County Historical Museum Banner House Museum, Beech Mountain Resort, Crossnore Fine Arts Gallery, Horn in the West, Mast General Store, Mystery Hill, Orchard at Altapass, Tweetsie Railroad

Recommended Restaurants: (For a complete list of all restaurants visit ashevilleguide book.com

Carolina Barbeque: (Barbeque) 500 Pineola St, Newland, NC 28657; 828-737-0700

Fabio's Restaurant: (Italian) 106 Pineola St., Newland NC 28646; 828-733-1314

Recommended Places To Stay: (For a complete list of all accommodations visit ashe villeguidebook.com

Newton

Newton is located in Catawba County in the foothills of Western North Carolina and is the county seat. Selected as the seat in 1843, Newton was incorporated in 1855. Today it is the second largest city in the county after Hickory. The city has experienced a steady rate of growth since 1970, expanding from 7,600 residents to the current population of over 13,600. Newton has a number of qualities that have contributed to this growth-challenging places to work, a low cost of living, diverse cultures, a strong array of recreational opportunities and a vibrant arts community. The city has earned a number of awards over the years, including seven Public Power Awards of Excellence in 2009.

Newton is home to the Catawba County Museum of History, located in the historic Catawba County Courthouse, an imposing National Register Renaissance Revival structure built in 1924. Other attractions in the area include the historic Newton Depot, the Newton-Conover Auditorium, the Green Room Community Theatre and the Hickory Motor Speedway. The City Parks & Recreation Department also maintain five parks that include numerous ball fields, tennis courts, walking & jogging trails, picnic tables & shelters, a swimming pool and two recreational centers complete with gymnasiums and a fitness center. One of the more popular is the 27-acre Southside Park located on Hwy. 3212 Business South.

Location: Foothills, 1 hour and 15 minutes east of Asheville

Town Hall: 401 North Main Ave., Newton NC 28658; 828-695-4300

Website: newtonnc.gov

County: Catawba County: County Offices, 100-A South West Blvd., Newton NC 28658; 828-465-8201

Elevation and Population: 1,001 feet, 13,000+

County Visitor/Welcome Center: Catawba County Visitor Information Center, 1055 Southgate Corporate Park SW, Hickory NC 28602; 828-328-6111

County Chamber of Commerce: Catawba County Chamber of Commerce, 1055 Southgate Corporate Park SW, Hickory NC 28602; 828-328-6111

Newspapers: The Claremont Courier, 3283 White Oak Court, Claremont NC 28610; 828-320-8450;

Hickory Daily Record: 1100 Park Place, Hickory NC 28603; 828-322-4510 and The Observer News Enterprise, 309 North College Ave., Newton NC 28656; 828-464-0221

Movie Theatres: State Cinema, 117 North College St., Newton NC 28658; 828-464-2171

High Schools: Fred T. Foard High School, 3407 Plateau Rd., Newton NC 28658; 704-462-1496; Newton-Conover High School 338 West 15th St., Newton NC 28658; 828-465-0920 and Newton-Conover Science High School, 605 North Ashe Ave., Newton NC 28658; 828-464-3191

Area Major Festivals: MayFest (May), Soldiers Reunion (Aug.), Newton ArtFEST (Oct.), Catawba Valley Pottery Festival (Mar.), Newton Light Up The Town Celebration (Nov.)

Area Natural Attractions: Pisgah National Forest, South Mountains State Park

Area Cultural Attractions: Bunker Hill Covered Bridge, Catawba County Museum of History, Catawba Science Center, Green Room Community Theatre, Harper House/ Hickory History Center, Hickory Furniture Mart, Hickory Motor Speedway, Hickory Museum of Art, Hiddenite Center, Historic Murray's Mill, Historic Newton Depot

Recommended Restaurants: (For a complete list of all restaurants visit ashevilleguide book.com

Blue Moon Tavern: (Grill) 100 N Main Ave, Newton, NC 28658; 828-465-6900

Tosaka Authentic Japanese Cuisine: (Japanese) 2725 Northwest Boulevard, Newton NC 28658; 828-465-9977

Recommended Places To Stay: (For a complete list of all accommodations visit ashe villeguidebook.com

The Peacock Inn: (B&B) 1670 Southwest Boulevard, Newton NC 28658; 828-464-5780

North Wilkesboro

North Wilkesboro, located in Wilkes County, was founded in 1891 when the Norfolk and Southern Railroad build a line into Wilkes County that ended on the northern bank of the Yadkin River opposite Wilkesboro, the county seat. The town of North Wilkesboro quickly developed around the railroad tracks and became home to many furniture, textile and leather factories. Lowe's Foods, one of the southeast's largest supermarket chains, and Lowe's Home Improvement Warehouse both started in North Wilkesboro, the former in 1954 and the latter in 1946. North Wilkesboro is also home to the Wilkes Regional Medical Center, the major medical facility in Wilkes County and the historic Kleeberg Liberty Theatre, still in operation, on Main St.

Due to the town's proximity to the nearby Blue Ridge Mountains, North Wilkesboro for many years was nicknamed the "Key to the Blue Ridge". Nearby Stone Mountain State Park and W. Kerr Scott Dam and Reservoir make North Wilkesboro a perfect spot to visit while enjoying these great outdoor attractions. North Wilkesboro recently opened the Yadkin River Greenway. The Greenway contains biking, jogging, and walking trails which follow the Yadkin River and Reddies River for several miles between the towns of North Wilkesboro and Wilkesboro. One of the most popular spots on the Greenway is a 156-foot-long bridge which spans the Reddies River at its mouth, where it joins the Yadkin River.

The major festival for the city is the Brushy Mountain Apple Festival, which is held annually to celebrate the local apple harvest. It is one of the largest single-day arts and crafts festivals in the South. Stretching from the North Wilkesboro and Wilkesboro area toward Lenoir along Hwy. 268 is the historic "Happy Valley." Located on the banks of the Yadkin River, Happy Valley was so named by the early settlers who described the valley as "a place of beauty, peace and tranquility" and the name aptly remains. A number of attractions are in the valley, including Fort Defiance, the Chapel of Rest and Whippoorwill Academy and Village.

Location: Foothills, 2.5 hours east of Asheville

Town Hall: 832 Main St., North Wilkesboro NC 28659; 336-667-7129

Website: north-wilkesboro.com

County: Wilkes County: County Offices, 110 North St., Wilkesboro NC 28697; 336-651-7346

Elevation and Population: 1,016 feet, 4,200+

County Chamber of Commerce: Wilkes County Chamber of Commerce, 717 Main St., North Wilkesboro NC 28659; 336-838-8662

County Tourism Development: Wilkes County Tourism, 203 West Main St., Wilkesboro NC 28697; 336-838-3951

Newspaper: The Record, 911 Main St., North Wilkesboro NC 28659; 336-667-0134

Movie Theatres: Kleeberg Liberty Theatre, 816 Main St., North Wilkesboro NC 28659; 336-838-4561

High School: North Wilkes High School, 2986 Traphill Rd., Hays NC 28635; 336-957-8601

Hospitals: Wilkes Regional Medical Center, 1370 West D St., North Wilkesboro NC 28659; 336-651-8100

Area Major Festivals: MerleFest (April), Carolina In The Fall Festival (Sep.), Brushy Mountain Apple Festival (Oct.)

Area Natural Attractions: Rendezvous Mountain Educational State Forest, Stone Mountain State Park, W. Kerr Scott Dam and Reservoir, Yadkin River Greenway

Area Cultural Attractions: Ben Long Frescoes in St. Paul's Episcopal Church, Happy Valley, Old Wilkes Jail Museum, Whippoorwill Academy and Village, Wilkes Art Gallery, Wilkes Heritage Museum

Recommended Restaurants: (For a complete list of all restaurants visit ashevilleguide book.com

Branciforte's Brick Oven: (Italian) 810 Main St., North Wilkesboro NC 28659; 336-838-1110

Brushy Mountain Smokehouse and Creamery: (American) 201 Wilkesboro Boulevard, North Wilkesboro NC 28659; 336-667-9464

6th and Main: (American) 6th and Main, North Wilkesboro NC 28659; 336-903-1166

Recommended Places To Stay: (For a complete list of all accommodations visit asheville guidebook.com

SEE Wilkesboro Recommended Places To Stay

Old Fort

In existence as a village since 1869 and originally a fort built by the colonial militia before the Declaration of Independence, Old Fort was a settlement that served for many years as the western outpost of the early United States. In the center of town at 25 West Main St. is a hand-chiseled rose granite arrowhead, 14 feet tall, erected in 1930 to honor the peace finally achieved between the pioneer settlers and the Native Americans. At the unveiling, over 6,000 people attended including chiefs from both the Catawba and Cherokee tribes. These two tribes had never smoked a pipe of peace together until that day.

Old Fort is also known for its weekly Mountain Music Concerts, which draw a large audience and many musicians from the surrounding areas to Old Fort's downtown each Fri evening at 7. The performances are held in the Rockett Building on Main St. Other historic and cultural highlights include the Appalachian Artisan Society Gallery, which showcases the work of over 60 local craft persons and artists, Davidson's Fort, a replica of the original, Revolutionary War-era fort built in 1776, the Mountain Gateway Museum & Heritage Center and the Old Fort Railroad Museum.

Of interest, located just outside of Old Fort is the locally famous man-made Andrews Geyser. The geyser's water comes from a lake located on a mountain high above it, and comes with enough pressure to produce a stream of water 80 feet high.

Location: Foothills, 30 minutes east of Asheville

Town Hall: 38 South Catawba St., Old Fort NC 28762; 828-668-4244

Website: oldfort.org

County: McDowell County: County Offices, 600 McDowell Dr., Marion NC 28752; 828-652-7121

Elevation and Population: 1,447 feet, 900+

County Visitor/Welcome Center: McDowell Tourism Development, Historic Depot, 25 Hwy. 70 West, Old Fort NC 28762; 888-233-6111

City Chamber of Commerce: Old Fort Chamber of Commerce, 25 West Main St., Old Fort NC 28762; 828-668-7223

County Chamber of Commerce: McDowell Chamber of Commerce, 1170 West Tate St., Marion NC 28752; 828-652-4240

Newspaper: The McDowell News, 136 Logan St., Marion NC 28752; 828-652-3313

High School: McDowell High School, 334 South Main St., Marion NC 28752; 828-652-4535

Area Major Festivals: Pioneer Day (April), Oktoberfest (Oct.).

Area Natural Attractions: Andrews Geyser, Pisgah National Forest

Area Cultural Attractions: Davidson's Fort, Historic Carson House, Mountain Gateway Museum and Heritage Center, Old Fort Arrowhead Monument, Old Fort Railroad Museum, The Appalachian Artisan Society Gallery

Recommended Restaurants: (For a complete list of all restaurants visit ashevilleguide book.com

Whistle Stop Pizza & Subs: (Café) 27 West Main St., Old Fort NC 28762; 828-668-7676

Recommended Places To Stay: (For a complete list of all accommodations visit ashe villeguidebook.com

The Inn on Mill Creek: (B&B) 3895 Mill Creek Rd., Old Fort NC 28762; 828-668-1115

Robbinsville

Located at the far western end of the state, Robbinsville, the Graham County seat, was incorporated in 1893. Robbinsville is a delightful small town that is a welcome stop for visitors seeking recreation in the vast wilderness areas that surround it. The village is located in a region of Western North Carolina that contains hundreds of thousands of acres of wilderness and one that is home to some of the highest and most remote mountains east of the Mississippi. Two-thirds of Graham County is National Forest. The county is the home of Joyce Kilmer Memorial Forest and the Nantahala National Forest, and borders the Great Smoky Mountains National Park. Robbinsville, as county seat, is home to the Graham County Courthouse, an elegant building constructed of locally quarried quartzite.

Robbinsville is close to a number of mountain highways that are famous for their scenic beauty and challenging drives: the Cherohala Skyway and the Tail of the Dr.agon, considered by many to be one of the world's best motorcycling and sports car roads. This extraordinary stretch of highway has 318 curves in just 11 miles. Just a short distance from Robbinsville is the beautiful Lake Santeetlah, a pristine mountain lake that features 76 miles of mostly natural forested shoreline and is over 3,000 acres in size. Nearby 10,230–acre Fontana Lake with its world-famous dam is also a major tourist destination. Fontana Lake is the largest lake in Western North Carolina and offers visitors an abundance of recreational opportunities. The village of Fontana Lake is also home to the Graham County Museum of Prehistoric Relics.

Location: Western Mountains, 2.5 hours west of Asheville

County: Graham County: County Offices, 12 North Main St., Robbinsville NC 28771; 828-479-7961

Elevation and Population: 2,044 feet, 2000+

County Visitor/Welcome Center: Graham County Travel and Tourism Authority, 12 North Main St., Robbinsville NC 28771; 800-470-3790

Newspaper: The Graham Star, 774 Tallulah Rd., Robbinsville NC 28771; 828-479-3383

High School: Robbinsville High School, 301 Sweetwater Rd., Robbinsville NC 28771; 828-479-3330

Colleges and Universities: Tri-County Community College, Graham County Center, 145 Moose Branch Rd., Robbinsville NC 28771; 828-479-9256

Area Major Festivals: Graham County 4th of Jul. Celebration and Fireworks (Jul.)

Area Natural Attractions: Appalachian Scenic National Trail, Cherohala Skyway, Fontana Lake, Great Smoky Mountains National Park, Joyce Kilmer Memorial Forest, Lake Santeetlah, Nantahala National Forest, Slickrock Creek Wilderness Area, Tail of the Dragon

Area Cultural Attractions: Stecoah Valley Cultural Arts Center, Graham County Museum of Prehistoric Relics.

Recommended Restaurants: (For a complete list of all restaurants visit ashevilleguidebook.com

El Pacifico: (Mexcican) 429 Rodney Orr Bypass, Robbinsville, NC 28771; 828-479-8448

Lynn's Place: (American) 237 E Main St, Robbinsville, NC 28771; 828-479-9777

Snowbird Mountain Lodge: (American-Fine Dining) 4633 Santeetlah Rd., Robbinsville NC 28771; 800-941-9290

Recommended Places To Stay: (For a complete list of all accommodations visit asheville guidebook.com

Blue Waters Mountain Lodge: (Country Lodge) 292 Pine Ridge Rd., Robbinsville NC 28771; 888-828-3978

Snowbird Mountain Lodge: (Country Lodge) 4633 Santeetlah Rd., Robbinsville NC 28771; 800-941-9290

Rutherford College

The village of Rutherford College began in 1853, when a small private academy known as Owl Hollow School was located in the eastern part of Burke County. The school received funding from local resident John T. Rutherford which allowed it to expand. Prior to the Civil War, the school taught military tactics and philosophy but it was forced to close its doors when the Civil War began. It later reopened in 1871 as a four-year college. The town of Rutherford College, originally named Excelsior, was founded 1871 and today is a bedroom community with approximately 1,300 residents. It incorporated in 1977.

The town is bordered by Lake Rhodhiss on the north, and by Mineral Springs Mountain on the south, and is home to the Rutherford College Summer Festival, held on the first Sat in Aug. The main street, Malcolm Boulevard, runs for approximately three miles, with numerous homes, Methodist and Baptist churches, banks, pharmacies, doctor's clinics, a car dealership, convenience stores, and a post office.

Location: Foothills, 1 hour and 15 minutes east of Asheville

Town Offices: 980 Malcolm Blvd., Rutherford College NC 28761; 828-874-0333

Website: rutherfordcollegenc.us/index.html

County: Burke County: Burke County Government Center, 200 Avery Ave., Morganton NC 28680; 828-439-4340

Elevation and Population: 1178 feet, 1,300+

County Visitor/Welcome Center: Burke County Visitor Center, 110 East Meeting St., Morganton NC 28655; 828-433-6793

County Chamber of Commerce: Burke County Chamber of Commerce, 110 East Meeting St., Morganton NC 28655; 828-437-3021

Newspaper: The News Herald, 301 Collett St., Morganton NC 28655; 828-437-2161
High School: East Burke High School, 3695 East Burke Blvd., Connelly Springs NC 28612; 828-397-5541 and Jimmy C. Dr.aughn High School, 709 Lovelady Rd. NE, Valdese NC 28690; 828-879-4200
Area Major Festivals: Rutherford College Summer Festival (Aug.)
Area Natural Attractions: Brown Mountain Lights, Lake James State Park, South Mountains State Park
Area Cultural Attractions: History Museum of Burke County, North Carolina School For The Deaf Museum, Old Burke County Courthouse Heritage Museum, Quaker Meadows Plantation, Senator Sam J. Ervin Jr. Museum
Recommended Restaurants: (For a complete list of all restaurants visit ashevilleguide book.com

No recommended restaurants currently available in Rutherford College. *See* Morganton and Valdese.

Recommended Places To Stay: (For a complete list of all accommodations visit ashe villeguidebook.com

No accommodations currently available in Rutherford College. *See* Morganton and Valdese.

Rutherfordton

Rutherfordton, the county seat of Rutherford County, was established in 1787, and is one of the oldest towns in Western North Carolina. Both the county and the town were named after General Griffith Rutherford, a popular Western North Carolina politician and general during the Revolutionary War. During that war the corps of Patriots known as the Over Mountain Men marched through present-day Rutherfordton on their way to the Battle of King's Mountain. The Patriots defeated British troops under the command of Maj. Patrick Ferguson on Oct. 7, 1780.

Rutherfordton has managed to retain many of its historic buildings, and the downtown district is listed on the National Register of Historic Places. Rutherfordton is home to the only remaining cluster of antebellum houses and public structures in the southern foothills of North Carolina. These include 1849 St. John's Church and 1932 "Holly Hill" on North Main St., the 1830's Bechtler family residence on Sixth St., the Gothic-Revival Rucker-Eaves home (circa 1858–1870) on North Washington St. and the Bynum House on Sixth and North Washington St. The village center is home to the Rutherford County Courthouse and an eclectic selection of stores and restaurants. Rutherfordton is also home to an innovative hands-on children's museum, the KidSenses Children's InterACTIVE Museum and the Rutherford Hospital Museum.

Location: Foothills, 1 hour southeast of Asheville
Town Hall: 129 North Main St., Rutherfordton NC 28139; 828-287-3520
Website: rutherfordton.net
County: Rutherford County: County Offices, 289 North Main St., Rutherfordton NC 28139; 828-287-6045
Elevation and Population: 1075 feet, 4100+

County Visitor/Welcome Center: Rutherford County Tourism, 130 West 6th St., Forest City NC 28043; 800-849-5998

County Chamber of Commerce: Rutherford County Chamber of Commerce 162 North Main St., Rutherfordton NC 28139; 828-287-3090

Newspaper: The Daily Courier 601 Oak St., Forest City NC 28043; 828-245-6431

Movie Theatres: Retro Cinema 4 2270 US 221 South, Forest City NC 28043; 828-248-1670

High School: Chase High School, 1603 Chase High Rd., Forest City NC 28043; 828-245-7668

Hospitals: Rutherford Hospital, 288 South Ridgecrest Ave., Rutherfordton NC 28139; 828-286-5000

Area Major Festivals: Mayfest Festival (May), Hilltop Fall Festival (Oct.)

Area Natural Attractions: Chimney Rock Park, Lake Lure

Area Cultural Attractions: Bennett Classics Antique Auto Museum, KidSenses Children's InterACTIVE Museum, Rutherford County Farm Museum, Rutherford County Museum, Rutherford Hospital Museum

Recommended Restaurants: (For a complete list of all restaurants visit ashevilleguide book.com

Gregory's Original Restaurant: (American) 211 North Main St., Rutherfordton NC 28139; 828-287-2171

Mi Pueblito Mexican Restaurant: (Mexican) 139 South Washington St., Rutherfordton NC 28139; 828-286-2860

Recommended Places To Stay: (For a complete list of all accommodations visit ashe villeguidebook.com

Carrier Houses Bed & Breakfast: (B&B) 255 North Main St., Rutherfordton NC 28139; 800-835-7071

The Firehouse Inn: (Village Inn) 125 West First St., Rutherfordton NC 28139; 828-286-9030

Saluda

Saluda, situated in the foothills to the south of Asheville, is a town of old-fashioned charm and beauty, with sixteen of its buildings listed on the National Register. Many years ago, before the railroad and the town existed, this area was known as Pace's Gap, a crossroad for traders and herders. The Pace's Gap community included separated homesteads and a Dr.overs Inn. The roads were used by traders who carried goods and by people who herded livestock through Pace's Gap from the western towns and villages.

Nestled peacefully in the mountains, Saluda became a railroad stop on the way to Asheville from the lowlands and, to this day, the steep climb up the mountains is called the "Saluda Grade." The historic railroad district allows visitors a chance to catch a glimpse of local railroad history. Main St. is also a National Historic District and offers restaurants, galleries and a variety of small shops. Saluda's main festival is Coon Dog Days held each Jul.

A noteworthy local attraction is nearby Pearson's Falls, located off Hwy. 176 between Tryon and Saluda. This botanical preserve is comprised of 268 acres of native forest, spring-fed streams and a 1/4 mile trail to a 90 ft. waterfall. There are over 200 species of fern, flowering plants, algae and mosses in the wildflower preserve.

Location: Central Mountains, 45 minutes south of Asheville
Town Offices: PO Box 248, Saluda NC 28773; 828-749-2581
Website: cityofsaludanc.com
County: Polk County: County Offices, 40 Courthouse St., Columbus NC 28722; 828-894-3301
Elevation and Population: 2,060 feet, 575+
County Visitor/Welcome Center: Polk County Travel and Tourism 20 East Mills St., Columbus NC 28722; 800-440-7848
County Chamber of Commerce: Carolina Foothills Chamber of Commerce 2753 Lynn Rd., Ste A, Tryon NC 28782; 828-859-6236
Newspapers: Tryon Daily Bulletin 16 North Trade St., Tryon NC 28782; 828-859-9151 and Polk County News Journal PO Box 576, Columbus NC 28722; 864-457-3337
High School: Polk County High School, 1681 East NC Hwy. 108, Columbus NC 28722; 828-894-2525
Area Major Festivals: Saluda Arts Festival (May)
Area Natural Attractions: Pearson's Falls, Pisgah National Forest
Area Cultural Attractions: Foothills Equestrian Nature Center (FENCE), Polk County Courthouse, Polk County Historical Museum, Tryon Fine Arts Center
Recommended Restaurants: (For a complete list of all restaurants visit ashevilleguide book.com

Green River Bar-B-Que: (BBQ) 131 Main St., Saluda NC 28773; 828-749-28773
The Purple Onion: (Mediterranean) 16 Main St., Saluda NC 28773; 828-749-1179

Recommended Places To Stay: (For a complete list of all accommodations visit ashe villeguidebook.com

The Orchard Inn: (Country Inn) 100 Orchard Inn Lane, Saluda NC 28773; 828-749-5471
The Oaks Bed & Breakfast: (B&B) 339 Greenville St., Saluda NC 28773; 800-893-6091

Sawmills

Sawmills lies between Hudson to the north and Granite Falls to the southeast in Caldwell County and is positioned on both Lake Rhodhiss and US 321. The name Sawmills was chosen in 1988 because of the many sawmills that supplied wood for local furniture plants. The town has the county's second highest population and is among the largest in land area. The town operates two parks, Veteran's Park on Lake Rhodhiss, which features a paved walking trail and fishing pier, and Baird Dr. Park, that features a picnic area, walking track, playground, and athletic fields. Caldwell County, known as the Furniture Capital of the South, is home to the "20 Miles of Furniture" where numerous outlets and stores offer deep discounts. Located along or near a stretch of U.S. Hwy. 321 between Lenoir and Hickory, the area, which passes through Sawmills, is a required destination for any serious shopper looking for furniture.

Location: Foothills, 1.5 hours east of Asheville
Town Hall: 4076 US Hwy. 321-A, Sawmills NC 28630; 828-396-7903
Website: townofsawmills.com
County: Caldwell County: County Offices, 905 West Ave. NW, Lenoir NC 28645; 828-757-1300
Elevation and Population: 1,247 feet, 4,900+
County Visitor/Welcome Center: Caldwell County Chamber of Commerce Visitor Center,1909 Hickory Blvd. SE, Lenoir NC 28645; 828-726-0616
County Chamber of Commerce: Caldwell County Chamber of Commerce, 1909 Hickory Blvd. SE, Lenoir NC 28645; 828-726-0616
Newspaper: News-Topic,123 Pennton Ave., Lenoir NC 28645; 828-758-7381
Area Major Festivals: Christmas Parade (Dec.)
Area Natural Attractions: Pisgah National Forest, Tuttle Educational State Forest, Wilson Creek
Area Cultural Attractions: Caldwell Heritage Museum, Chapel of Rest, Fort Defiance, Granite Falls History and Transportation Museum, Happy Valley, 20 Miles of Furniture
Recommended Restaurants: (For a complete list of all restaurants visit ashevilleguidebook.com

No restaurants currently available in Sawmills. *See* **Lenoir** and **Granite Falls**

Recommended Places To Stay: (For a complete list of all accommodations visit ashevilleguidebook.com

No accommodations currently available in Sawmills. *See* **Lenoir** and **Granite Falls.**

Sparta

Located at the center of Alleghany County and its county seat, Sparta is a classic southern small mountain town, with the historic Allegheny County Courthouse as the primary building. There is an older business district with overtones of years gone by and two shopping centers, a satellite campus of Wilkes Community College and Alleghany Memorial Hospital..

The town also features one of the most complete public parks for a community of its size, Crouse Park. The park features a basketball and volleyball court, horseshoes, walking course and exercise and play equipment for all ages from toddlers through adults. Near to Sparta are two state parks-Stone Mountain State Park and the New River State Park, home to the famous New River, the second oldest river in the world.

Nearby Lansing has a history of mining and dairy farming, both of which have been replaced by Christmas tree farming. Frazier firs from Lansing are shipped nationwide each Christmas. Lansing has a number of festivals each year, including the famous Ola Belle Reed Homecoming Festival which is held every Aug. and highlights folk and bluegrass music.

Location: Northern Mountains, 3 hours northeast of Asheville
Town Office: 304 South Main St., Sparta NC 28675
County: Alleghany County: County Offices, 348 South Main St., Sparta NC 28675; 336-372-4179
Elevation and Population: 2,939 feet, 1,800+

Visitor/Welcome Center: Alleghany Chamber of Commerce Visitor Center, 58 South Main St., Sparta NC 28675; 800-372-5473

County Chamber of Commerce: Alleghany Chamber of Commerce 58 South Main St., Sparta NC 28675; 800-372-5473

Newspaper: The Alleghany News, 20 South Main St., Sparta NC 28675; 336-372-8999

High School: Alleghany High School, 404 Trojan Ave., Sparta NC 28675; 336-372-4554

Colleges and Universities: Wilkes Community College, Alleghany Campus, 115 Atwood St., Sparta NC 28675; 336-372-5061

Hospitals: Alleghany Memorial Hospital, 233 Doctors St., Sparta NC 28675; 336-372-5511

Area Major Festivals: Alleghany County Fiddler's Convention (Jul.)

Area Natural Attractions: Blue Ridge Parkway, New River State Park, Stone Mountain State Park

Area Cultural Attractions: Allegheny County Courthouse

Recommended Restaurants: (For a complete list of all restaurants visit ashevilleguide book.com

Horizon Bistro: (Café) 38 South Main St., Sparta NC 28675; 336-372-7444

Recommended Places To Stay: (For a complete list of all accommodations visit ashe villeguidebook.com

Alleghany Inn: (Motel) 341 North Main St., Sparta NC 28675; 888-372-2501

Harmony Hill Bed & Breakfast: (B&B) 1740 Halsey Knob Rd., Sparta NC 28675; 336-372-6868

Spindale

Located midway between Forest City and Rutherfordton, Spindale features a diverse selection of specialty shops, long-established businesses, restaurants and service professionals. It is also home to Isothermal Community College, the cultural and learning center for the entire region. Concerts at The Foundation for Performing Arts and Conference Center, the college's new convention and performance facility, are among the highlights of every cultural season. Spindale also offers a stretch of the Thermal Belt Walking Trail, following an old railroad right of way, a well established Farmer's Market, and on Main St., Spindale House, the town Community Center. Spindale has gained fame in recent years as the home of Public Radio Station WNCW FM 88.7, which is licensed to Isothermal Community College. The station has a worldwide listener base and features programming of an eclectic blend of music styles.

Location: Foothills, 1 hour southeast of Asheville

Town Hall: 103 Revely St., Spindale NC 28160; 828-286-3466

Website: spindalenc.net

County: Rutherford County: County Offices, 289 North Main St., Rutherfordton NC 28139; 828-287-6045

Elevation and Population: 960 feet, 4,000+

Visitor/Welcome Center: Rutherford County Tourism, 2932 Memorial Hwy., Lake Lure NC 28746; 800-849-5998

County Chamber of Commerce: Rutherford County Chamber of Commerce 162 North Main St., Rutherfordton NC 28139; 828-287-3090

Newspaper: The Daily Courier 601 Oak St., Forest City NC 28043; 828-245-6431

High School: Chase High School, 1603 Chase High Rd., Forest City NC 28043; 828-245-7668

Colleges and Universities: Isothermal Community College, 286 ICC Loop Rd., Spindale NC 28160; 828-286-3636

Area Major Festivals: Spring Foothills Antique and Artisan Show (April)

Area Natural Attractions: Chimney Rock Park, Lake Lure

Area Cultural Attractions: Bennett Classics Antique Auto Museum, KidSenses Children's InterACTIVE Museum, Rutherford County Farm Museum, Rutherford County Museum

Recommended Restaurants: (For a complete list of all restaurants visit ashevilleguidebook.com

Barley's Taproom & Pizzeria: (Pizza) 123 West Main St., Spindale NC 28160; 828-288-8388

Recommended Places To Stay: (For a complete list of all accommodations visit ashevilleguidebook.com

No accommodations in Spindale. ***See* Rutherfordton.**

Spruce Pine

Located in Mitchell County on the banks of the Toe River and just off the Blue Ridge Parkway at mile marker 331, Spruce Pine is a vibrant mountain town with a past rich in gem mining history and lore. In the early 1900s, Spruce Pine was a booming mining town and the Clinchfield Railroad operated to bring materials and supplies to and from the growing community. Chartered in 1913, Spruce Pine was built around the Carolina, Clinchfield and Ohio Railroad Depot. The railroad is still going strong, and train enthusiasts continue today to come from far and wide to Spruce Pine to enjoy watching the frequent passage of CSX trains through the downtown area. Over 30 trains a day pass by, often blowing their horns in greeting.

Historically, the White House Christmas tree has come from the Spruce Pine region and with so many Christmas tree farms in the area, the town has appropriately become known as the "Christmas Tree Capital of the World," a title it shares along with "The Mineral City." Located in a region of the mountains that is known for gem mines, Spruce Pine is famous for the world-class rubies and emeralds that have been found in local mines. The surrounding mountains have a more concentrated wealth of feldspar than any other area on earth, supplying 60% of the United States production of the mineral. Additionally, almost 100% of the United States and the world supply of ultra-pure quartz, which is used in the production of semiconductors, comes from the Spruce Pine region.

Spruce Pine has the distinction of having two Main St., Upper St. (Oak Ave.) and Lower St. (Locust St.), with nicknames given because of respective altitudes. Spruce Pine also has two municipal parks, Riverside Park on Tappan St. with a wonderful walking path and access to the Toe River, and Brad Ragan Park on Laurel Creek Court.

Location: Northern Mountains, 2 hours northeast of Asheville
Town Hall: 138 Highland Ave., Spruce Pine NC 28777; 828-765-3000
Website: townofsprucepine.com
County: Mitchell County: County Administration Building, 26 Crimson Laurel Circle, Bakersville NC 28705; 828-688-2139
Elevation and Population: 2,517 feet, 2,000+
County Visitor Center: Located in the Museum of NC Minerals, Milepost 331, Blue Ridge Parkway; Spruce Pine NC 28777; 800-227-3912
County Chamber of Commerce: Mitchell County Chamber of Commerce: 11 Crystal St., Spruce Pine NC 28777; 828-765-9033
Newspaper: Mitchell News-Journal 291 Locust Ave., Spruce Pine 28777; 828-765-2071
High School: Mitchell High School, 416 Ledger School Rd., Bakersville NC 28705; 828-688-2101
Colleges and Universities: Mayland Community College, 200 Mayland Dr., Spruce Pine NC 28777; 828-765-7351
Hospitals: Blue Ridge Regional Hospital, 125 Hospital Dr., Spruce Pine NC 28777; 877-777-8230
Area Major Festivals: Fire on the Mountain Blacksmith Festival (April), Toe River Storytelling Festival (Jul.), Mineral City Heritage Festival (Oct.)
Area Natural Attractions: Blue Ridge Parkway, Grandfather Mountain State Park, Pisgah National Forest
Area Cultural Attractions: Emerald Village, Museum of North Carolina Minerals, North Carolina Mining Museum, Orchard at Altapass
Recommended Restaurants: (For a complete list of all restaurants visit ashevilleguide book.com

DT's Blue Ridge Java: Coffee Shop & Café: (Café) 169 Locust St., Spruce Pine NC 28777; 828-766-8008

Skyline Village Inn & Cavern Tavern: (American) Skyline Village Inn, 12255 Hwy. 226A, (Milepost 334 Blue Ridge Parkway), Spruce Pine NC 28777; 828-994-0027

Recommended Places To Stay: (For a complete list of all accommodations visit ashe villeguidebook.com

Richmond Inn Bed & Breakfast: (B&B) 51 Pine St., Spruce Pine NC 28777; 877–765-6993

Skyline Village Inn: (Country Inn) 12255 Hwy. 226A, (Milepost 334 Blue Ridge Parkway) Spruce Pine NC 28777; 828-994-0027

Sugar Mountain

Sugar Mountain is a small resort village nestled in the middle of the High Country located at the eastern end of Avery County and is a year-round vacation destination offering golf, hiking, tennis, skiing and other outdoor activities. The major attraction is the Sugar Mountain Resort located in nearby Banner Elk, a full-service alpine snow ski and snowboard area that features a 1,200-foot vertical drop and 18 slopes and trails with eight lifts. With an average annual snowfall of 78" and state-of-the-art snowmaking equipment, Sugar Mountain offers winter sports enthusiasts a fabulous white playground. Besides Sugar Mountain for skiing, the popular Hawksnest Tubing Park is located in nearby Seven Devils.

Location: Northern Mountains, 2 hours east of Asheville
Town Hall: 251 Dick Trundy Lane, Sugar Mountain NC 28604; 828-898-9292
Website: townofsprucepine.com
County: Avery County: County Administrative Building, 175 Linville St., Newland NC 28657; 828-733-8202
Elevation and Population: 4,432 feet, 250+
County Chamber of Commerce: Avery County Chamber of Commerce: 4501 Tynecastle Hwy., Unit #2, Banner Elk NC 28604; 800-972-2183
Newspaper: The Mountain Times PO Box 1815, Boone NC 28607; 828–264-6397
High School: Avery County High School, 401 High School Rd., Newland NC 28657; 828-733-0151
Area Major Festivals: Sugar Mountain Oktoberfest (Oct.), Sugarfest (Dec.)
Area Natural Attractions: Blue Ridge Parkway, Grandfather Mountain, Linville Caverns, Linville Gorge.
Area Cultural Attractions: Avery County Historical Museum, Banner House Museum, Crossnore Fine Arts Gallery, Horn in the West, Mast General Store, Mystery Hill, Orchard at Altapass, Tweetsie Railroad
Recommended Restaurants: (For a complete list of all restaurants visit ashevilleguide book.com
Bella's: (Italian) 3585 Tynecastle Hwy., Sugar Mountain NC 28604; 828-898-9022
Recommended Places To Stay: (For a complete list of all accommodations visit ashe villeguidebook.com
Sugar Ski & Country Club: (Resort) 100 Sugar Dr., Banner Elk NC 28604; 800-634-1320

Sylva

Sylva is a quaint town in Western North Carolina that is surrounded by beautiful mountains and conveniently located near many of the major natural and cultural attractions in Western North Carolina. The town has a delightful downtown area with many restaurants and shops, and is also home to the historic Jackson County Courthouse and Southwestern Community College. Recreational opportunities abound and nearby outdoor mountain attractions include the Cataloochee Ski Area, the Blue Ridge Parkway and three great forests and parks: the Great Smoky Mountains National Park, the Nantahala National Forest and the Pisgah National Forest. Sylva also has a state of the art children's playground, and a wonderful park, Pinnacle Park, that boasts hiking trails, waterfalls and a view of the town from 5,000 feet.

Of interest also is the famous Judaculla Rock, a large stone covered with cryptic markings that predates the Cherokee Indians and which are thought to be over 2,000 years old. The rock is the largest and best-known example of rock art in North Carolina and is open to the public. To get there, take Route 23 from downtown 1.3 miles to NC 107, then turn left onto 107. Dr. 8 miles south on 107 and take a left onto Caney Fork Rd., County Rd.

1737. Go 2.5 miles, then turn left onto a gravel road and drive 0.45 mile. The rock is on the right, with parking on the left.

Location: Western Mountains, 1 hour west of Asheville
Town Hall: 83 Allen St., Sylva NC 28779; 828-586-2719
City Websites: sylvanc.govoffice3.com
County Visitor/Welcome Center Website: mountainlovers.com
County: Jackson County: County Offices, 401 Grindstaff Cove Rd., Ste A-207, Sylva NC 28779; 828-586-4055
Elevation and Population: 2,036 ft, 2,600+
County Chamber of Commerce: Jackson County Chamber of Commerce 773 West Main St., Sylva NC 28779; 800-962-1911
Newspapers: The Sylva Herald 539 West Main St., Sylva NC 28779; 800-849-3193 and The Smoky Mountains News 633 West Main St., Sylva NC 28779; 828-631-4829
Movie Theatres: Quin Theaters East Sylva Shopping Center, Sylva NC 28779; 828-586-5918
High School: Smoky Mountain High, 100 Smoky Mountain Dr., Sylva NC 28779; 828-586-2177
Colleges and Universities: Southwestern Community College, 447 College Dr., Sylva NC, 28779; 828-586-4091 and Western Carolina University, University Way, Cullowhee NC 28723; 828-227-7211
Hospitals: Harris Regional Hospital, 68 Hospital Rd., Sylva NC 28779; 828-586-7000
Area Major Festivals: Greening Up The Mountains (April), Mountain Artisans Arts and Crafts Shows (Jul. and Nov.), Concerts on the Creek (Summer), Mountain Heritage Day (Sep.)
Area Natural Attractions: Judaculla Rock, Pisgah National Forest, Waterfalls in Western North Carolina, Great Smoky Mountains National Park
Area Cultural Attractions: Cherokee Indian Reservation, Fine and Performing Arts Center at WCU, Great Smoky Mountains Railroad, Mountain Heritage Center, Western Carolina University
Recommended Restaurants: (For a complete list of all restaurants visit ashevilleguide book.com

Guadalupe Café: (Tapas, Caribbean) 606 West Main St., Sylva NC 28779; 828-586-9877

Lulu's On Main: (American Gourmet) 612 West Main St., Sylva NC 28779; 828-586-8989

Nick & Nate's Pizzeria: (Pizza) Asheville Hwy., #38 The Overlook Village, Sylva NC 28799; 828-586-3000

Recommended Places To Stay: (For a complete list of all accommodations visit ashe villeguidebook.com

Grand Old Lady Hotel: (Country Inn) 68 Seven Springs Dr., Balsam NC 28707; 800-224-9498

Mountain Brook Lodge and Cottages: (Lodge, Cottages) 208 Mountain Brook Rd., Sylva NC 28779; 800-258-4052

The Freeze House Bed & Breakfast: (B&B) 71 Sylvan Heights, Sylva NC 28779; 828-586-8161

Tryon

The small mountain town of Tryon, located southeast of Asheville, is well-known for the equestrian events held at the Foothills Equestrian Nature Center almost every weekend from April through Oct. Incorporated in the late 1800s when the Spartanburg and Asheville Railroad came to the area, it is the largest town in its region. Tryon is also home to the famous Tryon International Equestrian Center, a year round venue located in Mill Spring, NC and is the world's premier Equestrian Lifestyle Destination showcasing some of the top riders in the Hunter/Jumper, Dressage, and Eventing disciplines. Many of the historic buildings on Trade St. were in place by 1900, including a general store, a pharmacy and a post office. Tryon quickly grew as a resort town, drawing tourists to the area to enjoy the mountain views and good climate. Over the years, Tryon has been home to many artists and writers including the stage actor William Gillette, most famous for his portrayal of Sherlock Holmes, and F. Scott Fitzgerald. This mix of locals, artists and retirees continues today, creating a vibrant, active community. The village also has a number of art and craft galleries, and a nice selection of restaurants and accommodations, and over the years Tryon has earned the reputation as one of the friendliest towns in the south. The premier event in Tryon is the running of the annual Block House Steeplechase, presented by the Tryon Riding & Hunt Club.

Nearby Pearson's Falls is located off Hwy. 176 between Tryon and Saluda. This botanical preserve is comprised of 268 acres of native forest, spring-fed streams and a moderate ¼ mile trail to a 90 ft. waterfall. There are over 200 species of fern, flowering plants, algae and mosses in the wildflower preserve.

Location: Central Mountains, 45 minutes south of Asheville

Town Hall: North Trade St., Tryon NC 28782; 828-859-6654

Website: tryon-nc.com

County: Polk County: County Offices, 40 Courthouse St., Columbus NC 28722; 828-894-3301

Elevation and Population: 1,100 feet, 1,750+

County Visitor/Welcome Center: Polk County Travel and Tourism 20 East Mills St., Columbus NC 28722; 800-440-7848

County Chamber of Commerce: Carolina Foothills Chamber of Commerce 2753 Lynn Rd., Ste A, Tryon NC 28782; 828-859-6236

Newspaper: Tryon Daily Bulletin 16 North Trade St., Tryon NC 28782; 828-859-9151 and Polk County News Journal PO Box 576, Columbus NC 28722; 864-457-3337

Movie Theatres: Tryon Theatre, 45 South Trade St., Tryon NC 28782; 828-859-6811

High School: Polk County High School, 1681 East NC Hwy. 108, Columbus NC 28722; 828-894-2525

Area Major Festivals: Block House Steeplechase (April), Blue Ridge BBQ Festival (Jun.)
Area Natural Attractions: Pearson's Falls, Pisgah National Forest
Area Cultural Attractions: Foothills Equestrian Nature Center (FENCE), Polk County Courthouse, Polk County Historical Museum, Tryon Fine Arts Center, Tryon International Equestrian Center
Recommended Restaurants: (For a complete list of all restaurants visit ashevilleguide book.com
Huckleberry's Restaurant: (American) 62 North Trade St., Tryon NC 28782; 828-436-0025
Recommended Places To Stay: (For a complete list of all accommodations visit ashe villeguidebook.com
1906 Pine Crest Inn: (Country Inn) 85 Pine Crest Lane, Tryon NC 28782; 800-633-3001

Valdese

Valdese, a town located about eight miles east of Morganton, ranks second in size for Burke County with a population of 4,600. The community has a heritage that dates back to the Middle Ages in Europe and was settled about 113 years ago by the Waldensians, a sect from the Cottian Alps located in northern Italy and southern France that found their way to Burke County where they could freely practice their religion. For centuries in Italy they had been persecuted for their religious beliefs. Sites to visit in Valdese include the Trail of Faith, the outdoor drama "From This Day Forward" and the Waldensian Heritage Museum.

Valdese today is a tourist destination, a city rich in history, and remains a town still linked by its roots to Italy. The Old Rock School, built in 1923 by the original settlers of Valdese, was renovated in the 1970's and remains the focal point of the town. The facility now houses art galleries and a 473-seat auditorium where bluegrass music, "Bluegrass at The Rock" is performed on a regular basis throughout the year. Valdese also has a Farmer's Market, held across from the town hall, on Wed and Fri during the summer season and also a great recreational park at McGalliard Falls Parks, complete with a restored grist mill. Not to be missed while downtown is the Village Park Mural, a stunning outdoor painting on Main St.

Location: Foothills,1 hour and 15 minutes east of Asheville
Town Offices: 121 Faet St., Valdese NC 28690; 828-879-2120
Website: ci.valdese.nc.us
County: Burke County: Burke County Government Center, 200 Avery Ave., Morganton NC 28680; 828-439-4340
Elevation and Population: 1,203 feet, 4,600+
Visitor/Welcome Center: Valdese Visitor Center, 400 West Main St., Valdese NC 28690; 828-879-2129
County Chamber of Commerce: Burke County Chamber of Commerce, 110 East Meeting St., Morganton NC 28655; 828-437-3021
Newspaper: The News Herald, 301 Collett St., Morganton NC 28655; 828-437-2161
High School: Jimmy C Draughn High School, 709 Lovelady Rd. NE, Valdese NC 28690; 828-879-4200

Hospitals: Valdese Hospital, 720 Malcolm Blvd., Valdese NC 28690; 828-874-2251
Area Major Festivals: Jul. 4th Fireworks (Jul.), Waldensian Festival (Aug.)
Area Natural Attractions: McGalliard Falls Parks, South Mountains State Park
Area Cultural Attractions: From This Day Forward, Trail of Faith, Waldensian Heritage Museum
Recommended Restaurants: (For a complete list of all restaurants visit ashevilleguide book.com

Myra's: (Italian) 155 Bobo Ave. NW, Valdese NC 28690; 828-874-7086

Recommended Places To Stay: (For a complete list of all accommodations visit ashe villeguidebook.com

No accommodations currently available in Valdese. *See* Morganton

Valle Crucis

Located high in the mountains near Boone, Valle Crucis is an historic community that has been around for 200 years. It is home to the famous Mast General Store, the Holy Cross Episcopal Church and the Valle Crucis Conference Center, as well as many shops, galleries and studios featuring handmade crafts and art, rustic furniture and pottery. The town is North Carolina's first rural historic district and the entire community is listed on the National Register of Historic Places.

Valle Crucis' name means "Vale of the Cross," a reference to a valley in the area where three streams converge to form a shape similar to an archbishop's cross. Valle Crucis began in the 1840's when an Episcopalian missionary, William West Skiles, came to the area. He founded the first Episcopal Church in the region as well as the Valle Crucis Mission School. Skiles also founded the first monastic order within the Episcopal Church in the United States, the Brotherhood of the Holy Cross.

During recent years, Valle Crucis has transformed from a little-known rural community to a popular destination for tourists and new residents. The valley's serene scenic beauty and protected location in the mountains proximate to the Pisgah National Forest have been factors in this recent development. The major attraction in town is the original Mast General Store, which offers visitors a true glimpse into bygone days.

Location: Northern Mountains, 2 hours east of Asheville
Website: vallecrucis.com
County: Watauga County: County Offices, 842 West King St., Boone NC 28607; 828-265-8000
Elevation and Population: 2,800 feet, 800+
City Chamber of Commerce: Boone Area Chamber of Commerce 870 West King St., Ste A, Boone NC 28607; 828-264-2225
County Chamber of Commerce: Boone Area Chamber of Commerce 870 West King St., Ste A, Boone NC 28607; 828-264-2225
Newspaper: The Watauga Democrat 474 Industrial Park Dr., Boone NC 28607; 828-264-3612 and The Mountain Times PO Box 1815, Boone NC 28607; 828-264-6397
High School: Watauga High School, 300 Go Pioneers Dr., Boone NC 28607; 828-264-2407

Area Major Festivals: Valle Crucis Creekside Bluegrass Festival (Jun.), Valley Country Fair (Oct.)

Area Natural Attractions: Blue Ridge Parkway, Grandfather Mountain, Pisgah National Forest

Area Cultural Attractions: Hickory Ridge Homestead, Horn in the West, Mast General Store, Turchin Center for Visual Arts, Tweetsie Railroad

Recommended Restaurants: (For a complete list of all restaurants visit ashevilleguide book.com

The Mast Farm Inn: (American) 2543 Broadstone Road, Banner Elk NC 28604; 828-963-5857

Recommended Places To Stay: (For a complete list of all accommodations visit ashe villeguidebook.com

The Mast Farm Inn: (American) 2543 Broadstone Road, Banner Elk NC 28604; 828-963-5857

Waynesville

Incorporated in 1871, Waynesville is Haywood County's oldest city, and the fifth largest city in Western North Carolina after Asheville, Hickory, Morganton and Hendersonville. It was founded in 1810 by Colonel Robert Love, who donated land for the courthouse, jail and public square, and who named the town after his former commander in the Revolutionary War, General "Mad" Anthony Wayne. Rich in history dating back almost 200 years and known for its southern hospitality and magnificent views of the surrounding mountains, Waynesville is a tourist destination in its own right and has a wealth of unique shops, arts and crafts galleries, restaurants and accommodations.

The Waynesville area began to see major development after the arrival of the railroad in the late 1800's, with agriculture, lumber and tourism becoming the major industries. The last passenger train to Waynesville was in 1949, but the railroad line is still active and today Norfolk Southern Railway freight trains still pass though the city on their way to Sylva in the west.

Waynesville has a number of distinct neighborhoods: Downtown, Frog Level, Hazelwood, Laurel Ridge, West Waynesville and Russ Ave. The downtown area, once the primary retail business center of the town, is now home to town government and administration buildings, Cafés, restaurants, shops, art galleries and professional offices. It is known for its lofty shade trees, brick sidewalks, benches, water fountains, and outdoor sculptures. Frog Level is an historic railroad district that was so named because of frequent flooding of nearby Richland Creek and as the early home of Waynesville's railroad depots. Today, Frog Level has experienced the same type of revitalization as the downtown Main St. area.

Hazelwood was primarily a working class town before annexation by Waynesville, and is similar to West Waynesville, the industrial part of city. The town is dominated by the Waynesville Commons shopping center which is anchored by a Wal-Mart Super Store. Russ Ave. is a newer business district of Waynesville and features restaurants, retail stores, auto dealerships, banks and grocery stores.

Waynesville has two outstanding recreational facilities: the Waynesville Recreation Center located at 550 Vance St., and the Old Armory Recreation Center at 44 Boundary St. These facilities serve the entire region and together offer an eight-lane pool, water playground, gymnasium, weight room and indoor and outdoor tracks. The Parks and Recreation Department also maintains an 18-hole disc golf course, five neighborhood parks, two dog parks, tennis courts, softball fields, a soccer field and a Greenway near Richland Creek.

Waynesville is also host every year to the world-famous FOLKMOOT USA, North Carolina's official international music and dance festival, as well as the Haywood Arts Regional Theatre, Museum of North Carolina Handicrafts, and the Red Barn Mountain Museum. Nearby outdoor mountain attractions include the Cataloochee Ski Area, the Blue Ridge Parkway and three great forests and parks: the Great Smoky Mountains National Park, the Nantahala National Forest and the Pisgah National Forest. Close by also is the famous Cherokee Indian Reservation as well as the Lake Junaluska Conference and Retreat Center. Lake Junaluska is notable as the site of the headquarters of the World Methodist Council, a consultative body linking almost all churches in the Methodist tradition.

Location: Central Mountains, 45 minutes west of Asheville
Municipal Building: 16 South Main St., Waynesville NC 28786; 828–452-2491
Website: townofwaynesville.org
County: Haywood County, 215 North Main St., Waynesville NC 28786; 828-452-6625
Elevation and Population: 3,600 feet, 10,000+
County Visitor/Welcome Center: Haywood County Tourism Development Authority Visitor Center, 44 North Main St., Waynesville NC 28786; 828-452-0152
County Chamber of Commerce: 28 Walnut St., Waynesville NC 28786; 828-456-3021
Newspapers: The Mountaineer, 220 North Main St., Waynesville NC 28786; 828-452-0661, Smokey Mountain News, 144 Montgomery St., Waynesville NC 28787; 828-452-4251
Movie Theatres: The Strand at 38 Main, 38 Main St., Waynesville NC 28786; 828-283-0079
High School: Tuscola High School, 564 Tuscola School Rd., Waynesville NC 28786; 828-456-2408
Area Major Festivals: Folkmoot USA (Jul.–Aug.), Smoky Mountain Folk Festival (Sep.), Church St. Art and Craft Show (Oct.)
Area Natural Attractions: Blue Ridge Parkway, Great Smoky Mountains National Park, Nantahala National Forest, Pisgah National Forest
Area Cultural Attractions: Cataloochee Ski Area, Cherokee Indian Reservation, Ghost Town In The Sky, HART-Haywood Arts Regional Theatre, Museum of North Carolina Handicrafts, Red Barn Mountain Museum, Wheels Thru Time Museum, World Methodist Museum, SEJ Heritage Center at Lake Junaluska
Recommended Restaurants: (For a complete list of all restaurants visit ashevilleguidebook.com

Bogart's Restaurant: (American) 303 South Main St., Waynesville NC 28786; 828-452-1313
Bocelli's Italian Eatery: (Italian) 319 North Haywood St., Waynesville NC 28786; 828-456-4900

Chef's Table: (American-Fine Dining) 30 Church St., Waynesville NC 28786; 828-452-6210

Clyde's Restaurant: (Country) 2107 South Main St., Waynesville NC 28786; 828-456-9135

Cork & Cleaver: (American-Fine Dining) Waynesville Inn, 176 Country Club Rd., Waynesville NC 28786; 800-627-6250

Maggie's Galley Seafood Restaurant: (Seafood) 49 Howell Mill Rd., Waynesville NC 28786; 828-456-8945

The Sweet Onion Restaurant: (American) 39 Miller St., Waynesville NC 28786; 828-456-5559

Recommended Places To Stay: (For a complete list of all accommodations visit ashe villeguidebook.com

Andon Reid Inn Bed & Breakfast: (B&B) 92 Daisy Ave., Waynesville NC 28786; 800-293-6190

Best Western Smoky Mountain Inn: (Motel) 130 Shiloh Trail, Waynesville NC 28786; 828-456-4402

Boyd Mountain Log Cabins & Tree Farm: (Cabins) 445 Boyd Farm Rd., Waynesville NC 28785; 828-926-1575

Oak Hill on Love Lane Bed & Breakfast: (B&B) 224 Love Lane, Waynesville NC 28786; 888-608-7037

Oak Park Inn: (Inn) 196 South Main St., Waynesville NC 28786; 828-456-5328

The Swag: (Country Inn) 2300 Swag Rd., Waynesville NC 28785; 828-925-0430

The Waynesville Inn Golf Resort & Spa: (Resort) 176 Country Club Rd., Waynesville NC 28786; 800-627-6250

The Yellow House on Plott Creek Road: (B&B) 89 Oakview Dr., Waynesville NC 28786; 800-563-1236

Weaverville

Located just 12 miles north of Asheville, Weaverville is a small vibrant community that was incorporated in 1874. It was the birthplace of Zebulon B. Vance, Civil War governor of North Carolina in 1862–65 and 1877–79, who was born in the nearby Reems Creek Valley. His birthplace, the Zebulon B. Vance Birthplace, is a state historical site and worth a visit if you are interested in North Carolina history and historical sites.

Weaverville in the 1800's was home to a number of grand hotels, all now gone. These included the Dula Springs Hotel and Blackberry Lodge, where Low Country visitors came to escape the heat of South Carolina summers. These destination hotels, as well as Weaverville's natural charm and mountain beauty, helped solidify the town's reputation as a resort destination. This continues to this day, although Weaverville as a destination is greatly overshadowed by nearby Asheville.

The town has a lovely park, Lake Louise Park, and a number of excellent restaurants and places to stay, including some world-class bed and breakfasts. The Reems Creek Valley, to the east of the town center, is considered one of the most scenic valleys in the greater Asheville area. Weaverville also has the distinction of being named a "Tree City USA" every year since 1990. Weaverville is home to many residents who work in nearby Asheville but also is hosts a number of manufacturing businesses, including a branch of Arvato Digital Services, the world's second-largest replicator of CDs and DVDs.

Location: Central Mountains, 15 minutes north of Asheville

Town Hall: 30 South Main St., Weaverville NC 28787; 828-645-7116

Website: weavervillenc.org

County: Buncombe County: County Offices, 205 College St., Asheville NC 28801; 828-250-4000

Elevation and Population: 2,176 feet, 2,600+

County Chamber of Commerce: Buncombe County Chamber of Commerce 205 College St., Asheville NC 28801; 828-250-4100

Newspaper: The Weaverville Tribune, 40 North Merrimon Ave., Asheville NC 28787; 828-252-5804

High School: North Buncombe High School, 890 Clarks Chapel Rd., Weaverville NC 28787; 828-645-4221

Area Major Festivals: Candlelight Tours at Vance Birthplace (Dec.), Weaverville Art Safari (Apr. and Nov.).

Area Natural Attractions: Blue Ridge Parkway, Mount Mitchell State Park, Pisgah National Forest

Area Cultural Attractions: Biltmore Estate, Dry Ridge Historical Museum, Pack Place Education, Arts and Science Center, Thomas Wolfe Memorial, Zebulon B. Vance Birthplace

Recommended Restaurants: (For a complete list of all restaurants visit ashevilleguide book.com

Stoney Knob Café: (Continental-American Fine Dining) 337 Merrimon Ave., Weaverville NC 28787; 828-645-3309

Recommended Places To Stay: (For a complete list of all accommodations visit ashe villeguidebook.com

Dry Ridge Inn: (B&B) 26 Brown St., Weaverville NC 28787; 800–839-3899

West Jefferson

West Jefferson is located in the eastern part of the North Carolina mountains in Ashe County, and is in an area known for the famous New River, spectacular views and Christmas tree farming. The town has a thriving business district and is noted for the murals that create an art and history focused walking tour. The murals are the works of local artists in North Carolina that depict the area's history.

As with many small towns, West Jefferson has a number of distinctive and unique festivals, one of which is Christmas in Jul., featuring the very best in traditional mountain music and handmade crafts. The Ashe County Farmer's Market, open seasonally, is also located in West Jefferson on the Backstreet in downtown and is considered one of the premier farmer's markets in the mountains. St. Mary's Church on Beaver Creek Rd. also features the Ben Long Frescoes of the Mystery of Faith, Mary Great with Child, and John the Baptist.

Overlooking West Jefferson is the Mount Jefferson State Natural Area, which occupies the summit of Mount Jefferson. Hiking trails, picnic tables and pavilions are some of the amenities offered there. The Ashe County Arts Council Gallery is located in the Ashe Arts Center at 303 School Ave., and has regularly changing exhibits of local artists and performances of music, poetry and literature.

Location: Northern Mountains, 2.5 hours east of Asheville

Town Hall: 01 South Jefferson Ave., West Jefferson NC 28694; 336-246-3551

Website: townofwj.com

County: Ashe County: County Offices, 150 Government Circle, Ste 2500, Jefferson NC 28640; 336-846-5501

Elevation and Population: 3,200 feet, 1100+

County Chamber of Commerce: Ashe County Chamber of Commerce 01 North Jefferson St., Ste C, West Jefferson NC 28694; 336-846-9550

Newspaper: Jefferson Post, 203 South Second St., West Jefferson NC 28694; 336-846-7164

Movie Theatres: Parkway Theatre, 10 East Main St., West Jefferson NC 28694; 336-846-3281

High School: Ashe County High School, 184 Campus Dr., West Jefferson NC 28694; 336-846-2400

Area Major Festivals: Christmas in Jul. (Jul.), Ola Belle Reed Homecoming Festival (Aug.)

Area Natural Attractions: Blue Ridge Parkway; Mount Jefferson State Natural Area, New River State Park

Area Cultural Attractions: Ashe County Arts Council Gallery, Ben Long Frescoes, Museum of Ashe County History

Recommended Restaurants: (For a complete list of all restaurants visit ashevilleguide book.com

Boondocks Brewing: (American) 108 South Jefferson Ave., West Jefferson NC, 28694; 336-246-5222

Mountain Aire Seafood & Steaks: (American-Seafood) 9930 Hwy. 16 South, West Jefferson NC 28694; 336-982-3060

Recommended Places To Stay: (For a complete list of all accommodations visit ashe villeguidebook.com

Buffalo Tavern: (B&B) 958 West Buffalo Rd., West Jefferson NC 28694; 877-615-9678

***See also* Jefferson Recommended Places To Stay**

Wilkesboro

Wilkesboro, founded in 1800 and incorporated in 1847, is the county seal of Wilkes County, and is located along the south bank of the Yadkin River, directly opposite the slightly larger town of North Wilkesboro. Wilkesboro is probably best known as the home to the celebrated MerleFest, an internationally acclaimed acoustic and bluegrass music festival held every April. Nearby outdoor attractions, including nearby Stone Mountain State Park and W. Kerr Scott Dam and Reservoir, the many downtown shops and galleries, and the multifaceted cultural life in this charming foothills town ensure a great visit. Wilkesboro's largest industry is the Tyson Foods poultry processing plant; it is one of the largest poultry plants east of the Mississippi River. The town also contains several textile and furniture factories; one of the largest is the Key City Furniture factory.

Noteworthy also is the fact that Daniel Boone, the famous explorer and pioneer, lived for several years where Wilkesboro and North Wilkesboro are located before moving west to Kentucky. Wilkesboro is also the place the Tom Dula saga took place. The incident was immortalized in song and legend, most notably in the murder ballad Hang Down Your Head, Tom Dooley recorded in 1958 by the Kingston Trio. Each summer the Wilkes Playmakers also present a popular play based on the legend. Visitors to Wilkesboro interested in local history may take a self-guided walking tour which includes stops at thirteen historic buildings.

One of the many artistic highlights of Wilkesboro are the beautiful Ben Long Frescoes in St. Paul's Episcopal Church, located at 200 Cowles St. These classically-executed frescoes of St. Paul the Apostle are open for viewing by the public. Wilkesboro is also home to Wilkes Community College, a public coeducational two-year college which has an enrollment of over 3,500 students. Located on the campus is The Walker Center, one of the major cultural arts and performance venues in the area. Also in Wilkesboro is the Wilkes Heritage Museum, located in the historic Old Courthouse.

Stretching from the North Wilkesboro and Wilkesboro area toward Lenoir along Hwy. 268 is the historic "Happy Valley". Located on the banks of the Yadkin River, Happy Valley was so named by the early settlers who described the valley as "a place of beauty, peace and tranquility" and the name aptly remains. A number of attractions are in the valley, including Fort Defiance, the Chapel of Rest and Whippoorwill Academy and Village.

Location: Foothills, 2.5 hours east of Asheville
Town Hall: 203 West Main St., Wilkesboro NC 28697; 336-838-3951
Website: wilkesboronorthcarolina.com
County: Wilkes County: County Offices, 110 North St., Wilkesboro NC 28697; 336-651-7346
Elevation and Population: 1,042 feet, 3,200+
County Chamber of Commerce: Wilkes County Chamber of Commerce, 717 Main St., North Wilkesboro NC 28659; 336-838-8662
County Tourism Development: Wilkes County Tourism, 203 West Main St., Wilkesboro NC 28697; 336-838-3951
Newspaper: The Record, 911 Main St., North Wilkesboro NC 28659; 336-667-0134
High School: Wilkes Central High School, 1179 Moravian Falls Rd., Wilkesboro NC 28697; 336-667-5277
Colleges and Universities: Wilkes Community College, 1328 South Collegiate Dr., Wilkesboro NC 28697; 336-838-6100
Area Major Festivals: MerleFest (April), Carolina In The Fall Festival (Sep.), Brushy Mountain Apple Festival (Oct.)
Area Natural Attractions: Happy Valley, Rendezvous Mountain Educational State Forest, Stone Mountain State Park, W. Kerr Scott Dam and Reservoir, Yadkin River Greenway
Area Cultural Attractions: Ben Long Frescoes in St. Paul's Episcopal Church, Chapel of Rest, Old Wilkes Jail Museum, The Walker Center, Whippoorwill Academy and Village, Wilkes Art Gallery, Wilkes Heritage Museum.
Recommended Restaurants: (For a complete list of all restaurants visit ashevilleguidebook.com

See also **North Wilkesboro restaurants**

Amalfi's Italian Restaurant & Pizzeria: (Italian) 1919 Hwy. 421, Wilkesboro NC 28697; 336-838-3188

Recommended Places To Stay: (For a complete list of all accommodations visit ashevilleguidebook.com

See also **North Wilkesboro accommodations**

Graystone Manor Bed & Breakfast: (B&B) 406 Woodland Boulevard, Wilkesboro NC 28697; 336-667-7282

Hampton Inn: (Motel) 1300 Collegiate Dr., Wilkesboro NC 28697; 336-838-5000

Leatherwood Mountains: (Resort) 512 Meadow Rd., Ferguson NC 28624; 800-462-6867

Wilderness Lodge: (Country Lodge) 185 Edmiston Lane, Boomer NC 28606; 336-921-2277

Woodfin

Located north of and adjacent to Asheville, Woodfin was named in honor of Nicholas Washington Woodfin, a former lawyer and statesman of North Carolina. Woodfin is the only municipality bearing the name Woodfin in the United States. Woodfin was incorporated in 1971, and has roots back to the mid-19th century.

The history of Woodfin is closely tied to manufacturing. Much of the remaining early housing stock is characteristic of early 20th century mill villages. Many neighborhoods within the community are easily recognized for the mill village style and bear names such as "Martel Village" and "Company Bottom." The decline of American industry in the 1970s and 80s brought a decline in the fortunes of Woodfin as well. The loss of many manufacturing jobs led to a decline in population and property values. During the 1990s and into the present, however, Woodfin has grown rapidly from an influx of new residential growth in the region, including the development of luxury private mountain communities, most notably Reynolds Mountain, and from its proximity to neighboring Asheville.

The Town of Woodfin has a number of superb parks: Woodfin River Park, located at 1050 Riverside Dr.; Roy Pope Memorial Park, located at 90 Elk Mountain Rd.; and South Woodfin Park, located at the intersection of Lookout Rd. and Midwood Dr. Woodfin River Park offers an ideal spot for a picnic by the meandering French Broad River which flows through the city.

Location: Central Mountains, immediately north of Asheville
City Offices: 90 Elk Mountain Rd., Woodfin NC 28804; 828-253-4887
Website: woodfin-nc.gov
County: Buncombe County: County Offices, 205 College St., Asheville NC 28801; 828-250-4000
Elevation and Population: 2,113 feet, 6,000+
County Chamber of Commerce: Buncombe County Chamber of Commerce 205 College St., Asheville NC 28801; 828-250-4100
Newspaper: Asheville Citizen-Times,14 OHenry Ave., Asheville NC 28801; 800-672-2472, 800-800-4204.
High School: Asheville High School, 419 McDowell St., Asheville NC 28803; 828-350-2500
Area Major Festivals: French Broad River Festival (May), Bele Chere (Jul.), Craft Fair of the Southern Highland Craft Guild (Oct.)
Area Natural Attractions: French Broad River, Blue Ridge Parkway
Area Cultural Attractions: Biltmore Estate, Dry Ridge Historical Museum, Thomas Wolfe Memorial, Zebulon B. Vance Birthplace
Recommended Restaurants: (For a complete list of all restaurants visit ashevilleguide book.com

See **Asheville restaurants**

Recommended Places To Stay: (For a complete list of all accommodations visit ashe villeguidebook.com

***See* Asheville accommodations**

Chapter Five

Western North Carolina Wineries

Many visitors to Western North Carolina are surprised at the number of vineyards and wineries that are found here. Out of the more than ninety wineries in the state of North Carolina as a whole, over twenty are found in the mountains. Commonly planted varieties include Cabernet Sauvignon, Cabernet Franc, Merlot, Syrah, Chambourcin, Chardonnay, Viognier, Sauvignon Blanc, Riesling, Seyval Blanc and Vidal Blanc.

The largest winery in the mountains is the world famous Biltmore Estate, in operation since May of 1985, when the Biltmore Estate Wine Company opened its 6.5 million dollar state of the art winery to the public. Small quantities of wine produced from experimental vineyards were first sold to Biltmore visitors in 1977. Current production averages 100,000 gallons of over a dozen varietal wines, utilizing grapes from the estate's 75 acres of vinifera grapes, other North Carolina vineyards and juice from California. For visitors to Western North Carolina who are interested in wines and wine making, a visit to this world-class winery is a must-see on any travel itinerary.

Western Mountains

Calaboose Cellars: 565 Aquone Rd., Andrews NC 28901; 828-321-2006; calaboose cellars.com

Notterly River Valley Vineyards: 1150 Old Culberson Rd., Murphy NC 28906; 828-837-7822; nottelywine.com

Central Mountains

Addison Farms Vineyard: 4005 New Leicester Hwy, Leicester NC; 828-581-9463; addisonfarms.net

Biltmore Estate Winery: Biltmore Estate, Asheville NC 28803; 800-543-2961; bilt more.com

Burntshirt Vineyards: 2695 Sugarloaf Rd., Hendersonville NC 28792: 828-685-2402; burnshirtvineyards.com

Ritler Ridge Vineyards: 5 Piney Mountain Church Rd., Candler NC 28715; 828-280-0690

Saint Paul Mountain Vineyard: 588 Chestnut Gap Rd., Hendersonville NC 28792; 828-685-4002; saintpaulmountainvineyards.com

Northern Mountains

Banner Elk Winery and Villa: 60 Deer Run Lane, Banner Elk NC 28604; 828-898-9090; bannerelkwinery.com

Thistle Meadow Winery: 102 Thistle Meadow, Laurel Springs NC 28644; 800-233-1505; thistlemeadowwinery.com

Foothills

Elkin Creek Vineyard: 318 Elkin Creek Mill Rd., Elkin NC 28621; 336–526-5119; elkincreekvineyard.com

Green Creek Winery: 413 Gilbert Rd., Columbus NC 28722; 828-863-2182; greencreekwinery.

Lake James Cellars: 204 East Main St., Glen Alpine NC 28628; 828–584-4551; lake jamescellars.com

McRitchier Winery and Ciderworks: 315 Thurmond PO Rd., Thurmond NC 28683; 336-874-3003; mcritchiewine.com

Mountain Brook Vineyards: 731 Phillips Dairy Rd., Tryon NC 28782; 828-817-4376; mountainbrookvineyards.com

Overmountain Vineyards: 2012 Sandy Plains Rd., Tryon NC 28782; 828-863-0523

Parker Binns Vineyard: 7382 Hwy. 108E, Mill Spring NC; 828–894–015; parker-binnsvineyard.com

Raffaldini Vineyards: 450 Groce Rd., Ronda NC 28670; 336-835-9463; raffaldini.com

Russian Chapel Hills Winery: 2662 Green Creek Dr., Columbus NC 28722; 828-863-0541; russianchapelhill.com

South Creek Vineyards and Winery: 2240 South Creek Rd., Nebo NC 28761; 828-652-5729; southcreekwinery.com

Waldensian Heritage Winery: 4940 Villar Lane NE, Valdese NC 28690; 828-879-3202; visitvaldese.com

Waldensian Style Wines: 2340 Quail Run, Connellys Springs NC 28612; 828-879-9271; waldensian.com/hone.html

Index

C

D

R

S

Made in the USA
Middletown, DE
15 August 2022

71402996R00265